**Conrad Totman** is Professor Emeritus in Japanese History, Yale University. Acknowledged as the leading Western authority on Japanese environmental history, his books include *Japan before Perry, The Green Archipelago, Early Modern Japan* and *A History of Japan* (3rd edn., 2010).

## ENVIRONMENTAL HISTORY AND GLOBAL CHANGE SERIES

Series Editor
*Emeritus Professor Ian Whyte, University of Lancaster*

Editorial Board
*Kevin Edwards, University of Aberdeen*
*Eric Pawson, University of Canterbury, New Zealand*
*Christian Pfister, University of Berne*
*I. Simmons, University of Durham*
*T.C. Smout, University of St Andrews*
*Harriet Ritvo, Massachusetts Institute of Technology*

This important new series provides a much needed forum for understanding just how and why our environment changes. It shows how environmental history – with its unique blend of geography, history, archaeology, landscape, environment and science – is helping to make informed decisions on pressing environmental concerns and providing crucial insights into the mechanisms that influence environmental change today. The focus of the series will be on contemporary problems but will also include work that addresses major techniques, key periods and important regions. At a time when the scale and importance of environmental change has led to a widespread feeling that we have entered a period of crisis, the *Environmental History and Global Change Series* provides a timely, informed and important contribution to a key global issue.

# Japan

## An Environmental History

CONRAD TOTMAN

**I.B. TAURIS**
LONDON · NEW YORK

New paperback edition published in 2016 by
I.B.Tauris & Co. Ltd
London • New York
www.ibtauris.com

First published in hardback in 2014 by I.B.Tauris & Co. Ltd

ISBN:      978 1 78453 743 2
eISBN:     978 1 78672 152 5
ePDF:      978 1 78673 152 4

A full CIP record for this book is available from the British Library
A full CIP record is available from the Library of Congress

Library of Congress Catalog Card Number: available

# Contents

# Illustrations

## ILLUSTRATIONS

# Acknowledgements

I thank the Yale University Library for having maintained the splendid book collection that enabled me to prepare this text. And I thank I.B.Tauris and its consultants for giving me an opportunity to write it. Finally, I thank my family and my fellow residents of Whitney Center for bearing with my absent-mindedness during the three years of the book's preparation.

# Notes on Japanese Terminology

The names of Japanese individuals are given in the customary Japanese manner, surname first.

The Japanese language employs both "long vowels" and "short vowels" for the sounds represented by the Roman letters "o" and "u". The long vowels are formally denoted by a "long mark" over the letter: ô and û. Following customary practice, however, this text omits the long marks for common geographical terms or terms that have been anglicized. Thus Kyûshû appears here as Kyushu.

Long marks have been omitted in the following terms: Hokkaidô, Ôsaka, Kyôto, Ryûkyû Islands, Kyûshû and Tôkyô.

# Glossary of Japanese Terms

| | |
|---|---|
| Ainu | the forager people of northeast Japan, ca. 1600ff |
| akamatsu | Japanese red pine (*Pinus densiflora*) |
| akutô | "evil group", outlaw bands of ca. 1250–1350 CE |
| amado | heavy, sliding, wooden exterior-wall panels |
| baito | secondary capitals (of *ritsuryô* era) |
| baiu | summer monsoon weather |
| bakufu | "camp government", denoting shogunal regimes, ca. 1180–1868 |
| bakuhan | an elision of *bakufu* and *han*; denoting the *shogun-daimyô* ruling system of 1603–1868 |
| bunbu | "the civil and military arts", the type of knowledge that rulers urged warriors to pursue, ca. 1600–1850 |
| bunmei kaika | "civilization and enlightenment", a slogan invoked by reformers after 1870 |
| chisan chisui | "management of mountains and waters", the Confucian term for protection forestry |
| chô | a measure of land (2.45 acres; 0.992 hectares) |
| daimyô | "great names", regional barons of ca. 1400–1870 |
| daizu | soybeans; an Asiatic legume (*Glycine soya*) |
| dekasegi | working away from home on a seasonal or temporary basis |
| egoma | an Asiatic mint (*Perilla ocimoides*) |
| Emishi | early name for the forager people of northeastern Japan |
| Ezo | a later name for the forager people from Tôhoku northward (and a term for that largely unknown region) |
| ezomatsu | Ezo spruce (*Picea jezoensis Carr.*) |
| fukoku kyôhei | "rich country; strong army", a classic Chinese phrase invoked by Japan's leaders after 1870 |
| fusuma | lightweight, opaque, sliding-door panels |
| gekokujô | "those below overthrowing those above", local warriors toppling their superiors in power struggles |

| | |
|---|---|
| gen'ya | barren or waste land; a moor |
| gunken | "district/prefecture", a term denoting a centralized, hierarchical political order |
| hageyama | "bald" or denuded mountains |
| hajiki | a type of earthenware |
| han | a baronial (*daimyô*) domain, ca. 1550–1870 |
| hayashi | forest or woodland |
| Hayato | a forager people of Kyushu |
| heimin | "commoner", a class label for non-titled people after 1870 |
| hinoki | Japanese cypress (*Chamaecyparis obtusa*) |
| hiratake | a mushroom (*Agaricus subfunereus*) |
| hôken | an enfeoffment or "feudal" system of hereditary rule by a suzerain and subordinates |
| hongawara | roof tile of thick, semi-tubular design |
| igusa | a rush (*Juncus effusus*) |
| ikki | a local protest or uprising, ca. 1400–1600 |
| iroha momiji | Japanese red maple (*Acer palmatum*) |
| itai itai | "ouch, ouch", popular label for a painful disease caused by cadmium poisoning |
| jikatasho | "farm manuals", agricultural writings modeled on Chinese and Korean precedents, ca. 1700–1850 |
| Jinmu | mythological founding emperor of Japan |
| jitsugaku | "practical learning", or knowledge promoted for its practical utility, ca. 1700–1850 |
| jôi | (see *sonnô jôi*) |
| jômon | "cord marking" of pottery used by a forager society; denotes that society and its pottery |
| kaki | persimmon (*Diospyros kaki*) |
| kamado | a squat, earthenware cooking stove |
| kami | the gods of *Shintô* |
| kan/min | "public/private" or "government/people", to distinguish between governmental and non-governmental property or other matters |
| kanji | "Chinese characters" (ideographs, pictographs), as used in Japanese script |
| kanpaku | "regent" to an adult emperor (*tennô*) |
| kanrin | "government forest", an official category of the 1870sff |
| karamatsu | larch (*Larix leptolepis*) |
| keyaki | zelkova (*Zelkova serrata*) |
| Kinai | the Nara-Kyoto-Osaka vicinity |
| kô | "mutual assistance" arrangements within and between villages |
| Kôfun | ancient tomb; denotes society of the era of giant-tomb building |
| koku | a measure of volume (4.96 bushels; 180 liters) |
| kokugaku | "national learning", an ethnically conscious scholarly development of *bakuhan* centuries |

| | |
|---|---|
| kokugaryô | "provincial domains", land claimed as imperial domain and administered by provincial governors during later *ritsuryô* period |
| kokujin | "provincials", local warrior leaders of ca. 1300–1500 |
| konbinato | an integrated industrial production facility |
| kôyûchi | "common-use land", an official category established in 1872 to denote village or other communal land |
| Kumaso | a forager people of Kyushu |
| kuri | Japanese chestnut (*Castanea crenata*) |
| kuroshio | Japan Current |
| -kyô | "capital", denotes the emperor's seat of government |
| matsu | pine tree (*Pinus spp.*) |
| matsutake | a mushroom (*Armillaria edodes*) |
| mikan | mandarin orange (*Citrus deliciosa*) |
| miso | bean paste |
| miyake | "crown lands", lands claimed as their own by imperial rulers of the early *ritsuryô* period |
| myôshû | "local overseer", a person of local influence recognized as a local leader by aristocratic landholders of the later *ritsuryô* period |
| nanushi | "village headman", using the same *kanji* as *myôshû* |
| nengô | a period of years as designated in the Japanese calendrical system |
| niguruma | two-wheeled carts for commercial transport |
| nôsho | "farm manuals" (see *jikatasho*) |
| oyashio | Chishima Current |
| rangaku | "Dutch learning", the study of things European, ca. 1700–1850 |
| ritsuryô | "government of laws and ordinances", formed in seventh to eighth centuries |
| sake | rice wine |
| sangawara | a flat roof tile, thinner and lighter than the *hongawara* that it replaced, ca. 1700ff |
| sankin kôtai | the "alternate attendance" system wherein *daimyô* spent alternate 12-month periods in residence in Edo, ca. 1630–1863 |
| sanrin | mountainous forests; high forest; well-stocked timberland |
| sasa | sasagaya, a dwarf bamboo (*Microstegium japonica*) |
| Sat-Chô | an elision of the domanial names Satsuma and Chôshû |
| seii-tai-shôgun | "barbarian-subduing generalissimo", initially an expeditionary commander appointed by *tennô*; later, successive hereditary military hegemons |
| sekkanke | "houses of *sesshô* and *kanpaku*", the dominant Fujiwara lineage of later *ritsuryô* centuries |
| sesshô | "regent" to a child emperor (*tennô*) |
| shi | "gentleman", samurai; the hereditary warrior retainers of *daimyô* and *shôgun* |
| shijuku | private schools for commoners, ca. 1700–1870 |

| | |
|---|---|
| shinôkôshô | "warrior (*shi*)-peasant (*nô*)-artisan (*kô*)-merchant (*shô*)", the four formally designated social classes of ca. 1600–1870 |
| Shintô | "the Way of the gods", mythology of the early ruling elite, later elaborated to a religion |
| shiso | an Asiatic mint (Perilla nankinensis) |
| shizoku | "of samurai ancestry", a class label assigned to de-classed ex-samurai after 1870 |
| shôchû | an alcoholic beverage made from available grains |
| shôen | "manorial land", land assigned to aristocratic households and fanes by imperial rulers of *ritsuryô* centuries |
| shôgun | (see *seii-tai-shôgun*) |
| shoin-zukuri | a Japanese architectural style, ca. 1400 ff |
| shôji | lightweight, translucent, sliding wall panels |
| shôyu | soy sauce |
| shûu | autumn rainy weather |
| sô | a self-governing village association, ca. 1350ff |
| sonnô jôi | "revere the emperor (*sonnô*); expel the barbarian (*jôi*)", a political slogan/ideology of the 1860s |
| sugi | cryptomeria (*Cryptomeria japonica*) |
| suiko | rice loaned to farmers to start a new crop |
| taisha | a "grand shrine" of *Shintô*, as at Izumo |
| tan | a square measure (0.245 acres; 993 square meters) |
| tatami | thick, spongy floor matting |
| tennô | "heavenly ruler", denoting emperors of Japan |
| tenshukaku | a castle tower or keep |
| terakoya | local schools for commoners, ca. 1700–1870 |
| todomatsu | white fir (*Abies sachalinensis*) |
| tôfu | bean curd |
| Tôhoku | northeastern Honshu |
| ton'ya | licensed wholesalers, ca. 1600–1870 |
| tsunami | tidal wave; seismic wave |
| unka | leaf-hoppers; a type of leaf-eating insect (*Cicadula sexnotata*) |
| urushi | varnish tree; a species of sumac (*Rhus verniciflua*) |
| Wajinden | "Commentary on the People of Wa"; ca. 290 CE |
| yakuza | a crime syndicate |
| yamase | the cooling effect of a northerly air flow down over northeast Japan |
| yen | Japanese currency since 1870s; value fluctuates over time |
| za | a guild or entrepreneurial trade group |
| zaibatsu | "clique of wealth", the industrial elite of pre-1945 decades |

# Preface

Today, as the global bio-system reels under the multifaceted impact of excessive and escalating human demand, we ask ourselves what – if anything – can be done to reverse the accelerating global die-off and disintegration. And as we seek to answer that question, we must perforce ask how we humans got ourselves and the global biome into this predicament.

This latter question shifts our attention from present and future to the past. But it does so in a way that focuses on those aspects of the past that have led to our present global ecological dilemma. Such a focus prods us to look at particular societies and situations not primarily in terms of what makes them distinctive or unique but, rather, in terms of what makes them part of the larger story that has eventuated in today's world.

A couple of factors make Japan a rather good "case study" of environmental history. For one thing, its history is relatively well documented. For another, that history has traversed much of the course of humankind in general, from a sparsely settled forager (hunter-gatherer) society through the process of agrarian development and elaboration to the present-day condition of a densely settled industrial society. In addition, because Japan is a set of islands clearly separated from other areas of human habitation, its boundaries are uncommonly clear, and the nature, timing and extent of external influences on its history are unusually identifiable.

Needless to say, there already exist well-established ways of presenting Japan's history. The Japanese have developed their own straightforward historical narrative that tells the story from "prehistoric" Jômon and Yayoi cultures on through the eras of successive ruling elites – identified by their headquarters sites of Nara, Heian, Kamakura, Muromachi and Edo – and, recently, dynastic eras such as Meiji and Shôwa. Or one can shoehorn Japan's history into categories derived from Europe – ancient, medieval, early modern and modern – in an apparent effort to "de-exoticize" it and legitimize it as "real" history in the eyes of "Westerners" (meaning Europeans and their descendants elsewhere?).

Of course Japan – like every society and every individual of every species – is indeed unique. And of course it – like every society – really does have characteristics

similar to some found in western Europe. But to focus on the agendas of unique-
ness or Euro-comparability perpetuates the image of Japan as a quaintly "different"
society or one that is noteworthy mainly because of its implied likeness to western
Europe. More to the point here, these agendas may disregard factors basic to the
broader human story and they illuminate poorly the background of today's critical
problems of the global bio-system.

Accordingly, this study of Japan's history employs a different organizing
framework, an environmental perspective. It is a universally applicable perspective
and one that highlights themes germane to the global ecological agenda of our
own day. Hence the title: *Japan: An Environmental History*.

That title reminds us, however, that words can be tricky. And the terms "Japan"
and "Japanese" (or "England" and "English", "Brazil" and "Brazilian" and so
on) exemplify the semantic problem. "Japan" can refer to a physical place, as in
"Japan, the archipelago", or "They went to Japan". It can refer to a polity, as in
"Japan capitulated to Perry's gunboats" or "Japan attacked Pearl Harbor". Similarly,
"Japanese" can refer to a language, an ethnic or "racial" group, an economy and
its products, or to allegedly distinctive cultural qualities of "the Japanese people".

In this book "Japan" refers mainly to a physical place, namely the island chains
currently recognized as the political entity of Japan (that is, the archipelago proper
and the adjoining Bonin and Ryukyu island chains). In the chapters on industrial
society, however, where Japan-outsider interactions become more central to
our inquiry, the term also refers to state and society. And "Japanese" refers to
phenomena found on those islands (or – on occasion – that originate on those
islands and remain identified with them, through choice or popular custom).

Similarly, the term "environmental history" requires clarification. An environmental history of Japan could entail a study of how the myriad variables in Japan's
environment interacted over the millennia. Or it could select a particular variable
in that environment (for example, climate, wolves, rice, humans and so on) and
yield a study centered on the interaction of that variable and its context. The
former approach, which sees the process of interaction as an integral whole, would
produce a "synecological" (syncretic or synthetic ecological) study. The latter
would yield an "autecological" (autonomous ecological) approach. If the variable
around which the story was constructed were the human population, it would be
a "human-centered autecological study". And such it is.

Perhaps the verb "interact" needs to be emphasized. We humans too often
choose to view ourselves as "in control", as independent actors, the sole source of
"agency" in history. But in fact, of course, our behavior and influence are shaped
by our context even as we have an impact on it. And this study will attempt to illuminate how the contextual variables of biology, climate, geography and geology
interplayed with the human initiatives to shape the archipelago's history.

Regarding those "human initiatives", we shall see that the human impact on
environment is shaped by three key variables: the density of human presence; the
level of material consumption per capita; and the technologies the humans employ
to provide themselves with those material goods. These variables determine how
much space they shift from "natural" to "unnatural" uses; how extensively they

deplete resources elsewhere in the ecosystem and how much they damage the bio-system through the production of pollutants and waste.

So, our story centers on the human occupants of the archipelago – on how they arranged their lives, how they interacted with their environmental context and how those processes changed as time passed. And we shall seek to examine the "why" and "so what" of those arrangements, interactions and changes in hopes of illuminating both the human experience and that of the archipelago's other constituent elements, both living and non-living.

This story extends through thousands – even tens of thousands – of years. In terms of the three basic phases of forager, agricultural and industrial society, however, we shall see that each is of decreasing duration but of increasing historical visibility compared to its predecessor. We shall also see that each of the successive stages displays more extensive and complex environmental ramifications, which trend has eventuated in today's accelerating rush to global ecological crisis.

# Introduction

The crucial variables in human-environment relations are global location, paleo-geological heritage, climate, the resulting biotic community and the character and scale of human society's impact on its environs. These variables have determined the layout of this book.

The first chapter examines the role of geography – meaning topographical, geological, climatic and biotic factors – in this history. As we shall see in that chapter, before humans altered Japan's bio-system, it was almost entirely a lushly forested realm. For that reason, the central environmental change in the archipelago has been a gradual displacement of woodland by other forms of land use. And in that process vegetational change has been – until very recent decades – more visible and more fully recorded than have changes, for example, in pelagic, coastal or inland fisheries or animal life in general. And that emphasis on forest vegetation is reflected in this book, although a few valuable studies of mammalian, piscine and microbial factors enrich later segments of the story.

Subsequent chapters examine the evolving human society of the archipelago, utilizing, as noted in the preface, the sequential phases of forager, agricultural and industrial society. The three terms denote three fundamentally different techniques by which humans acquire the energy and other materials needed to sustain themselves. In essence, foragers survive by taking what they need from what is available in the ambient bio-system. Agriculturists manipulate the nearby biome, nurturing favored plants and animals at the expense of "wild" biota.

Industrial society treats the entire planet as a legitimate target of exploitation. Insofar as technology permits, it radically increases the rate of per-capita energy cycling by humans, primarily through the consumption of fossil fuels – the accumulated remnants of millions of years' worth of biota. And its members regard the entire globe, rather than just their own locale, as an appropriate resource base. One consequence of this shift to a global resource base, as we shall see in Chapters 7 and 8, is that it renders the "nation state" inadequate as a vehicle for the study of industrial society's environmental interactions. However, for all but the most

1

recent few decades, this perspective will suffice for our task of studying the archipelago's environmental history.

Forager society in Japan lasted for millennia, but, as we shall see, data on its scale, character and environmental impact are very modest. So we treat that long era in a single chapter. Agricultural society prevailed for only some 2,500 years, down to the late nineteenth century. But it is far more fully documented than the forager era and occupies four chapters.

The third historical phase, industrial society, has been present in the archipelago for a mere century or so, but it is richly documented. Moreover, as we shall see, the basic characteristics of industrial society (consumption of fossil fuel and reliance on a worldwide resource base) lie at the heart of today's global ecological problems – namely, declines in biodiversity, bio-adaptability and biomass volume and productivity. Consequently, despite its brevity, Japan's industrial society occupies two chapters. Then an epilogue recapitulates our story and looks at the current situation and foreseeable prospects.

Such is the overall arrangement of this book. Now, however, let us look a bit more closely at two general problems. One is the question of how societies move from forager to agricultural and thence to industrial forms of organization. The other problem is the three categories themselves, because forager, agricultural and industrial societies are neither as distinct nor their end-points as clear as the labels and dates may seem to suggest.

Regarding the process of moving from foraging to agriculture and later to industrialism, in all societies both changes involve difficult tasks of learning and adaptation. A portion of the task entails innovation, but mostly it is a matter of adopting and adapting techniques developed by others, whether neighbors down the road or strangers from afar. However, not all the world's people have been equally well placed to learn or use the new techniques "from afar". Human groups in close proximity to one another quickly share – whether willingly or not – those new devices and arrangements that seem advantageous to the user, whereas those situated in deep jungles, on tundra or on isolated islands generally have been slower to hear about the new practices and/or to find ways of utilizing them.

In the case of Japan, "strangers from afar" played important roles in the shifts to both agricultural and industrial society. People from the Korea-China-Manchuria vicinity seem to have been crucial to the former shift. For the later shift, the strangers were mainly from Europe and North America. And in both cases, Japan's location off the coast of east Asia influenced the timing and character of its exposure to the new technologies.

Regarding the ambiguities imbedded in the three categories of forager, agriculture and industrial society, Japan's initial human inhabitants were foragers (or hunter-gatherers). They sustained themselves by consuming edible materials found in their ambient natural surroundings and their society endured for untold thousands of years. Gradually, however, those foragers learned about or devised ways to broaden their food supply and preserve foodstuffs for later consumption, and with those changes their numbers grew and their society gained complexity.

Eventually, too, the foragers learned how to encourage select plants (and a few animals) to grow more abundantly, thereby assuring themselves a larger and surer source of food and other necessities. Prior to about 3,000–2,500 years ago, those developments appear to have been only supplemental to the basic forager diet and lifestyle. However, from about that time, migrants, mostly from or via the Korean peninsula, began to introduce and disseminate a much more fully developed set of agricultural practices. And by some 2,500–2,000 years ago, those practices were well established, at least in southwestern Japan, as the primary source of foodstuffs.

Properly speaking, of course, the term "agriculture" refers to the cultivation (*cultura*) of fields (*ager*), but more generally it connotes the pre-industrial forms of purposeful manipulation of biota for human use, mainly to produce food. In this broader sense, it encompasses animal husbandry and orchardry as well as field cropping. In agricultural Japan, animal husbandry was practiced less extensively than in many societies. Orchardry had a more substantial role, but it was field cropping that became the predominant form of agriculture. And that agricultural configuration persisted for some 2,500 years, well into the nineteenth century.

By 1890, however, Japanese society was entering the third phase of environmental interaction, that of "industrial society". As adumbrated above, the basic characteristics that distinguish this phase from earlier ones are: (1) an immense expansion in the per-capita rate of humanly caused energy cycling; and (2) a shift from dependence on a local resource base to dependence on a global resource base.

These developments require a bit of clarification. First, regarding the stunning acceleration in human energy cycling, it was made possible initially by exploitation of so-called "fossil fuels" – notably coal, oil and, later, natural gas – which dwarfed the energy available from currently living biota. Combining that "new" source of energy with skillful manipulation of physics and chemistry, the Japanese (like members of other industrializing societies) soon developed other sources of energy, notably hydroelectric and subsequently nuclear. Combining those energy supplies with new scientific and industrial technology, they radically expanded their capacity to exploit almost all aspects of the ecosystem, thereby increasing many-fold the total demand they made on it. As a corollary, the trend reduced proportionally the space and other resources left available for use by the rest of the bio-system. In addition, the very processes of obtaining and utilizing these fossil fuels and other materials produced vast quantities of by-products, including waste that has polluted and cluttered the bio-system to an unprecedented extent.

Second, regarding the shift from a "local" to a "global" resource base, the people of Japan have from the beginning had contact with continental folk, as noted above. However, during forager millennia, that contact was extremely rare from the day-to-day perspective of inhabitants and it offered no significant supplement to the local resource base. Later, during agricultural centuries most of the contacts, although far more frequent, touched only the lives of the elite, providing little more than luxury goods, information and political complications.

Moreover, within the archipelago itself, as we shall see, complex inter-ethnic contacts did occur between Japan's agricultural society and forager societies in the southwest and northeast extremities. And while those interactions did generally entail hardship and losses for the foragers, whose territories were gradually overrun, they had only a modest impact on the agricultural people themselves, adding little to their resource base except as conquest and "settlement" extended the "local" area subject to their direct exploitation.

During these centuries of Japan's agricultural society, local interactions gradually became more far-reaching as domestic mobility and trade increased. However, most of the time those increases occurred within the context of a more-or-less stable socio-political order that was subject to control from above. The control was exercised by an elite that would – for obvious reasons of self-interest – try to referee disruptive disputes in a manner that would quiet discontents and sustain social order, thereby maximizing the extent to which the benefits of this expanding local resource base would continue flowing to themselves.

With industrialization, by contrast, the "resource base" quickly spread far beyond the reach of any supervisory body with the capacity to ensure orderly management of the system's rewards. Instead, it came to involve interactions of a competitive nature with outcomes determined by the self-interest and relative power of the players, whether they were organized as "political" entities – governments – or as "economic" entities – corporations.

So, for Japan, as for other industrializing societies, the stunning increase in demand for energy and other material goods enmeshed the society in transactions on a global scale. However, because that outcome has been shared by all industrial societies, it has meant that these societies have found themselves competing ever more intensively for resources and interacting in ways that are unprecedented in scale, diversity, complexity and difficulty.

In general terms, then, we can characterize Japan's history as moving through the three basic phases of forager, agricultural and industrial society. As we proceed, however, we shall note "sub-stages" of these basic phases.

We shall see that forager society moved from a long, scarcely visible, "pre-pottery" cultural phase into a shorter phase – roughly 15,000 years – of "pottery" culture. We shall also note that, during the 2,500 years of agricultural society, Japan seems again to have passed through two overall phases – an earlier one of "dispersed agriculturalists" practicing "extensive agriculture" and a later one (from around 1250 CE for a date) of more densely settled "intensive agriculture". And finally, Japan's century or so of industrial society can be viewed as consisting of an earlier phase when governmental initiative and priorities seemed to be the primary determinant of developments and, since 1945, a more recent phase when the agendas of industrial leadership seem to have played a more crucial role in shaping historical processes and outcomes.

Moreover, in both the early and later agricultural phases and in industrial society, we shall note periods of clear "growth", in both human population and total human demand on the bio-system. Each such period is then followed, however, by one of "stasis", when population appears to stabilize in size and when the rate of resource exploitation seems to cease growing or even retrench.

\* \* \*

For us today, who live in a global bio-system that is rapidly disintegrating (declining biodiversity and so on as noted above) as the consequences of excessive human demand on the ecosystem manifest themselves, the key historical questions that present themselves are these: what has been the pattern of human interplay with the rest of the bio-system through the millennia; and how has it changed to bring us to our present situation.

For the study of Japan's history, as for the study of all histories, this environmental situation compels us to look again, utilize more pertinent criteria and craft new interpretations that help us answer those questions. This book is an attempt to do so.

# 1 *Japan the Place*

On its face, Japan today is an easy place to describe. It is a lushly green, mountainous archipelago with densely settled, highly productive lowlands. However,
when one digs beneath the surface, one discovers that the physical (geomorphological) character of this archipelago is wondrously complex. Two basic – and
interacting – variables have determined that character: geological process and
global location. Together these factors have shaped the island chain's material
composition, topography, climate, biological population and, in recent millennia,
its human experience.

## JAPAN TODAY

Japan today consists of a main archipelago ("Japan proper") and two associated
island chains, those of the Bonin and Ryukyu Islands.[1] Japan proper consists of
four major islands – Honshu, Hokkaido, Kyushu and Shikoku, in descending
order of size – plus a host of nearby islets, notably Tsushima and Sado. This island
character has meant that almost from the outset of human habitation, seagoing
vessels have been part of Japanese life. The four main islands are close enough
together, however, so that today they are linked by bridges and tunnels that carry
both road and rail traffic.

The archipelago is situated in the temperate zone of the northern hemisphere,
just off the East coast of the Eurasian continent. The four main islands curve
northeastward from Kyushu in the southwest through Shikoku to the Kantô region
of Honshu and on northward to Hokkaido. They extend from 31° North latitude
at the southern extremity of Kyushu to 45.5° at the northern tip of Hokkaido, a
North–South distance of about 1,660 km (1,030 mi). They are bounded on the
West by the East China Sea, Korea Strait and Sea of Japan, on the North by the Sea
of Okhotsk and on the East and South by the Pacific Ocean.

The main islands come closest to continental Asia at their southwest corner,
where the northern end of Kyushu lies hard by the southwest tip of Honshu. From

**Figure 1.1:** Mountain ridges in central Tôhoku, 1955

**Figure 1.2:** Flood-plain valley of the Kitakami River near Hiraizumi in eastern Tôhoku, 1962

there it is only about 200 km to the southeast corner of the Korean peninsula. And the sheltering coves of the two sizeable islets that comprise Tsushima lie midway between the two. At the Kyushu-Honshu juncture, the short, slender Kanmon Strait leads eastward from Tsushima Strait into the Inland Sea.

The Inland Sea is a long, shallow, islet-strewn marine sea sheltered from the open ocean by Kyushu and Shikoku on its South and West and Honshu on its North and

**Figure 1.3:** Rocky coastline, which is prevalent in Japan; this one in western Kyushu, at the entry to Nagasaki Bay on left, 1963

East. In terms of human use, this sheltered sea has for two millennia proven to be one of the archipelago's most precious assets, facilitating travel, settlement and commerce, even as it yielded a rich supply of seafood.

Regarding the Bonin and Ryukyu island chains, the Bonins run some 1,050 km southward from the Kantô region. The Ryukyus curve southwestward from southern Kyushu, stretching some 950 km, almost to Taiwan.[2] Japan proper occupies some 375,000 km² (145,000 mi²) of land surface, while the two island chains add another 12,000 km². For comparison, Germany covers about 357,000 km², Iraq 435,000 and Montana, USA, 381,000.[3]

On its landed surface Japan consists primarily of mountain terrain. Much of that terrain is characterized by high ridges and peaks that thrust steeply up from narrow valley systems. Down those mountainsides into the valleys drain the waters that become myriad streams, which debouch onto the surface of coast-facing flatlands and a few inland basins. Most notable of the basins are Lake Biwa in South-central Honshu and the Yamagata-Shônai Basin in northern Honshu.

Whereas many of the world's great lowland areas are vast sheets of ancient, horizontal bedrock, Japan's lowlands consist almost entirely of deposited materials, some produced by erosion and some by volcanic activity. The major lowland surfaces of today are very recent, dating to about 5–6,000 years ago. As we note more fully below, however, many of them are lined by higher "terrace deposits". These are the remnants of more ancient lowlands that were formed many thousands of years earlier and subsequently eroded, the surviving margins having been slowly uplifted to their present levels, which range from 10 to 300 m above adjacent lowland. Roughly speaking, mountains occupy some 80 percent of Japan, while only 20 percent consist of lowland and terrace deposits.

Because Japan's mountainsides are so steep, much terrain has been minimally accessible to human exploitation. The mountains have served mainly as a source of fuel wood, timber, foraged foodstuffs and green fertilizer. In consequence, most of them – some 70 percent of the archipelago – are still more or less richly wooded. As a corollary, this topography means that Japan's human population is clustered on lowlands and the lower levels of hillside. Because these lowlands mostly consist of deep deposits of well-watered fluvial sediment and volcanic ash, they constitute fertile arable land and today, as during past centuries, they are the site of Japan's agriculture, as well as its cities, towns and industrial activity.

## GEOLOGICAL PROCESS

As the above comments indicate, the human experience in Japan has been fundamentally shaped by the archipelago's topography. And that topography, in turn, is a product of Japan's geological experience. Nonetheless, perhaps the most striking fact about that geological experience is its brevity. The archipelago that we humans know is, by planetary standards, an extraordinarily recent development.

### The Geological Pre-history

The planet Earth, after all, is roughly 4.5 billion years old and its earliest continental surfaces date to nearly 4 billion years before the present (4 byBP or 4,000 myBP). In contrast, as recently as 15 million years before the present (15 myBP), much of today's Japan was submerged beneath the waves. By 11 myBP, it was rising, but as of a mere 2 myBP its mountain ranges still stood at only about half their present height.[4]

The extreme newness of Japan's mountains contrasts with the agedness of the world's major mountain chains. The Rocky Mountains of western North America, the Andes of South America and the vast Alpine-Himalayan chain, running from Europe to Southeast Asia, all of which are relatively new, began to rise some 250 myBP and had taken most of their present shape by 25 myBP. Even sharper is the age contrast with the Appalachian chain of eastern North America and the Ural range of central Eurasia, both of which are much older, having already risen to great height by 250 myBP, only to erode to their present-day gently rolling shape during subsequent eons.

This is not to say that the physical material of the Japanese archipelago has no history antedating 15 myBP. Geologists have identified substantial areas of rock in Japan that trace to ancient origins.[5] These seem to place "paleo-Japan" on the edge of plates that eventually merged to form the continental area we know as northeast Asia (the China-Siberia environs). This process of merging occurred during the breakup of the planet's most recent "supercontinent", Pangaea. That breakup unfolded over the eons from about 250 myBP onward, forming the continents of today, which were largely in place by roughly 40 myBP.[6]

During those eons of Pangaea's breakup, the land we know as North America migrated northwestward, while the conjoined continental surfaces we know as

Europe and Siberia wheeled clockwise, causing the Siberian extremity to pivot southeastward from a high polar position. As it did so, it gradually collided with and accumulated other plate fragments, including two known as the North and South China plates. In the process it created the northeast Asian land mass of today.

By 40 myBP the continental and oceanic plates of today's northwest Pacific region were roughly in their present positions and in collision with one another.[7] From the northeast and east the North American continental plate and, later, the Pacific oceanic plate were pressing other plate fragments, notably an Okhotsk plate, southward and westward, pushing them up against the northeast Asian land mass.

Meanwhile, far to the South, the Indian continent's powerful advance northeastward out of the southern hemisphere and into Asia was creating the towering Himalaya-region mountain ranges and pressing the Asian area back northward. In addition, to the East and southeast of paleo-Japan, oceanic plates pressed West and northwestward, subducting under the Asian land mass and producing upward pressures as they were forced downward.

These several processes fostered intense volcanic activity and created other severe stresses, both horizontal and vertical, in the vicinity of paleo-Japan. Between about 35 and 10 myBP they evidently led to the formation of several "back-arc basins", one of which developed into the Sea of Japan – the East Sea as it is known in Korea.[8] Because of the lateral stresses created by inter-plate pressure, especially that of the India–Asia collision, an upward flow of subterranean molten material (magma) in that locality slowly shifted the continental edge (paleo-Japan) eastward, opening its West side to marine flooding. This opening occurred initially in what became the northern part of the Sea, pressing today's northeast Japan eastward. Later the upwelling of magma extended southward, pushing the continental edge there southeastward, thereby forming the southern half of the Sea and of today's Japan.

As millions of years passed and that dislodgement of continental edge slowly proceeded, the two segments gradually fractured, eroded and slipped downward. By 15 myBP the fragments were largely submerged. Subsequently, however, and especially after about 5 myBP, when the remnants were situated at about the site of present-day Japan, pressure from adjacent oceanic plates forced them to rise again. That process of uplift also filled the gap between the northeast and southwest segments with material that eventually became the archipelago's most mountainous region, as we note more fully below.

### Archipelagic History

By 5 myBP the planet Earth was essentially the same as today. The oceans and continents were those we know, and flora and fauna were mostly the species now extant. Thereafter the geophysical activity of greatest global significance was not tectonic movement but climatic fluctuation, especially during the most recent 2 million years, the so-called Pleistocene Ice Age.

This is not to imply that "ice ages" never occurred before the Pleistocene epoch. The planet's temperature had waxed and waned ever since it initially cooled enough to begin forming a continental crust some 4 billion years ago.[9] In the case of Japan, temperature fluctuations were evident from the outset, as its ancestral segments slowly migrated eastward during formation of the Sea of Japan. Thus, it appears that around 18–16 myBP that vicinity was experiencing tropical-subtropical temperatures. By 6 myBP, however, it was substantially cooler. It gradually warmed again by 4 myBP and then grew enough colder by about 3 myBP to be characterized as experiencing a glacial period. The most extreme and erratic shifts between cold and hot weather seem to have occurred, however, during the last million years.[10]

For Japan, of course, due to the archipelago's recent provenance, tectonic change has continued to be a major aspect of its history since 5 myBP. Indeed, it has been central to the creation of both the highlands and lowlands of today.

### 1. The Highlands

Two entwined geomorphological factors have been central to the formation of modern Japan's highlands: tectonic uplift and volcanism.

By about 5 myBP, as noted above, the nascent Japanese archipelago was being briskly uplifted by the force of colliding plates. "Briskness", of course, is relative. If, as earlier suggested, Japan's mountain chains rose some 1,200 m during the past 2 million years, they were rising at the rate of about 1 centimeter (0.4 inches) every 17 years. At that rate no human would have noticed it in the course of a lifetime.

That extreme slowness notwithstanding, the process of tectonic uplift gradually elevated old areas and created new mountain ranges, producing the high ridges and sharply pitched slopes of today, the greatest cluster of which are found in central Japan, today's Chûbu District.[11] At the heart of that cluster is the "central cordillera" or "Japan Alps". It is a set of three, roughly parallel, North–South mountain ridges (the Hida, Kiso and Akaishi ranges) that arose, as noted above, between the northern and southern sections of paleo-Japan after those had been separated from one another during the Sea of Japan's opening.

Many of Japan's ridgelines now stand 2–3,000 m high, with the highest non-volcanic peak being Mt Shirane (3,192 m) in the Akaishi range.[12] For comparison, Mt Mitchell, the highest peak in eastern North America (in North Carolina), stands 2,038 m high, and Scotland's Ben Nevis, the highest in the British Isles, rises 1,343 m.

The fact that millennia of tectonic uplift elevated remnants of paleo-Japan has been important to the archipelago's human experience. Those old areas contained various minerals and other ancient matter, including gold, silver, copper, iron and coal. The materials have proven useful for well over a millennium, but during the past century the most valuable subsurface resource has been the extensive seams of coal. They are mostly found in Kyushu and Hokkaido at sites that date to roughly 65–25 myBP.[13] So they were formed during warm eras prior to or in the early stages of paleo-Japan's eastward movement. They survived the trek and when uplifted became accessible to miners, thereby facilitating the development of Japan's industrial society.

Regarding volcanism, it has been an important aspect of global crustal activity for billions of years. In the case of Japan, it has been evident from the onset of the Sea of Japan's opening about 35 myBP.[14] A long period of particularly intense volcanic activity during 23–13 myBP gave way to a comparable period (13–2 myBP) of relative quiescence, and then to renewed volcanism during the most recent 2 million years, the Pleistocene epoch.[15]

Some 200 volcanoes have been involved in that activity, and the contents of their eruptions and outflows – notably, tephra, meaning lava, ash and various types of glassy rock-type debris, such as obsidian – eventually came to cover about 40 percent of Japan's land surface.[16] The volcanoes are found from one end of the archipelago to the other, but they have been concentrated in the areas of today's Kyushu, Hokkaido and the western periphery of the Kantô region in central Honshu.[17]

**Figure 1.4:** Diluvial terrace land opened to dry-field tillage southwest of Tokyo, 1981

Of these 200 volcanoes, some 60 are still considered active today, and that number constitutes about 7–8 percent of the world's active volcanoes.[18] The most famous of these is Mt Fuji, which stands West of the Kantô and at 3,776 m is Japan's highest peak today. It is also one of the newest volcanoes, having become active only some 80,000 years ago. It had a vigorous early phase and a more subdued later one, its most recent eruption occurring in the year 1707.[19]

## 2. The Lowlands

Both the volcanic and non-volcanic highlands have played key roles in the formation of Japan's numerous small and scattered but fertile lowland areas. The process of forming those lowlands has been complex, however, because of the continual interplay of two key variables: long-term tectonic uplift and short-term swings of global temperature.

Had global temperature – and consequently sea level – remained stable, the story of Japan's lowland formation would be quite straightforward. That is to say, because the archipelago's mountains are of such recent provenance, most of their slopes are steep and their surface cover of regolith (stones, gravel and soil) is easily disturbed. Snowmelt and heavy rainfall, especially the torrential downpours of typhoons, can produce a high rate of erosion and recurrent landslides. The waterborne material descends to the lowlands then settles out when stream flow decelerates, producing alluvial fans. Because the heaviest pieces of material drop first, these fans are characterized by rocky debris in their upper reaches, followed by phases of gravel, sand and silt as stream flow slows and ends its descent, whether on existing coastal plains or at the shore. Volcanic ash and other debris add to the material that composes these lowlands.

Because of the ongoing – although very slow – tectonic uplift, of course, streams must continually extend themselves to reach the shore. So, during periods of heavy flow they dislodge some of the sediments they had earlier deposited and move them farther downstream, thereby slowly extending the lowland seaward but not altering its basic pattern of deposition.

In the absence of long-term temperature fluctuations, that is to say, Japan's lowlands would simply have grown larger and larger as mountainsides slowly eroded, volcanoes ejected tephra, and the land ever-so-slowly rose. However, the making of those lowlands has not been that simple because they have mostly formed during the recent 2 million years of the Pleistocene glacial age.

To elaborate, because vast quantities of the planet's water were stored in polar and continental glaciers for long periods during the Pleistocene epoch, sea level dropped sharply and stayed low for millennia. Three major glaciations, which occurred around 500,000, 200,000 and 21–18,000 yBP, are all thought to have lowered sea level by more than 120 m.[20] Lesser cold spells between them caused lesser drops.

As glaciation advanced and sea level fell, streams that once flowed leisurely across the sedimentary lowlands they had previously created began to accelerate. As that happened, they loosened sediments and carried them further seaward. Because of the extent of sea-level drop, that trend gradually washed vast quantities of sedimentary material seaward, in the process carving new valleys out of former coastal flatlands whose outer flanks might survive as terrace deposits. Centuries or millennia later, as climate warmed again, glaciers would melt, oceans rise and sea-water flow back into these new valleys, forming estuaries into which rivers would drop their loads of sediment. That process created ever-thicker accumulations of submerged sediment, which would later emerge as dry lowland when climate cooling again caused sea level to drop and coastlines to recede.

Most recently this rhythmic cycle of global cooling and warming, and consequent erosion and rebuilding of coastal plains, occurred during the millennia from about 25,000 to 6,000 yBP. The depths of cold weather during 21–18,000 yBP, which had lowered sea level some 130–140 m, gave way to warming that gradually refilled the new valleys. The warming trend peaked around 6,000 yBP, shifting to a moderate cooling trend that by 4–3,000 yBP had again moved the shoreline seaward, re-establishing alluvial plains and giving Japan much of the lowland configuration it has today.

14

The terrace deposits, meanwhile, were being slowly etched with side valleys, while their more easily dislodged soil materials were washed from the exposed flanks. In consequence the terraces today tend to have drier, coarser and less fertile soil than adjoining alluvial lowlands. Accordingly, through the centuries of human habitation, many have remained wooded, have yielded fuel and fertilizer material or have been used for less intensive forms of agriculture, such as orchardry.

Glacial cycles have thus played a major role in shaping Japan's lowlands. The cycles have not, however, had an equivalent impact on high elevations. In striking contrast to northwestern Europe and much of North America, Japan was not buried under vast glaciers that scraped soil off uplands, wore down peaks and sharp ridges, and deposited the accumulated material in valleys and on plains as low hillocks and thick layers of glacial till (a jumble of boulders, smaller rocks, gravel, sand and clay). Rather, while the epochs of cold weather did transform much of Hokkaido and higher elevations of northern Honshu from temperate forest into tundra, they only produced a few field glaciers in high mountain valleys. So, most of Japan's high peaks and ridges and steep mountainsides have remained intact down to the present.

**Figure 1.5:** Extensively clear-cut mountainsides and terraced lower slopes, with deep snow cover, in central Nagano Prefecture, 1963

Finally, one other aspect of these glacial episodes deserves note because of its biological effect. Global cooling lowered sea level enough to produce long periods when Japan was rejoined to the continent by "land bridges" of dry, re-vegetated sea bed. One set of such "bridges" linked Honshu to Hokkaido, thence Sakhalin, and from there, Siberia. More important here, however, was the transformation of China's shallow coastal seas into a sprawling lowland – the "Yellow Plain" – that linked southwest Japan to Korea and eastern China.

**Figure 1.6:** Spring flooding within the levees of the Edogawa in northeast Tokyo, 1956

As we note more fully in Chapter 2, the existence of this lowland enabled plant species and their associated fauna, which had been forced southward during millennia of gradual cooling, to migrate northward again during the millennia of warming. As a consequence the rich biotic community of east Asia was able to re-establish itself in Japan, giving the archipelago sufficient biodiversity to cope with its great North–South length, its high and steeply pitched mountains, its pronounced seasonal changes, and, in recent millennia, the presence of an increasingly dense human population.

As is implicit in a number of the foregoing comments, the effects of geological process are strongly shaped by the global location in which they occur. So let us examine the ways in which Japan's global location has influenced life there.

## GLOBAL LOCATION

Japan's global location has been a major determinant of its climate and, as a corollary, its biotic composition. The key factor has been its position on the eastern flank of Eurasia in the northern temperate zone.[21] Two secondary factors – ambient ocean currents and the archipelago's North–South length – have shaped the specific ways in which its different regions have been affected by that position.

We can perhaps highlight the importance of Japan's position East of Eurasia by comparing the archipelago with the British Isles and then with eastern North America in the same latitudes, roughly 30°–45° North.[22]

As sites of human history, Japan proper and the British Isles are remarkably similar. Both societies were strongly shaped by nearby continental populations; both evolved through the same sequence from early forager to today's industrial society; and in many ways their social structures and values have been comparable through the ages.

In terms of environment, however, and despite their similarity as island clusters a few score kilometers off the same continent, the two are strikingly dissimilar in both climate and biotic communities. Although the British Isles at their southernmost point in Cornwall are some 500 km more northerly than Japan's most northern point in Hokkaido, Japan has far colder and far snowier winters. It also, however, has far hotter and wetter summers. And whereas Britain's native plant community is of very modest diversity, reflecting that of nearby continental areas, Japan's is very rich, reflecting the great biodiversity of east Asia.

Comparing insular Japan to continental eastern North America from Georgia to Maine, one is struck by the dissimilarity of the human histories. Whereas Japan's society evolved from forager to predominantly agricultural during the millennium or more before 700 CE, eastern North American society remained predominantly forage-based until about 1700 CE. And had there been no invasion, conquest and extirpation by Europeans, it probably would still be such. Nevertheless, in terms of both climate and biota, Japan proper is very comparable to that strip of eastern North America. The annual rhythms of rain and snow are similar, even to their autumnal maritime cyclonic storm systems (typhoons, hurricanes). And the biotic communities are much more similar in terms of diversity, durability and regional distribution.

So let us examine Japan's position on Eurasia's eastern flank to see how global location has helped shape the archipelago's history.

### Japan's Position in Eurasia

This position influences climate throughout the archipelago by making it strongly subject to easterly flowing air masses that traverse the continent. During winter months, dense, cold air flowing southeastward from Siberia sweeps out over the Sea of Japan and across the archipelago, maintaining a fairly stationary cold front to its southeast, and thereby assuring Japan relatively stable but cold wintertime temperatures.

As those cold Siberian winds sweep down across the Sea of Japan, they lift moisture from its relatively warm surface and proceed to drop it as snow when the winds ascend the high mountain chains of Honshu. That precipitation gives the region from about Fukui city northeastward a depth of snow that can range from a meter at lower levels to 3 m in the higher mountains. By the time those rising air masses clear the ridges, however, they have dropped most of their moisture, and as a result the winter months of Japan's eastern seaboard tend to be dry, sunny and cold.

As the orbiting Earth's northern hemisphere tilts sunward, the air in that hemisphere warms and winter passes. The Siberian air mass loses density and becomes unable to sustain its front southeast of Japan. As the front retreats, moist warm air from the southwest begins streaming across the archipelago. Powered by winds that the towering peaks of the Himalaya Mountains have steered eastward across the Arabian Sea, India and Bay of Bengal, this warm, water-laden monsoon air then flows across Southeast Asia, up over southeast China and its adjoining seas, and on to Japan and the northern Pacific.

During June and early July this monsoon weather (*baiu*) brings ample rain to Japan South of Hokkaido, fostering vigorous crop growth. By mid-July, however, the flow of Southeast Asian air has pressed further westward into continental east Asia, and then much of Japan, becomes subject to hot but drier air circulating over the northern Pacific region. In northern Honshu and Hokkaido, meanwhile, cooler air streaming down from the Sea of Okhotsk frequently displaces that hot air, cooling the region (the so-called *yamase* effect) and slowing the growth of agricultural crops.

By summer's end, as air masses over northern Eurasia begin to cool again, the Siberian cold front starts pushing back southeastward toward Japan. That change introduces a new period of rainy weather (*shūu*) by causing warm air from the South to cool and drop its moisture as it moves over the archipelago.

More strikingly, far to the south of Japan, westward-traveling cyclonic storms that form over the equatorial Pacific start turning northwestward over the Philippines and South China, arcing northward and eventually moving northeastward along the Siberian front. In the process they bring a few typhoons – 3–4 per year on average – to the southerly regions of Japan, usually during September/October. Despite the flooding and sporadic damage they do, these typhoons and other autumn rain also enable farmers in the archipelago's southern half to raise winter crops successfully despite the relative dryness of the winter period when the Siberian high again covers the archipelago.

In sum, Japan's position on the eastern flank of temperate-zone Eurasia gives it a pattern of clearly delineated seasons that usually provide ample, dependable precipitation. In the southern half of the archipelago, moreover, ambient temperature is warm enough so that farmers can engage in double-cropping, thereby increasing substantially their annual yield-per-acre.

### Ambient Ocean Currents

Two ocean currents flank Japan proper. The stronger, more consequential of the two is the Japan Current (*Kuroshio*), the local leg of the grand, clockwise-circling North Pacific current. It carries warm water from equatorial regions northward along the Ryukyu Island chain up to Kyushu. There a portion flows into the Sea of Japan, where it moves northward along its eastern flank. The warm water that it brings in helps sustain a rich and more warm-water-oriented population of marine biota. And, as noted above, by warming the surface waters, it helps maximize the snowfall on Japan's western seaboard.

The greater portion of the Japan Current bends eastward below Kyushu and moves along the archipelago's southern littoral. It flows past Shikoku, central Honshu and on eastward toward North America, where it loops south to start another circuit westward. As it flows by southern Japan, the Current adds warmth and moisture to the region, especially when warm air from Southeast Asia overflows the archipelago during early summer. Also, Japan's southern littoral is so richly endowed with shallow seas and bays that it has long sustained an uncommonly rich marine bio-system, and the Current contributes to that richness.

The Japan Current has also had a role in the long-term maintenance of Japan's terrestrial biodiversity. During the millennia of gradual warming that followed glacial periods, the vast Yellow Plain southwest of Japan would gradually re-flood. As that occurred, plant species found it more and more difficult to re-migrate northward. Some of those species, however, would have seeds, fruit or even rooted specimens dropped by wind, rain or flood into the ocean, and the Japan Current could then carry them northward and deposit some on coastal sites in the Ryukyus or Japan proper, thereby re-introducing them to the archipelago.

The other ocean current is the Chishima Current (*Oyashio*). It is a regional phenomenon of the northwest Pacific. A portion is cold current flowing south-westward from the Bering Sea. As that current descends the Kurile Island chain, it is supplemented by a current circling clockwise in the Sea of Okhotsk. A portion of the latter's southward flow passes through the Kuriles and on down the eastern seaboard of Hokkaido and northern Honshu, while a second outflow of Okhotsk water to the West of Sakhalin moves southward down the western flank of the Sea of Japan. In contrast to the Japan Current, the Chishima Current lowers ambient temperature, particularly in northeastern Honshu (Tôhoku), thereby lowering its agricultural productivity. Also, it fosters a marine community that is very different from that found on Japan's southern littoral.

Unfortunately, on all shorelines of Japan, industrial pollution and over-harvesting have decimated the natural maritime community. In some places it has been partially replaced by fish and seafood farms; many other marine areas simply survive, severely depleted of life forms.

### North–South Length

While all of Japan proper lies within the northern temperate zone, the archi-pelago's great length means that its climate ranges from sub-tropical in southern Kyushu to cold temperate in northern Honshu and Hokkaido. Accordingly, both its natural vegetation and its agricultural production show great regional variation.

As we note more fully in Chapter 2, Japan's natural vegetation varies greatly from North to South. It ranges from coniferous boreal forests in the North through a broad array of mixed, mainly deciduous broadleaf woodlands to sub-tropical evergreen broadleaf stands in the South.[23] These richly diverse forests have been the home of such signature "Japanese" trees as *akamatsu* (red pine), *iroha momiji* (Japanese red maple), *keyaki* (zelkova), *kuri* (chestnut) and *sugi* (cryptomeria). They have also supported a diverse population of tropical grasses (bamboos), which range from the ubiquitous and perdurable 2–3 ft tall understorey growth of *sasa* to the grand bamboos whose new shoots can surge upward to nearly their full height of 20–40 ft or so in a matter of weeks during the spring.

Besides being evident in its natural vegetation, Japan's great North–South length and corresponding range of climate is clearly evident in its agricultural experience. The cold winters of the archipelago's northern half have limited its crop variety to those that could sprout and fully ripen between spring and autumn frosts. One crop per year has long been the limit, and only in recent centuries have varieties of wet rice been developed that could be grown there even in summer. Along the southern littoral, on the other hand, double- and even triple-cropping has been possible, commonly with a summer rice crop being followed by a winter dry grain crop plus sometimes a vegetable crop. Tea plantations have mostly been found in south temperate regions, as have persimmon (*kaki*) and mandarin orange (*mikan*) orchards. During the past century apple growing has become established, and those orchards tend to be in more northerly regions, along with the dairy farming that is also a recent development.

### Some Human Consequences

Finally, let us focus briefly on some of the ways in which Japan's geography and global location have influenced its human history. As mentioned above, the basic patterns of human settlement and land use have been strongly shaped by topography and climate. In addition, the fact that northwest Kyushu and Tsushima lie closer to the mainland than any other place in the archipelago has surely been critical to their role as the major entry point for continental peoples and social practices, at least during the most recent 2,500 years or so.

New people and new technologies – such as those of agriculture, architecture, literacy, mining and warfare – have mostly entered there. And from there the key avenue of their dissemination has been the Inland Sea. As human groups acquired new capabilities, regional imbalances of social power developed, which found expression in diverse forms of conflict and interaction until the new capabilities were more fully diffused. That process surely was slowed by the archipelago's great length and by its mountainous character, particularly the central cordillera, which so firmly separated southwest from northeast.

For a long while political elites that were established on the margins of the Inland Sea, all the way from northern Kyushu to its eastern end, jockeyed for power. Gradually, however, the obstacles to travel presented by the central cordillera were overcome and social change spread northeastward into the Kantô and Tôhoku regions. As that occurred, the geography of conflict also shifted, with the East–West rivalry more and more pitting those in the Inland Sea vicinity against those East of the cordillera. And in recent centuries that long-lasting tension between northeast and southwest has periodically reared its head in political violence while finding enduring expression in semi-humorous cultural prejudices of diverse sorts.

The Japanese experience reminds us, that is to say, that though we may try to ignore the geographical factors that shape our lives, those factors will in the end have it their way.

\* \* \*

In summary, then, the archipelago we know as Japan is one of the world's youngest major parcels of terrestrial real estate. Basically it has the land forms, overall configuration and temporal rhythms we find there today because long-term geological processes have caused (and are still causing) it to rise as it has, when it has, and where it has. Because of its location, it has always been subject to the climatic patterns of the Eurasia-North Pacific region even as those have cycled through the grand changes that culminated in Pleistocene Ice Ages and the inter-glacial phase of today.

Glacial phases periodically transformed the archipelago into a chilly region of boreal and temperate conifer forest. Thanks to the existence of the Japan Current and the glacial-age presence of the Yellow Plain and other "land bridges" to the continent, however, when the world warmed again, the archipelago was able to recover its full array of warm-era vegetation and accompanying fauna. And it was in the context of those ice-age fluctuations that humans first encountered the archipelago, beginning that brief period of humanly influenced change that has helped give Japan its present-day character.

# 2  *Forager Society to ca. 500 BCE*

From the outset, human society in Japan – as everywhere – has been shaped by its environmental context. Conversely, as the millennia have passed, humans have played an ever-more powerful role in shaping that context. During the long era of foraging culture, human impact on the biome was severely limited, both spatially and temporally. Nevertheless, as we shall see, there were hints even then of the complex interactions that were to develop in recent centuries and emerge as the defining issue of our own day.

Archaeologists have long categorized forager society by the stone tools their members used. The earlier or more "primitive" form, called "paleolithic" ("old stone" age), was a society that utilized rough or chipped pieces of stone as implements for chopping, scraping, cutting and such like. Later, humans refined their tool production, selecting those raw materials that were more amenable to splitting and sharpening, and then polishing the stone to make sharper and more diverse stone points, blades and other objects. These "neolithic" ("new stone" age) people then went on to develop pottery and diverse other new technologies and social arrangements.

In Japan and its northeast Asian environs, however, it appears that paleolithic people learned to make and use pottery before they acquired polished-stone-tool technology.[1] So the temporal categories we use here are "pre-pottery" and "pottery". The latter period, commonly called Jômon, is so named because of the "cord markings" (*jômon*) that were impressed on the surface of pots in the course of their production.[2]

Regarding both phases of Japan's forager society, one wonders when and how humans reached the islands, from where, and why. One wonders how that development related to climate changes of the Pleistocene epoch. Once they were in Japan, how did those people live; how did their arrangements vary over time and from place to place; how did their presence affect the ambient bio-system and vice versa? And finally – to foreshadow Chapter 3 – how and why did those forager arrangements eventually give way to agricultural patterns of sustenance?

## ENVIRONMENTAL CONTEXT

Humans reached Japan late in the Pleistocene epoch, most likely doing so during cold phases when sea level was so low that the region was approachable on foot. However, the chronology of both climatic fluctuations and forager-culture developments is imprecise at best. And the early stages are unclear in the extreme. Nevertheless, one suspects that human developments of the era were firmly shaped by the ebb and flow of climate changes.

One can roughly plot the cycles of cold and warmth as follows:[3]

| Colder | Warmer |
|---|---|
| ca. 500–400,000 yBP | |
| | ca. 300,000 yBP |
| ca. 120–110,000 yBP | |
| | ca. 100–80,000 yBP |
| ca. 70–50,000 yBP | |
| | ca. 50–33,000 yBP |
| ca. 33–28,000 yBP | |
| | ca. 28–25,000 yBP |
| ca. 25–15,000 yBP | |
| | ca. 14,500–13,000 yBP |
| ca. 12,500–11,500 yBP | |
| | ca. 11,000–5,000 yBP |
| ca. 4,500–2,000 yBP | |
| | ca. 2,000 yBP ff |

It should be noted that within these phases, especially the earlier ones, there were intermediate fluctuations. Indeed, the "cold" phase 500–400,000 yBP may well have held as many oscillations as the period from 100,000 yBP down to today.

Also, each phase can be described in terms of earlier millennia of warming or cooling and later millennia of cooling or warming. For example, the "warm" period 50–33,000 yBP consisted of several millennia of gradual warming, which seem to have given way ca. 41,000 yBP to a renewed cooling trend. And the "cold" period 33–28,000 yBP (which should perhaps be dated from 35,000) may have started warming again about 31,000 yBP.

These climatic cycles played a role in human affairs in two ways. First, they altered sea level and thereby changed global shorelines, forming and subsequently destroying vast areas of lowland, and affecting the capacity of humans – as well as other fauna and flora – to move hither and yon. Second, they altered both mean temperatures and the levels and patterns of precipitation. These latter variables changed biotic communities, thereby altering substantially the types and quantities of food available for human consumption in particular localities.

*Sea Level*

Changes in sea level matter, of course, because Japan today is an archipelago separated from continental Asia by straits. Not all the separations are equal, however, as this table indicates.[4]

*Present-day Depth of Straits Around Japan*

| Name | Depth (meters) |
|---|---|
| Tartary (Mamiya) Strait | 15 m |
| *(between Siberia and Sakhalin)* | |
| Soya Strait | 60 m |
| *(between Sakhalin and Hokkaido)* | |
| Tsugaru Strait | 100 m |
| *(between Hokkaido and Honshu)* | |
| Tsushima and Korea Straits | over 100 m |
| *(between Kyushu, Tsushima and Korea)* | |
| Yellow Sea | less than 50 m average |
| *(between China, Korea and Japan)* | |

Regarding the Kurile Island chain, at about three places along its length, it is cut by channels more than 200 m deep. The Ryukyu chain is similarly cut by deep channels, and segments of the Bonins are separated by even greater ocean depths.

The sea floors of these several straits are regularly scoured by ocean currents, so their absolute elevations today may be little changed from what they were throughout the later Pleistocene epoch. It seems likely, however, that the floor of the Yellow Sea is appreciably higher today than in earlier times because of the immense volume of sediments deposited on it by the many rivers of the region, most especially the Huang Ho (Yellow River), which drains northwestern China, but also the Liao, which drains South Manchuria, and the Yangtze, which drains South-central China.

These differences in the depth of straits matter because they mean that Japan's dry-land connections to Asia during glacial ages were of extremely dissimilar duration. The durations differed so greatly because global climate change and resultant changes in sea level occurred so very gradually (see Appendix 1).

Thus, to look at Japan's continental linkages since the last glacial maximum, Sakhalin might well have been firmly linked to Siberia for tens of thousands of years, before, during and after that maximum, staying linked until roughly 10–9,000 yBP. Sakhalin and Hokkaido would have been joined for a considerably lesser term, perhaps until about 13,000 years ago. And the rest of Japan (today's Honshu-Shikoku-Kyushu) would have been linked to Asia via Sakhalin and Tsushima for a yet-shorter period, perhaps a few thousand years at most, until roughly 17–16,000 yBP.

In short, if any humans – or other creatures – on mainland Asia had reason to move by land into the area we call Japan, they would have had a considerably longer-lasting opportunity to get there – at least to Hokkaido – via the Tartary Strait than via the Tsushima vicinity. And even if they were equipped with small boats, whether dugouts, rafts or vessels made of animal pelt, the northern approach would have been easier because the straits there are narrower, even at high sea level.

*Temperature and Precipitation*

Besides creating and melting glaciers and thereby causing sea level to fall and rise, global temperature fluctuations caused striking changes in biotic communities. We noted in Chapter 1 the temperate-zone character of Japan's present-day bio-system and the crucial role played by the "Yellow Plain", the glacial-age flatland that linked southern Japan to mainland Asia, in maintaining the richness of that system.

During the most recent glacial maximum – let's say 20,000 yBP for a convenient date – when Japan was one long, unbroken "arcland" looping around the enclosed Sea of Japan, the distribution of plant (and hence animal) species was very different from that of warm periods, such as today.[5] Proceeding from North to South, the differences in vegetation may be summarized as follows:

(1) Treeless and scrub-brush tundra exist in Japan today only as "alpine tundra", which is found above the tree line on a few high peaks and ridges in northeastern Japan. However, 20,000 years ago tundra blanketed northern Hokkaido and dotted the higher elevations of mountain ranges in Honshu southward to the central cordillera.

(2) Boreal conifer forest (mainly select fir and spruce) is found today only on uplands of the northern half of Hokkaido and high ridgelines from the cordillera northward. But 20,000 years ago it reached southward from coastal regions of Hokkaido across all of northern Honshu and onward to cover the mountainous areas of central and southwestern Japan.

(3) Temperate conifer forest (fir, spruce, hemlock, pine) is limited today to a few higher elevations of Kyushu and Shikoku. But 20,000 years ago it covered nearly all the lower elevations of Japan from the Kantô Plain westward.

(4) Cool-temperate deciduous broadleaf forest (mainly oak or beech with mixed walnut, elm, linden, chestnut, horse chestnut) covers much of Japan today, extending from central Hokkaido South to the vicinity of Lake Biwa and to higher elevations southwest of there. At 20,000 yBP it existed only as mixed conifer/broadleaf stands situated on warmer coastal areas that today are mostly submerged beneath sea water.

(5) Finally, warm-temperate evergreen broadleaf forest (mainly evergreen oak with other non-deciduous species) covers the lower elevations of Japan today from the Kantô vicinity westward – insofar as those areas are not given over to agriculture and urban sprawl. Some 20,000 years ago, however, such stands were found only at the southwest tip of the arcland, mostly on land now re-submerged beneath the sea.

Temperature change was the key factor behind these radical shifts in forest composition. And the slowness of that change was a crucial consideration: had temperature changed too rapidly, plant life would simply have died in situ. Vegetative travel, after all, is mainly an inter-generational thing. Plants of a particular type – whether tree, vine, shrub, forb, grass or whatever – occupy a given range, and during a cooling phase those at higher elevations or on the northern edge of the range grow less well and produce fewer viable seeds, which in turn fare less well when they sprout.

Meanwhile, plants at lower sites or on the southern edge of that range fare better and produce more seeds. The seeds that sprout and mature on the southerly forest edge yield more seeds in turn and are scattered around, assisted by wind, rain and those creatures that deposit them hither and yon. Gradually, generation after generation, the species works its way southward and down to lower elevations, a few meters per generation. But given adequate time and circumstance, vegetation can travel thousands of kilometers in search of an optimal home.

During the millennia of Pleistocene cooling, southward movement of species within Japan was facilitated by the generally North–South alignment of ridges and valleys. Endangered species were able to escape even further South thanks to the re-emergence of coastal lowlands and the Yellow Plain. Then, millennia later, with warming renewed, that slowly shrinking plain, together with the Japan Current, facilitated the return of species to the archipelago.

Apart from temperature fluctuation and resultant shoreline movement, changes in rates and patterns of precipitation also play a role in forest adaptation. During the glacial maximum of ca. 21–18,000 yBP, the arcland received less than a third as much precipitation annually as Japan does today.[6] The vegetational impact of this reduced moisture level seems to have been most evident on the Sea of Japan littoral and in southwestern Japan.

On the Sea of Japan's East flank, both snow and rainfall were sharply diminished. This was so because when that Sea was closed off from the ocean and functioned as a giant lake, the warming effect of the Japan Current was nullified. So its water became colder and westerly winds blowing across it from Siberia picked up comparatively little moisture to deposit on the arcland's western flank.

Rainfall also diminished because global cooling altered monsoon patterns in the south Asian region.[7] The cooling caused drier winds from continental southwest Asia to sweep southward around the Himalayas, across India and Southeast Asia, and up to eastern China and the Japan vicinity. As a consequence, during glacial millennia the arcland experienced far less summer precipitation than in warmer times.

The glacial combination of coldness and dryness favored hardy conifers, such as fir and spruce. They handle coldness better than do deciduous broadleaf species thanks to their ample pitch, and they require less moisture because they do not have to replace their entire leaf system annually. In consequence, as noted above, most of the glacial-age arcland was covered with conifer forests, while the broadleaf stands found so widely today were almost non-existent.

When global warming enabled the Japan Current again to flow into the Sea of Japan and wet monsoons to flow across the region, the Sea of Japan littoral experienced heavy snowmelt in spring and ample rains during the summer. The run-off persistently leached and eroded hilly surfaces, reducing both soil fertility and stability. Under those circumstances the hardy conifer forests of colder millennia gradually gave way to cryptomeria, an evergreen that flourishes in warm, wet climates and on impoverished soils. Indeed, cryptomeria was so well suited that it could prevail over the beech and oak forests that were also reappearing with warmer weather.

A comparable pattern was evident along the southern littoral in Shikoku and Honshu. Although those areas did not lose topsoil to snowmelt, they lost it to monsoon downpours and typhoons. So there, too, as warming trends advanced, cryptomeria found favorable conditions on eroded hillsides, displacing boreal conifers and outlasting the reviving deciduous species. Most recently this cycle of cryptomeria revival accelerated during the warm millennia around 10–8,000 yBP, creating many of the lush stands that would later underwrite centuries of pre-industrial architectural grandeur.[8]

For the archipelago as a whole, the millennia of post-glacial warming witnessed a gradual re-establishment of the regionally varied natural forest of recent centuries, with its mix of tree species, variegated understorey, and diverse birds, mammals and other creatures.

## EARLY ARRIVALS (PRE-POTTERY)

These long-term changes in vegetation mattered to humans in the region because vegetation strongly influenced an area's animal composition, and humans relied heavily on animals as food. During glacial ages, northeast Asia supported an array of hardy beasts, notably Naumann's elephant, giant deer, bison and the woolly mammoth, which foraged on the region's tundra, scrub woodland and transitional grassland. Their presence, in turn, supported a predator population that included bears and wolves as well as humans. As climate gradually changed and forest composition evolved, the herbivores adapted their foraging territories, in general terms moving southeastward during cooling epochs and northwestward as the region warmed. Perforce, the carnivores followed them.

Humans of these pre-pottery millennia utilized fire for cooking and heating, and they had stone tools usable for cutting, scraping and digging. For most of the era, however, they apparently did not have weapons sufficient to capture and kill large animals, and they were ill-equipped to challenge hungry bears or wolves for a carcass. So, one suspects that they scavenged left-overs opportunistically, bringing meat home to their caves, rock shelters or – later – crude huts to cook on their fire. They supplemented that meat with such edible vegetable matter (nuts, berries, select tubers) and other nutrients as they might find, including fish or other seafood where available.

As the preceding section attempted to suggest, evidence regarding Pleistocene plant distribution is relatively rich, and the logic connecting it to climate trends is reasonably straightforward. Compared with that, the evidence of early human presence in the Japanese archipelago is very thin, and the logic of its relationship to environmental trends is debatable. The following comments attempt to sum up the implications of scholarly research.[9]

In Chapter 1 we noted that Japan's location was a key factor shaping its climate and biological community. Location also directly shaped its human experience. As one scholar succinctly put it:

> located at the easternmost reaches of the Eurasian continent, [the Japanese archipelago] was the last region of that part of the world to be reached by human settlers.[10]

That observation seems to have applied to earlier hominid forms as much as to Homo sapiens.

To start with the oldest evidence, around a million years ago, hominids classified as Homo erectus – and known from their discovery site as Peking Man or Sinanthropus pekinensis – lived in the vicinity of today's Beijing (Peking).[11] From whence they came, how many lived in the region and how widely they ventured in search of food are all unknown. However, they may well have derived from ancestors living to the North or West of there, who had gradually moved southeastward as the animals they sought adjusted their habitat in response to the migration of those plant species that sustained them.

Moreover, during phases of global cooling, these hominids could have followed game farther and farther out onto the Yellow Plain as coastline receded and more and more of the region evolved decade after decade from open sea to coastal shallows, brackish swamp, shrubby grassland, and eventually mixed woodland of one or another sort.

During the coldest millennia, Japan was an arcland firmly attached to the continent. But only along its more southerly coastlines and on lowlands to the southwest did it hold the mixed deciduous forests that would sustain a diverse fauna. It may well be, however, that hominids, as well as other fauna living on the Yellow Plain, could have crossed the river that drained the Sea of Japan, at least if its surface froze during winter months. And any creatures moving southeastward from Siberia could have reached Japan via Sakhalin.

In any case, although evidences of Homo erectus in the Beijing vicinity date to a million years ago, as well as a few more recent dates, whether any were in Japan during these millennia remains unclear. Signs of early hominid presence in the arcland are few and of uncertain import.[12]

There does seem to be firm evidence of a hominid presence in Miyagi Prefecture, in the vicinity of present-day Sendai, from around 130,000 yBP, when a warm phase was giving way to a new glacial age. Solid evidence of an earlier presence in Japan has not yet been found, but its absence does not settle the matter. After all, many of the most plausible areas of occupancy during cold periods – when the arcland was relatively accessible if not very hospitable – are now beneath the sea, having been destroyed by the erosion of lowlands and the subsequent flooding of glacial-age valleys and coastal plains.

Well before the time of the Miyagi occupancy, Homo erectus had given way on the continent to other, more "modern" humans. Most well-known are

Homo neanderthalis, who ranged across Europe, the Near East and west Asia. In addition, recent findings have established the presence of a group closely related to neanderthalis, "who lived in Asia from roughly 400,000 to 50,000 years ago".[13] Informally called "Denisovans" after a discovery site in Siberia, they ranged from Siberia to Southeast Asia. Therefore, it seems very likely they would have reached Japan at one time or another, and they probably were occupants of the Miyagi site.

Moreover, around 125,000 yBP, people of a similarly modern character were present in the Beijing vicinity, and their stone tools resemble those found at the Miyagi site. These similarities suggest another wave of migration as human groups responded to changing faunal and floral distributions and associated changes in sea level by moving southeastward in cooling eras or northwestward as climate warmed.

It seems likely that at least a few such humans – Denisovans, one suspects – were in Japan most of the time thereafter. An archaeological site in Kyushu that may date to some 100,000 yBP contained stone choppers and other items resembling those of the Beijing-area people. And a site near Tochigi City on the northern Kantô Plain indicates that comparable humans were present, at least periodically, during ca. 80–40,000 yBP.[14] The stone tools found at many sites of this era also resemble those found at Siberian sites, which may indicate that they were introduced via Sakhalin.[15]

By 40,000 yBP, however, yet another change was occurring in the Eurasian population of humans, and it would shortly reach Japan. Somewhat earlier, roughly 60,000 yBP, a species usually identified as Homo sapiens moved beyond eastern Africa onto the Eurasian continent. In following millennia they spread across the landscape. Precisely how they maneuvered between, co-existed or interbred with, fought and eventually displaced the other humans whom they encountered is unclear. It appears, however, that by 40,000 yBP descendants of those newest emigrants from Africa were present in the vicinity of Beijing.[16]

At the time a warm phase was beginning to cool, and during the following several thousand years, the region again moved into a cold period and Japan again became an accessible arcland. By about 35–30,000 yBP, Homo sapiens appear to have reached the arcland, their presence suggested by stone tool assemblages that differed from earlier ones but were similar to some found in both northeast China and the Amur River region.

The Amur flows eastward from Mongolia, looping around Manchuria in a grand zigzag and emptying into the Sea of Okhotsk near the northern tip of Sakhalin. Particularly if people in that region used boats, they could well have reached the arcland via the Amur and Sakhalin.[17] But even on foot, as they followed game adapting to climate change, they could have reached the arcland by either the northerly or southerly route during the coldest millennia.

It does appear that both entryways were used. During the millennia 30–20,000 yBP, when the arcland warmed somewhat and then cooled to its most recent glacial maximum, evidences of human presence became more pronounced. Even then, however, the total numbers of people at any given moment may have been very modest, perhaps a few thousand or even fewer.

Nonetheless, the evidence suggests that people were living there for enough consecutive generations that they were improvising locally. They devised techniques to use local types of rock in tool production, and they adapted to the changing environment sufficiently to assure their food supply. The broader regional diversity in stone tools suggests that migrants from the Yellow Plain region were prevailing in Kyushu and western Honshu, while migrants from the Amur region predominated from about the Kantô region northward.[18] And during the next several thousand years, those patterns persisted.

It is possible, too, that some humans reached Japan from more southerly regions. The Japan Current could well have carried sailing people from the Philippines northward past Taiwan and along the Ryukyu Islands to southerly Japan.

## JÔMON CULTURE (POTTERY)

Around 17–16,000 yBP, strange things began to happen in the arcland. They seemed to reflect strange things occurring on the wider Asian and even global scene. How these things related to one another is still unclear, but they eventuated by about 12,000 yBP in formation of the social order we know as Jômon.

In subsequent millennia, complexities were added to the initial perplexities. They are evident in the relevant archeological evidence, which is voluminous and varied, especially for the millennia from roughly 7,000 yBP onward.[19] For example, at the large, long-lived Sannai Maruyama site near Aomori, at the North end of Honshu, researchers have unearthed a wealth of diverse items. These include:

various kinds of hunting and food-processing tools, such as arrowheads, stemmed scrapers, grinding stones and stone mortars. [Also] various types of bone and ivory tools and ornaments, as well as wooden containers, lacquerware, basketry, cordage and textiles, [and an] abundance of exotic materials such as jade, amber, asphalt and obsidian.[20]

In its richness, evidence such as this reveals a complex but ambiguous picture. One can make a few generalizations about regional and temporal developments, but closer scrutiny reveals ample uncertainties. So let us examine the initial perplexities, the overall generalities and some of the ambiguities relating to Jômon society and changes therein, as evidenced in the surviving materials.

### Perplexities of the Onset

The key developments that invite attention seem to be these:

(1) Around 17,000 yBP the final Pleistocene Ice Age began to warm, probably doing so erratically.[21]
(2) A further influx of humans to the arcland seems to have occurred, most likely from the Amur River region and via Sakhalin, but also perhaps via the Yellow Plain.

(3) The migrants introduced a simple pottery and some new stone tools that evidently included spear points and arrowheads, which became prevalent across Japan over the next few thousand years.

(4) Large mammals (notably Naumann's elephant, the giant deer, bison and woolly mammoth) that had long been important to human diet in the region appear to have become extinct around this time.

(5) Even as these creatures were dying off, the human population seems to have begun growing in an unprecedented manner, with diet becoming more diverse and technology and social arrangements more complex.

\* \* \*

In terms of human-environment relations, the core questions provoked by the above developments seem to be these: why did humans evidently move southeastward rather than northwestward during a period of glacial warming, and why did the great mammals die off then, even as human numbers were rising? Are these unrelated trends or were they causally linked?

It is possible that climate change ravaged the mammals, but that seems very unlikely: they had survived how many prior cycles of cold and warm? Moreover, the die-off was a global northern-hemisphere experience. Was climate change in that hemisphere so radically different from that of the southern, where other large mammals continued to flourish?

Or perhaps a new micro-organism decimated the great beasts. But if so, why just the great herbivores, but evidently not other creatures, not even those – humans, for example – that ingested the great-herbivore meat?

If a trend such as either of these were decimating the large herbivore population in more northerly regions, that trend could well have prodded the humans to travel southeastward in search of alternative food and in flight from other hungry carnivores. Or if a micro-organism fatal to herbivores caused severe discomfort or illness among humans eating the meat, that situation could have prompted other group-members to try cooking other foods on their hot stones, perhaps discovering that boiling some otherwise inedible items in water would make them digestible. And in the process they might have stumbled on the technique of pottery-firing.[22] The resulting gradual change in diet could then have prompted movement in search of more of the new-type resources.

It seems more likely, however, that this mammalian die-off reflected the appearance of one new variable on the scene – humans equipped with bows, arrows and spears powerful enough to fell the great mammals and deter rival carnivores. Such weapons were new to northern Eurasia, it appears, and to North America, probably having crossed the Bering Straits during cold spells, much as they entered the arcland of Japan.[23]

Utilizing their new weapons, these humans were able to hunt, trap and kill the great beasts while keeping wolves and such at bay. With that food supply more sure – and perhaps supplemented by other foods cooked or processed in the new-fangled pottery – human numbers grew and their settlements became larger. However, the escalating demands on the giant-mammal population exceeded its reproductive capacity, and eventually the great beasts were so decimated that isolated survivors were unable to mate and produce offspring and simply died off. Insofar as smaller game and vegetable and marine foods were more prevalent in warmer areas, the loss of large game could have been the key factor propelling the well-armed humans southeastward and eventually into the arcland. There the process of great-mammal extinction seems to have played itself out by about 13,000 yBP.

Within the arcland, human weapons were not the only menace to the great mammals. The warming trend of those millennia gradually flooded its exposed straits, robbing them of escape routes to northern Eurasia. More importantly, perhaps, that trend also destroyed the vast flatlands of the Yellow Plain, the extensive ribbons of coastal lowland that bordered the arcland, and the sprawling interior lowlands that evolved into the Inland Sea. As those forested regions disappeared, the great mammals lost foraging range and became increasingly vulnerable to predators who could corner them in narrow, dead-end valleys – valleys from which smaller, more agile creatures could escape.

Even as the situation for great herbivores was deteriorating, however, the changing vegetation became more supportive of smaller animals and of the humans who increasingly preyed on them. Those trends enabled the humans, at least, to proliferate in the archipelago.

One scholar has characterized the invention of pottery as "the first deliberate use of chemical transformation by humankind".[24] Similarly, the use of bow and arrow may be considered one of the first complex applications of principles of physics. It is perhaps ironic that even from this early time, human manipulation of the ecosystem could have contributed to a pattern of unsustainable exploitation that eventuated in wide-ranging extinctions and forced the humans to develop alternative survival arrangements.

### Jômon Overall

Whatever factors spurred these northeast Asian people to develop archery and pottery technology and subsequently to move into the arcland, they had that effect. By around 16–14,000 yBP the new devices were widely employed. Evidence of their presence during these millennia has been found at archaeological sites stretching from Aomori in northern Honshu and Fukui on the Sea of Japan to the western edge of Shikoku and southern Kyushu.

During subsequent millennia, their descendants – and probably more immigrants via Sakhalin or other entryway – also developed other technical capabilities to accommodate their changing environment. They mastered the art of processing acorns and other nuts so as to remove their tannic acid and make them digestible. They constructed and deployed weirs to trap freshwater fish. And they learned how to catch and process various types of seafood, including fish, shellfish and such sea mammals as dolphins and beached whales. They also developed equipment and techniques for successfully hunting, capturing and processing smaller land mammals, including wild boar, Japanese serow, otter, marten, hare, weasel and deer.[25]

Thus well fed, the humans multiplied. No one knows, in fact, how many people were living on the archipelago at any moment during these millennia, but one scholar's intricate calculations yielded the numbers below. They suggest the success of human adaptation, especially in eastern Japan, to a post-great-mammal world.[26]

*Human Population Estimates for Jômon (and later) Japan*
*ca. 9,000–1,300 yBP*

| Period | Median Date | West Japan | East Japan |
|--------|-------------|------------|------------|
| Initial | 9,000 yBP | 2,800 | 17,300 |
| Early | 6,500 | 9,000 | 96,500 |
| Middle | 5,000 | 9,500 | 251,800 |
| Late | 3,800 | 19,600 | 40,700 |
| Final | 2,800 | 10,900 | 64,900 |
| | | | |
| Yayoi | 2,000 [AD 0] | 302,300 | 292,600 |
| Haji | 1,300 [AD 700] | 3,087,700 | 2,312,100 |

Certainly such population numbers cannot be taken literally; they may well overstate the scale of growth. However, they can reasonably be seen as suggesting both regional variation and temporal trends in Jômon society (as well as the later agricultural Yayoi and Haji societies).

Regarding the extreme regional variation in Jômon population, the numbers suggest that Japan from the Lake Biwa vicinity westward supported only a slender population prior to about 2,500 yBP [500 BC], while the area from Biwa northeastward displayed a long phase – roughly 3–4,000 years – of impressive growth. It is possible that the re-submersion of Tsushima Strait stymied migration from the continent to western Japan, whereas arrivals from the North were able to continue much longer. More importantly, perhaps, rising sea level affected southwest Japan far more than the northeast because it destroyed such vast lowlands and created such obstacles to travel within that part of the archipelago.

However, the most important factor in this regional variation likely was the change in vegetation. Whereas most of northeastern Japan came to be covered with deciduous broadleaf forest that supported a relatively rich and varied understorey of shrubs, forbs and grasses, woodland in the southwest came to be dominated by evergreen broadleaf stands that produced comparatively meager food for many herbivores, and hence for carnivores, as well as relatively little by way of berries, easily edible nuts and succulent shoots for humans.

Turning from regional differences to temporal trends, the trajectory of population growth prior to about 4,500 yBP reflects several factors: the long-term warming trend of those millennia; the human success in utilizing pottery, polished-stone tools and other devices to enhance their food supply; and the development of storage, housing and exchange arrangements that helped them maximize those successes. However, a cooling phase set in around 4,500 yBP, and that trend disrupted vegetation and hence the food supply. It affected the northeast, especially more mountainous regions, sooner, longer and more severely than the southwest, and resulted in the region's sharp drop in human numbers.

When that downward trend in population started to reverse around 2,500–3,000 yBP, it did so primarily because of another radical technological change. Most likely this one was introduced from the continent via the Tsushima Strait, and it affected the southwest centuries before it did the northeast. That change was the introduction by immigrants of well-developed agricultural techniques, which, as we note in Chapter 3, eventuated in remarkable changes in both the archipelago's human society and its bio-system.

### Regarding Ambiguities of Society and Culture

The era of "cord-marked" (*jômon*) pottery spanned some 10,000 years. Utilizing the population figures cited in the table above (and positing an average lifespan of 25 years), the archipelago's human population during those millennia might have totaled some 30–35 million people.[27]

That is an impressive total, but because it was spread over such a long era, it may conceal the sparsity of settlement at any given moment. Even around 5,000 yBP, when the Jômon population was at its peak, it numbered less than one person per square kilometer overall and fewer than four per square kilometer of lowland.[28] (For comparison's sake, Japan's population density in the year 2000 CE was about 340 people per km² of total area and 1,700 per km² of lowland.)

Whatever the numerical specifics, it was in toto a substantial human presence, and its passage is evident in the rich array of material artifacts that have survived and been recovered by archaeologists. Inferring social and cultural patterns from such artifacts is a tricky business, but let us look at the historical patterns suggested by the ceramic ware, stone tools, other artifacts, shell mounds and evidence on housing.

### 1. Ceramic Ware

The pottery of Japan is among the world's earliest and most elaborate "low-fired" ceramic ware. Dating from around 16,500 yBP or perhaps earlier, it initially consisted of cooking pots with simple surface decorations. By some 12,000 yBP, however, potters had developed a more elaborate decorative pattern of "cord-markings", which they achieved by rolling a strip of rope or cord across a pot's surface before firing it.

Perhaps because of their usefulness as cooking pots for converting diverse types of vegetable and maritime matter into palatable nutrients, pottery use spread across the arcland. And because clay usable in its production was quite widely distributed, local production appears to have become widespread, as suggested by the great diversity in pottery shapes and decorative styles.[29]

As millennia passed, pottery style became more decorative and even flamboyant, and ceramic products served more diverse functions. By around 7,500 yBP, pots were providing storage containers for acorns and other items as well as serving dishes for meals.[30] By 5,000 yBP, ceramic pieces were also serving as burial urns for infants and as lamp-oil containers for interior illumination, while clay figurines and phallic stones likely served ritual or spiritual functions that seem to have reflected growing socio-cultural complexity.[31] Finally, the presence of this elaborate and regionally variegated ceramic ware suggests that some people had acquired a special expertise in ceramic production, which they may have used to trade their output for other valuables and/or to serve as producers for higher-status figures.

### 2. Stone Tools

The stone-tool assemblages that archaeologists have meticulously salvaged and analyzed shed much light on Jômon society and its evolution. Together with the pottery, they suggest the linkages between occupants of the arcland/archipelago and adjoining continental regions.

They shed a much brighter light, however, on affairs within the archipelago. Thus, the dating, location, quantities, size, style and diversity of stone tools, together with temporal changes therein, reveal patterns of food acquisition, processing and consumption, and their variation through time and space. The raw materials from which stone tools were made, as well as other materials that were used with the stone, reveal aspects of social organization and regional interactions.

To elaborate some of these themes, the evidence shows early Jômon people modifying their hunting tools – shifting to smaller spear points and arrowheads – as the great mammals disappeared and smaller game became more central to their diet. The strong and persistent presence of grinding tools in western Japan suggests the greater dependence of people there on the acorns taken from their evergreen broadleaf woodlands, which they pounded and ground into meal, using pestles and stone mortars. In eastern Honshu, on the other hand, the large numbers of fish-hooks, spear/harpoon points and sinkers for use with fishing nets suggest that people there relied much more heavily on seafood.

Analysis of the tools' raw materials helps identify their probable sources and suggests the extent of trade or travel. Most notable, perhaps, was the widespread use of obsidian (a volcanic glass). It could be sharpened to make strong, hard tools with sharp edges, and hence was excellent for spear/harpoon points, arrowheads and scrapers. Being produced by volcanic activity, deposits of obsidian nodules were widely scattered about Japan and scores of sites were quarried to provide the raw material for flaking and polishing. It was utilized from early Jômon years onward, and as millennia advanced and its use increased, patterns of trade in obsidian grew more elaborate and extensive. Thus obsidian taken from quarries in today's Nagano Prefecture and from sites in the Izu vicinity was utilized in the Kantô region. The closer users were to a particular source, the more extensively they used stone from that site.

Most obsidian sources are found, however, in Kyushu and, especially, from the central cordillera northward into Hokkaido.[32] Between Kyushu and the cordillera, volcanic activity has been much less common and obsidian sites are rare. So dwellers in that large region had to obtain their material from relatively distant sources or make do with other, less satisfactory types of stone. Perhaps that dearth of obsidian was a factor limiting population growth in western Japan by restricting or reducing efficiency in hunting/fishing activity.

Jade was another type of stone that Jômon people were using widely by 5,000 yBP or earlier. Mainly employed as decorative beads, its use suggests a degree of luxury, at least among a portion of the Jômon community, and hence a degree of social stratification. Because the mineral is found at very few sites, mostly in the Niigata vicinity on the Sea of Japan coast, the wide distribution of these beads also suggests that an extensive trade network served at least the interests of the more well-off Jômon people.[33]

Another noteworthy item in the Jômon equipage was asphalt. This viscous black "fossil fuel" was found in beds associated with extensive oil deposits along stretches of the Sea of Japan coast in northeast Honshu and in central Hokkaido.[34] It was used mainly to glue points made of stone or bone to wooden hafts, forming arrows, spears, harpoons and axes. It was also used as glue to repair cracked clay pots, figurines and other objects.[35]

Whereas jade beads were distributed widely across the archipelago despite their very few sources, asphalt artifacts have been found almost solely northeast of the central cordillera despite the material's more extensive sources. That limited distribution may reflect the modest role of hunting and fishing in southwestern Japan. And it probably reflects asphalt's workaday function, exemplifying the general truism that trade is an indicator of social stratification, which enables a few to afford – or to impose on others – the costs of purveyance. Finally, in broader terms of human-environment relations, this use of asphalt appears to be one of the very early instances of human use of fossil fuels.

### 3. Other Artifacts

Items made of stone and baked clay are by far the most numerous of Jômon remnant goods. However, both bone and ivory objects, made from skeletal parts of mammals, have also been found. In addition, archaeologists have recovered traces of a few other, far more perishable items that Jômon people used in their daily lives. These include "wooden artifacts, baskets, cordage and textiles".[36]

"Wooden artifacts" include sections of tree trunk that had been hewn and burned inside to form "dugout" vessels measuring up to about 0.7 m wide by 7 m long.[37] These enabled users to travel between islands despite rising sea levels. Tree trunks and limbs were also hewn into posts and beams, which were cut and shaped by hand, some even being notched and grooved for structural use. Artisans also carved wood to create bracelets, combs, containers and other hand-held objects.

Baskets, woven from strips of fibrous material, were used to store nuts and for other storage and carrying purposes. Cordage – ropes of diverse sizes – were produced by twisting together strands of strong but pliable fiber, such as that of false nettle. These would then be used for various purposes, such as making fish net or securing or hauling items. Surviving pieces of fabric reveal that Jômon weavers wove together twisted fibers of false nettle, hemp or ramie to make sturdy textiles.[38]

Perhaps the most interesting aspect of these artifacts – and an aspect that helped them survive to the present – is that Jômon craftsmen coated many of their products with lacquer.[39] Throughout the Jômon era, lacquer was used despite the trickiness of its production.

To produce lacquer, one must first extract sap from the varnish tree (*urushi*), refine it and then add any desired color – such as red derived from iron oxide or cinnabar or black from particles of soot. It was a tricky task because the raw sap affects human skin in the manner of poison ivy and therefore had to be handled with extreme care. Moreover, the delicate task of refining sap to proper consistency required months of time. It seems likely that lacquer-making was something of a specialist's task. But once available, it could be – and was – applied to wooden items, ropes, basketry and fabrics, making them all more sturdy, durable and weather-resistant.

### 4. Shell Mounds (or Middens)

Shell mounds shed light on several aspects of Jômon society. They reveal regional and seasonal variation of diet as well as the probable presence of trading activity. And, most pertinent for our study, they show humans adapting to the circumstances of their environment, as on the Kantô shoreline.

The cold Chishima Current, as noted in Chapter 1, flows southward along Japan's eastern seaboard until it encounters the northeastward-flowing Japan Current. The two merge adjacent to the Kantô Plain, in the process bringing a richly diverse assemblage of sea creatures to the waters there.

**Figure 2.1:** Paddy tillage and stable forest edge in the upper reaches of a valley in eastern Tôhoku, 1955

During the millennia of Jômon society, as sea level rose and the convoluted bays and inlets of the Kantô vicinity gradually re-filled with sea water, they supported rich and durable populations of fish, shellfish and other marine life. These were accessible to humans in the area, and by some 7,000 yBP they were becoming a substantial source of seasonal nutrients. Thus, at one shell mound on lower Tokyo Bay, archaeologists have found remnants of such shellfish as oysters and granular ark shells, such fish as tuna, mullet, black porgy, sea bass and flathead, and also the animals wild boar, raccoon dog and hare.

People of the vicinity caught and processed those creatures for food as they became available. Thus they took shellfish especially during late winter and spring months when they were "one of the few food items [freshly available] in the Japanese archipelago".[40] One suspects, moreover, that while those who harvested and processed the shellfish consumed some of them, they used others in trade. By doing so, they could obtain other foodstuffs or such items as obsidian from the Izu and Nagano regions, which, as noted above, they used in their hunting and fishing activity.

### 5. Settlements and Dwellings

As one would expect, Jômon-era pottery, stone tools and other artifacts have mostly been found in conjunction with settlement sites. Even shell mounds are commonly in or adjacent to places where people lived.

Archeologists have excavated scores of settlement sites, and findings there convey the basic story we've already noted: a long-term increase and subsequent decrease in population, and hence in number and size of settlements that reflected the warming and eventual cooling trajectory of climate during those millennia. The sites also reveal regional differences, with appreciably more of them lying in eastern than western Japan. Patterns of village use, however, remain unclear.

Jômon people likely were more mobile during their early millennia, as suggested by their relatively small numbers, the comparative simplicity of their dwellings and other equipment, and the absence of storage pits for such food supplies as nuts. Their diets and lifestyles were firmly shaped by local resources, which also helped determine where they lived and for how long.

However, by 11–10,000 yBP or so, Jômon living arrangements were gradually changing. Simple huts gave way to round pit dwellings, with thatched walls and roofs supported by sturdy posts and framing. Commonly, 3 m or more in diameter, these dwellings provided sufficient space for indoor cooking and storage. Moreover, their floors were set into the ground, about knee deep, with the excavated soil laid up around the pit to prevent water from running in. That design also kept the dwellings warmer in winter and cooler in summer.

These new architectural practices first appeared in Hokkaido and southern Kyushu, and they probably reflected the continuing influence of immigrants. In southern Kyushu, however, volcanic eruptions appear to have destroyed human settlements in the area, enabling the Hokkaido precedents gradually to extend southward.[41]

Besides using more complex dwellings that better fitted their colder environment, these northerly people engaged in active fishing, employed storage pits for food and buried their dead near their dwellings. In some places they arranged several houses in a circular layout around a communal space that could be used for such purposes as food storage, burial or waste disposal. Eventually, too, some sites included larger structures that seem to have functioned as raised-floor storage sheds or may have served some other communal purpose. These developments suggest that Jômon folk were becoming less mobile, living instead for extended periods in their houses, and bringing home for storage and eventual use the foodstuffs gathered on foraging trips.

The decreasing mobility of the Jômon people is not surprising either. The construction of pit dwellings entailed a considerable investment of labor and materials: one would not vacate such a dwelling lightly. Once a residential site had been developed, moreover, there was much reason to use it over and over; replacing one dwelling with another when its posts rotted or it otherwise became unusable. Most importantly, perhaps, even with the best of hand tools, digging a pit in soil full of tree roots can be an exhausting task. It is far, far easier to dig again an area already free of such roots, and especially to reuse existing pits, even if one must adjust the pit's shape a bit to find firm soil in which to place the new posts. This impetus to use dwelling sites over and over is reflected in archeological excavations, which frequently show pits superimposed one upon another.[42]

One consequence of this practical reuse of cleared sites is that they commonly seem to have held large numbers of households. In general, however, it appears that even the larger settlements numbered only 5–6 dwellings at a time, with fewer at the many smaller sites.

By 5–6,000 years ago, such settlements were widespread. And particularly in eastern Japan, their occupants engaged in locally specialized production of select foodstuffs, such as seafood, salt or terrestrial plant and animal products. Specialists also turned out stone and pottery products for both practical and ceremonial uses. These goods were then exchanged locally and regionally, with such highly valued items as jade ornaments traveling long distances. These patterns of production and exchange, along with evidence of more elaborate burial arrangements and the use of ornate ceremonial pottery items, suggest that a substantial degree of social complexity and some degree of stratification had become quite widespread.

**Figure 2.2:** Farmer weeding young cabbages and fertilizing with night soil just North of Tokyo, 1955

Nevertheless, and despite the widespread presence of bows and arrows, spears, daggers and axes, archeologists have thus far found no evidence of Jômon warfare or comparable violence – as might be revealed by human skeletons with severed or punctured skulls, cracked ribs or missing arms or legs. If indeed such violence was absent, that may have been because population density remained very modest, as noted above, even during the Jômon heyday, ca. 5,000 yBP, and/or because even the larger settlements were small in scale. Especially striking is the lack of evidence for such violence during the difficult centuries of climate cooling around 4,000 yBP, despite the accompanying hardship that is suggested by sharp population decline.

## RECAPITULATION

In sum, then, the experience of Japan's forager society was fundamentally shaped by its environmental context. Because of the archipelago's global location, geomorphology, climate and resulting biological composition, it constituted a relatively lush environment for human habitation, except during millennia of severe glacial cold. Its extreme geological youth and resulting acutely mountainous character meant, however, that only a small portion of its land surface was actually suitable for such habitation.

Despite the obstacles presented by Japan's mountainous topography and its frequent separation from the continent during glacial warm periods, people did enter and reside in the arcland/archipelago. It seems most likely that they came from the Siberia-China region, though others could have come from Southeast Asia. They entered Japan from both North and South, but the northern entryway, via Sakhalin, seems to have been the more frequent and influential source of in-migration during the early millennia because it was traversable for longer durations during cold periods.

From about 35–30,000 yBP onward, the immigrants were Homo sapiens. In subsequent millennia, due to some interplay of in-migration and indigenous innovation, their culture evolved from a pre-pottery, paleolithic one to a much more populous, more complex, pottery-making, neolithic one. As time passed, this Jômon society employed an ever-richer variety of techniques – including some early agricultural practices, as we note in Chapter 3 – in dealing with its environment.

Several of these Jômon technical practices merit reiteration here. In terms of chemistry, besides the use of boiling and cooking to make certain foodstuffs edible, these foragers used heat to convert clay into ceramic ware. And they processed lacquer so that they could apply it to diverse materials and enhance their usefulness and durability. They created archery equipment and constructed durable housing. By smearing asphalt skillfully, they glued surfaces together. And by twisting together strips of durable fiber, they formed cordage of varying length, thickness and stiffness for use as rope, and to weave fabrics and basketry.

In short, these millennia of human life in Japan foreshadowed the patterns of innovation and change that humans would experience in subsequent centuries down to today. In some ways, too, that forager experience foreshadowed the later human impact on environment.

The most noteworthy instance of that impact probably was the extinction of great mammals. Although the dynamics of this die-off remain unclear, it seems likely that Homo sapiens' development of improved hunting technology was a key factor. But whatever the dynamics, the result was extinction of select species, which probably enabled a number of smaller mammals to increase their presence even as it forced the humans to modify their diet.

By utilizing new and improved technology to diversify diet and enhance foraging efficiency, Jômon society altered biotic species composition locally, in and around settlement sites and perhaps at some fishery sites. Also, they may have introduced a few exotic species – in addition to themselves – such as the dog or possibly select plants or microbes.

Nevertheless, any such changes were environmentally inconsequent compared to the changes effected by later (agricultural and industrial) societies. The Jômon peoples' impact was so slight because their population density and level of material consumption per capita – and hence their total material demand – were extremely low compared to those of later centuries. And those were low because the technology being used to manipulate the ecosystem was so modest by comparison with that of more "advanced" human societies.

So, while one certainly can point to the ways in which this forager society's performance foreshadowed that of later centuries, in terms of environmental impact it constituted only the faintest of a foreshadowing. As far as human impact goes, except for the loss of great mammals, the Japanese archipelago at the end of the forager millennia was essentially the same sort of place it had been a million years earlier, when Homo erectus may possibly have first ventured into the region. Ten thousand years of Jômon society had left Japan's ecosystem intact for the use of future generations.

# 3 *Early Agricultural Society to 600* CE

Diverse bits of archeological evidence suggest that very simple agricultural practices were present during later millennia of Jômon forager culture. However, it was from about 600 BCE (2,600 yBP) or earlier that the early phase of fully developed agriculture (field cropping, orchardry and animal husbandry) gradually became established in the archipelago, spreading slowly from southwest to northeast. Its establishment led, in turn, to radical changes in both human society and its environmental context. Clearly associated with these changes, as we shall see, were the introduction and diffusion of metal technology, which helped shape both the social and environmental impact of agriculture.

**Figure 3.1:** A series showing a paddy crop from seeding to harvest. The paddy fields not yet tilled, save for seedbed plot in left distance. (Pictures taken in 1962. Site is adjacent to ICU [International Christian University] in western Tokyo. Site subsequently was transformed into a golf course and thence a highway.)

**Figure 3.2:** Spring. Paddy plot of #3.1 serving as seedbed; seedlings to be planted in adjoining fields

**Figure 3.3:** Early summer. New rice crop transplanted and growing, with irrigation water obtained from stream on right border between fields and scrub woodland

**Figure 3.4:** Late summer. Paddy starting to ripen

**Figure 3.5:** Early autumn. Harvest begun, with cut stalks suspended for air-drying from wooden frames

**Figure 3.6:** Later autumn. Harvest complete, with all fields cleared
and stalks drying down, awaiting the threshing process

The most noteworthy changes in Japan's human society during these centuries seem to have been threefold: unprecedented population growth; unprecedented social differentiation and stratification; and the emergence of political elites. Conflict among these elites and their entanglement with elites in nearby continental areas produced a gradual consolidation of power by the victors. That process eventuated in the establishment, around 650 CE, of a hegemonic political elite, the imperial government, which claimed sovereignty over a realm that included Kyushu, Shikoku and as much of Honshu as it knew anything about, which probably extended its claim beyond the central cordillera into the southern Tôhoku region.

The key environmental change of this millennium was widespread deforestation due to land clearance, mainly on lowland areas and mostly for agricultural purposes. In addition, as lowland forest disappeared and human material demand kept growing, there occurred a slowly spreading harvest of hillside woodland, mainly for use as fuel wood and construction timber. These trends, together with forest fires – some of them accidental and some set for the purpose of land clearance – opened more and more terrain to sustained sunlight. Moreover, they created, mainly at the foot of steeper hillsides, long, convoluted stretches of more-or-less permanent "forest edge". These trends favored diverse smaller plants, animals and microbes at the expense of large mammals and trees.

The trends also replaced large areas of diverse natural growth with a select population of cultivated crops – with accompanying "weeds" and "pests", meaning plants and animals (including insects) unwanted by those humans utilizing the site. Besides altering the balance among species, the spread of land clearance may have led to some unrecorded extinctions. And it produced a substantial increase in the rate of soil erosion, which leached hillsides of nutrients even as it enlarged river deltas and nearby coastal lowlands.

In less than 1,000 years, agricultural society produced far more extensive changes in the archipelago's ecosystem than Homo sapien foragers had produced in 30,000. As we note below, the adoption of wet-rice cultivation was the most visible component of this agricultural change and one scholar has summed up its impact in this way:

Adaptation of land features in monsoonal Asia to the purpose of rice agriculture remains one of man's greatest impacts on the surface of the earth.[1]

Wet-rice tillage had some very distinctive characteristics, as that comment implies, and we shall note them more fully below, after examining characteristics of agri-culture as a whole.

## REGARDING AGRICULTURE

As adumbrated above, developments of the millennium to ca. 600 CE stood in striking contrast to Japan's Jômon-era experience and that difference reflected the basic difference between forager and agricultural dynamics. So let us examine the matter a bit further by looking at three topics: the forager/agriculture distinction; the distinction between "early" and "later" agriculture; and the special character-istics of wet-rice culture.

### Forager-Agriculture Comparison

Forager consumption, as we have seen, is based essentially on a system of direct appropriation by humans. It is limited to what people can acquire and utilize from that which grows naturally. Consequently human numbers and their level of consumption-per-capita are both limited by the skill with which they can extract (that is, take while offering no quid pro quo) from whatever is locally available.

Agrarian consumption, on the other hand, entails patterns of collaboration (mutuality or symbiosis) between humans and select other creatures – the so-called "domesticated" plants and animals.[2] In essence the parties agree that insofar as the human cares for the collaborator – protects it from predators, shelters it as needed, and enables it to grow and reproduce – the latter will in due course be available for human use, whether as food, servant or whatever.

More broadly, this transactional arrangement can be characterized as humans playing domesticated creatures off against the others, thereby empowering them-selves to engage in extensive manipulation and exploitation of the ecosystem. Doing so enables them to expand their environmental foundation, which makes possible the above-noted patterns of social growth and change.

However, this arrangement also enables the collaborators to multiply, diversify genetically and expand their spatial presence. So, agrarian culture seems more properly viewed as a set of alliances in which the collaborating species work together to advance their common interests. In this sense it exemplifies the widespread biological phenomenon of symbiotic relationships (such as those of bees and flowering plants, microbes and mammals, trees and select fungi).

### Early–Later Agriculture Comparison

This forager-agriculture distinction – between direct exploitation and collaborative mutuality – seems clear enough. Less clear is the distinction between "early" or "extensive" agriculture and "later" or "intensive" agriculture, which was mentioned briefly in the introduction. In Japan, as elsewhere, that distinction appeared as the centuries passed and it requires elucidation.

The "early–later" distinction can also be characterized as a "one-stage"-"two-stage" distinction. In "one-stage" agriculture the humans seek to nurture the collaborating plant or animal directly. In "two-stage" agriculture the humans nurture another category of organism, and the latter's vitality enables the collaborating creature to flourish. This distinction applies to both horticulture – field cropping in particular – and animal husbandry.

Looking first at animal husbandry, in its "one-stage" form, the domesticated animals forage for themselves, whereas in "two-stage" husbandry the humans purposely transform woodland or other sites into pasturage for the animals' use and, in colder climates, grow and harvest field crops as winter feed for them.

In Japan, however, animal husbandry always remained a small part of the agricultural scene. In Jômon times humans made some use of dogs, wild pigs and small horses. And subsequently, during agricultural centuries, horses served as mounts and pack animals, and both horses and bovines (oxen) came to be used as draft animals. However, the domesticated goats, sheep and birds (geese, ducks, chickens) so central to many agricultural societies were few or absent – with the corollary effect that relatively little land was devoted to feeding domesticated animals. And until much later in Japan's agricultural history, the animals mostly foraged for themselves in the "one-stage" manner.

So Japan's agriculture was primarily a matter of plant cultivation. And of the two forms orchardry and field cropping, the former was of comparatively modest significance during the centuries of early agricultural society. Consequently field cropping constituted the heart of this society's symbiotic arrangements.

In early or "one-stage" field cropping, humans simply presume to facilitate the collaborating plant's natural pattern of growth by sowing seed or planting "sproutable" plant parts in favorable locations, protecting them against competitors or predators as needed, harvesting the crop, and saving seed material for the next season. In "two-stage" nurturing, the crop is purposely fertilized. That is to say, the soil microbes are fed, which convert this food into nutrients that the plant can then absorb through its roots and put to use.[3]

Early agriculturists did not knowingly fertilize their crops. But in the absence of such fertilizing, their fields rapidly lost fertility and had to be abandoned and allowed to lie "fallow" for a few years until volunteer-plant growth and decay revitalized their soil.

In fact, of course, "one-stage" horticulture, whether field cropping or orchardry, may entail considerable unplanned and unrecognized fertilizing. The weeds that a tiller dislodges but leaves to die and decay, the stalks and roots of harvested crops that rot in place, the fallen leaves from nearby woodland that lodge and rot in fields, the undergrowth that lives and dies in an orchard, the various creatures that defecate or die in a field, and the water that enters a field from adjoining areas – they all provide nutrients for microbes and thence for crops.

However, in Japan, as in most early agricultural societies, much of this potential fertilizer material was used as fuel, thatch or otherwise. The nutrient value of whatever remained or accumulated in the field was usually far less than what permanent tillage required or what intensive agriculturists added to their fields in later centuries.

It appears that human societies have commonly practiced early or one-stage horticulture for centuries before they learned about and gradually mastered the intricacies of the later, two-stage techniques. In the case of Japan, it appears that this later form of horticulture gradually spread across the realm from about 1200 CE onward.

We must note, however, two forms of *de facto* two-stage agriculture that were found in Japan almost from the onset of fully developed agricultural practice. The less consequent form was that of silk production. The silk comes from silkworms, but their food is the leaves of the mulberry tree. Because the worms are raised where they can be controlled, the humans must provide their food. And because natural mulberry trees grow too large for harvesting, the silkworm farmer grows them as "bushes" in a managed plantation; that is, humans nurture the mulberry so it can feed the worm that produces the filaments of silk.

**Figure 3.7**: Diluvial terrace land opened to paddy tillage southwest of Tokyo, 1981

**Figure 3.8:** Well-to-do farmstead at edge of diluvial terrace southwest of Tokyo, 1981

The other, more important *de facto* two-stage crop was "wet rice" (paddy, from the Malay padi).[4] And because wet rice became the most visible aspect of Japan's agriculture, it requires more detailed examination. Two aspects of paddy tillage merit comment: how does it differ from other grain cultivation; and what portion of total field-cropping did it constitute in Japan?

### Paddy Culture: The Technique

Properly speaking, rice (*Oryza*) is a genus of grass (*Gramineae*) or grain, not an aquatic or swamp plant. However, the cultivated species (*Oryza sativa*) flourishes in saturated soils as other grains do not, and most varieties are much less tolerant of drought than are other grains. Cultivated rice also produces a larger number of seeds per plant than do most grains, yielding a greater harvest per acre and hence a smaller proportion of seeds that must be saved as seed-grain for the following year.[5]

Among the cultivatable species of rice, two types are predominant: *Oryza sativa indica* and *O. s. japonica*, each of which encompasses numerous varieties.[6] The former flourishes in tropical areas; the latter, *japonica*, prefers the longer days of temperate-zone summers and is more tolerant of cooler climates. So *japonica* is the predominant rice in Japan and has been for most of the time since the crop's introduction there some 2,600 years ago.

Regarding those varieties of cultivated rice that can be grown as dry-field crops, they yield far less harvest per hectare than do wet-field crops. And being "one-stage" crops unless fertilized, they can exhaust a field's fertility within two or three years. Probably for those reasons rice appears to have been grown primarily in flooded fields, almost from its initial cultivation, which seems to have occurred in the Burma-China-Vietnam border region more than 7,000 years ago.[7]

The great productivity of wet-rice cultivation reflects its intrinsic character as a *de facto* "two-stage" type of horticulture. To explain, the inflowing water – which humans purposely provide to keep the fields flooded – carries organic matter that feeds algae and micro-organisms in the water and topsoil. The life-cycle activity of these creatures produces nutrients that the rice plant's roots can absorb to sustain vigorous plant growth. Because this inflow, processing and production of nutrients occurs whenever paddy fields are kept flooded, those fields can be used year after year without periodic fallowing.

Irrigation water also serves two other important purposes: it suppresses many weeds, which cannot sprout or fare poorly in the water; and it lengthens and improves the growing season by absorbing solar heat during the day and releasing it on cold nights more efficiently than soil does, thereby protecting the rice crop against frost.

It is important to note, however, that not all paddy tillage is alike. There are various degrees of complexity and corresponding differences in yield-per-acre. In its simplest form, wet-rice cultivation entails a farmer spreading seed "broadcast" in a swamp, where it germinates and grows amidst the other swamp vegetation. The farmer may manage outlets to control the water's depth, but basically the plant is on its own until its seeds are mature. Then the cultivators step into the swamp, grasp the rice stems that thrust up among the other growth, and use their hand-held stone blades to snip off the ripened heads of grain, which they place in their gathering sacks. Later they dump and spread out the ripened heads to finish sun-drying. They save some as seed grain for the following year and eventually mill the rest to obtain edible grain.

However, swamp culture has shortcomings. Irregular weather can disrupt water flow and damage a crop, and competing vegetation limits the yield from such tillage. Also, the farmer's inability to drain the swamp makes the harvest process more cumbersome. Finally, swampland is limited in extent, and longer-term climate fluctuations can destroy usable coastal swampland by transforming it into brackish swamp, open sea or, conversely, dry land.

Because of these limitations, early rice farmers gradually developed other lowlands for cultivation. In Japan, however, they found that many of the broadest, most accessible lowlands were not amenable to paddy tillage.

To explain, as noted in Chapter 1, Japan is geologically so youthful that much of it is characterized by steeply mountainous terrain fronting on alluvial plains, and its global location exposes it to irregularly heavy precipitation, mainly during monsoon and typhoon seasons. As a consequence, hillsides frequently send large quantities of water gushing downward and out onto the alluvial flatlands, where they can overload rivers, causing them to flood adjacent acreage, depositing silt and debris.

For a farmer to open fields on these flood plains is to invite recurrent disaster. Moreover, the extreme variation in stream flow means that irrigation dams, dykes and ditches built along large rivers are vulnerable to destructive pummeling that can, in a few hours, undo years of laborious construction and maintenance.

As a result, when paddy farmers in Japan sought non-swampland to till, they initially gravitated toward such flatter surfaces as they could find within smaller valleys and along the inland edge of broader plains. There they could capture run-off directly, whether from the hillsides themselves or as it ran down small streams. At that stage irregularities of flow were much more manageable. Larger flatlands were left undeveloped or were used for other purposes that entailed less severe losses in the event of deluge.

Even in safe locations, non-swamp paddy tillage entails more work than swampland culture. It commonly requires careful leveling of the land and entails complex irrigation tasks – the construction and maintenance of ditches and dams for inflow and outflow, as well as embankments for holding water in the fields. And as these irrigation systems grow more elaborate, they require ever more labor and more extensive social organization.

Nevertheless, because paddy fields of this sort can be drained, they make it easier to regulate water supply, control competing growth, dry down the ripened crop for harvest and harvest without wading through the soggy swamp. So the payoff for the extra effort and discipline is a greater and more dependable yield-per-acre.

The other major technical improvement that adds to output is the adoption of seed beds. Seed beds can be started earlier in spring because, being small, they are easier to prepare and to shelter from frost. And when the seedlings are subsequently transplanted into pre-flooded – and hence pre-warmed – fields, they can root quickly. Such seedlings also can be transplanted in rows, optimally spaced to maximize growth while facilitating the task of weeding. Finally, row-planted rice in drained fields can be more efficiently harvested by cutting stems at the base with sickles, which secures more seed per swipe than does snipping of heads. Like the management of water supply, this use of seed-beds and row-planting increases productivity per acre.

These several types of agronomic improvement all seem to have appeared, at least in simple versions, during the early centuries of wet-rice cultivation. And while they did make it a more technically complex and extremely labor-intensive form of cropping, paddy tillage's waterborne fertilizer supply enabled farmers to harvest a substantially greater yield-per-acre and to do so year in, year out, provided the water supply was not seriously disrupted.

Finally, we should remember that even in its more elaborate forms paddy tillage is a seasonal employment. Rice farmers have substantial free time between autumn harvest and the following spring's planting tasks. They can – and did (and still do) – use that time for other purposes. They might work on behalf of social superiors, expand their arable acreage, grow a winter crop of some sort or handle other household tasks. Or the "off-season" work might – and often did – involve classic foraging activity, whether on land or sea, enriching the household diet and reducing the risk of hunger should the stored harvest prove insufficient.

As a result of these several characteristics, paddy farming enabled communities to grow to a size and complexity which communities of foragers and even dry-field cultivators could not equal. And that capability had substantial socio-political ramifications, as we shall see.

### Paddy Culture: Its Extent

It is much easier to discuss *how* wet rice was grown than *how much* of it was grown in Japan during the centuries of agricultural society. The heart of the problem is this: during the centuries when written records were kept (meaning ca. 600 CE ff), paddy was grown mainly on behalf of the ruling elite. So, record keepers paid close attention to rice production but relatively little attention to other forms of agricultural output. In consequence, the surviving records of land use and food production mostly pertain to wet rice.

Setting aside the question of land dedicated to orchards for fruit and nut trees or plantations for tea and mulberry bushes, let us focus solely on the acreage devoted to cultivated crops. The historical visibility of the rice crop notwithstanding, it does not necessarily follow that most tillage output in Japan was paddy or that most tilled fields produced it.

This is so for several reasons. First, scholars routinely point out that most rice was eaten by the elite. Insofar as the producer populace consumed rice, they ate it mixed together with other grains and in unpolished form as "brown rice" rather than as polished "white rice". (And while the brown is more nutritious than the white, that is another issue.) The rice-consuming elite were, however, only a small portion of the total populace: perhaps 5 percent during the early agricultural era, growing to 10–20 percent in the later pre-industrial centuries.

Now, surely the elite ate better and were more wasteful of food than were the producers. But an active work force burns more calories per capita than does a largely sedentary populace. So it may well be that total nutrient consumption per capita among hoi polloi rivaled or even exceeded that of the favored few.

It is true, too, that a portion of the rice crop was devoted to making alcoholic drinks – *sake* and *shôchû* – which seem to have been consumed quite widely through society. But their production also required a small amount of other grains, and, in any case, it is not at all clear what portion of the total rice crop was consumed in this way.

Finally, as noted in the preceding section, paddy yield per acre was far greater than that of dry-field grains. So, if most people mostly ate dry grains rather than rice, and if they had to till substantially more dry-field acreage to get the same caloric yield, it may be reasonable to postulate that, for much of Japan's agricultural history, most cultivated fields (possibly 60–75 percent?) grew dry-field grains rather than paddy. And if one includes non-grain crops, notably garden crops such as vegetables, in the estimate of total cultivated fields, then the percentage devoted to paddy was even smaller.

A second aspect of this conundrum is whether paddy acreage gradually became a larger portion of the total in later centuries, as "two-stage" cultivation of dry-field crops became established. Certainly the way rulers emphasized paddy-field development suggests that it did.

However, as centuries passed, cultivators spread ever farther into the northeast, a region too cold for paddy tillage until more cold-resistant varieties were developed in recent centuries. Moreover, as centuries passed, more and more commercial crops were grown – in both dry fields and inferior paddy fields that farmers ceased to irrigate – giving such fields greater relative value. Even as late as the 1880s or thereabouts, it appears that only about half the cultivated acreage was used for wet-rice tillage.[8]

Ultimately, however, the question may be largely semantic because with the spread of double-cropping from roughly 1200 CE onward, more and more dry-field crops were grown in winter on fields that grew paddy in summer. Still, as recently as 1854, only about 45 percent of paddy fields were double-cropped from the Kinai region westward, and only 15 percent or less in the northeast.[9] But in any case, whether to count such acreage as paddy land or dry fields – or both – is not obvious. One hopes that future research will clarify our understanding.

**Figure 3.9:** Dry-field farming on lower slopes of mountains in western Tokyo, 1982

## AGRICULTURE: EARLY MANIFESTATIONS

### General Observations

As the preceding section suggests, the shift from forager to agricultural society entailed some radical changes in the ways humans interacted with the ambient bio-system. Gradually, however, people mastered the broad array of new technologies that constitute agriculture. They learned which animals they could domesticate for use and how to care for them. They identified useful trees and low-growing plants (grasses, forbs, shrubs) and figured out how to nurture them and how to repel grazers and other predators. They learned how to recognize, till, and sustain fertile soil, how and when to sow seeds so that they would germinate with some reliability and grow as desired, how to suppress competing growth, and how to identify, acquire and preserve those seeds, sprouts and saplings essential to the next crop.

As mentioned in the introduction, people living in relatively isolated circumstances tended to acquire new techniques more belatedly, and that truism found modest expression in the Japanese archipelago. Whereas fully developed field cropping (of millet and rice) was practiced in China some 7,000 years ago and on the Korean peninsula some 3–4,000 years ago, the oldest solid evidence of its presence in Japan dates to some 2,600 years ago, when it appeared with immigrant communities in northwest Kyushu.[10] As field cropping did become established in Kyushu – followed in a few centuries by the use of metals – it spread eastward across the archipelago, in the process displacing or radically modifying Jômon sustenance practices. That change is commonly designated the transition from Jômon to Yayoi culture or from forager to agricultural society.[11]

This is not to say, however, that there were no signs of "incipient" agriculture in Jômon society. All three major forms – animal husbandry, orchardry and field cultivation – found expression there.[12]

### Jômon Agricultural Practices

As noted previously, animal husbandry was extremely limited in Japan. Recovered bones suggest that a few domesticated dogs were present during much of the Jômon era, whether for use in hunting, as food or both. Pony-sized horses may have been used for food or as pack animals.[13] Also wild boars appear to have been raised for food. Whether they were bred and raised domestically or captured as wild piglets, penned and raised is unclear.[14]

Orchardry, too, was minimal. The most valued tree appears to have been the native chestnut (*Castanea crenata*), whose nuts were much easier to process for eating than were those of other nut trees, particularly several oaks and buckeye (horse chestnut). Moreover, its wood made sturdy posts for construction purposes. However, the native chestnut did not compete well with other major tree species, easily being overgrown and shaded out. Evidence from Jômon sites suggests that people dealt with that limitation by nurturing chestnut trees around residential clearings while suppressing competing growth.[15]

Several types of smaller, cultivated plants are also evident in the archeological record, mostly dating from about 6–7,000 years ago or later. These included varieties of barley, barnyard millet, bottle gourd, buckwheat and burdock, as well as dry-field rice, select mints (*egoma, shiso*) and beans.[16] The evidence suggests, however, that as foodstuffs these items constituted a very modest part of the Jômon diet. And how well developed the tillage techniques may have been is unclear.

Villagers could have used fire purposely to clear woodland for cultivation, but doing so would surely have placed their settlements at great risk, and so it likely was a rare practice. It seems more probable that grains were grown in garden plots in the forest openings of dwelling sites, while seeds of other plants were scattered in vacant spots where available, notably sites enriched by rotted garbage. Such practices would have given the plants enough sunlight to mature, while the presence of people and dogs could have deterred or repelled foraging wild animals such as deer or serow. Or, conversely, such crops could have been grown to lure game in for the kill.

So, it appears that in Japan, as elsewhere, the members of forager society were gradually discovering the material advantages of agricultural techniques. The evidence also suggests, however, that in the absence of new influences from abroad, the rate and scale of such change would have remained modest and that

Japan's later history might well have unfolded in a manner more akin to that of pre-1600 eastern North America; that is, in the absence of new stimuli, Jômon society's discovery, refinement and elaboration of agrarian technique would have proceeded at a much slower pace than what actually did transpire in the archipelago.

## YAYOI: THE BEGINNING OF FULLY DEVELOPED AGRICULTURE IN JAPAN

The onset of fully developed agricultural practice in Japan is lost in the mists of time. Whether it was introduced once and the practice expanded thereafter, or whether it was repeatedly introduced before becoming established, is unclear. When that establishing occurred, by whom, how and why are all unknown, although evidence can be amassed to support various interpretations and speculation is rife.[17]

When developed agricultural practices did become established, however, they seem to have done so initially in northwest Kyushu, most likely having been introduced by emigrants from the nearby continent, although they could have come from the South via the Japan Current. What most distinguished this agriculture from the earlier plant-nurturing practices of Jômon society was the presence of paddy tillage. This agriculture, in turn, underlay a degree of social change so great that scholars, as we noted above, employ a separate term – Yayoi – to distinguish this society from the Jômon foragers it displaced.

Lest the emphasis here on paddy tillage be misconstrued, almost certainly it remained a secondary part of total agricultural activity in Japan. In both acreage and nutrient yield, it was far surpassed by that of dry fields, vegetable gardens and orchards, all of which were technically simpler undertakings that could be pursued on more varied sites. However, while the rice was of much less importance to hoi polloi than were other foodstuffs, paddy tillage left a much more durable physical imprint on terrain and had a disproportionate environmental impact throughout the centuries of Japan's agricultural society.

### Background and Beginnings

Archeologists have unearthed evidence of paddy tillage dating to about 2,600 years ago in the Fukuoka vicinity of northwest Kyushu. Lying about 200 km off Korea's southeast corner, this is the part of the archipelago closest to the peninsula.

The appearance of wet rice culture in that place at that time, and its subsequent spread eastward across Japan, reflects three developments of the day. One of the three was a set of major changes in northeast Asian society; the other two were developments in marine technology and in metallurgy.

### 1. Mainland Social Change

Regarding the changes in northeast Asian society, by 3,000 years ago, transformational developments and associated political turmoil on the continent had begun giving people in and around the North-central China region unprecedented impetus to move. As centuries passed, that trend eventually found expression in increasing cross-straits traffic.

To elaborate, by some 7,000 years ago, paddy tillage was being practiced in the Yangtze River basin of East-central China, while dry-field grain cropping and animal husbandry were becoming predominant in regions to the North and West of there.[18] With those changes in food supply came growth in population and the emergence of larger communities that gradually cleared more and more land for cropping, spun off satellite villages, and increasingly competed for resources with other communities. As the competition grew more harsh and violent, communities developed ever more complex social structures and hierarchies of power and privilege. By some 4,000 years ago these struggles for advantage had produced large-scale ruling groups whose power and prestige were enhanced by the addition of a new technology – bronze weaponry, tools and ornaments – to their earlier devices of stone and wood.

In subsequent centuries, political conflict and the continuing dispersal of agricultural communities and practices spread the accompanying social changes and disorder eastward and southward to China's Pacific coast, and northward onto the Manchurian plain and into the Korean peninsula. By 3–4,000 years ago, wet-rice tillage – whether introduced via Manchuria, the Shantung peninsula or elsewhere – was being practiced in the fertile lowlands of southwestern Korea, where warm wet summers favored it. And eventually, by some 2,600 years ago (600 BCE) these processes of population growth and movement began affecting the Japanese archipelago as migrant groups started traversing the straits and settling in areas amenable to paddy culture.

### 2. Marine Technology

As for developments in marine technology, it was changes in boat design that expedited such maritime travel. During Jômon millennia the boats used in northeast Asia appear to have been dugout canoes and rafts, and the dugouts constituted safe and sturdy vessels for maritime travel. Made from sections of tree trunk that could be, as noted in Chapter 2, up to about 0.7 m wide by 7 m long, these vessels were exceptionally rugged and stable. With their thick, largely unhewn, lower halves, they were very resistant to damage when slammed against submerged rocks or coral reefs, and they had enough ballast to resist flipping in heavy seas. On the other hand, their size was limited, and their very weight made them difficult to propel or steer.

Consequently, using these vessels for travel across the straits to Japan was a risky enterprise. For millennia occasional travelers had done so, going via Tsushima and Iki Islands, as evidenced by similarities of pottery found in those localities. However, given the difficulty of controlling these small vessels on the shallow and rough waters of those straits, such travel was risky and infrequent.[19] Moreover, one suspects that not all trips were intentional. The strong westerly winds of winter, the northeastward-blowing monsoon winds of summer, the cyclonic storms of autumn and the Japan Current, all could propel free-floating vessels into the Sea of Japan as easily as across the straits or toward any intended landfall.

During Yayoi centuries, however, mariners in the region gradually developed a new type of vessel that retained the dugout's advantages while overcoming its limitations. They began fastening plank superstructures to them, initially making simple walls but eventually elaborating them to form wider and longer decks. In some cases they attached large tree trunks end-to-end to make longer vessels. These changes gave them space for more oarsmen, eventually even allowing the installation of sails and rudders to assist in propulsion and steering. By ca. 300 CE, after a millennium of gradual development, their vessels were large enough to sport raised decks fore and aft, and vessels of this sort continued to be used – in Japan at least – for another millennium thereafter.[20]

From about 600 BCE, as these improvements in vessels slowly appeared, more migrants sailed to Japan and more and more wet rice began to be grown in northwest Kyushu, probably by members of immigrant communities. As centuries passed, the simple tillage of swampland gave way to the more complex forms of irrigation-based cultivation, and paddy cropping spread eastward to scattered sites on the Japan Sea coast and along the Inland Sea littoral and beyond, reaching as far as the Nobi Plain in central Japan.

*3. Metallurgy*

Even as the diffusion of paddy tillage was occurring in East Asia, it was facilitated by another major technical development: the use of iron. The earlier-known bronze devices were rather limited in their utility because the copper and tin that they contain were relatively scarce in East Asia, making the alloy too precious for widespread use by ordinary folk. Iron sand, by comparison, was plentiful, and it could produce far more tools and weapons. Lacking bronze's shininess, and being less easily shaped and more subject to rust, iron was much less useful as a decorative or prestige item. But its hardness meant it could handle more rigorous, practical tasks.

In consequence iron provided many more, and more effective, swords, axes, hoes and other weapons and tools. It expedited forest clearance, creation of paddy fields and irrigation ditches, tillage and harvesting, and diverse forms of construction activity, whether of boats, bridges, dams, dikes, houses or larger structures. It also facilitated more frequent and larger-scale warfare. So the use of iron contributed to the further spread of agricultural practice, the resulting population increase and socio-economic growth, and the accompanying social conflict, stratification and institutional elaboration.

In Japan, iron proved particularly influential after its introduction, which may date to about 200 BCE.[21] By then paddy culture was well established across western Japan. And it appears that with the improved boats, ever more regular contact was maintained between the agricultural communities of southern Korea and southwestern Japan. This mattered because the southern peninsula contained rich sources of iron sand and had developed – probably well before 200 CE – a smelting industry that provided iron ingots and tools to users in the China-Korea vicinity.

For the next few centuries iron from that area also provided the weapons and tools used in Japan. Initially, it appears, iron was used for weapons by those local hegemons in western Japan who had contacts in southern Korea. Consequently, assuring their access to that iron became a matter of politico-military importance. Later, as the iron supply became greater, more and more was used for agricultural tools, replacing stone knives and providing iron tips for wooden hoes and spades.[22] This trend made the Korean connection more important for society as a whole. Not until about 450 CE were iron sands found in Japan, as we note further on, whose discovery began reducing late Yayoi society's need for close ties to southern Korea.

### Some Socio-cultural Conundrums

So paddy tillage and other forms of field cropping did become established in the archipelago, most likely due to the arrival of people from the mainland, people who may have been fleeing violence or other harm or who were simply seeking more land to till. But, one wonders, who were they, what was their relationship to the Jômon populace they encountered, and how did the interaction among these groups play out as the years, generations and centuries passed?

It seems most plausible that the newcomers were rice-growers from southern Korea. But how long they (and their ancestors) had lived in that region is unknown. And from whence those ancestors came is similarly unknown. Also unknown are what language they spoke and whether they were somehow related to or had any sustained contact with, the Jômon-era residents of southwestern Japan.

However, the archeological evidence – or, rather, the lack of tell-tale evidence to the contrary – seems to suggest that for centuries the establishing of paddy tillage in northern Kyushu proceeded with little violence. Insofar as that perception is valid, it may suggest that the incoming and resident populations were able to communicate and accommodate one another. Or it may simply mean that the Jômon populace in Kyushu was so thinly dispersed and the land areas it utilized so distinct from those of the new arrivals that the two populations co-existed, at least for a few years or generations. And in time the less powerful Jômon residents may have adapted to the new ways, learned the newcomers' language and intermingled, moved away or perhaps been decimated by conflict or by some disease that the newcomers introduced. One suspects that all these forms of interaction occurred.

As this Yayoi agricultural population of northwestern Kyushu grew, spurred by both continuing immigration and on-site reproduction, the competition for arable land intensified. That competition appears to have been exacerbated in the centuries around 200–0 BCE by climate warming that raised sea level, inundating areas of swampland and forcing tillers to relocate to higher ground.[23] This relocation to higher, forested ground entailed more difficult land clearance and then development of the more complex irrigation systems mentioned above. The payoff came in terms of a higher yield per acre (i.e. it was a change that both required and sustained a more dense population of producers). These developments likely increased conflict with any residual foragers, even as it spurred the dispersal of Yayoi cultivators eastward across the archipelago.

Another striking result of this agronomic adaptation and social growth was the development, by 100 BCE or thereabouts, of fortified bastions controlled by local ruling elites that used iron weaponry in the battles they waged with rival elites. A celebrated example of such bastions is Yoshinogari, which flourished during ca. 100 BCE–250 CE. Situated a few kilometers inland from the northwest corner of Kyushu's Ariake Sea, it was easily accessible overland from the Fukuoka vicinity.[24] Local political centers of this sort housed a substantial, stratified population of producers. And their leaders exercised control over satellite villages – which generally numbered about 8–10 houses apiece – in the adjoining lowlands. They probably retained control by offering protection against intruding outsiders or by providing other forms of assistance in return for tribute and such labor service as they might need.

In addition to violent conflict between rival local elites, surviving skeletal evidence suggests that as the Yayoi people spread eastward along the Inland Sea, they encountered more resistance from local Jômon residents, causing the initial Jômon/Yayoi accommodation to disintegrate. Why this was so – whether because reports from Kyushu forewarned the foragers against acquiescence, because the two groups were competing more directly for use of the same acreage or because they were ethnically so separate as to be unable to communicate effectively – is unclear. In any case, Jômon foragers in the region gradually moved elsewhere, died out or adapted.

After a few centuries – by 100 or 200 CE, let us say – ethnic distinctions within the archipelago's population seem to have become more regionally delineated. In southern Kyushu, where paddy tillage did not thrive due to the vicinity's legacy of volcanic eruptions, people later known as Kumaso and Hayato seem to have preserved their own ways.[25] Some Yayoi agriculturalists may have tried to settle in the vicinity, only to find that the soil did not favor wet rice, prompting them to move on southward into the Ryukyu Islands.[26]

From northern Kyushu eastward to the mountains of the central cordillera and on along the Pacific littoral of the Chûbu District, where the influence of immigrants prevailed, the general populace came to be known as the Wa and later the Japanese. In Tôhoku and Hokkaido lived people later known as the Emishi, probably ancestral to those more recently known as Ainu.

The pre-agricultural peoples of southern Kyushu and northeastern Japan are all said to have been descendants of the Jômon people. So it may be reasonable to view Jômon society as a polyglot world of people whose ancestors had reached the archipelago from diverse places and at various times, but who nevertheless had found means of communication sufficient to sustain long-distance trade and a substantial degree of cultural sharing.

With the arrival of Yayoi agricultural society, however, that legacy of diversity began to yield to a process of social integration. The process would continue for centuries as Wa society became more highly structured and extended its presence across the archipelago, even while absorbing a persistent stream of immigrants from the continent.


## YAYOI AND BEYOND: CA. 200–600 CE


By 200 CE, then, agriculture had become well established in southwest Japan as a by-product of complex socio-political and technological developments in nearby continental areas. Along with the diffusion of agriculture in the archipelago came population growth, more complex patterns of social organization and stratification, more interaction with continental societies, new types of warfare and the gradual clustering of local elites in regional centers.

The way these several developments played out during the centuries to ca. 600 CE can be examined in terms of later Yayoi society, its successor, known as Kôfun ("ancient tomb") society, and the environmental ramifications of this human experience.

### Later Yayoi Society

By 200 CE, the character of Japan's early agricultural society was well established. Geographically, it reached from the northern half of Kyushu eastward across Shikoku and western Honshu to the southern littoral of Chûbu, with patches of settlement found in the Kantô region and a few scattered sites in northerly Honshu.

In spatial terms one might envisage this early agricultural society as consisting of irregular ribbons of open land, scattered households and small settlements. The ribbons meandered as topography dictated, mostly being bordered on one side by the steeper slopes of hills and mountains, and on the other by small streams or the forested flood plains of larger rivers. Both hills and flood plains still contained potentially arable land but, in both cases, careless clearance could prove disastrous.

In these ribbons of open land, paddy commonly was grown where feasible, with such dry-field grains as barley and millet planted on sites less amenable to irrigation. Diverse vegetables were grown in garden plots near housing settlements, and useful trees and shrubs grew on some of the nearby sites not convenient to tillage. Doubtless some foraging of edibles and hunting of meat continued, as did fishing and sea-food collecting, especially during the late winter and spring months of "spring hunger" when the supply of stored harvest ran low.

It was a system of provisioning that enabled the archipelago to sustain unprecedented growth in human numbers. In Chapter 2 we cited population estimates for 800 BCE of about 76,000 people and for 0 CE of some 595,000, nearly an eightfold increase in 800 years, with the bulk of that growth occurring from the Kinai vicinity westward.[27] During the next 700 years, as agriculture spread, the human population would grow even faster, expanding some ninefold to an estimated 5,400,000 people in 700 CE. Increase at such a rapid rate surely reflected the increased fecundity that a more reliable food supply permitted, but it also reflected the long-sustained in-migration of mainlanders.

As noted above, by 200 CE the growth in population, and the resulting competition for resources, had already given rise to inter-community conflict, social stratification and more elaborate community organization. Doubtless local leaders used that organization for mobilizing a labor force to clear yet more land, level more fields and build more extensive irrigation systems, as well as to construct the moats, barricades, watch towers and other wood and thatch structures of larger settlements. It seems likely, too, that these community organizations served as mechanisms for dealing with such local problems as floods, fires, other natural disasters or households particularly stressed by illness, food scarcity or other hardship.

The more Yayoi society grew, however, especially after the use of iron weapons became widespread, the more actively local elites found themselves engaged in larger-scale, inter-communal rivalries. The ever-greater scale of defense works and – as seen at archeological sites – the increasing presence of both weapons and skeletons showing violent injury reveal a long-term growth in the extent of warfare.

That trend was paralleled by growth in the number and size of burial mounds, which reflected the heightened presence, power, pretensions and prestige of the elite. These tombs were found widely across Japan, most of them situated on the larger agricultural basins of northern Kyushu, the Inland Sea littoral, the Sea of Japan coast of western Honshu and the Kinai and Chûbu regions.

Then, around 250 CE, there began to appear gigantic tombs – in the Kinai vicinity most notably – that reflected the heightened power of regionally dominant groups. The tombs contained more grave goods that reveal the occupant's high status, warrior power, increased connections to the continent and greater interaction with other regions of the archipelago. The scale and contents of these great tombs suggest such growth in the magnitude of elite power and pretension that archeologists use them to signify a new phase of history, that of the Kôfun age, with dates of about 250–550 CE, which we examine below.

The appearance of these great tombs also coincides roughly with the earliest written records pertaining to Japan, at least insofar as those are known today. Unsurprisingly, these written records, which were created by and preserved for the literate few within China's ruling class, shed light primarily on elite affairs. However, one of the earliest of these surviving sources, the *Wajinden* or "Commentary on the People of Wa", which dates to around 290 CE, does seem to shed some light on more general human affairs in the "mountainous islands" wherein dwell "the people of Wa".[28]

Scholars note the many ambiguities within and uncertainties about *Wajinden*, which purports to describe life among the people of Wa, but fails to make clear where Wa was situated.[29] Indeed, its discussion of travel directions and distances – both to and within the land of Wa and whether by land or sea – is thoroughly confusing.

These limitations notwithstanding, *Wajinden* does convey a sense of the land and of life among the people.[30] Thus, we are told that the people of Wa

cultivate grains, rice, hemp and mulberry trees for sericulture. They spin and weave and produce fine linen and silk fabrics. There are no oxen, horses, tigers, leopards, sheep or magpies. Their weapons are spears, shields and wooden bows made with short lower part and long upper part; and their bamboo arrows are sometimes tipped with iron or bone. Thus in what they have and what they lack, they are similar to the people of Tan-erh and Chu-yai.

The report continues: "The land of Wa is warm and mild [in climate]. In winter as in summer the people live on vegetables and go about bare-footed."

The reference to "warm and mild" climate and to people going barefooted year-round suggests that southerly Japan and likely northwest Kyushu is the area being described. The comparison to "Tan-erh and Chu-yai" reinforces that likelihood because they are sites on Hainan Island, off China's southeast coast.

*Wajinden* also reports that in Wa:

The land produces pearls and green jade. There is cinnabar in the mountains. The trees are mountain camphor, horse-chestnut, camphor tree, heath rose, *quercus serrata*, cryptomeria, *quercus dentata*, mulberry and maple; of the bamboo family there are *shino*, arrow bamboo and rattan bamboo. There are also ginger, citrus, pepper, prickly ash and *zingiber mioga*, the excellent flavor of which the people are not aware.

It also notes that in Wa "are monkeys and black pheasants". This botanically well-endowed realm supported a rather complex society that consisted of roughly 30 "countries", some of which were controlled by officials subordinate to "a Queen".

There are class distinctions among the people, and some men are vassals of others. Taxes are collected. There are granaries as well as markets in each province, where necessaries are exchanged under the supervision of the Wa officials.

Mainly, however, *Wajinden* describes lifestyles of the elite and summarizes details of political life and diplomatic relationships. It does so because Chinese rulers of the day had reason to learn about the ruling class of this distant and shadowy land of Wa. They had reason to learn because the politics of the day had prompted a leading figure of Wa, a woman identified as Himiko, to send embassies to Chinese authorities in 238, 243 and 247 CE to seek their goodwill, and in those embassies she evidently was identified as "the Queen of Wa".[31] Whether Himiko was in fact a "Queen" of some sort, where she was headquartered and how large a realm she ruled are all unknown, although both scholars and ideologues have – from the seventh century down to the present – expended immense amounts of energy trying to solve those riddles.

Whatever her precise political status, Himiko stands as a striking example of how agricultural production and the use of iron had, by 250 CE, sustained the rise of ruling elites in the Kyushu-to-Chûbu region and created ongoing interaction with the mainland, most intimately with the southern littoral of Korea. For the next 400 years, as we note more fully below, Japan's Kôfun-era rulers and would-be rulers continued the practice, engaging erratically in politico-military dealings with groups on the peninsula and adjacent areas. Such enterprises were made possible by the material resources and manpower those rulers controlled, and by the larger ships they were able to have constructed and deployed.

The Kôfun-era rulers pursued these ventures, it appears, mainly because of their interest in retaining access to iron supplies and other material goods. Probably as means to that end, they also sought favorable diplomatic relationships with one or another ruling group in the Korea-Manchuria-China region. Whether those considerations were reinforced by linguistic or familial connections between ruling groups in southern Korea and the archipelago is uncertain. But from time to time, at least, emigrants from the mainland clearly played important roles in shaping political and cultural developments on the archipelago.

### Kôfun

The three centuries ca. 250–550 CE are known primarily for their great burial tumuli, which, as noted above, scholars use to denote a new stage in the archipelago's political history. More broadly, these centuries witnessed a continuation of trends established during the preceding Yayoi centuries. There was continued expansion of cultivated acreage, agricultural population, and the portion of Japan occupied by that population. The extent of society's politico-economic stratification, the scale of politico-military operations, and the interplay between elites in Japan and those on the mainland continued to grow, although erratically.

These several trends all had environmental ramifications, as we note below. But first, some comments on Kôfun society. Even more than for later Yayoi, the surviving archeological and written evidence of these centuries sheds light almost entirely on elite affairs, but one can make a few observations about the general populace.

### 1. The Commoners

Most people continued to live in small clusters of a few houses, the number and location of dwellings essentially being dictated by daily logistics: people lived within reasonable walking distance of the fields they tilled and on sites that were reasonably level but not subject to flooding.

The dwellings themselves continued to be Yayoi-type, dirt-floored, thatch-roofed, post-and-beam houses. And the cost and difficulty of house construction and replacement – which probably rose as deforestation reduced timber availability even while population growth was increasing demand – caused people to use them fully.

Each house commonly sheltered several people, including adult siblings, because women seem customarily to have given birth to children in their parents' households, joining their spouses only after the children were old enough to be of service to their paternal households.[32] That arrangement – which maximized the role of the socially visible maternal relationship and minimized that of the socially unprovable paternal relationship – surely enhanced a child's security and strengthened cohesiveness among a household's members.

Two material developments of the Kôfun centuries did improve household life. A standardized type of earthenware, known as *hajiki* (Haji ware), came to be widely used in food storage, processing and consumption. Produced in volume by specialist potters, it was more readily and cheaply available as an item of barter.

More important, perhaps, was the adoption of the *kamado*, a squat cooking stove whose design was of continental origin. Made of high-fired clay, it replaced an open, stone-lined hearth above which a cooking pot was suspended. Whereas smoke from the hearth could eddy about a house interior until it exited via openings in the peak of the roof, the *kamado* had an exhaust port that could vent smoke directly through a hole in the wall, thus improving a house's air quality. Also, the *kamado*'s fuel chamber served to direct more of the fire's heat to the cooking pot, improving its fuel efficiency. As land clearance reduced the quantity of easily accessible fuel wood, that efficiency became ever more valuable. In cooler regions of the northeast, however, the *kamado*'s limited capacity as a room heater discouraged its use and open-hearth arrangements continued to prevail.

The other development in commoner life that seems worthy of note was growing exploitation by the ruling elite. As centuries passed, the rulers developed more elaborate mechanisms of tribute collection, taking a portion of the harvest that likely grew as fast as did productivity per acre or per man-hour of labor.

The elite's success in tribute collection had a couple of noteworthy consequences for commoners. Because the crop that most interested tribute takers was wet rice, villagers depended heavily on other foodstuffs, a situation that sustained dry-field cropping and other horticulture as well as diverse forms of foraging, as noted earlier. As a result, despite the prominence of paddy in the historical record, and despite the low harvest rates of dry-field crops, considerable upland acreage, and probably a swelling acreage near major rivers, was used for dry-field cropping, insofar as weather, topography and soil fertility permitted.

Also, because tribute collection was so effective, the problem of "spring hunger" was not ameliorated by increases in the output of paddy fields, with the result that desperate households found it difficult to save enough seed rice for the new season's planting. The rulers therefore regularized a practice (likely derived from the continent) in which a portion of the tribute rice was "loaned" back to needy villagers as "seed rice" (*suiko*) to sustain them and to assure that they could plant a new crop and thereby meet their next annual tribute obligation.

The other major form of exploitation was labor service. Commoners were conscripted to provide oarsmen on war vessels and portage crews for land transport of tribute goods and other materials. Moreover, they were assembled in huge numbers to work at construction of the giant tumuli, mainly during the agricultural off-season. Thus organized, those projects could continue seasonally year after year until final completion had properly glorified the deceased. By one calculation, for example, the construction of a giant tomb might entail 15 years of work as huge gangs of perhaps 2,000 laborers invested some 6–7,000,000 labor-days (200–230 days per year) moving hundreds of thousands of cubic meters of stone and soil.[33]

### 2. The Elite

Regarding the rulers, the basic story told by the archeological and written evidence is of the gradual rise to predominance of elites situated in the Kinai vicinity, at the eastern end of the Inland Sea. Of this development, one wonders why and how it occurred and with what consequences.

A key factor enabling Kinai elites to prevail was geography. Their cluster of lowlands constituted one of Japan's largest and most productive agricultural basins. It is true that during Kôfun centuries, much of today's Yodo River flatland was still coastal waters and wetland, a part of the Inland Sea. But at the time, so too were many of Japan's other present-day coastal lowlands. So even then, the Kinai lowlands as a whole were more extensive than any of the several basins lining the Inland Sea or Kyushu.

South of Tôhoku, only the Nobi Plain around Nagoya is of comparable size, and only the Kantô Plain around Tokyo is larger. But the Kantô, whose soil in most areas was much less amenable to paddy culture, remained largely forested until centuries later. And the Nobi Plain lacked convenient access to western Japan and mainland Asia because mountain ranges obstructed land travel westward, while ocean travel around the Kii Peninsula was extremely hazardous due to a harsh coastline and turbulent waters.

Kinai elites were able to use their larger agricultural foundation to offset their one major disadvantage. This was that they were situated much farther than their western rivals from the Korean iron that equipped their armies and facilitated their agricultural activity. Given their location, they could safely traverse the Inland Sea and Kanmon Strait to obtain that iron – or other continental goods and services – only by securing the cooperation or acquiescence of those rivals.

The political history of these centuries seems to consist primarily of maneuvering by elites seeking access to the continent and, secondarily, of local rivalries among neighboring elites. The *Wajinden* report on Himiko and Wa foreshadowed this later story. It appears that elites in the Kinai vicinity worked out their local rivalries long enough to battle and bargain their way westward, gradually establishing alliances with, or control over, groups situated along the Inland Sea, in northern Kyushu and on the Sea of Japan littoral.[34]

To secure their access to iron and other benefits on the Korean peninsula, they also found themselves becoming embroiled willy-nilly in peninsular politics, which were as riven as those on the archipelago. Korean records speak of active military involvement by forces from Wa from the 390s until 407, when they were severely defeated by the armies of Koguryô, a regime that controlled the northern half of the Korean peninsula and most of the South Manchurian region.

That defeat had been at the hands of horse-mounted fighters, and the lesson was not lost on Kinai leaders. For centuries, as noted earlier, pony-sized horses had been used as pack animals in the archipelago, and following the reversal of 407, leaders there began training men and mounts for horse warfare while fostering the importation and production of equestrian gear and associated armaments. Also, according to Chinese records, the leaders of Wa labored to rebuild useful diplomatic connections on the mainland.

The success of Kinai leaders in that diplomatic effort, together with their military "modernization", seem to have emboldened them again, and in about 450 CE they renewed their military activism on the peninsula. However, in 475 Koguryô again routed them, along with their southern Korean allies. That rout, which ended Kinai military activity on the mainland for another half-century, also brought a flood of political refugees to the archipelago. There their talents were put to use enhancing the regime by improving its system of administrative control and thereby expanding its political reach and fiscal foundation.

Not every local power holder acquiesced in Kinai ambitions, however. Most famously, perhaps, early in the sixth century a certain Tsukushi no Iwai emerged as the dominant figure in northern Kyushu. He is alleged to have allied himself with a Korean regime hostile to those favored by Kinai leaders, and during the 520s he reportedly obstructed a Kinai military force headed for the peninsula. Iwai's actions forced the Kinai army to redirect its effort and suppress him, which it finally did.[35]

In the following decades Kinai leaders consolidated their control over the seaway to northern Kyushu. However, rivalries among elite groups within the Kinai region itself occupied them well into the seventh century, thwarting any renewed military involvement on the mainland. During the 660s, when Kinai leaders did, as we note in Chapter 4, again engage in peninsular politics, the catastrophic results led to harsh conflict at home and to a period of reform and consolidation that yielded a substantially altered political order.

Earlier, the military reverses of 407 and 475 in Korea had deprived Kinai leaders of their original source of iron ingots and equipment. However, two other developments of that century enabled them gradually to overcome that loss. Probably during the decades after 450 CE, immigrant craftsmen in the Kinai area established furnaces that could smelt iron, enabling rulers to reuse old iron and cast new weapons. Not long afterward, it appears, those Kinai leaders learned that iron sands had been found within Japan, and this discovery offered them a new source of additional iron.[36]

To elaborate, as noted in Chapter 1, some 40 million years earlier, southwestern Japan had been attached to the continent in the vicinity of southern Korea. A portion of the geological formation that held iron sands in southern Korea had been pushed eastward when the Sea of Japan formed, becoming the northerly coast of western Honshu. Particularly in the Izumo vicinity, deposits of iron sand were discovered, perhaps by skilled immigrants. So, local leaders began having them processed and the iron smelted for use in trade with other groups in western and central Japan. That supply became a valuable substitute for Korean iron, but it also created a strong reason for Kinai leaders to seek control of the region. And that quest became an important part of the elite political narrative during the final Kôfun century.

### Environmental Ramifications to 600 CE

Turning, finally, to the question of Kôfun society's environmental impact, basically human activity during the centuries ca. 200–600 CE constituted a continuation of trends from the preceding Yayoi centuries of land clearance. However, those trends were shaped and intensified by several factors: namely, the greater use of upland cultivation and the growing complexity of irrigation technique; the introduction of iron mining and smelting; expansion in the scale of warfare and the use of cavalry forces; and the appearance of more grandiose construction projects.

### 1. Upland Cultivation and Complex Irrigation
Most obviously, perhaps, the opening of ever more upland to cultivation furthered the shifting balance of species in the archipelago, steadily expanding the portion of the biome dedicated to domesticated species at the expense of whatever plants and animals had hitherto occupied the areas.

The development of more complex systems of irrigation reinforced that trend by fostering the construction of dams and ditches that captured hillside run-off and diverted stream flow from established waterways, especially during the summer months so crucial to species maintenance. Moreover, as noted earlier, in non-swamp paddy tillage, flooded fields were drained during late summer so that the crop could ripen, and they generally remained unirrigated for the rest of the year. In consequence, whereas the use of swampland for paddy culture had inconvenienced many natural denizens of the swamp but allowed their survival, the wet-dry cycle of irrigated paddy cropping prevented such wetland communities from becoming established.

Moreover, upland tillage, especially of dry fields, increased substantially the rate of human-induced erosion. In the grand geological picture, of course, erosion is an essential part of the planetary surface's natural, sustainable rhythm. In an enduring *pas de deux*, tectonic movement creates mountain ranges and erosion then wears them down, so that they may be thrown up again and worn down yet again and again.

On the picayune scale of human affairs, however, erosion has two major effects of more immediate consequence. It reduces the fertility of eroded sites, in due course rendering them barren, as we shall note more fully in later chapters. And the soil materials that are washed away settle downstream, gradually filling in swamps, extending coastlines and modifying coastal biomes. In Japan, human-induced erosion became consequent with the introduction of field cropping, its effects mostly becoming visible in later centuries.

### 2. Iron Mining and Smelting

In Japan, as noted above, the mining of iron sands appears to have developed during the fifth century. One should not, however, confuse the mining of iron sands – "placer mining" – with the mining of ore.

Iron sands generally are found in stream beds or in near-surface deposits left by former rivers, and their extraction and processing tend to be much less disruptive of the ecosystem than is the pit-mining of ore. The process does, however, on a relatively small scale, produce waste, disrupt vegetation, foster erosion in the vicinity of the work site and damage the downstream ecosystem.

Moreover, the iron sands of Izumo had a very low percentage of iron, so they required extensive processing. To remove the excess of non-ferrous solids, miners erected a series of dams to form sedimentation pools along the stream below their work site. Sand-bearing water was moved from pool to pool, enabling the heavier, iron-bearing material to settle to the bottom, where workers could collect it for later smelting.[37]

Like placer mining, the smelting of iron developed in Japan during the fifth century. That process was substantially more destructive of woodland because it consumed such great quantities of fuel wood. And such burning produced air pollutants in ways and at rates that organic decay of dead wood did not, while also causing the nutrient value of the consumed wood to be lost to most forest areas.

In short, these processes of mining, sand-processing and smelting all disrupted local environments. And the heavy fuel requirements of smelting and forging spurred deforestation in nearby woodlands.

### 3. Expanded Warfare and Cavalry Use

Warfare is mainly destructive of human life and, one could argue, is thus of benefit to the larger biome. However, insofar as it creates demand for iron weapons, it is indirectly a cause of woodland damage and erosion. Moreover, in the case of Kôfun Japan, because warfare of the day did entail the occasional deployment of large water-borne forces along the Inland Sea and across the straits to Korea, it involved the construction and maintenance of substantial fleets of boats, which also consumed considerable standing timber.

Mounted warfare had a more substantial impact on the bio-system because it fostered the proliferation of horses, which required pasturage, thereby shifting more biome in the direction of horse-supporting grass monoculture. In the near-absence of most other animal husbandry practices, however, much grazing likely was done in and around settlements and along the edges of cropland. So the effect of horse pasturing may have been modest, at least until later centuries.

### 4. More Grandiose Construction

From early forager times, of course, insofar as humans created huts, they altered patches of bio-system. Not until millennia later, however, after early agricultural practices became established and population had multiplied, did the scale and style of settlement construction begin to have appreciable environmental consequences.

In the case of Japan, one could cite the Yayoi-era tombs, as well as settlements of the Yoshinogari sort with their large wooden buildings and stockades, as types of construction that at least foreshadowed significant long-term disruption of the archipelago's biome. And one could argue that the great Kôfun-era tumuli, with their surrounding moats, marked the onset of construction as a force that more-or-less permanently modified portions of the bio-system. As we shall see in Chapter 4, however, it was another set of developments – the introduction of a new, monumental style of wooden construction, initially in the later sixth century and the associated erection of major capital cities centered on an elaborate palace layout, beginning around 700 CE – that transformed construction activity into a force for substantial environmental change.

### RECAPITULATION

In sum, then, the early ("one-stage") form of agriculture came to southwestern Japan, probably from the nearby continent, around 600 BCE or earlier. From the outset, however, it included paddy tillage, which amounted to a de facto later ("two-stage") form of agriculture. Paddy culture's exceptionally high productivity per acre, together with the availability of exploitable acreage for other essential crops, made possible the rapid rate of population growth that reflected greater fecundity and continuing immigration.

Immigration and the agriculture undergirding it were but two facets of continental impact on the archipelago during these centuries. The use of metals, new forms and uses of pottery, new styles of warfare and new patterns of elite burial all reflected continental influence. Moreover, during the final decades of this period, as we shall see in Chapter 4, new concepts and ideologies of rule, new religious creeds, new architectural techniques and a sophisticated form of literacy were all introduced to the archipelago's dominant few, laying the foundation for further striking changes during later centuries.

Rapid social growth during the centuries to 600 CE fostered more elaborate social organization and stratification as well as more inter-communal competition for resources. This Yayoi-Kôfun capacity for both social growth and increasing conflict was heightened by the use of iron tools and weapons. And the task of assuring access to the sources of that iron became a significant purpose of such conflict. By 600 CE these trends had given southwestern and central Japan a complex society that sustained inter-regional conflict, but that was increasingly dominated by horse-mounted elites based in the topographically favored Kinai district.

We have noted the several ways in which these centuries of social growth and change modified the bio-system of affected regions, altering land use and species composition, and fostering erosion with its effects on both upland and lowland. In closing, it seems worth mentioning the other side of that relationship: the ways in which the geographical character of the archipelago shaped social developments.

As noted in Chapter 1, Japan's global position gave it a climate that favored biotic richness. And the fact that the warmer southern half of the archipelago was particularly favorable for field cropping in general and wet rice in particular was a crucial factor in its emergence as the heartland of this agricultural development with all its socio-political ramifications.

Less obviously, perhaps, paleo-geological factors continued to play a role in shaping this history. Topography determined the basic distribution of arable land and people, and hence of a locality's potential political clout. Also, the general eastward advance of this agricultural order, which had been facilitated by the Inland Sea and its bordering lowlands, was subsequently slowed by the existence of the central cordillera, which helped to sustain both forager society and a more pristine bio-system in the northeast. The cordillera's towering mountain ranges, as noted in Chapter 1, had been thrust upward by those processes of tectonic collision and uplift that had filled the space between Japan's northeastern and southwestern regions millions of years earlier.

More narrowly, the relative abundance of iron sands in the Izumo region, which, as we noted, played a role in shaping regional political relationships, reflected the region's paleo-geological connection to the mainland. Finally, the fact that soils of the Kantô region and southern Kyushu were relatively unfavorable to wet-rice culture, largely because of their volcanic heritage, made those regions less attractive to agriculturalists, helping Jômon descendants to continue living in southern Kyushu and much of northeastern Japan. That outcome, in turn, as we shall see, helped shape the archipelago's politics during later centuries.

# 4  Early Agricultural Society, 600–1250

In terms of agricultural technology and human-ecosystem relations, the centuries after 600 CE were basically a continuation of preceding ones. There were, however, a few striking social developments and one noteworthy technological development that had powerful effects on both society at large and the bio-system in much of Japan.

The key social development of the age was creation, and subsequent decay, of a powerful political regime modeled on continental precedents and centered in a sprawling capital city in the Kinai region of central Japan. In that city members of the ruling elite – a few thousand governing a population of millions – went on to produce a much-celebrated "higher culture" whose influence would echo down through subsequent centuries. One aspect of that culture was the key technological development of the age; namely, adoption of a radical new style of architecture for most elite buildings, both political and religious.

The crucial environmental point about the new architecture was that it made immense demands on woodland. Because the archipelago in pre-agricultural days had been essentially a fully wooded, temperate forest zone, human manipulation of woodland produced the most powerful human impact on the bio-system. And because of the ways deforestation for purposes of wood production and deforestation for purposes of agricultural land clearance differ and interact, the topic commands attention, much as the distinctive characteristics of paddy culture did in Chapter 3.

Besides burdening woodland with the demands of a new architecture, consolidation of a continental-style ruling elite entailed a series of other innovations and elaborations that eventuated in complex society-biome interactions. In toto the developments produced not only great privilege for the favored few and further changes in the bio-system but also widespread human hardship, intensified social conflict, gradual modifications in society throughout the realm, and eventually the first signs of a shift to intensive or "two-stage" agriculture.

## REGARDING DEFORESTATION

Because of their dissimilarities and interconnections, it is useful to distinguish deforestation to obtain timber (that is, logging) from deforestation for the purpose of agricultural land clearance.

### Logging

In "traditional" logging (meaning, in the absence of plantation forestry), Japanese loggers, like their fellows everywhere, functioned as scavengers. Like fishermen, they took what they wanted from what was naturally there and then left the ambient bio-system to rejuvenate itself.

What loggers take or leave, of course, depends on their purpose. They may be very selective, felling only the few desired trees and leaving the rest standing, or they may cut more completely, leaving the site stripped of its standing timber. Where a logging project calls only for large timbers or wide planks and boards, for example, or for wood of a certain tree species, fellers will cut only those trees that meet the specifications. If, on the other hand, the project requires diverse sizes of timber as well as firewood, all the trees may be taken.

Whatever the case, once the logging project is complete, the site is left to recover. Depending on how extensively it was cut over and how much secondary injury – damaged trees and undergrowth, dislodged and eroded soil or fire damage – occurred, an abandoned site will sooner or later begin to restock itself. Initially it will sprout grasses, forbs and scrub brush and later fast-growing trees. Eventually (in 50–100 years) the slow-growing but larger trees that constitute a climax forest will regain predominance.

**Figure 4.1:** Construction of temples, such as the Honganji in Kyoto, consumed much firewood and clay to make roof tiles, as well as timber for framing, flooring and paneling, 1962

**Figure 4.2:** Pillars for temples and temple gates required large, straight tree trunks, as at this site in Kyoto, 1962

As long as people do not use such logged sites for other purposes, such as tillage or pasturage, logging usually does not alter the long-term character of the woodland proper. However, given a logger's objective, he may deforest steep slopes, and there the process of removing logs may entail extensive disruption of the soil. As a consequence, logging may precipitate substantial amounts of erosion and flooding that can wreak long-lasting havoc downstream.

### Agricultural Land Clearance

A cultivator seeking land to till prefers relatively level terrain with good soil. And he (or she) much prefers sites that have few or no large trees. The larger the tree, the more difficult it is to cut down and remove, especially for people equipped only with simple axes and chisels. If one simply girdles the tree, to let it die, the large tree will stand dead for years, even decades. Equally bothersome, the bigger the tree, the larger and more solidly established will be its root system, which can obstruct tillage for years after the tree has died.

Farmers may simply burn forest to open it up, but that is a risky process, given the ability of wildfire to spread uncontrollably. It is not surprising, therefore, that deforestation to obtain lumber and fuel wood often leads to land clearance for agricultural purposes. This is so especially when loggers are working on relatively level land, which nearby farmers then clear of debris and commence to till – or when the loggers themselves are basically farmers who sell or use the wood and then clear and farm the land.

Whereas timber removal by itself has only a temporary impact on the affected bio-system, deforestation for agricultural land clearance, whether done for that express purpose or as a secondary result of logging activity, shifts acreage from the support of an indigenous biotic community to the support of "invasive species" – humans and their collaborators. And it does so for as long as the site is farmed or otherwise utilized.

Like logging, land clearance for agriculture also dislodges soil, producing erosion and downstream complications. However, in the case of pasturage and orchardry, the soil dislodgement is temporary and tends to be quite modest. And in the case of tillage, farmers generally work less steep hillsides and try to preserve soil fertility by preventing erosion. So, in and of itself, this form of land clearance probably produces fewer downstream complications than does intensive logging activity *per se*.

Given the intensity of logging pursued by the ruling elite during these centuries, and given their need for diverse types of wood for construction and fuel, it seems likely that logging had more substantial downstream consequences than did agricultural land clearance because it produced so much more erosion. On the other hand, whereas logging activity *per se* changed biotic composition only within the community of indigenous forest members, and then only temporarily, land clearance that increased the total farmed acreage sustained the long-term advance of humans, their collaborators and parasites at the expense of the indigenous biotic community. In combination, then, the two types of deforestation achieved a high level of both short-term and long-term change in Japan's bio-system, doing so initially in the Kinai vicinity and during subsequent centuries more widely across the archipelago.

## FORMATION OF A CENTRAL ELITE, 600–850

For several centuries prior to 600 CE, as noted in Chapter 3, Wa society had been gradually forming local elites, some of which developed into regional elites, with the pre-eminent one becoming established in the Kinai vicinity, perhaps by 400 CE or earlier. This trajectory had been shaped by geography, by the nature of agricultural society, by its interaction with the Jômon forager populace, and by precedents from – and interplay with – the mainland, from whence the Yayoi and Kôfun immigrants came.

From the mid-500s onward, this political consolidation seems to have accelerated. Doubtless the use of military force and other forms of political coercion were central to the process. However, one distinctive facet of Kinai political maneuvering was the use of indigenous mythologies, which were ancestral to what became known as *Shintô*, "the Way of the Gods". They were employed to help win, retain or regain the goodwill of those rivals who had submitted or been subdued. To that end, Kinai policy would define godly relationships in ways that honored those rivals and their legacies while situating them at a level of subordination that most likely reflected an estimate of their real power.[1]

Perhaps the most charming instance of this rhetorical maneuvering was the Kinai effort to establish favorable relations with stubbornly independent leaders in Izumo, and thus to secure access to their iron sands. In that effort, Kinai leaders declared the ancestral deity of the pre-eminent Izumo chiefly lineage to be a mischievous younger brother of – and thus almost on a par with – the primal deity of their own godly progenitors. The official ranks, titles and courtly honors they awarded to Izumo leaders were correspondingly high. Then, in about 659, the Kinai ruler Saimei initiated construction in Izumo of a "grand shrine" (*taisha*) that gave permanent expression to Izumo's high status. The Izumo *Taisha* was ranked just below the primary shrine of the Kinai rulers, which was situated in Ise, over the mountains from their headquarters, due East in the direction of "the rising sun".

As the scale of Wa politics had grown during the sixth century, interaction between elites of archipelago and mainland intensified. Especially from the mid-500s onward, immigrants introduced to members of the Kinai elite select Buddhist religious doctrines, Confucian principles of governance, Taoist thought and other concepts. They also provided instruction in the Chinese language and writing system.[2]

In political maneuvering of the day, factional groups within Japan employed these continental creeds and rhetoric, along with indigenous ones to define relationships and justify claims to power and privilege. Most famously, perhaps, the Soga family and its collaborators, who dominated affairs for much of the century after 550, promoted Buddhism, sent study missions to China and implemented Confucian governmental practices. Then in 645 they were toppled from power in a major domestic coup that led to a cluster of even more radical political changes, those known today as the Taika Reform.

During the 660s, after strengthening ties to Izumo, these Kinai rulers deployed an armada of vessels that ferried some 25,000 warriors to aid political allies in Korea. That military venture proved catastrophic when the armada was overwhelmed and destroyed by a superior Chinese force. The Chinese triumph drove the surviving Wa forces and their peninsular allies back to Japan, where they promptly set to work preparing defensive fortifications at strategic points all the way from Tsushima and northwest Kyushu eastward along the Inland Sea to the Kinai region.[3]

The feared Chinese invasion did not materialize, but stresses of the day precipitated another harsh domestic power struggle that ended in 672 with the triumph of a Kinai leader known to history as Tenmu *tennô* ("heavenly ruler") or Emperor Tenmu. He proved to be a ruthless but rational ruler. Skillfully avoiding continental entanglements, he pursued a vigorous policy of political consolidation that involved developing a more elaborate bureaucratic structure and fuller, more regularized control of the countryside, and, thus, of the regime's fiscal and manpower foundations. He also promoted extensive codes of law, rules of governance and articulations of myth and ritual to legitimize his rule.[4]

This Kinai drive to centralize power took much inspiration from Chinese precedents, and a major expression of royal domination in China was the ruler's grand capital city and palace compounds. Tenmu evidently envisaged such capital construction for his headquarters at Asuka, but never carried the project beyond erection of an elegant palace. However, around 690, his successor (and widow)

Jitô *tennô* launched the construction of Fujiwara-kyô, a sprawling, Chinese-style, governmental headquarters compound that would stand within a capital city of unprecedented size. Located near the edge of the plain some 20 km south of today's Nara, it was, as we note below, the first of several such projects that would use the new architectural style to ever-greater extent despite the social and environmental consequences of doing so.

This process of political consolidation yielded a regime – commonly known as the *ritsuryô* order or "government of laws and ordinances" – that flourished well into the ninth century and was not effectively replaced until centuries after that. For our purposes its major aspects are these: capital cities; the new architecture mentioned above; centralized control and exploitation of the hinterland; and consolidation of the margins.

## Capital Cities

The establishment of capital cities in Japan constituted one of the most striking changes in the history of the archipelago's human-ecosystem relations. The rise of large urban centers anywhere constitutes a noteworthy change, but the abrupt introduction of this particular urban form proved especially disruptive. Three aspects of the Chinese capital ideal were central to the impact that *ritsuryô* city-building had on Japan. One was the sheer size of the desired city and the grandeur of its official structures. Another was the notion of capital city as embodiment of the regime, which meant that the founder of every "new" regime should have a new capital. A third was the ideal of dual or multiple capitals and royal residences.

Before examining these aspects of *ritsuryô* city-building, however, let us consider some issues imbedded in the very notion of cities and the urban-rural dyad in particular.

### 1. On Cities and the Urban-Rural Dyad

Our sense that society consists of distinct urban and rural parts is a fixture of present-day social perception. And it is laced with emotion and judgmental content that can favor either side: city slicker vs. hick from the sticks; knowledgeable, urban sophisticate vs. backward, ignorant rube; or virtuous, hardworking countryman vs. sleazy, urban hustler, and so on ad nauseam.

More importantly, the rural-urban dyad envisions rural households and groupings that provide their own necessities of life, whereas urbanites mostly depend on strangers who provide those necessities from afar. And, similarly, households dispose of the waste that rural folks generate locally, whereas urban waste must be taken elsewhere by elaborate transport arrangements.

The reality, of course, is more ambiguous, not only in the obvious sense that simplistic moral judgmentalism is absurd but in the more subtle sense that urban and rural are not two neatly distinct categories. Even a simple triadic categorization of city-town-hinterland captures the human configuration of both agricultural and industrial societies far better than does the urban-rural dyad.

The basic distinction between self-sustaining rural life and deeply dependent urban life poses problems. In "mature" industrial societies, of course, the distinction is misleading because by then rural folks, too, are deeply dependent on providers other than themselves or their neighbors. But even in agricultural societies – and particularly in places such as the Japanese archipelago, where arable land and especially good paddy land is scarce and highly valued – the urban-rural dyad is deeply compromised by the durable mingling of urban settlement and arable land that is tilled by farmers who reside on site. In Japan, moreover, because of the way towns and cities expanded as society industrialized, extensive agricultural activities persisted in urban areas well into the later twentieth century.

Having noted these qualifications, however, the urban-rural dyad is still useful in examining the rise of *ritsuryô* capital cities because the Chinese urban model envisioned a capital city sustained by rural producers throughout the realm. Before looking at the *ritsuryô* case, however, let us briefly examine the way cities generally depend on the hinterland for provisions and waste disposal.

Regarding provisions, most obviously the food that urbanites consume is produced and, to greater or lesser extent, processed into consumable form elsewhere. The raw material of clothing, similarly, is produced and at least partially processed elsewhere, as are heating and cooking fuel, basic construction materials and other essentials. Especially in larger urban centers, the necessary water usually comes from elsewhere. Even the oxygen that urban populations breathe is produced by plants that grow, almost entirely, far beyond city limits.

Despite this pervasive dependency, urban populations manage to survive, doing so by using three mechanisms to secure those necessities. Most simply, they, like other human groups, rely on natural rhythms of the bio-system, as in the case of winds blowing oxygen in and carbon dioxide out or of water flowing nearby in rivers and subterranean waterways. Much more complex is the acquisition of goods produced by human effort. Urbanites may rely on coercive power, as in the case of taxation, or on transactional lures (material quid pro quos), as in the case of commercial exchange. In actual practice, of course, these mechanisms of coercion and enticement usually intertwine.

Regarding urban waste of myriad sorts, it must be disposed of somehow, somewhere other than at the site of its creation. In pre-industrial societies the task was greatly simplified by the fact that nearly all waste was organic and therefore subject to natural biological reprocessing. Ceramic shards and metal were the main exceptions, with the former commonly being dumped or buried and the latter, because of its high value, mostly being purposely recycled for further human use.

The organic waste was mostly deposited in latrines, dumped into garbage pits or heaps, or, in the case of human bodies, buried or cremated. At that point the organic material was recycled, whether by micro-organisms or larger animals. Or it was dumped into rivers or streams and washed away for biotic recycling downstream.

Turning now to the *ritsuryô* case, one finds all these urban characteristics. The several techniques of waste disposal were all employed. And as regards urban provisioning, the intertwining of coercion and enticement were well developed. Indeed, such intertwining seems to have been present even earlier, in the small headquarters towns of the late Yayoi period. Cultivators in nearby areas were assured protection against pillagers or competitors from elsewhere in return for fulfilling regularized corvée labor and tribute requirements.

Subsequently, the *ritsuryô* regime combined the two mechanisms in a grandly elegant rationale for its tribute (tax) claims. The realm, it was asserted, belonged to the emperor, but in a proper act of benevolence he (or she) bestowed certain "use rights" on subordinates in return for their fulfilling of certain quid pro quo obligations. Subordinate members of the elite were delegated governing authority of explicit sorts, with designated rewards in return for dutiful service. And below them cultivators were assured use rights to specified parcels of land in return for fulfillment of the associated corvée and tribute obligations.

So there was no "ownership" of real estate, no "buying" or "selling" of land. Instead, this mechanism of officially sanctioned use rights as quid pro quo for tribute goods and services became customary practice, underlying the provisioning of most of Japan's capital cities and regional political headquarters towns until the 1870s.

The use-rights mechanism could do so because even as new configurations of power appeared and disappeared and economic complexities proliferated, the mechanism allowed transfer and adjustment of rights and obligations as shifts in power and need occurred. Especially during the centuries of intensive agriculture, as we shall see in later chapters, that mechanism enabled rulers and ruled, rich and poor alike, to manipulate land-control arrangements in ways that helped accommodate changes of the day. Not until the year 1873 was the concept of real estate as "property" adopted from Europe and land ownership and the right to buy and sell it formally established.

On the other hand, as we note later in this chapter, while the notion of taxable real estate ownership did not develop, a system of commercial exchange arose to handle other goods and services during the later centuries of the *ritsuryô* period. That system proved central to the rise of durable small towns widely scattered about the realm, and it gradually became, as well, a factor in large-city provisioning.

For early *ritsuryô* capital cities, however, it was the system of official use rights linked to reasonably effective enforcement of control that enabled rulers to keep their great cities provisioned. Before looking more closely at how these urban rulers used this system to control their hinterland populace, and thus sustain their cities, let us examine the aforementioned aspects of the cities that were central to their impact on the archipelago's society and bio-system; namely, city size, city as symbol and multiple capitals.

## 2. City Size

Whereas Kôfun-era rulers lived in elegant thatch-roofed buildings situated among other buildings housing perhaps hundreds of kinsmen and subordinates, the builders of *ritsuryô* capitals envisaged great, rectangular cities that could house tens of thousands. They were to be laid out in meticulous checkerboard fashion, roughly 5 × 6 km in size, and surrounded by high, tile-covered walls pierced by grand wooden gates.

One could enter the city through one of its gates and traverse it South-to-North via the grand central boulevard, or in all four directions via numerous criss-crossing lesser avenues and streets. Some sections of the city were devoted to sprawling walled-and-gated compounds housing the palaces, mansions and administrative buildings of the ruling elite. Others held temples, shrines, warehouses, markets and scores of city blocks set aside for commoner use as residential space. Such a city might house 100,000 people or more, most of them commoners who, in one way or another, served the wants of the aristocratic few.

### 3. City as a Symbol of the Regime

The burden that such a city placed on the archipelago's bio-system was heightened by the notion that it symbolized the establishment of a "new" regime.[5] And because political rivalries among eminent lineages led to periodic coups, successive new capitals were erected.

To elaborate, during the Soga heyday before 645, Kinai rulers had mostly maintained their headquarters in the Asuka vicinity of the southern Nara Basin, where they built elegant palaces and temples. But in 667, after the military debacle in Korea, the ruler Tenji moved his court northward to Ōtsu at the South end of Lake Biwa, probably as part of the regime's earlier-noted defense preparations. He erected a fine palace and associated temples, but five years later, the newly triumphant Tenmu moved back to Asuka. There he pursued his own grandiose palace and temple construction and started planning a great capital city in the Chinese manner.[6] As mentioned above, his widow Jitō implemented those plans, building Fujiwara-kyō on the nearby plain.

Subsequently, as we note more fully below, a succession of new capital cities was erected, most famously Heijō-kyō (later called Nara) in the 710s and Heian-kyō (later called Kyoto) in the 790s. When such moves were made, buildings from the existing city were routinely disassembled and moved to the new one. But in the process, tiles and timbers were inevitably damaged, and rotted or otherwise defective pieces had to be replaced. Moreover, structures tended to be enlarged and additional ones erected, so each new urban project required new materials – as well as goods sufficient to support the vast army of laborers who did the work.

### 4. Multiple Capitals

The pressure on woodland was further heightened by the Chinese ideals of dual or multiple capitals and royal residences at other sites. During the 700s, when Heijō-kyō was the primary capital, a large, secondary capital (baito) was maintained at Naniwa, a port on the Inland Sea coast in the vicinity of present-day Ōsaka. Other secondary capitals were envisioned, and during those decades a number of separate royal residences were established here and there in the Kinai vicinity.

In combination these factors of lavish construction and city size and number meant that central Japan experienced a huge increase in logging activity. That work required thousands of laborers to work year after year as fellers, loggers, raftsmen, boatmen, road-builders, ox-cart operators, kiln operators, hewers and carpenters. And all those people had to be recruited, fed and housed for months on end. As became evident during the ninth century, capital construction as desired was an enterprise that could not be sustained; neither the human nor the material resources sufficed.

An especially noteworthy factor in that situation was the earlier-mentioned new architecture, which placed unprecedented demands on the archipelago's woodlands.

## The New Architecture

As one scholar has put it: "Japan experienced a veritable revolution in architectural production during the sixth century."[7] Jômon-Yayoi-Kôfun architecture, it will be recalled, had used posts set into the ground to support wooden-framed buildings with thatched walls and roofs. By Kôfun times buildings of the elite might be substantial, two-storey structures, but even then they required relatively little timber, mostly from trees of modest size.

The new architectural style – which in Japan was first used for Buddhist temples and then gradually came to be employed in more and more governmental buildings and aristocratic residences – replaced post-hole construction with hewn stone foundations upon which pillars were set or sills placed.[8] The use of heavy-duty mortise-and-tenon joinery instead of rope lashing enabled carpenters to construct far more sturdy and durable framing. They were enabled thereby to use much larger timbers as both pillars and cross-pieces, and so to construct vastly larger and more elaborate buildings.

Indeed, the largest pillars, such as those found in giant Buddhist temples, were simply huge tree trunks – preferably of *hinoki* (Japanese cypress). The trees were carefully selected from dense, old-growth stands in which they had grown straight and fast, shedding their lower branches quickly and producing straight-grained wood that was both sturdy and attractive. Smaller trees provided the framing timbers and floor, wall and roof boards.

This extremely sturdy construction permitted the replacement of relatively light thatch roofs with heavier wood, bark or tile. Of the three, tile roofs involved by far the most complex provisioning. To produce the tile, artisans had to locate and dig up adequate deposits of clay, shape it into tiles, bake the pieces in large kilns and later bundle them for eventual delivery and use. The baking process, which required sustained heat, consumed immense volumes of fuel wood.

Moreover, tile was by far the heaviest of the three types of roofing. All tile is heavy, of course, but the tile used in *ritsuryô* construction was especially heavy because it was a type known as *hongawara*. These tiles were thick, semi-tubular pieces that roofers aligned in overlapping rows running from peak to eaves. To help hold them in place and to improve water-tightness, roofers slathered a bed of clay on the boards of the under-roof and placed the tile on it.

The combination of heavy under-roofing, clay bed and overlapping rows of thick tile constituted an extremely heavy roof and required elaborate structural underpinning. To handle it, carpenters developed complex systems of wooden bracketing, bracing and joinery that could support their grandly designed tile roofs. These complications notwithstanding, tile roofs gradually came to prevail because they were more durable, offered greater protection against urban fire and remained available even after deforestation caused roofing-quality bark and wood to become scarce.

So the elegant new tile roofs consumed wood as both structural materials and fuel wood. The demand for fuel wood also rose because the logging and construction projects continually required iron tools and because the projects also involved production of other paraphernalia, as we note later on. In combination these timber and fuel-wood demands made all types of woodland targets of exploitation, and the scale and recurrent nature of such construction assured that the demand was immense.

The replacement of post-hole construction with stone foundations did, of course, reduce losses from posts rotting in the soil. And tile roofing reduced the ease with which urban fires could spread from building to building. However, those reductions in loss were of relatively little consequence in face of the massive increase in overall wood consumption fostered by the new architecture. That consumption was maximized by the earlier-noted ideals of grand cities, multiple capitals, awe-inspiring temples and additional royal residences.

### Control and Exploitation of the Hinterland

The unprecedented orgy of *ritsuryô* city-building obviously necessitated immense inputs of both energy and matériel. To obtain them required a well-organized system of control and exploitation, and for well over a century Kinai leaders were successful in operating such a system despite the various complications their enterprise produced and encountered.

To operate the system, they developed an elaborate bureaucratic structure. In the capital city alone, some 10,000 people worked as administrators, clerks, technicians and menial assistants of myriad sorts. Some 60-odd provincial governors, with their staffs and enforcement agencies, were stationed about the realm at sites designated provincial headquarters. They in turn oversaw some 550–600 district administrators with their underlings, who were charged with both keeping the peace in the 4,000 or so "townships" of the realm and assuring that tribute goods and services were provided to higher authorities as stipulated by law. The few thousand higher-ranking members of this sprawling apparatus were carefully fitted into an elaborate structure of aristocratic ranks, titles and privileges that helped assure their loyalty and performance.

To facilitate officialdom's task of extracting labor service and tribute goods, the regime undertook land surveys that attempted to locate and measure the acreage of all wet-rice fields. It also initiated censuses intended to determine the population of able-bodied producers in every household. And it elaborated regulations stipulating the rates of corvée labor and rice tribute per-acre and per-household-adult, as well as the climatic or other variables that would warrant adjustments in the burden. Other regulations specified the tribute rates on such handicraft products as salt, textiles, paper or charcoal.

Armed with these statistics and rules, provincial governors were to determine the quantity of tribute goods and services that every household and township in their jurisdiction could be required to provide, and thus the quantity of goods and labor they must forward to the warehouses and worksites of the capital city. And a portion of that service obligation was to provide manpower for a conscript army whose assigned tasks were to enforce the rules, suppress dissidents, guard against invaders and, as we note further on, expand the realm into the farther corners of the archipelago.

This whole enterprise depended, of course, on the existence of some system for transporting tribute goods from throughout the realm to the capital city.[9] It appears that the rulers initially intended all such goods to move along highways, perhaps in accord with their Chinese model, or because maritime travel seemed more risky and more difficult to control. Within a few decades, however, both waterways and highways were carrying tribute goods, probably because water transport was appreciably cheaper, easier and faster for many parts of the realm. Especially along the Inland Sea, official ports were designated or established and supervisory staffs were installed, with authority to mobilize corvée labor and vessels as needed to move goods and people.

More elaborate than waterways was the highway system. A few major routes were identified that would lead directly to the capital city from minor branch roads in all parts of the realm. Work crews were mobilized to improve existing routes so as to meet the new standards of width and slope and to build new roads as needed. They felled trees, cleared brush and graded hillsides to make smooth road surfaces. They constructed drainage systems to prevent flooding and erosion of the roads, and they established and maintained fording sites at rivers along the main highways. At major crossings they even maintained "pontoon bridges, ferries, and emergency lodgings" as necessary.[10]

A system of barrier gates was established to discourage unauthorized travel, while some 3,500 horses for official use were stabled at relay stations. About 400 post stations were erected at ten-mile intervals to provide traveling officials with overnight lodging.[11] The corvée obligations of nearby townships were specified, and supervisory personnel were assigned to the post stations to assure that tribute goods and official travelers moved along as per schedule.

In its entirety this elaborate system of control and exploitation served its purpose very well for a century or more. Indeed, one could argue that it worked too well, and that its very success helped assure its ultimate failure.

### Consolidation of the Margins

The same key factors that spurred other aspects of *ritsuryô* consolidation – concern about danger from the mainland and a desire to maximize the ruling elite's tribute base – shaped policies toward the realm's socio-geographical margins. The policies had two basic foci: regulating contact with mainlanders and extending the realm as far as possible across the archipelago.

#### 1. Regulating Mainland Contacts

The turmoil and dynamics of northeast Asia during the centuries of *ritsuryô* hegemony assured that an irregular stream of mainlanders – migrants, diplomats, the occasional missionary, castaways, traders and pirates – kept arriving on the islands.[12] As during Yayoi-Kôfun centuries, they mostly traveled the shortest, safest route, which was from southeast Korea via Tsushima to northwest Kyushu, although a few vessels entered ports elsewhere in western Kyushu and along Honshu's West coast.

Because most contacts continued to be via Tsushima, the *ritsuryô* regime designated Hakata Bay the authorized point of entry. After the military debacle of 663, as earlier noted, it had built a string of defensive fortifications that reached from

Tsushima to the Kinai region. In following decades it deployed coastal watchmen to report all suspicious marine activity, had foreign vessels directed to Hakata, issued regulations to control the movement of mainlanders within Japan, and established a large, well-manned and well-fortified regional bastion at Dazaifu, some 12 km inland from Hakata Bay.

As tensions with China eased during the 700s, *ritsuryô* leaders sought to renew official contacts by sending formal diplomatic missions. To do so without becoming entangled in Korean peninsular politics, they decided to send their delegates directly to China, sailing via the Ryukyus or straight from southwest Kyushu. That choice, however, required that they employ large, Chinese-style junks rather than the small dugout-based vessels of ordinary usage that we treated in Chapter 3. Probably utilizing immigrant craftsmen, a shipyard in the vicinity of today's Hiroshima produced large, flat-bottomed sailing junks equipped with 3–5 masts of up to 75-foot height, roughly the length of the vessel. These ships were able to carry well over 100 passengers and freight on the multi-day trip to China. The trip was sufficiently costly and risky, however, that only about eight such official voyages were made before they were abandoned in 894.[13]

As for the mainlanders who were formally permitted to enter Japan, they were to do so only via Hakata Bay, being housed and processed there at a government-operated center. Officials at that site also were to oversee all trading activity and supervise the movement of those few mainlanders who were permitted to travel elsewhere in the islands.

As mainland affairs stabilized after the 700s, the influx of migrants diminished. That stabilization also eased the fear of military invasion, and apart from the occasional pirate sortie, mainland contacts thereafter mostly involved cultural and material exchange that catered to the *ritsuryô* elite.

### 2. Extending the Realm

The system for regulating mainland contacts seemed to work well enough in areas occupied by the agricultural people of Wa. But on the peripheries North and South, control was not so secure, which prompted the regime to improve it, in a process that substantially enlarged the realm.

In the South, two aspects of Kyushu's history presented challenges to Kinai leaders. Agricultural society and ruling elites had emerged in northerly Kyushu well before they did in the Kinai vicinity, and for centuries members of this Kyushu elite had enjoyed closer relations with mainlanders than had those in the Kinai region. That heritage seems to have helped fuel periodic outbreaks of resistance to Kinai control, as in the earlier-noted rebellion of Tsukushi no Iwai in the 520s, and also in other incidents of the 730s and 860s. Kinai leaders were able to suppress those challengers, but, as we note further on, the process tended to involve concessions that gradually helped weaken Kinai rule.

The other complicating aspect of Kyushu's history was its older heritage of forager peoples known as Hayato and Kumaso, who had lived there for untold generations.[14] The Kumaso may have been overrun or assimilated during the later Yayoi-Kôfun period, but prior to the 700s the Hayato were largely able to rebuff attempts by Wa leaders to secure their submission. Subsequently, however, after *ritsuryô* leaders established the Dazaifu headquarters and consolidated their control of northern Kyushu, they were able to deploy forces sufficient to compel Hayato submission. Then, in the manner employed elsewhere, they awarded posts and titles to cooperative Hayato leaders, utilizing them in various guard-duty functions and thus integrating them into their own status hierarchy.

Substantially greater effort was required to secure the northern frontier.[15] The indigenous population there – the Emishi – was much greater and was spread across a much larger region. Moreover, the Emishi had acquired some of the agricultural and horse-riding skills introduced to Japan during the Yayoi period, and those skills made them more able to resist conquest. Nevertheless, the task of "pacifying" them seemed worthwhile because – quite apart from the possibility that Emishi leaders might align with one or another mainland regime – the northern region was so large and appeared to have such potential for development and exploitation.

Indeed, for generations agricultural settlers had been slowly spreading northeastward, circumventing the mountain chains of the central cordillera by crossing the southern coastal plain of Chûbu into the Kantô Plain, by traveling northeastward along the Sea of Japan littoral, or by trekking up the Kiso River and on through tortuous intermontane valleys into tillable regions of northeastern Honshu. And during the eighth century, government policy encouraged such settlement.

When the Emishi resisted this encroachment, the government dispatched military forces to subdue them, most notably during the 720s–730s and the four decades to 810. Also, as with the Hayato, it attempted to draw Emishi leaders into the *ritsuryô* order by awarding such titles and political roles as seemed helpful to the cause. The policy evidently worked, and as the century advanced, *ritsuryô* control extended ever further beyond the Kantô into the fertile valleys and coastal plains of northern Honshu, reaching roughly to the vicinity of Morioka.

The Emishi resistance was persistent and powerful, however, and when "pacification" armies were withdrawn, settlers in the Kantô and northerly areas had to develop and maintain their own defensive capabilities. An important factor in this Emishi capacity to resist was their military skill, which enabled them to challenge the government's foot soldiers. Living in a region where both climate and topography favored pasturage and horse-breeding, they had mastered the art of mounted warfare. As an official chronicler lamented in 839: "fighting with bows and horses is a custom of the barbarian hunters; one of them is a match for even ten ordinary men".[16]

Under these circumstances, settlers of necessity developed comparable military skills, and as decades passed, those "eastern warriors", whether of Emishi, settler or mixed ancestry, acquired a reputation as Japan's finest mounted fighting men. *Ritsuryô* leaders would later discover that, whatever their ancestry, they posed a vastly greater threat to elite privilege than the earlier Emishi ever had done.

\* \* \*

This process of expansion that brought people of Wa and their agricultural enterprises ever farther northeastward contributed, of course, to society's overall demographic growth. As noted in Chapter 3, the Wa population is thought to have grown roughly ninefold during the centuries 0–700 CE to an estimated 5,400,000 people. Other estimates, as we note below, place the number at about 6,000,000 as of 735 CE.

Needless to say, this long-term demographic increase involved an immense amount of land clearance and entailed ever-greater inroads on the archipelago's bio-system. So, while the demands of the elite and their new urban elegance placed especially intense burdens on the Kinai vicinity, this overall growth of early agricultural society had environmental ramifications that affected the entire realm.

## ENVIRONMENTAL RAMIFICATIONS OF THE RITSURYÔ ORDER

Creation and maintenance of the *ritsuryô* political order had some particularly noteworthy environmental ramifications. As noted above, changes in vegetational composition due to deforestation and more extensive tillage had their most severe effects at the center – in the Kinai vicinity. The greater frequency, regularity and volume of population movement about the realm had effects that were more widespread. And these two factors of vegetational change and human movement appear to have interacted with climatic fluctuations to produce other realm-wide consequences of note, both environmental and societal. Before examining these realm-wide matters, however, let us look at the Kinai experience.

### Regarding the Center

The erection and maintenance of a series of sprawling capital cities that employed the new style of architecture required immense amounts of timber.[17] And because the movement of heavy timber was a daunting task, given the technology of the day, builders obtained their material from the nearest sources that could satisfy their requirements.

From the outset, however, the nearest woodlands were already degraded. Thus, Jitô's 690s capital of Fujiwara-kyô was built in the southern Nara Basin, but prior construction, fuel-wood use and land clearance had already deforested the once lushly wooded areas nearby. So the builders had to obtain timber from elsewhere, mainly from Mt Tanakami in southern Ômi Province. They worked the logs from felling site down to river's edge; floated them from there down to and along the Uji River, and then dragged them back up the Kizu to a landing at Izumi (today's Kizu town). There the logs were laboriously hauled ashore, loaded onto ox-carts and sent slowly southward some 25 km to the construction site.

The next capital, Heijô-kyô, erected during the 710s, was situated at the Nara Basin's northern end. Its construction utilized buildings from Fujiwara-kyô and took what timber was available from the adjoining hills. But its builders also had to exploit Mt Tanakami and the Kôka hills, both in southern Ômi, as well as locations in Iga Province on the upper Kizu River.

During the century of Heijô-kyô's existence, the regime maintained a major secondary capital at Naniwa, which utilized timber taken from the surrounding region. And, as noted earlier, emperors also built "detached palaces" at other sites in the Kinai vicinity, notably at Kuni on the Kizu River; at Shigaraki, which was situated between the Kôka and Tanakami hills; and at Hora, near the southern tip of Lake Biwa. All of these sites offered relatively favorable access to standing timber.

Then during the 780s, Emperor Kanmu ordered construction of a new primary capital at Nagaoka, a site near the Yodo River that gave him better access to both the woodlands of the northern Kinai region and, via maritime transport, to Inland Sea locations. A decade later, when problems of flooding made Nagaoka-kyô untenable, Kanmu relocated yet farther northward to build Heian-kyô. In all these moves, buildings from prior sites were torn down and relocated, but each new project still required immense quantities of new timber and fuel wood.

In addition, these centuries witnessed massive projects that erected Buddhist temples – mostly in the Kinai vicinity – to promote the faith and benefit their aristocratic sponsors. And other projects yielded grand shrines intended to honor the indigenous *Shintô* gods and thereby the imperial family and its collaborators. As early as the 620s, during the Soga heyday, some 46 Buddhist temples had already been erected, and in following decades, construction was so frenetic that by the 690s there were some 545 government-supported temples in the Kinai vicinity alone.[18]

The religious building boom continued during the 700s, producing yet grander structures. The greatest of these later temples was the Tôdaiji, situated on the eastern edge of Heijô-kyô. Construction began there during the 740s and in the outcome yielded a remarkable assemblage of buildings. It has been estimated that the initial timber requirements of that temple alone would have denuded the equivalent of some 900 hectares (2,200 acres) of top-grade timberland, or, in more practical terms, of vastly more acreage of the mixed woodland that was common in central Japan.

These centuries of grand construction also proved particularly damaging to woodland because the crude tools of the day wasted much wood. Until the later 700s, it appears, saws were not used, and tree trunks and limbs were shaped by axe, adze, chisel and planing knife. By one estimate, "as much as nine-tenths of the lumber was wasted in the process of dressing".[19] Of course, much of the waste could be used for fuel, but that did not reduce the demand for larger trees.

By the time Kanmu undertook construction of Heian-kyô in the 790s, timber was so difficult to find and the social stresses of these great enterprises so great that he never completed the city's construction. And no new capital cities were built for centuries thereafter. Similarly, religious construction slowed as the difficulties of such tasks intensified.

By then, however, the damage had been done. Simply to maintain the city of Heian, logging crews had to press farther northward into the upper reaches of the Ôi River watershed, southward into the intermontane forests of Kii, across the Inland Sea into the Yoshino River valley of Shikoku and eastward into the Kiso River system that reaches northward from the Nobi Plain. And they did so even though the difficulties of transport sharply raised the cost – and sometimes reduced the value – of the timber acquired.

Exemplifying the difficulties of transport, to get timber from the Kiso watershed to Heian required that it be hauled some 25 mi overland by ox-cart to Lake Biwa, rafted another 25 mi to the lake's South end, and then floated more than 30 mi down the Seta-Uji and up the Yodo-Katsura rivers to the building site. The overland trek was so long and difficult, however, that all the timber had to be cut into five- or six-foot lengths and split into six or eight pieces for the trip. Thus processed, the pieces were of much more limited utility, but builders still deemed them worth the cost and effort.

The demand for woodland yield was heightened by the many other uses of wood – for boats and ships, for the giant-sized religious statuary of the day, for metal-smelting and ceramic-firing, for cooking-fuel and for the simple construction and maintenance needs of commoners. Because of this intensive demand, during the eighth century most of the remaining, accessible old-growth stands in the Kinai vicinity were cut off, and the ongoing demand for fuel wood and small timber was so great that harvested woodlands were unable to re-establish new stands of high forest.

Rather, logged-off sites that were not too steeply sloped commonly were utilized by cultivators for dry-field or "slash and burn" tillage, or for such orchardry as tea, mulberry, persimmon, lacquer or chestnut culture. Although some of the tillage practices were not especially productive, they and the orchardry served local interests and were less burdened by the rulers' tribute demands.

Of the woodland that survived in and around the Kinai region, much came to be characterized by scrub growth that was very flammable. The reckless use of fire for land clearance, other human sources of fire and lightning strikes seem to have produced a rash of wildfires in the region, and during the eighth century some ten major forest fires roared through woodlands there, threatening palaces and cities, terrifying the populace and eliciting attempts – generally ineffective – at fire-fighting.

The denuding of woodland also spurred erosion and downstream flooding and sedimentation. Indeed, at Nagaoka flood waters pouring down from recently denuded hills on the city's West flank are said to have been the key factor prompting Kanmu to abandon that capital after only a decade of use.[20] Because denuded hillsides were less able to retain rainfall and snowmelt, sudden flooding became more frequent and severe, with particularly destructive effects on irrigation systems and the paddy cultivation they sustained.

The long-term effect of such erosion and sedimentation is very apparent in the changing shape of the Kinai river system and the shoreline near present-day Osaka. The process of coastline change in that vicinity traces, of course, back to pre-Jômon millennia when the post-glacial rise in sea-level slowly transformed the central lowlands of southwest Japan into the Inland Sea. Initially that sea reached far into the Kinai vicinity, but gradually the upstream areas filled in. As recently as the eighth century, however, lowlands immediately South and East of the Nagaoka site still consisted largely of lakes and swampland, while much of today's Osaka Plain was coastal waters and estuaries of the Yodo and Yamato rivers. In following centuries, sediments brought down from eroding hillsides slowly filled in the marine areas, destroying and relocating coastal biomes even while creating more lowland for eventual tillage and settlement.

The scavenging, wildfire and erosion also caused more and more hillsides in the Kinai vicinity gradually to lose their fertility. As a result, more and more upland areas evolved into poorly vegetated scrub and grassland. Two main components of scrubland growth were Japanese red pine (*akamatsu*) and dwarf bamboo (*sasa*). The red pine is a somewhat scraggly tree that yields little valuable lumber. It fares poorly in healthy forest but grows much better than most competing trees on deteriorated soils, while the dwarf bamboo is a tough, rapidly spreading under-brush that stands about two-to-three feet high, suppresses other low growth and is highly flammable.

When hard-pressed residents repeatedly harvested this scrub growth for fuel or other uses, the denuded areas gradually evolved into barren areas known generically as "bald mountains" (*hageyama*). As uplands lost the capacity to sustain indigenous vegetation, they also lost the capacity to support humans. They provided less and less fuel wood and other produce, supported less game for foraging and contributed fewer nutrients to the run-off that sustained paddy tillage.

That downturn in woodland bio-productivity was substantially less pronounced elsewhere in the archipelago. Cumulatively, however, the trend in central Japan interacted with other trends of the day, as we note below, to produce ramifications of a more realm-wide sort.

### Regarding the Realm

Two key aspects of *ritsuryô* policy had particularly noteworthy realm-wide envir-onmental consequences. One was the implementation of tribute policies based on land surveys and population censuses; the other, development and utilization of a realm-wide system of travel with continental connections. The effects of those policies were complicated, however, by the role of weather in determining agricul-tural output, so that topic too requires a brief note.

### 1. Land Surveys and Population Censuses

As noted earlier, land surveys officially focused on paddy fields because their relatively high productivity enabled the rulers to skim off a sizeable tribute yield.[21] Dry-field crops did not regularly provide much excess, so government policy primarily encouraged the development and regular cultivation of more paddy acreage. The rulers appear to have expressed an interest in dry-field grains, notably barley and wheat, only when failures of the rice crop threatened to produce famine that would undermine the regime's supply of tribute and corvée labor.

The population censuses served two main purposes. They enabled rulers to locate exploitable corvée labor and to determine the labor force available to each household for rice tillage and hence the optimal level of tribute to require of each.

These survey and census policies sought to maximize, in an orderly and equitable manner, the level of exploitation to which the public would be subjected. The net effect, however, was nearly to eliminate any advantage that paddy tillage offered producers, with the consequence that they tended surreptitiously to open more land to dry-field cultivation and orchardry. Its yield was theirs to keep, and in the event of erratic weather, such land might yield a more usable crop. This practice led, however, to more "slash and burn" tillage and to cultivation of more fields on uplands and hillsides, which increased the rate of erosion and downstream complications.

Moreover, when producer households encountered crop failure or other misfortune, the tribute system's demands could spur individuals or even whole households to abscond, heading into the hills or toward frontier regions. There they would try to open new land secretly, resort to traditional forager practices, or pursue those intra-species forms of foraging called piracy and brigandage.

Overall, then, the survey and census policies served intentionally to increase the acreage devoted to paddy tillage and unintentionally to increase other tillage activity on hillsides, in intermontane areas, and on the frontier, particularly in the northeast.

As an environmental corollary, the policies contributed to the long-term shift in the archipelago's species composition, increasing arable land and the acreage devoted to scrub land and forest edge, while reducing the forest acreage in both intermediate and climax stands. The impact on fauna is unclear. The population of swampland-users, such as frogs, some snakes, mosquitoes or migratory water birds, may have gradually increased; some woodland creatures may have declined with habitat losses and intensified hunting.

### 2. Highways and Waterways

As noted above, *ritsuryô* rulers ordered the construction of both highways with post stations and seaports with shipping facilities to assure their control of the realm, and their access to the desired tribute goods and corvée labor.

Construction and maintenance of these facilities had local environmental effects, of course, but more noteworthy was the broader impact of their utilization. They not only linked the capital city and its privileged few, via provincial officialdom, to the rural masses who sustained them, but also linked them – mainly via Dazaifu and Hakata – to the mainland population. These travel facilities thus exposed much of the realm to the pool of micro-organisms and contagious diseases that was sustained by that mainland populace, most pertinently smallpox, measles and influenza.[22]

The more-or-less continual immigration of Yayoi-Kôfun centuries had surely brought various disease organisms to the archipelago. But no record of widespread epidemics prior to the *ritsuryô* period survives, and the relative immobility and intermontane isolation of the populace may in fact have prevented such outbreaks. However, once the highway system was established and its diverse users – officials, messengers, tribute bearers, corvée laborers in transit, military conscripts and army units – began traveling to and fro, outbreaks of smallpox and other illness began to occur, becoming irregularly recurrent experiences.

Surviving records suggest that the pathogens commonly were introduced at Hakata and then made their way eastward, having their greatest impact in and around the crowded capital city. The mortality rate tended to be high because the populace had developed no immunity. And because the epidemics occurred so irregularly, immunities were very slow to develop; with the consequence that during the eighth and ninth centuries, epidemics repeatedly took many lives, with noteworthy demographic consequences.

Regarding those consequences, censuses, of course – even present-day ones – are notoriously unreliable, generally doing a much better job of counting the socially prominent than hoi polloi. And surely *ritsuryô* censuses had their shortcomings. Insofar as they were reliable, however, they suggest that the long-term trend of population growth that Wa society had experienced during Yayoi-Kôfun centuries ended during the eighth century, peaking at 6 million or more people before a devastating smallpox outbreak in 735–737. For the next three centuries or so, the archipelago's population remained roughly static, perhaps declining to some 5 million by about 950, before commencing a gradual increase back to roughly 6 million by 1150.[23]

In part this cessation of growth during the 700s reflected the earlier-noted decline in in-migration. But in part it reflected the impact of recurrent epidemics, and thus of the *ritsuryô* system of travel and continental contacts. In addition, however, that lack of population growth reflected recurrent episodes of crop failure and starvation.

The dynamics of this crop failure and famine are unclear. However, part of the problem was that the tribute and corvée demands took so much of the harvest that villagers were chronically exposed to "spring hunger" after the last of the winter's food supply had been exhausted. The resulting malnutrition could incapacitate people or make them particularly vulnerable to disease organisms. When famine or epidemic did kill or immobilize family members, the necessary tasks of crop production might be inadequately performed, extending the hardship through another crop cycle.

In addition, irregularities of weather could have contributed to harvest failures and, thence, to malnutrition, illness, reduced fecundity, higher death rates and more absconding, piracy and other acts of desperation. Climate records of the *ritsuryô* period are sparse and mostly produced in the Kinai vicinity, and their implications are less than clear. They seem, however, to suggest that during those centuries unseasonably wet or dry, cold or hot weather quite frequently produced crop failures with all their malign consequences. The relationship of weather vagaries to crop yields is a complex one, however, and requires brief examination.

### 3. Weather and Agriculture

As noted in Chapter 1, Japan today has a temperate climate that ranges from hotter ("sub-tropical") in the southwest to colder ("cold temperate") in the far northeast. During the roughly 2,500 years of agricultural society, the archipelago experienced the modest long-term swings of temperature that characterized other regions of the planet, and it was as subject as other areas to the customary seasonal irregularities, whether of unusual cold or heat, wetness or dryness.

Whether modest swings of temperature or irregularities of precipitation will have an impact on crop production, however, depends on a number of considerations other than the extent of climate deviation itself. One factor is timing: inclement weather early in the growing season may have very different consequences from the same weather later in the season. Another factor, of course, is crop sensitivity, as mentioned in the Chapter 3 discussion of rice varieties.

Other aspects of the agricultural environment are also of consequence, particularly as they shape the impact of irregular precipitation. One of these aspects is deforestation; another is tillage itself, and, most pertinently here, aspects of paddy culture.

Deforestation can transform a modest excess or scarcity of precipitation into an agricultural disaster. Standing forest captures moisture from ambient fog and clouds, thereby reducing the atmospheric load and risk of downpour while making some of the moisture available for biotic use. When, however, hillsides are stripped of their high canopy of leaves and needles, they lose that absorptive capacity, and as moisture-laden air passes by, the denuded site simply remains dry, increasing the chance that unseasonal dryness in that locality may result in drought.

In the event of substantial precipitation, healthy forest canopy catches much of the falling rain (or snow), eventually dropping it to the ground. There, much of it will settle into the layer of forest litter and, on sloping terrain, slowly start moving downhill. A substantial portion will seep further into the soil and move through subsurface waterways, later becoming available for lowland plant use, whether agricultural or not.

When, however, deforestation strips an area of its canopy, the rain pounds the ground cover or soil surface directly, spurring erosion and rapid run-off. Intensive scavenging of woodland for fuel material can even deprive the soil of both its protective cover of litter and, before long, the subsurface binding effect of root systems. Such terrain is far more prone to torrential run-off and erosion than is a well-wooded landscape, which means, in turn, that downstream areas are at much greater risk of flooding, silting or other damage, while receiving far less water in a manner useful for plant growth.

Besides controlling precipitation, woodland can also moderate swings in ground-level temperature. The air that fills well-forested terrain is not easily blown elsewhere by passing atmospheric winds. In consequence, well-forested woodlands shelter nearby agricultural land from both abrupt rises and drops in temperature. Once those woodlands are denuded, however, they lose that sheltering capability and ambient areas become more subject to frost or wilting heat.

Regarding tillage practices, the opening of hilly land to dry-field cultivation obviously makes it more vulnerable to erosion, especially on steeper hillsides, which exacerbates the destructive effects of modest climatic irregularities. But paddy cultivation also presents complications because the capacity of an irrigated field to handle water efficiently is strongly influenced by the condition of the soil therein. Ideally a wet-rice field will have a subsurface layer of watertight clay hardpan. That layer holds the water in the flooded field, enabling roots of the growing crop to extract the nutrients they need. Where that clay pan is missing or badly fractured, a farmer must keep providing more water to replace the water that continually seeps down and away.

However, not all soils contain sufficient clay particles to produce a solid pan, so some paddy fields are routinely more susceptible to drying out in the event of drought than are others. Moreover, after a farmer levels an area to create a paddy field, the clay particles in the soil will only gradually flocculate to form the desired subsurface layer. Several years may have to pass before the layer is solidly in place, and until then the fields will require more water. Should that layer then be ruptured, whether by careless tillage, the intrusion of root systems, seismic shaking or other factor, the field will again require more water until the leaks are sealed.

In short, vagaries of weather can disrupt the harvest, but their capacity to do so is greatly shaped by human action. In the case of *ritsuryô* Japan, massive deforestation of the central region left it particularly vulnerable to irregularities of precipitation. And as land reclamation spread across the realm, and the demands of the ruling elite led to more deforestation and denuding of hillsides, the effects of minor fluctuations in weather became more pronounced. Also, when the elite undertook major projects to create more paddy fields, they created substantial acreages that were, for a few years at least, more at risk of yielding poor harvests should the weather prove less than optimal.

* * *

In sum, then, for the realm as a whole, and especially for the Kinai vicinity, the *ritsuryô* system led to changes in bio-system composition and performance due to logging, land clearance and their ramifications. It also disseminated through the archipelago deadly micro-organisms that altered the long-term trajectory of human population size, an alteration reinforced by crop failures and consequent famine. The stresses produced by these complications then precipitated social developments that undermined the *ritsuryô* order, as we note below. This fostered conditions in which Japanese farmers began adopting the practices of intensive (later or "two-stage") agriculture, with all their social and environmental ramifications.

## THE LATER RITSURYÔ CENTURIES, 850–1250

As the preceding sections have suggested, the *ritsuryô* system and its unintended complications severely overburdened portions of the archipelago's bio-system as well as its overall human productive capability. Consequently, by the ninth century the system was sustainable only through reductions in the scale of elite demand and changes in the mechanisms of control and exploitation. Those reductions and modifications did occur, but as centuries advanced, they eventuated in major changes in both intra-elite and elite-producer relations.[24]

With literacy still being a skill found only among the elite, the historical record largely illuminates travails and triumphs among the favored few. For the general populace, one must rely on snippets of information and buckets of inference.[25] It appears, however, that the most striking changes of these centuries occurred among the elite. And that is not surprising since they had been the primary – indeed, probably the only – beneficiaries of *ritsuryô* arrangements.

These changes undermined political cohesion within the elite, leading to turmoil that by 1200 had replaced the *ritsuryô* system with a new realm-wide structure of power and privilege. By the 1500s, as we note in Chapter 5, only the nominal apex of the *ritsuryô* system – the imperial household and its closest attendant courtiers – survived as a token remnant of past glory, a legitimizing device for real power holders. And in the later nineteenth century, as we shall see in Chapter 6, that token monarchy was elevated to symbol of "the nation", as Japan's leaders commenced developing its industrial order.[26]

For society more generally, the later *ritsuryô* changes in mechanisms of control and exploitation primarily entailed a fragmenting of political control, a gradual rearranging of local organization and the emergence of entrepreneurial commercial activity. Those changes in turn facilitated changes in agronomic practice that constituted the beginnings of intensive agriculture.

Finally, in broader bio-systemic terms, developments of these later *ritsuryô* centuries had two major aspects. One was a continuing extension, mainly to the East and northeast, of deforestation and land clearance, with their customary consequences. The other was a gradual, realm-wide change in the human/microorganism relationship as humans developed select immunities, which reduced substantially the rates of adult death and debility from the most fearsome communicable diseases.

These trends in turn fostered a renewal of demographic growth and a rise in material output, which increased the power potential available for exploitation by the elite. However, the gains in population and production accrued mainly to areas East of the Kinai vicinity, giving leaders from there – the so-called "eastern warriors" – a much more influential role in the expanded political activism that gradually replaced the *ritsuryô* system with a new military-dominated order.

These several trends can be examined in terms of intra-elite changes, changes in elite-producer relations, and changes in producer organization and practice.

### Intra-elite Changes

From its inception, the *ritsuryô* regime aspired – with considerable success for well over a century – to function as a single political pyramid with all players, whether civil, military or religious, integrated into the structure and subject to orderly control from above and sustenance from below. However, from the ninth century onward, as the inadequacy of the system's material foundation complicated elite life, that pyramid fragmented. At the top, rivals competed for supreme control. More broadly, as we note more fully in the next section, the civil, military and religious components evolved into a multiplicity of disorderly and competing interest groups, all of which developed more autonomous systems of linkage to the producer populations that sustained them.

The rivalry for supreme control reflected a pattern long evident within the Kinai elite, which had found expression over and over in competing claims to the chief position that had come to be known as *tennô*. However, during the ninth century, those rivalries found a new form as key figures in the powerful Fujiwara family exploited their long connection to the imperial lineage to secure familial control of the formal regency office, whether as regent (*sesshô*) to a child emperor or regent (*kanpaku*) to an adult emperor.[27] For nearly two centuries after about 870, Fujiwara regents controlled imperial decision making so effectively that their lineage became known as the *Sekkanke* ("houses of *sesshô* and *kanpaku*"). They commonly sustained their influence through skillful marriage connections and by inducing young emperors to retire in favor of their child-heirs, who could then be manipulated with relative ease.

Then, however, from about 1050 to 1180, a series of uncommonly resolute "retired emperors" reasserted royal power by building and maintaining political coalitions that could keep *Sekkanke* leaders under control. In their exercise of power, these retired emperors sought to restore the imperial glory, but they found themselves relying heavily on the support of military commanders who headed professional warrior families.

Retired emperors had to rely on such figures because the *ritsuryô* military system of conscript forces led by imperial appointees had long since been abandoned. That military system had proven excessively burdensome to sustain, difficult to deploy and not very effective in quelling dissidents or controlling Emishi. In its place rose an ad hoc system of "private" military forces personally commanded by aristocrats, career military men, temple leaders or others.

The most famous of these professional military men were of the Taira and Minamoto families. As they came into close proximity to high authority, they began playing a more active role in governmental decision making, doing so, of course, in ways that served their familial interests.

During the 1180s, collisions between rival warrior leaders led to full-scale civil war. One group, the Taira, used their landed base in southwest Japan, together with the Kyushu legacy of resistance to Kinai control, to mount a challenge to the leadership in Heian. That effort prompted another group, the Minamoto based in eastern Japan, to counter-attack. The latter enterprise succeeded, eventuating in victorious "eastern warriors" establishing their own ruling headquarters in their home territory at Kamakura on the South coast of the Kantô Plain.[28]

From there the Minamoto attempted to control affairs by a two-pronged strategy of using their own disciplined followers to control rivals throughout the realm while sustaining the imperial court in Heian because it legitimized Kamakura's control of those rivals. The court did so by awarding successive Kamakura chiefs the established military title of "shogun" (from *seii-tai-shôgun* or "barbarian-subduing generalissimo"), the grand title held in earlier centuries by *ritsuryô* commanders who had been deployed to subdue such "barbarians" as the Hayato and Emishi.

Commonly called dyarchy, this Kamakura balancing of civil and military interests was awkward, and it was further complicated from the 1220s onward when shoguns became the tools of their own regents. Nonetheless, the system managed to survive for about 150 years, until renewed realm-wide warfare of the 1330s destroyed it, ushering in a long era of overt military rule that was sanctioned by the merest of imperial fig leaves.

### Changes in Elite–Producer Relations

Even as these intra-elite adjustments were playing out, the later-Heian centuries were also witnessing major changes in the way those elites were linked to the producers who sustained them. The changes can be examined in terms of three key factors that shaped them: the origins and character of *ritsuryô* governance itself;

**Figure 4.3:** A view of Obanazawa Basin from Shin-Tsuruko dam

**Figure 4.4:** An island near Kyushu, with dry-field terraces ascending
from shoreline to hilltop, 1963

subsequent changes in mechanisms of control; and the changes, noted above, in intra-elite relationships.

### 1. Regarding Ritsuryô Origins and Character
*Ritsuryô* governance, as noted earlier, emerged from an intricate process of conquest and conciliation that Kinai leaders had employed as they expanded their realm.

They had applied that dual strategy in the control of land as well as people. On one hand, as they established control over new areas, they posted officials and deployed immigrants or others to open more land to tillage, granting them specified "use rights" in such "crown lands" (*miyake*), and in return claiming direct tribute-rights therein. On the other hand, they accorded collaborating regional leaders the right to continue collecting tribute from areas they had previously controlled, the level of such income being fitted to the recipient's newly ascribed official rank and office. And they assigned land and producers to fanes (Buddhist temples and *Shintô* shrines) to help them sustain their facilities and members.

To assure ultimate government control of all these categories of land and people, *ritsuryô* leaders had the earlier-noted land surveys conducted to determine their locations, acreage and producer populations. Moreover, regulations stipulated that government had the right to reassign such lands and producers at six-year intervals as seemed appropriate. And to assure that all tribute was handled acceptably, goods and personnel were required to move along the government-supervised transport arteries to approved storage facilities at the capital, where authorities could assure their proper allocation.

Undergirding this set of arrangements was the earlier-noted principle that the realm belonged to the emperor. It was his/hers to award, withhold, transfer or otherwise use as seemed proper. That principle meant, however, that subordinates had only such rights to land as higher authority had awarded to them. And such use rights were always accompanied by a quid pro quo, whether in the form of political cooperation, tribute or corvée service as stipulated in the original agreement or subsequent modifications thereto.

## 2. Regarding Subsequent Changes in Mechanisms of Control

For well over a century, this carefully formulated system worked reasonably well. However, in all systems of tribute and taxation, natural disasters and human disorder can disrupt operations and elicit changes. And because *ritsuryô* tribute and corvée obligations were so onerous, it appears that epidemic disease, crop failure and famine proved particularly disruptive to the entire system.

Moreover, some attempts to remedy problems of the day served ultimately to weaken the system. Thus, in an early attempt to re-activate abandoned fields and encourage more land reclamation, the court decreed that if a fane or aristocratic household restored such a property to production, the acreage would be designated manorial land (*shôen*), and the restorer could retain the tribute yield, subject to government oversight. Later, during the 800s, rural hardship and difficulties in tribute collection and delivery intensified, undercutting the government's capacity to fund its operations. In response, the government broadened its definition of *shôen* to include currently cultivated fields. That maneuver in effect placed on aristocratic households and fanes more of the burden of securing their own income even as it granted them more fiscal autonomy.

By then *ritsuryô* leaders were less and less able to maintain up-to-date land surveys and population counts. They had abandoned the original policy of periodically reassigning lands from one jurisdiction to another, and they relaxed controls on the reporting and handling of tribute income, in effect granting landholders still more autonomous control. By the tenth century the original, highly-centralized system of land control had been substantially modified in ways that left hitherto subordinate elements of the elite in more control of – and more responsible for – their own sustenance.

These several responses to problems of tribute collection gradually modified the original unitary pyramid of control, creating several parallel, increasingly independent lines of connection between elite groups and the producer bases that empowered them. And those trends, not surprisingly, became synergistically entangled in the earlier-noted changes in intra-elite relations.

### 3. Regarding the Later Changes in Intra-elite Relationships

From about the tenth century onward, the changes in elite-producer relations accelerated as intra-elite relationships became more fractious. Most notably, once *Sekkanke* regents had secured control of the throne, they engaged actively in "privatizing" landed property by having obedient emperors assign it as *shôen* to themselves, their allies and the temples they favored. Subsequently, when retired emperors regained control after 1050, they used their position even more vigorously to assign land as *shôen* to households of the imperial family and its collaborators.

By the 1100s, at least half of Japan's arable land was administered as *shôen* by retired emperors, civil and military aristocrats and fanes. And they controlled their properties with almost no governmental oversight.[29] What remained of the former *ritsuryô* tribute-producing "public" or government land became known as *kokugaryô* ("provincial dominions"). Those parcels were administered by provincial governors and their underlings, but with so little central control as to constitute a *de facto* system of "tax farming".

By then, that is to say, the *ritsuryô* system of land control was long gone. Nevertheless, the jerry-built *shôen/kokugaryô* arrangements that had replaced it continued to function because the most bothersome threats to *shôen* holders were conflicting territorial claims by others, whether those were other *shôen* holders, professional military men, energetic provincial governors or local officials. To resolve disputes peacefully, *shôen* holders had to appeal to higher authority and obtain favorable judgments that senior authorities would support. Consequently, as weakened as the imperial court may have been, it still played a useful role in the lives of these competing elite interests, prompting them to be moderately solicitous of courtly need for support and cooperation.

This clumsily balanced system kept the realm largely intact until the 1180s despite recurrent crop failures and hardship, some local insurrections, eruptions by organized groups at major temples and outbreaks of piracy and brigandage. And even after the major turmoil of the 1180s, as noted above, the shogunal regime at Kamakura left much of this fragmented elite-producer system intact into the fourteenth century.

During these centuries of *ritsuryô* decay, only one overt territorial loss to the imperial realm seems worthy of note. It occurred in northeast Honshu in the 1080s, when a regional leader headquartered at Hiraizumi, North of Sendai – a man whose lineage traced back to Emishi ancestors – broke away, declared himself the ruler of an independent realm, and proceeded to build a grand capital in the style of Heian-kyô. But even that loss proved temporary, for a century later Yoritomo, founder of the Minamoto shogunate at Kamakura, destroyed Hiraizumi and ended the region's claim to autonomy.

* * *

In sum, then, it appears that problems of crop failure, famine, disease and harsh tribute levies undercut *ritsuryô* effectiveness, fostering a series of ad hoc modifications in land-control that fundamentally altered both intra-elite and elite-producer relations. Those changes then contributed to modifications in the way producers handled their local affairs, modifications that had major effects on the broader trajectory of Japan's history.

### Changes in Producer Organization and Practice

The shift in real land control from imperial court to aristocratic households, fanes and provincial governors placed on the latters' shoulders the burden of supporting themselves, leaving them to deal with abandoned fields and a decimated producer population. Gradually they succeeded in doing so, thanks primarily to changes in producer organization and practice. These changes emerged from the symbiotic interplay of four major factors: reliance on local leaders; development of entrepreneurial commerce; population recovery; and agronomic change.

#### 1. Reliance on Local Leaders

The basic problem facing holders of *shôen* and *kokugaryô* in the later Heian period was the scarcity of labor and the danger that such workers as they had might abscond or be lured away. Accordingly, although such landholders might commonly resort to the "stick" of bullying to get tasks performed, as time passed, they seem to have relied more and more on the "carrot" of positive inducement to keep their workers at home.

To elaborate, elite landholders would designate a local person of influence, commonly the head of a well-established household, as local overseer (myôshu) of a particular locality and populace. Such overseers were responsible for delivering tribute as stipulated, and they were empowered to organize their communities, to arrange affairs in the way that best utilized their land and other resources, and to lead them in defense against outside threats.

Being local figures, however, and ultimately dependent on local support and cooperation, these overseers commonly had to maneuver between the landholder above and neighbors below. That very dependence on local goodwill seems to have given these overseers enough bargaining power *vis-à-vis* the holders to secure less onerous tribute rates or other special adjustments as circumstances dictated. It was an arrangement that helped keep demands from above at a level that was locally acceptable and therefore sustainable. In effect this local-overseer arrangement constituted a step in the direction of self-governing communities. Indeed, in later centuries the Chinese characters (*kanji*) for myôshu came to be pronounced '*nanushi*' and denoted the village headman.

## 2. Development of Entrepreneurial Commerce

A second factor that facilitated growth of more stable and autonomous local communities during later *ritsuryô* centuries was the development of trading venues that were not subject to effective control by the ruling elite.

As noted in earlier chapters, trade of one sort or another had existed in Japan since Jômon times and grown substantially during Yayoi-Kôfun centuries. However, *ritsuryô* leaders had sought to control commerce as fully as possible, and they incorporated most of it into the tribute system, with other transactions channeled through the hierarchy of district and provincial officialdom.

By the later 1000s, however, with the tribute system a shambles and rural production growing again, entrepreneurial artisans, merchants and itinerant peddlers began to appear, along with local marketplaces. Some of these entrepreneurs formed trade groups (*za*), which then served as licensed agents of temples or elite households, even as they nurtured broader producer and customer bases among villagers, village leaders, local warriors and others.

This trade activity was expedited by the appearance of a serviceable coinage. Early *ritsuryô* leaders had minted coins, but as copper supplies had grown scarce, they had re-minted them in devalued issues, and during the 800s those discredited coins gradually ceased to circulate. From the eleventh century onward, however, a burgeoning mainland economy fostered a revival of trade with Japan and with it a new source of coinage for the archipelago.

A modest trade with China and Korea had existed for centuries, of course, but *ritsuryô* rulers had regulated it as carefully as they could, even trying to carry it on their own vessels, as earlier noted. The trade had always catered to the elite, and it seems only to have involved a few ships per year. However, it did encompass diverse products from Japan, and as China's economy boomed, the trade prospects spurred more and more Chinese merchants to send trading ships to Hakata, in later years to ports along the Inland Sea, and during the 1200s even to Kamakura.

By then, more Japanese vessels were also engaged in the trade, as this thirteenth-century Chinese text reveals:

Japan, that is, Yamato, is situated in the far East, near the place where the sun rises. The trees of this country are of the very finest quality, having formed rings over the course of many years. Normally, the Japanese are skilled manufacturers of paper in five colors and, using gold leaf, they decorate it with orchids and other flowers in a manner still unmatched by the Chinese. They mainly use this paper for copying sutras. Their bronze craft also is more refined than that of China. Their trade ships arrive on our shores by a northeasterly wind, and they bring us all sorts of merchandise: products of high value – gold leaf, gold dust, decorative pearls, pearls for medicinal use, mercury, stag horn, and dichrocephala [*dichrocephala latifolia* D.C., a medicinal plant grown in southern Japan]; and second-class products – sulfur, mother-of-pearl shells, rush mats, pine wood, cryptomeria wood, and planks of Luo tree wood.[30]

As this report implies, artisans in Japan produced diverse craft items, for which they used such mineral resources as gold, iron, tin and sulfur and diverse plant and animal products, both terrestrial and marine.

In exchange for these products, the Chinese provided a variety of goods, mostly for elite consumption. These included numerous perfumes, medicines, dyes, ornaments, elegant fabrics, fancy ceramics, books and diverse exotica.[31] Then during the 1100s, Chinese coins began to appear, quite rapidly growing into the most prized import and one of value to a much broader public. They soon moved into the domestic economy, where they facilitated the growing scale of commercial exchange.

*3. Population Recovery*

Even as political power was diffusing more broadly through society and economic activity was growing more diverse, changes at the microbial level also were having an effect on archipelagic society.

As noted previously, by the eleventh century Japan's population appears to have developed enough resistance to contagious diseases, notably smallpox and measles, so that it recommenced slow growth. As it did so, the agrarian labor supply began to increase, and more and more fields were brought into full-time production. In particular, more dry-field crops, such as wheat, buckwheat, soybeans, millet and barley, were grown, along with more wet rice.[32] Doubtless elite landholders secured a portion of the gain, but enough remained in the village to sustain continued demographic growth and local stability through the twelfth century.

During the thirteenth century, that growth appears to have stalled temporarily, hammered by successive bouts of cold, wet weather.[33] This ruined crops, particularly in eastern Japan, where a recent surge of logging and land clearance may have created cropping conditions highly sensitive to erratic weather. Whatever the particulars, crop failures appear to have precipitated hardship and starvation that reached westward across much of the realm. Subsequently, however, the growth resumed, as we shall see in Chapter 5.

*4. Agronomic Change*

This socio-economic revitalization and demographic growth of the later-Heian period seems to have been sustained in large part by re-activation of fields that had lain abandoned and by the opening of additional acreage to tillage, mainly in eastern and northeastern Honshu. It was also abetted, however, by modest changes in agricultural techniques, which increased output-per-acre and per-producer, even as they fostered entrepreneurial trade. These changes mostly foreshadowed the emergence of later (intensive or "two-stage") agriculture.

The changes in agrarian technique mainly involved wet-rice and dry-field tillage. Orchardry did grow, but the most important factor in that growth seems to have been the rise of more extensive and flexible mechanisms of trade rather than any agronomic innovation. These mechanisms enabled producers in much of the realm to expand their output of such marketable products as fruit, nuts, silk and tea.

In field cropping, the appearance of more hardy varieties of rice seems to have facilitated the expansion of paddy tillage in cooler regions. More noteworthy was a technological development linked to expanded animal husbandry. This was the spreading use of animal-drawn, hand-held plows, which villagers used to prepare fields for planting.[34] Although equipped with iron shoes, the plows cut a sufficiently shallow furrow that they did not puncture the watertight hardpan of paddy fields, so they could be used for both wet and dry cropping.

At first these plows were used by larger-scale cultivators who could afford to maintain both the animals and equipment. And the adoption of these plows may initially have been a response to labor scarcity. Later, however, their use spread, mainly because of their demonstrated efficiency.

This increased use of plows was facilitated by the spread of horse-breeding. Initially favored as mounts and pack animals, horses gradually were employed as draft animals, pulling carts and farm implements. Oxen also were used for that purpose, and as the later *ritsuryô* centuries advanced, harnesses were modified and strengthened to facilitate such fieldwork.

Animal-drawn plows enabled farmers to work more land, and where the terrain favored paddy tillage, they enlarged irrigation systems to handle the increased acreage. By the twelfth century this need for more irrigation water was also prompting farmers to build more and larger dams and ponds to hold water for field use during the growing season.

Another consequence of utilizing animal power was that manure accumulated, and farmers began putting it to use as fertilizer. Ashes from stoves, hearths, tile kilns and other sources also were used, and gradually mulch began to be collected and spread on fields. In part, and especially in central Japan, nutrients from these sources simply replaced nutrients that had been lost to paddy fields by the denuding of woodland. But, in principle, they constituted an early expression of the emerging two-stage agriculture.

Finally, in lowlands along the Inland Sea, farmers began to double-crop, starting a winter crop on paddy fields that had just been harvested in the autumn. It was a practice that would spread widely in subsequent centuries.

## ENVIRONMENTAL RAMIFICATIONS OF LATER RITSURYÔ DEVELOPMENTS

During the early *ritsuryô* period, power and privilege had been so well centralized that the impact of society on the bio-system was much more pronounced in the Kinai vicinity than elsewhere in the realm. By late in the period, however, power was so diffused that the environmental ramifications of human performance were spread much more widely across the archipelago.

On the other hand, these later ramifications seem to have been much less dramatic than those of the earlier period. As a corollary, they are not as well recorded and less easy to examine. Let us treat them in terms of three factors that seem to have had particularly noteworthy environmental effects: renewal of agricultural growth; changing center-periphery relations; and two lesser examples of urbanism.

## Renewal of Agricultural Growth

The establishment of widespread adult immunities to smallpox and measles was a prerequisite to renewed agricultural expansion. Although childhood illness and death due to contagion persisted, those losses were much less disruptive of the work force, could much more quickly be replaced, and therefore had far less economic and demographic consequence than had the high rate of adult mortality during early *ritsuryô* centuries. And because the previously noted changes in elite-producer relations were enabling more and more locals to manage their own affairs more fully, this expanded pool of labor could be directed to more sustained and sustainable agricultural production.

Largely due to this improvement in workforce effectiveness, the renewed expansion in land clearance and cultivation persisted, especially in eastern Japan. The environmental ramifications of this increased tillage were, however, somewhat complex.

In overall terms, certainly, the expanded cultivation sustained long-term changes in the terrestrial bio-system by shifting more acreage to the task of sustaining humans, their collaborating ("domesticated") plant and animal species and opportunistic parasites (mice, house flies and so on), of necessity doing so at the expense of the indigenous biotic community. And the associated erosion and downstream sedimentation surely altered riverine and offshore biomes while enlarging lowlands, particularly in the Kantô Plain and coastal flatlands of the northeast, just as they had been doing in more westerly regions for centuries.

Diverse factors, however, tended to limit the broader effects of this agricultural growth. Expanded orchardry and pasturage for animals were a significant part of the growth, and their environmental impact was substantially less severe than that of regular tillage. For one thing, both types of land-use employ perennials, which obviate annual soil turnover, while their long-lived root systems help hold soil in place, and these characteristics sharply reduce erosion. In addition, some of the vegetation in both pastures and orchards decays on site, creating mulch, further stabilizing the soil and helping sustain its fertility. Hillsides used in this way thus met human needs, while disrupting the local bio-system and downstream areas much less severely than did either "slash and burn" or dry-field tillage.

Even on tilled land, as noted earlier, customary agricultural practices helped contain the damage. The partial terracing of hillsides for dry-field farming, which slowed the speed of water-flow and hence its capacity to carry solids, helped restrain erosion. And the bunds (embankments) around paddy fields effectively captured rainfall and run-off, holding nutrients and solids in place. Moreover, the opening of more land to tillage frequently created more "forest edge", a type of environment that favored more diversity and density of both plant and animal life.

Along the coast, where sedimentation slowly altered the shoreline, the process gradually relocated offshore biomes. However, there seems to be no evidence of basic injury. Information is extremely scarce, but fishermen and gatherers of shellfish, seaweed and such continued to pursue their work, evidently using the new avenues of trade to increase sales without overburdening local marine stocks.

Another coastal change that seems to have had little environmental effect was the growing use of "salt fields". Salt-makers had previously obtained salt for human use by boiling down the seawater. Due, perhaps, to increased scarcity of fuel wood, during later Heian they created more and more flat, shallow settlement basins back from the water's edge. These basins would be refilled by hand-carried bucket or by overflow at high tide, and the captured water would then evaporate. Although climatic humidity could make it a very slow process, eventually enough salt would accumulate on the basin floor to be scraped up, bagged and marketed, using much less labor and fuel wood than did the earlier boiling process.[35]

### Changing Center-Periphery Relations

The later-Heian decay of central political control notwithstanding, the environmental effects of *ritsuryô*-period land use mostly continued to be more pronounced in the Kinai vicinity than elsewhere. It is also apparent, however, that the activities of people in and around Heian were having a greater environmental impact on regions beyond the Kinai itself.

Certainly the earlier noted abandonment of new and multiple capitals and the severe slowdown in urban construction lowered the rate of deforestation. Nevertheless, the demand for fuel wood persisted, and the occasional elite construction project – usually necessitated by urban fire – did sustain logging activity. In consequence, the record reveals continuing deterioration of central Japan's woodland.[36]

As mentioned earlier, the intense and sustained harvesting of Kinai woodland had gradually but substantially altered species composition there. Numerous rich stands of prized conifers gave way to deciduous growth, scrub brush and red pine barrens, and during later *ritsuryô* centuries that trend continued, nicely illustrated by two developments.

One development was displacement in those woodlands of the mushroom *hiratake* by the mushroom *matsutake*. *Hiratake*, which had flourished there in earlier centuries, is a species that prefers moist, shaded sites. *Matsutake*, which had largely displaced the other by the 1200s, grows atop the shallow roots of pine trees in dry, comparatively sunlit soil.[37]

The pine trees were there, as noted earlier, only because the original woodland stands had been cut off and the desiccated hillsides could support only pine trees and scrub brush. Thus, in the provinces of Ômi and Yamato, folk wisdom that had once celebrated the region's glorious stands of old-growth evergreens (*sugi* and *hinoki*) evolved in later *ritsuryô* centuries into a folk wisdom that praised the area's firewood and charcoal, two products of deciduous scrub woodland. And as more and more of the high forest gave way to scrubland, a generic term – *gen'ya*, wasteland or moor – came into usage to distinguish such areas from true "forest" or *hayashi*.

Another development that reflected this forest deterioration was a gradual modifying of architectural standards. There occurred a "downsizing" of such structures as mansions and temples, together with an increased utilization of less-esteemed types of conifers and of lumber marred by knots, discoloration and irregular grain.

These trends appeared, moreover, despite a further expansion of the region being logged. More and more of the timber for use in Heian came from southern

Kii, Ise, more distant parts of Shikoku, deeper in the Kiso River watershed, further westward along the Inland Sea even to the Hiroshima area, and on a few occasions from Kyushu. As a corollary, construction projects required more labor, became much more expensive and proceeded much more slowly.

A richly documented instance of this quest for good timber survives from reconstruction of the celebrated Tôdaiji, the great temple on the East flank of Nara. Originally built in the 740s, it was incinerated during a battle in 1180.[38] Only through an appallingly difficult and costly effort during the 1180s–90s were some minimally adequate central pillars finally extracted from ancient forest in the upper reaches of the Saba River, near the far western end of Honshu. Many huge trees were felled at the site, and the few that proved to be sound were slowly, laboriously moved down to the sea for transport to the Kinai region, where ox-cart trains hauled them overland for erection at the building site.

Finally, one must consider the faunal community. The deer, boars and bears of Japan did not become extinct. However, the patterns of land abandonment and absconding that hard-pressed peasants had displayed over the centuries led to foraging activity as people struggled to survive, and the hunting/trapping activity of these displaced folk may well have exceeded the reproductive capacity of such animals in central Japan. At least the city experienced a declining sale of animal pelts and one suspects that it was scarcity more than any Buddhist injunctions against killing that reduced the trade.

### Urbanism: Two Lesser Examples

Turning to our third topic, the later-*ritsuryô* era's long-term changes in elite society and the consequent rise of new power centers also had environmental ramifications. This was evidenced most notably, perhaps, in the rise of Hiraizumi and, more significantly, Kamakura as urban centers. The former stood just beyond the northern edge of the Sendai Plain; the latter on the southern coast of the Kantô Plain.

#### 1. Hiraizumi
The earlier-noted construction of Hiraizumi in the 1080s entailed erection and maintenance of "several thousand structures, including scores of temples, shrines, and mansions".[39] The initial construction and subsequent maintenance of both buildings and urban population entailed extensive deforestation, especially along the northern edge of today's Sendai Plain and the Kitakami River network, which drains the region from Iwate southward. From the grand mountain ranges that line both flanks of the valley, the Kitakami carried run-off down to Sendai Bay, where the sediments settled.

Earlier millennia of erosion and centuries of agricultural land clearance had slowly enabled the Kitakami to extend Sendai Plain southward, of course, but in all likelihood the erosion fostered by this later-*ritsuryô* surge of logging and land clearance accelerated the Plain's enlargement, just as it was doing on coastal plains in the Kinai and other vicinities. The subsequent destruction of Hiraizumi in the 1180s and dispersal of its human population likely reduced the rate of damage to nearby woodland, enabling some to renew normal cycles of plant growth and succession, in the process stabilizing soil and minimizing downstream effects. However, the Plain, which provided extensive pasture for horse-raising, remained sufficiently short of timber-bearing forest thereafter, so that during the 1500s the regional baron who ruled the Sendai area was one of the first to adopt policies of forest protection.[40]

### 2. Kamakura

More fully recorded are the environmental consequences of Kamakura's emergence as a major urban center. The Minamoto rise to power and glory entailed the customary construction of grand temples and shrines, as well as governmental and residential buildings and other urban facilities for use by its large population of officials, their retainers, prelates and diverse plebian service people. In Kamakura's heyday, its population totaled some 60,000, making it second in size to Heian.[41]

The city's initial construction and subsequent maintenance – plus periodic reconstructions after urban fires – placed great stress on woodland in adjoining areas.[42] To meet the city's needs, timber and fuel wood (the latter increasingly in the form of charcoal) were brought from nearby Kantô woodlands, from the Izu Peninsula, and farther West from the lower reaches of the Tenryû River valley and even the Kiso region.

Timber consumption in these areas was increased by the earlier-noted appearance of Chinese traders in their large, seagoing junks. Because the accessible forests of China had been ravaged by centuries of heavy demand, it had become economically feasible for Chinese merchants to purchase large, high-grade timbers in Japan – cryptomeria (*sugi*) and Japanese cypress (*hinoki*) in particular – and haul them to China for sale. Initially such timber was obtained in Kyushu, but by the 1200s, woodland holders in the Kamakura vicinity were profitably selling large timbers to the Chinese traders. By the 1220s, shogunal timber sales filled 40 to 50 of these Chinese vessels annually, while sales by forest-holding temples filled other vessels.

In succeeding decades the trade grew, with Japanese shippers also carrying lumber to China. A Chinese record of about 1300 put it this way:

[The Japanese] grow a lot of cryptomeria and Luo trees, which reach heights of fourteen to fifteen zhang [41 to 44 m] and up to four feet [1.2 m] in diameter. The inhabitants of the regions concerned cut them into rectangular planks and load them onto large vessels to sell them at Quanzhou. The men of Quanzhou go to Japan only rarely.[43]

While these timber exports likely constituted but a small portion of total consumption in the Kamakura vicinity, they contributed to an overload of the bio-system. Already by the 1250s, Kamakura leaders were alarmed at the deterioration in lumber quality and the rising price of firewood and charcoal. Attempts at regulation notwithstanding, problems of wood quality and quantity persisted, reflecting an enduring demand that fostered bio-system change and deterioration. This may have been most visible on Izu Peninsula, whose relatively accessible stands of evergreen forest (*hinoki*, *sugi* and *matsu*) were largely reduced to coppice stands and brushwood, a condition that persisted for centuries thereafter.

The downstream effects of deforestation, land clearance and its resultant erosion in the Kamakura vicinity are not clear, but one suspects that they added to the coastal lowlands flanking sections of the region, such as the Numazu vicinity on the West side of Izu.

\* \* \*

For the realm as a whole, then, the environmental story of later *ritsuryô* centuries was essentially a continuation of the Yayoi-Kôfun-early *ritsuryô* story of defor-estation and land clearance, with their enduring impact on topography and biodiversity. Compared more narrowly to the early *ritsuryô* period, the later period involved a renewal of human population growth that combined with changes in social organization and other factors to push Japan toward a regime of intensive agriculture, whose ramifications appeared in the centuries after 1250.

## RECAPITULATION

The centuries 600–1250 unfolded initially as a continuation of Yayoi-Kôfun times. Population continued to grow, more land was brought into cultivation and the ruling elite continued consolidating its power. Continental contacts were sustained and immigrants continued to arrive, introducing new aspects of mainland culture, technology and society.

These trends culminated during the later 600s in formation of the *ritsuryô* regime, a highly stratified, realm-wide political order centered in a glorious capital city in the Kinai Basin and anchored in an elaborately structured system of producer-control and exploitation.

After the 660s, *ritsuryô* leaders successfully avoided debilitating involvement in continental turbulence of the day. Nonetheless, before many decades passed, problems within the archipelago began to confound their regime, setting in motion processes of change that gradually weakened it, opening the way for alternative developments.

Basically, it appears, the regime overloaded its foundation of producers and their yield. And a major factor leading to that outcome seems to have been the very system of controlled travel, transport and communication set up to acquire that yield. The elaborate and well-used system of highways and waterways proved an excellent means not only of moving goods and people but also of disseminating communicable disease, notably smallpox and measles, among a general popula-tion that lacked resistance to the pathogens.

The high rates of illness and adult deaths due to this onslaught of disease – combined with the onerous burden of tribute and corvée duty, the sharp decline in immigration, and the consequences of excessive deforestation and land clearance – led to widespread suffering, population stasis and decline, land abandonment and absconding. As a result, agricultural output declined, labor scarcity complicated transport, construction and policing activity, and the elite found its supply of essential goods declining.

The resulting difficulties in elite life fostered policy disputes. These spurred intensifying conflict, disintegration of political cohesiveness, and the gradual emergence of a new, more decentralized power structure. This new structure was better adapted to the limits of its resource base, and as biological resistance to the worst communicable diseases became widely established, the changed political circumstances facilitated a gradual demographic recovery and renewed cultivation of abandoned agricultural lands.

Those factors, together with increased settlement and land opening in eastern Japan, a spreading network of entrepreneurial traders and artisans, and the emergence of more mutually advantageous and durable linkages between producers, local leaders and the higher echelons of elite society, facilitated the rise of new "medieval" patterns of rule. And these benefitted from, even as they accommodated, the processes of agronomic change that characterized the rise of intensive agriculture.

# 5    Later Agricultural Society, 1250–1650

In overall terms, as we have seen, Japan's early agricultural society initially experienced a long era of growth, one that lasted well over a millennium to around 730 CE. With establishment of the *ritsuryô* order, however, that growth gave way to an era of demographic stasis that lasted, with fluctuations, well into the 1200s. Similarly, Japan's later agricultural society experienced centuries of growth, from the late 1200s until around 1700, after which, as we shall see in Chapter 6, it too entered a phase of stasis, one that lasted until the later 1800s.

Within this overall story of repeated growth and stabilization, an interesting dissimilarity of general process merits note. It can be argued that much as the modest scale of the Yayoi-Kôfun elite – and the correspondingly modest burden it imposed on the general populace – had allowed long-term development of early agriculture, so, too, weakness of the "medieval" ruling elite enabled agricultural intensification to advance. However, whereas the very strength of the early *ritsuryô* ruling elite, the changes it enacted and complications it introduced to the archipelago seem to have been instrumental during the 700s in halting that long era of demographic growth, the very strength and the policies of a newly consolidating elite during the 1500s sustained, indeed accelerated, agronomic expansion and population increase until the later 1600s. And after that, it was biological limits of the archipelago more than weight of the elite that halted further increase.

These centuries of later agricultural growth – ca. 1250–1650 CE – were perhaps the most complex in Japan's history. At the level of elite politics, they encompassed an era of extreme disorder, violence and confusion, and at the level of society more broadly, an era of substantial conflict and change in social organization and practice. Those developments were shaped by sustained growth in population and material production, and that trend, in turn, was enabled by the social and technical changes involved in agronomic intensification. And in the background, this overall experience was quietly, but fundamentally, shaped by its geographical context, which deserves brief mention.

## GEOGRAPHY

As noted in Chapter 1, Japan's geological history and global location determined its overall size, shape, topography, natural resources, climate and external relationships. These variables, in turn, shaped the archipelago's bio-system and the human society that developed therein.

During the centuries 1250–1650, southwest Japan's proximity to Korea and eastern China continued to sustain and shape wider social interactions, even as the realm's island character helped minimize its entanglement in continental affairs.[1] And at the archipelago's northern end, the proximity of Hokkaido to Sakhalin and thence the continent helped sustain a vigorous forager society (known as Ezo and later Ainu) that continued to slow the northward advance of Japan's agricultural society while sustaining trade and other contacts, much as the Emishi of Tôhoku had done for centuries.[2]

South of Hokkaido, the archipelago's highly mountainous and sharply incised topography continued to shape the character and configuration of agricultural lands and the distribution of human settlement. And its temperate climate enabled it to support an increasingly wide range of agricultural enterprises.

More specifically, the Inland Sea continued to play its role as central artery for human movement, helping sustain the pre-eminent social role of the Kinai vicinity.[3] East of there, the central cordillera continued to play its role as obstacle to movement between eastern and western Japan, thereby influencing the political history of the day. And the climatic differences between warmer, wetter southwestern Japan and the cooler, drier northeast continued to shape dissimilarities in the way agriculture, and hence society, developed in the two regions.

Even more specifically, when agriculturists first ventured into the sprawling Kantô Plain, they evidently found the most satisfactory lands to lie along its northern periphery.[4] In part this reflected the realm-wide pattern of "ribbon" settlements between hillsides and smaller streams, which avoided the risk of destructive flooding on the alluvial plains bordering large rivers. In part, however, the Kantô heartland, especially in its more southerly sections, was deeply covered with soil of volcanic origin that the Fuji and Asama volcanoes had spewed out sporadically through past millennia. Much of it lacked the clay necessary for paddy fields, and it could not be developed into rich soil for dry fields without sustained nurturing. Only with the adoption of intensive agriculture's fertilizing practices, that is to say, was the Kantô able to play the productive and influential role that its large size seemed to promise.

Finally, one wonders how Japan's geological heritage may have influenced the character and location of defensive fortifications that arose, mainly during the 1500s. The great castles of the day, as we note more fully near the chapter's end, utilized immense, elegantly formed stone walls and parapets. However, depending on its chemical composition, stone can be extremely difficult to work with. One wonders if Japanese masons of the day were able to extract and shape so many huge stone blocks because Japan had an ample supply of reasonably accessible and relatively workable sedimentary rock and volcanic tuff. And one wonders whether the location of workable stone influenced the selection of castle sites.

## THE ELITE: POLITICS OF DISORDER AND RECONSOLIDATION, 1250–1650

The disorderly politics of these centuries can be examined in terms of three phases. These are the final decades of dyarchy (1250–1330), when a comparatively stable political order fell apart; a long era of disarray and disorder (1330–1550), when attempts at political stabilization repeatedly faltered and failed; and the period of reconsolidation (1550–1650), which established a phase of exceptional social stability.

### The Final Decades of Dyarchy (1250–1330)

As noted in Chapter 4, the Kamakura shogunal regime had from the outset engaged in an awkward balancing act whose stability depended primarily on the continuing loyal support of the shogun's vassals, who were posted throughout the realm as peacekeepers and overseers. As generations passed, however, that vassal force grew and fragmented, losing its political commitment to the leaders in Kamakura. That trend was exacerbated after warriors repulsed the two Mongol invasion attempts of 1274 and 1281 and stood on guard for years afterward without, in their view, receiving adequate compensation.[5]

Meanwhile, Kamakura's attempts to maintain amicable relations with the imperial court and its associated civil aristocrats became more difficult after 1272, when a bitter rivalry developed between claimants to the imperial throne. Kamakura leaders tried to pacify the two factions by alternating succession between them, but that policy only allowed the quarrel to fester.

At a broader social level, periodic crop failures and the resulting hunger, illness and fiscal duress sustained public discontent, which found diverse forms of expression. One form was absconding by peasants; another, heightened protests against tribute levies and other elite demands. Two other forms of discontent were the emergence of lawless bands known as *akutô* and an expanded scale of piracy that even included plundering activity along the coast of Korea. As the disorder grew more widespread and intense, Kamakura's control of its vassal force, and through them of the countryside, became ever more tenuous.

By the early 1300s, warrior leaders in Kyushu and northeastern Honshu were defiantly exercising a high level of autonomy. Moreover, proponents of new religious dogmas were recruiting their own followers and securing their own material foundations, whether by shrewd political maneuver or blatant defiance of established authority. By 1320, the situation seemed primed for upheaval if some ambitious figure proved able to exploit the widespread tension and discontent.

### The Era of Disarray and Disorder (1330–1550)

Long before the year 1320, the ancient *ritsuryô* city of Heian-kyô, "capital of peaceful tranquility", had deteriorated in physical terms and lost its political pre-eminence. In a sweet instance of historical irony, however, it had also come to be known – whether as an expression of empty respect or wistful pretension – by the much more assertive name of Kyoto (Kyôto or "capital metropolis"). During the 1320s the inordinately ambitious emperor Go-Daigo (1288–1339) energetically recruited followers, and during the early 1330s he attempted to challenge the Kamakura regime militarily, with the goal of making Kyoto the real capital city of a fully rejuvenated imperial regime.

Then, however, a brash, young Kamakura official, Ashikaga Takauji (1305–58), seized the occasion of Go-Daigo's challenge to launch his own insurrection and quest for power. He attempted to establish in the Muromachi section of Kyoto a new shogunate that would, in the Kamakura manner, control the realm through warrior subordinates while protecting the interests of court, aristocrats and fanes in return for their acceptance of his rule.

From the outset, however, the several groups refused to work together, and the realm was engulfed in decades of sporadic warfare that served primarily to sustain broader social conflict and change. For some 50 years, warrior groups repeatedly took to the field, commonly in the name of one or the other of two rival lineages claiming the title of emperor. One of those lineages was headquartered in Kyoto as a puppet of the new shogunate. The other – the "Southern Court" of Go-Daigo, his successors and supporters – was ensconced in the Yoshino Mountains South of Nara (the renamed Heijô-kyô) and aspired to real power and authority in the manner of *ritsuryô* founders.

Finally, in 1392, the third Muromachi shogun, Ashikaga Yoshimitsu (1358–1408), was able to induce the imperial rivals to abandon their struggle and re-establish a single, essentially powerless, imperial court in Kyoto. He was able to do so, basically, because shogunal collaborators had gradually secured control of much of the realm, in the process depriving the Yoshino court of its material and military foundation.

This Ashikaga success was, however, never complete, and it proved to be short-lived. Neither Kyushu nor the Kantô vicinity was effectively brought under shogunal rule. And most of the territory in between was controlled by regional barons (*daimyô* or "great names") that commonly paid only opportunistic allegiance to the shogun. Ashikaga leaders had to rely on those barons because only they had power sufficient to command the local warrior leaders (*kokujin* or "provincials") who exercised some real control over the local population that actually produced the food and other necessities of life.

These *kokujin*, in turn, commonly found themselves agreeable to baronial leadership, in considerable part because their own positions often were threatened by rival *kokujin* or by organized groups of producers. The latter could withhold tribute payments or other services, engage in protest demonstrations (*ikki*) or otherwise undercut a *kokujin*'s position.

As the 1400s advanced, organized groups of villagers, artisans and minor warriors became more and more resistant to the burdens imposed by members of the elite, whether baron, aristocrat, cleric or the wealthy moneylenders who hobnobbed with the favored few. In attempts to preserve or enhance their material bases, barons, *kokujin* and others increasingly came to blows, seizing one another's estates and villages where possible, plundering elsewhere, in the process destabilizing the whole structure of power.

In 1467 the baronial tensions erupted in major battling within Kyoto itself. That struggle – known as the Ônin War – went on sporadically for a decade, gradually reducing much of the already-shrunken city, including its great fanes and handsome mansions, to ashes and rubble.[6]

With the city destroyed, and with most aristocrats and imperial family members, as well as many temple groups, reduced to penury, the warring armies retreated to their bastions in the countryside. There, the warfare became more widespread. In a savage process commonly called *gekokujô* ("those below overthrowing those above"), local warrior groups battled for advantage, with winners gradually consolidating control of the areas they seized, in the outcome toppling their former superiors.

In this political free-for-all, new religious movements, most notably the Jôdo Shin and Hokke Buddhist groups, continued to grow, thanks to their own military muscle and mobilizing mythology.[7] And across the country, more able or fortunate warrior leaders gradually established more stable control of their domains. By the later 1500s, as we note more fully further on, a number of these barons had established sufficiently secure control of both their retainer bands and their producer populations so that they could aspire to rebuild a unified and peaceful realm, a worthy replacement for the long-gone *ritsuryô* system.

### The Period of Reconsolidation (1550–1650)

In overall terms, as well as in eventual outcome, the process of political consolidation during the decades after 1550 can be likened to that of the later Kôfun centuries, which had culminated in creation of the *ritsuryô* system. In both cases the leaders of local political units jockeyed for power, with those who enjoyed advantages of geography, leadership and luck prevailing. Utilizing muscle and maneuver, the ambitious forged ahead, gradually forming fewer but larger units, until the process culminated in establishment of a hegemonic center that kept the peace through a hierarchical structure of subordinate personnel and political units. The cooperation of these subordinates was secured by a mix of "carrots" and "sticks", all nicely rationalized by enforceable rules and elegant rhetoric. Known as the *ritsuryô* system in the early agricultural instance, this later agricultural instance of hegemonic rule is commonly called the *bakuhan* system, baku being short for *bakufu* (shogunate) and *han* denoting the domain of a baron (*daimyô*).

One can examine this later-agricultural process of political consolidation in terms of three phases: an initial phase to about 1570, during which regional leaders established effective control over their domains; an intermediate phase to 1600, in which major regional barons battled for realm-wide supremacy; and after 1600, a final phase of routinization and tidying up that yielded a durable order.

### 1. Local Stabilization

The initial forging of stable local domains can be viewed as an implementation of lessons learned. Especially from the 1420s onward, as we note more fully below, the lowly – whether villagers, artisans, merchants or minor warriors – had repeatedly disrupted governance by those above and gradually came to exercise more local autonomy.[8] By the early 1500s, more and more local military leaders seemed to recognize the necessity of accommodating the interests of those groups as the quid pro quo for securing their cooperation. That strategy enabled those leaders to deploy larger military forces, which could then protect their producer base against outside marauders. By the mid-1500s a number of these relatively stable baronies were found throughout the realm, from southern Kyushu to northeast Honshu.

### 2. Realm-wide Dominion

From about 1550 onward, new military technology gave warfare greater potential and greater risk, which fostered larger military enterprises and greater political ambitions. Most notably the firearm – an early type of matchlock and, a bit later, small cannon – increased offensive capability, which led to changes in battlefield tactics and construction of much more elaborate defensive fortifications.[9] These developments spurred a trend away from reliance on small forces of mounted warriors to the use of massed infantry, whether equipped with matchlocks or pikes and halberds. And that trend combined with the grand castle-building projects to increase the total scale and cost of warfare, giving barons ever more reason to seek control over larger, more productive domains.

By the 1570s, these trends were encouraging a few major barons to pursue the goal of realm-wide domination. The scale of warfare escalated, and as years passed, barons from one end of Japan to the other became entangled in the struggle for supremacy.[10] The showdown came in the autumn of 1600 when the armies of rival alliances-of-convenience assembled in central Japan for what proved to be the decisive battle at Sekigahara, on the western edge of the Nobi Plain. In the outcome a coalition of lords mainly from eastern Honshu defeated a coalition mainly from the Kinai region and westward, prodding the latter to return home, regroup and prepare for a later day.[11]

The victors, under command of Tokugawa Ieyasu (1542–1616), then established a new shogunal regime with its headquarters in his castle at Edo (today's downtown Tokyo, North of Kamakura in the Kantô). They also maintained a major presence in Kyoto, where the court and aristocracy were again assured a powerless life of cultured comfort.[12]

### 3. Routinization

The peace that came to prevail after Sekigahara was essentially a military truce that became routinized into a stable order, the *bakuhan* system. It was, in both fact and theory, a much less centralized regime than that of the *ritsuryô* founders. But it was more firmly grounded in effective control of the realm's productive resources. And given the much greater material output of the realm, it sustained a scale of elite luxury exceeding that of even the most self-indulgent *ritsuryô* ruler. And it did so while still allowing the general public a material level of living and a sense of security that probably surpassed those of any prior time in Japan's history.

The process whereby savagely bloodied armies of the day were transformed into orderly keepers of the peace had several dimensions. By 1650 or so, a number of inept or uncooperative barons had been replaced and a good many discontented warriors and religious enthusiasts had been suppressed. The 200-plus barons who remained in control of their domains had accepted a set of rules and regulations that assured their dignity and security in return for their acquiescence in shogunal rule – provided they kept the peace in their own domains. In addition, foreign relations had been regularized in a manner that controlled disruptive influences from abroad while permitting orderly trade relations with continental merchants – including, from the 1550s onward, a few Europeans.

Most importantly, perhaps, as war-free years passed, both shogunate and barons demobilized their armies and slowly converted warriors into functionaries or commoners. The many warriors who resided in the countryside were gradually ordered to settle in the headquarters town of their lord. There they were easier to control and could be used as stipended administrators, police and guardsmen, all nicely fitted into a highly stratified, realm-wide social order that was noteworthy for both the clarity of its categories and its success in finding places for people in most sectors of society, from emperor to outcaste.

This process of demobilization merits particular attention because it echoed – even as it radically differed from – a *ritsuryô*-era development. Back then, as noted in Chapter 4, early *ritsuryô* rulers had attempted to maintain an army of foot soldiers by ordering the general public to provide and provision conscripts as needed. That system had proven disastrous, as we noted, and it finally collapsed of its own weight, to be replaced by small forces of mounted warriors with attendants. These were much less costly to maintain and more effective in combat. However, they were poorly integrated into the command structure, and as decades passed, they proved less and less amenable to central control. In the end they became key players in the *ritsuryô* order's dissolution.

In this second era of political consolidation, when large armies of foot soldiers again appeared, barons made greater effort to provision them in a sustainable fashion. And after peace was restored in 1600, they gradually moved to demobilize them, carefully storing the firearms and other weapons, and replacing the masses of pikemen and musketeers with much smaller – and effectively controlled – forces of mounted swordsmen and attendant foot soldiers.

That process of demobilization substantially reduced the war-making potential of barons, but it left them in control of the armed forces that survived. The process also trimmed their costs of domanial operation, and thus reduced a major aspect of their burden on the producer populace. The process also released large numbers of able-bodied men for other employment. Given the technological changes of the day, these men were able to find productive work back in the villages from whence most had originally come or in the castle towns and other urban centers that were rapidly expanding.

By 1650, most facets of the process of routinization were complete. Warfare was largely a distant memory of the elderly, and peacetime habits of productive, pedestrian daily life were largely in place.

## THE PRODUCER POPULACE: GROWTH IN SCALE AND COMPLEXITY

For humans, as for other biota, demographic growth requires access to an expanding supply of nutrients and other necessities – or, in extreme circumstances, reduction in specimen-size. Humans generally achieve population growth by obtaining those necessities from a greater acreage of supply or by deriving more usable yield per acre, whether terrestrial or maritime. During the centuries 1250–1650, both strategies were employed in Japan.

Nevertheless, determining the size of Japan's population during these centuries, and hence the extent of its growth, is practically impossible because the disorder of the day meant that censuses were not undertaken or records preserved. Even the most careful estimates can vary greatly, depending on one's premises. However, it appears that the archipelago's human population held at about 6 million during the famine-torn 1200s, only resuming its growth again during the 1300s. In one estimate, it reached some 10 million by 1450 and 15 million or more by 1600, after which it spiked to some 30 million by about 1700.[13]

Even allowing for substantial error, those figures denote a major change in post-*ritsuryô* demographic trajectory, and that change entailed a commensurate change in food supply. During the Yayoi-Kôfun millennium of early agricultural growth, as noted in Chapter 3, the increase in harvest had been mostly a result of bringing more land into production. During the centuries of later agricultural growth to 1650, more land did continue being opened to tillage, especially in northeastern Honshu and southern Kyushu. However, the overall gains in output, and the resulting demographic increase, seem to have stemmed primarily from developments in agronomic technique that permitted a substantial expansion in yield per acre.

Before examining these technical developments, however, we should explore other variables that facilitated their utilization. The factors that invite scrutiny are human-pathogen relations and elite-producer relations, both of which need only brief comment, and producer organization and practice, which require much fuller examination.

### Human–Pathogen Relations

The later-Heian development of heightened resistance to epidemic disease persisted during the centuries of later agricultural development.[14] The patterns of human mobility that had spread disease about the realm in preceding centuries also persisted, but deadly new forms of pathogens seem rarely to have appeared. Consequently, although outbreaks of smallpox and measles continued to be reported, they were largely illnesses of childhood, reflecting their endemic character.

Influenza viruses mutate easily, and occasionally flu outbreaks were harsh. Then, in about 1512, syphilis was reported in Japan, with some fatalities resulting, particularly during the first few decades of its presence. On balance, however, perhaps because of improvements in housing and diet, fatalities from the various contagious diseases were sufficiently modest that they did not thwart the larger trend of population growth.

### Elite–Producer Relations

The key point about the relationship of those above to those below during these "medieval" centuries seems to have been that those above became weaker and

**Figure 5.1:** Winter wheat ripening just North of Tokyo, 1955

**Figure 5.2:** Farmer cutting a row of double-cropped winter wheat amidst young summer corn growing just North of Tokyo, 1955

those below stronger. A second point to note is that the hierarchy of power and privilege became much more convoluted and disorderly, with more people falling into intermediate roles – political, economic, religious, cultural – that were neatly linked to neither elite above nor producers below.

The heightened social weakness of the ruling elite, which had been foreshadowed in developments of the later Heian centuries, was a by-product of the political disorder adumbrated above.

**Figure 5.3:** Farmer staking summer-crop cucumbers after removing winter wheat crop in southwestern Tokyo, 1962

Rulers and their warrior supporters still could – and did – kill, maim, abuse and harass commoners. But much of the time they lacked the stabilized power structure necessary to either extract goods from them in an orderly manner or win their goodwill by protecting them from other abusers.

Advantaged commoners, whether functioning as merchant chiefs, pirate chiefs or community leaders, were the greatest beneficiaries of this change in power relations. But in overall terms, the change enabled producers as a whole to control their own situations more fully and to strike more favorable bargains with those above. Their success in doing so reflected not only the disorder among their superiors, but also changes in the organization and practice of commoner affairs, both urban and rural.

### Producer Organization and Practice

One can identify a number of intertwined aspects of organization and practice that facilitated the widespread adoption of intensive agricultural techniques. They include the diffusion of literacy, the emergence of monetized commerce, the rise of new religious patterns, and the appearance of larger, more well-organized villages.

### 1. Literacy

A quietly important development of these centuries was the spreading awareness that written documents – especially when combined with a readiness to argue one's case verbally and to act forcefully if necessary – could serve one's interests. Gradually literacy spread among local leaders of various sorts, and some people with literate skills found employment writing petitions and complaints, other correspondence, commercial documents and such like on behalf of ordinary commoners.

The use of documents in disputes is nicely illustrated by a petition for legal redress, dated 1275, that was submitted to their landlord by residents of Ategawa *shôen* in northern Kii province. The landlord was a major temple that relied on the *shôen* for essential timber. However, the local overseer (steward) insisted that the residents give priority to other work, which thwarted their logging efforts. The residents described their dilemma this way:

> *Item on the timber:* in the capital as well as in the nearby region, we have to serve the steward unrelentingly. Just when the few remaining workmen set off to the mountains to transport the timber, the steward calls them back: "Sow wheat on the fields of the peasants who have fled," and he threatens further: "If you do not sow this wheat, I will lock up your wives, cut off their ears, shear off their noses, cut off their hair, make them look like nuns and tie them with ropes. That is how I will treat them." Therefore, the delivery of timber is behind the schedule. Moreover, the steward pulled down one of the houses belonging to the peasants who have fled.[15]

When reinforced by oral testimony of the aggrieved, documents of this type could help those below challenge and constrain those above. And as generations passed and towns and larger villages proliferated, more and more producers became adept at using these literate skills to advance their individual and group interests.

### 2. Monetized Commerce

A much more visible trend, the emergence of a monetized economy, had been foreshadowed, as noted in Chapter 4, by developments of the later *ritsuryô* period. As the original tribute system had broken down, ad hoc provisioning arrangements had developed to move goods between hinterland and town. These arrangements gradually were sorted out, with the surviving ones eventually functioning as regularized markets and as artisan/merchant groups whose dealings with the elite were based more and more on mutual advantage rather than top-down authority.

This trend was expedited by the China trade that flourished during those centuries. The crucial role of that trade was in providing the coins that facilitated long-term expansion of domestic trade within Japan. How Chinese coins could play such an important role requires comment, however, because the role of money is not as self-evident as we denizens of industrial society tend to assume.

Money is actually very tricky stuff. We use it in part because of its easy portability and marvelous fungibility. However, its utility also depends on its credibility; that is, its capacity to maintain a generally stable purchasing power. And that capacity is based on two key variables that may function singly or in combination.

Money may maintain its value because – as in the case of gold and silver coins – it is produced from a material that is relatively scarce, that is quite persistent in its level of scarcity and that has alternative uses, which can soak up excess supply or make more of the raw material available during periods of excessive scarcity. Or money may hold its value because – as in the case of paper currency – the supply is so regulated by a stable socio-political order as to maintain its overall purchasing power and hence its credibility.

*Ritsuryô* Japan in its latter years hardly seems a place for money to have acquired credibility. As noted in Chapter 4, even when the early, and reasonably stable, *ritsuryô* regime had issued gold coins of good quality, those had failed to gain much traction, and they lost even that due to later, debased minting, which ended their circulation. After that experience, it seems remarkable that coins could acquire credibility when they were produced by a foreign regime, made of copper, and introduced by entrepreneurial traders.

One suspects that this second *ritsuryô*-era experience with coins succeeded in part because the disorder of the day made both barter and verbal promissory arrangements difficult and unreliable. For trading activity to replace the disintegrating tribute system, some sort of credible exchange mechanism was essential, and coinage performed that function.

These foreign coins could do so because they retained their value even after domestic forgers tried to replicate them. The fact that they were coins from the "Middle Kingdom" during the flourishing Sung Dynasty may have given them a special air of excellence and credibility. But in addition, copper deposits in China gradually had become exhausted, creating scarcities that led governments there to oppose all coin exports.[16] Nevertheless, Chinese merchants seeking high-grade timber and other valuable items were able to acquire the coins they needed, ship them to Japan and use them to pay for at least a part of their purchases. In addition, because demand for the coins was sustained in Japan by the continual growth in both domestic and foreign trading activity, their persistent scarcity – despite vigorous smuggling – helped sustain their value.

Finally, one could argue that the very absence of a stable political order in Japan helped preserve the value of these imported copper coins by preventing the appearance of a domestic coinage with sufficient credibility to displace them. When political order was finally restored during the later 1500s, domestic coins did reappear and the Chinese coins shortly ceased to circulate.

This foreign trade was a very small part of the total commercial picture, but its trajectory does suggest the scale and scope of overall economic growth during these centuries.[17] Whereas such trade during the *ritsuryô* period had involved only a few ships per year, by the 1400s, scores, even hundreds of vessels, both Japanese and foreign, carried goods between archipelago and mainland annually.

Moreover, the diversity of trade grew along with its volume. Although imports, other than coins, continued to be goods for elite consumption, as Japan's elite grew larger and more diverse, the imports too tended to become more varied. More importantly, the exports, once mainly gold dust and silk, had by the 1200s come to include not only timber but various artisan products and exotic items for elite consumption, as noted in Chapter 4. In subsequent centuries, the exports diversified yet further, encompassing large quantities of swords, other manufactured goods, such raw materials as copper, sulfur and gold, and substantial numbers of horses. And, in one last quirk that was indicative of the expanded maritime trading activity, some goods of Southeast Asian origin, which had been traded to the Ryukyus and Kyushu, were re-traded as exports to Korea.

These changes in the scale and contents of trade were accompanied by changes in the trading arrangements. Whereas foreign trade had been controlled by government in the *ritsuryô* heyday, by the 1300s, it was mostly handled by nearly unregulated Japanese and continental merchants. The former commonly worked as agents of one or another temple, baron or other elite figure, but as the medieval centuries advanced, they acted more and more autonomously, sometimes even functioning as pirates.

This foreign trade thus reflected – even as it fostered – the rise of organized groups of merchants and artisans. And as these groups grew, they became more and more influential in both urban and rural affairs.

In terms of urban life, commercial provisioning activity gradually replaced much of the older tribute system. The buying, selling, transporting and warehousing activity of merchants spurred the growth of numerous port towns and trading centers as well as transport networks. And their profits became a source of monetized tribute income for their political superiors, whether temple, baron or shogun, supplementing or even replacing *ritsuryô*-type tribute-in-kind.

By the 1500s, merchants, artisans and their guilds (*za*) – such as the guilds of rice dealers, *sake* brewers, silk weavers or moneylenders in the case of Kyoto – commonly constituted neighborhood leaders and administrators even in the largest towns. Then during the later sixteenth-century reconsolidation of elite rule, collaborating merchants played crucial roles in the provisioning of officialdom, their armies and the castle towns and other governing facilities they created.

In terms of rural affairs, the most well-known aspect of merchant activity may have been moneylending and the bouts of organized anti-usury protest by debtors (whether farmers, packhorse operators, rural warriors or others) that erupted periodically.[18] More important in the longer run, however, was the role of merchants and artisans in providing useful avenues of exchange.

Thus, during the 1200s–1300s, local periodic markets – usually held three times a month, but more frequently in later centuries – became established throughout the realm. There, local cultivators could offer such foodstuffs as soybeans, sesame seeds, string beans, rice or barley for sale or in exchange for the goods being sold by itinerant merchants. These included such things as "lamp oil, paper, knives, iron hoes, fresh fish, salt and sometimes fabrics".[19] By thus enabling producers to sell their output, these markets facilitated sustainable agricultural production, thereby aiding the rise of intensive agriculture.

Finally, this trend to commercialization was evident in other types of primary production.[20] These included the continuing development of fisheries, with the harvest being sold not only in local periodic markets but also in the trading and port towns that were proliferating across the realm. This growing urban consumer population also increased market opportunity for those who scavenged such "wild" foodstuffs as fruit, nuts, berries and game. And it offered market opportunities for those who produced sea salt or processed iron sands and other raw materials to meet the growing demand for iron, gold, silver and other minerals.

*3. Religious Trends*
The spread of both literacy and monetized commerce fostered – and was fostered by – the new Buddhist sectarian movements that we noted earlier. These movements

were directed much more toward the general public than were the old elite sects, and they served as mechanisms for organizing local groups. Although they were promoted in the name of one or another doctrinal teaching, their social role was to create organized interest groups that could challenge established authority locally and, in a few instances, regionally. They flourished in both urban and rural settings, and while their actions did often contribute to disorder and violence, the net effect of their rise was a further disrupting of the old elite structure, creating social space for new arrangements at intermediate and lower social levels.

The other religious trend that merits note was the increasingly visible social role of local shrines anchored in the long-established indigenous tradition known today as *Shintô*, "the way of the gods (*kami*)". These shrines often became the focal point of community life, providing a place to meet, a site for celebratory and ritual events, a basis for communal organization and a symbol of communal identity. They were particularly important in the development of organized villages, providing a solid basis for social cohesion and offering a justification – one is serving, even defending, the *kami* – for vigorous village action.

*4. Villages*

The factors noted above – disorder among the elite and trends in disease, literacy, commerce and religion – all facilitated the development of larger, more organized and self-controlled villages.

To elaborate, the disintegration of elite rule into endemic disorder pressured villagers into developing alternative mechanisms of communal governance and self-defense. That elite weakness and turmoil also facilitated village development by reducing the overall tribute drain on local resources, although the recurrent warfare certainly could present savagely brutal, if sporadic and localized, demands.

Immunity to killer diseases obviously helped sustain village vitality, and the gradual spread of literacy empowered more and more villagers to advance their interests. Concurrently, merchant-artisan activity gave more and more of them access to iron tools, other useful materials and markets for their output. And religious groupings, whether sectarian Buddhist or centered on the local village shrine, provided one form of local organization and a basis for local cohesion.

Abetted by these factors, from the later 1200s onward, villagers under the leadership of locals began developing systems of communal self-government and self-defense, doing so initially in the conflict-ridden Kinai vicinity and later in outlying regions. Because such larger villages (known as *sô*) could repulse marauders more effectively than could small ones, the long-established pattern of scattered dwellings and small settlements gradually gave way to more densely packed villages that might number dozens of dwellings. By the 1500s, as one scholar has put it, such villages were "the basic units of the social system".[21]

The marauders who menaced these villages were diverse. One venerable type, of course, was the pillaging warrior; another, the predatory tribute-taker. Yet another, more recent type was the ruthless debt collector. As the monetized economy had grown, especially in the Kinai vicinity, indebtedness and usury had become widespread, and during years of poor harvest or other hardship, debtors found it especially difficult to meet their obligations. During the 1420s, organized villagers in the Kyoto vicinity became increasingly resistant to the demands of debt collectors, and in 1428 they erupted in the first of numerous forceful protests against the wealthy moneylenders (mostly *sake* brewers) of Kyoto. As one dismayed observer put it:

> The peasants in the country are in revolt. They are demanding a "virtuous government" [an edict abolishing debts] and destroying earthen storehouses, saké brewers' houses, and temples. They are seizing anything they want and taking back the cash they owe in debts. ... This is the first time that we have heard of peasant revolts in Japan.[22]

Whereas moneylenders could infuriate, marauding warriors could – and did – slaughter, so substantial village efforts went into defending against them. Especially in the Kinai vicinity, more and more villagers encircled their settlements with mud walls and sturdy gates. And they channeled irrigation water around them to form ditch-barriers against the marauders. They also used other techniques of self-defense, even equipping themselves with such weapons as swords or pikes.

As villagers became accustomed to managing their own affairs, they discovered more and more benefits in doing so. Not only could they work together in self-defense, but they could also collaborate on land reclamation, development and maintenance of larger, more complex irrigation systems and joint management of shared resources such as woodland. Then, as expanded use of land and water resources brought more and more villages into contact – or collision – the organized villages had mechanisms in place to negotiate inter-village agreements on resource use or, if necessary, to defend their interests against aggressive neighbors.

One factor facilitating intra-village cooperation was long-term trends in agricultural practice that fostered gradual "egalitarianization" of village households, particularly in central Japan. By the 1500s, output-per-acre of farmers in that region had improved sufficiently that households commonly could support themselves on about one hectare (2.47 acres) of tilled land. Cultivating that much land fully utilized the household labor pool, so those with that much arable tended not to open more land, while those with less land sought more. As a result, more and more village households came to utilize roughly similar-sized holdings and to share comparable standards of living.[23]

In sum, then, one can point to several socio-economic developments that fostered the rise of larger, internally more cohesive villages. But in the end, that trend depended on the development of intensive agricultural techniques for the simple reason that farmers of necessity must live within reasonable walking distance of their fields. Only by increasing output-per-acre could more and more people live together in large, defensible villages.

## TRENDS IN AGRICULTURAL TECHNIQUE

As foreshadowed in Chapter 4, the techniques of intensive agriculture began to appear in the later *ritsuryô* period. Specifically, we noted that horses and oxen began to pull plows for turning the soil and their manure was used as fertilizer. Tillers also developed more elaborate irrigation systems and the double cropping of paddy fields began to be practiced along the Inland Sea.

By 1250, it appears, the basic techniques of intensive or "two-stage" agriculture were in use, at least on a small scale and mainly in central Japan. During the next four centuries their use spread widely across the realm, an outcome facilitated by the contextual social developments discussed above. In addition, although the basic techniques were evident by 1250, numerous refinements were made there-after, and a few new practices merit note. The subject can be examined in terms of three facets: fertilizer use, water management and noteworthy new crops.

### Regarding Fertilizer

During medieval centuries, cultivators applied more and more fertilizer material to their fields. One factor spurring this increase in use was the disappearance of fallowing. As population grew and labor became more available, abandoned and idle arable was returned to full-time tillage. That change meant, however, that the natural processes of "weed" growth and decay on such sites ceased, and only by purposeful application of fertilizer material could the soil's nutrient level be maintained for recurrent cropping.

Fertilizing a crop is not, however, a simple matter of "you provide it; the plant uses it". To elaborate a point adumbrated in Chapter 3, plant roots can utilize bio-fertilizer materials only after those have been processed by bacteria and other micro-organisms, which digest the material and convert it to chemical forms that the roots can absorb.

That processing can be done in the field or elsewhere. When farmers stir fresh green material into the soil, the process of converting it to usable plant-nutrients ensues, making them available weeks later. Those micro-organisms may, however, do their processing work in the gut of an animal, in a pile of rotting mulch or manure, in the woodland soil through which water percolates en route to a paddy field or in the water itself. In such cases, the fertilizer material – whether manure, well-rotted mulch or nutrient-laden irrigation water – is "pre-processed". That makes it ready for relatively rapid absorption into the roots of the growing crop when it reaches them.

Summer cropping on both dry and paddy fields was enhanced by the use of fertilizers, whether pre-processed or not. However, it was the use of such pre-processed types as manure, ashes and well-rotted mulch that greatly aided a major agrarian advance of the medieval era; namely, the widespread use of double-cropping, which required that fertilizer materials become quickly available for use.

A portion of this double-cropping, as noted above, consisted of growing a winter crop, usually a dry grain, on paddy fields that had been drained and dried for the autumn harvest. Such fields would then be fertilized and tilled again and re-seeded. The new crop would start but then grow little during the coldest weeks of winter, only to spurt to maturity during the longer, wetter, warmer days of spring. Once that crop was harvested, the farmer could then start his summer crop of rice by fertilizing, tilling and re-flooding his fields and transplanting the rice seedlings from their seed-bed. By 1550, perhaps a quarter of the paddy land in central and western Japan was being double-cropped.[24]

Probably a greater portion of the double-cropping was done on dry fields that could grow two crops or, under the right conditions, three, of which at least one would be faster-maturing garden vegetables. Commonly the second crop – the winter crop – would be a legume, such as soybean, pea, string bean or broad bean.[25] Certainly the heavy yield of these plants made them attractive to growers, as did the likelihood that they would be taxed minimally, if at all, by higher authority. A less obvious advantage of these legumes was their habit of producing nitrogen-fixing nodules on their roots. After the beans had been harvested, these nodules would decay in the ground, releasing their nitrogen into the soil where it could spur growth of the successor summer crop.

### Water Management

The total acreage of both dry and paddy fields expanded during these medieval centuries. In considerable part this expansion simply consisted of more land clearance in less developed regions, notably northeastern Honshu and southern Kyushu. In the more developed areas of central Japan, however, the opening of additional paddy fields entailed a complicated process of constructing more elaborate irrigation works that utilized larger and longer sluices, and more and larger holding ponds for water storage.

This expansion in tilled acreage gradually brought farmers closer and closer to large streams, whose irregular flooding had deterred earlier projects of land-clearance. Increasingly, however, organized villages (and as the 1500s advanced, baronial rulers seeking to enhance their domanial output) were mobilizing work crews to erect streamside levees that could contain high water. Such crews might also clear rocks and debris from streams so as to improve their flow.

Another innovation that helped transform the floodplains of larger rivers into more dependable farmland was the practice of "field-leveling". Long used to give paddy fields the necessary table-top flatness and to make dry fields less susceptible to erosion and water loss, the technique was cleverly employed to make flood-plains more usable. Soil from one part of a field would be piled up in another and both parts smoothed, thus creating a lower level that could function as a paddy field and a raised section that could grow a dry-field crop, whether grain or something else. That arrangement gave some protection against unusual drought or wetness and helped reduce the impact of any river overflow.

Besides enhancing their control of river flow, villagers found a new way to put river water to work. They adopted and adapted mainland types of water wheels. One type was set up so that stream-flow itself would turn the wheel, lifting water in its tilted water trays, from which the water emptied into a plank chute that carried it across the embankment to the nearby irrigation ditch. The other type utilized human power to lift the water, with workers peddling on an axle that caused an inclined chain of water trays to transport water up from the stream, over the embankment and into the irrigation ditch.

## Noteworthy New Crops

Finally, two new crops merit note. One, which came from the mainland sometime after 1100, was a variety of wet rice known as Champa rice.[26] A type of Southeast Asian long-grain (indica) rice, it was noted for its hardiness, being particularly resistant to both drought and flooding, and to select diseases and insect pests. Especially where paddy acreage was recently created or in areas exposed to flood-prone rivers, Champa rice was a wise choice.

Moreover, being a long-grain variety, it was deemed less tasty than the short-grain japonica and so was less valued by the elite. In consequence, the grower of Champa rice might find himself less burdened by high-status seekers of tribute. So, while the grower might have to settle for a slightly lower market price for his crop, he may have found his own food supply less at risk of confiscation. In any case, the agronomic advantages of Champa rice were such that its cultivation had spread widely across the archipelago by 1400. And it continued to be grown in much of the realm into the 1700s, by which time a more fully stabilized agrarian order made japonica rice a sufficiently reliable crop for general use.

The other new crop was cotton. For centuries the elite had worn silk clothing, but most Japanese still wore hemp or ramie, stiff material that offered little insulation against cold air. So a broad market existed for a better type of cloth at an affordable price and cotton met those criteria. It had been grown in Korea during the later 1300s, with cloth eventually being exported to Japan. Then at some point in the 1400s, its cultivation was introduced to Kyushu, from where it gradually spread eastward as far as climate permitted during the next century or two. To grow cotton requires intensive fertilization of the field, but by then farmers were familiar with the practice, and they grew the new crop successfully. Imports continued to enter until the later 1500s, but for the three centuries thereafter, domestic producers met Japan's cotton needs.[27]

## SOCIAL AND ENVIRONMENTAL EFFECTS OF TECHNOLOGICAL CHANGE

The multifaceted developments of this era of growth, 1250–1650 – notably, population growth and the agricultural and other technological developments that sustained it; the socially broader (but certainly not universal) rise in material standard of living; growing social complexity; and politico-military disorder – had substantial and diverse effects on Japan's ecosystem and human-ecosystem relationship.

Most obviously, the human impact penetrated the archipelago more fully than ever before, extending and intensifying the effects that we noted in Chapters 3 and 4. There were, in addition, some noteworthy new developments, in terms of both the way human actions affected the bio-system and how humans responded to the resulting bio-system changes.

These themes can be examined in terms of three general topics: deforestation and its ramifications; the effects of agrarian intensification; and, insofar as information is available, such other matters as the effects of hunting, mining and fishery development.

**Figure 5.4:** Paddy land on the Sendai Plain in eastern Tôhoku, 1955

### *Effects of Deforestation*

The social and environmental effects of deforestation depend on its purpose, techniques and intensity. During these medieval centuries, Japanese loggers continued to function as scavengers, taking what they wanted and then leaving the ambient bio-system to rejuvenate itself. But later, during *bakuhan* centuries, as we shall see in Chapter 6, they gradually shifted from scavenging to "farming" the forests, planting and nurturing new crops of the desired trees, much as cultivators nurtured field crops. And much as the medieval shift to intensive agriculture was foreshadowed by later *ritsuryô* developments, so this *bakuhan* shift to plantation forestry was foreshadowed by late medieval efforts at forest management.

Plantation forestry developed, of course, only because natural regeneration no longer met the human demand for timber. This timber shortage manifested itself in several ways: in some notable architectural adaptations; in the extraction of timber from ever more difficult sites; and, eventually, in attempts at forest management. And lest we overlook the obvious, one long-term factor that contributed to the growing timber scarcity: the continuing process of land clearance, which permanently converted terrain from tree-growing to other uses. So let us examine those topics seriatim.

### 1. Logging and Elite Architecture

During the *ritsuryô* period, as earlier noted, logging had primarily served to provision the capital cities of the Kinai region, and even after 1250 that region remained the primary site of timber consumption. However, the regional barons and temple organizations of the 1300s–1500s, as well as the proliferating commercial towns of those centuries, increased the total demand for timber and spread it much more widely about the realm.

**Figure 5.5**: Hewn stone provided walls for warrior residences,
as here in Shimabara in Kyushu, 1963

One other factor that substantially increased the demand for lumber was the warfare and social conflict of the age, which involved both arson and accidental conflagrations that destroyed countless fortifications, temples, mansions and other structures. Replacing such buildings was immensely burdensome. Two of the most well-known instances – rebuilding the Tôfukuji and Nanzenji, grand Zen Buddhist temples in Kyoto, during the 1440s – exemplify the issue.

To restore the Tôfukuji in 1442, packhorse operators transported some 6,000 horse loads of Mino lumber overland from the Nagara River to Lake Biwa, from whence they were rafted to the city. Five years later eight-horse teams hauled 1,000 cartloads of Mino and Hida timber from the Nagara to Biwa and Kyoto to rebuild the Buddha Hall of the Nanzenji.[28]

Not only did arson sharply increase the demand for construction lumber, but it also led to innumerable wildfires that raced up dry hillsides and through the scrub brush-covered areas commonly found in the vicinity of towns, villages and other sites of human activity, in the process ravaging future timber and fuel-wood stands.

Whether spurred by the need to rebuild, the demand for fuel wood or other factors, medieval logging continued to eat further and further into Japan's forests, especially in central Honshu. The environmental consequences were essentially escalations of trends noted in Chapter 4; that is, as old growth forest fell to the axe, it was replaced by scrub brush and fast-growing tree species. Because of persistent human demand for this young growth (mainly for fuel wood and small-scale construction), old-growth stands of cryptomeria, Japanese cypress and other valued trees mostly failed to re-establish themselves, transforming ever more areas

**Figure 5.6:** Stonework provided the towering walls of castles,
as here at Kumamoto in Kyushu, 1963

of formerly coniferous forest into mixed, mostly small-scale, deciduous and red pine growth.

Gradually these changes in forest composition exacerbated timber shortages and created other difficulties that generated an array of responses. One of the most well-known developments was a set of architectural innovations that have the earmarks of adaptation to problems of lumber scarcity, costliness and deteriorated quality.

One aspect of this adaptation to lumber scarcity was the earlier-noted process of "downsizing". During the *ritsuryô* heyday, it will be recalled, elite construction had favored grand buildings supported by large framing timbers and equipped with wooden floors, walls and doors, all of them visible to the naked eye. During these medieval centuries, those structural elements all changed, doing so initially in the Kinai region, where timber scarcity was most acute. Buildings tended to become more modest in size and used other materials in place of high-quality wood.

To elaborate, with large, straight, attractively grained trees hard to find, medieval builders settled for smaller pillars. Or they used composite posts made of unattractive wood concealed by a thin veneer of high-grade lumber. Similarly, as attractive planks of sufficient size for floorboards became too costly or simply unattainable, elegant wooden flooring gave way to crude wooden under-flooring that was concealed beneath *tatami*. These were large, slightly spongy mats (nowadays standardized at about 5 centimeters thick and 1 × 2 m surface measure) that consisted of firmly bound straw covered with a thin but attractive surface mat made of the rush *igusa* (*Juncus effusus*).

In place of bare plank walls, carpenters formed plaster walls by slathering mud onto mesh frames of woven sticks or brush and then applying an attractive finish coat. Instead of sliding wooden doors between rooms, they utilized *fusuma*, lightweight sliding panels created by pasting attractive, stiff fabric or cardboard-like material onto a frame made of slender wooden sticks. And handsomely paneled wooden doors facing the outdoors were replaced by *shôji*, similarly lightweight sliding panels made of translucent paper glued to a frame of delicate wooden sticks. These were supplemented, for night-time security or inclement weather, by exterior "rain doors" (*amado*), crude wooden panels that slid aside into storage pockets where they were concealed from view when not in use. In combination, these changes yielded an architectural style known as *shoin-zukuri*. It is associated with the tea ceremony and has come to be viewed as the quintessential "Japanese-style" architecture.

So the adoption of shoin-style construction eased demand for large, high-quality timber from prized conifer species. It also, however, increased other types of demand on the bio-system.

For one thing, the new *tatami* floors and paper walls were easily flammable and difficult to clean. To use open hearths for heating or cooking in such a setting became dangerous and bothersome because of the sparks and smoke they emitted. For centuries, higher ranks of the elite had used charcoal, which produced almost no smoke or sparks, and during these medieval centuries, as intermediate classes of warriors and merchants proliferated and acquired the wealth to pay for charcoal, its use spread widely, replacing open hearths with charcoal-burning heaters and stoves.[29]

The resulting expansion in charcoal use added to demand on woodland because, whereas the fuel used in wood-burning stoves and hearths could be wood scraps of all sorts, charcoal was made from solid pieces of hardwood. Moreover, a portion of the wood's heating potential was consumed in the process of converting it into charcoal. As a consequence, charcoal production required select trees and yielded less usable heat per unit of woodland growth than did firewood.

Besides increasing the pressure on hardwood stands, shoin-style buildings elevated the demand for both desirable clay for wall plaster and plants that would yield paper or other material of the type used in *fusuma* and *shôji*. Most significantly, perhaps, the use of *tatami* created a substantial demand for straw-like materials, and particularly for the *igusa* rush, which grows in swampland and can be grown in flooded fields in the manner of wet rice. It thus created a new farm crop but also added to the demand for usable lowland.

Even as the favored few were learning to make do with inferior lumber, the overall demand for timber and fuel wood was continuing to escalate. Especially after 1550, with changes in warfare and the emergence of baronial competition for realm-wide domination, the earlier-noted boom in giant-castle construction created an immense new, realm-wide demand for timbers large and small, a level of demand far in excess of that during the *ritsuryô* heyday. That boom continued into the 1600s, being supplemented by the associated construction of 200-odd castle towns, which dotted the archipelago from the northern end of Honshu to southern Kyushu.

The scarcity of timber was reflected in the castle construction, in which much of the woodwork consisted of smaller or inferior pieces hidden by tile, plaster or veneer. Nonetheless, within a century that surge in castle and castle-town construction had consumed most of the remaining accessible, high-quality timber throughout the realm.

Because of the magnitude of their environmental impact, these baronial castles merit further comment. They were expressions of power and hubris that matched the great tumuli of the Kôfun era and surpassed even the grandest mansions and temples of the *ritsuryô* heyday. Besides consuming immense quantities of timber, their use of stone, as we note later, was unprecedented in scale and had environmental effects of unknown character and scope.

An extreme example of baronial ambition in this construction activity was Toyotomi Hideyoshi (1536–98), key figure in the political reconsolidation of the day. Besides building immense castles, he sought to restore Kyoto's glory, and one such project involved erection of a huge new temple, the Hôkôji, which would glorify his own accomplishments.

To elaborate, in temples the ridgepole was both a crucial load-bearing timber that supported the heavy tile roof and a visible piece that could convey a sense of elegance or tawdriness, depending on its quality. So Hideyoshi wanted a huge, handsome timber, and in 1586, Tokugawa Ieyasu, lord of the Tôkai region and one of Hideyoshi's supporters-of-convenience, undertook to provide it. After a long search,

his loggers found a tree of sufficient size and quality growing at the foot of Mt Fuji. They felled it, cut it to form a timber exceeding 80 ft in length, and carefully worked it downriver to Suruga Bay, from where crewmen hauled it by ship around to Osaka and up the Yodo River to Kyoto. The project required three months of effort, 50,000 man-days of corvée labor and 1,000 *ryô* in gold.[30]

As fate would have it, an earthquake destroyed the temple a few years after its completion, and when Hideyoshi's heir tried to rebuild it, three years passed before he finally located a replacement ridgepole in southern Kyushu. The forests of Japan, it appears, could no longer support the grandeur of yore.

### 2. Issues in Timber Transport

Besides causing forest composition to change and forcing humans to adapt, the processes of excessive felling and log removal presented other environmental complications. As loggers pursued their work onto more, higher and steeper mountainsides – such as those that lined the Kiso and Tenryû rivers and their tributaries in the central cordillera – the costs and difficulties of timber removal became greater, leading to innovations in transport.

Thus, to extract logs from steep hillsides, lumbermen utilized heavy-duty winches that could drag them down and out of the forest. And for longer distances, they laid out logs to form elaborate wooden chutes, down which they could skid the timber to an assembly point.

Increasingly, too, they used streams in place of pack animals and carts to transport logs yet longer distances overland. In the precipitous, ledgey, upper reaches of streams, they built temporary wooden dams designed to collapse when triggered. They would fill the reservoir with carefully aligned logs, trigger the collapse, and send the logs surging downstream to the next temporary reservoir and so on until the stream was large enough to float them.

Where sticks would float, medieval loggers sent their newly felled pieces free-floating downstream, to be snared at a convenient landing. There they would be beached and then hauled overland by cart or packhorse – as in the above-cited rebuilding of Tôfukuji and Nanzenji. Or, if the landing were near the coast, they would be loaded onto ships for delivery by sea, as in the case of Tenryû timber bound for Kamakura or even China.

Such free floats posed problems, however. They sometimes entailed substantial losses of timber, whether to thieves en route, to stranding, or to freshets that carried the sticks pell-mell into the ocean, where only a portion would beach and be retrievable. Accordingly, from around 1600 onward, loggers resorted to supervised mass floats of logs and, later, to the use of elaborate rafts made of logs lashed together, which raftsmen steered downstream to landings.

Obviously, almost every stage of this logging activity fostered erosion, and the eroded materials silted up stream beds, which led to more flooding of adjacent lowlands. And such mud and other material as reached the sea contributed to long-term changes in marine wetlands, shorelines and offshore fisheries.

The silting of stream beds also complicated the logging operations by making stream use more difficult. In response to this problem – and also to clear streams of their boulders and other obstacles – loggers and their baronial employers began to dredge streams, and in places even to reroute or straighten them. It was an immensely labor-intensive task that became increasingly common from the later 1500s onward. It was doubly worthwhile, however, because it also facilitated the development of cultivation in adjacent lowlands.

### 3. Towards Forest Management

With good timber becoming ever more scarce, difficult to locate and costly to obtain, forest users began to undertake measures of forest protection and rehabilitation. Back during the *ritsuryô* heyday, as the consequences of reckless deforestation had become apparent in the Kinai vicinity, emperors had issued edicts intended to restrain excessive wood cutting, but with little evident success. And temples similarly attempted to preserve their woodlands, but to little effect.

During the 1500s, as barons maneuvered to strengthen their realms, they began taking steps to protect their woodlands. One of the first to do so was the baron (named Go-Hôjô and headquartered at Odawara) who controlled the Kamakura vicinity, including Izu Peninsula. The peninsula, exploited for centuries to sustain Kamakura and its elite establishments, had long since lost most of its coniferous cover, as mentioned in Chapter 4, and mostly grew a mix of smaller deciduous growth and large bamboo. Because the baron attached great value to both standing bamboo groves as barriers against enemy attack and bamboo as a harvestable commodity, he took steps to control the treatment of both bamboo groves and standing timber. He appointed forest overseers to regulate woodland use and gave them powers of effective enforcement.

Other lords, too, mostly those in central Honshu and further West, but even some on Shikoku and in northeastern Honshu, also began pursuing policies of forest control and protection. They did so in part because of their desire for timber and in part to control the downstream damage that complicated governance in so many ways. And from the 1600s onward, this trend to purposeful forest management gradually accelerated, as we note more fully in Chapter 6.

Moreover, forest management evinced the first signs of purposeful reforestation. A very few records of *ritsuryô* centuries mention attempts at tree-planting, specifically through the use of cryptomeria (*sugi*) cuttings (slips), which root relatively well in humid soil. There is no evidence of sustained planting, however, until the 1500s, when overseers of woodland that catered to the elite used cuttings to start *sugi* plantations. They did so at a few scattered sites in Kyushu and Shikoku and, more famously, on woodland in the Kitayama area North of Kyoto, which had long serviced the imperial court.[31] Gradually, as the 1600s advanced, such planting projects became more common.

In sum, as logging stripped accessible hillsides of desired wood, loggers moved deeper and deeper into interior mountains, which made lumber ever more difficult, costly and damaging to obtain. Those trends fostered substitution in architectural design, changes in techniques of lumber acquisition, and eventually efforts at forest regulation and rehabilitation.

*4. Agricultural Land Clearance*
As noted in Chapter 4, deforestation to obtain lumber and fuel wood often led to land clearance for agricultural purposes. That process shifted acreage permanently from the support of an indigenous biotic community to the support of humans and their collaborators. Like logging, moreover, it produced some degree of erosion and downstream complications.

During medieval centuries, more and more of the land clearance was on hilly sites, which often were used for swidden ("slash and burn") culture. Commonly such tillage involved sporadic land use, with sites being abandoned after one or two crops and months of erosion had consumed such nutrients as the soil initially held. But forest recovery on these abandoned sites was a very slow process, as successive generations of vegetation gradually restored the site condition to where it could support large timber trees.

## Effects of Agricultural Intensification

Turning from forests to farmland, of the several aspects of agricultural intensification discussed above, two had the most substantial environmental impact: widespread use of fertilizer and expansion of irrigation works.

### 1. Fertilizer: Manure and Mulch

The purposeful use of fertilizer – the key factor in "two-stage" agriculture – affected the broader ecosystem in a couple of ways, depending on whether the material being used was manure or mulch.

Manure from domestic animals, mainly horses and oxen, was especially valuable for double-cropped land because it had been "pre-processed" by the animal's digestive system and hence its nutrients were more quickly available for plant uptake. However, that very process of digestion meant that a substantial portion of the animal's original food intake – mostly grass and other pasture growth – was consumed by its metabolic processes. Only a portion of its nutrient value survived in the manure. This meant that a substantially greater acreage of pasture was required to generate a given fertilizer impact on the farmer's crop via application of manure than would have been the case had the pasture growth been used directly as mulch; that is, the advantages of labor saved and faster nutrient availability were achieved at the cost of more land lost by the indigenous woodland community.

If, however, one compares Japan's animal husbandry with that of some other parts of the globe, such as Europe, one sees factors that minimized the environmental impact of domesticated animals and their manure. For one thing, in Japan, horses and oxen were used as mounts and draft or pack animals, and while they likely were eaten in the end, animals were not raised expressly as sources of meat or milk. So their total numbers, and hence their pasturage requirements, remained far lower than in many places.

Even more significantly, sheep and goats were not kept. Whereas horses and oxen are selective eaters of grass and forbs, sheep – and especially goats – are much more ravenous and can eat so assiduously as to denude pasture land, making it vulnerable to erosion and desiccation. So, while manure is a somewhat wasteful form of fertilizer, the archipelago was spared the destructive impact that intensive animal husbandry, of goats and sheep in particular, inflicted on some regions of the world.

Turning to mulch, mostly it consisted of forest undergrowth, litter and harvest waste that could be stirred directly into the soil, rotted for use or burnt to form ashes. As agriculture intensified – with once-fallowed land coming under full-time cultivation, more and more acreage opened to tillage, double-cropping more widespread, nutrient-gobbling cotton crops more prevalent, and ever more paddy and dry fields purposefully fertilized – the demand for mulch rose sharply. That trend had notable environmental consequences.

The basic issue is this: when mulch removal was pursued in moderation, it tended to promote the growth of grasses and forbs at the expense of trees and other slower-growing woody species; that is, it altered biotic composition but had little downstream impact. When pursued more intensively, however, it had more drastic effects. It would gradually strip a surface of its vegetational cover, fostering erosion, drying the soil and robbing it of fertility.

During the *ritsuryô* era, as noted in Chapter 4, those trends had gradually produced "bald mountains" (*hageyama*) in the Kinai vicinity. During the medieval centuries of agricultural intensification, the sharp increase in land clearance, fuel-wood use and mulch gathering led to the appearance of such desiccated terrain elsewhere; notably, the Inland Sea vicinity, the Tôkai region and scattered sites elsewhere about the realm where humans were most densely settled.

This spread of *hageyama* had several consequences. It furthered the shift in bio-system composition and the decline in biomass. It reduced the nutrient value of run-off that farmers used to irrigate fields and heightened an area's vulnerability to drought. And it increased the volume of flood waters that a rainstorm would produce, hence the degree of erosion and downstream silting and damage.

### 2. Expanded Irrigation Works

The enlarged scale of irrigation works had a couple of impacts on the bio-system. Insofar as it expedited the conversion of major flood plains to agricultural usage, it constituted a major step in the long-term transformation of the forest-clad archipelago into a bifurcated realm, with lowlands and valley floors occupied by humans and their collaborators, and mountainsides mostly occupied by indigenous flora and fauna. Today that bifurcated character still persists, except that a sizeable portion of the upland is now plantation forest rather than self-seeded mixed growth.

Less grandly, the proliferation and enlargement of irrigation systems meant that more land was occupied by ponds holding water for summertime use and by ditches of diverse sizes and lengths shunting water from river to field.

More complex than this shift in land use were downstream ramifications of the expanded systems. By removing water from the river, these irrigation networks reduced stream flow below the points of diversion. During post-monsoon summer months, when precipitation was relatively low, this diversion of water lowered river levels enough so that more vegetation could establish itself here and there within the river bed. This riverine growth would gradually anchor soil more firmly and enable sediments to accumulate, creating shallows and even small islands along the stream. Then, when torrents cascaded downstream during typhoons, other heavy downpours, snowmelt or monsoon, the racing water was less able to scour the river bed and instead was more prone to overflow the riverbanks and flood adjoining areas.

The need to keep river beds clear as a way to minimize flooding meshed nicely with the earlier-noted wish to maintain river flow for floating and rafting logs. In response villagers and – mainly after the 1550s – barons organized dredging and riverbank building projects that utilized vast swarms of manpower in off-season work, and did succeed in improving stream flow and reducing flood damage.

Finally, one other development of these centuries also may be attributable to this irrigation-induced change in patterns of stream flow. Rather as the scarcity of large, attractive timber may explain the rise of shoin architectural characteristics – the aforementioned *tatami, fusuma* and *shôji* – so the difficulties in maintaining a stable river flow downstream from major areas of paddy farming may explain a change in the style of aristocratic ornamental gardening, in Kyoto most notably. Back in the *ritsuryô* heyday, elite gardens had involved graceful ponds and streams with delicate footbridges, well-manicured islands and grassy vistas. During the medieval centuries, a new "quintessentially Japanese" garden style, the "sand garden", replaced water with carefully raked areas of sand. This seascape of sand was interspersed with rocks of diverse sizes and select trees, shrubs or other greenery to represent terrain of various sorts.

*Other Matters*

Logging, land clearance and agricultural intensification were the human activities that had the greatest environmental impact during these centuries. However, a few other matters also seem to merit attention: castle stonework; mining and hunting; salt-making, fishing and coastline changes.

*1. Castle Stonework*

As noted above, the timber used in castle construction constituted a major drain on standing forest, especially during the decades after 1550. The stonework involved in those castles also had an environmental impact, although its scale and character are unclear.

Stonework had been utilized for bases of pillars and for horizontal building foundations ever since the *ritsuryô* heyday. However, the scale of such use had been modest and remained so for a millennium. Fortifications did proliferate during the centuries of *ritsuryô* decay and medieval disorder, but their construction relied on timber for both buildings and defense works. It appears, however, that from about 1500 onward, some fortified temples began using stone walls as defense works.[32] Still, it was after the earlier-noted changes in warfare in about 1550 that the gigantic stone walls of castle defenses emerged and became established as standard military technology.

Generally those castles were built on hill sites that improved their defensibility. Some of those sites were irregular projections or remnants of bedrock mountain. More commonly, however, they were segments of elevated terrace deposits, the diluvial residue of Pleistocene glacial phases, as discussed in Chapter 1. Overlooking arable plains or river basins, they provided defensible sites that were relatively convenient to both transportation and sources of manpower and material goods.

More relevant here, the soil of terrace deposits was also manipulable, even if low in fertility and sometimes laced with stones. It was, that is to say, relatively easy to sculpt as needed to form the flat surfaces and steep drop-offs required by a defense bastion. However, the terraces eroded easily once the soil was exposed or disturbed, so to keep them stable, one had to shelter them from rain and run-off. Those considerations shaped the way castle walls were constructed.

Lacking mortaring compounds, masons built with loose stones. To prevent them from shaking loose in earthquakes, the builders sloped their walls so the stone rested against the supporting hillside. And to prevent the soil of that hillside from slowly washing out through cracks and holes between large rocks, they placed a thick layer of pebbles and rock shards between the original hillside soil and the stone face of the castle wall.

It proved to be a remarkably durable type of construction. And in subsequent decades, when triumphant barons added more walls and towering keeps (*tenshu-kaku*) to their castles, they used the same basic architecture: heaping up and pounding soil as needed to form the core fill, facing it with a layer of pebbles, and covering those with the final rocks of the exterior wall.

The projects were immense. Depending on a castle's size, each one consumed tens to hundreds of thousands of rocks, which commonly measured a cubic foot or more in volume. And a roughly equal volume of smaller stones, pebbles and rock shards were used for the cushioning layer behind the face rocks.

Such vast projects could not come without environmental cost. We earlier noted the burden on forests imposed by the timber consumed in castle work. And, lest we forget, that burden was heightened by the volume of fuel wood used in such tasks as sustaining the work force, forging iron goods, and firing the tile that covered the sprawling roofs of castle buildings and parapets. But what of the immense amount of stone work? Where did the stone come from and what effect did its removal, transport and use have on the ecosystem?

The question is easy to pose but difficult – perhaps impossible – to answer satisfactorily. So, one speculates. The rock used to face castle walls was of two basic types: rock that was quarried and hewn to shape; and well-worn stones, many plucked from streams, which could be used with little or no processing.

The act of quarrying obviously disrupted the quarry site. And the removal and transport of large rocks certainly disrupted ambient biota. But once the quarry ceased to be exploited, vegetation would reclaim access routes and ever-so-slowly re-occupy the site.

The larger rocks gathered from stream beds would most likely have come from the upper reaches of rivers, where flood waters had deposited them, with smaller ones being found farther downstream. The act of removing them from stream beds would have dislodged soil and grit, creating more sediment for downstream deposition. Many of the smaller stones and pebbles to be placed between hillside and wall proper also likely came from river beds with similar effects. Depending on how the work was handled, it could have exacerbated the larger problem of erosion, sedimentation and river flooding. Or, conversely, it could have helped in the processes of dredging and straightening rivers that were undertaken to reduce flooding and improve log-floating.

The other way in which stone use had an environmental impact was in its transport. Much of the rock was moved by boat or raft on both rivers and sea, depending on the location of quarry and castle. To get rocks from quarry to raft and from raft to building site used animal power, carts, sledges, rollers and human labor. Such transporting of stone, like that of logs, disrupted ambient growth and generated loose soil, with resulting erosion and sedimentation. But there, too, once a project was finished, the natural processes of environmental repair would gradually have restored vegetation to most disturbed areas.

So, a tentative assessment may be that the riparian effects of castle-wall construction were mixed. Depending on how careless or attentive the project leaders were to the effects of their enterprise, they could have added to the environmental disruption and injury caused by logging and land clearance, or they could have ameliorated it by using the process of rock and pebble gathering to improve river flow.

## 2. Mining and Hunting

The medieval centuries witnessed a substantial increase in mining, notably of iron, gold and silver. Until the 1600s, however, it seems to have been placer mining of near-surface mineral-bearing sands, such as the earlier-noted iron sands of Izumo. So it did not involve the deep pits, heavy timber demands and mountains of slag and waste that one associates with industrial-age mining. It did, however, add to local disruption of streams and woodlands for at least the lifetime of the mineral deposits, and it probably left scars for at least a few decades after a site was abandoned.

Hunting also had an impact on the woodland faunal community. But how extensively deer, boar or other game were hunted is unclear. It is likely that the Buddhist doctrinal objections to such killing and eating were diffusing as the earlier-noted medieval Buddhist movements spread among the producer populace.[33] That trend presumably would have reduced the market for meat, undercutting the value of hunting as an occupation. However, some of those who were displaced by disorder of the day took shelter in woodland areas, and doubtless many of them relied on hunting and trapping to help sustain themselves. Whether habitat changes – less mature woodland, more scrub brush, forest edge, pastureland and open fields – helped or hindered deer, boar or other species is unclear. In any case, on balance it seems likely that the social growth of these centuries did not produce a commensurate increase in damage to most woodland fauna.

## 3. Salt-making, Fishing and Coastline Changes

As noted in Chapter 4, the development of coastal salt fields – in which seawater was impounded and gradually evaporated by solar heat, with the deposited salt then raked up and processed for use – seems to have had minimal effect on nearby biota. Moreover, insofar as natural evaporation of the water replaced boiling, it reduced the consumption of fuel materials.

These medieval centuries also witnessed development of more extensive fisheries.[34] Some were marine fisheries; others, freshwater, most famously those of Lake Biwa, just northeast of Kyoto.

Three factors encouraged fishing on Biwa. First, being a big lake, it held a large and relatively diverse fish population. Second, being near Kyoto, it gave fishermen favorable market access. Third, being a major travel link between the Kinai area and regions East and North of there, the lake enabled fishermen to generate income as boatmen, hauling both people and goods. Exploiting these advantages, residents of a number of villages along Biwa's shore developed organized systems of fishing. They caught fish mainly with nets and weirs, processed them, and delivered them to market.

Fishing villages also developed along sea coasts, particularly in the Inland Sea. Others developed on the shores of Ise Bay, on Wakasa Bay in the Sea of Japan (which was reached via Lake Biwa) and at other coastal sites with access to markets. Using weirs, as well as nets cast from the shore or from small boats, these fishermen gathered fish from coastal waters. They also gathered and processed shellfish and seaweed. However, they evidently did not extend their fishing activity into deeper waters, so it may be safe to infer that their efforts had only a modest impact on inshore biota.

Regarding the coastlines themselves, those near river mouths continued to change as upstream erosion produced soil and other debris for deposition along the shore. Such deposits were particularly pronounced near the mouths of rivers impacted by lumbering, land clearance and construction activity. By the 1500s, such sites were found from one end of the realm to the other, as exemplified by the Sendai Plain in the northeast, the Kasumigaura vicinity in the Kantô Plain, coastline near the mouth of the Kiso/Nagara River complex in the Nobi Plain, scattered sites along the Inland Sea and the shoreline at Hakata in northern Kyushu.

Datable markers for such changes in shoreline seem to be few, but one exists on the Kinai coast: Sumiyoshi Shrine. Dating back to around 400 CE, the shrine was built on a bluff (Uemachi Plateau) directly overlooking the coast at Naniwa, on the Inland Sea. It was situated there to provide sailors with a landmark as well as with godly protection during their dangerous ventures. As centuries passed, however, silt that was brought down primarily by the Yamato and Yodo rivers filled in the large bay northeast of the Plateau and gradually extended the beaches to its West. Today the shrine stands roughly 10 km inland, and while part of that distance is a product of industrial-age port construction for Osaka, already by the 1500s the shrine stood well back from the shore to its West.

Gradually, shoreline changes of this sort relocated coastal wetlands and their biotic communities. However, except in the wake of major storms and huge down-flows of debris, such changes seem generally not to have been destructive of local marine bio-systems. Indeed, the nutrient inflow surely helped some biota to flourish, even as it slowly altered the coastline.

**Figure 5.7:** The harbor and town of Hirado in far northwestern Kyushu. The harbor sustained both fishing and commercial sailing activity, 1963

## RECAPITULATION

For Japan, then, the 400 years to around 1650 were an age of wide-ranging growth. But they were equally marked by complexity. Those qualities were evident in the ruling elite, society more broadly, the agriculture and technology that sustained this society, and the interactions between humans and the rest of the bio-system.

As we noted at some length, the gradual disintegration of the old *ritsuryô* political order prompted recurrent efforts by career warriors and others to re-impose order on society. Although some of those efforts were partially successful for a time, not until the later 1500s did would-be rulers succeed in controlling their domanial subordinates and producer bases well enough to engage in a fight for realm-wide hegemony. As it worked out, the Tokugawa winners of that fight then stabilized the whole society during the early 1600s, doing so, in effect, by leaving the losers with enough benefits so that they chose not to risk all in a renewed quest for supremacy.

Whereas the ruling elite of the *ritsuryô* order – essentially a few thousand aristocrats and associated clerics and senior subordinates headquartered in a single imperial city – had constituted the very narrow, sharp-pointed peak of a vertically elongated population triangle, the "early modern" or *bakuhan* ruling elite constituted a fatter, less sharply pointed peak of a much more broadly based population triangle. That elite consisted of a few hundred powerless aristocrats and senior clerics in Kyoto and other sites, a shogun with thousands of comfortable subordinate officials and senior attendants in the gigantic city of Edo, some 200 barons (*daimyô*), each with scores-to-hundreds of officials and attendants in their castle towns throughout the realm, and thousands of lesser landed warriors and opulent merchants scattered among its many towns and cities.

This large and comfortable elite could exist because of the growth and change in the producer populace whose numbers grew from some 6 million in the *ritsuryô* heyday to upwards of 30 million by about 1700. That population growth reflected the reduced impact of the "three horsemen of the apocalypse" – famine, disease and war. Although the three centuries to 1600 were scarred by endemic warfare, the fighting was sporadic, its scale small until the later 1500s, and in consequence its demographic impact less than one might expect. Disease also was less lethal because the major epidemic forms had become endemic and their lethality mostly limited to children. Finally, famine was less prevalent, due in part to the elite's weakened powers of expropriation, but mainly due to improvements in agriculture that enabled food production to both increase and become more immune to routine irregularities of weather.

So the medieval centuries witnessed a substantial increase in the producer populace. However, even that demographic increase, mostly achieved after 1300, could not possibly have supported the huge *bakuhan* elite without major changes in its per-capita capacity to produce material goods, food most basically.

That gain in human productivity was facilitated by the elaboration of more effective transport and transaction arrangements, which linked producers to consumers with unprecedented flexibility. And that development accompanied the emergence of a large and variegated populace of middlemen, the so-called "merchant class", who developed the elaborate monetary system that handled their transactional activities.

Undergirding this whole socio-economic transformation, of course, were the various technological changes that constituted intensified agriculture. And those in turn were facilitated by technical improvement in such areas as riparian management and shipping.

As is standard bio-system practice, needless to say, gains by one species are achieved at the expense of other species, and the increased scale of land clearance, logging and other extractive activities led to further changes in the archipelago's biotic composition. Basically, more and more of the realm was devoted to sustaining sapiens and its collaborators; less and less to other species. Most famously, perhaps, the tree species most prized by builders – notably *sugi* and *hinoki* – were decimated, their place taken by other plant species and, in more and more areas, by desiccated "bald mountains".

Those changes, in turn, led to others. They altered riverine patterns and coastal configurations. And they affected human behavior, fostering modifications in architecture and heating arrangements as well as in woodland and riparian management. Eventually, as we shall see in Chapter 6, they led to an elaborately developed system of resource sharing and management, purposeful reforestation and other innovative measures to broaden and sustain society's finite resource base.

# 6 Later Agricultural Society, 1650–1890

The centuries from 1650 to 1890 have a charming deceptiveness about them.[1] On the face of things, they stand in striking contrast to the preceding medieval centuries as a time of stability and order vs. that earlier time of turmoil and disorder. When, however, we dig beneath that orderly surface, we discover a richly documented era of complicated trade-offs, tricky balances, grievous hardships and radical changes that remind us of those earlier centuries.

In overall terms, these centuries encompassed two major transitions. The first was a difficult transition from burgeoning socio-economic growth prior to 1700 to an era of general stability that lasted to the mid-1800s. At a basic level, this transition constituted an adaptation to the archipelago's ecological limits. The islands simply could not sustain further growth of intensive agricultural society.

This transition entailed a number of changes in social structure and relationships. Also involved were changes in human-ecosystem relations, most notably sharp declines in logging and land clearance but also changes in mining and fisheries.

Subsequently, even within the context of demographic stability and overall political order, diverse changes continued within society at large. Rural-urban relations and class relations within villages both continued to evolve. Agricultural practices modified slowly and extraordinary changes occurred in the handling of woodland, changes that foreshadowed core trends of the twentieth century. Some of the developments in both mining and fisheries could be characterized as forerunners of industrialization. And associated with these trends were continued developments in public literacy and learning, which also could be so characterized.

Then in the mid-1800s, a second major transition commenced. In that process the *bakuhan* political order (of shogun and barons) was sharply disrupted by foreign complications. That disruption led to the most radical reorientation of Japan's society since the introduction of agriculture some 2,500 years earlier; namely, the shift to industrialization. And whereas the earlier change, from basic forager to predominantly agricultural society, had occurred slowly over a millennium or so, the shift to a heavily industrial society occurred within a century or so, as we shall see in Chapters 7 and 8.

From about 1860 onward, these foreign complications led to basic changes in relations with external societies and the beginnings of radical changes in domestic political structure, socio-economic arrangements and the uses of technology. With those several developments came more diversified and intensified exploitation of the ecosystem, the demographic growth made possible thereby, and the environmental ramifications of those trends. By the 1890s, those changes were having a broad socio-economic impact at home, even as they empowered Japan's elite to launch a new era in their international relationships.

Let us examine this intricate story in terms of developments within the *bakuhan* elite; the changing situation of the general populace and trends in technology as they pertained to human-ecosystem relations. The environmental ramifications of these diverse developments can then be summarized briefly in the Recapitulation.

## THE ELITE: POLITICS OF STABILITY, RUPTURE AND REORIENTATION

The two centuries from 1650 to 1850 were, when compared to the three preceding ones, an era of remarkable political stability. And within the elite, stability was maintained despite the intrinsic limitations of the *bakuhan* power structure and the socio-economic difficulties associated with the shift from demographic growth to stasis, difficulties that had so bedeviled the *ritsuryô* system nearly a millennium earlier.

During the nineteenth century, however, disorderly politico-economic developments elsewhere in the world impinged with intensifying severity, creating unprecedented political stresses within Japan's ruling class.[2] Those stresses led in 1867–68 to violent collapse of the *bakuhan* system and formation of a new regime nominally centered on the emperor. The leaders of this new regime undertook to consolidate its position and defend it against aggressive foreigners by learning and utilizing the technologies and concepts that had enabled the Euro-Americans to threaten Japan in the first place. By 1890 they appeared to have fully succeeded.

Accordingly, the elite politics of these centuries from 1650 to 1890 can be examined in terms of three topics: *bakuhan* structure and limitations; the foreign menace and its effects from about 1790 to 1860; and the radical changes of the decades 1860–90.

### Bakuhan *Structure and Limitations*

As we noted in Chapter 5, the *bakuhan* system emerged after 1600 from a *de facto* truce between rival armed barons (*daimyô*), the victorious Tokugawa and their allies from the East and unsuccessful rivals from the West. The truce endured, in essence, because the barons accommodated one another and maintained a social order that was sufficiently advantageous to all the elite so that the risk, cost and difficulty of trying to alter it by force made such efforts seem counter-productive.

Even more than the *ritsuryô* order, this new *bakuhan* order entailed an intricate, official hereditary ranking of people. The imperial court nobility and clerics were neatly ranked, and barons were carefully categorized by size of their domain and by their relationship to the shogun – as kin, vassal or outsider. Lesser warriors were pigeonholed in terms of rank, salary and duty, and commoners were similarly identified by status and function as peasant, artisan or merchant.

From first to last, the new order's unstated understanding was that Tokugawa shogunal authorities would not pursue a purposeful policy of centralizing power and usurping baronial authority, and in return, barons would not plot to overthrow the Tokugawa. That understanding endured despite the dispossession of several barons during the 1600s and even though small-scale political maneuvers and manipulations for local advantage went on almost without pause thereafter.

Perhaps the most visible – and most famous – expression of that understanding was the "alternate attendance" (*sankin kôtai*) system.[3] It required every baron to spend, as per fixed schedule, alternate 12-month periods at his domanial residence in the shogunal city of Edo, where a portion of his staff lived permanently, along with his family members. In return for this expression of submission, he was allowed to spend the other half of his time in his own castle town, where most of his retainers stayed, governing his domain.

Given this basic understanding of shogun-baron relations, rulers were able to deal with gross malfeasance that might threaten the political order. Shogun could disempower disruptive or inept barons by pressuring baronial advisors to install a successor or to "rectify" policy. Similarly, baronial regimes could – and felt pressured to – control the behavior of subordinate officialdom, who in turn kept their subordinates in line and so on. Also, as the decades passed, more and more of the rules and regulations issued by shogunal authorities in Edo were adopted or emulated by baronial authorities in their castle towns. As a result, the meticulous political parcelization notwithstanding, by the 1700s and 1800s, there existed throughout the realm a high degree of overall similarity in the rules and routines of life, despite myriad, small variations.

Like regimes everywhere, the *bakuhan* leadership faced recurrent fiscal difficulties, along with problems of factionalism within the elite and hardship and discontent among the lower social orders. And at times those problems were exacerbated by severe irregularities of weather, crop failure and resulting public distress, most notably during the 1730s, 1780s and 1830s.

Well before those notorious calamities played out, however, natural and man-made disasters had already placed severe strains on the polity. The catastrophic Edo fire of 1657 followed a harsh famine in the 1630s, which we note more fully below. Then during subsequent decades, a series of earthquakes and other misfortunes befell the realm.

Most horrifically, an earthquake in 1703, "the strongest recorded in Japanese history", ravaged the southern Kantô vicinity. It killed an estimated 380,000 people and triggered a conflagration that again destroyed much of Edo, thereby imposing vast new reconstruction costs on occupants of the city as well as other towns and villages in the region. Then, only four years later, Mt Fuji erupted in an immense explosion that dumped several inches of ash across much of the Kantô region, crushing buildings, clogging rivers, ruining arable land, and in the process presenting *bakuhan* leaders with a huge new set of costs and complications.[4]

Even as these events were saddling society with vast new burdens, the end of rapid economic expansion during these decades was ushering in an era of sustained fiscal shortfall and institutional economizing. Baronial retinues were reduced in size, stipends of subordinates trimmed, construction projects simplified or abandoned, and myriad small expressions of luxury modified or discontinued.

By then only about 5 percent of households in Japan were headed by hereditary warriors (samurai or *shi*), the retainers of shogun and barons. And roughly half of those household heads, mainly lower-ranking warriors, were men on standby duty, sustained only by their modest hereditary stipend. When *bakuhan* leaders trimmed those stipends, low-ranking warriors faced real hardship, spurring many to pursue supplemental income-generating careers, usually as teachers or artisans.

The stresses experienced by these poorer warriors were severe, but by themselves they did not destroy the basic order of the *bakuhan* system. Rather, that outcome resulted from unprecedented escalation of the foreign menace during the decades after 1790.

### *The Foreign Menace (1790–1860)*

As noted briefly in Chapter 5, early *bakuhan* leaders regularized Japan's foreign relations during the early 1600s. To assure orderly management of the realm's margins, they charged the Satsuma domain in southern Kyushu with handling Ryukyuan affairs; the Tsushima domain in the straits facing Korea with handling Korean affairs; and the Matsumae domain at the southwestern tip of Hokkaido with handling Ezo affairs. As quid pro quo for handling those tasks peacefully, the domains were granted monopoly rights to trade there. Shogunal leaders retained for themselves the control of Nagasaki and the Dutch and Chinese trade that went on there.[5] Until around 1800, these arrangements seemed to function satisfactorily despite recurrent tensions and occasional squabbles.

By 1800, however, the European powers had established a solid history of invading other societies, seizing land and resources, and using them for home advantage. Japan, being in the "far East", on the opposite side of the planet from western Europe, was one of the last areas of the globe to come under European pressure, following that early-1600s stabilization of foreign relations.

When the European threat did finally materialize, it did so initially as a by-product of the Napoleonic wars, which had entangled the Dutch and thus their trading position in Nagasaki. Particularly troubling was the fact that the menace took the form – or so it appeared – of a two-front pincer-like movement that threatened the realm from both Kyushu in the South and Ezo (the Hokkaido-Kuriles-Sakhalin vicinity) in the North. In essence it was Russians who, from 1796 on through the 1810s, sought trade, areas for settlers and other concessions in the Ezo region. And it was Britons, from about 1800 to 1818, who posed the threat from the South, sometimes in the Ryukyus but mainly at Nagasaki.

Despite a few violent incidents of bombarding, burning and pillaging in the North, and coercive demands for supplies in the South, Japanese authorities were still able to insist that all European contacts be limited to Nagasaki, as in the past.

To avoid unnecessary trouble, however, they quietly instructed coastal barons to provide foreign ships with emergency provisions if necessary.

For a short while the problem seemed to ease, but then during the 1820s it escalated again. This occurred after European and American whalers began appearing here and there off Japan's coast seeking, or sometimes demanding, provisions and assistance. The whalers – hundreds of them – were there in the northern Pacific because, in their quest for lamp oil for industrializing Euro-America, they had so severely depleted the Atlantic population of preferred whales that it had become worth their while to make the long, dangerous trek around South America and up across the Pacific to the rich whaling grounds of the Aleutian-Kurile region.[6]

Whalers' occasional demands for supplies or aid proved troublesome in part because they upset local people and authorities and violated the Nagasaki-only regulation. In addition, they provided ammunition for a newly emerging body of ideological rhetoric about foreigners as a menace to the realm.

To elaborate, back in the decades before 1600, when rival barons had battled for supremacy, select groups of doctrinally inspired Buddhists had been seen as particularly incorrigible menaces to a stable baronial order. Then, Christian missionaries and converts, with their doctrinal certitude and connections to Iberian military power, came to be viewed as similarly dangerous. However, by the 1660s all these groups had been brought under control one way or another.

Over a century later, with the foreign collisions of the 1790s–1810s, that old fear of religious subversion gained a new life. By then, too, a body of scholarship (called *kokugaku* or "national learning"), which had been developing for a century or so, asserted the importance of distinguishing between what was "Japanese" and what was "Chinese" in the culture of the day.[7]

For centuries, of course, some among the elite had been aware of the differences – linguistic, at least – between Japanese and Chinese or Korean societies, and some (but not all) had developed a keen sense of admiration for things Chinese in particular. As commerce, literacy and mobility increased during medieval centuries, and especially during the *bakuhan* era, awareness of a non-Japanese "other" spread more widely among the elite and those associated with them.[8] That awareness had been reinforced, needless to say, by the arrival of Europeans in the later 1500s and by the presence of Dutch traders at Nagasaki thereafter.

This consciousness of us-them differences among the literate few was nicely expressed in 1706 by the Confucian scholar and teacher Kaibara Ekiken:

Our Japan surpasses other human realms in the mildness of its climate, the richness of its soil, the refinement of its people, and the wealth of its resources. But many of our people are not mindful of these facts ... We are like "insects surfeited with luxurious grasses heedless of good fortune".[9]

Especially during the 1800s, this emerging sense of ethnic or "national" distinctiveness and worth was employed by writers to explain what was at risk when foreigners – such as whalers – approached.

Under the circumstances of the day, and with an "us-them" framework already established, it proved easy to move beyond the earlier notion that Christianity and its proponents were a menace to the *bakuhan* political order, and to present outsiders in grander terms as a "foreign" or "alien" threat to the very essence of the ethnic Japanese "self".[10] In effect this formulation, like *kokugaku*, was an early expression of national self-consciousness. We should note, also, that it foreshadowed industrial society insofar as it consciously sought to engage a broader public in "affairs of state".

During the 1830s, domestic hardships caused by famine shifted attention away from the foreign issue, but during the 1840s it returned to center stage, this time as a more sharply etched military threat. The precipitating event was the Anglo-French attack on China, the so-called First Opium War, which brought large European naval forces into the region and demonstrated that they could defeat even mighty China, forcing it to accept the opium that European merchants were selling. Reports that the Europeans would also demand major concessions from Japan led leaders in Edo to adopt tentatively conciliatory policies even as they attempted to strengthen defenses. But then the Europeans became engaged in matters elsewhere, and the danger did not actually materialize until 1853.

When it did reappear, it was Americans, not Europeans, who made it clear by military deployment that if *bakuhan* leaders failed to adopt the trade and diplomatic policies being demanded, they would be bombarded and the city of Edo with its shogunal castle would be burned to the ground. With the Chinese example fresh in mind, and aware that their own defenses were utterly inadequate, shogunal leaders capitulated. In a series of treaties signed during 1854–58, they abandoned two centuries of relationships that had been regulated as the shogunate preferred.[11] By the new arrangements, Americans and Europeans gained the right to trade at several ports, maintain diplomatic legations and restrict Japanese tariffs on foreign trade. They also were allowed to travel about Japan, practice their own religions there, and enjoy immunity from Japanese law.

Needless to say, the concessions unleashed a wave of domestic outrage, especially among those sensitized by *kokugaku* to the notion of ethnic identity. From about 1857 onward, a mix of ethnic conviction, moral outrage and political opportunism interplayed with recurrent foreign imbroglios and domestic hardships to produce a decade of political disorder that radically reoriented thought among both those in control and those seeking to rule.

### Political Restructuring (1860–90)

As leaders and would-be leaders struggled for control during the decade after 1857, they gradually realized that, no matter who won the contest, the *bakuhan* system, with its policy of restricting foreign interactions to a few sites (Ryukyus, Nagasaki, Tsushima and Ezo) was no longer tenable. Rather, a radically restructured order capable of standing up to Euro-American military-commercial power must be established. The main questions to be answered, therefore, were who would lead the formation of that new order and how the necessary policies would be implemented.

Such tacit agreement among senior figures notwithstanding, implementing the new understanding proved to be an immensely difficult task, in great part because it involved so much unknown terrain and such unprecedented complications.

Already by the early 1860s, the political wrestling in Japan displayed unfamiliar as well as familiar qualities. The disputants had gradually sorted themselves into two very familiar core groups: the "easterners", who supported the shogunate; and "westerners", who sought to topple it. Most of the barons, however, gingerly tried to mediate or avoid entanglement. In one sense, then, the contest was a rerun of the 1600 struggle, and, more broadly, another expression of the age-old East–West division, with all sides claiming to speak on behalf of the imperial interest.

Another familiar quality – to those with long memories, at least – was the need of those above to heed the views of those below. We earlier noted how medieval politics had come to involve eruptions of lower-class discontent and how the emergence of stable baronies during the 1500s had depended in part on constructive responses to those eruptions. During the 1860s, the contestants for power similarly found that the anger of subordinates, in this case, mainly lesser warriors, had to be accommodated if they were to enjoy political success.

This time, however, the nature of the discontent was different. This time it was not domestic difficulties but foreigners who spurred the unrest.[12] And it was the *kokugaku*-inspired sense of ethnic identity that found vigorous voice in a new rhetorical slogan, *sonnô jôi* ("revere the emperor; expel the barbarian"), which gained great popularity among political activists. The proponents of *sonnô jôi* aspired to drive away the recently arrived Euro-Americans and, in some ill-defined way, to restore the Emperor, who now seemed to serve as a symbol of ethnic Japanese-ness, to his rightful place, whatever that might be.

Not surprisingly, it was westerners – primarily *Sat-Chô* baronial forces (from Satsuma, in southern Kyushu, and Chôshû, in today's Yamaguchi Prefecture in far western Honshu) – who were able to turn this emergent ethnicity to advantage as they challenged the shogunate. Although *Sat-Chô* leaders may have fully realized that the old *bakuhan* foreign policy was no longer tenable, they also recognized the political utility of denouncing Tokugawa capitulation to foreigners as a display of traitorous cowardice that justified the regime's utter destruction.[13]

This posture of outrage proved very useful. The gains in both manpower and motivation that *sonnô jôi* ideology provided *Sat-Chô* leaders proved sufficient, and during 1867–68 they were able to defeat the easterners in a series of savage battles that reached from the Kinai vicinity eastward into Tôhoku. In the process they added a harsh new chapter to the long legacy of domestic East–West distrust.

Even as they savored triumph, however, the *Sat-Chô* victors faced a dilemma. Some of their most avid *sonnô jôi* supporters had already moved to implement the expulsion concept by directly attacking foreigners in the Osaka vicinity. In response, foreign authorities demanded apologies and retribution, which presented the new leaders with a choice: stand by their most fervid supporters, or repudiate them and accommodate the foreigners, just as the shogunate had done. The new regime chose the latter course, thereby avoiding disaster. But doing so meant that a substantial number of its supporters were severely embittered. Over the next decade the resultant domestic tensions would seriously complicate political life, even as the new leadership wrestled with the question of how to restructure the polity so as to sustain itself, while mastering the technologies necessary to keep the foreigners at bay and, eventually, to regain Japan's sovereign independence.[14]

The *Sat-Chô* victors had repudiated the *jôi* "expulsionist" portion of their rhetoric, but that very action gave them all the more reason to cling to the sonnô "imperial loyalist" portion, lest they alienate too many more supporters. In that spirit they initially made Kyoto their headquarters, and a few months later they had the customary calendrical year period (*nengô*) changed, with the new period being designated Meiji, an auspicious term that conveyed the notion of a bright new era of rule.[15]

By then, however, they had decided to move their headquarters to Edo, a city most of them knew well. Unlike Kyoto, it had good port facilities, a powerful castle and nearby office and housing facilities of proper elegance despite a spate of fires during 1866.[16] The city's occupancy would constitute irrefutable evidence of Tokugawa defeat, and it was, moreover, a good location from which to keep an eye on any "easterners" who might harbor revanchist ideas. To give Edo an imperial aura, they renamed it Tokyo (Tôkyô, or "eastern capital"), a name that nicely evoked *ritsuryô* precedents. They then brought the boy emperor – he turned 16 while en route eastward – and his retinue to his new capital, thereby transforming the Tokugawa castle into the new imperial palace.

So, the new leaders stayed close to their emperor in part to retain and recruit as many supporters as possible. In addition, as they looked ahead, the imperial institution gained importance as a key piece of their larger vision for the future – a future that, they hoped, would give their regime all the elements of power that European governments seemed to have.

That future was imbedded in the concept of a *gunken* or "district/prefecture" system of rule, meaning a centralized political structure such as that of the *ritsuryô* era. It was contrasted with the *hôken* or "enfeoffment" system of the *bakuhan* era.[17] During their first months in power, the new leaders actually attempted to restore the old *ritsuryô* arrangements. However, the effort fared poorly, and as the years passed, they made change after change, gradually devising an effectively consolidated *gunken* political structure that formally was centered on the imperial household but, in fact, was controlled by themselves, senior officials outside of that household.

Those officials headed the central administrative offices that appointed and oversaw governors who controlled prefectural governments, which in turn supervised district administrators and, thence, towns and villages. That chain of command was then used to help keep the peace, promote new policies, conduct new land surveys and population censuses and implement the taxation programs that generated income for the treasury.

As part of this basic restructuring of the polity, during the 1870s leaders abolished all baronies. They pacified the barons with handsome ranks, titles and stipends, thereby transforming them into a new aristocracy in the *ritsuryô* – or contemporary European – manner. They also abolished the several ranks of warriors, commuted their hereditary stipends meagerly, and employed many of them in their new military, police and civil administrative organs. They granted these disestablished warriors the empty honorific title *shizoku* ("of samurai ancestry") to distinguish them from all the lesser people, who were lumped together as *heimin* or "commoners".

Such radical changes inevitably created new surges of dismay and unrest, which leaders tried to counter by further strengthening their ideological claim to rule. A key aspect of that policy was implementation of more measures to glorify the imperial household, to strengthen its role as the center of a "national" ideology, and to link that glory to themselves. The ancient religious customs of *Shintô*, which had acquired more ideological heft in recent centuries, were "purified", elaborated and tied tightly to the regime, giving it a "church-state" linkage as solid as that of any European regime of the day. In addition, imperial palaces, graves and shrines were spruced up, and as a national system of education developed, it was used to teach the glories of the imperial legacy and the virtue of imperial loyalism.

By then the regime had begun modernizing its military forces, obtaining more up-to-date weaponry for land forces as well as ships for a new navy. They had instituted a system of universal military conscription to replace hereditary warriors with an industrial-age "national" military, and they used the military training program as another occasion to promote loyalism.

The regime also utilized new slogans to replace the discredited *jôi* rhetoric. One slogan that exploited the nascent sense of national pride was *fukoku kyôhei* or "rich country, strong army", a classic Chinese phrase that Confucian scholars of the *bakuhan* era had popularized.[18] Besides helping to legitimize the new systems of taxation and conscription, it helped to foster the ethnic sense of self as "Japanese" rather than as merely the member of such and such a domain or region, village, class, family or other group.

Another slogan, one that sought to put a positive spin on the repudiation of *jôi*, was *bunmei kaika* or "civilization and enlightenment". It implied that there really were good things to be learned from the foreigners, things that would advance the wisdom of the people and thus enhance the power and glory of the realm. As one leader of reform put it, policy aimed to

> make good Japan's deficiencies by swiftly seizing upon the strengths of the western industrial arts; to construct within Japan all kinds of mechanical equipment on the western model, including shipbuilding, railways, telegraph, mines and buildings; and thus with one great leap to introduce to Japan the concepts of enlightenment.[19]

*Bunmei kaika* proved an invaluable slogan for promoting new ways, encouraging study abroad, legitimizing both the hiring of foreign experts and the adoption of diverse alien practices, and helping to justify the time and money people were being urged to spend on schooling.

As the 1880s drew to a close, the Meiji leaders, as they came to be known, brought this project of radical political restructuring to completion. In 1889 the Emperor formally promulgated their new Constitution, which in effect declared the permanency of the new order's basic principles and arrangements.[20] Those included a bicameral legislative body, the Diet, with its upper house of Peers chosen from the new aristocracy, and a lower house elected by a small propertied electorate. The first elections were scheduled to occur in 1890.

Also in 1890, to guide the people in their lives and learning, the Emperor issued an imperial rescript on education. Grounded in Confucian and imperial loyalist ideals, it called upon all Japanese to be virtuous, to learn, to be lawful, and "should emergency arise, offer yourselves courageously to the State", so as to preserve the "Imperial Throne coeval with heaven and earth".[21] Clearly, the agricultural ideal of a general populace productive, peaceful and apolitical had given way to the industrial ideal of a populace actively engaged in support of the government and its leaders in the happy belief that they were all equal members of an ethnic community, the "nation".

## THE PRODUCER POPULACE: GROWTH, STASIS AND CHANGE

For the elite, then, these centuries constituted a long era of general stability that yielded during the 1800s to decades of escalating turbulence and change, which culminated in an unprecedented burst of socio-economic and geopolitical reorganization and redirection.

For the rest of the population, the rhythms of change were rather different. In quantitative terms, several decades of rapid demographic growth gave way around 1700 to nearly two centuries of stasis.[22] The overall population numbers remain uncertain, but much less so than for prior centuries. As noted in Chapter 5, the 15 million or more of 1600 approached 30 million by about 1700. The subsequent stability entailed substantial shrinkage in the northeast, which was offset by a continuing, modest growth in the southwest. Rather similarly, a phase of urban expansion in the 1600s gave way to a longer period of urban churning, with the population of many domanial cities and towns declining while that of commercial towns mostly grew or held steady.

When the Meiji regime completed its first census in 1872, it recorded some 33 million people. That was the first census to attempt a count of Japan's entire populace. *Bakuhan* counts, which were made frequently after the 1720s for fiscal purposes, sought to determine the population of commoners and intentionally disregarded the entire elite and its in-house servant populace. Moreover, as per custom, families commonly did not record the presence of young children because death rates among them were so high.[23] In consequence, demographers now estimate that the *bakuhan* census figures, which fluctuated between 26 and 27 million during the years 1721–1846, omitted some 5–6 million people, giving society of the day a total number of 31–33 million, or nearly that of the early Meiji years.

From about 1870, however, Japan's population started growing, commencing the huge and rapid increase associated with industrialization. Initially the growth was most evident in Hokkaido, where the government promoted settlement, and in eastern Honshu, where Tokyo's population grew apace and that of its hinterland grew along with the booming foreign trade in silk goods.[24]

These demographic changes of the *bakuhan* era reflected qualitative changes in the lives of people, mainly those of the producer populace, who still constituted some 90 percent of the total.[25] To examine those changes in commoner life, let us again employ the three general topics: human-pathogen relations, elite-producer relations and producer organization and practice.

## Human-Pathogen Relations

Basically the role of contagious disease during these centuries was an extension of their medieval role. Most notably, measles, smallpox and influenza outbreaks sickened people, with smallpox in particular continuing to claim the lives of many children.

As in the past, cities and large towns, with their crowded, mobile populations, continued to be the loci of disease outbreaks. And because a larger portion of the total population – upwards of 20 percent by 1700 – lived in urban settings, at least part of the year, conditions there had a greater effect on the overall demographic pattern.

These contagious diseases tended to be more lethal, of course, during periods of crop failure and famine. In part this was so because the undernourished had less resistance to disease, but in part it was so because more of the famished headed for the cities in search of help, thereby exposing themselves to more pathogens. Because famines became more severe and common during the 1700s, contagious disease was able to play a role in the demographic stabilization that was occurring by then.

Another disease, dysentery, was not new to Japan, but it became a more widespread affliction, especially after 1700. One suspects that its spread was facilitated by the substantial increase in collection and distribution of "night soil" (human excrement) for use as a crop fertilizer. If so, there is a rich irony in the situation because this assiduous removal of night soil was one aspect of Japan's cities of the day that drew praise from visiting Europeans, who found them markedly cleaner than European cities. Also, since night soil as fertilizer contributed substantially to agriculture's continuing capacity to feed a large populace, it is ironic that the process of making it available may also have helped sustain a higher death rate. In more recent times, of course, the techniques of handling night soil have improved, eliminating most dissemination of pathogens.

As for new afflictions, epidemics of typhus evidently date from 1783. Cholera was introduced in 1822, and in following years it resulted in numerous fatalities and severe illnesses. Then, after the treaties of the 1850s brought more foreigners to the archipelago, bubonic plague also appeared, and it, typhus and cholera, "raged in the late 1850s and 1860s".[26] Subsequently, in a foreshadowing of industrial-age disease, when factory production started developing during the Meiji period, tuberculosis also appeared, especially among employees of the new and dusty cotton mills. Tuberculosis' social impact became pronounced, however, only after 1890.

On the other hand, well before then an early expression of industrial-age medicine, with its scientific intervention in the human-pathogen relationship, had made its appearance. The new medicine appeared initially as an aspect of *rangaku*, or "Dutch learning". This *rangaku* – the study of things European – had developed mainly through scholarly contact with Dutch residents of Nagasaki. By the later 1700s, a small number of dedicated scholars and physicians were studying European medicine, and as the 1800s advanced, they pursued their studies and began applying the new medical knowledge. Most notably, they started to use vaccination as a means of controlling smallpox.[27]

Converting expert knowledge into social practice proved difficult, however, and this was so in part because it was appearing, as noted above, in the context of an emerging ethnic consciousness. A century earlier the celebrated shogun Tokugawa Yoshimune (r. 1716–45) had been an enthusiast for learning about European medicine and other *rangaku* matters. But during the early 1800s, shogunal leaders sought to distance their regime from such foreign things lest they be smeared for betraying the realm. Most strikingly, perhaps, in 1849, during the brief post-Opium War lull in foreign crises, private physicians, with the support of many barons, engaged in a remarkable countrywide program using Jennerian (cowpox) vaccine to inoculate children (mostly of barons and their retainers, it appears) against smallpox. Even senior officials of the shogunate favored the program, but officially the regime offered it no support, and it did not give formal approval to such vaccination for another decade.[28]

In any case, decades would pass before these practices bore measurable demographic results. By 1890, however, Meiji leaders had made the study and use of European medicine an important facet of their broader program of *bunmei kaika*, and the new medicine was becoming widely accepted.

Indeed, that new medicine helped solve one of the most worrisome diseases to accompany Japan's nascent industrialization. During the 1880s, doctors reported an alarming proliferation of coal miners, textile workers and soldiers suffering from a "wasting" illness that gradually left them weaker, anemic, paralyzed and in extreme cases dead. Thus an army report of 1885 tallied 69,224 such cases among soldiers during 1878–85, of which 1,655 had proven fatal.[29] During the 1890s, doctors discovered that changing diet to include whole grains eased the illness. And eventually it was diagnosed as beriberi, caused not by some pathogen but by a deficiency of thiamine (vitamin B$_1$).

What had happened, it appears, was that a populace once largely rural and nurtured on brown rice, other whole grains and diverse vegetables had found employment in situations where they lived and ate in dormitory-like settings. There they were fed "up-scale" polished (white) rice but insufficient foods that were rich in thiamine – notably whole grains, meats, legumes and nuts. Therefore, healthy people gradually became unhealthy, but once the problem was identified, diet was improved and the workforce regained the productivity that employers valued.

### Elite–Producer Relations

During the medieval centuries, as noted in Chapter 5, Japan's ruling elite became weaker vis-à-vis the producer populace, which became much more diverse and more complexly organized due to centuries of economic and agricultural change. However, during the 1500s, regional barons reversed that weakening, devising more reliable ways of turning commoner energy to advantage and thereby being able to create and dominate the *bakuhan* order.

*Bakuhan* leaders draped their regime in Confucian rhetoric, and one of their constructs was an official ranking hierarchy that encompassed commoners as well as the elite. Called the *shinôkôshô* or "warrior-peasant-artisan-merchant" order, it sought to link rulers closely to their peasant producer base while relegating intermediate "processors" to more subordinate statuses.

In fact, of course, each of these four categories encompassed a range of people from wealthy to poor, cultured to crude. However, by erecting a clear ideological distinction between those above, the *shi* or rulers, and those officially farthest below, the shô or merchants, the formulation may have helped the new rulers to distance themselves from the collaborating merchants who had assisted them in their rise to pre-eminence during preceding decades.

Lying outside these four official categories were the residual civil nobility of the imperial court in Kyoto, a widely scattered population of clerics, and a diverse population of entertainers, hereditary pariahs and non-hereditary outcasts.[30] Rules and regulations sought to govern these groups. But in practice, control of the diverse marginal people was fragile, and as centuries passed, their numbers grew because they provided services – such as sanitation work or disposal of corpses – that others needed or welcomed but chose not to perform.

During the centuries after 1650, the ruling elite retained its primacy despite complex changes within the producer populace, which we note below. The elite did so in part, of course, by using its police power to prevent or quell civil unrest, which became more common during the 1700s and 1800s.[31] In addition, rulers continued the medieval practice of trying to accommodate and utilize those within the producer populace – successful merchants and the largest rural landholders – that were best placed to present a threat to the regime. They did so, in essence, by imbricating them in the power structure as local leaders of both urban and rural hoi polloi.

That strategy had a price, however, insofar as it allowed more wealth to reside outside the elite while serving to deprive low-ranking warriors of an advantageous peacetime function. And one suspects that the hardships and resentment associated with that shift of gainful roles to members of lower-status groups may help explain why, during the nineteenth century, it was such warriors who provided the bulk of supporters for *kokugaku* and *sonnô jôi* activism. And while some commoners did find that type of ethnic rhetoric energizing, for the most part, as earlier noted, the disorder that toppled the *bakuhan* regime in the 1860s was a warrior phenomenon.[32]

Then, when the Meiji leadership pursued its radical new policies during the 1870s–80s, it found that discontented warriors posed a far greater challenge than did any part of the general populace. This discontent reflected the fact that changes of the day disrupted warrior lives far more than they did those of commoners, rural folk in particular.

It is true that some members of the merchant community eagerly pursued new commercial ventures in line with the regime's goals, and some rural folk headed cityward to pursue new opportunities there. However, most rural folk stayed put. As of 1700, about 80 percent of the populace was rural, and in 1870 the figure was about the same. Thereafter, it changed slowly, not dropping to some 60 percent until around 1920.[33] Prior to 1890, then, it seems fair to say that all the *sturm und drang* notwithstanding, most rural people found their lives only moderately changed, although tax reforms and other policy innovations did at times weigh heavily on poorer villagers, reduce more of them to tenantry, and provoke local outbursts of resentment or alarm.

## Producer Organization and Practice

In Chapter 5 we examined producer affairs in terms of four topics – literacy, religious trends, commerce and villages – before focusing more closely on trends in agricultural technique. Those four topics plus "cities and towns" will serve for examining the period 1650–1890, but we shall see that the factors functioned somewhat differently than during medieval times.[34]

### 1. Literacy

During the medieval centuries, literate skills began to spread beyond the ruling elite. Nevertheless, as of the early 1600s, literacy in Japan still remained the skill of a small minority, perhaps 5–10 percent of the populace. That minority included members of the old courtly and religious elites, middle- and higher-ranking warriors, urban merchants and village leaders, especially in central Japan.[35]

However, by the mid-1800s, it has been estimated, approximately 40 percent of boys and 10 percent of girls throughout the realm were attending school of some sort, where they received instruction in reading and writing as well as other skills. And by 1890, as a result of Meiji-era reforms, some 70 percent of school-age boys and 35 percent of school-age girls were enrolled in four-year elementary schools, where they received basic instruction in reading and writing.

This Meiji-era surge in schooling and literacy reflected the government's pursuit of "civilization and enlightenment". By comparison, the dynamic that led to increased schooling and consequent literacy during the preceding *bakuhan* era is not readily apparent. Perhaps it was a response to the later agricultural shift from growth to stasis in the years around 1700. With that shift came fiscal difficulties for the elite and recurrent hardship among the producer populace, conditions that spurred people to seek solutions and gradually to see in literacy and learning a way of doing so.

To elaborate, scholars of the day found in Confucian thought a concept that proved particularly fruitful.[36] This was the notion of *jitsugaku* or "practical learning", which stressed the utility of learning, rather than its aesthetic or esoteric pleasures. Especially from about 1700 onward, the wish to acquire knowledge of practical use spurred interest in two noteworthy fields of study.

One of those fields of study was the earlier-noted "Dutch learning", with particular focus on medicine, astronomy and – during the 1800s – military technology.[37] The other, more important field was further study of Chinese and Korean learning.[38] Some of the most valuable information from those sources pertained to agriculture, writings known as "farm manuals" (*nôsho* or *jikatasho*).

Especially from 1697 onward, farm manuals began to be written in Japanese, published and disseminated for use. As the 1700s advanced, they came to be widely utilized, with itinerant scholars and local leaders employing them to foster more productive farm practices. Although the manuals dwelt at length on matters of right behavior and diligent work, they also conveyed much practical information on optimal techniques of tillage, animal husbandry and arboriculture.

This dissemination of practical writings was made possible by two other developments of the day: the utilization of printing technology and the spread of schooling.

During earlier centuries, reading material in Japan had been handwritten with copies produced manually one at a time. Then, in the decades around 1600, moveable-type presses of Korean and European invention were brought to Japan and utilized by the elite for a few years. However, it was woodblock printing that soon prevailed, perhaps because it permitted an easier combining of text and illustrations and could thus be pitched to a broader range of readers, from the fully literate to those with little or no reading skill.

Using woodblocks, a printer could produce scores of copies of a work and then store the blocks for later use as demand warranted. It was a technology that radically increased the availability of reading materials and, because of it, by the 1700s Japan had a well-established printing industry. The most celebrated publishers were situated in Kyoto, but others were scattered widely about the realm.

Even those printed books remained too costly for any but the wealthy. However, the practice of book-rental became widespread during the 1700s, with peddlers traveling around neighborhoods, providing loan copies that made the works as widely accessible as literate skills permitted.[39]

The other development that facilitated this spread of practical learning was the earlier-cited gains in access to schooling. From the outset *bakuhan* leaders had urged their retainers to acquire an education, arguing that as members of the ruling elite, they all had a moral duty to master *bunbu*, "the civil and military arts". To that end the shogunate and barons established domanial schools to train their warriors in the ways of a proper life.

In addition, a few scholars and some temples operated schools to serve other sectors of the elite. Initially, authorities did not deem the lower classes needy of formal education, but even so, during the 1700s schooling began to spread among both urban and rural commoners. At first it reached the more well-to-do merchants and the village wealthy, but gradually more and more of the broader urban artisan class and landholding peasantry sent their heirs to school.

Some of this schooling of commoners was fostered by rulers who, in response to public hardship and outbursts, sought to use it as a vehicle for moral indoctrination as well as practical instruction. Much more education of commoners occurred, however, in the scores of private schools (*shijuku*) operated by individual scholars and the thousands of small local schools (*terakoya*) that provided basic instruction for youngsters in villages and towns about the realm.[40] These two types of school became important mechanisms for promoting literacy and the spread of knowledge about agriculture, medicine, finance and other practical matters.

The value ascribed to learning was nicely conveyed in 1831 by the son of a village headman in the eastern Kantô:

Possessing a variety of skills is like having a treasure. Developing these talents provides a livelihood for one's entire life. In other words, learning is the seed of a prosperous life ... Rather than turning over money to [one's children], it is wiser for parents to impart basic literacy to [them].[41]

Nevertheless, as the cited literacy figures for the mid-1800s suggest, the majority of commoners still did not attend school. Instead, they learned the skills they needed at home or as shop apprentices, maids or other sorts of servants. They could do so, in part, however, only because their employers or other acquaintances could read and share knowledge, whether of a useful or simply entertaining sort.

*2. Religious Trends*

During the centuries of medieval disorder, as noted in Chapter 5, religious organizations had played a substantial role in political affairs. They did so, moreover, not only among the elite, as in *ritsuryô* times, but also among both urban and rural commoners.

By the 1660s, however, the last of the troublesome religious organizations had been stripped of their capacity to exercise autonomous political power. During the centuries to 1890, religious institutions abided by the rules of the secular elite. Apart from major temples, which functioned as self-contained monastic communities and as pilgrimage destinations, religion functioned mainly as a household or neighborhood matter. Local temples were supported by income from assigned lands, gifts and dues paid by their members, and their activity focused on the routines of daily life and death.[42]

In broader socio-political terms, religion (or at least philosophical thought) served primarily as an intellectual force. And the most noteworthy expression of that role was the aforementioned *kokugaku* movement of the 1700s–1800s, which gave voice and content to the sense of Japanese ethnic self. In that form a religious sort of conviction helped shape nineteenth-century politics. It complicated the study and utilization of *rangaku* and during the 1860s provided a foundation for the *sonnô jôi* movement. After the *Sat-Chô* victors of 1868 repudiated *jôi*, as earlier noted, they redoubled their sonnô posturing. And in following decades, even as the study of things foreign flourished, a countervailing sense of ethnic self continually asserted itself, becoming deeply imbedded in the new socio-political order and educational system that was emerging by 1890.

*3. Commerce*

As noted in Chapter 5, during the decades of baronial consolidation, ca. 1500–70, successful barons had found it advantageous to have merchant collaborators organize provisioning operations, supervise construction projects and mint money for commercial use. Subsequently, shogunal leaders moved to standardize commercial practices throughout the realm. To that end, they unified the currency system, controlled the weight and fineness of both coins and bullion, and standardized weights and measures.

A particularly valuable policy, and one with *ritsuryô* antecedents, was the creation and maintenance of a realm-wide system of highways and secondary roads. Established to facilitate military deployment and the transport of tribute goods, the system was later sustained by the annual comings and goings of baronial retinues on their *sankin kôtai* trips. As commercial traffic developed, however, those highways also became important factors in economic growth. They facilitated movement to and from cities and towns, and eventually even enabled a large population of pilgrims and recreational sightseers to get about the realm safely.[43]

Along these highways, the authorities maintained post stations that facilitated overnight stays. They also eliminated tariff barriers, fostered messenger services, and encouraged development of coastal shipping, ports, canals and river-clearance projects.

Together with the restoration of peace, these improvements in commercial arrangements helped sustain burgeoning economic growth during the 1600s. That was evident in the overall demographic increase as well as the growth of urban centers, which we note more fully further on. It was also evident in the proliferation of entrepreneurial merchants, who competed with and, in a few decades, largely displaced the earlier generation of merchants with official connections. These newer merchants gradually developed their own business organizations and became key figures in transactions throughout the realm. Their importance was particularly evident in the towns and cities. There, except for the neighborhoods and affairs of the ruling elite, community life was largely supervised by organized groups of merchant households. And they generally handled affairs with enough sensitivity to elite interests – for example, showing proper deference and providing "loans" as requested – to retain official approval and avoid destructive conflicts.

This economic flowering was encouraged, as we also note below, by some changes in mining technique. Those increased dramatically the supply of precious metals, which not only facilitated the blossoming of domestic commerce but also the foreign trade that brought luxury goods to the privileged classes. To considerable extent that trade involved elegant imports paid for by export of specie, a reversal of the earlier pattern of exporting goods and importing Chinese coins.

Well before 1700, however, the boom in gold and silver mining was over, and bullion scarcity was beginning to pose serious economic problems. In response, shogunal policy tried to halt the outflow of specie. One strategy was simply to restrict or forbid its export. Another was to encourage domestic production in place of items that had been imported.

Gradually these policies reduced the volume of foreign trade. By the late 1700s, most of the official trade with Korea via Tsushima was ended, although illicit trade did continue. In the North, trade with the indigenous Ainu population of Ezo, and through them with the adjacent continent, continued. But while it did provide animal pelts, birds and other ceremonial goods of value to the elite, its larger impact on the domestic economy was minimal – although it did generate serious complications for the Ainu themselves.[44]

Most visibly, trade with the Dutch at Nagasaki and with the Chinese in Nagasaki and the Ryukyus declined. Thus, whereas about 100 Chinese and Southeast Asian vessels per year traded at Nagasaki during the peak years 1685–90, by the early 1700s, the number was about 30 vessels per year, and after 1735 only about ten. And there, as at Tsushima, much of the surviving trade was "unofficial".[45] Such illicit trade notwithstanding, the authorities did largely succeed in stemming the outflow of bullion. By the 1700s, however, economic activity in the realm was so extensive and so highly monetized that scarcity of specie still remained a chronic problem.

Therefore, starting in the 1730s, the authorities turned to devaluing their currency, producing gold and silver alloys for use in coinage, minting copper – and even iron – coins and printing paper money. And from the 1760s onward, they imported silver and gold in exchange for copper exports. Those exports were sufficiently vigorous so that Chinese ships carried away about half the annual copper output of Japan's mines, while another fifth or sixth went out on Dutch vessels.[46] These measures were never fully satisfactory, but they sufficed to keep the economy functioning, leaving most merchant houses intact and accepting of their situation.

The decline in mine output, shrinkage of foreign trade and manipulation of domestic currency were but facets of the overall commercial change that Japan was experiencing around 1700 as the era of growth ended. The process of stabilization also fostered more tension between interest groups, and as the eighteenth century advanced, shogunal and domanial authorities developed more business regulations in the hope of easing difficulties of the day. To ease their own fiscal difficulties, they devised excuses for levying fees on merchants. And to ease pressure on the cities while also, it was hoped, sustaining rural production, they attempted to regulate the movement of people, mostly by sending migrants back to their villages of origin.[47]

The century or so leading up to 1840 – with its aforementioned crop failures and public hardship – was for many people a very difficult time. Nevertheless, the commercial system did continue to function without much further change until foreign complications upended affairs. Then, following the establishment of new treaty relations during the 1850s and the political reorientation of the 1860s, both domestic and foreign commercial affairs began a process of radical transformation.

Domestic economic change gradually accelerated during the 1870s and 1880s. More elaborate mining techniques were adopted; shipyards were enlarged and new ones erected, and factories of diverse sizes were established to process ore and to produce textiles, metal goods and other items. Railroads, telegraph lines, bridges, brick and ferroconcrete buildings began to appear, and coal-fired steamships and other steam-powered equipment began to be put to use.[48]

These developments clearly marked the commencement of Japan's industrialization, as did the increase in foreign trade, notably a sharp growth in silk-thread exports and machinery imports. During the decades to 1890, however, that trade bore all the earmarks of colonialism: besides being conducted according to treaties dictated by the imperial powers, it consisted mostly of raw material exports and finished-product imports.[49] That is to say, Japan was serving as part of someone else's global resource base.

From about 1890, however, that pattern began to change, as we note more fully in Chapter 7. In part this change occurred because Japan's renewed population growth gradually eliminated most of the surplus in domestic agricultural production, starting Japan on the way to net food imports, which have characterized the country ever since. Additionally, foreign trade changed because, by the 1890s, Japan had established enough factories and other industrial facilities to consume most of its other raw material output, therein foreshadowing an eventual need to import those materials. These same developments also began equipping Japan to produce finished goods for export, further marking its emergence as an industrial society deeply grounded in a global resource base.

## 4. *Cities and Towns*

By 1650 urban centers had existed in Japan for over a millennium. They appeared initially, as we have seen, in the form of late Yayoi-Kôfun political headquarters and then in the grand capital cities of the *ritsuryô* era. Urban centers based on commercial activity began developing later, during the transition from early to later agriculture.

Then came the immense surge of urban construction, mostly during 1550–1650, that produced the headquarters towns of barons scattered throughout the realm. Eventually numbering some 200 in all, the 80 or so towns belonging to the most richly enfeoffed barons had mighty castles – stone-walled bastions whose size and grandeur matched the baron's rank and wealth – at their center. Surrounding the castle were residences of retainers, as well as the lesser dwellings, warehouses and commercial establishments of the commoners who served them.

By the 1650s, these baronial headquarters towns were being supplemented, and in some ways supplanted, by proliferating small commercial towns, most of which developed in conjunction with improvements in transportation. Coastal port towns appeared or expanded, as did river ports and highway towns. Besides serving as warehouse and trans-shipment points, such towns also functioned as centers for artisanal production and as market sites for the producer populace in surrounding hinterlands.

By 1700, these baronial and entrepreneurial cities and towns came to house some 15–20 percent of the *bakuhan* population, or roughly 4–6 million people. It was a number roughly equivalent to the archipelago's entire population some 700–800 years earlier.

To examine this urban experience more closely, let us first consider the basic arrangements for city provisioning, then look at some instructive particulars of Edo and Osaka, and then note how changes in the wider economy eventually undermined the era's urban vitality.

*A. Provisioning the Cities.* We noted in Chapter 4 the relative fragility of cities as sites for human life because of their dependence on outsiders for life's necessities. And we saw how *ritsuryô* leaders achieved the provisioning of their great capital cities by implementing an elegant, enforced scheme of imperial benevolence – the granting of "use rights" – with tribute in goods and services as quid pro quo.

Founders of the *bakuhan* system sought to provision their cities by revitalizing the *ritsuryô*-era notion that the realm belonged to the Emperor, who designated successive shogun as responsible for keeping the peace and enforcing the legal principles of use rights and tribute obligations. In return for this token grant of authority, the shogun assured the imperial nobility of its privileges. Successive shogun also assured barons their domanial "use rights" in return for dutiful subordination and so on down the social hierarchy to villagers, whose right to till the land was quid pro quo for timely payment of tribute goods and such corvée service as might be required.

This use-rights mechanism generated a tribute yield of rice, other goods and money that the warrior elite could then distribute to their retainers, and exchange via merchants for other necessities and luxuries. In the process they sustained their headquarters cities and towns, most visibly the three greatest: Edo, Kyoto and Osaka.

The process of bringing goods into the city meant, of course, that waste had to be removed from them. The *ritsuryô*-era task of urban waste disposal had been handled simply by burying and dumping refuse or sending it away via stream flow. Although problematic in aesthetic terms, those practices seem to have sufficed, given the modest scale of urban settlement, because the waste was organic and would reprocess biologically.

During *bakuhan* centuries, a major change occurred in urban waste disposal. Organic waste – both the refuse from food processing and night soil – acquired a great new market value as agricultural fertilizer. As suggested above, the widespread collection and transport of night soil may well have fostered dysentery. However, from about 1700 onward, the fertilizer trade also enabled cities and towns to dispose of vast quantities of waste in a profitable manner, thereby eliminating much trash accumulation, improving urban aesthetics, minimizing the waste dumped into nearby rivers and streams, and accommodating the vast increase in urban population.

These waste-disposal practices may also help explain the survival of vibrant marine fisheries in the waters around large port cities. Most famous, perhaps, was Edo (later Tokyo) Bay. Its rivers, such as the Tamagawa, and its coastline supported rich stocks of fish, shellfish and edible seaweed, resources that helped feed the city while providing some trade goods for exchange with the hinterland.

*B. Regarding Edo and Osaka.* As noted previously, the three greatest *bakuhan* cities were Edo, Kyoto and Osaka.[50]

To note Kyoto briefly, at its height (as Heian) during the early *ritsuryô* era, it may have numbered some 100,000 residents, but it generally held fewer than that during later centuries. By the late 1400s, it had shriveled to a linked pair of small urban areas, one where surviving aristocrats clustered (Kamigyô) and, to its South, another where merchants prevailed (Shimogyô). Then, after 1570, Kyoto revived under baronial auspices, grew very rapidly, and by 1650 attained a peak population of some 400,000. After that date, however, it gradually lost residents again, in part because of the rise of nearby Osaka, which numbered some 400–500,000 by the later 1700s. By then Edo, which had numbered perhaps 30,000 as of 1600, is said to have reached well over a million.[51]

The extraordinary seventeenth-century growth of these three central cities had been sustained, to a great extent, by regularization of the earlier-noted *sankin kôtai* ("alternate attendance") system, which funneled into them goods, wealth and people from throughout the realm. However, by the late 1600s, as the era of agricultural expansion passed, the tribute income of rulers had ceased growing, and castle towns across the country were starting to experience stagnation or decline in both population and elegance. In due course, even Osaka and Edo went into decline, with Osaka shrinking to some 310,000 by 1860 and Edo experiencing a dramatic drop during the 1860s to some 600,000.

The initial rise of Edo – today's downtown Tokyo – deserves special note because in a sense it arose on what was a preposterous site for a city.[52] As a castle site, it was very sensible. It consisted of low bluffs overlooking Edo Bay to the East, but it was shielded from naval assault by a wide strip of brackish swamp. It was guarded North and South by rivers that constituted natural barriers, while flat areas to the West were easily watched from towers on the bluff. That very layout meant, however, that urban growth would require filling in swamps, leveling hillocks and bridging rivers or else sprawling westward across potentially valuable farmland.

In recurrent feats of monumentally labor-intensive urban construction, work crews were mobilized and sustained, streams re-routed and bridged, swamplands filled, canals dredged, wharf areas constructed, streets laid out, and castle, mansions and city blocks erected. Even as the city grew, however, a critical problem became apparent. There was no adequate water supply. Wells in low-lying areas produced salt water. Adjacent streams carried silt and debris from upriver.

To cope with this water-supply problem, Edo's leaders undertook two major waterway construction projects. The first one, in the early 1600s, took water from Inokashira Pond, some 12 km west of the castle, transporting it via a surface aqueduct much of the way but nearer the castle utilizing a pipe made of hollowed-out tree trunks fitted end-to-end. Near the castle, an array of underground branch lines carried the water to neighborhood outlets. However, by 1650 this water supply was proving insufficient, so an even grander engineering project was launched. It involved constructing a larger aqueduct that snaked its way some 35 km eastward from the clean, upper reaches of the Tama River, following contours of the land carefully enough to carry huge quantities of clean water smoothly to the city. There, a reported 3,662 wooden tubular branch aqueducts distributed the water through the city.[53]

That aqueduct, the Tamagawa Jôsui ("Tama River Waterway") – which still flows today, paralleled by highways and city streets – sufficed, helping Edo grow into the world's most populous city of the day. But while it was an admirable feat of engineering, it was also a vulnerable system. Most notably, perhaps, the aforementioned great earthquake of 1703 damaged it severely, requiring extensive repairs before the city water supply could be restored.[54]

Turning to Osaka, when the *bakuhan* period began, it was a quintessential political center. It was a castle town with a strongly warrior-dominated population centered on its huge castle, from which a shogunal deputy kept an eye on affairs in central and western Japan. However, as the *sankin kôtai* system of baronial visits to Edo became routinized during the 1630s, Osaka's canals and its location at the eastern end of the Inland Sea and mouth of the Yodo River transformed it into a transportation and warehouse hub for barons throughout western Japan.[55]

Initially these barons used collaborating merchants in this work of transporting, warehousing and marketing the rice and other materials that they required to sustain their Edo residences – as well as the lesser residences that some of them maintained in Osaka and Kyoto. As decades passed, however, more and more of that baronial provisioning was handled by independently organized merchants, with the result that, by 1700, Osaka seemed to be primarily a merchant-dominated city, with a population consisting mainly of artisans and laborers. Employing most of these people – and administering much of the city – were the merchants, whose number included some 4,500 licensed wholesalers (*ton'ya*).[56]

In effect, Osaka had been transformed from a giant castle town into the realm's predominant commercial center. It was an evolution that prepared the city for a major role in Japan's industrialization.

C. *On Urban Decline.* During the 1700s, as noted earlier, even the central cities began to experience the stabilization and eventual decline in size and economic vitality that most baronial towns were already facing. Two factors seem to have been particularly influential in those downward trends. One factor was biological, the other, economic.

The biological factor was inability of the urban commoner populace to reproduce at a rate that would sustain its numbers. One reason for this inability was the aforementioned role of cities as loci of contagious disease: too many urban infants and children died of smallpox and other illnesses. The other reason was the gender imbalance in this population. A large number of urban working-class people were rural men, single or married, who had families in the village and who traveled to the city only for temporary work (a practice called *dekasegi*), doing so most commonly during the agricultural off-season.

As a consequence of these biological constraints, cities were dependent on the continual inflow of rural people seeking employment, people who might not carry immunity to those diseases present in the city. And during the later *bakuhan* period, even that inflow slowed, in considerable part because of the economic factor, which was the outflow of artisanal jobs to the countryside.[57]

To explain this outflow, in the early *bakuhan* period, artisanal skills and whatever literacy skills they required were mainly found in the cities, where craftsmen produced goods mostly for urban elite consumption. As the decades passed, however, the ruling elite found its tribute income, and hence its capacity to sustain an urban consumer populace, becoming less adequate and more unreliable. Meanwhile, small towns were proliferating about the realm; literacy was spreading, and more wealth was coming to reside among merchants and well-to-do village landholders. With those changes, more and more of the artisanal market shifted away from the elite and the cities in which they dwelt.

Craftsmen found also that in addition to this shift in their consumer market, there were economic advantages to producing in the hinterland. For one thing, as literacy spread about the realm, more and more rural folk were becoming capable of handling or overseeing artisanal tasks. As a result, more and more of those villagers who once trekked to the city for off-season, temporary work found that they could stay at home and do piece work that was more gainful for themselves even at lower wage rates.

Also, for many artisanal jobs – such as production of *sake*, soy sauce or cotton or paper items – it was more economical to have them done near the sources of raw material and to transport the finished goods to market than it was to haul the raw materials to an urban work site. This was especially true as the supply of raw materials near cities became depleted, to be replaced by materials in more distant places.

The upshot of these later *bakuhan* trends was that cities were unable to sustain their commoner population as they gradually lost jobs to the countryside. The

**Figure 6.1:** Ripping timber to produce boards near a logging site; a print by Hokusai Katsushika (1760–1849) in the series "Thirty-six Views of Mt Fuji", in author's collection

**Figure 6.2:** Stacking shingling, producing boards and storing bamboo at a lumberyard in northeast Tokyo; a print by Hokusai Katsushika (1760–1849) in the series "Thirty-six Views of Mt Fuji", in author's collection

trend would not reverse until post-1870 policies introduced new societal goals and new technologies that were centered in and near the cities. Those changes created powerful new magnets to lure rural people back into town. In addition, the adoption of industrial-age techniques of medicine and public health helped urban populations to reproduce and grow with greater safety despite the earlier-noted appearance of beriberi and tuberculosis.

### 5. Villages

As we saw in Chapter 5, during Japan's medieval centuries, villagers were subjected to disruption and exploitation by the political turmoil of the times, especially in the Kinai vicinity. They also, however, used more and more of the techniques of intensified agriculture, which increased output per acre, enabling their villages to grow in size, develop more elaborate social organization, counter outside threats, manage communal resources more effectively and deal with the rising commercial economy more advantageously.

These general trends gradually spread across the realm, and they continued during *bakuhan* centuries but with some noteworthy changes.[58] By 1600, as mentioned previously, the baronial elite were moving their warrior forces into castle towns, leaving villagers more fully in control of their own localities. Concurrently the restoration of peace spared villagers many of the abuses endured by earlier generations. But it also exposed them to a gradually more regularized and rigorous control from above.

To elaborate, in the *bakuhan* order, this control of villagers was exercised via a hierarchy of baronial appointees that extended downward to include formally designated village leaders, who generally were the largest landholders. Utilizing the earlier-noted concept of use rights, shogun and barons deployed land-surveying teams to determine who tilled what fields, and what their estimated yield and consequent tribute obligation would be.

Initially, during the 1600s, these land surveys were conducted annually, and the intended tribute burden (some 40–50 percent of estimated paddy yields) was adjusted in accordance with the condition of the crop, the rice crop in particular. Rulers also sought to encourage more land clearance by setting the tribute rate for new fields at a lower level, gradually raising it in subsequent years as the output of those new fields rose.

For much of that century, as we note more fully further on, the process of additional land reclamation continued. That trend, together with improved techniques of cultivation, increased total output and sustained an expanding population. And since at least 80 percent of that swelling populace was in villages, it meant that many villages grew larger and many new villages were formed, by one estimate giving Japan some 63,000 villages in the 1700s.[59] Around 1720, one village headman succinctly described the process of village formation and growth:

> As to the origin of villages, one or two families usually settle where the land is good, and fields are brought under the plow surrounding the dwellings of the settlers. Gradually a village forms; new houses are built among the existing ones, new fields are opened up, and land previously neglected, such as valley bottoms

and marsh, is filled in, ditches and embankments are built and new fields are developed until not an inch of land is left.[60]

For most of the realm, the era of such village creation and growth was petering out by 1700. By then, however, the trends noted above – the removal of warriors from villages and the imposition of more standardized higher control – had combined with the growth and proliferation of villages to undermine much of the control that large-scale landowners had acquired during preceding centuries. So, small-scale landholders had grown more numerous.

This proliferation of independent smallholders, which accompanied the century of overall agricultural expansion, began to reverse during the 1700s. Increasingly, such holders discovered that with no more land to reclaim and with such burdens as river maintenance becoming more onerous, their circumstances were deteriorating. Measures to boost yield per acre only postponed difficulties, and as decades passed, more and more smallholders abandoned their lands or negotiated agreements with well-to-do neighbors that transferred to them the use rights and tribute obligations, thereby transforming themselves into rent-paying tenants.[61]

By the 1860s, roughly half of Japan's farm households were tenants or partial tenants.[62] And in following decades, tenantry continued to grow: whereas tenants tilled about 27 percent of the arable land in 1873, by the 1890s, they were tilling over 40 percent – and constituted about 70 percent of farm households.[63] Many of these poorer villagers also found themselves in more-or-less permanent debt to their landlords, who advanced them monies to pay for seed, fertilizer and other necessities.

Two factors served to blunt the harsh social effects of this re-stratification of villages. First, by 1700 government had largely abandoned its annual re-survey

**Figure 6.3:** Paddy-field terracing on lower slopes of mountains in central Kyushu, 1963

of crops because with little additional land becoming tillable, the costs of re-surveying outweighed the benefits. Therefore, insofar as villagers were able to open additional bits of land to tillage or increase the yield of their existing arable, most of the increment stayed in the village. Indeed, by one estimate, whereas the early *bakuhan* tribute burden had actually been some 50–60 percent of output, by the mid-1800s, it had fallen to 30–35 percent.[64]

Second, as villagers used ever more intensive techniques of tillage, their interdependence grew, especially in terms of irrigation water, woodland and green-fertilizer sources, as well as the use of draft animals and scheduling of labor. Particularly where double-cropping and handicraft enterprises created complex and tightly scheduled work cycles, cooperation among villagers became crucial.[65] Accordingly, the village elite had compelling reason to try to help their poor neighbors stay afloat, especially in hard times. Villagers established "mutual assis-tance" organizations (*kô*), and developed inter-village systems of cooperation that enabled them to help one another and, in especially hard times, to petition the authorities for relief or even to organize protest movements.[66]

Helping to sustain these local social arrangements was a rural ethos that encour-aged diligence. As the headman of a village in mountainous Shinano Province put it in 1760, one's duty was to

Protect the "household occupation" more than anything else ... Protect the properties and farmlands entrusted to you by your ancestors from being dimin-ished, and be frugal in all matters.[67]

Such advice, obviously, was easier to follow for landlords than for tenants and marginal smallholders.

These tenants and smallholders also tried to cope with straitened circumstances in other ways. They took secondary employment in town (*dekasegi*) or in the village, as noted earlier. And they devised ways to limit family size by outplacing children or by preventing their appearance through reduced pregnancy rates, abortion or infanticide.

This management of reproduction had a number of effects. Besides helping to stabilize overall population size, it appears to have reduced the female death rate, helping average human lifespans increase from an estimated 30 years overall in the later 1700s to some 42.8 years for men and 44.3 years for women by about 1880. In addition, with less time consumed by pregnancy and infant/child care, women had more time and energy for other tasks. So as handicraft production, such as silk-thread spinning, spread through the hinterland, women were more available to handle the work.[68] Consequently, smallholders were able to increase household output (and income) without a commensurate increase in household expenditures.

These several responses to the changing times continued to be practiced throughout the latter half of the *bakuhan* period, giving Japan a fairly uniform village pattern that consisted of a small populace of well-to-do, commonly literate village leaders and a large populace of subordinate villagers who pieced their lives together by combining small-scale or tenant farming with such by-employments as they could secure.

These long-term trends toward tenantry, greater dependence on by-employments and more disciplined family management also had political ramifications. They created an overall situation, especially during times of crop failure and hardship, in which – the virtues of mutual assistance notwithstanding – vulnerable, poorer villagers found it rather easy to see the rent-collecting village elite as the heartless villains of the situation. In consequence, when hardship translated

**Figure 6.4:** Clearcut and restocked mountainsides in central Tôhoku, as seen from a small aircraft, 1955

**Figure 6.5:** The port of Nagoya, in Aichi prefecture, is the busiest port in Japan

**Figure 6.6:** Plantation forests on edge of lowland in eastern Tôhoku, 1955

into social protest, it usually was in the form of assaults on the local commoner privileged rather than attacks on the ruling elite. Only in extreme circumstances did it expand into assaults on the urban merchant class and baronial elite.

The situation was nicely analyzed by a senior shogunal official in 1815:

> When it comes to peasant revolts, there is no need to be concerned just because a lot of people are involved. And that they are bitter about headmen and lower officials and start riots to demonstrate about that doesn't amount to much either. But when they're close to starvation because of famine and decide to rise up rather than starve to death, and attack the homes of the wealthy and the rice dealers, or start setting fire to everything, it's time to look out. They are strongest when the fief holder's government is bad, for then they make him out to be the enemy. Moreover these risings are worst when there are additional complaints because of long-standing despotic government with heavy demands for taxation, transport, corvée, and forced loans.[69]

As that assessment suggests, by the 1800s, rulers were aware that severe stress among the general populace could pose a threat to the established order. But as a general rule, it did not. And in the end, as we noted above, it was foreign-policy-related discontent within the warrior class that destroyed the *bakuhan* order.

Subsequently, during the decades to 1890, village life followed much the same rhythms as before.[70] With rather few exceptions, the changing patterns of politics, trade, technology and elite culture had only a gradually escalating impact on more and more villagers, mostly after that date, as elements of industrialization began to affect their lives.

## TRENDS IN TECHNOLOGY [71]

In preceding chapters, the principal technologies of interest related to agriculture, although both mining from the Kôfun era onward and architecture of the *ritsuryô*, medieval and castle-building eras also commanded some attention. For these final centuries of intensive agriculture, notable new developments in mining, forestry and fisheries all require note, along with agriculture, because they all played a role in the growth and stabilization phases of the *bakuhan* era and in Japan's subsequent reorientation toward industrial society.

### Mining

The mining examined in preceding chapters was mining of metals – iron, copper, gold and silver mostly. During the *bakuhan* era, metal mining experienced some notable changes and, more strikingly, coal mining made its appearance.

### 1. Metal Mining

Mining of iron and other metals dated back at least as far as the Kôfun era. However, that was placer mining, which mainly processed sand deposits containing the desired minerals. The sand deposits commonly were in or near stream beds, although they might have been shallowly buried. As described in the early 1600s, those engaged in placer mining would divert the water in a stream bed

> and then dig into the sand which remains, until they reach the living stone and rock beneath the river bed. And in the sand lodged in the rents and fissures of the rock is found gold as fine as beach gravel.[72]

Extracting such deposits thus did not entail the complex excavation work of pit mining.

Until around 1600, miners continued processing such surface and near-surface deposits. During the following decades, however, the pursuit of metal-bearing sands and more solid deposits of ore took them farther into the ground. They followed the ore deposits by tunneling. Loosening material with hand tools as they advanced, they then hauled it to the surface in baskets slung across their backs. As the tunnels grew deeper, they began devising ways to drain or pump out water and to improve ventilation with hand-cranked fans.[73]

Mine output also expanded as more and more ore deposits were found. Silver mines had been discovered on Sado Island in the 1520s, and others were found in Kyushu in the 1590s and North of today's Kôbe city in the 1610s. Gold mining was so highly valued that stream bed placer-mining operations even extended across Hokkaido during the 1600s, intruding into regions of Ainu settlement and severely damaging many of their fisheries.[74]

New copper mines were discovered in the northeast Kantô in the 1590s and in the northwest Kantô in 1610. Over the following century other metal mines were found scattered across the realm from Tôhoku in the northeast to Shikoku and Kyushu in the southwest. Thus, an official report of 1703 spoke of 243 active copper mines, and during the decades 1708–1843 the most productive ones were in Tôhoku and Shikoku.[75]

During the early 1600s, with the technical improvements and additional mines, miners were able to produce a short-lived – but world-famous – boom in gold and silver production that lasted until about 1630, after which output rapidly declined. From the 1660s onward, as noted earlier, bullion scarcity began to produce a range of economic complications, but in the absence of further changes in mining technology, output continued to shrivel.

Copper mining, on the other hand, continued its growth in output into the 1690s, and it remained robust well into the late 1700s, while iron mining was sustained into the 1800s, enabling those metals to supplement or replace gold and silver in numerous functions.[76] When, however, *bakuhan* leaders of the 1800s began casting more large cannon for coastal defense, they found that even the iron supply was insufficient to their needs.

Long before then, Japanese society had discovered another major problem with mining – its downstream destructiveness. The placer-mining activity of pre-*bakuhan* centuries seems to have generated comparatively few problems, although it could disrupt stream-flow and damage downstream fisheries. The problems were relatively few mainly because the scale of such mining was modest, but also because the ore being removed had long since been leached of many chemicals and its extraction and processing did not produce large quantities of waste. With the newer, deep-mining techniques, however, the scale of production grew sharply, and the ore, the mine residue and the associated refining processes produced much more gaseous and liquid pollution.

Because of Japan's steeply mountainous topography and seasonal irregularities of precipitation, large volumes of effluent from these mining operations would occasionally race downstream to the densely settled farmlands lining rivers in the valleys below, flowing from there on to the coastal plains and bays with their fishing operations. As the pollutants advanced, they rendered potable water poisonous for humans and animals, fouled irrigation systems, thereby poisoning rice crops, and killed fish and diverse coastal marine life.[77]

Unsurprisingly, these intensified mine operations soon developed into a social problem. As early as the 1640s, effluent from a copper mine in northeast Kantô was doing so much damage to nearby farm lands that farmers protested and the authorities finally ordered it closed. At the same time, contaminants from some of the gold mines in northeast Japan were damaging enough paddy fields so that authorities ordered them closed too.

In following decades, as gold and silver output dropped, it was the poisonous effluent from copper mining and the noxious gases from its smelting that produced most of the protests, although occasionally iron or sulfur mines were the source of trouble.[78] By the 1700s the damage caused by metal mining was well enough known so that villagers in some areas would mobilize protest movements to prevent the opening of mines at nearby sites. But in a foreshadowing of future developments, *bakuhan* authorities commonly sided with mine operators, who provided the government with the metal it needed. And when damage occurred, farmers commonly received compensation designed to still the complaints, although on occasion a mining operation would be shut down or required to alter procedures one way or another. But still the problems – and the protests – persisted, outliving the *bakuhan* regime itself.

Given this legacy of intensifying resource-scarcity and enduring pollution, it is unsurprising that after the 1860s, improvements in mining technique became an important aspect of Meiji regime-strengthening. The government hired foreign experts who during the 1870s introduced such new devices as forced-air ventilation, steam-powered pumps to remove water, blasting powder to loosen ore and winches to haul it out by the cartload.

The resulting increase in mine production was stunning, as this table suggests.[79]

| Year | Gold (troy oz.) | Silver (troy oz.) | Copper (long tons) | Coal (long tons) |
|------|------|------|------|------|
| 1874 | 3,129 | 87,890 | 2,078.5 | 204,864 |
| 1884 | 8,630 | 736,321 | 8,758.3 | 1,123,330 |
| 1894 | 25,260 | 2,328,131 | 19,622.5 | 4,214,253 |
| 1904 | 132,814 | 1,977,756 | 31,653.0 | 10,619,026 |

*Output of mines, 1874–1904*

For comparison, at its earlier peak around 1680–1700, copper mining had yielded a bit over 5,200 long tons of metal per year, with output declining to about 2,500 by the late 1700s and 1,000 by the mid-1800s.[80] The post-1868 gains in iron mining, as well as gold, silver and coal output, were similarly unprecedented.

Predictably, this vast increase in mine output was accompanied by increasing pollution and protest. During the 1870s–80s, metal mines on the Izu Peninsula, near Nagoya, and in northwestern Shikoku and eastern Kyushu, all were causing enough downstream damage to generate protests of varying intensity. The most disastrous operation, however, was that of the Ashio mine in northwestern Kantô, which by 1890 was producing about a quarter of Japan's copper.

The Ashio mine had been discovered in 1610, but during *bakuhan* centuries its copper output was so modest that it evidently created few serious problems downstream along the Watarase River. During the 1870s, however, new deep-mining and industrial-smelting techniques were introduced. These led to such a sharp increase in fuel-wood consumption and waste production that by 1880 run-off from the mine and the denuded mountains around it was poisoning downstream areas. The arsenic, heavy metals and copper sulfate destroyed river fisheries, flooded and ruined paddy fields, sickened people and devastated villages. By 1890, the metastasizing disaster was even threatening Tokyo with both pollutants and angry marchers, turning it into Japan's first major pollution crisis of the industrial era.[81]

## 2. Coal Mining

In addition to these changes in the mining of metals, the centuries after 1650 experienced one other major development in the mining industry: the emergence of coal mining.

For centuries, charcoal for various uses had been produced from sticks of wood by anaerobic combustion in kilns. However, thanks to massive land clearance, the associated population growth, construction boom and concurrent increases in fuel-wood consumption, by the later 1600s, reasonably accessible woodlands across the realm were no longer capable of meeting current demand for either construction material or fuel. So the need – and market space – for another fuel existed.

Back in 1469 farmers in Kyushu had discovered ground coal in a shallow seam at Miike, hard by the Ariake Sea in the vicinity of today's Ômuta City.[82] Later, other deposits were found elsewhere in Kyushu, but they seem to have been little used. During the 1600s, however, as fuel wood became scarce, villagers living near such seams began digging the coal out for use, perhaps in response to some foreigner's suggestion. Whatever the initial inspiration, as the 1700s advanced, the use of ground coal spread eastward across Shikoku and Honshu, at least as far as the Nagoya vicinity. The coal was bituminous ("soft") and was used primarily for three purposes: to evaporate seawater for salt-making, to fire pottery and to process sugar cane.

From the outset, however, this coal use presented a wide array of major problems. The mining process itself produced waste and run-off that polluted downstream rice fields and compelled villagers to pursue preventive riparian maintenance work. By the 1780s these problems were generating protests in Kyushu and prompting authorities to investigate and shut down some mining operations.

In many places smoke and ash produced by the burning of coal generated neighborhood protests because they damaged crops and sickened workers. During the 1830s, protesting villagers near Hiroshima explained the problem this way:

> the soot and smoke stick to the fruit and leaves of rice, wheat, soy beans, red beans, cow peas, buckwheat, tea, and everything else, smearing them with oily smoke, and causing them to wither or ripen poorly, much like a general crop failure.[83]

Even the users of coal mostly employed it from necessity rather than choice. Quite apart from the social conflict it generated, it had intrinsic limitations compared to wood. For example, perhaps the most widespread use of coal was to produce sea salt, but the salt-makers preferred to use pine boughs, as in the past, because those generated a less intense heat that yielded fine, white crystals of salt. Even the soft coal burned more fiercely and produced larger, irregularly sized and cloudy crystals. The product was not marketable as table salt but it could be used in commercial food processing, where it sold for a lower price.

Despite the problems and shortcomings of coal production and use, as well as the protests they inspired, coal consumption kept growing because of fuel wood's chronic scarcity. By the 1820s, annual coal output was roughly 150,000 long tons. Then, when Japan's post-1850 transformation began, this prior experience in coal mining facilitated the early stages of society's shift to a fossil-fuel energy foundation, as the previous table suggests.

Not surprisingly, however, the Meiji era's stunning gains in coal production were paralleled by increases in pollution and other forms of damage at both the mining sites and places of use. Most notoriously, the accelerated removal of coal from the shallow seams of the Miike mine and from mines on Takashima, an islet

**Figure 6.7:** View of Shinjuku skyscrapers and Mount Fuji as seen from the Bunkyo Civic Center in Tokyo

near the mouth of Nagasaki Bay, set in motion a series of destructive trends. Thus in 1882, villagers on Takashima petitioned for the mine's closure because it was causing "land subsidence, tilting of houses, drying up of water sources, and decline of fishing catches".[84] In following decades, problems of this sort were to multiply.

### Forestry

We noted in Chapter 4 how the unprecedented construction boom and urban fuel consumption associated with early *ritsuryô* city-building and maintenance ravaged woodland and led to destructive environmental consequences in the Kinai vicinity. For all its severity, however, that experience was dwarfed by ramifications of the realm-wide deforestation and land clearance that swept across Japan during the construction and population boom of the century to 1650 or so. Here let us examine forestry developments of the era 1650–1890 in terms of the initial situation, early and later responses to deforestation, and post-1860 developments.

### 1. The Initial Situation

The logging enterprise of the century to 1650 had such far-reaching consequences because it was so eclectic in character, so extensive in territorial scope and so entangled in the process of agricultural expansion.

The logging was eclectic because even though cryptomeria and Japanese cypress (*sugi* and *hinoki*) remained the preferred wood of the elite, lumber was being used for so many diverse purposes that all types and sizes found a market. Moreover, the demand for fuel wood was rapidly expanding due to increased metallurgy, ceramic and tile production and salt-making, as well as the cooking and heating demands of a swiftly growing population.

All sorts of wood were utilized, and it was obtained from throughout the realm. This was made possible by the improved transport technology of the day, the consolidated powers of the ruling elite and the organizational capacity of merchants. Even the greatest timbers found in any accessible corner of the realm could be transported to where builders wanted them. Thus, we see the builders of Edo, Kyoto and Osaka requisitioning timber from throughout the realm: from Kyushu, Shikoku and all parts of Honshu.

The one place where accessible timber remained in rich supply throughout the *bakuhan* era was Hokkaido, most of which was still occupied by Ainu and was, for political reasons, almost completely off-limits to lumbermen. But even there, surreptitious logging was pursued at various sites, mostly from the 1700s onward.[85]

So lumber was taken from accessible places everywhere. Furthermore, because this logging activity was accompanied by rapid, realm-wide expansion of arable acreage, many of the most fertile woodlands disappeared or were prevented from growing replacement stock. Commonly logging was but the first step toward complete deforestation as gentler hillsides and wooded areas near large rivers were converted to arable. In addition, more and more tillers terraced ever-steeper hillsides, producing stunning vistas of steeply terraced farm lands soaring skyward. Moreover, hard-pressed cultivators utilized for swidden ("slash and burn") culture innumerable sites that were too steep to terrace or too difficult to reach for regular use.

Finally, as arable acreage grew, so too grew the need for fertilizer material. Recently logged areas that could not be tilled became a major source of green fertilizer because they initially produced grasses, forbs and other low growth that could be harvested for mulch. It was in the farmer's interest to keep those areas free of large trees as a way to assure their supply of fertilizer material and other small growth. Consequently, if tree seedlings did start, they too became targets of the sickle.

As a result of this full-throttle assault on woodland, by 1650 the archipelago South of Hokkaido had almost no surviving construction timber in accessible areas. The large trees that survived were mostly high on steep interior mountains or otherwise far from usable waterways or roads. What the realm had, instead, was a surging problem of erosion, proliferating wasteland and downstream damage.

The extent of the archipelago's timber loss was brutally revealed early in 1657 (year three of the Meireki year-period). A few days after New Year's (in mid-February by the Gregorian calendar), a fire erupted in a temple just North of the shogun's castle in Edo – just nine years before the Great Fire of London ravaged that newly plague-ridden city. Whipped by the cold, dry winds of winter, the temple fire rapidly spread in all directions, raging for three days. It finally died down for lack of fuel, having consumed most baronial mansions, most of the castle's buildings, some 300 temples and shrines, 60 bridges, 9,000 rice granaries and some 500 blocks of densely crowded commoner neighborhoods; that is, most of the city. It killed more than 20 percent of Edo's half-million residents.[86]

This notorious "Meireki fire", perhaps the worst urban catastrophe of the *bakuhan* era, sharply exposed the extent of Japan's lumber scarcity. Thus, shogunal calls to barons for building supplies were repeatedly met with apologetic explanations that the requested materials were no longer available. And as building projects were undertaken, they yielded smaller structures made of inferior materials. Most famously, the immense main enceinte of the shogunal castle – the towering symbol of the regime's might and glory – was simply never rebuilt.

The temple in which the fire had erupted was one of scores situated near the city's center. To reduce density of settlement, make space for more government buildings and remove one source of future fire danger, authorities required all temples to be relocated to the outer sections of the city, beyond the castle's outermost moat.[87]

More importantly, when the city was rebuilt, tile roofing – which had been widely used by the elite ever since *ritsuryô* days because it was a mark of status, was more durable, and also helped protect against fires caused by flying sparks – was proscribed. The practical problem that led to its proscription was that the type of tile then in use was still the thick, semi-tubular *hongawara* that we encountered in Chapter 4 when discussing *ritsuryô* architecture.

There were good reasons to prohibit the use of *hongawara*. First, it was a type of roofing which, with its clay bed, consumed much raw material. Where clay deposits were scarce, tile-kiln operators would sometimes use clay dug out from the hardpan of paddy fields, thereby compromising the fields' effectiveness as cropland. Moreover, firing such thick tile required a lot of fuel wood, which already was scarce. In addition, *hongawara* and its clay bed required both thick under-roofing and extremely sturdy framing – that is to say, good timber from large trees that were no longer available.

The logic of tile's prohibition notwithstanding, it meant that the rebuilt city, with its wood and thatch roofing, was more fire-prone than ever, and urban fires became a recurrent problem in following decades. *Bakuhan* society, it seemed, had exceeded the biome's carrying capacity.

Technology, however, brought a reprieve. By 1700, a new type of tile – *sangawara*, a thinner flat tile whose pieces fitted together with minimal overlap to make a much lighter roof – had been developed, and from the 1720s onward shogunal leaders encouraged its use in all sorts of urban construction, thereby gradually helping ease the city-fire problem.

*2. Early Responses*

As noted in Chapter 5, baronial efforts at forest management and rehabilitation began to appear during the 1500s, and during the 1600s those efforts gradually intensified.

These early responses to deforestation were inspired in part by military needs and in part by the urban demand for lumber and fuel wood. But as the 1600s advanced and the situation worsened, the issues of concern increasingly pertained to villages situated downstream from logged terrain. The heart of the problem was that disturbed and denuded hillsides were producing erosion, flooding and sedimentation that clogged streams, wrecked irrigation facilities, ruined fields and occasionally flooded the villages themselves. These developments directly threatened local well-being and broader social stability, as well as the elite's food supply. Consequently, when rulers started to address the problems of realm-wide deforestation, their policy efforts initially focused on what is commonly called "protection forestry" rather than "production forestry".[88]

Protection forestry – or "management of mountains and waters" (*chisan chisui*) in the Confucian terminology of the day – sought to preserve stable, richly wooded uplands and smoothly flowing streams that would help protect the arable lowlands against flooding and silting. Its proponents found, however, that effective measures were exceedingly difficult to implement.

Fundamentally, of course, the woodland problem was so intractable because the humans were simply removing biomass faster than the terrain could replace it. The problem was substantially complicated, however, by the fact that different groups wanted different types of yield, and the types were mutually exclusive. Basically villagers wanted understorey – grasses, forbs, brush – for mulch, fodder, fuel and small-scale construction projects. Rulers wanted timber from large trees. It was only through elaborate systems of regulated access and multiple-use arrangements that these biologically irreconcilable sets of demands were enabled to co-exist peacefully.

During the 1700s, these complex systems of woodland management did gradually become established, a process facilitated by the earlier-mentioned "mutual assistance" organizations that were appearing. Ultimately, however, such management became possible only because the intensifying difficulty of land reclamation was causing that practice to peter out. As woodland ceased being converted to cropland, its boundaries – both legal and biological – stabilized, and then regulated multiple-use practices could and did become routinized.

### 3. Later Responses

This elaborate system of protection forestry helped stabilize the countryside, enabling villagers to manage their resources in a reasonably orderly manner. However, the system did little to increase woodland production of timber. Rather, in that regard it sought simply to assure some natural forest regeneration by preventing villagers from using designated areas in ways injurious to such regeneration.

An increase in gross timber yield only commenced during the early nineteenth century, following the development of timber plantations. With the adoption of these plantations, logging, which hitherto had been a classic forager enterprise, began its evolution into an "agricultural" enterprise in which humans collaborated with select species of tree to foster their growth at the expense of other species, so that the favored trees could mature to produce the desired goods.

This plantation forestry was grounded in the earlier-noted "farm manuals", which devoted substantial space to the art of growing trees and shrubs. Appearing from the later 1600s and proliferating during the 1700s, these manuals provided woodland managers with rich detail on seedling and slip culture, plantation aftercare, the principles of rotation cutting, and other aspects of woodland maintenance, repair and use.

During the 1700s, as literacy spread through the hinterland and villagers gradually worked out stabilized, multiple-use systems of communal woodland management, these labor-intensive, time-consuming plantation-forestry techniques gradually began to be practiced – even though they would pay off only decades later. They were employed most extensively in central Japan, but appeared in more rudimentary form at other places throughout the realm.

Thus even in Tsugaru, in far northern Honshu, where natural reseeding and modest aftercare remained the dominant practice, a forester could write about the merits of careful aftercare this way:

The art of forestry is different from that of paddy or dry field. Though one may be spared flood, drought, frost, or snow, he still must give general care to the area for about ten years before withdrawing human effort. If this is done, the forest will be as though filled with a treasure whose virtue is so immense it will reach to one's children and grandchildren. Truly, one's prosperity will be eternal.[89]

As a result of this spreading appreciation of forest nurturing, during the 1800s the volume of timber production began slowly to push upward and the condition of woodland to improve.

### 4. Post-1860 Developments[90]

Then the Euro-Americans had things their way and the realm was turned upside down. During the 1860s, as defense construction soared, timber consumption began to grow and downstream damage to intensify. During the 1870s those woodland trends accelerated, mainly for two reasons. The simpler reason was a surge in demand for lumber. As new technologies were adopted, they were utilized in more and more ships, wharves, bridges, telegraph poles, railroad ties, mine timbers and buildings for new factories and other uses. And this lumber use was facilitated by changes in logging technology, most notably adoption of the cross-cut saw and sawmill.

The more complex reason for accelerated logging was the Meiji regime's early-1870s decision to scuttle the hoary tradition of land-use rights. It declared all land, including woodland, own-able and alienable property, and proposed to tax all privately owned parcels on the basis of their estimated market value. Initially formulated in 1871 in simple dyadic terms of a public/private (*kan/min*) division, the proposal promptly elicited widespread protest because so much land, especially woodland, served multiple local purposes. Accordingly, in 1872 the government devised a third land category: that of *kôyûchi*, "common-use" land. It was to encompass those areas subject to multiple uses by diverse users and to be placed under local communal control.

Even that adjustment failed to still the discontent, however, because much of the woodland that locals had long used with lordly assent was officially recorded as baronial property and so was automatically designated government forest (*kanrin*). Objections notwithstanding, the government forged ahead, and the decision to establish property rights on land was followed by a countrywide program of land surveying and ownership determination.

On arable land, where most boundaries and use-rights were already clearly identified, the surveying proceeded rapidly, being completed in 1881. On woodland, however, boundaries were commonly unclear and use-rights were complex and deeply entangled. Consequently, the woodland-surveying project went on for decades. From Hokkaido to Kyushu, the process sustained intense fear among villagers that they would lose long-standing use-rights in woodland essential to their livelihoods.

To avoid the loss of standing timber or other items that they had nurtured or to which they had a customary right of use, villagers throughout the realm began cutting down and selling trees or otherwise harvesting yields before the authorities could prevent it. And because government policy called for turning over to villages parcels that seemed to hold no value as timberland, local people engaged actively in woodland arson and timber theft, hoping thereby to gain local control of the destroyed areas.

The scale of this woodland devastation was stunning. For the decade 1878–87, government foresters reported annual damage that totaled as follows.[91]

*Trees Damaged on Government Forest (kanrin) 1878–87*

| | |
|---|---|
| By Arson | 5,373,545 |
| By Illegal Felling | 1,826,783 |
| By Natural Causes | 2,010,957 |

Thus natural damage – mostly due to high winds, heavy snowfall or lightning strikes – ruined less than a third as many trees as did humanly caused injury. By far the worst damage was wrought by arson, which villagers employed to clear land for other uses or simply to render it so worthless as timberland that the government would turn it over to villagers as private or communal land. And they engaged in illicit felling so as to obtain timber or fuel wood, or to devalue the land and thereby induce government to reassign it to local people.

Even as these push and pull factors were causing the woodland situation to deteriorate at an alarming rate, Meiji leaders were launching other forest-related initiatives, and these included the study of European forestry. The investigators discovered, however, that – in contrast to medicine, mining, transport and many other technical fields – the "best practices" of Japan's existing silviculture were, in their day-to-day techniques, largely appropriate to the new age.

Nevertheless, the study of European forestry (German forestry in particular, because it was Europe's most advanced) provided two valuable lessons. First, Japan's existing silvicultural practices were "scientific" and therefore up-to-date and worthy of promotion. Second, the government could properly take a leading role in woodland rehabilitation so as to maximize the public good. By 1890 this "new" perspective on woodland management was becoming well established, in the process perpetuating or refining most of the silvicultural techniques that had emerged during the two preceding centuries. Thus revitalized, those techniques were vigorously applied and, as we shall see in Chapter 7, over the next few decades they gradually reversed much of the earlier woodland damage, leading to extensive rehabilitation of Japan's forest land.

### Fisheries

Fishing has a long history in Japan. It was a part of forager culture and continued to function as a forager-type enterprise thereafter, until around 1700 when the first signs of "agricultural" fisheries appeared.[92]

During the centuries of early agriculture, the amount of fishing activity had grown as the population rose. Boats became larger and other fishing equipment – notably hooks, lines and nets – improved. However, two factors constrained that growth. One was the seasonality and unpredictability of the marine fish supply; the other, the irregularity of the market because so much of the fish catch tended to be consumed as a ceremonial dish for holiday feasting or other special occasions.

Gradually, however, fishing communities overcame the market irregularity by learning how to dry or salt fresh fish for storage and shipment. Those techniques also helped them make fuller use of more types of fish and other sea life, including seaweed, shellfish and sea mammals. And with the proliferation of entrepreneurial merchants during medieval centuries, fishermen gained access to a much broader market place.

During the early 1600s, when *bakuhan* leaders issued regulations to govern the realm, they applied to nearby waters the same *ritsuryô*-era principle of use rights that they applied to land. So, when coastal communities were surveyed, boundaries were delineated offshore as well as on, and residents were granted use rights there in return for stipulated tribute goods and services. However, given the mobility of fish and the difficulty of identifying watery boundaries clearly, disputes within and between villages occurred often enough during the 1600s to produce litigation and settlements that created diverse systems of shared usage, rather as in the earlier-noted handling of woodland.

During the growth surge of that century, fishing villages had participated in the overall process of expansion. Subsequently, however, when society as a whole was shifting to a pattern of stabilized terrestrial output during the 1700s, a couple of developments enabled the coastal fishing industry to experience a striking surge in the scale of production.

Most importantly, even as deforestation, land clearance and expanded agricultural output were creating an endemic scarcity of green fertilizer material, fishermen were discovering that dried fish could be pulverized, pressed into fishmeal cakes and sold as high-yield fertilizer. For fishermen the profit margin in such fishmeal was modest, but it was a dependable market. When their catches could not be sold more advantageously for human consumption, at least they could be disposed of as fertilizer material. By then, moreover, maritime transport and the mercantile infrastructure were sufficient to give fishmeal producers reliable access to a very broad market.

The demand for fishmeal became particularly intense because its high nutrient content made it an optimal fertilizer for two voracious commercial crops. One was cotton, which by then was widely grown and in continual demand. The other was tobacco, a crop recently introduced from abroad and grown with particular success in southwestern Japan. During the eighteenth century fishmeal fertilizer for cotton, tobacco and other crops became a major product of fisheries, consuming countless tons of sardine and other fish.

In fact, because fishmeal could be produced from almost any type of catch, it became worthwhile to deploy more and bigger boats, with work crews numbering up to 50 members or thereabouts. They would spread huge nets that could then be maneuvered in diverse ways to trap the fish. The catch would then be hauled in, sorted out, the fish set aside that would sell for food, and the rest processed in bulk for fertilizer use.

The other major development in marine fisheries pertained to whaling. Although salvage harvesting of beached whales had long been practiced, active whaling dated from the 1500s. Initially it was a small-scale enterprise that simply used harpoons to kill the whales. However, during the 1600s, whalers developed the use of nets to snare their prey – preferably humpback and right whales – and hold them long enough to harpoon them and then haul them to shore for processing. The whales provided meat for human consumption, as well as oil, made mainly from the blubber.

Whale oil gained a valuable new market during the mid-1700s when it was discovered – following the disastrous crop failure and famine of 1732–33, which was caused by an infestation of leaf-hoppers (*unka*) that devoured crops throughout southwestern Japan – that whale oil was an effective insect repellent. Indeed, not only blubber but also whale bones that were pulverized to produce oil could serve this purpose.

With a good market for whale oil established, enterprising coastal merchants deployed whaling fleets with hundreds of men on numerous ships. The flotilla would steer migrating whales toward the proper shore, where they would be netted, slain, processed and marketed. Compared to contemporary Euro-American whalers with their great, masted, ocean-going ships, this coastal whaling industry was still a small and local operation. But it meant that most of the technical skills and organizational ingredients of open-ocean whaling were in place. After the forced redirection of life in the 1860s, it was only a matter of years until Japanese whalers set forth in large ships to compete with others in harvesting the seas around Japan.[93]

Finally, during the 1700s, freshwater fishermen began to raise carp in ponds, along with catfish, freshwater shrimp and other edible creatures.[94] And while the scale of such production was modest, it marked the start of fishing's transformation from a forager enterprise into an agricultural one, much as plantation forestry was doing at about the same time.

By the later *bakuhan* period then, fisheries had become important to overall Japanese well-being. They not only provided a substantial volume of foodstuffs directly, but indirectly as well by compensating for the loss of terrestrial fertilizer material. By the 1800s, fishmeal was sustaining a significant portion of the agricultural production that fed and clothed the archipelago's human population.

### Agriculture

In most particulars the transition from early to later (intensive or "two-stage") agriculture had been accomplished during the medieval centuries. During the *bakuhan* era, the key techniques of later agriculture – purposeful fertilizer use, double-cropping, greater crop diversity and more complex irrigation arrangements – were applied extensively and with great discipline throughout the realm, as more and more villagers were inspired and guided by the earlier-noted "farm manuals". In addition, these techniques were supplemented by a few noteworthy new practices.

The vigorous agricultural growth of the 1600s was grounded in widespread land reclamation.[95] Most famously, baronial muscle was used to mobilize huge crews of corvée labor to dredge rivers, erect sturdy embankments, construct elaborate irrigation systems and clear land to produce extensive new areas of paddy field on the larger flood plains. Less visibly, myriad villagers throughout the realm pressed ahead with the laborious task of opening new patches of woodland to tillage, in the end hacking out tiny parcels that might measure only 50–100 square feet in land surface, roughly the size of an automobile parking spot or two.

This century of intense land clearance brought costs as well as benefits. Even as the last usable areas of lowland were being opened to use in the late 1600s, the problems of green-fertilizer scarcity and conflict over woodland use-rights were becoming pronounced. Those trends led to the earlier-noted woodland system of multiple-use arrangements sustained by local programs of communal collaboration, regulation and punishment of offenders.

Meanwhile, the baronial river improvements, some of which were meant to facilitate log-rafting as well as land clearance, had the effect of making rivers less adaptable to torrential downpours and rapid snowmelt. Many of the carefully diked rivers had lost natural overflow areas, so it became imperative that they not be allowed to silt up. As a consequence, river dredging, debris clearance and dike maintenance became burdensome tasks that villagers were repeatedly obligated to perform under baronial supervision lest disaster befall them.

As these adaptations to the realm-wide boom in land reclamation were being made, a number of new developments altered agricultural practice. Most notable were the use of new fertilizers and new crops. In addition, a rabies epidemic among wolves and wild dogs in northeastern Japan led to complications there.

### 1. New Fertilizers

One of the new fertilizers was fishmeal, as discussed above. The other, also noted above, was human bio-waste. A part of that waste was the refuse generated by producers of such goods as soy sauce, *sake* and vegetable oils, but the most widespread, voluminous and valuable waste was night soil.

As a "preprocessed" fertilizer, night soil was particularly valuable for its rich nutrient content and rapid availability to plants. In consequence it became highly sought by tillers. Whereas early-*bakuhan* city dwellers had to pay people to remove their night soil, by the 1700s, its acquisition and distribution to users was developing into a substantial entrepreneurial business.

That business probably profited the middlemen more than it did the cultivators. Indeed, in the Kantô vicinity, at least, during the 1800s fertilizer constituted the farmer's greatest expense, "costing as much as 70 percent of the total income from the crop".[96] But, however the economic advantages of fertilizer were distributed, it played a key role in achieving long-term gains in agricultural output. Thus, rice output-per-acre roughly doubled between the 1600s and 1800s.[97] As a result, the shift of arable land from production of food to non-food goods such as cotton did not reduce total food output proportionately.

The new fertilizers were not of equal benefit to all farmers, however. Because so much commercial waste and night soil came from cities and towns and was bulky material to transport, most went to farmers in nearby areas, although part of Edo's vast output went by sea to commercial farmers in the Kyoto vicinity. Similarly, because fishmeal came from coastal sites and was mainly distributed by boat, it was most readily available to farmers near the shore, larger rivers and coastal towns and cities. Thus, the many villagers living in interior valleys far from these sites still found themselves largely restricted to such fertilizer material as they could extract from nearby woodland or their own household waste.

Moreover, the cost of these marketed fertilizers gave poorer farmers, tenants in particular, much incentive to continue relying on local materials, in the process gradually converting ever more woodland to other growth. In 1888, when the government completed a countrywide survey of land use, it found some 1,338,000 hectares of land – about one-third as much acreage as was in cultivation – which it categorized as "grassland". This consisted of parcels and patches of land covered with diverse wild grasses or other low growth that provided fodder for animals but was used primarily as mulch for fertilizer material.[98]

*2. New Crops*

For cultivators on the broader lowlands and nearer transportation routes, however, the new fertilizers were a great boon. The fertilizers enabled them not only to double-crop extensively, but also to grow some valuable but highly fertilizer-dependent commercial crops.

One of those crops was the earlier-noted cotton, which came to be grown widely across the southern half of the realm but especially in the Kinai vicinity, making cotton a commonly used material in clothing.[99] Another new crop, also cited earlier, was tobacco, whose tillage slowly spread beyond southern Kyushu. More important than tobacco was sugar cane, initially grown in southern Kyushu and, from the 1730s onward, more widely across southern Japan.

Also new was ginseng, an east Asian herb valued for its medicinal qualities, which was grown in Japan from the 1730s onward. The cultivation of ginseng was encouraged by shogunal leaders as a way to save silver by reducing dependence on imports from Korea. Similarly, a substantial increase in silk production – and hence in the acreage of mulberry orchards – occurred as the government encouraged domestic development of high-quality silk goods to replace imports from China.

Silk production was not new to Japan, of course, having been practiced at least from the later Yayoi period onward. However, it grew into a much more extensive and highly skilled enterprise during the *bakuhan* era. Silk imports had persisted through the centuries because mastery of the skills necessary to produce high-grade silk thread and cloth is difficult, and Chinese silks continued to be judged much superior to domestic ones.

Raising the skill level was not easy. It was rural households that had the land to grow mulberry bushes and the building space for use as larval nurseries. They grew and harvested the mulberry leaves, which they then fed to the larvae hatched from eggs of the moth Bombyx mori. When whose larvae reached maturity, they would enclose themselves in cocoons of silk that they produced as they pupated, preparatory to evolving from chrysalis into adult moth.

The cocoons thus created in rural households were too delicate to transport very far, so the thread had to be spun nearby.[100] This meant that many rural households had to acquire the equipment and know-how necessary to produce high-grade thread before domestic silk products could compete with top-quality imports.

A couple of factors made that effort worthwhile. For one thing, the basic spinning of thread from cocoons could be done by family members. And if a farm household ventured into weaving, it was a task that could be pursued during those weeks when other farm work was less pressing.

In addition, silk production required little arable land and so did not displace other crops. As a farm manual of the early 1800s put it:

> The immediate benefit which silk farming brings to society is that it enables unused land along river banks, in the mountains and by the edge of the sea to be planted with mulberries, and silk spinning and weaving to flourish. Needless to say, when the products of the region are exported to other areas, the domain will become rich and its people prosperous. This is called "enriching the country".[101]

As a result of these considerations, as the 1700s and 1800s advanced, that capability gradually became widespread – in another reflection of spreading literacy and "farm manual" expertise. As silk output grew, imports declined, and by the 1850s, Japanese silk was of such high quality that, once the new treaty system was in place, it quickly emerged as the realm's most lucrative export item.

With the rush to fill foreign orders, however, quality control suffered, and considerable inferior silk thread did get exported. In response, during the 1870s, standards were tightened and new equipment and techniques introduced and disseminated. As a result, quality improved, and the export business continued to flourish well into the 1900s.[102]

Finally, less celebrated than silk, but more important than ginseng, sugar cane or tobacco was the sweet potato, which diffused northward from the Ryukyus, through Kyushu and into western Honshu by the 1720s. After the 1730s famine, when sweet potatoes were credited with saving some villages from starvation, their cultivation spread widely across the realm. The sweet potato proved particularly valuable because it would grow on small, open patches of unused ground, could withstand climate irregularities and produced nutritious edible tubers in the soil, where they were protected from many insects and other menaces.

As a whole, this array of crops meant that agriculture had developed crop specialties better fitted to regional climatic differences as well as to patterns of population distribution. Together with the social adaptations discussed in earlier pages, these horticultural changes enabled the realm to continue sustaining its human population of roughly 30 million despite periodic climate perturbations and even the volcanic eruptions of Mt Fuji in 1707 and Mt Asama in 1783, both of which devastated much of the Kantô vicinity.

Not all regions fared equally well, however. As earlier noted, the population of southwestern Japan managed to sustain a slow growth whereas that of the northeast fell substantially. Those trends were directly related to these agricultural changes.

To elaborate, one factor that had spurred the cultivation of some of these crops – cotton, sugar cane, ginseng and mulberry in particular – was, as noted above, government attempts, by the shogun Yoshimune most notably, to reduce silver exports by reducing imports through domestic substitution. The result, however, was that crops of a more tropical character were being encouraged. And that trend favored agriculture in southwestern Japan.

Meanwhile, with the stabilization of elite rule, the cultivation of rice changed. The tastier, short-grain japonica varieties gradually displaced the more hardy, long-grain Champa rice that had come to prevail during medieval centuries. That development, too, favored growers in the warmer parts of Japan, where japonica grew more reliably.

Lastly, an important aspect of agricultural intensification was the spread of double-cropping, and due to climatic differences, such multi-cropping was much more feasible in the warmer southwest. Lest the extent of double-cropping be overstated, however, even in the southwest, much paddy land grew only one crop per year, mainly because of difficulty in drying the soil adequately for a dry-field winter crop. Thus, as of 1884, only about 45 percent of paddy area from the Kinai vicinity westward was double-cropped, and in the northeast a mere 15 percent.[103]

In combination, these trends in agricultural production helped sustain the *bakuhan* population of southwestern Japan, even as that of the northeast shrank. And after 1870, as Japan commenced industrializing, those agricultural gains facilitated renewed growth of society at large.

*3. Difficulties in the Northeast*
As noted above, the colder climate of the northeast (both northern Honshu and Hokkaido) made crop-raising there a more problematic enterprise than in more southerly regions. Farming there was also complicated during *bakuhan* centuries by changes in the wild-animal population, changes precipitated by harsh difficulty in the lives of wolves and wild dogs.[104]

Japan's wolves, originally from Siberia, probably were present in the archipelago long before humans, and through the millennia they may well have maintained a reasonably stable predator-prey relationship with deer, wild boar and other resident herbivores. However, as the population of humans – foragers and, later, agriculturalists – multiplied, they and their domesticated dogs became competitors for prey and subsequently for living space. How well the two groups got along in the centuries prior to ca. 700 CE is unclear. But during the *ritsuryô* era, when periodic epidemics of smallpox or other illness left human corpses scattered about, wolves began scavenging in urban settings, and humans there experienced occasional wolf attacks. Nevertheless, insofar as the general populace held a shared opinion of wolves, it appears not to have been an aggressively hostile one during either *ritsuryô* or medieval centuries.

By the later 1600s, however, with ever more areas being opened to tillage and pasturage, wolf populations found themselves under unprecedented stress, and attacks on humans and farm animals seem to have proliferated. Then from the 1730s reports began appearing of dogs, badgers, foxes and wolves behaving erratically, and randomly biting people and other creatures. The behavioral evidence suggests that an epidemic of rabies, a fatal viral infection that somehow had been introduced from the mainland, was spreading through the wild and occasionally affecting domesticated dogs.[105]

As illness spread through the still-substantial wolf population of northeast Japan, attacks on humans and dogs proliferated, shortly leading to efforts at control by hunting. In combination, illness and hunting rapidly decimated the wolf numbers. As that occurred, however, their prey populations of deer, wild boar and serow proliferated, leading to an intensified search for edible vegetation. By the mid-1700s, the herbivores were overcoming their fear of humans sufficiently to feed on gardens and other cropland, especially such upland crops as soybeans, which commonly grew in relatively isolated sites. Fencing, trapping and guard-posting helped to protect crops, but at substantial costs in labor and other expense. So, for people in northeastern Japan, the later *bakuhan* problem of an unbalanced predator-prey population added to the risks of climate instability to make life more difficult.

Then during the 1870s, as Japan's leaders pursued the "opening" of Hokkaido to agriculture and other forms of exploitation, the rabies virus was introduced to that island's still-substantial population of wolves. Meanwhile, hunters using firearms were killing so many deer for their pelts that by 1880 the deer population had been severely reduced. Loss of that food source prompted wolves, whether healthy or diseased and demented, to attack domesticated animals, in particular horses on recently created horse farms, and the occasional human.

As advised by American consultants, farm operators responded to this problem by scattering bait soaked with imported strychnine. It so effectively killed off the wolves that its use spread southward, and the creatures evidently became extinct throughout the archipelago by about 1905. So, a predator-prey imbalance that initially had been precipitated by a virus had produced complications in human life that eventuated in the use of "modern" technology, mainly firearms and poison, to eradicate the problem by eradicating the animals, thereby sustaining gains in agricultural output at the expense of biodiversity.

## RECAPITULATION

As the preceding sections have shown at some length, the years from 1650 to 1890 displayed a wide array of difficult and changing human-ecosystem relationships. In overall terms, the period encompassed two notable watersheds. One was the transition from the growth phase of later agriculture to its phase of demographic stability; the other was the ending of that phase of stability with the onset of industrial development.

The transition to stability during the decades around 1700 indicated that the archipelago could sustain no more than the 30 million humans then resident, given their levels of material consumption and the technology and social organization of the day. That the realm had reached its carrying capacity was shown in several ways, social and environmental. It was apparent in: (1) the recurring evidence that the food supply was severely vulnerable to irregularities of weather and other natural perturbations; (2) the many signs of social stress and the complexity of mechanisms society used to maintain order; (3) the set of unwelcome procedures that kept the population from growing; and (4) the severe constraints under which most of the ruling elite operated, *faute de mieux*.

More specifically, the transition to demographic stability occurred because nearly all the land (South of Hokkaido) that could be put to human use, whether as agricultural land or for other purposes, had been developed. In essence, by 1700 the lowlands of Japan sustained humans and their collaborators; the uplands sustained what remained of the indigenous bio-system. And as we have seen, only complex social management and an immense, ongoing process of river maintenance could sustain that much lowland use.

Insofar as the humans made use of the uplands, moreover, we have seen that by 1700 they had exploited them about as much as was possible. The demand for fuel wood, fodder and fertilizer material ravaged woodland in the vicinity of towns and villages throughout the realm, leading to scarcities, to complex systems of use-control, and to the widespread appearance of desiccated scrubland and "bald mountains" (*hageyama*). In short, woodland, when left to its own devices, could no longer meet human demand.

Further reflecting that situation, the timber supply ceased to meet human needs. That development forced the adoption of forest protection and regeneration policies that were developing by the late 1700s into programs of plantation forestry – beginning Japan's transition from forager-type to agricultural handling of woodland.

That application to woodland of agricultural techniques of crop nurturing was echoed in the application of agricultural technique to fishery production. During the *bakuhan* centuries the technique seems to have been used only in the raising of carp and other freshwater creatures, but it did foreshadow the future.

Even more instructively, *bakuhan* society began to show early signs of Japan's industrial future in two forms of substitution for depleted resources. As we noted in this book's introduction, industrial society differs from agricultural society in two basic (and numerous secondary) ways: (1) in the use of fossil fuels as a major energy source; and (2) in viewing the entire globe, rather than one's own communal territory, as one's legitimate resource base.

During the *bakuhan* centuries, coal began to be used as a substitute for firewood in select industrial processes, and from the 1870s onward, with new markets and mining technology, coal output increased rapidly. In terms of global resource base, the fishing industry began to extend its operations as far from shore as its equipment permitted, maximizing yield to provide fishmeal fertilizer as a substitute for terrestrial nutrients. And one might argue that the largely hidden exploitation of Hokkaido East of the Oshima Peninsula, a region perceived as lying outside the *bakuhan* realm, or "beyond the pale," constituted another way of extending one's resource base abroad.[106]

Then, during the 1800s, as the foreign threat escalated, more and more aspects of industrial technology began to be adopted, mainly for military purposes at first. However, after 1870, new techniques began to be adopted for the whole gamut of social and technological changes that characterize industrial society. By 1890, those changes were reshaping the daily lives of more and more people throughout the realm, as well as their relationship to the bio-system of both the realm and the world beyond it.

# 7  *Imperial Industrialism, 1890–1945*

Historically, humanity's relationship to the environment has evolved through the three phases of forager, agricultural and industrial society. As earlier noted, the transitions from one phase to another are temporally ill-defined, and each of the three has sub-phases, notably those of growth and subsequent stabilization.

Regarding industrial society, we noted in the introduction that it is distinguished from agriculture by two basic characteristics and myriad secondary factors. Basically, industrial society grounds itself in a global resource base, not the local resource base used by foragers and agriculturalists. Moreover, whereas the latter two sustain themselves almost entirely by utilizing energy extracted from living biota, industrial society extracts what energy it can from the living biome but obtains much of its energy from the global fossil fuel supply that has accumulated over hundreds of millions of years, plus such other sources – nuclear, hydroelectric, wind and solar – as industrial technology makes available.

With these basic characteristics in mind, let us examine the history that unfolded during the half-century or so after 1890, as evidenced in "affairs of state", developments in society and the economy, and changes in technology, with their environmental ramifications. Before doing so, however, it seems worthwhile to consider some preliminary matters. One of these was foreshadowed in the introduction – the inadequacy of the "nation state" as a vehicle for examination of industrial society's environmental impact. Another matter is a characteristic common to all industrial societies – namely, human "packing and stacking" – that has seemed particularly evident in Japan's case. Two others relate to the dating and terminology used in these two chapters – 7 and 8 – on Japan's industrial society.

## SOME PRELIMINARIES

### On the Global Resource Base

In a number of ways industrial society in Japan, as everywhere, has had an unprecedented impact on the biome beyond its boundaries. Most obviously, perhaps, the exploitation of pelagic fisheries disrupts the global marine bio-system. But in addition, all items of transnational exchange, both exports and imports, whether of raw materials or manufactured products, as well as their mechanisms of transport, have diverse impacts on bio-systems wherever those items are produced and utilized.

So it is reasonable to argue that an adequate understanding of industrial Japan's environmental history requires an evaluation of environmental developments in Japan's global resource base. Unfortunately, a couple of factors make study of that base and assessment of Japan's impact on it very difficult.

For one thing, the process of interchange between societies has become so complex and entangled and so variable over time that sorting out the role of a single participant, such as Japan, is practically impossible. For another, as decades have passed, the scale of global transactions has become so immense that even if adequate information were available, disaggregating it to identify Japan's contribution would be an overwhelming task. Consequently, this study will make only a few passing observations on the environmental history of that global resource base. As we shall see in Chapter 8, however, that base – mainly as a source of raw materials and as a market for finished products – only became a major part of Japan's economic history in the later decades of the twentieth century. During the decades covered in this chapter, that base was only a modestly growing factor in that history.

### On "Packing and Stacking"

Japanese travelers abroad frequently note how much space is "wasted", especially in American suburbia. Their perception reflects one of the key mechanisms employed in Japan's industrialization, especially after 1945.

To elaborate, forager and agricultural societies are essentially "single-storey" societies, in which nearly everyone walks, works and lives on a single, shared physical level. Industrial society, on the other hand, is intensively multi-storeyed. Thanks to the development of technologies that use sturdy framing and cementing materials to form large, multi-storey structures, people can be "packed and stacked", cheek-by-jowl and one atop another.

The stacking is seen in skyscrapers, multi-storey apartment houses, office-buildings, factories, even transport systems with their subways, elevated lines, multi-level bridges and highways, and airplanes coursing through the sky. Similarly, the packing is evident in factory and office work places, auditoriums, barracks, dormitories, prisons, schoolrooms, stadiums and wherever else people crowd together.

In a crucial way, however, the immense space-saving quality of this industrial packing and stacking is utterly deceptive. Although the humans physically are cheek-by-jowl and one atop another, their survival (thus far, at least) has depended almost entirely on material goods supplied by an old-fashioned, single-storey world of farmland and forests, which provides the essential oxygen, water, food and clothing, as well as innumerable amenities. Somehow, therefore, this old-style world must generate enough of these goods to meet the requirements of this vastly increased "ant-hill" population of people. (Certainly the yield of "multi-storey" pelagic fisheries has helped sustain industrial society – at least for a few decades – but its future appears problematic.)

In Japan's case, both packing and stacking have been particularly important because, as noted in Chapter 6, the lowlands that were most amenable to human settlement and utilization were nearly all (South of Hokkaido) being used even before industrialization commenced. But because industrial society can fit large numbers of additional people into little more land area, Japan's population has been able to grow substantially despite this geographical constraint.

The problem, of course, has been how to provision all those extra bodies from an already-utilized single-storey supply base. Intensifying the exploitation of that base has been part of the solution, as we shall see. To a significant and growing extent, however, the answer has been found in that other aspect of industrial society – the global resource base. And the question of how to secure that global base has been a crucial and grimly fraught issue, particularly during the decades of Japan's imperial industrialism.

Let us now turn to the less ominous, semantic issues of dating and terminology.

### On 1890 as a Starting Date

Certainly one can point to the "foreshadowing" or even beginning of industrial society well before 1890, doing so in terms of both "basic characteristics" – namely, global resource base and fossil-fuel use.

Regarding the former, in earlier chapters we noted the long-established luxury trade with Eurasia, the gradual extension of *bakuhan*-era commercial activity into the Ainu regions of Hokkaido, and the spread of fisheries' activity out into coastal waters as far as technology of the day permitted. However, both the Eurasian trade and Japanese activity in the Ainu region of Hokkaido remained modest in both scale and domestic impact. Neither spurred significant changes in Japanese perceptions of Japan-world relations. So those activities seem best viewed as a continuation of the long-term luxury exchange between Japan and the continent and the equally long-term advance of agricultural Wa society into the adjoining terrain of foragers, whether Emishi, Ainu or others. From the 1860s onward, of course, those relationships did change, and in following decades, even as Japan's Euro-American trade was increasing, Hokkaido was opened to further agricultural settlement and exploitation. Before the 1890s, however, those two trends were significantly affecting the lives of only a modest portion of Japanese society.

As for marine fisheries, they remained near-shore during *bakuhan* centuries. Even after the 1860s, change came slowly because coastal fisheries still sufficed and the cost of acquiring and deploying large sailing or steam ships was prohibitive. From about the 1890s, however, the industry started to make that change as more and more coastal fisheries were depleted by over-fishing or by pollution from factories and mines (and subsequently by multiplying oil spills). Under these circumstances Japan gradually became an active participant in the industrial-age exploitation of deep-sea fisheries.

Turning to the issue of fossil-fuel consumption, Japanese use of ground coal dates from the 1600s, as noted in Chapter 6, but it grew only slowly thereafter.

Prior to the 1860s, such coal use was very limited in scope, and its problems notwithstanding, it did not entail the broader process of technological change associated with industrial development. Also, while the sharp increase in coal mining during the 1870s–80s did facilitate technical change, its ramifications in terms of mine accidents, pollution incidents and new routines of daily life did not become pronounced until later. As part of the "fossil fuelization" basic to industrial society, that is to say, before the 1890s, coal use still did not yield a transformative experience for most Japanese people or for society as a whole. And oil and natural gas only came into use decades later.

In a couple of other ways, as well, the 1890s mark Japan's transition to industrialism. For one thing, during that decade the government finally succeeded in revising the foreign-imposed treaties of the 1850s, thereby securing for Japan legal equality with the industrial "Powers" in terms of inter-state relations. Also, during the 1890s, Japan's leaders felt emboldened to adopt the diplomatic policies used by the Powers: namely, making coercive demands of others and, where necessary, using military force to secure them – that is to say, "imperialism" as a means of securing one's global resource base. That strategy, in turn, made great demands on the general populace and elicited an unprecedented level of public attention. It thus engaged the general populace as never before in "affairs of state" and helped give them a sense of self as a participant in the "nation".

Finally, in terms of foreign trade, during the 1890s, Japan began displaying the basic character of an industrializing society. That is to say, the early-Meiji "colonial" pattern of mainly raw material exports and finished-goods imports began its shift in the direction of the "imperial" pattern wherein essential raw material imports are largely paid for by manufactured exports.

### On "Imperial Industrialism" as a Temporal Category

As a sub-phase of industrial society, "imperial industrialism" clearly fails to encompass either of the environmental sub-phases, growth or stasis. Although catastrophic military defeat in 1945 did ravage the realm, it only produced a temporary reversal in Japan's trajectory of industrial growth, which, in the form of "entrepreneurial industrialism", continued for decades following the recovery from war.

However, one could liken this imperial/entrepreneurial distinction to the early/later (extensive/intensive) distinction we used in examining Japan's agricultural society. At least, in both cases a less productive, smaller-scale, and technically simpler, early phase gave way to a more productive, larger-scale, later phase. And certainly the later industrial phase was characterized by more complex technologies – jet engines, nuclear power, "super tankers", electronic gadgetry, an array of new chemicals and pharmaceuticals and so forth.

In other ways, too, the 1945 breaking point is useful. Most obviously, it marked a major – indeed, the most traumatic, even if temporary – disruption in Japan's history. In addition, as the imperial/entrepreneurial distinction suggests, it also marked a noteworthy change in the organizational dynamics of its industrial growth. In essence, growth that had been promoted by the ruling elite to benefit the "state" gave way to growth that was promoted by the entrepreneurial elite to benefit the enterprises they controlled. As a corollary, the strategy of using political empire as a mechanism for securing a global resource base gave way to the strategy of using entrepreneurial maneuver as a mechanism.

In fact, of course, this tidy imperial/entrepreneurial distinction is a bit deceptive. In all industrial societies, political and commercial elites are closely linked, each needing the cooperation of the other to flourish. However, the balance of power between the two can favor either side, and the rhetoric that legitimizes their undertakings will reflect that balance.

In the Japanese case, the Meiji political elite and its successors enjoyed the predominant position until 1945, and Japan's accomplishments were celebrated in "national" terms of "imperial" virtue and achievement. After 1945, the entrepreneurial elite enjoyed government cooperation that enabled the economy to revive and flourish, as we note in Chapter 8. And that cooperation helped major Japanese industries evolve into world-girdling enterprises, whose achievements were celebrated in terms of enlightened "free enterprise" and ascribed ethnic virtues, such as dedication, diligence and frugality.

### On "State" vs. "Elite"

In preceding chapters, when discussing agricultural society, we employed the basic categories of "elite" and "producers". The terms seemed apt because rulership and high status were quite firmly hereditary, while hoi polloi, or "those below", were purposely excluded from any sense of participation in the business or privileges of rulership. Their task was to "shut up and work"; that is, to be grateful for the "benevolence" of those above and peacefully to provide the tribute goods and services they desired.

Of course, neither "elite" nor "producers" was a rigid category through the centuries. We have seen how the elite developed from the relatively simple, hereditary *ritsuryô* ruling class to the more complex elite of medieval and *bakuhan* centuries, which came to include civil and military figures of high status as well as high-ranking clerics, those merchants who collaborated with the rulers, and an ancillary intelligentsia.

Rather similarly, "producers" in the *ritsuryô* era had essentially been peasants. Besides producing the elite's food and other necessities, they provided the corvée labor that hauled them to the cities, and built and maintained the roads and physical structures utilized by the privileged few. With the emergence of intensive agriculture, however, we saw the producer populace diversify to include many more specialized fishermen, boatmen, carpenters, other urban craftsmen, and an array of entertainers and other providers of goods and services.

With that increase in diversity of both elite and producers came more variation in the distribution of wealth. The trend was evident in growing numbers of relatively wealthy "commoners" and relatively poor members of the elite. Even then, however, the notion of "above" and "below" was retained, finding firm expression in the *bakuhan* hereditary status system.

In industrial society, the tidy distinction between those above and those below is thoroughly obfuscated by the diversity and complexity of institutional arrangements, with their myriad functions and intermediate positions, and their various patterns and criteria of personnel promotion and reward. Even the hoary labels "blue collar" and "white collar" tend to obscure as much as they illuminate about the hierarchy of power and privilege. In place of the elite/producer categories, industrial society's dependence on a global resource base sustains a new foundational social dyad, that of the ethnic or "national" "us" and the alien "them." And "the state" – that is to say, the government and its rhetoric of legitimacy – becomes the institutional expression of that dyad and the mechanism of its articulation.[1]

The state performs this function for a couple of reasons. Most directly, perhaps, industrial technology permits the creation of highly complex, large-scale military systems for use in securing a society's global resource base. But those systems require (in "pre-robot" days, at least) a large and enduring supply of menial military labor (so-called "cannon fodder"), which only the erstwhile "producer" populace can provide. To help secure a willing supply of such "fodder", the leaders of industrial society promote "patriotism" (meaning state-based ethnic consciousness) as the basis of self-identity, the "us" in the new "us/them" dyad.

Less obviously, leaders of industrial society use this "national" sense of self to help maintain a base of support among non-military people, both high and low. Regarding the high-born, rulers of agricultural society utilized the sense of elitism, and the rewards that came with it, to retain the support of their fellow aristocrats. Then, however, the rise of industrial society undermined that elite sense of identity and collaboration because its complexity gradually rendered the old hereditary elite irrelevant, replaced by new holders of power and privilege whose status was based on a complex and ambiguous combination of wealth, connections and position.

The new "national" sense of self provided an alternative identity that the new holders of power and privilege could share regardless of their origins. It could accommodate the remnants of the old elite as well as the newly prestigious. And, more importantly, it provided space for hoi polloi – both the rural and industrial masses – successors to the old "producer" class. In short, nationalism transcended the complexities of the new society, making it easier for leaders to mobilize society-wide support against any "foreign" rivals for access to the global resource base.

This "national" sense of identity appears to be crucial to industrial society. We need to keep in mind, however, that while it does marginalize the old notion of a hereditary elite, it supplements – but does not supplant – the many other forms of identity long found in agricultural society. The "self" as defined by age, gender, family, social role, community, class or caste, religion and region persist. Indeed, they are supplemented by new categories of identity, such as one's school, profession, military service, political party or dogma, or the rural-urban dichotomy that finds expression in such terms as "country hicks" and "city slickers".

Of these many categories new and old, one that remained particularly noteworthy in Japan was that of region. Long established as a southwest/northeast dyad, it was reaffirmed by the *Sat-Chô* conquest of 1868–69 and retained vitality thereafter.[2] Nevertheless, in post-1890 Japan, as in other industrial societies, all these forms of identity were politically subordinated to the "state" and its legitimizing notion of "nationhood".

Leaders of industrial society use several mechanisms to sustain this "national" sense of identity, in essence relying on a complex system of propaganda and indoctrination. They utilize "national anthems" and other patriotic songs and stories; they encourage flag-saluting and other rituals; they erect and maintain "national memorials", and they mount diverse other propaganda offensives. In addition, they rely on the educational system to instill "proper" values; they use political authority to taboo "seditious" behavior; and they equate "nation" with language, religious group, cultural heritage or "race", when that seems advantageous. Most interestingly, perhaps, they employ mechanisms of "election" and "representative government" to foster the belief among hoi polloi that they really are participants in the state, and that it serves their interests as well as those of the holders of power and privilege.

Cumulatively, these techniques constitute a policy of "social mobilization" that transcends the old elite/producer distinction, replacing it with a new, state-based "we/they" dyad that gives "nations" a useful degree of cohesiveness in their competition for global resources.

In Japan, as noted in Chapter 6, a national-level sense of "us" and "them" had begun to develop among the intelligentsia during *bakuhan* centuries. It found expression in *kokugaku* thought and, as the nineteenth century advanced, was redefined and strengthened by foreign complications and domestic responses.[3] After 1868, the new ruling group vigorously employed an array of propaganda devices to promote both the ethnic sense of "we Japanese" and their own claims to leadership of the "nation". Then, with the adoption of the Meiji Constitution in 1889, they used the electoral mechanism and the notion of representative government as institutional expressions of this ethnic identity, and as devices that presumably would help sustain public support for their efforts to "modernize" Japan and secure its global resource base.

The "state", that is to say, played a key role in Japan's industrialization, so let us examine "affairs of state" before exploring the socio-economic dimensions of Japan's industrial society and considering the environmental ramifications of industrial-age technology.

## AFFAIRS OF STATE

During the decades 1890–1945, policies relating to domestic issues – health, education, employment and so on – were the political matters of most day-to-day consequence to the public. However, given the international political turbulence of the era and Japan's deepening dependence on a global resource base, foreign affairs emerged as the most traumatic policy arena.[4]

### Domestic Politics

From the 1870s onward, political activists had organized groups to lobby and agitate on behalf of one agenda or another. And after the Meiji Constitution was promulgated in 1889, groups quickly formed into political parties that promoted agendas for government action and candidates for election to the Lower House of the national Diet (Kokkai, or parliament). From then until World War II, elections determined the composition of that House; parties waxed and waned; and agendas changed as situations evolved.

As the Constitution stipulated, top civil and military officials were appointees of the Emperor, who, in naming them, followed recommendations of his senior advisors, headed by the Prime Minister. In consequence, a more-or-less chronic power struggle between the Prime Minister and Lower House persisted during these decades. But gradually, and especially after World War I, the Lower House's influence grew and the voting franchise broadened. Then, during the early 1930s, with domestic society racked by the global depression and Japan's diplomatic situation severely complicated by military adventurism in Manchuria and other developments abroad, domestic politics grew more turbulent.[5] By the late 1930s, military leaders had established a dominant role in policy making, retaining that role until 1945.[6]

### *Foreign Relations*

As noted in Chapter 6, Japan was ushered willy-nilly into the age of industrialism as an accidental by-product of Euro-America's imperialist heyday. The take-home lesson of that experience was unambiguous. The world consists of winners and losers; empires and colonies; "Great Powers" and places of use to them in their quest for markets and resources with which to sustain their burgeoning industries and populations.

Japan's leaders had learned that basic lesson decades before 1890, but not until the 1890s were they in a position to turn it to their advantage. They then enjoyed nearly three decades of success in securing a global resource base. The three were followed, however, by two decades of ultimately disastrous misadventure.[7]

**Figure 7.1:** Extensively clear-cut mountainsides and terraced lower slopes, with deep snow cover, in central Nagano Prefecture, 1963

**Figure 7.2:** Diluvial terrace land opened to dry-field tillage southwest of Tokyo, 1981

**Figure 7.3:** A farmstead near Sendai, with vegetable crops in farm compound, paddy seedbeds to its right, and paddy fields in stages of preparation for flooding and transplanting, 1955

## 1. Years of Triumph

The geographical area that most interested these leaders was Korea because of its close proximity, long relationship and utility as a bridge to elsewhere. During the 1880s, even as Japan's politico-economic involvement in Korea began to grow, China's leaders sought to tighten their own ties to the peninsula lest Japan or some Euro-American power secure a strong colonial base there. By 1894, Tokyo leaders were so alarmed by the success of this Chinese effort that they resorted to warfare to drive the Chinese from the peninsula. That venture succeeded, and in the ensuing settlement Japan obtained China's withdrawal from Korea, a substantial indemnity, and Taiwan as a colony.[8]

During 1900 – two years after the USA ousted Spain from the Philippines, crushed a Philippine independence movement and made the islands a US colony – Japan sought again to demonstrate its standing as a Great Power. It did so by cooperating with Europeans in suppressing the Boxer Rebellion, an armed uprising in China that attempted to end the "unequal treaties" and expel the Powers from China. Japan's role in that suppression proved very effective, and the existing treaty system survived, with Japan as one of its beneficiaries. Two years later, Great Britain and Japan signed the Anglo-Japanese Alliance, which added to Tokyo's stature as a Great Power and gave it an ally in the problem that seemed to be looming.[9]

That problem was Russia. Of the Euro-American Powers, Russia had proven to be most persistently interested in the Korea/Manchuria vicinity, and, after 1900, Japanese concern with Russia's deepening involvement there rapidly intensified. Negotiations failed to resolve the differences, and during 1904–05 the two fought a brutal, exhausting war. The near-stalemate ended when an American-mediated settlement led the Czar to cede to Tokyo both Karafuto (the southern half of Sakhalin) and the Kurile Islands, while also recognizing Japan's primacy in Korea and ceding to Tokyo all of the treaty concessions that Russia had enjoyed in southern Manchuria.[10]

These military accomplishments not only brought Tokyo substantial colonial assets, but also gave Japanese entrepreneurs better access to China. On the other hand, the exhausting struggle with Russia also threw into sharp focus the high cost to hoi polloi – mostly rural villagers – of industrial-age military systems, with their immense fiscal expenditures and heavy reliance on "cannon fodder". Even in peacetime, the conscription system bore heavily on rural families because they lost productive young men to poorly paid military service. As a village report of 1903 put it:

> It is very hard indeed for those left behind by the conscript to continue the work of the house without trouble. Moreover, it is necessary to send to each conscript a minimum of ¥30 per year in spending money. In spite of the fact that the household is shorthanded and its income declines, they must pay these expenses. Truly it is hard for them.[11]

The pent-up frustration and anger caused by these burdens and the pain of losing loved ones, especially in the Russo-Japanese war (when some 81,000 were killed and many more crippled in various ways), exploded in domestic turmoil during 1905–06. However, the regime survived this turmoil, and in following years political and economic leaders pursued the development of Taiwan, Korea and southern Manchuria, while expanding their trading activity in China.

Rather few mainlanders welcomed those activities, however. In Korea, especially, resistance to Japanese influence persisted, and in 1910, Tokyo abolished the Korean monarchy and formally "annexed" the country, placing it under direct Japanese rule. Resistance within Korea was not thereby ended, but the Great Powers found the outcome agreeable. American leaders acknowledged Japan's claims to Korea in return for Tokyo's acceptance of US claims to the Philippines, and London and Tokyo agreed to recognize one another's position in Korea and India.

Then in 1914, European rulers blundered their way into full-fledged warfare among themselves. That development provided Tokyo leaders – naval leaders in particular – with immediate new opportunities. But in the end Europe's self-inflicted wounds also destroyed the very foundation of Tokyo's recent foreign-policy successes.

Regarding the new opportunities, they were facilitated by the Anglo-Japanese Alliance, which provided justification for Japan to declare war on Great Britain's enemy, Germany, and on those grounds to seize German imperial assets in China and the Pacific before the British or others could do so. Those assets consisted of the port of Tsingtao on the Shantung Peninsula of China and the northern portion of German Micronesia in the western Pacific (Australia and New Zealand seized the portion South of the Equator).

Then, in 1917, even as the war in Europe was grinding on, the Russian Revolution and Soviet triumph ended Russian cooperation with the Anglo-French military. In an attempt to reverse that outcome, the anti-German allies launched a two-pronged invasion of the new Soviet Union. Japan's military leaders, with unprecedented disregard for civilian authorities, cooperated in that venture, seizing the opportunity to invade Siberia in the hope of securing the rest of Sakhalin Island and somehow enlarging their presence in the continental Manchuria-Siberia vicinity. Before that project could be realized, however, the war in Europe ended and the other Powers withdrew from Soviet territory.

## 2. Years of Tribulation

With the end of the war in 1918, the global diplomatic climate changed. In an explicit repudiation of the old rules of imperialism, leaders in Washington promoted the notion of "self-determination" as a basis for drawing state boundaries (except within the USA and its "possessions"). Working through the newly formed League of Nations and modestly influenced by this new idea, the Powers allowed China – which also had sought to advance its interests by declaring war on Germany – to reclaim the Tsingtao vicinity from Japan. But they assigned northern Micronesia to Japan as a League "Mandate".

In Siberia, meanwhile, Japanese forces stood fast long after the other invaders had departed. However, the Soviet leadership refused to compromise, and finally, in 1925, Japan's frustrated military leaders agreed to withdraw their forces, having utterly failed to attain their goals.

By then, other problems were also muddying the waters. In Korea, resistance to Japanese rule continued. And at the League of Nations, American and Australian delegates succeeded in persuading the League to reject a Sino-Japanese proposal that the principle of racial equality be affirmed. American anti-immigration policies, and in particular a 1924 immigration bill that explicitly prohibited Japanese entrants, further poisoned the atmosphere. Evidently only "white folks" could be Great Powers. Therefore, as one Japanese commentator put it:

The mission of the Japanese nation is to become the leader of Asia, and restore the rule over Asia which has been usurped by the white race, and to teach the white race the essence of the justice and humanity they constantly talk about by putting these principles into practice.[12]

Becoming "the leader of Asia" was easier said than done, however.[13] As the 1920s advanced, Chinese political consolidation made progress, and by 1928 the armies of Chiang Kai-shek, leader of the Chinese nationalist movement, were reunifying the realm and presenting a challenge to the tenuous Japanese position in southern Manchuria. With that development, an important piece of the Japanese military leadership's legacy of empire-building became vulnerable, and with it, the entire record of Tokyo's post-1890 triumph.

By 1929, then, Japan's leaders had been repudiated by the "white" Powers, had been thwarted by the Soviet Union and faced a burgeoning challenge in China. Adding to these diplomatic reverses were real socio-economic injuries arising from global economic disorder.

To explain, during World War I, Japan's economy had flourished, providing goods and services both at home and abroad in place of those that European economies could not provide because of the war. But that boom collapsed in 1919, to be followed by years of widespread difficulty. Most dramatically, the Kantô Earthquake of 1923, while less deadly than that of 1703, did kill some 140,000 people and brought much suffering to millions more in the Kantô.[14] And because it ravaged much of the Tokyo-Yokohama vicinity, seat of the national government, it proved very disruptive to society as a whole.

Then abuses by the global financial industry precipitated the stock market crash of October 1929 and the Great Depression that ensued. By then the Japanese economy was so firmly enmeshed in the global one that, starting in 1930, it too was hammered by trade ruptures, burgeoning job losses and severe public hardship. And the government's attempt in January 1930 to protect Japan by pegging its currency to the Gold Standard only worsened the situation.

At that juncture, diplomacy added yet another grievance. During 1930, the three "Pacific Powers" (Britain, Japan, the USA) negotiated an agreement on the size of their naval forces as a way to halt an ongoing and senseless naval arms race that none of the three wanted or could afford. The problem was that their agreement permitted the British and American navies to remain substantially larger than that of Japan. This outcome was widely perceived as further evidence that only whites were acceptable as Great Powers.

Then, during 1930–31, as the world depression deepened and various countries established tariff barriers, import restrictions and other measures of economic self-defense, the combination of intense hardship at home and the growing Chinese threat to Japan's position in Manchuria prodded more military men to consider radical measures.

In the autumn of 1931, leaders of the army in southern Manchuria, operating without prior approval of the government in Tokyo, launched an armed conquest of the entire Manchurian region – an area nearly half the size of India and larger than Britain, France and Germany combined. The effort succeeded, and as the decade advanced, those military leaders worked with select businessmen to build a thriving Manchurian industrial economy based on mining and heavy industry. In seizing Manchuria, however, they had angered the Euro-Americans, who saw their own interests in China being threatened, and their denunciatory response to the venture prompted Tokyo in 1933 to announce its withdrawal from the League of Nations.

That withdrawal left Japan isolated among the Powers, and one thread of diplomacy during following years was Tokyo's quest for new connections to replace the earlier Anglo-Japanese Alliance, which had expired in 1922. In November 1936, in response to Soviet support for international Communist activities, Japan's leaders negotiated "anti-Comintern" pacts with Germany and Italy.[15] And in September 1940, by which time Japan's relations with the USA were under severe strain, Tokyo agreed to a Three-Power Pact of "mutual assistance" with Germany and Italy.[16]

As with the Anglo-Japanese Alliance, these agreements in fact amounted to very little, serving mainly to antagonize others while offering few material benefits in return. The more consequent developments were occurring on the ground.

Most importantly, the Japanese seizure of Manchuria had deepened Chinese anger, and as the 1930s advanced, Sino-Japanese relations worsened. The trend was propelled by growing Chinese strength on the one hand and, on the other, by intensifying Japanese efforts to extend their influence farther and farther into China.

Finally, in July 1937, a minor "police" incident near Beijing rapidly escalated into an all-out Sino-Japanese war. Over the next three years, Japan's military gradually extended its control across northeastern and coastal China. However, China's leaders refused to capitulate, and the farther Japanese forces pressed ahead, the more severely over-extended they became. By 1940 the demands of that seemingly endless war were creating serious hardships and unrest at home.

Meanwhile, global affairs were again growing turbulent as Europe again slipped into inter-state conflict. During September 1939, Germany's invasion of Poland provoked an Anglo-French declaration of war against the invader, and subsequent German advances westward across Europe heightened the American government's concern with global trends. That concern led Washington in July 1940 to announce a program of accelerated re-armament, including the construction of a "two-ocean" navy.

Japanese gains in China were also prompting Washington, as well as the British and Soviet governments, to provide the Chinese military with material support, policies pursued in hopes of keeping Japan's forces bogged down there and unable to threaten the interests of other Powers. Then, in September 1940, in a desperate attempt to defeat the Chinese regime by cutting off foreign sources of supply, Japanese troops moved into northern French Indochina (today's northern Vietnam). That development prompted the US government to cut off all exports of scrap iron and steel to Japan. With European trade disrupted by war, that move threatened to cripple Tokyo's long-term war-making capability.

By the spring of 1941, Japan's leaders had concluded that Washington's support of the Chinese military constituted a more serious obstacle than did Moscow's.

So they negotiated a non-aggression pact with the Soviet regime, hoping thereby to secure their northern perimeter and free resources for use in the South. The resulting Japanese military advances into southern Indochina in July led US and British leaders (and Dutch expatriate leaders in London) to freeze all the Japanese assets they controlled and to halt all oil exports to Japan.

With the oil cut off, Tokyo's fate was sealed. Either it must secure replacement supplies or it must abandon its entire China venture, thereby jeopardizing a half century of accomplishment. The necessary supplies of oil were in the Dutch East Indies (today's Indonesia), so policy debates focused on the question of how best to bring that region under secure control while current oil reserves lasted.

The decision that emerged called for measures to expel US and British forces from the Western Pacific and to do so by the end of 1941, in time to secure the necessary new oil supplies. On 8 December (7 December in the Americas) the effort commenced. For several months thereafter, matters developed as Tokyo intended, but by the end of 1942 the enterprise was stalled. During 1943–45 reverses followed one after another, and finally in August 1945, after American fire bombs had incinerated most Japanese cities and nuclear bombs had destroyed Hiroshima and Nagasaki, and after Russian forces had begun an advance from the North, the Emperor was authorized to denounce his military leaders for "erroneous and untimely" planning, and he ordered the government to accept the enemy conditions of surrender.[17]

And so, at horrific cost to common people throughout east and Southeast Asia, Tokyo's great venture in imperial industrialism had come to a disastrous end. In the ensuing diplomatic settlement, all of its colonies were lost and the ravaged remnants of the homeland were subjected to military occupation. The basic question at hand seemed straightforward: was Japan to become again an agricultural society sustained by its own resources, or was there some other way to establish the durable global resource base that would support an industrial order in the densely settled archipelago.

\* \* \*

Before leaving this melancholy story of imperial triumph and tragedy, let us consider a basic contradiction that sooner or later would surely have assured the utter failure of Japan's industrial-age empire. As earlier noted, the rise of industrial society entailed the rise of widespread public participation in "affairs of state" – that is, "national" self-consciousness. Given the rich history of pre-industrial Chinese and Korean societies, it is difficult to envisage them industrializing, even within the context of a Tokyo-centered empire, without development of a broad public consciousness of self as "Chinese" or "Korean" that would eventually demand a "state" of the same name. Indeed, one suspects that awareness of that potential may have underlain Tokyo's vigorous promotion of "Pan-Asian-ism" as a means of forestalling such a development.[18] The horrors of the 1940s, that is to say, may have been the merest foreshadowing of what lay in store had Japan's strategy of imperial industrialization prevailed at the time.

## SOCIETY AND ECONOMY

Even as imperial Japan's 50-year quest for a satisfactory global resource base evolved from success to failure, the many domestic dimensions of industrialization continued to develop. Let us examine them in terms of trends in demographics, commerce and industry, and urban and rural society.

### Demographics

Both the dimensions and dynamics of demographic change merit note, so let us ask of population trends during 1890–1945 what was the magnitude of growth, where did it occur, and what factors made it possible.

### 1. Population Estimates

As noted in Chapter 6, the later *bakuhan* population of an estimated 31–33 million rose past 33 million during the early 1870s to an unprecedented 40 million by 1890. By 1914, and the outbreak of World War I, it had surpassed 50 million, and by 1940, even as Tokyo and Washington were stumbling toward war with one another, it passed 70 million. By then, too, over 3 million Japanese were living in the colonies or elsewhere abroad, while more than a million non-Japanese, mainly Koreans, lived in Japan.[19]

This growth in the archipelago's human population was unprecedented in both rate and scale. However, it did not manifest itself everywhere to the same extent. It showed regional variation and, more importantly, a strong rural-to-urban trajectory that reflected the growth of urban commerce and industry.

In terms of regional growth, of the four main islands, Honshu, with its large cities, gained the most in absolute numbers. However, Hokkaido experienced the most rapid rate of expansion, even though the small population of surviving Ainu remained stable at some 18,000.[20] Due primarily to in-migration from Honshu, Kyushu and Shikoku, the island's "Japanese" (Wajin or "people of Wa") population grew 15-fold from some 111,000 in 1873 to 1,800,000 in 1913. It then nearly doubled to 3,300,000 by 1940.[21] Because of Hokkaido's relatively large size, however, it remained far less densely settled than were Honshu, Kyushu or even Shikoku, the least densely populated of the three.

### 2. Urbanization

More important than this regional variation was the trend everywhere of rural-to-urban movement. In part that shift was a statistical deception that resulted from the widespread incorporation of villages and towns to form larger towns or to be absorbed by nearby cities.

Thus, Tokyo as originally defined in 1871 was the former city of Edo, which consisted of area well to the East of Musashino. As the city grew and its need for potable water increased, it became more important to control the watersheds of those rivers that provided the water. So, in 1893, Tokyo took control of the Tama River watershed by appropriating areas to the South and West of Musashino. That maneuver greatly expanded Tokyo's area and absorbed a host of small towns and villages, as well as a substantial area of forested mountain terrain that included several peaks 1–2,000 m high.

When incorporation of this sort occurred, many villagers were instantly redefined as urbanites even though they remained on their farms, tilling their fields. Thus, whereas only about 16 percent of Japan's total populace was recorded as living in towns with more than 10,000 people in 1893, the figure had grown to 31.9 percent by 1920, and it reached 50.4 percent in 1940.[22]

Statistical sleight-of-hand notwithstanding, however, movement to urban sites and livelihoods was both real and sustained during these decades. That trend is evident in the burgeoning number of factory workers.[23]

| *Factory Workers* | |
|---|---|
| 1886 | 75,000 |
| 1900 | 387,000 |
| 1914 | 854,000 |
| 1919 | 1,777,000 |
| 1931 | 2,045,000 |

Conversely, even though agricultural output slowly increased in absolute terms, as a portion of total domestic production, it steadily dropped – from about 46 percent in 1890, down to 30 percent by 1920 and 19 percent by 1940.[24]

However, the geography of this urbanization was not random. Although the workers at mining and smelting operations mostly resided near sources of coal and ore, and many paper mills were located close to stands of timber, the key geographical factor shaping urban development was accessibility to transport. And given Japan's geographic character as a cluster of steeply mountainous islands, this meant that good port facilities were particularly valuable. From Naha in Okinawa to Wakkanai in northern Hokkaido, most of industrial Japan's urban growth occurred along the coast, in port towns and cities.[25]

Nor were these coastal cities spread evenly about the realm. Rather, the core of this burgeoning population and commercial life came to be concentrated on the coastal plains from Tokyo to Osaka. The Inland Sea littoral westward to northern Kyushu constituted a substantial secondary industrial region, while a number of good ports elsewhere in the archipelago developed into local industrial centers.

Most notably, Tokyo, which had numbered some 580,000 in 1872, regained its *bakuhan*-era million around 1890, surpassed 2 million in 1905, and stood at 6.7 million as of 1935.[26] By that year, the city held twice as many people as all of Hokkaido, which meant that nearly 12,000 people were packed and stacked into each km² of land, as against 38 people per km² in Hokkaido.

### 3. Factors in Demographic Growth

How was it possible for the Japanese archipelago, which for two centuries had sustained a maximum human population of some 32 million, to more than double its numbers in some 60 years? Basically the explanation is twofold: improvements in public health and increases in the food supply. Together they enabled more people to live longer and beget more healthy progeny.

*A. Public Health.* Regarding public health, more widespread vaccination and other improvements in medical treatment reduced losses to contagious disease, notably smallpox and especially in cities. As a result, while the *bakuhan*-era pattern, with mortality rates clearly higher in cities than in the hinterland, persisted until around 1900, by the 1930s, urban and rural rates were about on a par.[27] Well before then, changes in diet had overcome the 1870s–80s scourge of beriberi, noted in Chapter 6. And improvements in communication and transportation reduced the incidence of famine and malnutrition. So, everywhere the rates of fetal, infant and childhood mortality dropped and lifespans rose. By the 1920s, Japanese women were averaging over five live births per capita. And where average lifespan during the *bakuhan* centuries may have been around 30 years, by 1935 it had risen to 47 years.[28]

Perhaps the most impressive aspect of these gains in human survival rates and lifespan is the fact that they were being realized despite the rapid spread of industrial illness, injury and death – as we note more fully below – which previous generations had largely been spared. The other notable new source of disablement and death was industrial-style warfare, with its consumption of "cannon fodder" and creation of civilian casualties, most harshly during World War II, when American fire bombs and atomic bombs proved especially brutal destroyers of urban civilian populations. For all their grimness, however, these trends in industrial illness, injury and death were firmly offset by the burgeoning rates of childbirth and survival.

*B. Food Supply.* The benefits of public-health improvements could translate into sustained population growth, of course, only because the food supply also developed proportionally. That it could do so seems, in hindsight at least, quite remarkable. After all, as earlier noted, by the late *bakuhan* era, Japan's tillable lowlands had (except in Hokkaido) been almost entirely converted from natural biome to terrain that sustained humans and their collaborating species. Within Japan, there was little more land to be brought under cultivation. So its occupants could not simply sprawl across the realm to open up "virgin territory" or settle a "wild west". And being on islands situated offshore from a densely settled continent, they could not easily migrate to a receptive land nearby.

Within the firm constraints of this mountainous island context, the sustained gains in Japan's supply of foodstuffs were a result of two factors: increased domestic production per acre and importation from Japan's new global resource base.

Prior to the 1890s, Japan had been self-sufficient. Early-Meiji food imports and exports (except for tea) had constituted an almost inconsequent portion of the realm's total food production or consumption. And in that slender exchange, foodstuffs sent abroad had exceeded those brought in. In other words, from the 1860s to the 1890s, increases in food production had been sufficient to feed a growing domestic population, while leaving a bit for export.

During the 1890s, however, gains in domestic food output ceased to keep up with demographic growth. The export-import balance began to shift, and rice rapidly became a substantial import. By the eve of World War I, it totaled some 3 million *koku* (16.8 million bushels) per year, with the colonies of Korea and

Taiwan providing nearly 60 percent of that volume. Subsequently, that import dependency continued to grow, reaching some 10 million *koku* per year by the early 1930s, with nearly 90 percent of it coming from the two colonies.[29]

In terms of total food consumption, whereas domestic production prior to 1914 had still met nearly 98 percent of total demand, by 1935 it met only 82 percent, with most of the other 18 percent coming from the colonies.[30] Moreover, as we note more fully below, a growing portion of the "domestic" harvest was actually made possible by imported fertilizer material, which constituted an additional supply of nutrients derived ultimately from the global resource base.

Let us now look more closely at the nature of actual increases in domestic food output. Part of the gain was, until about 1918, a result of increased land utilization. The introduction of dairy and beef production and new forms of orchardry enabled farmers to exploit hitherto unused and under-utilized bits of land. And the vigorous "opening" of Hokkaido to tillage added new arable land. Thus, dry field tillage on the island, which in 1890 utilized 45,000 *chô* of land, had mushroomed by 1920 to 740,000 *chô* and continued to grow thereafter.[31]

A more important factor in the expansion of domestic food output was continuing changes in agricultural technique. Thus, development of more cold-resistant varieties of rice permitted its cultivation even in Hokkaido, where paddy acreage rose from some 2,000 *chô* in 1890 to 83,000 in 1920.[32] Together, these gains in dry-field and paddy-field acreage gave Hokkaido roughly 15 percent of Japan's total arable land.

For the country as a whole, agricultural gains were spurred by a combination of factors. One was pressure from above – from the government to fulfill one's tax obligations and from landlords to pay one's rent. Another was growing awareness of the gains to be achieved by adopting new techniques. This growth in awareness reflected the spread of education ever more widely through the population, with the accompanying notion of "science" as a key to "progress". It was an orientation that reflected the early-Meiji rhetoric of *bunmei kaika* noted in Chapter 6.[33] In 1908 the mayor of a village on the East flank of Mt Fuji put it this way:

> The main purpose of creating this council in our village is to insure that our tax obligations are fully met. It is obvious that the ability to pay taxes stems from economic enterprise. Therefore, to improve agriculture we will establish plots for testing alternative strains of rice and encourage seed selection by the saltwater method. To promote by-employment, we will have training courses on how to improve mulberry yields. I urge you to support progress by this means.[34]

Besides improvements in seed varieties, gains in yield per acre were achieved by better techniques of seed and harvest storage and transport and continuing improvements in paddy-field layout and handling. However, the single most important factor in these gains was the intensive use of fertilizer, which became much more common, with farmers of the realm tripling their fertilizer use between 1912 and 1939.[35]

Due to these several factors, rice production (which held steady at some 50 percent of total agricultural output by value) rose from about 29 million *koku* per year in 1880 to nearly 40 million by the mid-1890s and to 60 million by 1930. This doubling of both rice and other food output was obviously a major factor in enabling Japan's population to spurt upward.

Most strikingly, perhaps, this growth in output was achieved even though the agricultural producer populace remained essentially unchanged, holding at some 5.5 million households numbering some 14–16 million workers during the decades to 1940.[36] That is to say, the farm workers who produced about 2 *koku* of rice per person per year in 1880 were producing about 4 *koku* apiece by 1930.

This evidence of gains in domestic farm output notwithstanding, in a couple of ways the increased use of commercial fertilizer – which undergirded it – was also an expression of Japan's growing dependence on its global resource base. First, the empire provided raw material. In particular, Manchuria's soybean industry generated waste that was processed and shipped to Japan for use as fertilizer. Moreover, when Japan seized northern Micronesia in World War I, it acquired islands that for uncountable millennia had been roosting sites for sea birds. As a consequence, they held immense accumulations of guano, a phosphate-rich fertilizer material that Japanese entrepreneurs mined and shipped to the homeland.[37]

Second, pelagic fisheries – primarily in the seas around Hokkaido – became an important source not only of food but also of fishmeal fertilizer. To backtrack briefly, abolition of the *bakuhan*-era "use-rights" system in 1873 had compelled users of both riverine and inshore fisheries to work out new guidelines for allocation of their resources. But with consumer demand continuing, indeed growing, they had good reason to resolve disputes and sustain their output. They gradually did so, but despite the market incentive, fish farming does not appear to have grown noticeably. Probably that was so initially because it was less profitable than regular harvesting; in later decades it was discouraged by damage to water sources caused by industrial pollution, which we examine more fully below.

Prior to World War I, Japan's maritime fishing fleet had continued to depend heavily on the harvest from coastal waters. But as those fisheries declined one by one due to industrial pollution and overfishing, the industry acquired more and more large vessels for use on the high seas. By 1930 the total marine catch was some 3 million metric tons, and as of 1938, 38 percent of it had pelagic origins.[38] With that shift to deep-sea sources, the fishing industry was able to increase its production of fishmeal for fertilizer. So in two ways – with guano from the Marianas and fishmeal fertilizer from deep-sea fishing – the Pacific Ocean came to play an important role in sustaining the homeland's agricultural production.

These pelagic fisheries also fed people directly, of course, and in that way, too, they were facets of Japan's growing dependence on its global resource base. Thus, some 90 percent of the marine harvest was consumed at home, and while the remaining 10 percent was exported, other seafood imports as a whole exceeded those exports.

* * *

Unsurprisingly, several basic trends of the day – a high birth rate, rapid population growth, job losses and hardships during the 1920s–30s, more and more people living in the cities where they were heavily dependent on rural folk for basic sustenance, and ever more foodstuffs coming from foreign sources – gave rise during the 1920s to a rich discourse on the "problem" of over-population in a realm lacking additional "usable" space. Ideas flourished on how to cope with it or, conversely, on how it might be used as a tool in the world of empire-building and Great-Power politics.

One idea plucked from global discourse of the day was the notion of voluntary birth control. Other voices said that the solution was more economic "growth". Yet others saw emigration as the optimal solution – that, after all, was what other industrial Powers were doing with their surplus people. And such emigration would be most valuable to Japan, it was argued (especially after the anti-Asian immigration policies of the Australo-Americans were officially affirmed), if it were directed to the colonies.[39] Through the 1920s and 1930s, this last option enjoyed the most widespread support, being reflected in a burst of migration to Manchuria. But after 1945, as we shall see in Chapter 8, the field of discourse and action on population control was radically transformed.

### Commerce and Industry

The rapid growth of Japan's industrial-age urban population was made possible, then, by improved public health and an expanding food supply.

In addition, of course, orderly demographic growth depended on a commensurate increase in gainful employment. And that increase, in turn, was made possible by the rapid expansion of industrial output, which depended on a global resource base that provided the natural resources and reliable markets essential to orderly production and disposal of factory output.[40] So let us look at the foreign trade that linked Japan to its global resource base and then at the industrial activity that this base helped sustain.

### 1. Foreign Trade

The empire-building discussed above constituted a mechanism for trying to secure at least a portion of that global resource base. However, overseas commercial exchange (foreign trade) constituted the main mechanism of that base's utilization. During the decades to 1890, as earlier noted, foreign trade had grown gradually, but subsequently both the scale and composition of the trade experienced striking change. Also, the means of its transport underwent noteworthy alterations.

In terms of scale, the growth in this overseas commerce was stunning. Thus the trade, which in 1893 had a total value of 174 million yen, rose nearly ninefold by 1913 to 1.5 billion. And subsequently – despite the post-World War I recession and later Great Depression – its yen value rose more than fourfold to 7.2 billion in 1936.[41]

In terms of composition, the trade evolved from an essentially "colonial" trade with raw-material exports paying for manufactured imports, to an "industrial" trade with manufactured exports paying for raw-material imports. However, that shift in character proved to be a mixed blessing.

Prior to the 1890s, the trade had primarily involved the export of silk thread, tea, other foodstuffs, coal, copper and other raw materials in exchange for diverse manufactured products, including ships and machinery, and scores of hired foreign advisors. Of the exports, silk thread dominated, and it was produced mainly by farm households and small shops situated in villages scattered about central Japan. However, a newly built silk-reeling works of the 1870s (situated near sources of silk cocoons in the town of Tomioka in foothills of the northwestern Kantô) foreshadowed the future large-scale textile industry.[42]

Thanks to silk's strong market appeal, silk thread production increased rapidly, and by the 1890s it constituted some 42 percent of Japan's total exports by market value. Subsequently, however, even though silk production continued to grow vigorously – nearly tripling between 1894 and 1914 – its share of the burgeoning foreign trade gradually declined to about 33 percent of total exports before World War I disrupted the market.

After the war and on through the 1920s, cultivation of mulberry bushes and production of silk cocoons continued to expand, and silk remained a significant export item despite the development of rayon as a substitute. But then the Great Depression ravaged the global silk market, so exports shriveled, and cocoon production started a rapid and permanent decline.[43] It was a change that hurt rural society widely and severely, especially in the hilly regions West and North of the Kantô Plain.[44]

What had been slowly replacing silk's dominance in foreign trade since the 1890s were cotton goods and other diverse manufactured products, as new textile factories and other industries came into operation or were retooled for the export market. Due to the rapid expansion of cotton-mill production, cotton goods not only displaced silk as the dominant textile export but also sustained the key role of textiles in the rapidly expanding export trade as a whole. Thus, in 1936, even with silk thread nearly absent, textiles still constituted 58 percent of total exports by value.[45]

These massive cotton exports, however, were a mixed blessing. They were not nearly as advantageous to Japan's international "balance of payments" as were tea and silk. Nor did they prove beneficial to the rural populace.

To elaborate, the balance-of-payments problem was that whereas tea and silk came from home-grown materials, the domestic output of raw cotton was utterly insufficient to satisfy the burgeoning cotton mills. So manufacturers started importing raw cotton for processing in their new mills, and they discovered that the imports were cheaper than domestically produced raw cotton. By 1914, when imports as a whole consisted of about equal portions of industrial and primary products, raw cotton was the single largest import item, constituting some 65 percent of the primary category.[46] And reliance on foreign sources of raw cotton continued to grow in following years.

This heavy and growing dependence on raw-cotton imports reduced the net exchange value of cotton exports. More visibly, it injured the agricultural populace, doing so in two ways. First, in the same way that raw sugar imports were destroying domestic sugar production, raw-cotton imports undermined a valuable rural business, forcing farmers to abandon cotton growing and replace it with other, less profitable land uses. Second, the expanding cotton industry gave hard-pressed farm households a seriously hurtful "solution" to their more general economic predicament – that of permitting, or even encouraging, their daughters to leave home and take badly paid jobs in cotton mills, where far too often they contracted tuberculosis. What was good for the cotton-mill magnate, in short, rarely was good for the villager.

Finally, changes in maritime transportation merit note. Ocean transport, obviously, was essential to Japan's exploitation of global resources and markets. Insofar as the goods traveled on Japanese rather than foreign ships, their transport improved the balance of trade. In addition, that arrangement helped signal Japan's shift from "colony" to "imperial power".

*Bakuhan*-era foreign trade had mostly sailed on ships owned and operated by foreigners. But during the 1860s–90s, both Japan's government and entrepreneurs acquired larger vessels – warships for the government and cargo ships for merchants – buying most of them from foreign shipyards.

At the time, more costly and technically complex steamships were rapidly replacing sailing ships, and wooden-hulled vessels were just starting to give way to iron-hulled ones. Adapting to this set of technological changes was a costly, complicated process. Consequently, as of 1894, only 169 steamships sailed under Japanese registry, and nearly all were of foreign origin. Moreover, they carried only 8 percent of the country's foreign trade.

By 1913, however, the figures had swollen to 1,514 steamships carrying 50 percent of the trade. And in following years the numbers grew yet more, with most of the new vessels being built in Japan. By the mid-1930s, a vastly larger fleet carried nearly all the rapidly expanding colonial trade and about 70 percent of Japan's other foreign trade.[47]

### 2. Domestic Industry

The decades to 1940 witnessed the establishment in Japan of a vast array of new industries. Of the many types, certain ones – textiles, shipbuilding, steel mills, metal and coal mines – seem particularly noteworthy, along with the production of petroleum and electricity and the creation of a rail network.

A. *Textiles.* As noted above, silk and later cotton goods were Japan's most important export commodities. They were also important elements in the overall domestic economy. In terms of manufacturing output, textiles constituted between a quarter and a third of the country's total during the half-century, 1888–1938.[48] And because the textile industry was more labor-intensive than were others, such as metal and chemical, it was the single most important employer after agriculture. Indeed, as late as 1930, it accounted for about 50 percent of the industrial workforce, a portion that dropped rapidly thereafter as the Depression-era export market declined and, subsequently, as heavy industry expanded during the later-1930s drift to war.[49]

Textiles also played a unique role (except for the "water trades") as a major industry whose manual-labor force consisted largely of young women.[50] They handled nearly all the silk-reeling, much of which occurred in small, rural-household shops. Also, prior to World War I, young women (mostly in the 12–20 age range) had provided over 70 percent of the total workforce in cotton spinning and weaving. More broadly, the industry's prominence in the urban economy meant that women even constituted a majority of employees in larger-scale private industry as a whole.[51] In following years, however, as other heavy industries multiplied, the role of women in the industrial work force declined, and by the late 1930s, men had come to predominate.[52]

B. *Shipbuilding.* The rapid expansion of Japan's commercial fleet after 1895 reflected the rise of a modern shipbuilding industry. During *bakuhan* centuries, ship size had been limited by law, and only coasting vessels were allowed. From the 1850s onward, ship size increased, but for some years thereafter, most ocean-going vessels continued to be purchased abroad.

Gradually, however, Japanese shipyards scaled up and added steam-power capabilities.[53] Especially from the 1890s onward, the need for up-to-date warships and transport vessels spurred rapid development of shipyards, notably commercial shipyards in the Osaka vicinity and naval shipyards at Kure (near Hiroshima) and Yokosuka (near Tokyo). By the 1930s, Japan's shipbuilding technology was on a par with that of other industrial powers.

C. *Steel Mills.* Iron manufacture had a long history in Japan, as noted in previous chapters. By European standards, however, the technology had become outdated by the 1800s. During the 1890s, the emerging shift to iron-hulled vessels, together with myriad other growing military and civilian uses of iron and steel, prompted the government in 1896 to commence construction of an up-to-date steel mill. It situated the mill at Yahata, in a sheltered inlet (Dôkai-wan) on the north-Kyushu coast, just West of the Kanmon Strait. That location placed the mill relatively close to coal and iron mines, and gave it easy access to both the Inland Sea and ocean routes to the continent. The Yahata mill commenced production in 1901, and by 1913 it was meeting about a third of Japan's total pig iron and steel needs by producing upwards of half a million tons, mostly of pig iron, annually.[54]

Subsequently, steel mills at Yahata and elsewhere continued to expand production, increasing steel output some 18-fold between 1913 and 1936. By then domestic steel output alone stood at 4.5 million tons. And whereas imports had met some 70 percent of Japan's steel needs as late as 1913, by 1930 they had dropped to 30 percent or less despite the vast growth in total steel consumption.[55]

D. *Metal and Coal Mines.* To produce the pig-iron and steel, as well as other needed metals, two types of raw material were essential: ore from which to extract the metal and a fuel capable of refining the ore as desired. Metal and coal mines provided those materials.

Regarding iron ore, the archipelago's iron mines proved woefully inadequate despite a striking expansion of output. In 1900, they had yielded some 28,900 metric tons of ore, and by 1930 that figure had grown more than eightfold to 246,000. A decade later, as the war in China dragged on, iron ore production had, by ruthless force of will and at great risk to miners, been pushed sharply upward to 1,123,000 metric tons.

Meanwhile, however, domestic consumption of iron ore had grown so much more rapidly that by 1930 imports from the colonies and elsewhere dwarfed domestic production, having surged upwards to 2,261,000 metric tons. And by 1940 the ore imports had more than doubled to 5,129,000.[56] Industrial success was only deepening Japan's dependence on its global resource base.

These basic trends in iron mining – of expanding output that lagged ever farther behind demand – were representative of the mining industry as a whole. As noted in Chapter 6, during the 1870s–90s, entrepreneurs also undertook to modernize copper and other metal mines. These ventures, and particularly the copper mines, produced severe environmental problems, as we note later. However, industrial growth required metals, and copper output grew rapidly, with a yield of nearly 20,000 metric tons in 1894, rising to 66,500 by 1913 and 78,000 in 1936. Copper was also involved in foreign trade, initially as a valued export, but as years passed and domestic demand escalated, the balance shifted from export to import. As late as 1913, net exports of copper were some 40,000 metric tons per year, but by 1936 imports exceeded exports by about the same tonnage.[57]

As for coal mining, which was found mainly in Kyushu and Hokkaido, it showed an even more striking trajectory of growth, as this table indicates.

*Coal Production, 1874–1940*[58]

| | |
|---|---|
| 1874 | 208,142 metric tons |
| 1894 | 4,281,681 " " |
| 1913 | 21,000,000 " " |
| 1930 | 31,375,000 " " |
| 1940 | 56,313,000 " " |

That immense increase notwithstanding, coal output, too, displayed growing insufficiency.

Because of Japan's geological youth, much of its domestic coal was soft (bituminous) and did not yield the intense heat of hard (anthracite) coal. In consequence, it did not meet some basic industrial needs, and for several decades substantial quantities were exported in exchange for imported anthracite or other goods.

Up through 1913, coal exports greatly exceeded imports, but the wartime boom changed that balance. From then onward, more and more of the domestically mined coal was used at home, while imports also grew rapidly. During the 1930s, that growth in imports continued, nearly doubling by 1940 to some 5,000,000 metric tons – roughly 9 percent of Japan's total coal needs. And that final surge in coal imports occurred despite the big increase in domestic output that resulted from intense government pressure.

*E. Petroleum and Electricity.* Even as coal output, imports and consumption all escalated, new technology was also creating demand for other types of fossil fuel. Most importantly, the internal combustion engine came into use, especially during the 1920s and 1930s. It was utilized in motor vehicles, oil-fueled ships, airplanes, army tanks and stationary motors that served diverse purposes. In terms of motor vehicles, for example, in 1917, Japan recorded 3,856 vehicle registrations, but by 1937 the number was 128,735, mostly trucks and buses.[59]

Some of the petroleum for this fleet came from domestic oil and natural gas wells, most of them found along the Sea of Japan coast North of the Noto Peninsula. But demand so vastly exceeded domestic production that as of 1932, about 80 percent of need was met by imports. And nearly 40 percent of what was recorded as "domestic" production actually came from Karafuto. During the 1930s, production of domestic crude scarcely grew, but imports continued rising, nearly quadrupling during the decade.[60]

Despite this surging consumption of coal and petroleum, industrial Japan's appetite for energy could not be met by fossil fuel alone. Coal-powered generation of electricity had commenced in the later 1880s, and by 1910 the first small hydroelectric plants were in operation. As years passed, more and more electricity came to be used as electric motors replaced horses on streetcars, and as factories, offices, stores of myriad sorts and households shifted to electric lights, motors and other devices. Especially after World War I, electrification advanced rapidly, with electricity output increasing more than sixfold during 1919–37. By the mid-1930s, Japan was one of the world's most thoroughly electrified societies, with 89 percent of households having access to electricity, even if only for one or two light bulbs.[61]

To make the transition from coal-based electric generation to hydroelectric power, more and more rivers were dammed, intermontane valleys flooded, and larger-scale power plants put into operation. By 1936 hydropower generated some 75 percent of the total electricity being consumed, with coal-fired turbines being held in reserve, for use as needed during periods of reduced water flow.

*F. Railroads.* The countrywide growth and maintenance of mining, manufacturing and product distribution depended, of course, on the presence of an adequate transportation system. Just as *ritsuryô* leaders had seen highways as essential to their polity and *bakuhan* leaders had seen highways and waterways as necessary to their much more complex social order, so the leaders of industrializing Japan, whether entrepreneurs or officials, saw the need for up-to-date means of linking mines, ports, factories and other facilities together for the movement of goods and people.

What was different from earlier centuries, besides the scale of the system, was its basic technology. Railroads were the new highways, and from the 1870s onward, they were built.[62] The impact of railroads proved particularly dramatic because during *bakuhan* centuries, inter-city wheeled traffic had been forbidden. Back then, goods were moved by boat, raft, packhorse or porter, and people traveled by boat, or they rode horses or walked (excepting the senior elite, who were carried in palanquins). In consequence, railroads allowed a stunning increase in human mobility, and that increase enabled much of the socio-economic change that ensued during the twentieth century.

To create the rail lines, land was bought or "taken", terrain leveled, tunnels dug, bridges built and track laid. By 1895, Japan had over 2,000 mi of railroad, much of it built and operated by entrepreneurs. In following years, construction continued apace, reaching some 4,500 mi by 1904, with a core trunk line that ran the length of Honshu, from Aomori in the North through Tokyo to Shimonoseki on the Kanmon Strait.

The Russo-Japanese War made it clear how essential the railway network was to military deployment and provisioning. So, in 1906, the government moved to overcome problems of shoddy construction and maintenance as well as poor connections and coordination by nationalizing some 5,000 mi of railroad, including all the main inter-city lines.[63]

Subsequently, both government and entrepreneurs continued building lines throughout the realm, more than tripling their mileage by the 1930s. Then, in the late 1930s, when tunneling began under the Kanmon Strait to build a rail line linking Honshu and Kyushu, the new technology took its first step in transcending the water barriers that had always separated Japan's main islands from one another.

### Urban and Rural Society

This massive development of commerce and industry underwrote the earlier-noted population growth and urbanization. It also became the central fiscal pillar of government: whereas land taxes had constituted 82 percent of total government tax receipts in 1885, by 1920 they had fallen to 10 percent, replaced by other, mainly commercial sources.[64] In addition, industrialization produced major changes in both urban and rural society.

Before examining those changes, however, let us recall that in discussing the rise of *ritsuryô* cities in Chapter 4, we noted how the simple dyad "urban/rural" was a bit deceptive, because "urban" sites retained so many "rural" characteristics and remained so dependent on the hinterland for survival. As Japan industrialized, those patterns persisted. At the same time, however, the radical technological and institutional changes associated with industrialization reshaped urban society in ways that distinguished it from rural society even more than in pre-industrial times. So let us look at some of the ways urban and rural society changed during the decades 1890–1945.

#### 1. Urban Society

In industrial Japan's burgeoning cities, perhaps the most striking segment of society was the newly rising industrial elite, a plutocracy known as the *zaibatsu* (the "clique of wealth"). The most successful of them developed into giant combines, such as the well-known Mitsui and Sumitomo corporations, both of which grew out of *bakuhan*-era entrepreneurial operations, or Mitsubishi, established by an ally of the *Sat-Chô* founders of the Meiji regime. These *zaibatsu* conglomerates engaged in a broad array of enterprises – financing, manufacturing, marketing, mining and shipping – while striving to maintain mutually advantageous relationships with government organs and leaders.

Below the leadership of these conglomerates were the armies of "paper pushers" or "white-collar" workers of company administration, and the "blue-collar" or manual laborers who produced the goods that generated the wealth. For all their visibility, however, these *zaibatsu* firms employed only a small portion of the urban work force, relying instead on machinery to maximize output and profit.

Consequently, most of the urban workforce, both blue and white collar, found employment elsewhere. Government, the media and the growing educational and medical systems employed many, but small-scale businesses of myriad sorts provided the bulk of urban jobs.[65]

Because *zaibatsu* firms did use complex technology, they required relatively skilled labor, and their salary scale reflected the scarcity of such workers. For the rest of the urban workforce, however, the instability of much small business, along with the ample labor supply of a rapidly growing population, served to keep wages low and working conditions difficult.

Even before the 1890s, harsh working conditions were generating urban discontent. Its intensity fluctuated with ups and downs in the economy, but overall its scale grew in tandem with the growth of industrial production. The escalating problems of workplace pollution, poisoning, injury and death in mines, factories and other enterprises, which we note more fully below, combined with the issues of low wages and long hours to create and sustain a nascent labor movement. During the 1890s–1900s the movement began to grow, and labor leaders and advocates agitated for factory legislation. Meanwhile, both unionists and non-union workers mounted numerous industrial strikes and engaged in a few instances of violent attack on brutal employers, most famously against the Ashio mine operation in 1907.

Industrialists tried to prevent such activism, and one technique was to remind workers of their social obligations as "patriotic Japanese". That strategy was nicely expressed by a silk manufacturer in 1911:

> If you do not work thus [but instead] stay idly at home, the country of Japan will become poorer and poorer. Therefore, work with all your might for the country's sake, enabling Japan to become the greatest country in the world.[66]

Meager wages and unhealthy working conditions gave menial laborers ample reason not to be inspired by such patriotic rhetoric, but work they did, though not happily.

The labor unrest finally spurred government leaders in 1911 to override industry's objections and enact some weak factory legislation aimed at regulating work hours and child labor. Specifically, the law, which became effective in 1916, made 12 years the minimum age for employment and 12 hours the maximum working day, with some exceptions favorable to employers.[67] These minimalist reforms failed to address many workplace problems, however, and labor unrest continued to grow, prompting the government to tighten factory regulations during the 1920s, despite the continuing objections of industry. Later, however, during the 1930s, as Tokyo's diplomatic situation grew more worrisome, government became less receptive to labor demands and more accepting of factory owners' arguments about the need for labor-management "harmony", so as to hold down labor costs and maximize output.

### 2. Rural Society[68]

Two aspects of rural society command attention. First, despite the striking new characteristics of imperial Japan – rapid socio-economic growth and urbanization, technological change and shift to a global resource base – its urban society remained heavily dependent on the rural populace. Thus, the countryside was still the source of most food, most people, and many non-food products. Second, the rural populace traced a trajectory of growing success and good fortune, followed by difficulties and misfortune that coincided with the state's experience in empire-building.

*A. On Urban Dependency.* Regarding the food supply, we noted earlier that, the striking growth of rice imports notwithstanding, as late as 1940 most of Japan's food was still produced at home. And while a portion of that domestic output was consumed locally in the village, as agricultural output per work-hour increased, ever more of the yield moved into commercial markets: some 77 percent around 1920, rising to 85 percent by the mid-1930s.[69]

As for urban demographic growth, even after medical improvements raised urban survival rates, the hinterland continued to produce many of the people who populated the cities and towns. Thus, prior to World War I, some 80 percent of growth in the non-agricultural workforce came from the farm. That figure dropped to 40 percent during the 1920s–30s, by which time cities and towns contained upwards of half the total population. But even then, rural people were still leaving the agricultural labor force to take other types of work at the rate of 100,000–250,000 per year.[70]

This rate of departure from farming could be sustained because of the rising birth and child-survival rates and because of the continuing gains in agricultural labor productivity. These latter gains, as earlier noted, enabled a stable workforce of some 15 million men and women, which had been able to feed some 40 million people in 1890, to meet about 80 percent of the food needs of some 70 million in 1940. And they could do so even though the rate of food consumption per capita gradually rose as decades passed.

Finally, the hinterland provided urban centers with diverse products other than food. We noted in Chapter 6 how during the later *bakuhan* period much artisanal production – of textiles, wood and paper products, ceramics and so on – had shifted from urban sites to rural. That shift had enabled many villagers to combine the seasonal work of crop production with by-employments, thereby increasing their overall household productivity.

This pattern of combined employment persisted through the imperial era. Indeed, the role of rural by-employments grew as years passed. In 1890, income from such work, which varied regionally, had provided some 11–21 percent of total rural household income. By the early 1920s, it stood at about 30 percent, boosted, most famously, by increased output of silk cocoons.[71]

*B. On Changes in Rural Conditions.* This boom in farm by-employments – together with the concurrent adoption of more intensive agricultural practices and growing work opportunities in town – enabled a stable rural population to keep provisioning a rapidly growing urban populace.

That boom was also a central factor in changes affecting rural communities themselves. It did so by helping to create a comparative scarcity of rural labor.

That trend enabled wage rates in the countryside roughly to double between the 1880s and 1920, even as it caused rural work-hours per year to increase.[72] Larger landowners found, as a result, that it was more advantageous to rent out their land than to hire their own workforce. Consequently, whereas tenants had tilled some 28 percent of Japan's arable land during the 1870s, by 1910 the figure had risen to some 45 percent, where it stabilized until after World War II.[73] Thanks to these patterns of more work opportunities and more household income, as a whole the three decades to 1920 were, in one scholar's words, "the golden age of the Japanese rural economy".[74]

A couple of other factors, political and social, also lay behind these material gains. First, the rural population was still a sufficiently large portion of the total so that rural interests – mainly those of landlords – were well represented in the national Diet, and government policy on such matters as price controls and tariffs served rural interests. Second, while landlords may have been the major beneficiaries of this situation, the fabric of local society, with its *bakuhan* legacy of communal resources and mutual help, remained largely intact during the "golden age". So the benefits of government policy tended to trickle down even to tenants.

During the 1920s–30s, however, even as Japan's phase of foreign-policy triumph gave way to escalating difficulty, the rural situation also changed for the worse. That change was already being foreshadowed before World War I, but it was not fully realized until about 1930.

One can point to several factors that fostered this deterioration. In response to changes in the rural economy, both tenants and landlords adopted new practices that altered social relationships within the village, undermining communal cohesion. And broader socio-economic changes led to a major shift in government agricultural policies. By the 1920s, these factors were giving rural Japan a new and harsher social configuration.

Regarding the change in village social relationships, during *bakuhan* centuries, it will be recalled, the customs of local paternalism and mutual help had co-existed with a readiness on the part of tenants and other poor villagers to view landlords, at least during hard times, as cruel exploiters. That tension persisted, and from about 1905 onward, tenants began using a new technique, the tenant union, as a mechanism of local cohesion to counter landlord power. As years passed, the number of tenant unions increased, and they mounted a slowly growing number of legal disputes with landlords over rent and other issues.

By 1917 there were a reported 173 tenant unions in Japan, but it was after World War I and the postwar economic collapse that both tenant unions and tenant-landlord disputes really proliferated. And when they did, they appeared mainly in central Japan, from the Kantô region westward to the Inland Sea periphery, being most prevalent in regions hurt by turbulence in the silk market. By 1921 there were 681 tenant unions, the number surging upward to 4,582 in 1927, when they counted 365,331 members, or "9.6 percent of all tenant farmers".[75] Thereafter, the number of unions fluctuated in the 4–5,000 range, depending on economic and political conditions.

To consolidate the activities of these local groups, in 1922 a national peasants' union was founded with 14 local chapters numbering 253 members. By incorporating more and more pre-existing local tenant unions, it grew rapidly, in 1926 numbering 957 chapters with 72,794 members. In response to this show of "underclass unity", landlords founded their own organizations, thus changing the traditional local tensions between individual tenants and landlords into more of a realm-wide contest.[76] And that division was reflected in the rate of conflict.

Thus, whereas there had been some 400 tenancy disputes in 1920, they multiplied in following years, peaking at over 6,000 in 1937.[77] Initially occurring in central and southwest Japan, moreover, these disputes gradually spread to the northeast. There, landlordism remained more solidly entrenched, crops were more vulnerable to weather irregularities, urban by-employments were less accessible, and consequently rural hardship was more pronounced.[78]

This deterioration of tenant-landlord relations was also fostered by a fundamental change in landlord orientation. Prior to about 1910, as noted above, rising rural wage rates had encouraged landlords to put out more of their land to tenantry. But from about that year onward, they found rental rates stagnating. With rental income stalled and farm wages continuing to rise, landlords, especially in central and southwest Japan, turned more and more to urban investment. And in due course, many moved to town to supervise their enterprises there, becoming absentee landlords with little emotional connection to former fellow-villagers.

After World War I, these trends toward heightened village conflict and alienation accelerated due to a cluster of factors. Most strikingly, the economic collapse that came with war's end and the widespread and violent urban rice riots of 1918 spurred the government to shift its agricultural policy. Instead of trying to support domestic rice prices against imports, and thus protect landlords and other rural folk, policy sought to reduce rice prices and facilitate imports. That change in priorities was possible, of course, because by then demographic trends had increased the clout of urban voters in the Diet, doing so at the expense of rural folk.

This shift in government policy gave more landlords reason to redirect their attention and resources to urban areas. And that shift, in turn, left poorer rural folk more vulnerable to market and weather fluctuations, and more ready to form tenant unions and engage in legal disputes.

Rural hardship was also exacerbated by changing wage patterns that undercut the earning power of rural labor in both agricultural work and local by-employments. As noted above, rural wages had risen nicely before the 1918 collapse, and during the 1920s they revived and continued to gain a bit. But then the Great Depression turned them sharply downward – most notably in the silk-cocoon region North and West of Tokyo – and they did not regain their 1920s level until the late 1930s. Meanwhile, however, urban wage rates, which overall had stayed on a par with rural rates prior to World War I, rose much more rapidly after 1920 than did the rural rates, gradually luring more workers into town while undercutting rural purchasing power.[79]

The effects of this disparity in wages were nicely exemplified in 1922 when the landlord-mayor of Aihara village in the southwest Kantô described his village's situation:[80]

Many tenants in the [neighboring] Hashimoto and Aihara areas are giving up on farming in this time of low prices, and returning their land. Due to these conditions there are no new renters, and so it's not hard to imagine that in future there will be many overgrown fields. If a laborer goes to work in a factory or on the railroads, he can earn ¥70 or ¥80 a month, or he can earn ¥250 to ¥300 a year as a hired laborer on a farm. And so the number of self-employed farmers is declining and agricultural business is shrinking and the farmers present a miserable sight. This distress will not easily be dispelled in the next year or two.

Two years later he reiterated his lament about the lure of city wages, noting also that urban work "does not require such heavy physical labor so of course everyone is heading off to the cities". He went on:

Nobody is having a harder time than the landlords. This spring, many fields were returned to me. All of them are just going to turn into woodland. Next spring, it looks as though it's going to get even worse.

Woodland, he realized, would eventually yield a profitable timber harvest while involving minimal labor costs. But decades would pass before those savings could convert into actual income.

As the mayor's lament suggests, landlords too suffered when tenants did. That situation was highlighted after 1929 when the silk market collapsed. Resident landlords operated most of the local silk-spinning shops, and when the market collapsed, they lost that income. Moreover, the tenants who provided most of the cocoons that sustained these shops – and most of the women who did the spinning – found themselves unable to pay rent on the land once they lost the income from cocoon sales and daughterly labor. So landlords found their rental income declining along with income from silk sales.[81]

Landlords were so vulnerable in large part because most of them were actually very small-scale landowners. In the 1930s, over 90 percent of Japan's approximately 1 million non-farming landlords owned fewer than 5 hectares (12.4 acres) of land. And of Japan's roughly 1.28 million farmers who rented out part of their land, nearly 98 percent owned fewer than 5 hectares.[82] So, significant fluctuations in the market could seriously disrupt their lives, even if less harshly than those of tenants.

Cumulatively these trends and hardships had served by 1940 to undermine the old social structure and its forms of local mutual assistance. With so many landlords having departed the countryside, especially in central and southwestern Japan, many rural areas were left in the hands of small owner-renters. The latter mostly cultivated parcels ranging from 0.5 to 2.0 hectares in size (approximately 1–5 acres).[83] Such small acreages had long been favored because they constituted about as much land as household members could till, given the time they had available.

By 1940, however, much of the work on these small farms was being handled by the elderly and by household women while family males served in the military or worked elsewhere in better-paying non-farm jobs.[84] This reduced labor force was able to handle its tasks in part because of labor-saving technology – such as gasoline- or electricity-powered pumps for irrigating paddy fields and machines for threshing and polishing rice. As we note later in this chapter, when discussing the environmental impact of industrial technology, their use mushroomed during the 1920s and 1930s.

Two factors fostered this surge in mechanization. First, although the Great Depression hammered farm communities during the early 1930s, from about 1935 onward, the rural economy began to revive, spurred largely by urban industrial revival and a resulting growth in demand for both laborers and rural production. The renewed outflow of able-bodied workers and inflow of wages gave villagers both reason and means to acquire more of the new equipment. Second, and especially after 1937, as the army's need for "cannon fodder" escalated, the machines were adopted to replace the lost labor of sons drafted for military service.

We must note, however, that the apparent speed with which new machinery proliferated was somewhat deceptive. As of the early 1940s the new equipment was still benefitting only a small portion of the village populace, mostly in the central part of Japan. Small-scale farmers could not afford many of these items, and most were purchased by relatively affluent landowners, local farm cooperatives or other village groups.[85] The machines commonly served more than a single household, but throughout the country, much of the work that these machines could do was still being done by hand.

Then, after 1940, even those rural gains in well-being began to reverse. Two materials central to later-1930s farm production – chemical fertilizers and the fuel for motorized farm machinery – became unavailable due to wartime demands. With so many people away in military service or factory work, however, there were no workers available to gather natural fertilizer materials or replace the machines, so many farmers were forced to abandon production, and some 500,000 hectares of land that had been tilled became inactive.[86] Especially after 1942, agricultural output dropped precipitously, with the total yield in 1945 being only about half of that during 1938–40.

By 1940, then, even before a disastrous war upended affairs, new patterns of local organization had come into play, some of them with government encouragement. These replaced the old landlord-tenant mutual help arrangements with new forms of tenant unions, local cooperatives and government extension-service activities. By 1940, that is to say, although a substantial amount of agricultural land was still owned by absentee landlords, the old *bakuhan*-era system of village organization was largely gone. It had been replaced by a realm of smallholders dealing with urban markets through new arrangements.


## TECHNOLOGY AND THE ENVIRONMENT

Compared to the millennia of forager society or the centuries of agricultural society, the decades of industrial society have been stunning in their rate and variety of technological change and the ensuing environmental consequences.[87]

And in Japan, as everywhere, the way those consequences have played out has been firmly shaped by geographical context. Most basically, by the 1700s, as noted earlier, the archipelago (South of Hokkaido) displayed a strong bifurcation in function, with lowlands devoted to human affairs and steep uplands to affairs of the surviving natural biome.

Consequently, since most industrial development occurred in the lowlands, its impact mainly affected humans and their collaborating ("domesticated") plants and animals.

There were, however, some notable exceptions to this last generalization. During the decades to 1945, mining and railroad construction and tunneling damaged the natural biota of numerous "undeveloped" interior valleys. The installation of hydroelectric plants permanently flooded a number of vibrant, inter-montane valleys. The establishment and operation of various industries had a destructive impact on numerous riverine and coastal marine biomes. The logging industry extended its activities into vast tracts of old-growth forest, especially in Hokkaido, enabling farmers to transform much of that island's remaining lowland into agricultural acreage. And throughout the archipelago, logging facilitated the eventual conversion of much upland into even-aged monoculture stands.

These diverse hinterland impacts notwithstanding, industrial development weighed most heavily on long-utilized lowlands. We can examine these developments in terms of mining, manufacturing, fisheries, agriculture and forestry.

### Mining

Both metal and coal mining, as noted earlier, were developed into major industries in the half century before World War II. That growth entailed the expansion of existing mines, opening of new mines widely about the realm, and adoption of new technologies that enabled far deeper tunneling and much more rapid excavation and processing of ore.

There were, however, basic differences between metal and coal mining, and in consequence their environmental impacts were dissimilar. Besides the basic chemical difference between coal, which is organic material (that is, carbonaceous), and metal ores, which are inorganic, the deposits tended to be found in very dissimilar geological strata and geographic contexts.

In the case of metal mining, the ore came mainly from seams within bedrock mountain ranges. Consequently, the environmental problems mostly appeared downstream and were caused by flooding that resulted from the deforesting of nearby hillsides – done to obtain wood for mine timbers, other on-site construction and fuel. Such flooding then washed mine tailings and their chemicals downstream to areas of human habitation and use. In addition, the smelters that converted raw ore to useable metal were mostly located near the mines, and they emitted noxious gases that ambient airflow blew into nearby areas, where it damaged both plant and animal life, humans included.

Of the diverse metal mines, those for copper proved to be the most poisonous. Their effluent, as well as smelter emissions, spewed especially noxious chemicals, sulfur dioxide in particular, across adjoining areas, damaging crops, farm animals, natural vegetation and fisheries, causing human illness and generating intense protests. The Besshi mine complex in northern Shikoku, with its refinery on nearby Shisaka Island in the Inland Sea, proved particularly destructive and generated intense and persistent protests in the region.[88]

However, the most famous – or notorious – copper mine and refinery was at Ashio on the northern fringe of the Kantô. During the 1870s–80s, as noted in Chapter 6, poisonous effluent from its tailings and denuded hillsides had ravaged several agricultural villages downstream along the Watarase River. By 1890 the poisons were approaching Tokyo via the Watarase-Tone-Edogawa watershed, forcing authorities there finally to pay attention. During the 1890s, thousands of villagers from the Watarase region mobilized marches on the capital, only to be stopped by military force. By then the government was attempting to arrange a settlement, but decades of bitter conflict were to pass before the ravaged region partially recovered and grew quiet again.

Coal mines, on the other hand, and in Kyushu most notably, lay mainly at a shallow depth near or beneath lowlands that were already being used for agriculture and human settlement. The mining process entailed tunneling under these surfaces, removing the layers of coal, and using timbers or other material to hold the ground in place. Gradually, however, and sometimes abruptly, surface areas would crumble and settle, ruining topsoil and field layouts, sometimes enabling polluted water to rise and poison the fields. Where the settling occurred under villages, houses slumped, tilted and sometimes collapsed. The mining also disrupted underground water supplies, poisoning some wells, draining others and disrupting irrigation systems. As the scale of coal mining grew, so too did these consequences, giving rise by the 1920s to recurrent incidents of damage and protest.

Thus, some 20–30 km southwest of Yahata in northern Kyushu, coal mines that were linked to Yahata by riverine barge service and later by rail were vigorously exploited. By 1920 the cumulative damage done by that mining activity was reported as follows:[89]

200 hectares of paddies no longer fit for cultivation, 220 hectares sustaining more than 50 percent decrease in yield, 320 hectares showing more than 30 percent decrease, subsidence of housing land in 1,874 places, contamination and drying up of wells in 384 places, drying up of rivers and ponds in 25 places, and subsidence of roads in 16 places.

Four years later, a report for all of Fukuoka Prefecture stated that, due to coal mining, "about 4,500 hectares of farmland have been harmed by cave-ins and ... about 1,400 hectares have been contaminated by polluted mine water". If we postulate an average of about 1.5 hectares of arable land per farm household, then, with this much land damage, some 4,000 of Fukuoka's farm households would have found their fields damaged and hence their very survival put at risk.

Besides injuring surrounding areas and people, mining of all sorts was dangerous to the miners. As long as mining had remained a small, local business pursued in distant corners of the realm, the illness and injury of miners had been a nearly invisible social problem. However, dust was ubiquitous in all types of mines, and lung ailments (mainly silicosis or "miner's disease") became endemic, especially after the use of dynamite and industrial machinery dramatically accelerated the rate of ore extraction. The proliferation of mine illnesses was matched by growth in miners' accidental injuries and deaths. Those trends were sustained by the rapid expansion of mine employment: some 36,000 miners in 1886; 131,000 in 1900; 434,000 in 1917; probably well over 500,000 by 1940.[90]

Beyond the general mining problems of dust and accidents, metal and coal mines posed dissimilar health risks to the miners. Metal mines were dangerous primarily for the poisons they produced, such as copper or arsenic compounds, lead or sulfur dioxide. Coal mines, on the other hand, were dangerous primarily because the coal dust could explode, killing mine crews. And every year during the decades to 1945, scores or even hundreds of miners were killed by such explosions.[91]

## Manufacturing

Prior to 1914, mining activity seems to have been the predominant source of industrial pollution and environmental damage in Japan, although reports of factory-caused damage had appeared regularly. Then, however, the World War I industrial boom, and the continuing growth thereafter, altered that balance, making factories the primary new source of environmental injury. Like mines, factories were injurious to workers within and to the general bio-system without, humans included. And because the city of Osaka epitomized the problem, it warrants particular notice.

### 1. Impact on Workers

Among workers, factories generated illness, injury and accidental deaths. The most widespread source of illness was factory dust. And the most well-known disease was tuberculosis, with an annual mortality rate that rose to the range of 180–200 per 100,000 from about 1910 until after war's end in 1945.[92] Tuberculosis mainly killed young adults, and women working in cotton mills were especially susceptible because of their youth, their dusty workplaces and the dormitories they shared, in which they could transmit the disease to one another.

In addition, a vast array of other illnesses and disabilities were contracted by workers in nearly all types of industry – paper mills, metal works, match factories, all types of textile operations, cement plants, munitions factories, paint and glass works, shipyards, rubber works, chemical and pharmaceutical plants, battery factories and oil refineries.[93] Throughout the decades to 1945, the proliferation and diversification of factories sustained a growing incidence of such industrial poisoning despite extensive medical reporting and treatment, sporadic protests and the eventual implementation – usually in the face of industry resistance – of regulations to reduce the dangers of factory employment.

### 2. Impact on the Bio-system

Regarding manufacturing's external environmental impact, in a couple of basic ways it differed from that of mines. First, factories were so diverse in function that they produced a much wider array of noxious gases, liquid effluents and solid wastes than did mines.

Second, whereas most mines were located in the hinterland, in relatively sparsely settled areas and usually some distance from the coast, most factories were situated in or near major cities with good access to ports and marine shipping. There were exceptions, of course. Indeed, as we note in Chapter 8, a chemical plant established in 1908 at Minamata, on the rural Kyushu coast some 40 mi south of Kumamoto, went on to acquire, in post-1945 Japan, great notoriety for devastating chemical pollution, both gaseous and liquid.

Because of their diversity and their customary siting in or near cities, factories tended to pose much more danger to human populations than did mines. Also, because these factories commonly were near the coast, their effluent tended to be particularly destructive of marine life in both estuarine and coastal biomes, as we note more fully below.

Moreover, factories also damaged considerable farmland because so much agriculture continued to be practiced in and near cities. Exemplifying this last point, as recently as 1929, 23.9 percent of the land within Tokyo city boundaries was arable, while 33.6 percent of that in Osaka was, with most of Tokyo's used for dry-field crops while most of Osaka's grew wet rice.[94] In subsequent decades, for diverse reasons, nearly all of that farmland was gradually converted to urban uses.

Factories and their effects appeared in and near cities throughout the realm. However, the considerations that led entrepreneurs to place their factories at such sites – for example, optimal access to domestic customers and workforce and transport links to raw materials and foreign markets – gave them a particularly strong incentive to build in the vicinity of Osaka and Tokyo. So, let us see how industrial development affected Osaka.

### 3. The Osaka Experience [95]

As noted in Chapter 6, although Edo (Tokyo) as the political hub of *bakuhan* society grew to be much more populous than Osaka, the latter served as the mercantile hub, linking East and West Japan. After 1868 it retained its commercial centrality, and in following decades the Osaka vicinity also led in the development of industrial production. Indeed, not until 1938 did industrial growth in the Tokyo vicinity surpass that of the Osaka area, giving it a larger labor force and greater industrial output.[96]

Problems of environmental pollution had appeared in Osaka as early as the 1880s.[97] For several decades thereafter, the main complaint was air pollution, which injured both human residents and agricultural crops. Water pollution did gradually increase, but as of 1911, human waste was still a greater source of liquid pollutants than was industrial waste.

Factory activity kept growing, however, and in 1925 the city counted 15,388 factories employing 268,794 people. That growth was expedited by the city's rapid territorial expansion. Primarily by absorbing adjacent towns and villages, but also by filling in coastal shallows, Osaka increased its administrative area more than tenfold between 1889 and 1929, thereby adding substantially to its farmland acreage and raising its population from less than half a million in 1890 to more than 2 million in the 1930s.[98]

By the 1920s, the city's environmental problems due to factory production were generating both public protests and diverse efforts at remediation. But the issues persisted, and in 1928 it was estimated that the city's activities were consuming 2,668,000 tons of coal per year and generating 20,100 tons of coal dust that blanketed the city. The situation prompted one critic to declare:

> Smoke and soot must no longer be symbols of Osaka. A sure way to clear smoke and soot out of the city is to stir up public opinion – today's democracy hinges on citizens taking the initiative in government.[99]

The rhetoric of virtue carried little weight, however, and problems of both air and water pollution continued to worsen. Thus, an analysis of 1934 indicated that by then factory effluent had displaced human waste as the principal source of water pollution despite the city's demographic growth.[100]

In response to this water pollution, during the 1920s–30s the city built a new water treatment plant to improve drinking water. And it gradually installed an elaborate system of underground sewer lines that totaled some 1,200 km in length by 1939.[101]

By the 1930s, Osaka was also experiencing ground subsidence, as factory extraction of underground water lowered the water table, permitting land to settle. The process damaged agricultural acreage as well as buildings and other surface facilities. And near rivers and shoreline it led to submersion and flooding of factories and other structures. By the late 1930s, in the words of one scholar, the city's "canals and rivers were littered with refuse and chemicals. Its air became gray and noxious. And its surface area creased and cracked because of subsidence."[102]

\* \* \*

The rapid expansion of mining and manufacturing output in Japan had clearly benefitted the *zaibatsu*. And it helped assure the state's role as an imperial Power. For lower echelons of the general public, however, it was proving a decidedly mixed blessing. And for the bio-system, it was almost universally damaging, nowhere more so than in riverine and coastal fisheries.

### Fisheries

The basic story of fisheries development during the half-century to 1945 was a story of shift from coastal to pelagic fisheries. That shift was strongly driven by overfishing and pollution, both resulting from technological changes that gradually destroyed inshore marine stocks, forcing fishermen to assume the vast new financial and human risks of deep-sea fishing or simply quit the business.

The way that "improved" technology could increase a fish catch and lead to collapse of a natural resource is nicely illustrated by the herring fishery of Hokkaido.[103] During *bakuhan* centuries, organized fishing operations had regularly harvested the annual herring run, which brought huge schools of fish from the

Sea of Okhotsk down along the Hokkaido coast to the Sea of Japan. Merchants marketed most of the catch as fishmeal fertilizer sold in central Japan. However, during the 1800s, and especially from the 1860s onward, larger and better-designed pound nets enabled herring fishermen to increase greatly the volume of their catch. During the 1870s, they roughly tripled it to some 600,000 metric tons per year, and during the 1890s it exceeded 700,000 per year.

In this process of expanding their catch, the fishermen overtaxed the fish run and started its depletion. After 1902 the herring catch fell sharply to some 450,000 metric tons per year, reviving briefly during World War I through intensified effort, and then declining erratically through the 1920s. As the harvest fell, fishmeal production costs rose, and during the 1930s, development of factory-made fertilizer presented a major new form of market competition that essentially wiped out the struggling fishmeal industry by 1940. Although it revived to a pre-1870s level during World War II and the postwar recovery, during the 1950s it petered out again, one last herring run being fished with little effect in 1958.

Turning to the impact on fisheries of industrial pollution, both mine and factory effluent poisoned streams in many areas.[104] During the 1870s–80s, Ashio copper-mine waste produced massive fish kills on the Watarase, leaving the river nearly barren of fish by 1890. And by 1896 fish dead and dying from the Ashio waste were starting to show up in the Edogawa in Tokyo.

From the 1890s onward, reports also began appearing of fish kills on other rivers about the realm. In Hokkaido the most common source of river poisoning was paper-mill effluent, which generated problems from the 1910s onward. South of there, both mine and factory waste poisoned freshwater fish in numerous rivers from northern Honshu to southern Kyushu. Worse yet, the rivers flowed into estuaries and bays, where their poisons killed saltwater fish, shellfish and edible seaweed, as well as diverse organisms of less interest to fishermen and consumers.[105]

The experience of the Tokyo vicinity merits closer scrutiny as a major example of the problem. Back in *bakuhan* days, Edo Bay and its rivers, such as the Tamagawa, were celebrated for their rich stores of fish, shellfish and high-quality seaweed. Their natural production sustained a vigorous fisheries industry that catered to the city's huge population while also sending high-quality produce to elite consumers in Kyoto and elsewhere.

From about 1875 onward, however, new industrial processes in Yokohama began to produce waste that killed marine life offshore, and starting about 1900, the problem began to spread around the Bay. For another decade or so the Ashio *cause célèbre* pushed other Tokyo-area pollution issues into the shadows, but the spurt of industrial development during World War I brought a number of new industries to the region, and with them came intensified troubles.

Especially Kawasaki, a slender, largely rural area between Tokyo and Yokohama, acquired new factories. The town became an industrial area in part because of its convenient location on the coast and between major urban centers. Besides that, however, in 1912 the Town Assembly – which surely feared being gobbled up by its dynamic neighbors – voted to recruit manufacturing companies, urging them to build factories in town, thereby enabling it to "grow" right alongside those neighbors. The policy worked, and in following decades Kawasaki did indeed evolve into a major manufacturing center, even as Yokohama, Tokyo and other towns in the region also added new factories and expanded existing ones.

During the 1920s, the predictable (in hindsight at least) effects of this trend became visible. As the 1920s and 1930s progressed, the Tamagawa, which flows between Tokyo and Kawasaki, became a site of repeated fish kills due to industrial pollutants, and gradually its fishing industry withered. Other rivers that emptied into the Bay also experienced some extent of fish kill, but the major losses were to the marine fisheries of the Bay itself.

Initially, it was estuarine and coastal fish, shellfish and seaweed populations in the Kawasaki-Yokohama area that were devastated by factory effluent, oil spills from storage facilities and shipping accidents. But as the 1920s advanced, poisons from various factories in Tokyo proper spread the damage northward all the way to top of the Bay, while other spills and outflows extended the losses southward along the Miura Peninsula.

Fishermen's associations and others protested the damage, and various gestures of legislation appeared here and there. However, their effects seem to have been minimal. During the 1930s, the destruction spread, as marine currents carried the pollutants about the Bay and further southward toward the open sea. By the 1940s, the once-splendid fisheries and seaweed fields of Tokyo Bay's western side were largely destroyed, and in following decades the combination of pollution and landfill would complete the Bay's biological ruination.

### Agriculture

In preceding chapters the topic of agriculture-environment relations had two basic aspects. One was the way in which ecological context – climate, topography, geology – shaped agriculture, influencing what was grown, where, how and how much. The other aspect was the way agricultural practice affected the bio-system in terms of biotic distribution, diversity and vitality.

With industrialization, a major new variable came into play – the impact of industrial practices and technologies on agriculture, which led in turn to environmental complications. So, in looking at agriculture during the decades 1890–1945, let us first examine the direct impact of agriculture on the environment and, then, the indirect impact of industry via agriculture.

### 1. The Direct Impact of Agriculture

For the most part agriculture during these decades affected the bio-system in the same way as during earlier centuries. The processes of intensification continued to advance, as mentioned earlier, yielding increases in output, but also making further inroads on the indigenous bio-system. In addition, there were particular developments in all three main sectors of agriculture – animal husbandry, orchardry and field cropping – that merit fuller comment, as does their exceptional impact on Hokkaido.

Regarding animal husbandry, it was expansion of the dairy and beef industries that had the greatest environmental impact, but for a few decades horse-raising also became a flourishing business.

Dairy and beef farming were new enterprises to Japan, and they expanded rapidly during these decades. Bovines could be pastured – or tethered – on areas of hillside, upland or stretches of forest edge that hitherto had been of little use, and that process gradually transformed more and more areas of mixed growth into hardy grassland. And in winter they could be stabled and fed indoors, which permitted dairy farming to flourish even in colder regions. When the animals were stabled, they consumed such grasses and other materials as their keepers could harvest or purchase. Unless imported, most of that feed came from woodland or marginal areas or from former forestland converted to pasture and hay fields, all of which shifted to human use terrain that otherwise would have helped sustain the natural bio-system.

Similar in effect was a major expansion in horse-raising. Long practiced to furnish warrior mounts and draft and pack animals, horse-raising experienced a sharp expansion during these decades in response to changes in transport technology, which we examine briefly below.

Turning to orchardry, a number of new varieties of fruit trees were introduced, but the predominant new practice was apple growing. Because apple trees are more cold-resistant than citrus, they could be grown in northern Tôhoku and Hokkaido, providing a way to utilize many hillsides that hitherto had sustained native biota.

Another major development in orchardry was a vast expansion in mulberry culture – which produced the leaves that fed the silkworms that spun the cocoons that yielded the thread that foreign markets craved. Particularly from the Kantô area westward, the development of foreign silk markets encouraged farmers to bring substantial areas of moderately hilly or marginal land into agricultural use as mulberry orchards, doing so, of course, at the expense of diverse natural growth.

In terms of field-cropping, major expansion was made possible by the development of more cold-resistant crops, in particular new varieties of japonica rice. As we have seen in preceding chapters, during earlier centuries, and especially when "farm manuals" provided agricultural guidance during the *bakuhan* era, farmers had gradually acquired and developed new rice varieties. Then, with the new "scientific" agriculture of post-1870 decades, yet more varieties appeared. These enabled farmers in northern Honshu to grow rice with greater confidence of a full harvest and, as noted earlier, even enabled lowland in Hokkaido to be used for paddy tillage once it had been cleared of natural forest growth.

As that last comment suggests, during these decades, the "opening" of Hokkaido constituted agriculture's greatest assault on the archipelago's bio-system. By 1940, that process had transformed several million acres of pristine woodland into agricultural land, a far more rapid rate of conversion than at any time in Japan's history. As a result, most of Hokkaido came to share the basic characteristic we have noted elsewhere in the archipelago – lowlands support sapiens and its collaborators; uplands sustain the surviving natural biome.

## 2. Industry's Impact via Agriculture

Industrial developments had an impact on agriculture, and thence the ecosystem, in a couple of ways. Most visibly, perhaps, where farmland stood close to, or downstream from, industrial operations, the impact of both gaseous and liquid pollutants could be devastating, ruining crops and fields and forcing farm production to move elsewhere. In addition, industry had a farm-mediated impact on the bio-system through changes in transport technology and through agriculture's utilization of diverse new industrial technologies.

A. *Gaseous and Liquid Pollutants*. Numerous gaseous and liquid pollutants injured natural biota directly, of course, but as noted earlier, much of that damage was inflicted on lowlands already converted to human use, whether for agriculture or other purposes.

Regarding gaseous pollutants specifically, as discussed above, factory production generated a variety of noxious gases that damaged downwind trees, shrubs and other vegetation, causing leaves to wither and blossoms to fail. As for liquid pollution, much poisoning of farmland via liquid effluent occurred in and near cities, where new factories were established amidst farms. It also occurred, however, in the hinterland, either downstream from paper mills or metal-mining operations or on the land surface above coal mines. Especially during the 1920s–30s, such poisoning episodes generated protests by farmers' organizations and modest efforts at remediation by governments and some factories.

The most severe damage to farmland occurred near the major industrial centers, especially Osaka and Tokyo. In the case of Tokyo, for example, factory effluent in the Tamagawa poisoned so many nearby paddy fields during the 1920s–30s that by 1940 most of the once-rich rice production on the Kawasaki side of the river had been abandoned.

Finally, factory water-use damaged farmland in an indirect way. The volume of that use became so great that more and more factories pumped their water directly from underground aquifers. As they did so, they lowered water tables, sometimes causing land subsidence that ruined fields and in other cases wrecking water sources that nearby farmers had used for generations.

These several forms of industrial injury to agriculture affected the broader bio-system in two main ways. They could spur farmers to move elsewhere and open hitherto-undeveloped areas to farm production. Or they could lead farmers to abandon agriculture altogether, which could contribute to Japan's growing dependence on foodstuffs derived from its global resource base, which would mean relying on land elsewhere that had been converted from natural biome to agricultural production.

B. *Transport Technology*. We noted above how the construction of railroads had a direct impact on areas of natural biota. The sharp increase in use of horse-drawn vehicles affected the bio-system indirectly by increasing the demand for pastureland and fodder to sustain the surging number of animals.

To elaborate briefly, during the decades after 1885, cities laid down trolley lines, initially using horses to haul the cars. A substantially greater demand for horses arose as two-wheeled carts (*niguruma*) proliferated to haul the multiplying products of industry, carrying goods between factory and train depot, wharf and market place.[106] Concurrently, the military had use for ever more horses as cavalry mounts and for artillery and other cartage tasks. And in the hinterland, more and more horses were used to pull carts and other new equipment used in farming and logging. Not until the 1920s did the gradual spread of gasoline- and electric-powered conveyances start to ease the demand for more horses and the fodder to feed them.

*C. New Agricultural Technologies.* Of the diverse new technologies adopted by farmers during these decades, three seem to merit comment here because of their environmental impacts: new types of fertilizer; new types of machinery; and concrete construction.

Regarding fertilizer, as we noted earlier, forest litter, other mulch, night soil and other bio-waste were initially supplemented by guano from the Marianas and soymeal from Manchuria. During the 1920s, however, chemical fertilizers produced in factories in Japan started to displace the natural organic fertilizers that had sustained agricultural output for centuries.

Chemical fertilizers gained popularity for several reasons. For one thing, the supply of mulch was limited, and more and more was being used as animal feed instead of fertilizer. Second, night soil was becoming scarce. As cities grew during the decades after 1890, they gradually installed underground sewage systems. These collected more and more of the raw sewage that previously had been removed as night soil, transporting it to nearby rivers for discharge or, eventually, to sewage treatment plants. When released into streams, the sewage, which contained more and more industrial waste, proved increasingly toxic and destructive to downstream biomes. And later, when processed at sewage-disposal plants, it left a chemical stew that could not safely be employed as fertilizer material and instead was used for landfill.

In addition, chemical fertilizers had some strongly attractive features. They had the advantage of being faster-acting in the soil and therefore more useful for multiple-cropping. As their production expanded, moreover, they became competitive in price with the guano and soymeal brought from afar. And perhaps, most importantly, they were easier to apply, saving farmers many, many hours of labor. In consequence, as the 1930s advanced, their use spread rapidly. For Japan as a whole, some 70 percent of nitrate and phosphate fertilizers were factory-made by 1940.[107]

That extensive use of chemical fertilizers created new environmental problems, however. When raw material was processed in the factory into forms of potash, phosphates or nitrates, the product would be water-soluble, which made it quickly accessible to plants. That very quality meant, however, that the material also became subject to easy dispersal into nearby lowlands or streams, where it could seriously disrupt natural bio-systems.

Much more visible than these changes in fertilizer use was the adoption of new types of farm machinery. As this table shows, the use of such machinery skyrocketed during the 1920s–30s, steadily improving farmers' productivity.

*Agricultural Machines in Use, 1920–42* [108]

| | Electric motors | Oil-powered motors | Power tillers | Irrigation pumps | Powered threshers | Powered hullers |
|---|---|---|---|---|---|---|
| 1920 | 683 | 1,785 | | | | |
| 1927 | 11,603 | 39,406 | | 17,413 | 29,820 | |
| 1931 | 28,306 | 63,459 | 98 | 26,940 | 55,954 | 88,637 |
| 1937 | 66,718 | 125,583 | 537 | 44,189 | 128,620 | 117,738 |
| 1942 | 144,649 | 316,544 | 7,436 | 92,512 | 357,129 | 204,548 |

The use of this machinery meant, however, that more factories and follow-up facilities were needed to produce, sell and maintain the machines, facilities that occupied space and generated diverse sorts of environmental pollutants. Moreover, the machines were mostly powered by gasoline, which came from pollutant-spouting refineries and produced noxious exhaust when burned. Or else they were powered by electricity that was mostly generated by hydropower plants, whose presence had transformed lush interior valleys into reservoirs of relatively little biotic value.

Finally, less noticeable than farm machinery was the use of cement in concrete, which served diverse purposes of value to farmers. Employed mainly in urban construction, cement also came to be used in such riparian structures as dikes and irrigation inlets, dams and canals. During the 1920s–30s, cement plants near cities generated noxious dust that poisoned nearby vegetation and sickened people, leading to a number of forceful protests. But its use in river management proved very effective, enabling farmers to use more riverside lowlands without risk of sudden floods ruining their crops.

The scale and extent of concrete construction required to contain seasonal surges of flood water created wide, straight, totally "unnatural" stream beds that might stand nearly barren for much of the year and that troubled the aesthetically sensitive. More seriously, in environmental terms, this channeling of rivers reduced yet further the natural overflow areas that had constituted swampland along the lower reaches of so many Japanese rivers, thereby reducing another portion of the surviving indigenous bio-system.

In sum, then, industrial agriculture extended human domination of the archipelago's lowlands and furthered human inroads into the surviving upland bio-system, doing so, of course, at the expense of natural biota. That trend in uplands was fostered even more vigorously by developments in forestry.

### Forestry

Forests and forestry in imperial Japan experienced changes that were at least as complex and disruptive as those of agriculture. They were initiated around 1870 by a booming lumber market and by the changes in woodland-control – the replacement of "use-rights" with land ownership – discussed in Chapter 6. The reckless logging precipitated by those developments was sustained in later decades by continuing vigorous demand for timber and by adoption of new logging technologies.

That persistent demand was met in part, but only modestly and belatedly, by increased imports. Mostly it was met by domestic woodlands, which in the outcome were badly overcut, with the result that their condition deteriorated sharply. That trend, in turn, spurred implementation of long-range programs of reforestation, and by the 1920s–30s, those were reversing the trend toward upland devastation.

Before looking at those matters, let us note again the basic geography of these woodlands, which fundamentally determined how they were treated. Forests were found on uplands, not lowlands, and they covered some 80 percent of the realm. They generally were identified as either *sanrin* or *gen'ya*, "high forest" or "scrubland". Healthy *sanrin* was understood to consist of good stands of timber, and it was mostly found on steeply sloped bedrock mountainsides that lay beyond convenient walking distance of nearby villages. Healthy *gen'ya* consisted of diverse grasses and scrub growth, and was mainly found on terrace deposits adjacent to agricultural plains or on lower hillsides near villages. Woodland so badly denuded that it survived as eroded, desiccated wasteland was known as *hageyama*, or "bald mountains".

Let us examine the experience of this variegated woodland in terms of four topics: land-control arrangements; pertinent technological developments, patterns of overuse; and processes of rehabilitation.

### 1. Woodland Control

As noted in Chapter 6, in the early 1870s the government in Tokyo – which was operated by urban samurai with little understanding of village life – had abandoned the hoary custom of landed use-rights, replacing it with the "modern" principle of land ownership. On farmland, that policy was implemented quite easily within a decade. On woodland, however, the process of establishing boundaries, and thereby the limits of ownership, proved a gargantuan task because of the immensity of wooded tracts, their location on predominantly steep hillsides, and the fact that most of them had never been carefully surveyed.

The task was made even more difficult by widespread, angry and enduring resistance and sabotage. In consequence, its implementation advanced only slowly and with great difficulty, dragging on for half a century. By the 1920s, however, the surveying and resurveying of woodland was largely complete, and most disputes had been resolved or gone into sullen abeyance.

Woodland then totaled some 24 million hectares. About 37 percent of it was "government" (national and imperial household) forest; about 44 percent was "private" (household) woodland; and about 18 percent was locally owned as communal land.[109] Most of the *sanrin* was governmental; most of the *gen'ya* was communal and private property.

This division of forest types reflected the dissimilarity of village and governmental needs. Most villagers and communities wanted *gen'ya* for diverse local purposes. In many places *gen'ya* sites were usable for orchards, pasturage or dry field crops. And most of their vegetative cover – forbs, small bamboo, other grasses, scrub brush and oak or other types of coppice growth – served numerous farm needs, notably as fodder and fertilizer material.

Government, on the other hand, wanted for use or sale the large timber found in *sanrin*. And eventually, as excessive deforestation gradually produced unprecedented downstream damage, government control of most steep mountainsides also provided a basis on which programs of flood control and sustained forest rehabilitation could be pursued.

### 2. Logging Technology

New technologies made the felling, transport and processing of timber much, much faster than ever before. Their use began in 1868 when loggers were permitted to use the cross-cut saw to fell trees and cut them to log length. Such saws had been used in the decades around 1600, but during *bakuhan* centuries they had been outlawed to stop the timber theft that their speed and silent operation had facilitated.

Around 1870, sawmills were introduced to Japan, with water-powered mills gradually being erected near cities and at the foot of logging sites. They increased dramatically the speed with which logs could be converted to boards, planks and framing timbers. Where the sawing was done near the logging site, moreover, mills greatly facilitated lumber transport. Then, from about 1910 onward, the use of electric lighting allowed longer working days at sawmills, especially during winter months. By then, Japanese mills were processing some 8–10 million meters of logs per year.[110]

Additionally, in 1886, the pulpwood mill was introduced. Before then, Japanese paper had been made from various fibrous materials, but little came from timber. From that year onward, pulpwood paper rapidly displaced older types, meaning that a huge new demand was placed on woodland. Thus, by 1913, pulpwood output measured some 80,000 tons annually, a level that grew rapidly thereafter.[111] Besides consuming upstream forest growth, pulpwood mills also became a major source of downstream pollutants wherever they were established.

In 1907, the first plywood factory was put into operation. It, too, created a new way to use timber, thus adding to total demand on the forest. Moreover, both pulpwood and plywood could be produced from inferior wood and smaller trees, so their production gave loggers more reason to practice clear-cutting, with all its destructive downstream ramifications.

Another major area of technological change was timber transport. Change in that area proceeded more slowly, however, because it threatened powerful social interests.[112] To explain, during *bakuhan* centuries, logs had been transported from felling site to market via river and sea. They were moved along by an elaborately organized system of professional fellers, skidders, trestle and river-chute operators, raftsmen, boatmen and others. When railroads started to be built during the 1870s, these groups soon realized that flatcars could move logs and lumber to market faster and more cheaply than could river rafting, and would, therefore, destroy their own professions and livelihoods.

Consequently, they organized strong resistance to the introduction of rail lines into forested mountain areas, and not until after 1900 did railways begin making substantial inroads into the river-rafting transport system. But as they did, both entrepreneurial and governmental logging operations rapidly extended permanent rail lines into forested valleys, installed temporary forest railways and set up motorized tramways to move logs down to railhead loading sites.

As years passed, more and bigger sawmills and other devices were installed. Water power gradually gave way to steam engines, and, by 1930, to gasoline power. By then, too, Caterpillar tractors were being imported for use in pulling trains of logging sleds through woodland to railheads. As of 1940, the technology of timber extraction and processing had thus been utterly transformed, with the changes sharply increasing the rate at which woodland could be stripped of trees.

### 3. Effects of Woodland Overuse

Thanks to this evolving combination of factors – social pressure to harvest timber while one could, expanding and diversifying demand for wood products, and faster techniques of timber extraction and processing – Japan's forests, and *sanrin* in particular, experienced severe overcutting during the decades to 1910 or so. From Hokkaido to Kyushu the consequences became ever more worrisome: disappearance of accessible timber, the necessity of logging ever more difficult terrain, erosion and escalating downstream damage and gradually rising prices of wood products.[113]

These trends had two major effects: they spurred timber imports and – as we shall see in the next section – they fostered the development of forest-rehabilitation programs for use on *sanrin*. Concurrently, *gen'ya* also experienced deterioration followed by gradual recovery.

Regarding timber imports, their growth was a result of both a hungry domestic timber market and government success in creating an empire. In topographic terms, Hokkaido's vast expanse of virgin lowland forest constituted a new "colonial" region for exploitation. But in more strictly legalistic terms, the most important source of timber imports was Karafuto, which Japan acquired from Russia in 1905.

Karafuto gave the realm a rich new source of old-growth fir and spruce (*ezomatsu* and *todomatsu*) that had many uses. Especially during the 1920s–30s, the colony produced vast quantities of timber (nearly 20 percent of total consumption), while other colonies and foreign areas, notably North America, also yielded substantial volumes (over 10 percent of the total).[114] Then, however, World War II closed off most of those imports as trade shriveled and the country's cargo fleet was pressed into military-related tasks. Nevertheless, as the war dragged on, demand for timber became frenetic. Even useable trees in city parks were cut down to meet wartime needs. And *sanrin* was ravaged throughout the realm, a process that continued until around 1950 as the country struggled to rebuild the cities destroyed by fire bombing.

Even in the heyday of pre-1940 timber imports, then, foreign wood met at most a third of Japan's needs. The rest came almost exclusively from domestic *sanrin*. And the technological changes cited above – as well as the rehabilitation practices that we note below – had their impact mainly on those woodlands.

*Gen'ya*, on the other hand, was primarily affected by other, previously cited changes of post-1890 decades. That is to say, tea, mulberry and apple orchardry, as well as animal pasturage, ate away at *gen'ya* and woodland margins. In addition, farmers demanded more fertilizer and harvested their *gen'ya* aggressively to get it.

During the 1920s, however, imported fertilizers – guano, fishmeal, soymeal – started easing the demand for mulch, because their application was so much less labor intensive. Then, during the 1930s, the development of factory-made chemical fertilizers further relieved the pressure on *gen'ya*. By then, too, coal and gasoline were easing demand for fuel wood. So the deterioration of *gen'ya* slowly reversed – until around 1940, when wartime scarcities again led to harvesting whatever was available for food, fuel or fertilizer.

### 4. Forest Rehabilitation

As noted in Chapter 6, regenerative forestry had developed during *bakuhan* centuries as an aspect of the "practical learning" found in "farm manuals". And after 1870, it was given valuable legitimization by the "scientific" forestry developments then occurring in Europe. Mainly applied to *sanrin* by government foresters, "modern" programs of reforestation began taking shape during the 1890s.

By then, woodland surveying was making good progress despite persistent disputes with villagers, and government foresters began developing general management plans for the woodland they supervised. The plans would regulate logging, guide programs of seedling development, afforestation and aftercare, and control such construction programs as creation and maintenance of woodland roads and railroads, flood-control dams and river-management projects. Foresters were trained and deployed, and from the 1910s onward, programs of reforestation gradually revitalized Japan's woodlands.

Given the vast extent of woodland needing attention, much of the reforestation work continued to rely on natural reseeding and selective aftercare to restore mixed stands. But as time passed, more and more woodland was planted to preferred species – notably *sugi* and *hinoki*. Seedlings were set out in plantation stands and given sustained aftercare, and in consequence *sanrin* gradually evolved from diversified, multi-aged forest to even-aged monoculture stands.

Despite the "unnaturalness" of this trend and its negative impact on biodiversity, the basic condition of woodland gradually improved. Downstream damage abated, and by the late 1930s, timber output was increasing without creating new downstream problems. Then, of course, wartime and postwar demand ravaged the realm. By then, however, the advantages of reforestation had again been demonstrated, and as we note in Chapter 8, after 1950, Japan entered a complex new era of forest revitalization and change.

## RECAPITULATION

In sum, then, the decades 1890–1940 were for Japan a time of change unprecedented in both speed and scope. This was so in terms of rate and scale of population growth, degree of social complexity, extent of human mobility and relocation to urban centers, and scope and impact of technological diversification.

Clearly, Japan had moved from the age of intensive agriculture into the age of industrial society, although in terms of rural/urban balance it was only "half-way there" as of 1940. It had become deeply reliant on fossil fuel as well as other industrial energy sources and the technology that made them available for use. And it had shifted from a resource base grounded in the archipelago to one that depended in essential ways on goods and services from elsewhere, the global resource base.

The strategy of empire-building, which had been adopted in emulation of the other "Great Powers" as a means to help secure that base, ultimately failed at horrific cost. By then, however, it had helped to enmesh Japan deeply in the global arrangements of industrial society.

Unsurprisingly, change of this scale and speed had major environmental ramifications. Most obviously, it transformed the island of Hokkaido from an almost completely forested realm sporting a rich population of "wild" animals and plants into a realm modeled on the other main islands of the archipelago. Thus, lowlands were given over to human affairs while uplands retained most of the surviving indigenous bio-system.

For the archipelago as a whole, by the 1930s even mountain biomes had been substantially modified by intensive and widespread logging and the planting of ever more even-aged evergreen monocultures in place of self-seeded, mixed forest. And while lowlands still served humans and their collaborating species as in the past, they did so at an unprecedented level of intensity. Agricultural yield was higher per acre of tilled land than ever before, and it included a greater variety of products. In consequence, it could still support most of the much larger human population that was packed and stacked as never before in sprawling urban agglomerations.

The industrial techniques that enabled this rapid and far-reaching growth and change also produced pollutants and other side-effects that damaged terrestrial biota. More seriously, they substantially altered both riverine and inshore saltwater biomes, sharply diminishing their biodiversity and vitality. The loss of nearby marine harvest helped foster the rise of pelagic fishing. And that trend was part of the larger growth in reliance on a global resource base.

It is worth keeping in mind that just as the shift to industrial technology had environmental ramifications within the archipelago, so too it had consequences for the global resource base. Because our inquiry focuses on the archipelago, the impact of deep-sea fishing on the areas where it was practiced do not receive the attention they deserve. Similarly, the consumption of goods extracted from terrestrial sources elsewhere in the world had impacts similar to those in Japan, but they lie even farther beyond the scope of this study.

# 8 Entrepreneurial Industrialism, 1945–2010

Military defeat in 1945 ended Japan's brief experience as a major player in the global politico-military realm. Then, however, its rapid economic recovery and expansion in subsequent decades transformed it into a major player in the global economic realm.

As the terms "politico-military" and "economic" suggest, the sharp 1940s break in Japan's history also entailed a rebalancing of its domestic power structure. Whereas the political elite had dominated the commercial elite in pre-1945 decades, after defeat the latter became more influential in shaping both foreign and domestic policies, while the former seized upon economic successes of the day to help rebuild and sustain its own credibility at home and abroad.

During those postwar decades, Japan's presence in the global economy gradually became so pronounced that the society's performance – both its years of rapid growth into the 1980s and its years of sharp slowdown after 1990 – has received a vast amount of attention in foreign-language studies, English most particularly.[1] Here we must focus on those facets of this richly documented story that pertain to the realm's environmental experience.

In "big picture" terms of human history, developments of these decades bring us back to the "growth and stasis" patterns that we have already noted in both early and later agricultural society. In those cases, centuries of population growth and socio-economic expansion gave way to periods of population stasis or even decline and growing social stress and adaptation – at least among the holders of power and privilege, whose condition can be inferred from the historical record.

In broader environmental terms, we shall note, *en passant*, how the character of the archipelago has continued to shape human affairs. And we shall note more fully the diverse ways in which industrial development has continued to generate poisons damaging to the human populace. But ultimately we seek to understand the broader impact this society's activities have had on the ecosystem of the archipelago – Japan's domestic resource base – and on the ecosystem of the rest of the planet – its global resource base. We shall see, however, that because Japan's impact on the global ecosystem is totally entangled with the impact of other industrial societies, only a few rough generalizations can be made.

As mentioned in the preface to this book, the key variables determining human impact on the bio-system are the density of human presence, the level of material consumption per capita and the technologies employed to provide those goods. These factors determine: (1) the amount of space that gets shifted to "non-natural" functions (for example, agriculture, buildings, highways, golf courses, waste-disposal sites); (2) the extent to which other resources – both renewable (for example, forests, fisheries) and non-renewable (for example, fossil fuels, metal ores) – become depleted; and (3) the extent to which the surviving bio-system is damaged (for example, by scattered structures, high-energy transmission facilities or pollutants, which can damage terrain, maim and poison vulnerable species, spur others to excessive proliferation that disrupts sustainable biotic balances, or alter climate in ways that destroy biota, disrupt bio-systems and undermine bio-vitality).

So let us look briefly at the overall socio-economic history of the decades since 1945 and then address more closely the issues most relevant to our environmental focus – trends in demography, in material consumption and in technological development and change as those relate to mining, manufacturing, fisheries, agriculture and forestry.

## SOCIO-ECONOMIC HISTORY: A SUMMARY

The history of these decades is commonly, and with good reason, presented in three phases.[2] The first, which may be dated 1945–55, encompasses Japan's recovery from defeat and return to global economic activity. The second, dated 1955–85, covers the period of economic boom when Japan's imprint on the world economy became most pronounced, when the level of domestic material consumption reached unprecedented heights, and when the malign effects of industrial growth and pollution became most evident. The third phase, from the late 1980s to the present, consists of the post-boom decades when growth slowed substantially and the signs of historical "stasis" became more evident.

### The Years of Recovery, 1945–55

The years 1945–55 seem most noteworthy for their confusion and difficulty, particularly in terms of leadership organization and policy, but also, for two to three years after the war, in terms of basic public health. On the other hand, in some ways those postwar years were more striking than the post-1955 decades for both the extent of socio-economic change and the eventual gains in social well-being that they witnessed.

#### 1. Postwar Accomplishments and Perplexities
Regarding the magnitude of change and improvement during the years to 1955, it was rooted, of course, in the scale of disaster that befell the realm in 1944–45. For example, from 1947 to 1952, overall industrial production grew at an average rate of nearly 30 percent per year, and rapid growth continued through the 1950s.[3] Yet

by 1955 these gains in the overall economy had only restored Japan to its prewar level of output and given the general public a level of well-being comparable to that of prewar years.

Nevertheless, the accomplishments seemed so gratifying that they prompted the media to characterize the country's first official postwar boom (sustained from summer 1956 into the spring of 1957) as the "Jinmu Boom", in honor of the country's mythological founder.[4] Japan had been born again!

Nor were the good feelings unwarranted. The improvements since 1945 were suggested not only by the economic recovery but also by a sharp drop in tuberculosis deaths, broader trends of reduced mortality rate and increased life expectancy, a baby boom, and a resultant rapid increase in population, which we note more fully further on.

Accomplishments apparent in retrospect were not so obvious at the time, however. Far more evident, in the aftermath of defeat, was the confusion in leadership. Most obviously, military leaders and their agenda had been discredited, replaced by a foreign (essentially American) occupying authority with dictatorial power, strong opinion and its own agenda. In addition, party politicians and officials in the various government ministries were facing uncharted territory; the old *zaibatsu* were under attack and in disarray, and new forces, most notably labor unions, were beginning to exercise unprecedented influence.

With empire gone, merchant fleet sunk and industry ravaged, the crucial economic question facing this jumbled leadership was what policy would enable it to rebuild devastated cities and infrastructure and secure even the most basic necessities for a population that was more than twice as large as that which the archipelago had sustained during *bakuhan* centuries. No one, in fact, knew the answer. However, from even before the surrender, planning by various groups had commenced, and as the years 1945–50 advanced, a number of plans, often at odds with one another, appeared and were applied with mixed success.[5]

The root of the planning problem was that two irreconcilable truths were apparent. One truth was that, given the population's size and its surviving urban and industrial facilities, the archipelago could by itself never meet all its people's basic needs, much less their diverse wants. So some alternative to empire must be found, some new version of the global resource base. The other, more immediate truth was that, with empire gone, export markets almost nil and industry able neither to produce nor ship much with which to pay for imports, society was, at least in the short term, forced to rely heavily on that domestic resource base, its inadequacy notwithstanding.

Given this fundamental contradiction, planners focused on basic issues of the short term. Accordingly, plans and policy during the immediate postwar years strove to maximize Japan's domestic energy sources. Two types of energy were needed: that to sustain human activity and that to fuel industrial machinery.

### 2. Regarding Energy Policy

Above all else, human activity required an adequate food supply, of which farmers produced fully 90 percent and fishermen nearly 10 percent. The severe shortages of 1945–46 were eased by relief supplies from abroad, and in following years both farm and fishery output grew. By 1950 agriculture had regained its mid-1930s level, and by 1952 it was higher yet, some 85 percent above its low point in 1945.[6] And fisheries recovery was not far behind, reaching prewar levels in the early 1950s. For about 30 years thereafter, this food output continued expanding, until increases in imports and other trends reversed the gains.

The postwar increases in agricultural output were not easily achieved because little potentially arable land remained. Moreover, imported and maritime fertilizers were no longer readily available, and accessible woodland was too denuded to yield substantial mulch. So planners sought to maximize farm output by increasing the production and use of chemical fertilizers and also by expediting their renewed importation. Thanks to these focused efforts, the use of potash and nitrate fertilizers regained their prewar level by 1949, while phosphate use did so in 1950.[7]

Due to the rapid post-1945 population growth, however, simply regaining the 1930s level of output was insufficient. So, food imports remained essential, and of necessity they did continue. Indeed, they grew, in terms of value, volume and proportion of total food consumption. Thus, whereas imported food constituted about 8 percent of a person's annual food expenditure in 1950, by 1955 it exceeded 10 percent.[8] Together with the increase in domestic production, these imports sufficed to feed the realm's growing population. But they also reconfirmed the inadequacy of Japan's domestic resource base.

Turning to the problem of energy for powering industry, there too planners faced hard choices. With accessible woodland already severely overcut, fuel wood – which had very limited industrial utility in any case – was not an option.

Moreover, known petroleum sources were negligible. And during the 1950s, exploration confirmed – despite a brief surge of great optimism – that domestic oil and gas supplies, nearly all on the Sea of Japan coastal shelf, were very limited. Within a few years nuclear power would emerge as a long-term solution, but it would require immense investment and would, in any case, ultimately depend on foreign sources of uranium. And with Hiroshima and Nagasaki still reeking of radioactivity, it was not a real prospect in the immediate postwar years.

Then, of course, there was electric power, and after war's end, its production recovered rapidly (see Table 32). By maximizing the output of existing generator capacity and gradually adding new facilities, producers were able to double the output of 1945 (and surpass prewar levels) by 1950 and nearly triple it by 1955.[9]

There was, however, a basic problem with electricity as a "domestic" energy source. Proponents of hydroelectric production spoke enthusiastically about Japan's rich supply of rushing streams that could generate it, but by 1955 careful studies had revealed that the most promising sites were already in use. One could add new hydro plants only by sacrificing vast acreages of arable land or by damming intermontane streams that were distant, difficult and costly to reach and utilize, and subject to sharp seasonal fluctuation.

So, instead of hydroelectric power, of necessity coal- and oil-fired thermal generators came into favor. As the 1950s advanced, more thermal plants were built, mostly powered by domestic coal. Very quickly, however, imported oil emerged as the fuel of choice. Before 1947 such imports had been minimal, but during the early 1950s they grew sixfold, reaching some 8.5 million kiloliters per year by 1955 – a quantity roughly four times the prewar peak level.[10] In the end, then, increased electricity usage, far from enhancing Japan's energy independence, only confirmed the necessity for a global resource base.

Lacking both domestic petroleum and the exports necessary to pay for vast oil imports, postwar energy planners had to focus on the archipelago's coal – most of which was bituminous – as the key source of domestic energy. As noted in Chapter 7, however, by 1945 the mines had been harshly exploited. Coal seams were relatively thin, their working faces situated at the end of long tunnels, and many of them located beneath coastal waters. So coal production was very dangerous and highly inefficient. Nevertheless, coal appeared to be the only domestic energy source that could be substantially expanded, given the technology and funding available.

So the government moved to boost coal production, doing so with a key purpose of fostering more steel production. Steel was necessary not only to rebuild industry as a whole and provide farm machinery to increase food output, but also to produce export goods that could eventually generate funds to pay for imported oil and other raw materials. And the planners' efforts enjoyed some success. Starting in 1946 at well below half of late-1930s production, coal output began to recover, and by 1955 it had doubled to some 42 million metric tons per year.[11] That increase, together with expanded steel output and other advances, enabled mining and manufacturing as a whole to grow more than fivefold by 1955, nearly reaching their pre-1945 maximum.[12]

### 3. Recovery: A Narrative

By 1955, Japan had thus enjoyed considerable success in reviving and expanding its domestic resource base sufficiently to sustain most of its people and rebuild its economy. However, the grand figures of overall growth notwithstanding, for society as a whole, it was a tough slog to the later-1950s rewards.

During 1945–47, most people were able to survive the ongoing food shortage, myriad other scarcities, raging inflation and massive dislocation thanks to relief supplies, diligent foraging, and a pervasive black market that responded opportunistically as needs appeared. Gradually, bomb craters were filled, streets cleaned up and charred remnants of buildings removed. City provisioning arrangements revived, and by the autumn of 1948 malnutrition had ceased to be a widespread urban problem. As cement production revived (more than tripling during 1946–49), construction of plain concrete buildings accelerated, replacing temporary shacks and other accommodations as basic dwelling and business structures for urban populations. Railroad service improved; other infrastructure gradually recovered; and slowly people returned to the cities.

From 1947 onward, the escalating US-Soviet "cold war" led to a basic shift in American policy toward Japan. Instead of simply viewing Tokyo as an immoral enemy to be punished and rectified, American leaders saw it as a potentially valuable asset best kept on Washington's side of the new global game. That shift facilitated more expansive economic planning, faster growth in Japan's foreign trade, an increase in oil and machinery imports, and faster and less restricted industrial development.

Then, in summer 1950, the outbreak of the Korean War abruptly escalated American military demand for Japanese-made goods and services, and the economy began to thrive. Thus, between 1949 and 1953, Japan's "export" trade more than doubled, with most of the growth being due to "special procurement" by US forces engaged in the Korean War and by the personal spending of American soldiers who were in Japan because of that war.[13]

With the necessary foreign currency newly available, crude oil imports spurted ahead, as noted above, helping power the revival of industry. Thanks to that "Korean War boom", business improved broadly: "leather, rubber, textiles, steel, trucks, cement, and lumber all reported brisk sales".[14]

For planners, of course, the Korean War boom was merely a stopgap solution, and longer-term concerns still had to be addressed. The signing of a multi-nation peace treaty on 28 April 1952 formally ended the occupiers' authority and restored Japan's formal autonomy, but the core tasks remained – namely, maximizing self-sufficiency and generating long-term exports to pay for sustained imports from a slowly redeveloping global resource base.

In sum then, by 1955, Japanese society had not only regained its prewar level of industrial activity and social well-being but also was moving beyond the postwar attempt to anchor its future in domestic resources, returning instead to the prewar vision of a global resource base. But whereas the prewar base had been grounded in politico-military empire, in the manner of nineteenth-century Euro-American empire builders, the new base was being built on entrepreneurial activity.

*The Boom Years, 1955–85*

The boom years from 1955 to the later 1980s are striking for their rate of sustained economic growth and for the extent to which that growth benefitted society at large, rather than just the favored few. Indeed, those decades have served as a sort of poster child for the ideology of "growth is good".

Even then, however, not everything went well. For one thing, as time passed and human consumption grew, the domestic resource base proved less and less adequate. Both the food production for human energy and the fuel production for industrial energy required more and more supplementing with imports. And while Japan did have striking success in re-establishing the needed global resource base, it also encountered unnerving reminders of how unreliable such a base can be.

More destructively, as we shall note at some length when discussing technology and the environment, the stunning industrial expansion of those boom years produced a rash of pollution problems. These did grievous, even irreparable harm to many people and places, mainly fishermen and their coastal biomes but also farmers, industrial laborers and diverse others.

Finally, the very vigor of the economy bred elite corruption and speculation that culminated in major scandals and financial collapse in 1988–89. That outcome ended the boom and ushered Japan into an era of comparative socio-economic stasis that continued past 2010. Before looking at the problems of resource base and economic abuse, however, let us consider the overall story of socio-economic boom.

*1. On Economic Vigor*

Because Japan's domestic resource base was proving inadequate, industrial production had to serve two core purposes. Most crucially, it had to generate exports to pay for imports from the global resource base. Second, it had to provide goods and services for a domestic demand that grew exponentially in response to population increase and escalating material expectations. So manufacturers had to produce high-quality goods for those types of growing global demand in which they could produce at prices that were competitive both at home and abroad. And that task required mastering – and becoming creators of – the newest technologies, as well as organizing production so as to maximize its efficiency.[15]

The effort was strikingly successful. As Table 18 shows, whereas gross tonnage of exports in 1955 was less than 8 million metric tons, by 1985 it exceeded 94 million. Those exports included industrial supplies and equipment (such as chemicals, electrical machinery and precision instruments) as well as popular consumer goods (such as household appliances, musical instruments and automobiles), which sold in growing quantities. Those exports in turn paid for the imports (notably foodstuffs, fossil fuel, metal ore and timber) that sustained the expanding production.

Initially, exports failed to cover those import costs. Thus, in 1955 exports were valued at 724 billion yen, as against imports of 890 billion. However, by 1965 the balance had shifted in Japan's favor, and after 1980, there was a large and persistent export surplus that generally fluctuated in the 10–20 percent range.[16]

Sustained by these gains in trade, both overall industrial production and, more specifically, that of consumer goods grew about 12-fold during the decades 1955–85.[17] Because the population grew only from 89.3 to 121.0 million during those three decades (see Table 1), that gain in consumer-goods output enabled per-capita consumption to rise substantially.

The gains in domestic standard of living, which were evident in improved health and longer lives, also showed up in numerous other measures, such as better housing and greater leisure-time expenditures as well as increased consumption of diverse consumer goods (see Tables 14, 15, 17). For an extreme example, as Table 24 indicates, whereas passenger cars registered for private use numbered some 167,000 in 1955, they numbered 25.6 million in 1985.[18] However, these striking material accomplishments notwithstanding, there also were worrisome countervailing developments.

*2. On Problems of the Day*

As mentioned above, two troubling developments of the day deserve note here. One was growing evidence of Japan's deepening vulnerability to the vagaries of a global resource base. The other was escalating financial abuses that were fostered by rapid economic growth. A third, more grievous set of problems that accompanied this growth – worker injury and illness and environmental pollution – are treated later in the chapter.

*A. Resource Issues.* The vagaries of a global resource base were particularly worrisome because that base became the primary source of society's primary energy supplies.

So reliability was important to everyone's daily life. However, this resource base, unlike the empire-centered base of pre-1945 years, was an entrepreneurial base over which Tokyo had essentially no control. Rather, it was subject to the will of foreign elites, whether political or economic, who pursued their own agendas.

It was an aspect of foodstuff vulnerability that proved particularly alarming, although issues of fossil-fuel dependence ultimately proved more damaging in socio-economic terms. Ever since the 1860s, as noted in Chapter 7, Japan had been both exporting and importing foodstuffs. However, from about the 1890s food imports had begun to exceed exports, and by the mid-1930s, only about 80 percent of Japan's total food consumption was met by domestic production. Nearly all of the other 20 percent came from empire.

Following the turmoil of defeat and recovery, foodstuff imports began to grow again. By the later 1980s, as Table 22 shows, Japan had become so dependent on them that national self-sufficiency in calories had dropped from around 80 percent in the late 1950s to the vicinity of 50 percent.[19]

Basically, of course, this century-long downward trend in food self-sufficiency reflected the growth in Japan's population. However, as we note more fully later on, in part it reflected growth in individual height and weight and changes in culinary taste, as well as a sustained decline in acreage devoted to food production.

It was a "traditional" food source – soybeans (*daizu*) – that became emblematic of Japan's foodstuff vulnerability in the new global resource base. Soybeans were the raw material from which consumers obtained such basic dietary items as soy sauce (*shôyu*), bean paste (*miso*) and bean curd (*tôfu*). Back in the 1930s, large quantities of soy products had been imported from the empire, and after the war other sites, most notably the USA, became the foreign source. By 1970, as Table 21 indicates, those imports constituted nearly the entire supply – fully 96 percent – of Japan's soybeans.[20]

The "soybean problem" erupted suddenly in 1973. At the time, the American president, Richard Nixon, was responding to harsh political issues of the day with a set of bold moves that became known as the "Nixon shocks". One of those moves was an abrupt freeze on the export of soybeans to Japan. In fact, the issue passed quickly because Nixon soon lifted the ban in response to pressure from US soybean producers and marketers. For a short while, however, the freeze – so reminiscent of the US-imposed freeze on oil imports back in 1941 – provoked great alarm in Japan because of society's heavy consumption of the imported beans. The move threw into sharp relief the realm's vulnerability to such "trade retaliation".

That vulnerability showed up much more disruptively in the area of fossil fuel supplies. By the later 1950s, when domestic coal was still the primary source of industrial energy, the task of maximizing energy self-sufficiency was looking more and more challenging. Coal remained the planners' fuel of choice, but the character and condition of Japan's coal seams, together with aspects of the "culture" of this mining industry, made increased production dangerous and difficult and yielded a fuel that was relatively inefficient to use.[21]

Primarily because of these factors, attempts to increase coal output ultimately proved disappointing. Production never regained its pre-1945 maximum of some

56 million metric tons per year. And after output did peak at some 51 million tons in 1960, it began a sharp and sustained decline – to 22 million tons in 1973, 16 million in 1985 and 3.1 million in 2000, essentially ceasing by 2005.[22]

In the face of this massive shrinkage in production, imports of coal increased dramatically. Indeed, they grew so much in response to industrial demand that the country's total coal supply grew from 46 million metric tons in 1955 (of which over 92 percent – 42.7 million – came from domestic mines) to more than 110 million tons in 1985 (of which only about 15 percent was produced at home). And in following years, those trajectories continued to diverge: for example, in 2005 all 180.8 million tons of coal were imported.[23]

More strikingly, the crude oil supply, almost entirely imported, grew some 30-fold from 10 million kiloliters in 1955 to 306 million in 1973, after which it dropped back, thereafter mostly fluctuating in the 240–90 million range. Also, by the 1980s, natural gas was being imported, adding substantially to the total energy supply.[24]

A major function of coal and oil imports was to power thermal electricity generators. During the boom decades that demand escalated so rapidly that it spurred the adoption of nuclear power generation despite the widespread safety concerns evoked by that technology. As Tables 31 and 32 show, between 1965 and 1985 some 16 commercial nuclear power plants were put into operation, and by the latter year, those plants were providing about a quarter of Japan's electricity.

Even as nuclear power eased the need for imported fossil fuel in electricity-generation, a burgeoning use of cars and trucks was creating a huge new demand for it, as we note more fully later on. The upshot was that Japanese industry was becoming ever more hostage to foreign energy sources, mainly in the Middle East. Regimes in that region recognized that their oil reserves could serve as useful diplomatic bargaining chips, and in 1973 and again in 1978–80 they played them. They reduced output and sales, in the process creating temporary scarcities that sent global oil prices surging. The disruptions, which Tokyo was powerless to control, spurred industry to improve fuel efficiency, and in the outcome those adjustments sufficed to sustain Japan's global economic position for the nonce. However, the basic vulnerability to uncontrollable foreign variables endured.

B. *Economic Abuses.* Economic abuse is so pervasive among industrial elites as to seem unworthy of note except that at times its social effects can be broadly harmful. In 1980s Japan, the speculation and corruption became so pronounced that they led to abrupt deceleration of industrial growth and the end of a three-decade boom.

That particular surge in abuse illustrates nicely the interplay of geography, politics and industrial growth. The geographical factor was straightforward. Because of Japan's highly mountainous character, areas that were fit for industrial utilization were very limited. Most of them were situated along the coastline, and most were already in use as agricultural or residential land or in conjunction with nearby fisheries. By 1970, however, the sites most attractive to general industry – notably the Tokyo and Osaka vicinities and other places along the Inland Sea – were becoming packed with industry. And in response to the pollution, noise,

JAPAN: AN ENVIRONMENTAL HISTORY

land subsidence and other injuries associated with industrial production, urban protests proliferated during the later 1960s, leading in turn to political agitation and lawsuits of various sorts.

This escalating discontent worried the government, which clearly identified its own interests with those of industry. Thus, in June 1970, the Prime Minister (Satô Eisaku) warned: "We must not let concern about pollution go so far as to hamper economic growth."[25]

The problems persisted, however, and slowly the government began seeking ways to sustain industrial growth without exacerbating the urban discontent. Most notably, in January 1972, the Ministry of International Trade and Industry (MITI) began exploring strategies for decentralizing industry by dispersing plants to outlying localities.[26] And in following years, various measures were adopted to encourage the spread of industrial production about the realm. For the ruling political party (the Jiyûminshûtô or Liberal Democratic Party: LDP), which was heavily dependent on rural support, that policy also seemed a way to channel jobs to their main constituency.

The most well-known scheme was MITI's plan of 1980 to foster technological activity at a number of select sites about the realm. In doing so, MITI proclaimed, the plan aimed to

infuse the energy of high technology industry into the culture, traditions and natural abundance of the regions, and to achieve the creation of urban communities by harmonizing industry (advanced technological production), learning (academic and experimental research institutions), and lifestyle (a rich and comfortable living environment).[27]

The plan achieved less than MITI hoped, but together with other factors it did help spread industry about the realm.

Regarding those other factors, in the well-developed cities, the growing problems of industrial pollution, injury and consequent unrest spurred local governments – often reluctantly – to reject industry protests and start issuing rules and regulations that would counter the various problems and to limit industrial expansion. That trend raised the costs of production and prompted industrialists to seek other, more welcoming locations.

They could find them because in hinterland areas that lacked industry, many local leaders wished to entice companies to build. For them it was a way to develop new sources of property-tax income while providing employment that would slow the departure of local residents to cities where better-paying jobs were available.

Some local leaders, whether responding to local opposition or due to awareness of industry-caused problems elsewhere, did assiduously oppose the establishment of industries within their jurisdiction. But overall, the process of spreading industry widely about the realm made substantial gains, mostly to sites along the coastline. However, one result, as we note more fully later on, was that the process also spread pollution and environmental damage. More pertinently here, it soon became apparent that hinterland real estate was gaining unprecedented value as potential industrial sites with their accompanying residential and commercial development.

Investors, speculators and organized crime syndicates (*yakuza*) moved vigorously to reap the benefits, while patterns of collusion between industrial and political elites flowered as deals were brokered to secure and develop new sites.

The resulting speculative boom flourished well into the 1980s. During the years 1985–89 the Japanese stock market average roughly tripled and urban land prices quadrupled, gains based on the most reckless speculation.[28] Those upward trends abruptly reversed, however, after the underlying corruption and regulatory irresponsibility were exposed, and during 1989–90 the bubble burst and the economy slumped, leaving a demoralized, discredited political leadership to muddle through the difficult years that ensued.

### After the Boom, 1985–2010

The era of sustained postwar growth came to an end, then, in the later 1980s in a laissez-faire speculative boom and bust. By 1990, the boom years were history, and the long, difficult process of adaptation began. Regarding society, predictably, the rich and powerful suffered least; the weak and poor bore the brunt of hardship. In terms of Japan's dependence on a global resource base, the changed economic situation failed to reverse the trend to growing dependence. On the other hand, the sharp slowdown in industrial expansion did help ameliorate environmental damage at home.

#### 1. On Social Issues

The LDP, which had dominated the political scene since the 1950s, was, with good reason, held responsible for the bubble and its bursting. Nevertheless, despite embarrassing scandals, internal fissures and a brief loss of majority control in the mid-1990s, the party managed to remain in charge of the government until 2009. It could do so thanks largely to the absence of an effectively organized and cohesive rival force.

From 2005 onward, however, reverses in a series of elections gradually weakened its control, in the process strengthening an ad hoc rival coalition called the Democratic Party of Japan (DPJ). Then the economy was hammered again, this time by the global effects of the American copycat bubble and bust of 2007–08. By 2009 that disruption had led to a 30 percent drop in Japan's exports and a nearly 10 percent drop in gross domestic product. One scholar has succinctly summarized the social effects of this sharp downturn:

> There was a spike in suicide-related train delays; bankruptcies and homelessness increased; once-thronged stores and restaurants were quiet; and the nation collectively lost confidence.[29]

In that context, the LDP was trounced in elections, and in 2009 the DPJ took control. Its leaders have pursued modest reformist policies in hopes of revitalizing the economy, restoring socio-economic growth, and thereby consolidating their control of affairs. However, as of early 2011, their success remained limited and intra-party problems undercut their popularity.

Industrial magnates strove to protect their interests as vigorously as did the political elite. Whereas the rapid growth of the boom period had been immensely beneficial to them, however, the bust ended that era. During the 1990s manufacturing output sagged, instead of growing, and while it did regain its overall pre-bust scale by 2000 or so, it did not regain its earlier vigorous growth. Nevertheless, as during the boom years, manufacturers continued trying to produce high-quality goods in areas of growing demand. So production in some areas grew while that in others declined. With domestic demand down in many sectors, they sent more goods to overseas markets. And they tried to improve their competitive position by cutting prices enough to undersell the competition.[30]

A key strategy in price-cutting was the trimming of production costs. And a major aspect of this cost-cutting was reduction in labor expenses. Not only manufacturers but also wholesalers and larger-scale retailers responded to the bust by trimming their workforces, and replacing full-time employees with part-time workers who were excluded from various insurance and pension benefits. Through these measures, industrial profits, leadership bonuses and investor dividends recovered from their 1990s decline, regaining or surpassing pre-bust levels.[31]

On the other hand, this policy produced a major increase in the rate of unemployment – rising from the 1–2 percent range before 1980 to 4.1 percent in 1998 and persisting in the 4–5.5 percent range at least until 2008, as Table 13 indicates.

By the standards of most industrial societies, these rates are still very low, but for Japan they have been dismaying. They mean, after all, that whereas 1,140,000 job-seekers had been unable to find work in 1980, some 3,200,000 faced the same problem in 2000. Moreover, an ever-larger portion of positions was being filled on short-term and part-time bases, mainly by younger people.

Some demographic factors exacerbated the unemployment situation while others ameliorated it. On the negative side, for much of this period, the overall population continued to grow. As Table 1 shows, it kept growing until 2004, when it peaked, and after which it began a slow decline that continues today.

More directly pertinent here, due mainly to the postwar baby boom and improved survival rates (see Tables 7 and 8), the overall working-age population (ages 15–64 years) continued growing – from some 54.7 million in 1955 to 82.5 million in 1985 and 86.2 million in 2000.[32]

The pool of working-age people interested in employment was further increased by two other factors. First was growth in the number of registered aliens who entered Japan to work – a twofold increase between 1985 and 2000 (from about 850,000 to 1,686,000). Second was a modest rise in the percentage of workers who were women, a gain that reflected in part the higher rate of job-loss by male employees and in part an increase in the percentage of women in the job market.[33]

On the other hand were factors that ameliorated the growth in joblessness. One of these was a declining number of people of early-employment age. That trend reflected the long-term decline in the number of children born to Japanese mothers. As Table 5 shows, the fertility rate declined throughout the postwar years, doing so with sufficient speed to more than offset both the increase in number of women of child-bearing age and the improved survival rate of offspring. In consequence, by 1970, as Table 11 indicates, this sustained decline in birth rate was translating into fewer people in the age range 15–24. Especially after 1990, the shrinkage became noteworthy, such that by 2005 there were some 5,000,000 fewer young people available for the workforce than there had been in 1990.

More broadly, in Japan, as in other industrial societies, these unemployment figures represent only those people actively seeking jobs. However, given the relatively low number of Japan's homeless, imprisoned and otherwise non-job-seeking people, the overall rate of non-workers has remained low by comparison with many other countries, most notoriously the USA. Nevertheless, by indigenous standards, the rate of joblessness and the degree of job insecurity have been distressful, unmatched since the 1940s.[34]

Favorable international comparisons notwithstanding, under these post-boom circumstances, the disparity in well-being between those above and those below continued to increase. Between the 1980s and 2000s, households at all levels, from wealthy to poor, cut back most forms of expenditure. However, the poor cut back much more sharply in some categories, notably education but also travel and eating out.[35]

In part these reductions reflected the trend to smaller households with fewer children, but reduced spending on travel and eating out surely reflected a greater sense of prudence, or even necessity, in the face of diminished income. More substantially, the reduction in educational expenditure by the poor, even as the more well-to-do were sharply increasing theirs, reflected the greater difficulty the poor faced in paying for school, especially as such schooling came to seem a less sure avenue to employment.

The difficulty of life during the post-boom decades has also shown up in personal and family stress. Personal stress is reflected in a substantial increase in the suicide rate, which by the 2000s was roughly 33 percent above the boom-decades norm, as Table 10 indicates.

The difficulties of the day have also been suggested by a heightened divorce rate. As Table 4 shows, it began inching upward during the 1970s, growing rapidly from the 1990s onward and by the 2000s standing at more than double its average for the half-century to 1970. Doubtless this trend, like the trends in fertility and women working, has been to some degree a reflection of changing attitudes toward gender issues. But surely, too, it has been spurred by the same deepening hardship that has fostered suicide.

### 2. On International Issues

A number of international issues merit note. First, immigration has been an issue of concern not only in terms of jobs – and the more nebulous emotional issue of "ethnicity" – but also, at times, in terms of foreign relations. Overall, however, it has been a relatively minor diplomatic matter, mainly serving to "build bridges" but on occasion creating small-scale imbroglios.

In foreign affairs as a whole, Japan's leaders continued to adhere to the "low posture" policy that followed defeat in World War II. During the boom decades, they successfully turned to advantage the USA's wish for a quiet supporter in the Cold War, using that connection to rebuild their global resource base. However, that commercial success gradually generated tension with trade rivals.

Also, while the US military involvement In Vietnam during 1965–73 resulted in some commercial gains for Japan, its main impact was to generate widespread public dismay and hostility, in considerable part because it so resembled the Japanese military debacle in China three decades earlier. Then, when Washington responded to the 2001 "terrorist" attack on key symbols of American military-industrial power by launching and becoming bogged down in wars in the Near East – the key source of Japan's oil supply – leaders in Tokyo sought to minimize their entanglement.

Closer to home, a recurrent source of modest political concern, which grew more worrisome after 1990, has been the performance of the North Korean regime. At the time of writing, that situation remains fraught with uncertainty, which worries other regimes as well as Tokyo and may prompt Japan's leaders to strengthen their political ties to the South Korean government in Seoul.

A larger-scale issue has been China. During Japan's post-boom decades, China's burgeoning economy and growing global influence have spurred leaders in Tokyo to try to strengthen their own ties to their east Asian neighbors while avoiding harsh rivalry with China and defusing issues as they have arisen.

As in preceding decades, the most important and worrisome aspect of foreign relations has remained trade – notably, Japan's dependence on a global resource base for essential raw materials and the markets to pay for them. As noted earlier, the post-boom domestic downturn prompted manufacturers to ship more "high-tech" and other goods abroad. As a result, even though domestic consumption stabilized in many areas and showed substantial decline in a few, foreign trade continued its vigorous growth in the new century, with more exports paying for more imports, as Table 18 indicates.[36]

The immense gap between export and import tonnages reflects, of course, the fact that most of the imports were bulky raw materials, while the exports were highly machined items whose cash value per ton was several times that of the imports. Thus the exports of 2008 were valued at 81,018 billion yen while the much heavier imports had a value of 78,955 billion yen.[37]

Central to these increased imports have been the basic energy and other materials for industry and – in the form of foodstuffs – for human consumption. As Tables 19 and 20 show, the tonnage of imported materials for industrial-energy uses continued to grow throughout the boom years and after, the rate of growth slowing significantly (except for coal) only after 2000. And even some foodstuff imports continued to increase after the bust, or at least remained above pre-1985 levels, even though population growth had slackened substantially and unemployment-related hardships had trimmed household budgets.

The growth in these energy imports, which offset stagnating or declining domestic output of foodstuffs and fossil fuels, served to continue the century-long trend of declining energy self-sufficiency, as we note more fully below. In addition, the fabrication of new technological devices, particularly electronic gadgetry, created a need for new types of raw material, notably scarce metals and so-called "rare earths". Because of their intrinsic rarity and the costliness of their extraction, these materials tended to be available from only a few sources globally, making users more vulnerable to foreign manipulation.

For Japan, a particularly alarming – and widely reported – instance of such vulnerability occurred in 2010 when China, nearly the sole source of rare earths at the time, froze its export to Japan in retaliation for a previous dispute over control of an area in the East China Sea that was suspected of holding substantial undersea oil reserves. Although, like the 1973 soybean affair, it proved to be only a brief imbroglio, the incident reminded Japan again of its great vulnerability to such foreign maneuvers.

\* \* \*

To sum up this overview of socio-economic history, by 1955, Japanese society had largely recovered from the disastrous misadventures of the 1930s–40s. It then went on to a full three decades of unprecedented growth and prosperity, before entering a period – still unfolding as of this writing – of sharply slowed growth that has displayed social and demographic characteristics of a classic shift from long-term growth to stasis.

Throughout those decades human activity has had noteworthy effects on its environmental context, even as that context shaped the human experience. As noted earlier, human impact on an ecosystem is shaped by population size, patterns of material consumption and the technology utilized to obtain those goods. So let us examine those three topics – demography, material consumption and technology – more closely to see their environmental impact.

## DEMOGRAPHIC TRENDS

Throughout the decades 1945–2004, the basic trends of population growth, urbanization, and the factors that shaped them, continued to unfold, as before World War II. Gradually, however, the declining birth rate slowed that growth, finally tipping the demographic trend toward reduction.

### Population Estimates

As noted in Chapter 7, Japan's population, which had stabilized at 31–32 million during *bakuhan* centuries, grew thereafter (see Table 1). It more than doubled its 1925 level by 1985, giving Japan a total population about four times as large as that of the *bakuhan* heyday. As the table shows, after the 1945–50 surge in numbers, about 10 million more were added each decade until 1985. After that, however, the growth rate began to decelerate noticeably and growth ceased by 2005.

During the decades of growth, the increase occurred widely about the realm but was not equally distributed. As in prewar decades, regional disparities persisted. Honshu remained the most densely settled, then Kyushu, Shikoku and Hokkaido, the last with only one-sixth the density of Honshu in 1975.[38]

More noteworthy were two other general trends. One was the gradual depopulation and even abandonment of small settlements in numerous intermontane valleys, as marginal farming and logging operations failed. That trend led to net population declines in several mountainous prefectures and to near-stasis in several others, mostly in peripheral regions of the realm.

Offsetting those declines was the other notable trend – the immense growth of major urban centers, especially in the Tokyo-to-Osaka corridor. Most striking was the nearly 97 percent growth of Tokyo and its adjoining lowland prefectures (of Chiba, Kanagawa and Saitama) between 1955 and 1985 (from 15.4 to 30.3 million), even as the national population increased by only about 34 percent (from 90 to 121 million).[39] This meant that by 1985, nearly a quarter of the Japanese population – almost equal to the entire *bakuhan* populace – was "packed and stacked" as never before, crowded into the lowland portions of just four of the realm's 56 prefectures. And in following years that Tokyo-vicinity percentage continued to grow, exceeding 27 percent of the total (for example, 34.99 million) by 2008.

### Urbanization

The growth of Tokyo and its suburbs in adjoining prefectures was an extreme expression of the continuing national trend of urbanization. The precise extent of this trend was still obscured by the administrative integrating of rural communities into city and town units. However, if one distinguishes between urban centers officially defined as cities (most of which numbered 30,000 people or more) and those categorized as towns and villages (most with fewer than 30,000 people), the change over time is striking, as Table 2 indicates.

The wartime evacuation of people from incinerated cities, together with the postwar baby boom, actually swelled the town/village population briefly, but between 1950 and 1990 that population dropped rapidly – from 63 percent of the national total to less than 23 percent. Meanwhile, the city populace grew commensurately, from 37 percent to more than 77 percent of the total. And, as the table shows, the basic trend continued thereafter.

As in prewar decades, these trends in residency reflected trends in employment. As of 1955, when the dislocations of war and defeat were largely past, some 36 percent of employed people (male and female) were still in agriculture and forestry, while 64 percent had other employment. By 2008, only 3.8 percent had agriculture/forestry jobs, with the other 96.2 percent working elsewhere, as Table 12 indicates.

That huge drop in rural employment resulted from a combination of factors: import competition, changing urban dietary preferences, continuing mechanization of agriculture and the adoption of chainsaws and other new devices by the shrinking timber industry. It also reflected the heightened lure of urban jobs, which often paid better and offered socio-cultural advantages, especially for the young.

### Factors in Demographic Growth

As in prewar years, the key factors in Japan's overall demographic growth were public health and food supply.

## 1. Public Health

War's end, as noted above, left Japan with a populace desperate for food, shelter and other necessities. However, local communal help, together with opportunistic scrounging and relief measures by higher governmental levels, did suffice to get most people through the critical months of 1945–46.

A longer-term issue that required attention was tuberculosis (TB).[40] Having developed with the rise of textile and other industries after the 1870s, TB mortality rates reached the vicinity of 180–200 per 100,000 people during the 1920s–30s, and then rose yet higher during World War II and the postwar months of hardship. Soon thereafter, however, recently developed antibiotics became available. Together with improved labor conditions, the new medical practices led to a dramatic drop in the TB mortality rate: whereas 121,769 people died of TB in 1950, only 2,296 did in 2005, as Table 9 shows.

The new medicines and improvements in living conditions had a comparably dramatic impact on diverse other infectious diseases – such as cholera, diphtheria, dysentery, Japanese B encephalitis and typhoid fever – reducing their overall prevalence more than 97 percent during the decades to 1985, to a level so low that they later ceased to be recorded as distinct categories in government records.[41] And, of course, Japan's avoidance of warfare after 1945 eliminated the "cannon fodder" and "civilian casualty" factors in mortality rates.

On the other hand, pell-mell expansion and diversification of industry led to many more cases of industrial poisoning and injury as well as environmental pollution. In terms of human mortality, however, their statistical impact was sharply limited by two factors.

For one thing, during the 1960s, there emerged vigorous and widespread public protests against industrial poisoning and injury, as we note more fully below. As the decade passed, that effort succeeded in prodding reluctant governments (local, prefectural and national) to oppose industrial plans for expansion, and to legislate measures to control both environmental pollution and workplace injury and poisoning. As the 1970s advanced, industry's resistance to change was gradually overcome and companies began installing equipment and procedures to limit the damage.[42]

The other, statistically more important factor that reduced workplace danger was the major shift in employment patterns. By sharply reducing the numbers of those working at the most dangerous jobs, this shift substantially lowered overall workplace injuries and deaths. Most dramatically, the phasing out of coal (and most other) mining nearly eliminated the single most dangerous form of work. Also, decline of the logging industry sharply reduced another source of relatively frequent accidents.[43] And while farming remained a comparatively accident-prone occupation, and the greatly expanded use of pesticides generated numerous cases of user-poisoning, mechanization sharply reduced the farm-labor population and hence the broader statistical impact of farm accidents.

Many of the workers who lost these rural jobs ended up in other employment that was nearly as dangerous, notably the construction, transport and basic wood- and metal-working industries. But so many more people went into other, much safer lines of work – precision manufacturing, food service, retail sales and myriad other "white-collar" jobs – that the net result was a substantial drop in the overall rate of employment-related accidents. Consequently, despite the growing total number of workers, by the 1980s the absolute number who died in workplace accidents was actually dropping – from 3,155 in 1975 to around 2,000 annually by the later 1980s. In following years the decline continued, abetted perhaps by the industrial slowdown.[44] Concurrently, the industrial injury rate (per work-hour) also dropped – by more than 75 percent between 1960 and 1980, and by another 50 percent between 1985 and 2007.[45]

These several gains – in nutrition, medical care, control of communicable disease and workplace safety – all contributed to decades of declining death rates. Most stunning was the decline in infant mortality, as Table 7 reveals. In addition, during the postwar decades, survival rates in later years also improved sharply, as the selected figures of Table 8 indicate.

These reductions, especially in the mortality rate of younger people, translated, of course, into longer average lifespans, accelerating a trend that had emerged in prewar decades (see Table 6). The trend is noteworthy for both the overall long-term gains – from a life expectancy at birth of about 52 years in 1947 to about 82 years in 2007 – and the slightly greater gain by women. This latter reflects the declining pregnancy rate and improved maternal survival rates in pregnancy and childbirth.

The observant reader will recognize, however, that by itself the sharp drop in death rate, especially that of infants, should translate into a vastly greater rate of population growth than Japan actually experienced during the later twentieth century. The offsetting factor was the substantial decline in the overall birth rate, as mentioned previously (see Table 5).

To elaborate briefly, during the 1920s–30s, as noted in Chapter 7, the issue of "over-population" had generated considerable discussion, including calls for the adoption of birth-control policies. Following defeat, with food supply severely restricted and the prospect of mass starvation looming, the government finally legalized voluntary abortion.[46] Initially, abortions may have been the key factor in post-1945 fertility decline, but in addition, better techniques of birth control made it easier to avoid pregnancy in the first place. Then, as the economy thrived during the boom decades, changes in lifestyle led ever more young people, women in particular, to prefer fewer or no children.

By the 1980s, the elite – whether due to belief in the "growth is good" ideology, out of concern for "national power" or simply from worry about their looming retirement years – had shifted from favoring fewer births to favoring more, and in consequence it was 1999 before the government finally legalized the sale of contraceptive pills. However, as Table 5 indicates, long before then, women had reduced their reproductive rate enough to substantially offset the population gains resulting from improvements in public health, thereby contributing to the demographic trajectory Japan has experienced.

## 2. Food Supply

The best public health in the world is of no value, of course, if people do not have food to eat. Fortunately, during the decades of entrepreneurial industrialism, as during the preceding ones of imperial industrialism, Japan's food supply kept abreast of population growth and dietary change through a combination of gains in domestic food production and foodstuff imports. However, whereas the overall gains of pre-1945 decades had been primarily due to increased domestic output, the gains since 1945 have been mainly a result of increased imports.

As noted earlier, domestic farm and fishery production recovered quite briskly after World War II. During the boom years, overall foodstuff output continued to grow (subject, of course, to weather-induced annual irregularities), peaking during the 1980s but thereafter gradually dropping back to pre-1970 levels, as Table 40 indicates.

Even during the years of increasing output, however, domestic food production failed to keep up with demand because of population growth and greater intake per capita. The latter was due in part to increased indulgence, perhaps, but also to the gains in average human height and weight that Table 3 reveals. The result of these trends was greater total food intake and a consequent decline in the level of national food sufficiency (see Table 22).

So, in place of domestic foodstuffs, the public relied more and more on imported food. In terms of rice, potatoes and highly perishable foods – eggs, raw milk, fresh vegetables – domestic sources continued to prevail. But in such areas as meat, fishery products, wheat, coffee and soybeans, imports outpaced population growth, especially during the boom decades, as the earlier-cited Tables 20 and 21 indicate.

In sum, then, industrial-age medical care, together with access to a growing global food supply, enabled the people of Japan to recover from military defeat, experience an era of notable demographic growth, and then enter a period of demographic stabilization while encountering only modest levels of nutritional or medical distress. Given the extent of decline in foodstuff self-sufficiency, however, Japan's society today finds itself in a precarious position, more dependent than ever on essential resources over which it has no effective control. The situation is all the more worrisome because it seems so abnormal by comparison to other industrial societies. As one scholar has put it, unlike Japan, with its declining self-sufficiency:

From the 1970s through the end of the twentieth century, every Western industrial nation increased its food self-sufficiency rate, both calorie-based and grain-based, to either approach or greatly exceed 100 percent.[47]

The overall socio-economic growth that has eventuated in today's foodstuff situation also found expression in diverse other forms of material consumption.

## MATERIAL CONSUMPTION

When we think of material consumption by humans, we commonly think of food-stuffs and other products – textiles, automobiles, household appliances and so on. But a major form of consumption is spatial – the areas we utilize, converting them from support of the natural biome to support of humans and their collaborating ("domesticated") plants and animals. So let us look at trends in land use before considering other forms of consumption.

### Space Usage

In earlier chapters we noted that in Japan the most noteworthy change in human-environment relations associated with the shift from forager to agricultural society was the massive conversion of natural woodland into farm land, mostly for paddy- and dry-field tillage. The process transformed an almost totally forested realm into a bifurcated one in which, essentially, the lowland 20 percent of the realm sustained the humans while the upland 80 percent sustained natural biota.

To follow upland usage briefly, we noted that during *bakuhan* centuries, more and more upland areas also were modified, being converted from natural mixed forest to plantation (meaning even-aged monoculture) stands, primarily of *sugi* and *hinoki*. Then, as we saw in Chapter 7, the shift to industrial society from the late 1800s onward led to widespread deforestation followed by further conversion of natural forest to even-aged monoculture stands.

After 1945, as we note more fully below, another surge of logging and subsequent reforestation gave way from the 1970s onward to a gradual decline in the lumber industry, ageing and decay of plantation stands and an accompanying revival of natural woodland. That revival was also fostered by the earlier-noted depopulation of intermontane areas and abandonment of scattered plots of relatively poor and inaccessible arable land, which reverted to scrubland (*gen'ya*) and, eventually, forest (*sanrin*). Offsetting this trend to forest re-naturalization was the conversion to urban usages, mainly recreational, of more and more upland that had once sustained forest or other vegetation. According to one study:

> By the end of 1989, up to 19.2 percent (7,250,000 hectares) of the nation had been covered by resort developments.[48]

That acreage – nearly 2.5 times the total area devoted to paddy fields – included some 3–4,000 golf courses.

Turning to the lowland, the main change that accompanied industrialization was conversion of food-producing agricultural land to more direct human uses as a result of urban sprawl and the growth of industrial production and distribution. After 1945 these trends continued, shifting ever more arable land to other uses. In addition, landfill projects at many coastal sites, such as Tokyo Bay, added marginally to the archipelago's total land area, doing so at the expense of coastal fisheries.

This newly created coastal land was used for diverse urban and industrial purposes, as was most of the abandoned arable. Thus, the decades after 1945 witnessed growth in acreage devoted to roads, railroads, airports, recreational uses and industrial parking and storage.

Both roads and railroads experienced growth in terms of length, width and durability. Many roads were widened and paved, and beginning with the construction of an expressway linking Osaka and Kôbe in 1958, the government gradually laid out a country-wide network of limited-access expressways comparable to the US interstate highway system. Similarly, railroads were upgraded, and starting in 1959 the government laid track for what became Japan's celebrated "bullet train" system of high-speed rail lines. This growth in transport lines consumed space, of course, with acreage devoted to railroads growing modestly from 652.85 km$^2$ (65,285 hectares) in 1960 to 664.68 km$^2$ in 1984, and later declining somewhat as motor vehicle usage rose. Roads, being far more numerous, occupied much more land, with some 10,474 km$^2$ in 1980 growing to 14,940 by 2005.[49]

Even more substantial in terms of space usage was the increased use of land for housing and other building types.[50] Whereas some 5,700 km$^2$ of privately owned land was devoted to buildings of diverse usage in 1960, the area so used more than doubled to 12,763 km$^2$ by 1985, and it reached 16,062 km$^2$ in 2005.

The land for those buildings, as for other urban usages, mostly came from what had been arable acreage, causing the latter to shrink by about 12,570 km$^2$ between 1960 and 2005.[51] Most of the loss, it appears, was experienced by dry-field cropland. At least the area devoted to paddy fields held steady at some 30–31,000 km$^2$ during the boom decades, only dropping to 26,982 by 2005.

In short, industrial society's use of land for non-biotic functions, which dwarfed such uses in earlier societies, continued to grow. It provided the space necessary for production, distribution and consumption of the myriad material goods that also characterize industrial society, goods that derive in large part from raw materials found elsewhere in the ecosystem.

### Other Material Consumption

The increase in land devoted to housing partly reflected the rapid growth in the number of ordinary Japanese households, with the 16.4 million of 1950 growing to 38 by 1985 and to 49 by 2005.[52] It also, however, reflected a modest increase in the average size of housing. Whereas the average occupied dwelling in 1963 had 72.5 m$^2$ of floor area, by 2003 floor space measured 94.8 m$^2$ (see Table 14).

One distinctively Japanese measure of housing space that will illustrate both the gain in standard of living and the greater use of space is the number of *tatami* per occupant. A *tatami*, as mentioned in Chapter 5, is a thick, spongy floor mat made of tightly bound straw and covered with an attractive layer of neatly woven stems from the rush *igusa*. Each *tatami* measures about 1 × 2 m in size, and they are laid out atop rough under-flooring in standard patterns of 3, 4.5, 6 or 8 *tatami* to make rooms ranging in size from small to large.

The number of *tatami* per household occupant more than tripled during the half-century after 1950, as Table 15 indicates. In part, this trend to more floor space per capita reflected the declining number of members per household as the average family size shrank from more than four before 1960 to fewer than three after 1990 (see Table 16). It was possible to have fewer persons per household despite overall population growth, of course, because the number of households grew so rapidly, as noted previously.

In addition, those fewer household members were occupying larger houses with more rooms (Table 14). And a major reason for having more rooms and larger houses was to accommodate the growing variety and quantity of appliances, furniture and other durable goods that families were acquiring. That trend was evident in many ways, some of them shown in Table 17.

Finally, this growth in material consumption was also revealed by the burgeoning domestic demand for textiles of all sorts, a trend that also highlights Japan's growing dependency on a global resource base. During 1960–2005, while the population was growing by some 25 percent, domestic textile consumption nearly tripled. Enabling that increase were imports, which had been essentially nil in 1960 but gradually rose to almost 2 million tons annually, thereby meeting most of the demand. That huge growth in imports was facilitated by tariff adjustments that rendered domestic producers uncompetitive, with a resulting sharp post-boom decline in domestic output, as seen in Table 23.

\* \* \*

In sum, then, the decades since 1945 have enabled the general populace to enjoy more spacious housing and more material goods than ever in their past. One suspects that a well-informed emperor from the agricultural era would have been dumbfounded and envious. The cost, of course, was borne by the ecosystem, with Japan's global resource base bearing more and more of the burden as decades passed.

## TECHNOLOGY AND THE ENVIRONMENT

The third major variable shaping human impact on the environment – after human numbers and per-capita consumption – is the technology employed to extract and process materials for human use. This variable can be examined, as it was in Chapter 7, in terms of mining, manufacturing, fisheries, agriculture and forestry.

### Mining

The environmental issues pertaining to mining during the decades after 1945 were essentially those of the prewar years – workplace poisoning and injury and ambient environmental pollution. By 1970, however, most of Japan's metal and coal mines were past their prime, becoming less and less able to compete with imports. As a result, in following decades production in most of them dropped substantially, in the process sharply reducing mining's impact on health and environment.

#### 1. Impact on Workers
In terms of workplace injury, the nadir of coal mining came in the mid-1960s. On 9 November 1963, in Japan's worst mine disaster of the postwar era, an explosion in the Miike mine in central Kyushu killed 458; on 22 February 1965, an explosion at the Yûbari mine in Hokkaido killed 61; and on 1 June of that same year, a coal mine explosion near Fukuoka in northern Kyushu killed 237.[53]

In following years, mining, especially for coal, remained a dangerous occupation, but the number of injuries and fatalities dropped dramatically, substantially faster than the shrinking workforce, as Table 27 shows. Thus, whereas 6 percent of miners suffered serious injuries in 1960, only 1 percent did in 1985, and far fewer in later years, while the fatality rate dropped less radically and more slowly. In part these improvements were a result of improved safety policies; in part, a shift away from the most dangerous and toxic types of mining; and in part, a reflection of the much increased use of machinery, which reduced worker exposure to injury.

Those machines also helped sustain output in the mines that still yielded ore or other desired materials. Thus, whereas coal mining had shriveled by 1980, as had iron and copper mining (and lead and zinc by 2000), Japan's slender output of crude oil and natural gas was sustained, along with that of various non-metallic minerals, notably limestone, even though the required workforce was very small.[54]

*2. Impact on the Bio-system*
The problem of environmental pollution due to mining followed a similar, if somewhat later, curve of exacerbation followed by gradual amelioration. As in prewar decades, several trends – worsening conditions near a number of mines, some resulting public protests, eventual government regulation and reluctant mining company remediation – gradually improved mining and refining procedures, substantially reducing the run-off of polluted liquid waste and the release of noxious gases. Even the copper mine at Ashio, so well-known as a polluter from the 1880s onward, elicited only infrequent protests for its damage to the Watarase River region.

Before matters improved, however, they worsened. The forms of environmental injury due to mining were diverse, including poisoning of fish and other downstream biota, withering of trees and other vegetation downwind of refinery smokestacks, and poisoning of humans and domesticated animals. One notorious case illustrates with particular clarity how the postwar industrial boom injured people near mines. That was the case of Kamioka metal mine and refinery on the Jinzu River, which runs northward out of Gifu Prefecture through Toyama to the Sea of Japan.[55] The cadmium pollutants that their operation released, it was discovered, caused a painful illness popularly known as *itai itai* ("ouch, ouch" or "it hurts, it hurts") disease by disrupting bone calcium, especially among pregnant women.[56]

By the late 1950s, numerous women in a few downstream localities were suffering from *itai itai* disease. In 1961, a medical study of patients in the vicinity of the mine, which was operated by the Mitsui Mining and Smelting Corporation, concluded that cadmium was causing the illness. That report spurred Toyama prefectural authorities to start an inquiry, and then in 1964 more victims were identified on Tsushima Island, where the Tôhô Zinc Corporation operated a mine.

As the 1960s advanced, more and more *itai itai* cases appeared, some of them men, and more studies of the illness were made. Early in 1968, Toyama victims launched a lawsuit against Mitsui. Then in March a research unit in the national government's Health and Welfare Ministry affirmed that cadmium from the Kamioka mine was "the acting substance" in *itai itai*. Mitsui promptly responded, asserting that the report constituted "a hasty conclusion hard to understand".[57] However, hoping to still the protest, Mitsui also donated 10 million yen to the Red Cross to aid sufferers. But then in early 1969 – after the number of claimants had proliferated and a second lawsuit had been filed – the Mitsui operator of the Kamioka mine flatly denied that cadmium had poisoned anyone.[58]

By then, however, cadmium and numerous other industrial chemicals were found so widely about Japan, most dangerously in rice and drinking-water supplies, that the Health and Welfare Ministry was moving to address the problem by setting maximum allowable levels of contaminants. And other agencies took steps to assure that industry installed adequate filters and other mechanisms of contaminant control.

In the case of cadmium, in September 1969, the Ministry established maximum cadmium levels of 0.01 ppm (parts per million) in drinking water and 0.4 ppm in rice. Evidently buffeted by objections from agriculture and industry, in July 1970, the Ministry loosened its rice requirement, raising the level to 1 ppm for unpolished rice and 0.9 ppm for polished rice. Nevertheless, the city government of Tokyo, which by then was substantially more engaged in the pollution struggle, decided to adhere to the initial 0.4 ppm standard.[59]

Those rules notwithstanding, with so much cadmium already released into the soil, harvested rice continued for years thereafter to include cadmium quantities that exceeded even the relaxed limit and therefore had to be withdrawn from the market and stored in government warehouses at taxpayers' expense. Furthermore, industry kept adding cadmium and other pollutants to the environment by failing to install proper safety equipment. Thus a Labor Ministry report of September 1970 stated, "only 34 percent of plants handling cadmium are equipped with dust collectors and 73.5 percent with waste liquid treatment facilities".[60]

Finally, in June 1971, the primary lawsuit against Mitsui for its Kamioka pollution resulted in a conviction, which prompted Mitsui's president to deny that the ruling had a "scientific justification". Supported by a scholar who asserted cadmium's innocence, Mitsui lawyers appealed the judgment, claiming that the "cadmium theory" of *itai itai* disease was unproven.

In July 1972, as the legal appeal advanced, Mitsui Mining and Smelting and the Japan Mining Industry Association tried to defend their interests by informing prefectural medical associations and governments that cadmium pollution was totally unrelated to *itai itai* disease. The following month, however, the court affirmed the earlier ruling. A day later, in negotiation with the *itai itai* patients, Mitsui acknowledged that cadmium was indeed the cause of the disease, and two weeks later agreed to settle all remaining lawsuits accordingly.

So the ten-year struggle for compensation and for acknowledgement that the problem must be addressed was finally settled. And two years later, in 1974, the president of Tôhô Zinc Corporation, which had been sued over cadmium pollution at its mines on Tsushima Island and at Annaka in the northwestern Kantô, admitted that the company had engaged in a cover-up and agreed to pay compensation to its victims.

The legal issues may have been settled, but actual cadmium levels would decline only slowly and over many years. Nor did Mitsui really accept the outcome. By

1974–75, Japan's economy was in recession following the earlier-noted 1973 crisis in oil imports, and that situation enabled opponents of anti-pollution policies to mobilize support by arguing that such policies were economically damaging to Japan. In that context, pundits revived themes such as the notion that *itai itai* was really an illusory disease. That mood inspired Mitsui leaders in the spring of 1975 to assert once again that a host of doubts remained about the "so-called pollution ailment", *itai itai* disease.[61]

So, while the legal issue was settled, the more basic tension between the mining industry's short-term interests and the long-term interests of the public and the broader environment persisted. Ultimately, it was the exhausting and shuttering of mines that gradually led to elimination of the pollutants and their damage.

### Manufacturing

As bruising as the struggle over mine pollution may have been, a far greater source of environmental damage during postwar decades was manufacturing. Its impact essentially continued prewar patterns, with industry's unprecedented expansion during the boom decades leading to commensurate countrywide injury, which only slowly mended in subsequent years.

Table 28 reveals two key aspects of this industrial growth. One was manufacturing's employment, which nearly doubled during the 1955–85 boom years, even as the general populace grew by only about a third, thus helping assure younger people of more urban employment opportunities. The other key aspect was the stunning increase – roughly 14-fold – in the value of manufacturing's output during those 30 years.

That disparity between trends in labor input and value of output reveals the importance of machinery and market appeal in this industrial boom.[62] The way that industrial output could grow – but also fluctuate with market changes – is evident in the varying trajectories of Japan's many industrial products, as the slender sampling in Table 29 suggests.

In environmental terms, this substantial increase in productivity per worker meant that the gains were achieved with relatively little growth in demand for foodstuffs and the acreage to produce them. Rather, they required a substantial growth in consumption of fossil fuel, mainly oil, to drive the machinery that produced the goods, in the process generating more and more waste pollutants.

This extraordinary growth in manufacturing output also was central to another major difference in the environmental impact of mining and manufacturing. Whereas mining had its impact almost entirely on Japan's domestic environment, manufacturing's scale and function meant that it had an impact both in Japan and on its global resource base.

Regarding that global resource base, as noted in Chapter 7, of necessity it lies beyond our purview. Nevertheless, the environmental impact of industrial Japan – as of every industrial society – does extend across the globe, so let us note briefly the several major ways the impact of manufacturing has been manifested globally.

First, Japan's importing of raw materials has contributed to the overall consumption of worldwide supplies, most notably of fossil fuels and minerals. In addition, the extractive and refining processes that have provided this material have contributed to global pollution and environmental degradation.

Second, Japan's export of finished goods has contributed to humankind's increased use of space. And the utilization of those goods – whether automobiles, electronic devices or whatever – has consumed energy supplies and generated waste and pollutants. Moreover, insofar as Japan's industries have exported their actual processes of production by operating factories abroad, they have contributed to industrial pollution abroad rather than in Japan.

Third, the process of transporting goods and materials to and from Japan has consumed the resources necessary to construct and operate the transport vessels. And it has contributed to both air and water pollution. Finally, although not directly a result of manufacturing, Japan's pelagic fishing fleet, with its modern technologies, has contributed to the global decimation of fisheries and other marine resources.

Turning to the domestic environmental effects of manufacturing, as in prewar decades, it had an impact on its workforce through injury and poisoning. And it had an impact on the ambient bio-system, including its human component, through production of noxious goods and waste and through disruption of terrain.

*1. Impact on Workers*

As noted in discussing postwar demography, changes in employment, particularly the declines in mining, forestry and agricultural work, helped reduce workplace hazards by eliminating vast numbers of the most dangerous jobs. Those advantages were partially offset, however, by the pell-mell construction and opening of new industrial facilities, most especially chemical plants, during the 1950s.

Already by 1953, cases of chemical poisoning and industrial accidents were generating worker protests and government inquiries, and during the next 20 years those issues and responses grew in intensity.[63] Gradually the interplay of labor union protests, local hardships and lawsuits by the aggrieved prodded local, prefectural and eventually the national governments to legislate rules and restrictions. Those measures, in turn, goaded factory operators to install safety equipment and improve manufacturing procedures.

Cumulatively, these changes contributed to a long and sustained decline in the rate and severity of industrial accidents. As Table 30 indicates, between 1960 and 1990, the frequency of manufacturing accidents dropped by an impressive 86.6 percent while their severity dropped by 82.7 percent.

*2. Impact on the Ambient Bio-system*[64]

As in prewar decades, industry hurt the surrounding biome in three ways: by poisoning its occupants, human as well as other fauna and flora; by shifting more and more areas to non-biological uses; and by disrupting yet other areas. Also, as in prewar years, the damage was concentrated in lowland areas, but far more widely than before. Finally, industry did particularly extensive damage to riverine and coastal biomes, as we note more fully later when discussing fisheries.

Three major factors made industry's impact during these postwar decades so much greater than it had been before World War II. One, as noted above, was the vast increase in scale of production. The other two factors were proliferation of new chemical products and diffusion of manufacturing ever more widely about the countryside.

In terms of damage to "natural" biota, the most widespread, persistent and grievous injury was to fish, shellfish, seaweed and other life forms of rivers, estuaries and inshore coastal regions. In addition, reports proliferated of ill and dead birds, mostly victims of airborne pollutants, but some oil-smeared and others poisoned by polluted fruit, seeds, and other feed.[65] And of course the polluted waters that flooded paddy fields and other lowlands poisoned a vast array of natural flora and fauna, as well as the domesticated plants and animals that absorbed or ingested them.

Much more visible in the historical record is industrial pollution's impact on the ambient human populace. As in prewar years, the social group most severely injured by the spread of manufacturing was fishing folk because so much industry was located near rivers and coastlines, and because so much waste was disposed of by being flushed and dumped into the water. Consequently, the postwar popular opposition to industrial growth and proliferation was initially centered in fishing communities.

By the later 1950s, however, industry had grown so much that it was posing complex problems for most other sectors of society, both rural and urban. As a consequence, as the 1960s advanced, local protests against factory construction and operation proliferated. Investigatory reports of various sorts were prepared, and local and prefectural governments began issuing regulations to control pollution, require better safety practices and slow factory expansion within their jurisdictions.

The national government, meanwhile, was reluctant to intervene. Its posture did shift gradually, however, the change symbolized by a study of industrial waste that MITI completed and announced in the spring of 1970. The Ministry reported that current output of industrial waste, which measured some 58.5 million tons per year, could well rise to some 120 million tons by 1975. The report noted that while about 30 percent of the waste was currently being treated before disposal, some 40 percent of the total was being dumped into rivers and seas.[66] Following that acknowledgement of the problem's magnitude, the government began slowly to develop regulations designed to address the issue.

Rather similarly, most labor unions, while actively critical of dangerous working conditions, had initially opposed environmental measures that seemed to threaten job growth. But from the late 1960s onward, they reversed course, beginning to demand better pollution control.

In unions, as in government, the change came locally at first in response to local problems. Thus, the first time that organized labor formally made "pollution prevention" an official rallying cry was at a May Day rally of 1967 in Okayama Prefecture.[67] The declaration was spurred by a severe pollution problem in the vicinity of Mizushima, a nearby industrial port on the Inland Sea. There, factory effluent had for some time been poisoning fields and streams and spreading devastation into the Sea, while governments failed to take adequate measures to stop the damage.

Three years later, in 1970, the "first anti-pollution strike by a labor union" occurred at the Chisso Corporation's chemical plant at Minamata Bay in Kyushu. Chisso was perhaps Japan's most notorious polluter, and in earlier years the local union had actively opposed environmental critics of the company, so this action reflected a major shift in attitude. Indeed, the union action prompted Chisso to create a new, pro-company union. In 1973 it cooperated with the company in defying and disrupting Kyushu fishermen who were protesting the factory's damage to their fishing grounds.[68]

Whereas unions were torn by conflicting interests, industry took a firm stand against "excessive" regulation. Its leaders tried to quiet some protest movements with "voluntary" compensation for injuries and damage, while using their political muscle to woo support among government officials at both local and higher levels. And as anti-pollution lawsuits proliferated during the 1960s, they doggedly denied that harm had been done or, if it had, that their own operations were to blame.

Escalating marine pollution was one problem that elicited such industrial denial. Oil spills from coastal oil refineries, storage facilities, oil tankers and other ships were a major and growing source of the problem due to the massive increase in use of imported crude oil – up from some 8.5 million kiloliters in 1955 to 84.1 million in 1965 (see Table 19) – and the growth of technical facilities to transport and process it.

Most famously, perhaps, this immense growth in oil imports fostered the use of more and larger tankers. Whereas such vessels had been able to carry some 20,000 tons of oil apiece in the early 1950s, by the late 1950s new tankers were hauling 45,000 tons, and in 1962 the first "supertanker", the Nissho Maru, was put into operation, with a capacity of 132,000 tons.[69]

As the scale of oil importation, processing and use grew, however, so too did the scale of oil spillage. According to one study, for example, during 1966, oil pollution in the Inland Sea resulted in damage totaling 578 million yen to 73 fishery groups.[70]

Unsurprisingly, leaders of the oil industry were reluctant to address the pollution problem. Thus, about the time the 1966 report on Inland Sea pollution appeared, Idemitsu Kôsan, a major operator of tankers and refineries, was negotiating for permission to construct a new refining facility at Himeji, midway between Osaka and Okayama. The company president, Idemitsu Sazô, when speaking to new employees in January 1967, said of the oil-spill problem:

> The oil spills from supertankers and the foul-smelling fish that those in the opposition movement talk about are just trifling matters.[71]

Mr Idemitsu had a strong personal reason to defend the honor of supertankers. Just four months earlier, the world's largest tanker at the time, the Idemitsu Maru, had been newly launched.[72]

By 1969, the damage being wrought by oil refineries prompted MITI to consider a policy of having refineries situated within the oil-producing countries rather than in Japan.[73] Whether because of industrial opposition to this potential loss of a profitable business or because of the added pressure it would put on international balance of payments, the policy was not adopted, and in subsequent years nearly all of Japan's petroleum imports (for example, over 87 percent in 2007) continued to be refined after arrival.[74]

Although that MITI proposal went nowhere, the government pressed ahead in developing an array of pollution standards and considering bills to establish punishments for those convicted of polluting the environment. And in November 1970 the Diet met in special session to address the national pollution problem. In response, the two major voices of industry, Keidanren (Federation of Economic Organizations) and the Japan Chambers of Commerce and Industry, both stated their opposition to any punishment for those convicted of such crimes.[75]

Industry's position was surely not helped, however, by a Labor Ministry report of 1 December. It said that, of some 13,000 establishments handling harmful substances, "over 70 percent had no installations to eliminate toxic gases and 17.6 percent were discharging cyanides without the required treatment".[76]

Even without that pointed reminder of industry's culpability, the tide of public attitudes had turned. By 1967 schools were teaching their pupils about pollution problems, and in following years, books, films and lectures about pollution, its causes and consequences proliferated. By the spring of 1975, even as the economy was struggling out of recession, a survey by the government's Environmental Agency found that "90 percent of the Japanese question the benefits of large-scale development projects".[77] Reflecting that public mood, regulations to control industrial pollution proliferated, along with environmental lawsuits that slogged through the courts, usually ending in convictions and compensation for victims.

By the final years of the boom decades, then, environmental problems and protests directly traceable to manufacturing were in decline. In part, as we note more fully further on, that decline reflected two unfortunate facts: that many fisheries had already been destroyed and abandoned; and that much of the poisoned farmland had been sold and converted to urban uses.

In part, however, the decline in factory-targeted protest reflected implementation of anti-pollution regulations as more and more companies acquired the needed pollution-control devices. Due to that trend, during the 1970s the production and installation of such devices grew by leaps and bounds, with the market value of new pollution-control equipment hitting some 374.6 billion yen in 1973 and even more in subsequent years.[78]

Even as pollution problems directly attributable to industry were easing, however, other sources of damage were growing more pronounced, which sustained the overall level of public protest. The major complaints were about air pollution, noise pollution and arbitrary land-taking, and they related mainly to the proliferation of automobiles and the expansion of roads, railroads and airports. In addition, protests of diverse sorts attempted, with little success, to prevent the construction of nuclear power plants.[79]

Most pervasive and serious of these issues was air pollution generated by motor vehicles. That was primarily a consequence of their immense proliferation, as Table 24 indicates, but also the lack of up-to-date pollution control devices. As the table's figures suggest, the highway distance traveled by the "average" Japanese also grew. Indeed, as Table 25 reveals, it increased nearly eightfold during the years between 1950 and 1995.

That growth in vehicle use obviously entailed a huge increase in gasoline consumption, outracing other types of demand and devouring an ever-greater proportion of the growing crude-oil imports, as Table 26 suggests. That immense increase in gasoline use translated, of course, into a huge increase in air pollution. And as the disproportionate growth in use of passenger cars suggests, much of the increase was in commuting and recreational driving, with automobiles replacing buses and trains while permitting more, and more convenient, travel per capita.

By the later 1960s, authorities were discussing the problem of motor vehicle pollution and proposing regulations to control exhaust emissions, and in 1972 an advisory board recommended to the Environment Agency that it adopt the 1970 auto-emissions standards established by the USA. That proposal spurred the Japan Automobile Manufacturers' Association to issue a pamphlet denying that auto exhaust was a major component of air pollution. Two years later, in 1974, as the government neared completion of its exhaust regulations, automobile manufac-turers launched a rear-guard action to delay their implementation.[80] Nevertheless, by decade's end the rules were in force and being implemented. However, the continuing growth in motor vehicle usage meant that auto pollution persisted as an environmental problem.

*Fisheries*

The overall story of Japan's fisheries during the years from 1945 to the present is a story of recovery, struggle, adaptation, growth and subsequent decline. Its dimensions are suggested by the data assembled in Table 41.

Although figures on total catch vary a bit, depending on one's source, by the mid-1950s, Japan had regained its prewar level of catch, some 3 million metric tons per year. Overcoming various obstacles, fishermen raised the annual harvest to nearly 9 million tons by 1970 and more than 11 million by the mid-1980s, doing so even though the number of fishermen dropped throughout the postwar period – from about a million in 1955 to some 400,000 in the mid-1980s. After that, however, the harvest declined to some 5–6 million by the 2000s, when fishermen numbered fewer than 250,000.[81] That is to say, per-capita productivity rose from some 3 tons per fisherman-year to around 27 tons before falling back to the lower 20s.

This fishery topic can be examined in terms of problem and responses. The most devastating problem that fishermen faced in the postwar era was the rampant pollution of their fisheries as industrial development roared ahead, spreading ever more widely about the realm. And most of the innovations and changes in fishery activity constituted a direct or indirect response to that problem.

*1. The Problem*

Fisheries bore the brunt of Japan's industrial development because of society's dependence on a global resource base and because most lowland, the site of human settlement, fronted the coast. These factors led most industry to locate as near to deep-water ports as possible, and where the desired space was not available, landfill projects created new areas on which to build. Also, in laying out facilities, substantial effort was made to maximize the efficiency with which imported raw materials could be directly off-loaded, stored and processed into goods for domestic use or for re-loading onto vessels for shipment abroad.

Perhaps the most sophisticated expression of this strategy was the *konbinato*. A *konbinato* was an integrated production facility erected on specially designed coastal sites where ships could off-load raw materials directly into storage facilities adjacent to factories that would process them into finished products. These could then be directly packed into shipping containers and loaded onto freighters for re-export or onto railroad cars for domestic distribution.[82] As the efficiency of these *konbinato* became apparent, they proliferated, adding to the proportion of industrial activity whose waste products ravaged fisheries widely about the realm, from Hokkaido to the Ryukyus.

The deteriorating condition of coastal waters was evident in Tokyo Bay. As noted in Chapter 7, pollution in the Bay and its feeder rivers was already severe by the 1930s. Subsequently, the problems there accelerated.[83] In the later 1950s, pollutants from the Edogawa, mainly produced by a paper mill of the Honshu Paper Company, poisoned the Chiba side of the Bay, which had escaped most of the prewar pollution. That development spurred energetic protests and sit-ins during 1958, which led the Company to compensate the fishermen for their losses with a solatium of 19 million yen. The turmoil also spurred government to require the paper mill to install proper water-purification equipment.

That effort reduced the paper company's pollution impact, but various other industries continued dumping other poisons into the bay, even as landfill projects destroyed more and more patches of fishing ground. So the condition of the bay's fish and shellfish continued to deteriorate, and four years later, in 1962, fishermen operating out of Tokyo gave up the fight, surrendering all fishing rights in return for an indemnity.

By then, too, the adjacent Kawasaki and Yokohama fisheries were largely gone, and reports of 1970 indicated that marine fisheries outside the mouth of the bay were being ruined by the offshore dumping of industrial waste. Also, by the 1970s high levels of PCBs (polychlorinated biphenyls) were showing up in the bay, along with other chemicals, and in 1972 this worsening pollution led the fishermen of Sodegaura, across the bay from Yokohama, to abandon their fishing rights. By then a joint study by the prefectural governments of Chiba, Kanagawa and Tokyo had concluded that the bay was becoming a "dead water body".[84]

In following years, reports continued to appear of dead fish and other evidence of pollution, even as Tokyo Bay steadily shrank due to the continuing landfill projects. But in any case, for fishermen the bay had by then ceased to be an area of great concern; their futures lay elsewhere.

Unfortunately, other bays and inshore areas fared poorly as well. Far to the West, pollutants from the notorious Chisso chemical plant at Minamata ravaged the small Minamata Bay and spread mercury and other poisons into Yatsushiro Sea.[85] The nearby Ariake Sea also experienced sharp losses in fishery production, as did other seas, bays and coastal areas of Shikoku, Kyushu and western Honshu.

Thus, in northern Kyushu, where the Yahata steel mill and associated industries had for decades been polluting the long estuary known as Dôkai-wan, a newspaper asserted in 1956 that the bay was "a dead sea with the dirtiest water in Japan".[86] In fact, fishing did continue there for a few more years, but industries continued to proliferate and expand along the estuary's shores. Indeed, the vigor of that growth prompted Yahata and several other small cities there to consolidate in 1963 and form "Kitakyûshû", making the area one of Japan's ten largest and most fully industrialized cities.

Also reflecting that dynamic growth, pollution in the estuary and its adjoining sea continued to worsen and fishing catches kept dropping. By 1970, Dôkai-wan was virtually lifeless, even as governments in the area finally tried to revive it by establishing acceptable levels of pollution and requiring industry to install the equipment necessary to reach those levels.[87]

Elsewhere, too, belated attempts to preserve fisheries appeared. The most important struggle involved the Inland Sea, which was being poisoned from one end to the other by polluting industries and proliferating maritime traffic.

At its far eastern end the struggle was lost. Osaka's burgeoning growth before World War II, as noted in Chapter 7, had generated much water pollution. After the war, already by 1948 reports were speaking of serious pollution in fisheries of Osaka and the nearby city of Sakai. By 1960, the only river passing through Osaka that still supported fishing was the Yodogawa. And in 1969, Osaka fishermen settled for an indemnity in return for abandoning their fishing rights in the coastal port area, which was being obliterated by landfills.[88]

West of there, a sustained struggle continued. During the 1960s, oil and other pollutants were swept into the Inland Sea from all sides, as well as from ship traffic, their effects becoming ever more frequently visible in "red tides". These were massive blooms of plankton that killed fish and other marine creatures, whether living in the wild or being cultured on fish farms. By 1968 fishery damage in the Inland Sea was estimated to total some 3.4 billion yen.[89]

As the problems worsened, fishermen's protests intensified, and by 1970 local, prefectural and national governments were undertaking studies to identify the particular sources and scale of problems and to develop remedies. Thus, Yamaguchi Prefecture reported in June 1970 that a study it had just completed found the Inland Sea so severely deoxygenated that several areas, including the Iwakuni-Ôtake vicinity of Hiroshima Bay, were turning into "dead sea".[90]

Through such studies, those Inland Sea sites that were barren of living organisms were identified, and remedial measures were proposed. Countrywide studies revealed that during the early 1970s, as oil spills and other polluting events became more and more frequent, nearly half of them were occurring in that sea.

Then in December 1974, a huge oil leakage at the Mitsubishi refinery at Mizushima unleashed some 40,000 kiloliters (about 245,000 Imperial or 335,000 US barrels) of oil in four days. The oil spread eastward from Mizushima via the Kii Channel into the Pacific Ocean. The fishery damage from that spill alone was initially assessed at 4.4 billion yen. However, in following weeks and months the oil continued to wreak havoc, damaging the sea's bio-system and causing fish catches to drop. During May 1975 federations of fishermen reached settlements with Mitsubishi that totaled some 13.4 billion yen.[91] It was a sum roughly 700 times that of the 1958 settlement in Tokyo Bay.

As oil spills proliferated and worsened in the Inland Sea, so too did red tides, fish-kills, restrictions on fishing and fisherman protests. By 1975, some fishing groups were turning to lawsuits to secure indemnification for losses caused by red tides. And spurred by the Mizushima spill, mayors and governors in the Inland Sea vicinity drafted remedial proposals for the national government to consider.[92] In following years those measures gradually reduced the rate of destruction, and while a pristine Inland Sea was never restored, at least much of it was able to sustain a much-reduced fishing industry.

Elsewhere around the country, the same pattern played out, with ports on all sides of Kyushu, Shikoku, Honshu and even Hokkaido experiencing similar, if usually less disastrous, pollution.[93] And yet, as noted above, the output of the fishery industry continued to grow.

### 2. The Responses

The fishing industry sustained itself despite the destruction of resources by following three basic strategies in addition to the use of social protest and compensatory lawsuits. One strategy was to acquire the equipment that would make more pelagic fishing possible. The second was to shift nearby harvest efforts to less-polluted coastal fishing grounds. The third was to expand output of cultured fisheries.

In terms of equipment, the small oar- and wind-powered vessels of earlier generations were rapidly abandoned in favor of fishing boats powered by diesel and other engines (see Table 41). Thus, whereas over 65 percent of all registered fishing boats had been oar- and wind-powered in 1955, less than 6 percent were by 1985. And in following years, the proportion kept dropping, hitting 2.5 percent in 2005.[94]

These larger vessels, and the larger nets and other equipment that came with them, enabled fewer and fewer fishermen to produce ever-larger harvests – as long as the fish supply lasted. They did so by shifting more of their activity to more distant pelagic fisheries, in the northern Pacific at first, and then elsewhere around the globe, as regional fish populations shrank under the onslaught of industrial technology.

More locally, insofar as smaller-scale fishermen continued to harvest fish, shellfish and other yield in the vicinity of the archipelago, they focused more and more on those parts of the island chain least damaged by industrial pollution. In particular the waters around Hokkaido became a favored fishing area, even though the island accounted for only 15 percent of Japan's total coastline. Thus, whereas in 1983 about 17 percent of the wild marine harvest came from fishermen operating out of Hokkaido, by 2006 they produced over 27 percent of that catch.[95]

The third strategy for coping with the decline of natural riverine and inshore fisheries was to develop cultured seafood production.[96] Roughly 90 percent of this was saltwater culture; the rest, freshwater. And cultured production grew steadily as decades passed; rising from some 166,000 tons in 1955 to 1,390,000 in 1995, dropping somewhat after that. As a portion of the total fish catch, it also rose slowly, from about 3.5 percent in 1955 to nearly 11 percent in the 1980s, and reaching some 20–25 percent by the 2000s, as overall fishing production declined.

That post-boom decline appears to reflect international competition. As global fish stocks shrank, fishermen closer to the surviving supply and/or utilizing cheaper labor were able to undercut the comparatively high-wage fishermen who had to travel from Japan southward across the Pacific to the remaining fisheries. As a result, whereas Japanese fishing exports exceeded imports during the 1960s, by 1975 imports were the larger figure, and the disparity kept growing. By 2005, with domestic production at about half of its 1980s peak level, Japan was importing some 5,782,000 metric tons of fishery production – roughly equal to total domestic output – while exporting only 647,000 tons.[97]

Finally, as indicated in Table 42, Japanese whaling grew briskly during the 1950s, peaking in the 1960s at roughly 20,000 whales per year and shrinking thereafter to less than a thousand annually from the 1990s on.

* * *

In sum, then, Japan's fishermen recovered from World War II, subsequently coped with the damage wrought by industrial pollution, but finally were forced to retrench when global over-exploitation of the seas undercut their capacity to compete with fishermen who enjoyed economic advantages.

*Agriculture*

As with fishermen, the basic story of agricultural activity after 1945 was that of recovery, modest growth and eventual shrinkage in production. Within that context the story entailed striking processes of social change as well as mechanization and changes in crops grown. Less striking in overall impact were the effects of industrial pollution and the gradual shift of agriculture away from major industrial centers.

*1. On Rural Society*

Agricultural production recovered quickly after 1945 thanks to the ample labor supply generated by burned-out cities and demobilized armies. Moreover, one of the major social issues of prewar days – peasant-landlord conflicts – was eliminated by the American victors, who did so through a policy of *de facto* expropriation – forcing landlords to sell their rental land to the tenant operators at pre-inflation prices. By 1955 nearly all farmland (91 percent) was tilled by its owners.[98]

By then agricultural output had surpassed prewar levels. And thereafter, although increases in total yield were modest and sparse, sharp gains in output-per-capita made possible one of the most striking rural changes of those decades – a huge drop in the number of people engaged in farm work. Figures differ, depending on one's criteria of inclusion, but they all reveal the same trend. As Table 34 indicates, some 36.3 million adults farmed in Japan in 1955 whereas only 8.4 million did in 2005 – amounting to a 77 percent drop in farmworkers, from 61.1 percent of the total adult population down to only 7.6 percent of that population. As the table also shows, moreover, even in 1960, only about 38 percent of those engaged in farmwork pursued it full-time. The full-time percentage then dropped to less than 27 percent by 1985, increasing subsequently as the urban economy soured, and exceeding 38 percent in 2008.

In terms of households, as well as individuals, a rapidly dwindling number actually engaged in either full- or nearly full-time farming. Back in 1906, some 71 percent of Japan's 5.4 million farm households had been engaged in farming full-time, and in 1935, 74 percent of 5.5 million still were.[99] After the war, however, both trends reversed, as Table 33 shows. Moreover, while the total number of farm households dropped by some 28 percent between 1950 and 1984, the number of full-time farm households plummeted by nearly 80 percent. And of the many shifting to part-time farming, by the later boom years most were only modestly involved in agricultural production. In effect they were non-farm households that clung to the old homestead more from choice than economic necessity.

This sharp shift to part-time farming puts one in mind of *dekasegi*, the village practice of *bakuhan* centuries, noted in Chapter 6, in which farm folk worked part-time in town, mostly in the agricultural off-season. In both cases it was possible for ordinary folk to do so because of Japan's geographic patterns of dense settlement and urban-rural intermingling on the archipelago's lowlands, which enabled people to commute to other, frequently more lucrative jobs.

Following the late 1980s bust, however, many of the most marginal farming households – nearly 2 million between 1984 and 2005 – completely abandoned agriculture, whether voluntarily in response to generational change or by selling their land in response to economic need or opportunity. The more fully engaged in agriculture a household was, the better it survived the urban downturn, as many working members of those households gave up urban jobs and turned to full-time farming.

### 2. On Agronomic Trends

The large, long-term postwar decline in the number of farms and farmers was only marginally paralleled by the trend in arable acreage. From a low point in 1946, it grew moderately until around 1960, after which it gradually declined, as Table 36 shows.

That up and down trend in acreage was more closely linked to the trajectory of overall agricultural output, particularly in field crops. As a whole, gradual declines in some areas of production were substantially offset by gains in other areas, resulting in overall stability of agricultural output. That stability was maintained despite the sharp reduction in farmworkers by major gains in output-per-worker. And those gains were achieved primarily by mechanization and secondarily by a gradual shift to more consolidated production of foodstuffs that remained relatively safe from foreign competition.

Regarding mechanization, it advanced most rapidly during the 20 years 1965–84, as suggested by the select implements listed in Table 39. That trend reflected government policy – in 1961 it had promulgated the "Basic Agricultural Law", with the goals of promoting mechanization and the use of farm chemicals, policies that obviously appealed to the government's industrial supporters.[100]

This mechanization was a central factor in the rapid drop in farm labor requirements. As Table 37 reveals, however, it did not lead to a sustained increase in gross output of field crops despite the rapid growth in Japan's overall population and per-capita food consumption. Rather, after years of modest but widespread gains in output during the 1950s–60s, extensive declines in crop production became evident, starting in the later boom years. In general, crops that could be grown more cheaply abroad, harvested and then shipped to Japan in good condition – notably grains and pulses – did poorly in domestic farming, while those that were most perishable, such as lettuce and spinach, did better. Rice production fared relatively well, thanks mainly to special tariff arrangements, but it too declined substantially during the post-boom decades.

Turning to the second factor, consolidation of food production, it was especially pronounced in the area of animal nurturing, where the most striking absolute gains in food output were achieved. In essence, Japan was undergoing the shift from family farming to factory farming, especially in terms of pigs and chickens, as Table 38 reveals.[101]

Regarding raw milk production, whereas in 1950, 133,000 farm households (on average milking 1–2 cows apiece) produced 367,000 tons, by 1975 the output of 160,000 farms (averaging some 11 cows apiece) was 4.96 million tons. And in 2005, the surviving 27,700 large dairy farms (with some 60 apiece) sent 8.29 million tons to market.[102] Note also that whereas the average cow produced 1.85 tons of milk per year in 1950, by 2005 its output was 5 tons per year.

Finally, on the downside, perhaps the most stunning agricultural victim of technological change was the horse. In Chapter 7, we noted how demand for horses grew during the early decades of the twentieth century. After the war, their utility faded. Thus, whereas some 905,000 farm households were raising about 1,071,000 horses in 1950, by 1985 the figures had shriveled to 9,300 households and 23,000 horses. Thereafter the number of horse farms continued to shrink – to some 5,000 in 1993 – although the number of horses stabilized and then rose slightly to 27,000.[103]

### 3. On Environmental Issues

In a couple of ways agriculture during the decades after 1945 had less of an impact on the environment than in prior centuries. First, whereas farmers in earlier times had relied heavily on woodland for wood, fertilizer and other items, after recovering from World War II, they had less and less use for it, leaving the woodland much more free to pursue its own regeneration.

Second, whereas the long-term story of human-forest relations down through the "opening" of Hokkaido had entailed the conversion of ever more lowland from forest to arable acreage, post-1945 farming changed very little woodland to farmland. Indeed, as decades passed, overall farm acreage (meaning, the total of pasturage, orchards and cultivated land) shrank substantially – from a peak of about 6 million hectares around 1960 to some 5.4 million in 1985, and down further to 4.6 million in 2005.[104] And while most of the lost farmland shifted to other human uses, as we noted earlier, a portion – especially bits and pieces of hard-to-use land at the forest edge – reverted to natural growth.

On the other hand, in two ways, rural technological change had a negative environmental impact on farmers, farmland and adjoining areas. The adoption of fossil-fuel-powered farm equipment obviously added to air pollution, although urban fossil-fuel usage dwarfed its impact. More visibly, the widespread use of biocides, mainly insecticides but also herbicides, contributed to both water and air pollution.[105] And their victims included not only marine life, birds and nearby vegetation, but also farmers who applied the poisons and those consumers who encountered their residues in foodstuffs.

Thus, a medical report of early 1967 asserted that "more than 40 percent of farmers using insecticides and other farm chemicals show symptoms of chemical poisoning". And three years later, tests revealed that some green tea from Shizuoka Prefecture – one of Japan's most highly esteemed sources of such tea – had ten times the permissible level of the poison, DDT.[106] Findings such as this led government agencies to tighten their regulation of farmers' use of chemicals, and in following years the problems gradually eased.

Much more damaging than the chemicals used by farmers were the myriad others produced and used by industry. Industrialists were sometimes well aware of the damage caused by their chemical pollutants, as in earlier-noted cases relating to fisheries, but bottom-line considerations inhibited their readiness to address the issue.

One aspect of the industrial-chemical problem was harm done to farmers and farm operations. Another was harm done to consumers by poisons transmitted via the food they produced. A particularly tragic case of the latter appeared in 1955. That June, many babies in western Japan began to sicken and some even to die from severe and painful stomach illness. By August, official investigations in Okayama had established that the babies had been poisoned by arsenic in powdered milk, and it was determined that the lethal milk came from the Tokushima plant of Morinaga Milk Industry. The plant had been using "a cheap substitute product as a stabilizer for its powdered milk", and the substitute, which was labeled "for industrial use", was found to contain arsenic.[107]

Morinaga then corrected its mistake, but the case precipitated vigorous demands for compensation. The company refused on the ground that it could not afford to pay. Within a few months, most of the victim families accepted a government-sponsored token compensation. Others, however, persisted, mounting a lawsuit that dragged on for years. In October 1963, a lower-court ruling exonerated the accused Morinaga executives, but plaintiffs appealed to the Supreme Court. Six years later, in February 1969 – by which time the problems of industrial pollution were much more widely recognized – that court rejected a request for dismissal by the two executives accused of negligence, sending the case back to the Tokushima District Court. There the case dragged on for another four years, until November 1973, when that court found the Morinaga section chief who authorized the use of the arsenic-bearing material guilty of criminal negligence and sentenced him to three years in prison.[108]

Regarding the damage done to farming by industrial chemicals, food poisoning was not limited to humans. To cite some notable examples, in 1968, about a million chickens were made sick in western Japan by contaminated feed, and half of them died. In 1972–73, in the southern half of Japan, large numbers of cows sickened and died and calves were born deformed due to consumption of a synthetic feed. A few months later, it was contaminated pig feed that caused deformed and stillborn litters.[109]

More "traditional" types of industrial damage also continued to afflict farmers. As noted in Chapter 7, for farmers in hinterland regions, mining, smelting and pulp-mill operations had for decades presented the most widespread industrial problems because of their locations, usually upstream from paddy fields and other farm land. After the war, those problems continued to appear.

One of the most notorious instances appeared in the vicinity of Annaka in northwest Kantô. There the Tôhô Zinc Corporation's mining-smelting operation produced gas and liquid pollutants that from the mid-1950s onward severely poisoned farm lands, injuring fruit and mulberry trees, as well as silkworms. Later, during the 1960s–70s, as dairy farming expanded in the area, pollutants from the company's mine, cadmium most notoriously, poisoned pastures. From there they got into milk and sickened consumers, in the process becoming part of the rapidly expanding nationwide *itai itai* problem that we noted earlier.[110]

More troublesome than mine and pulp-mill wastes were the consequences of that other longstanding agricultural pattern – the geographical mingling of farm lands and urban development. That entanglement exposed more and more farms to the polluting impact of proliferating factories of all sorts. At the same time, however, that very industrial growth pushed up property values and created new job opportunities. So near-city farming was made more difficult, but abandoning it became easier.

Within that context, as more and more farmers found poisoned water, air and soil damaging their crops and even rendering some unfit for sale, they organized protests and law suits and, in some instances, received "voluntary" compensation from polluters. As the years passed, however, more and more of them abandoned farm production, especially when generations changed, with elders retiring and offspring selling the land and taking other jobs.

Over time this trend eliminated a lot of farmland from cities and towns, facilitating urban sprawl and causing a gradual countrywide redistribution of agricultural production. Much as fishery activity in Tokyo Bay and the Osaka area had collapsed even while that around Hokkaido expanded, so farming in those and other urban areas shrank far faster than did that of Hokkaido, which became – together with several other, largely rural prefectures, in Tôhoku mainly – the source of a greater portion of national farm output, as Table 35 suggests.[111]

* * *

In sum then, the demographic story of agriculture during the decades since 1945 has been one of sustained shrinkage, primarily due to farm mechanization. The economic story is one of product types evolving in response to changing public food preferences and foreign competition. That foreign competition has become more pronounced in recent decades as the rural sector's shrinkage has translated into declining political clout, with the consequent erosion of protective tariffs due to foreign pressure.

In terms of environmental impact, agriculture has been of relatively modest consequence. Mainly it has constituted a victim of urban industrial pollutants or has served as a vehicle for their transference to the broader ecosystem.

*Forestry*

Overall, the story of forestry in Japan since 1945 follows the same basic line as that of fisheries and agriculture: recovery from war, a period of boom and then retrenchment. The boom period was shorter, however, and the subsequent retrenchment longer and more substantial. There were other dissimilarities as well, ones that reflected differences in the biological character of the three biomes and in their uses by humankind.

Reflecting the fact that these forests mostly stood on steep hillsides for which humans had little other use, the total acreage of forest (*sanrin*) area and its pattern of distribution among public and private owners changed little over the decades after 1945, as Table 43 indicates. Indeed, as we earlier suggested, and as the table shows, the area of forestland actually grew a bit between 1960 and the 1980s, before starting a slow decline.

Let us examine this lush forest realm – roughly five times the acreage of cultivated land – in terms of three topics: natural threats to trees; woodland's role as a protection forest for human society; and, at greater length, issues relating to material provisioning, of timber in particular.

### 1. On Natural Threats

Humans, obviously, are the biggest threat to natural biomes, but forests, like fisheries, are also vulnerable to damage by other invasive biota. The one natural threat that has done major damage to Japan's forests in recent decades is the insect-borne pine nematode disease.[112] Introduced from abroad into southern Kyushu in the 1860s–70s or thereabouts, it has gradually spread northeastward, by the 1980s infecting stands of pine even in northeast Honshu. In the process it has decimated many such stands, by the 1970s–80s killing several million pines per year and leading to the gradual replacement of pine with other species of trees or other plants. The loss has been felt in terms of ruined timber but also in terms of weakened protection forests because some pines are very useful as anchors of desiccated soils.

### 2. On Protection Forests

Given the nature of Japan's woodland as temperate-zone forest mostly situated on steep hillsides that tower above the alluvial plains where humans live, one of its crucial functions has been to control the flow of rain and snowmelt so that they do not ravage those lowlands. As noted in earlier chapters, that function has long been evident, and from *bakuhan* centuries onward, protection forestry became a major aspect of society's forest policy.

That tradition continued after 1945. Whereas some 2.4 million hectares of forest were designated protection forest as of 1951 and managed accordingly, by 1980 the area had grown to 7.3 million hectares, and by 2006 to 11.8 million – nearly half of the archipelago's total woodland.[113] About half of the acreage designated protection forest and subject to its policies is government forest, and about half is owned privately.[114] Roughly 60–70 percent of that area serves to protect head-waters, and most of the rest is intended to prevent the erosion of vulnerable soils.

Implementing policy on protection forests has entailed a substantial and growing cost to the government, mainly for the construction of dams and retaining walls designed to reduce flooding and other damage. And while government receipts from lumber sales once covered a good portion of that cost, in recent decades the decline in logging income has shifted the burden to taxpayers.

These protection-forest areas have been subject to logging as long as it proceeded in accord with protection-forest regulations. And the rest of Japan's woodland has served primarily to generate wood products. Indeed, for most woodland owners, these have been the uses that mattered, and it is in such provisioning activity that forestry's most dramatic ups and downs have occurred.

*3. On Material Provisioning*

For some forest products the key determinant of their market value and volume has been the extent of displacement by other materials. Most notably, three of the products with the longest history of use – bamboo, charcoal and fuel wood – have experienced a large and sustained drop in usage from around 1960 onward, as Table 47 shows.

To elaborate, the bamboo was mostly replaced in diverse uses by metal and plastic. The charcoal and fuel wood, being used for various heating purposes, gave way to fossil fuel and electricity. Charcoal production peaked in 1951, started dropping rapidly in the later 1950s and by 1965 was below output levels of the 1880s.[115] Similarly, by one account, fuel-wood production peaked at some 32 million cubic meters in 1951.[116] Subsequently, as the table indicates, it plummeted as other fuels became available. Even imports of wood for use as fuel, which were massive in the early postwar years, had dropped to a very modest level by 1980. Yet even at that level, they dominated the surviving market-place thereafter.

Most wood, meanwhile, was timber material, and it was used primarily for construction purposes. Compared to fuel wood, the demand for timber proved more durable. As Table 45 shows, the overall production of logs rose sharply from some 20.3 million cubic meters in 1950 to 48.5 million in 1960, peaking soon after and then starting a sustained decline to 34.1 million in 1980 and on down to the 16–17 million range after 2000. That trajectory reflects the vigorous construc-tion activity of the postwar recovery and boom decades, as well as the subsequent slowdown. The growth in demand would have been even greater except for the increasing use of ferro-concrete construction, which flourished during the boom decades as large factories, skyscrapers and huge apartment buildings arose, the apartments gradually reducing demand for wooden housing.[117]

The trajectory of these figures also reflects other factors, namely the availability of timber, new technology, changes in production costs, supplies from the global resource base (that is, imports) and, finally, recycling.

*A. On Timber Availability.* The availability of harvestable wood was shaped by both biology and geography. The biological factor that distinguished forest yield from that of fisheries and agriculture was the simple fact that it takes several decades to grow a tree that will yield large-diameter logs, whereas fisheries and meat-producers can replace harvested stock in just a few years. And crop-growers usually can do so annually. Consequently, even when logged areas were diligently replanted, as they were from the 1950s into the 1970s, the reforested acreage would not begin to provide another rich timber crop until around 2000 or later.

The long wait for replacement stands mattered, even when ample old-growth forest remained, because not all timber stands were equally accessible. As years passed and trees were cut, loggers found themselves having to press ever farther into steeply pitched intermontane valleys, where wood extraction was increasingly difficult and costly.

The extent of logging and reforesting since 1930 – and most notably the formation of "artificial" or plantation (even-aged monoculture) stands during the 1940s–50s – is indicated by Table 44. It also reveals the great degree of shrinkage in both activities since the 1960s.

Regarding the great effort to expand plantation stands, the availability of cheap labor after 1945, together with the badly overcut condition of the country's woodland and the government's policy goal of maximizing self-sufficiency, gave rise to widespread reforestation. Some 70,000 hectares of plantation forest were established annually during the later 1940s, and during the 1950s the rate leaped to more than 300,000, but it slowed significantly from the later 1960s onward. As a result of this surge in planting activity, whereas in 1940, Japan had some 4 million hectares of plantation forest, by 1965 the figure was 7.6 million, and from 1985 onward a bit over 10 million hectares at varying stages of maturity. About 80 percent of that acreage was planted to conifers – *sugi, hinoki* and *karamatsu* (larch).[118]

Also, because dense plantation stands, and especially the evergreen *sugi* and *hinoki*, are very vulnerable to snow damage, most of the plantations were formed in southern Japan, notably on Shikoku and Kyushu, while most reforesting in Hokkaido and northerly Honshu was by natural regeneration.[119] Stand recovery on these latter sites was commonly assisted by programs of aftercare, which for a few years would suppress competing growth and help desirable stock to mature.

By the late boom years, more and more of these plantation stands were in need of thinning. However, due to the increased cost of labor, the declining demand for fuel wood and small-diameter lumber, and the availability of cheaper imported wood, such thinning proved uneconomic. Even such measures as vigorous expansion of the forest-road system, enhanced government assistance, and the introduction of three-wheeled, motorized thinning machines failed to make the work worthwhile.[120] As a consequence, since the 1980s, plantation stands have grown ever more crowded and more vulnerable to wind-throw and snow damage.

*B. On Technological Change.* Given the increasing difficulty of extracting logs as fellers worked ever farther into the mountains, Japan's capacity to sustain such a high level of production into the 1970s seems remarkable. Technology played an important role in that outcome, even though key mechanisms of industrial lumber production – the sawmill, forest-railway and tractor-drawn sled – were all introduced before 1940.

After the war, government policy, in its quest for self-sufficiency, encouraged vigorous use and technical updating of all those devices. In the case of forest railroads, however, "updating" during the boom years meant their displacement by forest roads as trucks became the dominant means of cargo transport. The availability of trucks led to a surge in construction of such roads despite the difficulty and costliness of building and maintaining them in Japan's mountainous terrain. Thus, by the year 2000, the effort had yielded a network some 128,000 km in length.[121]

More specialized devices for moving logs were also adopted to improve efficiency in the face of a shrinking and ageing labor pool and intensifying foreign competition. By the 1990s, more and more "high-tech" machines were being used to fell trees, saw them into logs, and skid, gather and load them for shipment.[122]

More consequential for forestry as a whole during the postwar decades was the widespread adoption of the chainsaw. As noted in Chapter 7, the re-utilization of cross-cut saws after 1868 had greatly increased loggers' productivity compared to that of *bakuhan* days. The next "great leap forward", adoption of the chainsaw, occurred after 1945, and mainly during the 1950s–60s. Its use proliferated, sharply increasing log-output per hour. Indeed, by 1965, some 45,000 of the saws were in use, and their presence surely was a key factor enabling loggers to continue increasing output even as they worked ever more difficult terrain.

As the 1960s advanced, however, a major problem with chainsaws emerged. The intense vibrations that they produced were severely damaging some of their users by giving them Raynaud's Disease, an injury of the nerves that could cause damaged fingers and hands to become "cold, pale, and painful, sometimes gangrenous".[123] By 1969, the union of national forestry workers was making the problem a focus of attention, and in response the government ordered that the saws be used no more than a specified number of hours per day. The problem persisted, however, and by 1973 the government's Forestry Agency had agreed to pay compensation to certified victims – who by the end of 1975 numbered over 1,000 in the national forests alone.[124]

Those national-forest workers were only a portion of the total injured by chainsaws, however, since forests not controlled by the Forestry Agency were more extensive and produced more timber than did Agency forests. Chainsaw injuries could be particularly hurtful to households logging their own woodland because most of those combined forestry and farm work, and injury from one enterprise would also hinder pursuit of the other.

The problem of chainsaw vibration notwithstanding, those saws, together with trucks and truck roads, the "high-tech" felling and processing equipment, and other technological advances, helped compensate for the topographical disadvantages of Japan's mountainous woodland, enabling the rapidly declining force of woodsmen to continue extracting logs for shipment to the mill.

*C. On Rising Production Costs and Foreign Competition.* All the technological advances notwithstanding, the long-term rise in labor and other production costs gradually undercut the capacity of domestic producers to compete with imported timber. Furthermore, the latter's price dropped as larger cargo ships – and elaborate sawmill facilities built in ports specifically to process off-loaded logs – lowered substantially the cost of imported wood.

Moreover, because the Philippines, Indonesia and Malaysia, which were major timber suppliers to Japan during the boom decades, employed less costly labor, imports from there also had a significant price advantage in terms of initial cost.[125] As Table 45 on wood production and imports shows, postwar imports were virtually nil before 1955, but their volume rocketed upward during the boom years, surpassing domestic output by 1970. They rose almost tenfold between 1960 and 1980, while domestic log production dropped by 30 percent. And imports remained high thereafter, even as domestic production continued its decline.

The drop in domestic log production drove large numbers of farm-and-forestry households out of the logging business. Thus the 2.5 million families so employed in 1960 had dropped below 2 million by 1980 and stood at about 1 million by 2000.[126] And burgeoning imports were the key factor in that decline. As a farmer-woodsman in a hamlet near Lake Biwa explained the problem:

> During the decade between 1965 and 1974, there was a period when forestry was strong. Then, after they started importing foreign lumber, many non-brand-name local lumbers became almost unsaleable. Cutting down and planting trees makes no profits. You can get at least some money if you are hired by the day for such jobs as logging or pruning, which are contracted to the forestry coopera-tive. So this is how we make a living. I'd rather have the national or prefectural government purchase all my forests on the mountains and be employed and work for them than owning and having to maintain all this. I think this is more or less the case with most forests on the mountains in Japan.[127]

*D. On Recycling.* The recycling of lumber has a long history in Japan, as we noted in earlier chapters. Reusable timbers of good quality went into new construction while damaged pieces became fuel wood. Since World War II, however, as fossil fuel displaced fuel wood, it has been in the new area of wood pulp that recycling emerged as a major activity.[128]

As noted in Chapter 7, the use of wood pulp for making paper dates to around 1890, and thereafter pulp mills became major users of wood – and, as a corollary, major polluters of rivers. For the forest owner, wood pulp was valued as a market for sticks too small for use as lumber. Larger tree limbs and, especially, the stems of young trees removed in the process of thinning plantation stands could be sold to pulp mills, helping recoup the woodsman's expenses.

After the war, pulp production revived during the 1950s and rose briskly into the 1970s, with most demand being met by domestic production. However, by 1980, even though total demand for pulp continued its brisk but irregular growth – having exceeded 30 million cubic meters annually in 1971 and nearly reaching 40 million in 1991 – two factors were combining to drive down the use of domestic wood in meeting that demand. One factor was continuing rapid growth of pulpwood imports, as evident in Table 46. The other was the growing extent of recycling. By 2000, wastepaper recycling supplied over half of the raw material used by paper mills, and the recycled quantities kept growing in subsequent years.[129] By then, too, other waste wood, including construction scrap and the residue of saw mills and plywood mills, was being recycled, further reducing demand for small-size timbers.

These trends of the past half-century – growth of wood imports and recycling of waste – reflected both the declining availability of raw material (as harvestable forest gave way to newly planted seedlings) and the rising cost of timber production (as wages and other logging costs rose). The net result has been a further decline in domestic forest yield and further growth of Japan's dependence on its global resource base. In the absence of recycling, however, that growth in import dependency would have been much greater.

\* \* \*

In sum, then, for Japan's forests since 1945, humans remained the chief menace. The scale of the postwar human assault was unprecedented, its magnitude a reflection of three factors: the great demand for timber created by postwar reconstruction; population growth and gains in living standards; and advances in logging technology.

As the boom decades advanced, however, human pressure on the archipelago's woodland eased. The shrinkage and abandonment of numerous intermontane villages and much marginal farmland enabled some areas to reforest, offsetting losses to recreational and other usage. The demand for forest products was eased by the use of ferro-concrete construction, by increased recycling of wood products and by the influx of imported wood. In terms of environmental impact, of course, that influx meant only that the demand on woodland had been shifted from archipelagic forest to that of the global resource base.

Cumulatively, these developments enabled Japan's forests to make a substantial recovery from the 1970s onward, with vast acreages of logged woodland gradually regaining forest cover. Much of that was re-growth as mixed, multi-aged woodland, but another large portion was even-aged monoculture stands. Because of the sustained drop in demand for domestic timber, however, and the prohibitive cost of plantation maintenance, as years have passed, those monoculture stands have become increasingly subject to wind-throw and snow damage.

From the perspective of the lumber industry (or the urban aesthete), this decay of plantation stands is a lamentable development. However, because the breakage on monoculture stands opens up forest floor to sunlight, it facilitates the growth of understorey and, eventually, other species of trees. Over time, that is to say, decay of plantation stands will lead to revitalized "natural" forest with a much richer diversity of both flora and fauna. How fully that outcome will be realized, of course, will depend on how diverse global and domestic trends play out in future.

## RECAPITULATION

By 1940, as we noted in summing up Chapter 7, Japan was "halfway there" in the transition from intensive agricultural to industrial society. During the half-century that followed, it completed the transition.

To do that, it had to overcome the archipelago's severely limited resource base so as to meet society's need for foodstuffs, fossil fuel and most of the other basic raw materials of advanced industrialization. And that requirement meant developing a global resource base to replace the empire-centered one it lost in 1945.

The entrepreneurial system of production and trade that was utilized – with particularly striking success during the boom decades 1955–85 – produced the finished goods that paid for those needed raw materials. In doing so, it also provided a vast array of jobs that absorbed a rapidly growing workforce, including millions of erstwhile farmers, fishermen and loggers. In addition, it enabled the general populace to experience gains in material well-being utterly unprecedented in the society's history.

On the other hand, that very process of industrial growth and diversification also produced a surge of environmental pollution. The pollutants proved particularly damaging to people, both in and near the workplace, leading to vigorous protest and eventual counter-measures that brought much of the problem under control.

The processes of industrial expansion, pollution and social adaptation also had broader environmental consequences in terms of farmland, fisheries and forestland. Regarding farmland, a combination of factors – industrial growth and pollution, agricultural mechanization and intensification, and competition from cheaper imports – produced a major, sustained decline in cultivated acreage, and a shift of farmland away from cities and poorly accessible intermontane areas to less hilly and more accessible rural areas, particularly in the colder, more recently developed northeastern section of the country.

Fisheries were the biome most savagely injured by industrial development, and much of Japan's coastal fishery activity died out, largely replaced by big-boat pelagic fishing. Initially, Japanese fishermen produced this oceanic catch, but as the boom decades ended, imports grew until the two sources yielded roughly equal quantities.

As for Japan's grand expanses of forestland, they were severely cut over during the early postwar years. Government-sponsored projects of protection forestry minimized the downstream damage of this deforestation, while vigorous programs of replanting gave the realm a vast acreage of new, even-aged, monoculture stands sporting a few preferred timber trees. By 1965, however, the logging and refor-esting activities had passed their peak, and in following years import competition gradually undercut the commercial utility of those plantations. So, many of them have been left to age and decay, slowly evolving into natural diversified woodland.

These trends in farmland, fisheries and forests were all visible by the 1980s. By then, too, a major decline in the total fertility rate of the human populace was outweighing gains in public health and workplace safety, thereby slowing popula-tion growth and by 2000 ushering in a phase of demographic stabilization. That trend was accompanied by stabilization in other demographic variables and also in measures of economic activity – such as employment, manufacturing output, foreign trade and consumer demand. In toto, these trends suggest that industrial society in the archipelago may be in the process of moving from the era of growth to the era of stability, much as intensive agriculture did in the decades around 1700.

Finally, in terms of Japan's global resource base, the decades of rapid growth after 1945 meant that the archipelago's society shared responsibility with other industrial and industrializing societies for the escalating consumption of both global biota – forests and marine fisheries in particular – and the accumulated global supply of fossil fuel and other raw materials, as well as for the polluting effects of their use.

As Japan's industrial society has moved from growth to stability, however, the trend lines in archipelagic consumption of imports have begun to shift. Rates of growth in fossil fuel and other raw material usage have slowed; some foodstuff imports have declined. But as of 2010, given the technological arrangements and per-capita consumption level of the archipelago's 127 million human residents, it continues to be heavily dependent on the yield of that global resource base.

# Epilogue

## A Recapitulation and Final Thoughts

In broadest terms the human (*Homo sapiens*) experience on the Japanese archipelago has constituted a microcosm of the global human experience. It has consisted of a long-term evolution through the three standard phases of human organization – those of forager, agricultural and industrial society. The three phases are clearly dissimilar in terms of their durations, their demographic scale and the nature of their human-environment relationship.

Regarding duration, as we have seen, the three differ greatly. Forager society in the archipelago lasted for roughly 25–30,000 years, giving way to the continental east Asian type of early agricultural society some 2–3,000 years ago. This agricultural society, in its earlier and later (or extensive and intensive) forms, survived to near the end of the 1800s, when it commenced a rapid evolution into the Euro-American type of industrial society found there today. So, whereas the archipelago has thus far been home to a form of industrial society for about 100 years, it sustained agricultural society for about 25 times as long and sapiens foragers for some 250 times as long.

Turning to demographics, both the size and the material culture of human population during these three stages merit note because both experienced striking growth and change. Demographic increase was primarily the product of more live births per mother and longer lifespans per person, although immigration was a significant factor at times. Increase in material culture entailed growth in the quantity, scale and variety of goods per capita.

To note first the size of this human population, it has been estimated that the forager populace grew from a few thousand during earlier millennia to a peak of some 250,000 as of 5,000 years ago. Most of this Jômon population was found in the northeasterly half of the archipelago, where mixed deciduous woodland provided a much richer array of floral and faunal foodstuffs than did the evergreen forests of the southwest. Consequently, when several centuries of colder weather ensued, shrinking the food supply even as it increased the human need for warmth, shelter and caloric intake, the overall population dropped rapidly to some 60–70,000.

Then, however, following the introduction of field cropping to southwestern Japan some 2,500 years ago, the population began to grow again, a trend abetted by substantial in-migration from nearby continental areas and gradual eastward relocation. In the course of roughly 1,200 years (to around 700 CE), it rose to the vicinity of 5,000,000, which it held for more than 500 years until around 1300 CE. Subsequently, with the diffusion of intensive agricultural techniques, that population grew again, peaking at about 30–32,000,000, whose level persisted for nearly 200 years after 1700. Then, with the shift to industrial society, the populace commenced a rapid and sustained demographic increase, coming to exceed 125,000,000 by about 2000, when it appeared to be entering a new period of stabilization.

These striking demographic changes – roughly a 100-fold gain over 5,000 years from maximal forager to maximal agricultural society and (as of today) a fourfold gain over 130 years from agricultural to industrial society – were accompanied by equally striking changes in scale of material culture. Whereas foragers in the archipelago utilized simple huts or caves, along with rudimentary clothing, cooking devices and hunting tools, the general populace of agricultural society lived in larger, structurally more complex houses, and had more elaborate clothing and bedding, cooking facilities and tools for work. In addition, agricultural society sustained a small but very privileged elite class that enjoyed much grander buildings, fancier clothing and diverse other possessions.

Most remarkable, however, is the difference between the material culture of agricultural and industrial society. The general populace of industrial Japan has become surrounded by material goods and services of myriad sorts and in quantities that their pre-industrial ancestors would find incomprehensible. For the elite, material possessions are essentially vastly elaborated and fancy versions of those found in hoi polloi culture.

These stunning changes in population numbers and material culture are reflections of the basic differences in techniques of sustenance utilized by the three stages of society. As we noted in the text, the archipelago's forager populace utilized the classic hunter-gatherer strategy of capturing and harvesting such indigenous foodstuffs as were locally available. Japan's early agricultural society adopted and adapted complex symbiotic relationships between humans and such "domesticated" plants and animals as rice, other grains, vegetables and horses. Later it maximized the yield from those relationships by employing more intensive techniques of field cropping, orchardry and animal husbandry that substantially increased the archipelago's food-production.

In two basic ways Japan's industrial society has made a sharp departure from the sustenance practices of both forager and agricultural societies. First, these latter based themselves on local yields from within the archipelago, whereas industrial Japan – in the manner of all industrial societies – has grounded itself in an ever more essential global resource base, whether that base was made accessible by primarily political (pre-1945) or economic (post-1945) arrangements.

Second, whereas the earlier societies relied for energy and sustenance on the yield of living biota, industrial society has increased its resource base radically by utilizing the energy stored in hundreds of millions of years' worth of accumulated biomass in the form of fossil fuel, whether found in the archipelago or – mainly

– elsewhere. By combining these (and other) new energy sources with the extraordinary array of industrial-age technologies, Japan has in a very short time achieved the above-noted demographic growth even as it has increased dramatically the level of material consumption per capita.

The immense growth and change experienced by the archipelago's human society as it has moved from forager to agricultural to industrial arrangements has been matched by the scale of change in its environmental relationship. As we have seen, that environmental context – the archipelago's global location, topography, climate and biotic composition – has always shaped peoples' lives, influencing where they lived, what they ate, what crops they raised, and what resources they used in producing food, clothing, buildings and other material goods.

To note briefly the impact of the archipelago's global location, it has played a major role from Pleistocene times to the present. It has determined the archipelago's biotic composition – humans included – as well as its weather patterns. Ever since the last glacial phase passed some 15,000 years ago, submerging the Yellow Plain and transforming arcland Japan into a set of islands, the nearby continent has continued to influence affairs.

Not only was it the source of the farming practices and most of the people of early agricultural society, but it also was the source of the metal-using technology and the political order that sustained an elite culture with its associated types of warfare. In addition, it was the source of the pathogens that played a key role in stabilizing and at times reducing the population during the later of those early agricultural centuries. And later yet, it was the source of techniques used in intensive agriculture and plantation forestry.

More recently, that global location off the coast of northeastern Asia helped insulate Japan from the imperialist marauding of Europeans. The Iberian surge of global activism passed with minimal impact, and not until the Anglophone surge of the later nineteenth century did European influence replace that of the nearby mainland as the principal outside factor in archipelagic history (for at least 150 years, anyway). Its brevity notwithstanding, that European impact was transformative, moving the realm into the phase of industrial society with its nation state political form and its associated shift to a global resource base and heavy fossil-fuel usage. So, from its beginnings to today, Japan's global location has shaped its human experience.

Conversely, in terms of human influence on the environmental context, as archipelagic society has changed through the millennia, so too has its impact on the ecosystem.

Regarding forager society's impact, the surviving evidence is very modest. In the immediate environs of small settlements, of course, the presence of simple houses and storage, waste and burial sites would have disrupted the local biome. And the occasional human-caused forest fire could have done more extensive damage. But such impacts would have been short-lived and had little if any lasting effect on the broader biome and its constituent elements.

The one lasting environmental impact that foragers of the archipelago may have had was destruction of the great mammals, notably woolly mammoths and giant deer, once the glacial melt-off of ca. 18–15,000 yBP had raised sea level and deprived them of the broad coastal lowlands on which they had once been able to roam freely. Their disappearance then led to other changes in the faunal community, which may have spurred the changes in forager hunting tools that replaced large spear-points with small points and arrowheads.

Agricultural society – being vastly larger, utilizing more elaborate technology and working together with its "domesticated" faunal and floral collaborators – had vastly greater impacts, both temporary and permanent, on the archipelago. Basically, agriculturalists transformed a single, integrated biome into a bifurcated one. Initially, Japan had constituted a forested archipelago whose woodland character ranged from sub-arctic to subtropical in accordance with its extended North-to-South orientation. Agriculturalists converted it into a bifurcated biome whose mountainous regions sustained forests, while its lowlands sustained humans, their collaborating species and such "parasites" as were able to find durable homes there.

As this basic transformation of the realm gradually spread from southwest to northeast through the centuries, it radically changed lowland species composition and probably led to various local extinctions. The hill country did not escape the impact of agricultural society either. Upland cultivation, whether done as permanent tillage or as sporadic "slash and burn" (swidden) tillage, disrupted local biomes and fostered erosion and downstream sedimentation. Moreover, the demand for construction timber, fuel wood and fodder denuded more and more diluvial terraces, especially near urban centers. The process fostered erosion that gradually transformed once-verdant hillsides into barren wasteland while producing downstream flooding and the gradual sedimentation of estuaries and bays, in the process altering coastal marine biomes.

Subsequently, during the centuries of intensive agriculture, collection of mulch for use as fertilizer added to upland denuding and erosion. Also, the techniques of plantation forestry that were introduced in the 1600s led slowly to species alteration and reduced biodiversity in ever-larger areas of forested mountainside. And on the lowlands, more elaborate techniques of cultivation and river management permitted more complete conversion of alluvial plains to agricultural usage.

By the 1800s, that is to say, Japan – with its few large cities, numerous towns and myriad villages scattered about productive agricultural lowlands that mostly abutted the coastline or nestled among mainly verdant hillsides – was a very different land from the one that Jômon foragers had known a few thousand years earlier.

Then came industrialization, and it has had an unprecedented impact on woodland, lowlands, coastal fisheries and other resources. Because of industrial society's dependence on a global resource base, moreover, industrial Japan has been integrally involved in altering the bio-system beyond the archipelago.

*1. Woodland*

Japan's forests, as we have seen, were subjected, ca. 1870ff, to ferocious logging activity in conjunction with the legal reforms and construction boom of initial industrial development, and, later, ca. 1935ff, in conjunction with military adventurism, defeat and reconstruction. In response to the severe deforestation and resultant erosion and downstream damage, widespread and sustained programs of protection forestry were developed. These used diverse measures, notably durable techniques of concrete construction, to help stabilize hillsides and riverbanks, thereby minimizing the lowland damage from heavy run-off caused by snowmelt or intense rainfall.

Concurrently, vigorous programs of tree-planting and aftercare transformed ever more of the realm's woodland into densely planted, even-aged monocultures consisting of two or three preferred species of tree. However, since the 1970s, the global timber market has rendered much of that plantation growth uneconomic to sustain. That development has created conditions in which plantations have been allowed to deteriorate, enabling areas to begin the reversion to mixed forest growth capable of supporting a more diverse biotic community.

### 2. Lowlands

In the meantime, lowlands of the realm have experienced two main trajectories: one involving agriculture, and the other, industry-related activities. As the site of agriculture, lowlands witnessed a full century of notable increases in acreage tilled (mainly in the northeast), in the use of machinery and fertilizer, in foodstuff output per acre, and in output per hour of human labor input. There also occurred equivalent reduction in the number of agricultural households and workers. The gains in production peaked during the 1970s–80s, however, and after that, overall food output went into decline as imports undersold more and more of the domestic produce. That trend, in turn, has been accompanied by a rapid decline in the acreage devoted to agriculture, especially in central and southwestern Honshu, and an accelerated reduction in the number of farm households.

Two aspects of industry-related activity merit note for their impact on the lowlands and their occupants. One of these aspects has been "urban sprawl" – the gradual spread outward from cities, towns and ports of factories, other commercial establishments, urban residential structures and diverse transport and recreational facilities. This sprawl has absorbed most of the lowland abandoned by farmers, and it has also made inroads into upland areas.

Closely related to this sprawling proliferation of industrial facilities has been the other, much more complex trend – that of environmental pollution.[1] The topic can be treated in terms of solid, liquid and gaseous pollutants, although the three in fact tend to be thoroughly entangled.

Solid pollutants of the environment, known commonly as waste, trash and junk, are amazingly diverse. As the material goods of industrial society have proliferated, so, too, has the discarded material. In Japan, as elsewhere, some has ended up cluttering the landscape, more has gone to "the dump", but most has come to be processed by compactor or incinerator, the solid residue then ending up as landfill, some on the land surface, some as material for coastal landfill projects, and some dumped further offshore. As the scale of material consumption mushroomed during the postwar boom decades, however, with resultant increases in imports and declines in trash-disposal sites, more and more material came to be recycled, slowing the rate of growth in pollution by solid waste.

Liquid pollutants have been less visible but more destructive. Throughout the century prior to the 1980s, liquid effluent from mines and paper mills, but especially from industrial activity in and near cities and ports, polluted ever more areas of farmland, as well as other lowland sites and poisoned water supplies used by both farmers and urban people. The trend eventually elicited such strong reactions that by the 1980s the worst problems were gradually being reduced. By then, however, numerous areas of contaminated lowland had been lost to agricultural usage.

One response to the problem of liquid pollutants was construction and expansion of elaborate urban water-supply and purification systems. These have had positive effects on public health even as they have disrupted local watersheds and biomes. Another response has been the construction of complex sewer and sewage-treatment systems. Those systems have substantially reduced the volume of untreated waste. However, because the overall volume of waste has continued to grow, the quantity of treated residue has increased substantially. By filtering and concentrating the pollutants so that they could be disposed of as solid waste, this solution has increased the volume of landfill and offshore dumping. Also, it has deprived farmers of vast quantities of night-soil fertilizer, compelling them to rely on alternative nutrient sources.

Gaseous pollutants from industry, as well as those from incinerators, also proved damaging to farm crops and animals as well as to other exposed creatures on both uplands and lowlands, including humans. As with liquid pollutants, public protests finally forced industry to control its gaseous wastes during the 1970s–80s. Whereas that source of such gases as carbon dioxide ($CO_2$) has since declined, however, $CO_2$ emissions from other major sectors of the economy – the energy-producing, commercial, residential and transport sectors – have continued to increase. Probably for that reason, the number of public complaints about pollution has also continued to grow over the past two decades.

Most stunning has been the increased pollution from motor vehicles. The nearly 60-fold increase in motor vehicles between 1955 and 2005, combined with the increase in miles-per-vehicle, make vehicle-exhaust pollutants a major problem, especially in and near urban areas. Efforts to improve gasoline mileage and reduce emissions may have slowed the rate of increase from the 1970s onward, but because of the immense growth in vehicle use, pollution by motor vehicles has continued to worsen. As in other industrial societies, the internal combustion engine remains one of the most polluting of mechanical inventions.

*3. Coastal Areas*

Fisheries also have been harshly impacted by aspects of industrial development. The first major factor was development of larger and technically more sophisticated fishing boats and equipment that enabled fishermen to make much greater inroads into the populations of fish, shellfish, seaweed and whatever other biota they harvested. Later, and especially after the 1950s, industrial pollutants ravaged both freshwater and coastal saltwater fisheries. Concurrently, landfill projects designed to foster industry and maximize the value of foreign trade cut into coastal fishing sites.

The human response to these fishery trends has been twofold. Where sufficient clean water could be found, artificial fish-culture (fish farming) has been established, mainly for saltwater species. Quantitatively much more important has been the shift to deep-sea fishing and, since the 1980s, to reliance on imports. These last two trends, of course, constitute shifts of provisioning from the domestic to the global resource base.

### 4. Other Resources

Besides having substantial impacts on woodland, lowland and coastal fisheries, industrialization has had unprecedented effects on other natural resources of the archipelago, most notably subsurface minerals and fossil fuels.

From early agricultural times onward, as we have seen, a few minerals were extracted by placer mining. And coal began to be mined and used for fuel from the 1600s onward. By then, damage due to poisonous mine effluent had appeared, and during the 1700s, problems caused by coal smoke also were being reported, although they remained few and widely scattered.

Then, however, with industrialization from the 1870s onward, new mining technologies and the opening of more mines yielded massive increases in both mineral and coal output. With those changes came major increases in pollution problems and mining accidents. During the later twentieth century, however, the mines gradually became exhausted, and by century's end most had been shut down, their yield replaced by expanding imports. The trends in mining-caused environmental pollution and workplace accidents rose and fell accordingly.

As coal-mine output commenced its decline during the 1960s, and as the severely limited extent of domestic hydroelectric potential and oil and natural gas reserves became apparent – even while energy consumption was spiking – industry sought new sources of energy that would not entail costly imports of raw material. The one source that seemed to hold great promise was nuclear power, and during the 1970s–80s, a succession of nuclear power plants came into operation. During the 1990s, their output came to account for about a quarter of the electricity generated in Japan.

Nuclear power thus helped (despite reliance on imported uranium) to hold down the amount of imported fossil fuel required by Japan's industrial expansion. Nevertheless, in all these areas – of forest, farm, fishery and other resource production – the long-term trend of industrial society (in the archipelago as elsewhere) has been to maximize domestic yield and, after it has peaked, to become more dependent on society's global resource base.

Unsurprisingly, therefore, with the passage of decades, Japan's industrial society has made ever-greater inroads on material resources found elsewhere about the globe. In terms of biota, the greatest impact has been on forests and pelagic fisheries. In addition, the realm's demand for fossil fuels – which continued to grow despite the use of nuclear energy – and its continuing need for iron ore and diverse other minerals has assured that Japan (along with other industrial societies) has continued to play an active role in the escalating competition for, and consumption of, the world's finite and shrinking supply of raw materials.

\* \* \*

So where does this leave Japan today, as the second decade of the twenty-first century unfolds?

The demographic evidence suggests that the archipelago's industrial society is moving beyond its era of growth into an era of stability or possibly contraction. One could also interpret the economic patterns of the past 20 years or so as signaling the shift from growth to stasis. Particularly in agriculture, forestry and mining, the extent of decline in activity suggests this shift. But also many areas of urban industrial and commercial activity suggest the shift, with slow growth in some sectors being offset by modest declines in others. That implication is also suggested by a modest decline in the level of household expenditures, which reverses the sustained rise of earlier decades.

International trade also signals this shift. Imports of many sorts – foodstuffs, most pertinently – have ceased to grow or have declined, although imports of industrial raw materials and advanced chemicals and machinery generally continue to increase. Exports, on the other hand, have grown or held steady in major areas, which suggests that the function of imports had become more fully than before to facilitate exports rather than to enhance domestic consumption.

All of which is to say that archipelagic society, whether knowingly or not, seems to be addressing two of the key variables involved in human impact on the global ecosystem – the density of human presence and the level of material consumption per capita. During pre-industrial centuries, of course, any reduction in total human consumption meant reduced demand on the archipelagic bio-system. Given industrial society's heavy reliance on the global resource base, such a reduction today obviously eases demand at a more global level.

However, because all industrial societies are engaged in shared exploitation of that broader resource base, reduced demand by any particular user may in fact have no significant impact on the overall rate of extraction. And given the evidence of continuing rapid global population growth and aspirations for more material consumption per capita, the rate of global resource consumption seems destined to increase for the foreseeable future.[2]

Rather similarly, although measures to reduce the rate of environmental pollution by Japan's industrial society may have local benefits, the global benefits of those reductions may be more than offset by increased pollution from other sources. Nor is the archipelago itself immune to the effects of increased pollution elsewhere. Pollutants reaching Japan from elsewhere via air and water currents have gradually increased in recent decades and seem likely to continue doing so.

Also, insofar as pollutants foster global warming that melts glaciers and raises ocean levels, that trend threatens Japan's extensive coastal lowlands. It also alters the distribution of the planet surface's weight, shifting the patterns of stress on tectonic fault lines. Because Japan is situated near major active fault lines, it is particularly subject to fault slips and any resulting earthquakes and tsunami (tidal waves). Indeed, such a slip seems to have triggered the major quake that ravaged the East coast of Tôhoku in March 2011.[3]

That quake also exposed again the dangers inherent in the use of nuclear power. Because such power can now provide about a quarter of Japan's electricity, however, replacing nuclear with other energy sources would be an immensely costly enterprise that would only add to archipelagic dependence on its global resource base, whether for fossil fuel or for the rare metals and other materials used in solar- and wind-power equipment.

Insofar as the replacement of nuclear power plants leads to new intrusions on woodland or coastal waterways, moreover, the process would add to the dangers facing vulnerable species in the island chain's bio-system. Although record-keeping on such matters is recent and longer-term significance of the statistics is unclear, trends to date suggest that the number of vulnerable and endangered species of plants and animals continues to grow, in Japan as elsewhere.[4] To accelerate that trend is hardly in the interests of either the archipelago's bio-system as a whole or its human component.

In sum, the trends to date suggest that life in the archipelago would be well served if indeed its human population and level of material consumption per capita do continue to decline. Given the extent of industrial society's dependence on the global resource base, however, such trends would hold solid promise only if they were also occurring widely about the globe, which they are not. Otherwise, stresses elsewhere would eventually impact Japan, whether in terms of migration activity, foodstuff acquisition or other considerations.

Moreover, it is difficult to imagine a scale of retrenchment that would make the archipelagic populace self-sufficient again. Far too many of the raw materials required by the lifestyle and material culture of present-day society come from elsewhere. For good or ill, Japan's future is inextricably linked to that of the rest of the world.

Most basically, the continuing shrinkage in Japan's arable acreage and the general stabilization of both domestic food production and food importation are patterns that can be sustained only as long as global food supplies suffice to meet the wants of the world's more well-to-do populations. When global demand for food exceeds supply – whether due to population growth or decline in global food production due to climate change or other factors – Japan's cost of food importation will rise. With the archipelago's populace about 60–70 percent dependent on food imports, that rise will generate pressure to produce more at home, and then the issue of land usage will acquire a harsh new urgency. Even as it does, however, the ancillary issue of fertilizer sources will become acute, underscoring industrial Japan's elemental dependence on its global resource base.

All of which is another reminder of a final irony. As we noted earlier, for Japan, as for the rest of the world, the "nation state" with its "nationally conscious" ("patriotic") populace and its "national" government is a recent invention, an institutional and ideological construct that developed in conjunction with industrialization. But the very process of industrial development that sustained the rise of nation states has also rendered them obsolete by making human life a globally interdependent experience. The situation suggests that a supra-national political order capable of regulating exploitation of the global resource base is needed. However, given the nature of the short-term self-interest of nearly every political and economic interest group of consequence, the emergence of such an order seems thoroughly unlikely. So the next few decades may prove to be a fascinating, if brutally uncomfortable period for humans as well as for other biota everywhere on this little planet.

# Appendix 1

## On Rates of Temperature and Sea-level Change (ca. 18,000–6,500 yBP)

Chapter 1 of the text noted the "brisk" snail-pace rate of geological uplift in Pleistocene Japan – an estimated 1-centimeter rise every 17 years. One can similarly suggest the rates of temperature change and ocean rise and fall.

It is estimated that the mean temperature in Japan during the final glacial maximum of ca. 21–18,000 yBP was 7–9° Centigrade lower than during the 1900s.[A] Keeping in mind that the area was probably a few degrees warmer around 6,000 yBP than during recent decades, let us say that the region warmed up 10°C during the 12 millennia 18–6,000 yBP. That equals an average change of about 0.08°C (0.17° Fahrenheit) per century, a trend so slow that no human of the day would have been aware of it. Even when climate was fluctuating "wildly", as it may have done during the Dryas oscillations of ca. 15–12,000 yBP, the changes would have been hard for people of the day to detect.[B]

Given the irregularity of this warming process, it is unlikely that the long-term rise in sea level occurred at a steady pace. Rather, the rate seems to have been very erratic and much faster in the millennia around 13,000 yBP. It has been argued that global warming did not really impact Japan before 16,500 yBP, but that by 11,600 yBP, enough warming had occurred so that sea level was only about 20–30 m lower than at present.[C] If, as noted in Chapter 1, sea level had been some 130–40 m lower than today when warming commenced ca. 18,000 yBP, then during the roughly 6,400 years to 11,600 yBP, it may have risen at an average rate of some 1.7 centimeters per year.

After 11,600 yBP the rate of rise would have slowed. It is said that during the warm era 7,400–5,900 yBP, sea level stood some 2–6 m above today's level. Assuming a 6-meter rise at the warmest point ca. 6,500 yBP, sea level had risen roughly 30 m during the preceding 5,000 years (or 0.6 cm per year).

During the millennia before 11,600 yBP, then, a person living near an estuary or shoreline could very well have noticed, in the course of a lifetime, the change in water level (85 cm, or nearly a yard, in 50 years). But in subsequent millennia the rise (30 cm, or about 1 ft, in 50 years) might well have gone unnoticed.

## NOTES

A    Yoshinori Yasuda, "Monsoon Fluctuations and Cultural Changes During the Last Glacial Age in Japan", in *Nichibunken Japan Review*, No. 1 (1990), p. 123.

B    Junko Habu, *Ancient Jômon of Japan* (Cambridge: CUP, 2004), pp. 42–43, treats the Dryas-era oscillations. For comparison's sake, it is reported that industrial-age climate warming in the 130 years after 1880 raised average global temperatures about 1.5° Fahrenheit (0.8° Centigrade), or roughly six times as fast as the general rate during the millennia of forager society in Japan. And most of that increase has occurred during the past 30 years, 1980–2010, when temperature has been rising at about 0.36° (0.2°C) per decade, some 20 times as fast as during the final Pleistocene warming. *The New York Times*, 22 January 2010, p. A8.

C    The following calculations are based on figures found in Habu, *Ancient Jômon of Japan*, pp. 36, 45.

# Appendix 2

## Tables

This assemblage of 47 tables derives from information found in annual books of the *Japan Statistical Yearbook* (*JSY*). *JSY* is a publication of the government's Statistics Bureau that consolidates myriad sets of data accumulated by various government agencies. First published in 1882 but discontinued in 1941, it was revived in 1949 as a grand, 7" × 10", 1,058-page assemblage of 610 tables. The following year it was revised and rationalized to form a 525-page tome consisting of 275 tables. Subsequent periodic revisions have expanded its coverage and pagination, and the 2009 book, which numbers 940 pages of the same size, contains 661 tables.

As years have passed and situations evolved, numerous analytical categories have been modified, which makes some longer-term analyses more difficult. And because different record-keeping practices can yield different figures for seemingly identical topics, care in the selection of tables is necessary. Nevertheless, for a vast array of topics in recent social and economic history, *JSY* provides a remarkably rich source of information.

### POPULATION AND SOCIETY

**Table 1:** Population of Japan (1895–2008) (in thousands)

| | | | | | | | |
|------|--------|------|--------|------|---------|------|---------|
| 1895 | 41,557 | 1935 | 69,254 | 1965 | 99,209 | 2000 | 126,926 |
| 1905 | 46,620 | 1945 | 72,147 | 1975 | 111,940 | 2004 | 127,787 |
| 1915 | 52,752 | 1950 | 84,115 | 1985 | 121,049 | 2005 | 127,757 |
| 1925 | 59,737 | 1955 | 89,276 | 1990 | 123,611 | 2008 | 127,692 |

*Source: JSY, 2010, pp. 34–35, Table 2-1.*

**Table 2:** Population by Urban Categories (1920–2005) (in millions)

|                   | 1920 | 1940 | 1950 | 1955 | 1975  | 1990  | 2005  |
|-------------------|------|------|------|------|-------|-------|-------|
| Towns & Villages  | 45.9 | 45.5 | 52.7 | 39.0 | 27.0  | 27.9  | 17.5  |
| Cities            | 10.1 | 27.6 | 31.4 | 50.3 | 85.0  | 95.6  | 110.3 |
| Japan, total      | 56.0 | 73.1 | 84.1 | 89.3 | 111.9 | 123.6 | 127.8 |

*Source: JSY, 1985, p. 28, Table 2-4; JSY, 2007, p. 38, Table 2-4.*

**Table 3:** Human Height and Weight (1935–2007) (of 18 year-olds)

| Year | Male | | Female | |
|------|-------------|-------------|-------------|-------------|
|      | *Height (cm)* | *Weight (kg)* | *Height (cm)* | *Weight (kg)* |
| 1935 | 162.9 | 55.0 | 152.0 | 49.6 |
| 1950 | 162.6 | 53.9 | 152.7 | 49.8 |
| 1970 | 168.6 | 59.3 | 156.6 | 51.3 |
| 1990 | 170.8 | 62.5 | 158.2 | 51.5 |
| 2000 | 171.7 | 61.7 | 158.6 | 51.5 |
| 2007 | 171.4 | 63.4 | 158.5 | 52.4 |

*Source: JSY, 1961, p. 502, Table 289; JSY, 1985, p. 616, Table 18-3; JSY, 2007, p. 672, Table 21-22; JSY, 2010, p. 674, Table 21-22.*

**Table 4:** Divorce Rate (1925–2007) (per 1,000 population)

| 1925 | 0.87 | 1970 | 0.93 | 1995 | 1.60 |
|------|------|------|------|------|------|
| 1940 | 0.68 | 1975 | 1.07 | 2000 | 2.10 |
| 1947 | 1.02 | 1980 | 1.22 | 2002 | 2.30 |
| 1955 | 0.84 | 1985 | 1.39 | 2005 | 2.08 |
| 1965 | 0.79 | 1990 | 1.28 | 2007 | 2.02 |

*Source: JSY, 2007, p. 61, Table 2-22.*

**Table 5:** Total Fertility Rate (1930–2007) (select years)

| 1930 | 4.70 | 1970 | 2.13 | 1995 | 1.42 |
|------|------|------|------|------|------|
| 1947 | 4.54 | 1980 | 1.75 | 2000 | 1.36 |
| 1950 | 3.65 | 1985 | 1.76 | 2005 | 1.26 |
| 1960 | 2.00 | 1990 | 1.54 | 2007 | 1.34 |

*Source: JSY, 2010, p. 66, Table 2-25.*

**Table 6:** Life Expectancy at Birth (1891–2007)

| Year | Male | Female | Year | Male | Female |
|------|------|--------|------|------|--------|
| 1891–98 | 42.8 | 44.3 | 1980 | 73.4 | 78.8 |
| 1935–36 | 46.9 | 49.6 | 2000 | 77.7 | 84.6 |
| 1947 | 50.1 | 54.0 | 2005 | 78.6 | 85.5 |
| 1955 | 63.6 | 67.8 | 2007 | 79.2 | 86.0 |
| 1960 | 65.3 | 70.2 | | | |

*Source: JSY, 1985, p. 55, Table 2-28; JSY, 2010, p. 68, Table 2-27.*

**Table 7:** Infant Mortality Rate (1921–2007) (per 1,000 live births)

| 1921 | 168.3 | 1971 | 12.4 |
|------|-------|------|------|
| 1931 | 131.5 | 1981 | 7.1 |
| 1941 | 84.1 | 1991 | 4.4 |
| 1951 | 57.5 | 2001 | 3.1 |
| 1961 | 28.6 | 2007 | 2.6 |

*Source: JSY, 1985, p. 51, Table 2-23; JSY, 2010, p. 63, Table 2-22.*

**Table 8:** Death Rate by Age (1935–2007) (per 1,000 population per year)

| | 1935 | 1950 | 1960 | 1970 | 1985 | 2000 | 2007 |
|---|------|------|------|------|------|------|------|
| **Age 25–29** | | | | | | | |
| Male | 8.1 | 5.6 | 2.3 | 1.4 | 0.8 | 0.7 | 0.6 |
| Female | 8.2 | 5.1 | 1.5 | 0.9 | 0.4 | 0.3 | 0.3 |
| **Age 50–54** | | | | | | | |
| Male | 19.5 | 13.6 | 10.2 | 8.0 | 6.2 | 4.6 | 4.1 |
| Female | 13.5 | 10.2 | 6.6 | 4.8 | 2.9 | 2.3 | 2.1 |
| **Age 80–84** | | | | | | | |
| Male | – | 177.9 | 173.6 | 151.2 | 108.0 | 80.5 | 70.1 |
| Female | – | 142.9 | 132.0 | 115.5 | 71.7 | 43.3 | 36.0 |

*Source: JSY, 1949, pp. 95, 97, Table 49; JSY, 1950, p. 19, Table 10; JSY, 1985, p. 54,*
*Table 2-27; JSY, 2010, p. 67, Table 2-26.*

**Table 9:** Tuberculosis Mortality (1926–2007) (all forms of TB)

| Year | Deaths per 100,000 (all) | Deaths from TB | | Year | Deaths per 100,000 | Deaths from TB (all) |
|------|------|------|------|------|------|------|
| | | Male | Female | | | |
| 1926 | 186.1 | 54,503 | 58,542 | 1950 | 146.3 | 121,769 |
| 1930 | 185.6 | 59,148 | 60,487 | 1955 | 52.3 | 46,735 |
| 1935 | 190.8 | 67,238 | 64,913 | 1970 | 15.4 | 15,899 |
| 1940 | 212.9 | 80,599 | 72,555 | 1985 | 3.9 | 4,692 |
| 1947 | 188.7 | 80,219 | 67,195 | 1995 | 2.6 | 3,178 |
| 1949 | 168.9 | 74,267 | 63,846 | 2000 | 2.1 | 2,656 |
| | | | | 2005 | 1.8 | 2,296 |
| | | | | 2007 | 1.7 | 2,194 |

Source: JSY, 1949, p. 114, Table 55; JSY, 1985, pp. 630–31, Table 18-18; JSY, 2010, p. 687, Table 21-15. The great majority of cases were respiratory tuberculosis.

**Table 10:** Suicide Rate (1930–2007) (per 100,000 population)

| | | | | | |
|------|------|------|------|------|------|
| 1930 | 21.6 | 1965 | 14.7 | 1995 | 17.2 |
| 1940 | 13.5 | 1970 | 15.3 | 2000 | 24.1 |
| 1947 | 15.7 | 1975 | 18.0 | 2002 | 23.8 |
| 1950 | 19.6 | 1980 | 17.7 | 2003 | 25.5 |
| 1955 | 25.2 | 1985 | 19.4 | 2005 | 24.2 |
| 1960 | 21.6 | 1990 | 16.4 | 2007 | 24.4 |

Source: JSY, 1949, p. 38, Table 24, and pp. 102–3, Table 52; JSY, 1985, p. 631, Table 18-18; JSY, 2010, p. 687, Table 21-15.

**Table 11:** Population of Age Group 15–24 (1960–2008) (peak years and after – in 1,000s)

| | | | |
|------|------|------|------|
| 1960 | 17,771 | 1990 | 18,807 |
| 1965 | 20,076 | 2000 | 15,909 |
| 1970 | 19,897 | 2005 | 13,537 |
| 1980 | 16,113 | 2008 | 13,260 |

Source: Calculated from figures in JSY, 2010, p. 50, Table 2-8.

## EMPLOYMENT

**Table 12:** Employment Trends (1947–2008) (male and female – in thousands)

|      | Total  | Agriculture and Forestry | Non-agricultural |
|------|--------|--------------------------|------------------|
| 1947 | 33,881 | 17,102                   | 16,779           |
| 1955 | 40,900 | 14,780                   | 26,120           |
| 1970 | 50,940 | 8,420                    | 42,510           |
| 1985 | 58,070 | 4,640                    | 53,430           |
| 1995 | 64,570 | 3,400                    | 61,160           |
| 2005 | 63,560 | 2,590                    | 60,970           |
| 2008 | 63,850 | 2,450                    | 61,400           |

*Source: JSY, 1949, p. 694, Table 381; JSY, 1985, p. 72, Table 3-4; JSY, 2010, p. 496, Table 16-4.*

**Table 13:** Unemployment Numbers and Rate (1947–2008)
(1,000s of labor force totally unemployed)

| Year  | Number | Rate (%) | Year | Number | Rate (%) |
|-------|--------|----------|------|--------|----------|
| 1947* | 900    | 2.8      | 1990 | 1,134  | 2.1      |
| 1955  | 1,050  | 2.5      | 1995 | 2,100  | 3.2      |
| 1960  | 750    | 1.7      | 2000 | 3,200  | 4.7      |
| 1970  | 590    | 1.2      | 2002 | 3,590  | 5.4      |
| 1980  | 1,140  | 2.0      | 2005 | 2,940  | 4.4      |
| 1985  | 1,560  | 2.6      | 2008 | 2,650  | 4.0      |

*The 1947 figure is an approximate average derived from monthly figures.

*Source: JSY, 1949, p. 698, Table 382 for 1947; JSY, 1986, p. 70, Table 3-1 for 1955–80; JSY, 2010, p. 492, Table 16-1 for 1985ff.*

## HOUSING

**Table 14:** Size of Dwellings (1958–2008)

| Year | A<br>Dwelling Rooms<br>per House | B<br>Floor Area<br>per House (m²) | C<br>Persons<br>per Room | D<br>Floor Area<br>per Person (m²) |
|------|------|-------|------|-------|
| 1958 | 3.60 | –     | –    | –     |
| 1963 | 3.82 | 72.52 | 1.16 | 16.37 |
| 1982 | 4.73 | 85.92 | 0.71 | 25.27 |
| 2003 | 4.77 | 94.85 | 0.56 | 35.52 |
| 2008 | 4.68 | 94.34 | 0.54 | 37.33 |

Column D = B divided by (A times C).

*Source: JSY 1985, p. 518, Table 15-4; JSY, 2010, p. 577, Table 18-1.*

**Table 15:** Household *Tatami* (1950–2008) (per person)

| | | | | | |
|------|------|------|-------|------|-------|
| 1950 | 3.7  | 1980 | 8.4   | 1998 | 11.24 |
| 1955 | 3.8  | 1983 | 8.55  | 2003 | 12.17 |
| 1960 | 4.3  | 1988 | 9.55  | 2008 | 12.87 |
| 1970 | 6.1  | 1993 | 10.41 | | |

*Source:* Figures for 1950–80 are from *JSY*, 1985, p. 512, Table 15-1; for 1983–2003, from *JSY*, 2010, p. 579, Table 18-1.

**Table 16:** Members per Private Household (1950–2005)

| | | | | | |
|------|------|------|------|------|------|
| 1950 | 4.97 | 1970 | 3.41 | 1995 | 2.82 |
| 1955 | 4.97 | 1980 | 3.22 | 2000 | 2.67 |
| 1960 | 4.14 | 1990 | 2.99 | 2005 | 2.60 |

*Source: JSY*, 1961, p. 40, Table 20; *JSY*, 1985, p. 47, Table 2-17; *JSY*, 2007, p. 57, Table 2-16

**Table 17:** Select Household Possessions (1964–2004) (number per 1,000 households)

| Year | Beds | Room Air Conditioners | Cameras | Cars | Washing Machines | Wardrobes |
|------|------|------|------|------|------|------|
| 1964 | 211   | 23    | 799   | 68    | 786   | 970   |
| 1979 | 759   | 643   | 1,238 | 670   | 1,054 | 1,480 |
| 2004 | 1,228 | 2,347 | 1,401 | 1,446 | 1,086 | 1,622 |

*Source: JSY*, 1985, pp. 544–45, Table 15-27; *JSY*, 2007, p. 620, Table 19-11.

## TRADE ISSUES

**Table 18:** Tonnage of Foreign Trade (1948–2004) (1,000 metric tons)

| Year | Exports | Imports | Year | Exports | Imports |
|------|---------|---------|------|---------|---------|
| 1948 | 1,837  | 7,378   | 1980 | 83,853  | 612,992 |
| 1950 | 3,130  | 10,503  | 1985 | 94,307  | 603,684 |
| 1955 | 7,712  | 36,713  | 1990 | 85,062  | 712,494 |
| 1960 | 14,039 | 89,540  | 1995 | 116,636 | 771,892 |
| 1965 | 22,758 | 198,684 | 2000 | 131,482 | 808,168 |
| 1970 | 42,008 | 435,924 | 2004 | 177,764 | 830,166 |
| 1975 | 70,209 | 549,547 | | | |

*Source:* Figures for 1948–55 from *JSY*, 1961, p. 239, Table 136; for 1960–80 from *JSY*, 1985, p. 352, Table 10-11; for 1985–2005 from *JSY*, 2007, p. 470, Table 15-10.

**Table 19:** Select Raw Material Imports (1950–2008) (by metric quantity)

| Year | Iron Ore (1,000 tons) | Coal/Coke (1,000 tons) | Petroleum (1,000 kl) | LNG (1,000 tons) |
|---|---|---|---|---|
| 1950 | 1,435 | 832 | 1,466 | – |
| 1955 | 5,459 | 2,862 | 8,502 | – |
| 1960 | 15,036 | 8,292 | 31,121 | – |
| 1965 | 39,018 | 17,080 | 84,143 | – |
| 1970 | 102,091 | 50,173 | 197,108 | 848 |
| 1980 | 133,721 | 68,228 | 254,447 | 16,841 |
| 1984 | 125,372 | 87,818 | 213,201 | 25,892 |
| 1990 | 125,290 | 107,517 | 225,251 | 35,465 |
| 2000 | 131,733 | 145,278 | 249,814 | 53,690 |
| 2005 | 132,285 | 180,808 | 248,822 | 58,014 |
| 2008 | 140,351 | 193,510 | 241,766 | 69,263 |

LNG = Liquified Natural Gas.

*Source:* Figures for 1950–60 from *JSY*, 1961, pp. 248–49, Table 142; for 1965 from *JSY*, 1976, p. 288, Table 210; for 1970–84 from *JSY*, 1985, pp. 346–47, Table 10-7; for 1990–2005 from *JSY*, 2010, p. 467, Table 15-6.

**Table 20:** Select Foodstuff Imports (1950–2008) (1,000 metric tons)

| Year | Meat | Shrimp etc. | Wheat | Coffee/Cocoa |
|---|---|---|---|---|
| 1950 | – | – | 1,573 | – |
| 1955 | – | – | 2,287 | – |
| 1960 | – | – | 2,678 | – |
| 1970 | 233 | 57 | 4,685 | 129 |
| 1980 | 543 | 148 | 5,682 | 219 |
| 1984 | 695 | 177 | 5,978 | 290 |
| 1990 | 1,289 | 304 | 5,474 | 394 |
| 2000 | 2,405 | 260 | 5,854 | 491 |
| 2005 | 2,380 | 242 | 5,472 | 536 |
| 2008 | 2,310 | 202 | 5,781 | 489 |

*Source:* Figures for 1950–60 from *JSY*, 1961, pp. 248–49, Table 142; for 1970–84 from *JSY*, 1985, pp. 346–47, Table 10-17; for 1990–2005 from *JSY*, 2010, p. 466, Table 15-16.

**Table 21:** Soybean Supplies (1930–2006) (in 1,000 metric tons)

| Year | Production | Imports | Year | Production | Imports |
|------|------------|---------|------|------------|---------|
| 1930 | 343 | 672 | 1975 | 126 | 3,334 |
| 1940 | 354 | 527 | 1980 | 174 | 4,401 |
| 1945 | 267 | 930 | 1985 | 228 | 4,910 |
| 1950 | 217 | 311 | 1990 | 220 | 4,681 |
| 1955 | 376 | 808 | 2000 | 235 | 4,829 |
| 1960 | 426 | 1,128 | 2005 | 225 | 4,181 |
| 1970 | 126 | 3,244 | 2006 | 229 | 4,002 |

*Source:* Figures for 1930–60 from *JSY*, 1961, p. 201, Table 103; for 1965–83, from *JSY*, 1985, p.160, Table 5-19, and p. 346, Table 10-7; for years 1980–90, from *JSY*, 2007, p. 241, Table 7-15 and p. 464, Table 15-6; for years 2000–08, from *JSY* 2009, p. 243, Table 7-15 and p. 464, Table 15-6.

**Table 22:** Food Self-sufficiency (1960–2007) (% from domestic sources)

| Year | Calories | Cereal | Year | Calories | Cereal |
|------|----------|--------|------|----------|--------|
| 1960 | 79 | 82 | 1990 | 48 | 30 |
| 1970 | 60 | 46 | 1995 | 43 | 30 |
| 1975 | 54 | 40 | 2000 | 40 | 28 |
| 1980 | 53 | 33 | 2005 | 40 | 28 |
| 1985 | 53 | 31 | 2007 | 40 | 28 |

*Source:* For 1960–90, *JSY*, 1995, p. 276, Table 6-73; for 1995–2007, *JSY*, 2010, p. 282, Table 7-61.

**Table 23:** Textile Supply and Demand (1960–2006) (in 1,000 metric tons)

| Year | Domestic Production | Imports | Domestic Demand | Exports |
|------|---------------------|---------|-----------------|---------|
| 1960 | 1,270 | 3.7 | 743 | 487 |
| 1975 | 1,776 | 63 | 1,444 | 610 |
| 1985 | 1,983 | 466 | 1,784 | 631 |
| 2000 | 1,089 | 1,692 | 2,353 | 439 |
| 2004 | 781 | 1,913 | 2,286 | 436 |
| 2005 | 734 | 1,865 | 2,184 | 417 |
| 2006 | 743 | 1,913 | 2,288 | 391 |

The numbers (production + imports = demand + exports) do not tally due to surviving inventory from year to year.

*Source: JSY*, 1985, p. 250, Table 6-29; *JSY*, 2009, p. 318, Table 8-22.

**Table 24:** Registered Motor Vehicles and Distance Driven per Year (1952–2008)

| Year | Passenger Cars (1,000s) | Automobile Distance (million km) | Trucks (1,000s) | Truck Distance (million km) |
|---|---|---|---|---|
| 1952 | 90 | 1,766 | 419 | 4,034 |
| 1955 | 167 | 4,137 | 693 | 6,764 |
| 1960 | 441 | 8,725 | 1,322 | 17,445 |
| 1970 | 6,777 | 120,582 | 5,460 | 100,040 |
| 1985 | 25,848 | 275,557 | 8,306 | 146,533 |
| 1995 | 39,103 | 649,646 | 8,858 | 267,128 |
| 2004 | 42,776 | 698,232 | 7,280 | 248,728 |
| 2005 | 42,747 | 685,996 | 7,160 | 242,091 |
| 2006 | 42,229 | 677,354 | 7,014 | 241,849 |
| 2008 | 40,799 | – | 6,568 | – |

*Source: JSY, 1961, pp. 215–16, Tables 114, 115; JSY, 1985, pp. 302, 304, Tables 8-5, 8-7; JSY, 2007, pp. 386, 388, Tables 12-5, 12-7; JSY, 2010, pp. 390, 392, Tables 12-5, 12-7.*

**Table 25:** Traffic Volume and Distance Per Capita (1950–2007)

| Year | Passenger Distance (million km) | National Population (millions) | Kilometers per Person |
|---|---|---|---|
| 1950 | 117,000 | 83.2 | 1,406.25 |
| 1960 | 243,000 | 93.4 | 2,601.71 |
| 1970 | 587,000 | 104.6 | 5,611.85 |
| 1985 | 858,000 | 121.0 | 7,090.91 |
| 1995 | 1,388,000 | 125.6 | 11,050.96 |
| 2000 | 1,420,000 | 126.9 | 11,189.91 |
| 2004 | 1,418,000 | 127.8 | 11,095.46 |
| 2005 | 1,411,000 | 127.8 | 11,040.69 |
| 2007 | 1,413,000 | 127.7 | 11,065.00 |

*Source: JSY, 1985, p. 302, Table 8-4; JSY, 2010, p. 390, Table 12-4. Travel by air and water, which are omitted here, accounted for less than 1 percent of total distance traveled, shrinking from 0.97 percent in 1950 to 0.24 percent in 2000.*

**Table 26:** Gasoline Consumption as Import Burden (1960–2004)

| Year | Gasoline Consumption (1,000 kl) | Crude Oil Imports (1,000 kl) | Gasoline as % of Oil Imports | Crude Oil Production (1,000 kl) |
|---|---|---|---|---|
| 1960 | 5,280 | 32,879 | 16.06 | 593 |
| 1970 | 21,643 | 204,871 | 10.56 | 899 |
| 1985 | 54,709 | 197,261 | 27.73 | 625 |
| 1995 | 80,784 | 265,526 | 30.42 | 861 |
| 2004 | 79,504 | 241,805 | 32.88 | 834 |

*Source: Calculated from data in JSY, 1985, p. 284, Table 7-15 and p. 304, Table 8-7; JSY, 2007, p. 348, Table 10-12, p. 388, Table 12-7.*

## MINING AND MANUFACTURING

**Table 27:** Mining Employment and Accidents (1950–2008)

| Year | Number of Miners | Number Killed | % Killed | Seriously Injured | % Injured |
|------|------------------|---------------|----------|-------------------|-----------|
| 1950 | 528,801 | 933 | 0.18 | 42,414 | 8.02 |
| 1955 | 453,505 | 850 | 0.19 | 26,021 | 5.74 |
| 1960 | 451,554 | 760 | 0.16 | 27,174 | 6.02 |
| 1970 | 162,611 | 266 | 0.16 | 11,251 | 6.92 |
| 1985 | 55,516 | 92 | 0.17 | 562 | 1.01 |
| 2000 | 18,305 | 5 | 0.03 | 57 | 0.31 |
| 2005 | 13,658 | 2 | 0.01 | 26 | 0.19 |
| 2008 | 12,953 | 3 | 0.02 | 26 | 0.20 |

*Source: JSY*, 1961, p. 524, Table 305; *JSY*, 1985, p. 746, Table 23-11; *JSY*, 2010, p. 817, Table 26-21. A more detailed breakdown of the mine workforce is given in *JSY*, 1985, p. 210, Table 6-2; *JSY*, 2010, p. 289, Table 8-1.

**Table 28:** Two Trends in Manufacturing (1950–2007)

| Year | Number of Employees (1,000s) | Index of Output (2,000=100) | Year | Number of Employees (1,000s) | Index of Output (2,000=100) |
|------|------------------------------|------------------------------|------|------------------------------|------------------------------|
| 1950 | 6,000 | – | 1991 | 14,096 | 101.6 |
| 1951 | 6,290 | – | 1995 | – | 95.6 |
| 1955 | 7,570 | 5.7 | 1996 | 12,930 | 97.8 |
| 1965 | 11,500 | 21.6 | 2000 | – | 100.0 |
| 1975 | 13,460 | 48.7 | 2001 | 10,956 | 93.2 |
| 1980 | 13,670 | 67.5 | 2004 | 11,500 | 100.2 |
| 1984 | 14,380 | 77.4 | 2005 | – | 100.8 |
| 1985 | – | 80.1 | 2006 | 9,922 | 105.3 |
| 1990 | – | 99.9 | 2007 | – | 108.3 |

*Source:* The "Index of Output" is a measure of "value added" and derives from the tables of "Key Statistics" in *JSY*, 1985, 1995, 2007 and 2010, with all figures adjusted to the 2000=100 index used in the 2010 edition. Employee numbers for 1950–51 derive from *JSY*, 1961, p. 46, Table 24. Later ones are from *JSY*, 1985, p. 72, Table 3-4; *JSY*, 2007, p. 183, Table 6-1; *JSY*, 2010, p. 188, Table 6-1. The absolute figures for employee numbers given in Table 8-4 of *JSY* 2010 and predecessor books differ from those given here but reveal the same employment trajectory.

**Table 29:** Trends in Select Manufacturing Output (1960–2007)

| Year | Automobiles (1,000s) | Construction Excavators | AC Electric Motors (1,000s) | TV Receivers (1,000s) | Microwave Ovens (1,000s) | Fax Machines (1,000s) |
|------|------|------|------|------|------|------|
| 1960 | 165 | 1,217 | 5,506 | 3,578 | 0 | 1.4 |
| 1980 | 7,038 | 57,063 | 30,389 | 16,327 | 1,876 | 100.4 |
| 2000 | 8,363 | 91,089 | 20,986 | 3,130 | 2,868 | 3,212.0 |
| 2007 | 9,945 | 180,599 | 15,167 | – | 575 | 130 |

*Source:* Selected from large sets of items listed in tables of *JSY*, 1985, pp. 234–41, *JSY*, 2007, pp. 304–8; *JSY*, 2010, pp. 308–13.

**Table 30:** Accident Rates and Severity (1955–2007)

| Year | All Industries | | Manufacturing | |
|------|------|------|------|------|
| | Frequency* | Severity** | Frequency* | Severity** |
| 1955 | 24.49 | 2.59 | – | – |
| 1960 | 17.43 | 1.83 | 9.70 | 0.81 |
| 1970 | 9.20 | 0.88 | 6.07 | 0.66 |
| 1980 | 3.59 | 0.32 | 2.68 | 0.27 |
| 1990 | 1.95 | 0.18 | 1.30 | 0.14 |
| 2000 | 1.82 | – | 1.02 | – |
| 2004 | 1.85 | 0.12 | 0.99 | 0.11 |
| 2005 | 1.95 | – | 1.01 | – |
| 2007 | 1.83 | 0.11 | 1.09 | 0.10 |

\* Frequency = cases per million man-hours of work.
\*\* Severity = work days lost per 1,000 man-hours of work.

*Source:* JSY, 1961, p. 529, Table 306; JSY, 1995, p. 779, Table 24-9; JSY, 2007, p. 814, Table 26-20; JSY, 2010, p. 816, Table 26-20. "All Industries" include forestry, mining, construction, transport and other services, and all types of manufacturing.

**Table 31:** Trends in Electricity-Output Capacity (1930–2005)

| Year | Total Capacity (1,000 kw) | Hydro | | Thermal | | Nuclear | |
|------|------|------|------|------|------|------|------|
| | | Plants | Capacity (1,000 kw) | Plants | Capacity (1,000 kw) | Plants | Capacity (1,000 kw) |
| 1930 | 4,500 | 1,376 | 2,948 | 432 | 1,552 | – | – |
| 1940 | 9,073 | 1,434 | 5,126 | 458 | 3,947 | – | – |
| 1945 | 10,385 | 1,424 | 6,435 | 293 | 3,950 | – | – |
| 1950 | 10,771 | 1,415 | 6,763 | 271 | 4,008 | – | – |
| 1955 | 14,512 | 1,458 | 8,909 | 407 | 5,603 | – | – |
| 1960 | 23,657 | 1,532 | 12,678 | 491 | 10,979 | – | – |
| 1965 | 41,005 | 1,558 | 16,275 | 415 | 24,717 | 1 | 13 |
| 1975 | 112,285 | 1,536 | 24,853 | 693 | 80,817 | 9 | 6,615 |
| 1985 | 169,399 | 1,629 | 34,337 | 979 | 110,161 | 16 | 24,686 |
| 1995 | 226,994 | 1,702 | 43,455 | 2,559 | 141,665 | 18 | 41,356 |
| 2005 | 274,468 | 1,739 | 47,357 | 3,341 | 175,767 | 17 | 49,580 |

*Source: JSY, 1961, pp. 189–90, Tables 94, 95; JSY, 1976, pp. 277–78, Tables 146, 148; JSY, 1985, pp. 348–49, Tables 7-1, 7-3; JSY, 2009, pp. 345–46, Tables 10-1, 10-3.*

**Table 32:** Trends in Electricity Production (1930–2005) (in million kilowatt hours)

| Year | Total | Hydro | Thermal | Nuclear |
|------|------|------|------|------|
| 1930 | 15,773 | 13,431 | 2,346 | – |
| 1940 | 34,566 | 24,233 | 10,331 | – |
| 1945 | 21,900 | 20,752 | 1,148 | – |
| 1950 | 46,266 | 37,784 | 8,482 | – |
| 1955 | 65,248 | 48,509 | 16,739 | – |
| 1960 | 115,497 | 58,481 | 57,017 | – |
| 1965 | 190,250 | 75,201 | 115,024 | 25 |
| 1975 | 475,794 | 85,906 | 364,616 | 25,125 |
| 1985 | 671,952 | 87,948 | 423,164 | 159,578 |
| 1995 | 989,880 | 91,216 | 604,206 | 291,254 |
| 2005 | 1,157,112 | 86,350 | 761,826 | 304,755 |

*Source: JSY, 1961, pp. 189–90, Tables 94, 95; JSY, 1976, pp. 277–78, Tables 146, 148; JSY, 1985, pp. 348–49, Tables 7-1, 7-3; JSY, 2009, p. 346, Table 10-3.*

## AGRICULTURE AND FISHERIES

**Table 33:** Farm Households (1947–2008) (in 1,000s)

| Year | Total of Farms | Full-time Farming | % Doing Full-time | Part-time Farming | |
|------|------|------|------|------|------|
| | | | | Mainly Farming | Mainly Other Work |
| 1947 | 5,909 | 3,275 | 57.4 | 1,684 | 951 |
| 1950 | 6,176 | 3,086 | 50.0 | 1,753 | 1,337 |
| 1965 | 5,665 | 1,219 | 21.5 | 2,081 | 2,365 |
| 1984 | 4,473 | 605 | 13.5 | 689 | 3,179 |
| 1985 | 4,376 | 626 | 14.3 | (3,750) | |
| 1990 | 3,835 | 592 | 15.4 | (3,243) | |
| 1993 | 2,835 | 447 | 15.8 | 429 | 1,959 |
| 1995 | 2,651 | 428 | 16.1 | (2,224) | |
| 2000 | 2,337 | 426 | 18.2 | (1,911) | |
| 2005 | 1,963 | 443 | 22.6 | 308 | 1,212 |
| 2008 | 1,750 | 410 | 23.4 | (1340) | |

*Source:* Figures from *JSY*, 1961, p. 71, Table 36; *JSY*, 1985, p. 149, Table 5-1, *JSY*, 1995, pp. 223–4, Tables 6-1, 6-3; *JSY*, 2010, pp. 235–6, Tables 7-1, 7-3.

**Table 34:** Adult Population of Farm Households (1950–2008) (in 1,000s)

| Year | National Adult* Population | Adult* Farm Population | Farm Population as % of National | Doing Farmwork Only | Farmwork Only as % of Farm Population |
|------|------|------|------|------|------|
| 1950 | 53,872 | (37,700 est.) | 70.0 | – | – |
| 1955 | 59,478 | 36,347 | 61.1 | – | – |
| 1960 | 65,352 | 34,411 | 52.7 | 13,096 | 38.1 |
| 1985 | 94,974 | 19,839 | 20.9 | 5,276 | 26.6 |
| 1995 | 105,425 | 12,037 | 11.4 | 3,732 | 31.0 |
| 2000 | 108,224 | 10,467 | 9.7 | 3,549 | 33.9 |
| 2005 | 110,193 | 8,370 | 7.6 | 2,746 | 33.0 |
| 2008 | – | 7,295 | – | 2,784 | 38.2 |

* "Adult" denotes age 16 and over for farm figures 1960–85; 15 and over for figures 1950–55 and for 1985 ff. In national figures (from *JSY*, 1961, p. 26, Table 11; *JSY*, 1985, p. 44, Table 2-13; and *JSY*, 2010, p. 56, Table 2-12), adult denotes age 15 and over.

*Source:* Percentages calculated from figures in *JSY*, 1961, p. 78, Table 37; *JSY*, 1985, p. 151, Table 5-4; *JSY*, 2010, p. 237, Table 7-4.

**Table 35:** Changes in the Location of Farm Activity (1960–2005) (by select prefectures)

| Prefecture | 1960 | 1985 | 2005 | % Remaining |
|---|---|---|---|---|
| **A. Farm Population (in 1,000s)** | | | | |
| All Japan | 34,546 | 19,839 | 8,370 | 24.2 |
| Hokkaido | 1,435 | 472 | 212 | 14.8 |
| Akita | 767 | 490 | 263 | 34.3 |
| Fukuoka | 977 | 553 | 229 | 23.4 |
| Kôchi | 425 | 193 | 78 | 18.4 |
| Shizuoka | 1,095 | 613 | 78 | 18.4 |
| Kanagawa | 463 | 229 | 74 | 16.0 |
| Osaka | 460 | 232 | 52 | 11.3 |
| Tokyo | 320 | 124 | 32 | 10.0 |
| **B. Cultivated Land (in hectares)** | | | | |
| All Japan | 6,375,084 | 5,379,000 | 4,692,000 | 73.6 |
| Hokkaido | 1,231,574 | 1,185,000 | 1,169,000 | 94.9 |
| Akita | 156,497 | 161,600 | 151,300 | 96.7 |
| Fukuoka | 130,775 | 111,000 | 88,300 | 67.5 |
| Kôchi | 55,684 | 39,300 | 28,900 | 51.9 |
| Shizuoka | 129,632 | 96,000 | 73,500 | 56.7 |
| Kanagawa | 57,693 | 28,200 | 21,100 | 36.6 |
| Osaka | 38,956 | 19,900 | 14,500 | 37.2 |
| Tokyo | 35,094 | 12,500 | 8,340 | 23.8 |
| **C. Paddy Fields (in hectares)** | | | | |
| All Japan | 2,940,003 | 2,952,000 | 2,556,000 | 86.9 |
| Hokkaido | 185,755 | 258,100 | 227,700 | 122.6 |
| Akita | 107,540 | 137,200 | 131,200 | 122.0 |
| Fukuoka | 96,993 | 83,300 | 68,900 | 71.0 |
| Kôchi | 31,733 | 28,300 | 21,700 | 68.4 |
| Shizuoka | 53,057 | 33,300 | 24,200 | 45.6 |
| Kanagawa | 16,667 | 6,630 | 4,280 | 25.7 |
| Osaka | 29,609 | 14,200 | 10,700 | 36.1 |
| Tokyo | 6,590 | 782 | 325 | 4.9 |

*Source:* For section A, percentages are calculated from data in *JSY*, 1961, p. 78, Table 37; *JSY*, 1986, p. 152, Table 5-6; *JSY*, 2009, p. 234, Table 7-3. For sections B and C, percentages for both cultivated land and paddy fields are calculated from *JSY*, 1961, p. 80, Table 38; *JSY*, 1986, p. 155, Table 5-12; *JSY*, 2009, p. 238, Table 7-9.

**Table 36:** Area of Cultivated Land (1935–2005) (in 1,000 hectares)

| Year | Total | Paddy Fields | Dry Fields | Year | Total | Paddy Fields | Dry Fields |
|------|-------|--------------|------------|------|-------|--------------|------------|
| 1935 | 6,009 | 3,193 | 2,816 | 1980 | 4,706 | 2,769 | 1,475 |
| 1946 | 4,945 | 2,836 | 2,109 | 1985 | 4,577 | 2,665 | 1,493 |
| 1955 | 5,140 | 2,847 | 2,001 | 1990 | 4,361 | 2,542 | 1,465 |
| 1960 | 5,324 | 2,965 | 2,035 | 1995 | 3,970 | 2,293 | 1,380 |
| 1965 | 5,134 | 2,968 | 1,770 | 2000 | 3,734 | 2,162 | 1,315 |
| 1970 | 5,109 | 3,046 | 1,600 | 2005 | 3,450 | 2,002 | 1,225 |
| 1975 | 4,783 | 2,800 | 1,486 | | | | |

*Source:* Data for 1935–46 from *JSY*, 1961, p. 80, Table 38; for 1955–75, from *JSY*, 1985, p. 154, Table 5-11; for 1985–2005, *JSY*, 2007, p. 235, Table 7-8. Different data sets yield different figures, and changes in analytical categories alter figures as years pass, but the figures given here seem to be reasonably consistent, if more conservative than in some tables.

**Table 37:** Crop Production (1930–2007) (in 1,000 metric tons)

| Year | Rice | Other Grains | Dried Red & Kidney Beans | Chinese Cabbage | Lettuce | Spinach |
|------|------|--------------|--------------------------|-----------------|---------|---------|
| 1930 | 10,031 | 1,683 | | | | |
| 1940 | 9,131 | 2,662 | – | – | | – |
| 1950 | 9,651 | 2,546 | 128 | 423 | | 82 |
| 1955 | 12,385 | 2,895 | 291 | 587 | | 156 |
| 1960 | 12,858 | 3,831 | 312 | 998 | – | 231 |
| 1975 | 13,165 | 2,521 | 155 | 1,607 | 258 | 346 |
| 1985 | 11,662 | 1,252 | 141 | 1,478 | 459 | 383 |
| 1995 | 10,748 | 662 | 138 | 1,163 | 537 | 360 |
| 2004 | 8,730 | 1,059 | 118 | 888 | 509 | 289 |
| 2005 | 9,074 | 1,058 | 105 | 924 | 552 | 298 |
| 2007 | 8,714 | 1,105 | 88 | 918 | 544 | 298 |

*Source:* Data gleaned from extensive entries in *JSY*, 1961, pp. 90–91, 94–95, Table 44; *JSY*, 1985, pp. 160–61, Table 5-19; *JSY*, 2010, pp. 244–45, Table 7-15.

**Table 38:** Livestock Farming (1950–2008) (in 1,000s)

| Year | Milk Farms | | Beef Farms | | Pig Farms | | Egg Farms | | Broiler Farms | |
|------|------------|------|------------|------|-----------|------|-----------|------|---------------|------|
| | Farm House-holds | Milk Cows | Farm House-holds | Beef Cattle | Farm House-holds | Pigs | Farm House-holds | Egg-layers | Farm House-Holds | Hens |
| 1950 | 133 | 198 | 1,986 | 2,252 | 459 | 608 | 3,754* | 16,545* | | |
| 1960 | 410 | 824 | 2,031 | 2,340 | 799 | 1,918 | 3,839* | 52,153* | | |
| 1975 | 160 | 1,787 | 474 | 1,857 | 223 | 7,684 | 560 | 154,504 | 12 | 87,659 |
| 1985 | 82 | 2,111 | 298 | 2,587 | 83 | 10,718 | 124 | 177,477 | 7 | 150,215 |
| 1995 | 44 | 1,951 | 170 | 2,965 | 19 | 10,250 | 79 | 193,854 | 4 | 119,682 |
| 2005 | 28 | 1,655 | 90 | 2,747 | 7 | 8,088 | 68 | 145,704 | 3 | 102,520 |
| 2008 | 24 | 1,533 | 80 | 2,890 | 7 | 9,745 | 3** | 181,664 | 2 | 102,987 |

\* Chicken-farm figures for 1950 and 1960 combine layers and broilers.
\*\* After 2005, all farms with fewer than 1,000 adult hens are excluded.

*Source: JSY*, 1985, p. 164, Table 5-23; *JSY*, 2007, p. 244, Tables 7-17, 7-18; *JSY*, 2010, p. 248, Table 7-17.

**Table 39:** Select Agricultural Implements (1955–1993) (in 1,000s)

| Year | Riding Tractors | | | Powered Rice Planters | Farm Trucks |
|------|-----------------|-------|-------|-----------------------|-------------|
| | All | Small | Large | | |
| 1955 | – | – | – | – | – |
| 1965 | 19 | – | – | – | 418 |
| 1971 | 267 | 188 | 79 | 46 | 1,015 |
| 1976 | 721 | 372 | 349 | 1,498 | 1,246 |
| 1984 | 1,650 | 469 | 1,181 | 1,672 | 2,051 |
| 1990 | 2,142 | 643 | 1,500 | 1,983 | – |
| 1993 | 2,041 | 402 | 1,639 | 1,866 | – |

*Source: JSY*, 1985, p. 158, Table 5-17; *JSY*, 1995, p. 232, Table 6-17.

**Table 40:** Indexes of Agricultural and Fishery Output (1945–2005) (year 2000 = 100)

| Year | Agricultural Output | Fishery Output | Year | Agricultural Output | Fishery Output |
|------|---------------------|----------------|------|---------------------|----------------|
| 1945 | 32.9 | 25.4 | 1980 | 105.0 | 114.6 |
| 1950 | 54.9 | 33.5 | 1985 | 115.8 | 131.8 |
| 1955 | 72.4 | 53.2 | 1995 | 106.0 | 112.6 |
| 1965 | 89.6 | 78.4 | 2000 | 100 | 100 |
| 1970 | 100.6 | 114.6 | 2005 | 95.3 | 92.0 |
| 1975 | 106.3 | 124.5 | | | |

*Source: JSY*, 2010, p. 4, Key Statistics. The index figures given here for 1945–65 are recalculated from data in *JSY*, 1985, p. 785, Key Statistics, using the 2007 basis year of 2000 = 100.

**Table 41:** Fishery Statistics (1930–2007)

| Year | Persons Engaged (1,000s) | Registered Fishing Boats | Non-Powered Fishing Boats | Total Catch (1,000 t)** | Exports* (1,000 t)** | Imports (1,000 t)** |
|------|------|------|------|------|------|------|
| 1930 | – | 359,285 | 323,228 | 3,136 | 93 | – |
| 1940 | – | 354,215 | 279,018 | 3,428 | 130 | – |
| 1946 | – | 297,273 | 237,099 | 2,075 | 0.1 | – |
| 1950 | 670 | 480,340 | 351,421 | 3,256 | 52 | – |
| 1955 | 540 | 415,588 | 271,167 | 4,659 | 159 | – |
| 1960 | 620 | 380,728 | 212,258 | 5,818 | 308 | – |
| 1965 | 612 | 403,250 | 181,875 | 6,382 | 410 | 667 |
| 1970 | 570 | 391,789 | 120,600 | 8,598 | 457 | 760 |
| 1975 | 478 | 414,745 | 53,260 | 9,573 | 465 | 1,113 |
| 1980 | 457 | 449,847 | 32,781 | 9,909 | 513 | 1,744 |
| 1985 | 432 | 437,150 | 24,302 | 10,425 | 369 | 2,315 |
| 1990 | 371 | 416,067 | 20,586 | 10,278 | 1,147 | 3,891 |
| 1995 | – | 386,067 | 13,977 | 6,768 | 285 | 6,755 |
| 1998 | 277 | – | – | 6,044 | – | 5,254 |
| 2000 | – | 358,687 | 11,545 | 5,736 | 264 | 5,883 |
| 2004 | 231 | 330,807 | 8,274 | 5,178 | 627 | 6,055 |
| 2005 | 222 | 325,450 | 8,118 | 5,152 | 647 | 5,782 |
| 2006 | 212 | 321,017 | 8,487 | 5,131 | 788 | 5,711 |
| 2007 | 204 | 313,397 | 8,622 | 5,079 | 815 | 5,161 |

\* Seafood export figures that include seaweed are substantially higher than the fish/shellfish figures cited here.

\** t = metric tons.

*Source:* This composite set of statistics derives from the following sources. (1) "Persons Engaged" from *JSY*, 1961, p. 46, Table 24; *JSY*, 1985, p. 182, Table 5-51; *JSY*, 2010, p. 264, Table 7-40. (2) "Fishing Boats" from *JSY*, 1949, p. 244, Table 150; *JSY*, 1961, p. 122, Table 60; *JSY*, 1976, p. 140, Table 99; *JSY*, 1985, p. 185, Table 5-54; *JSY*, 2010, p. 267, Table 7-44. "Non-powered"(for example, sail or oar-powered) boats include vessels for both marine and freshwater use. (3) "Total Catch" from *JSY*, 1961, p. 124, Table 62, and Key Statistics in *JSY*, 1985 and 2010. "Total catch" includes fish, shellfish, other marine animals and seaweed. (4) "Export and Import" data from *JSY*, 1961, p. 246, Table 141; *JSY*, 1986, p. 344, Table 10-6; *JSY*, 2009, p. 279, Table 7-60; *JSY*, 2010, pp. 281–82, Table 7-60.

**Table 42:** Whaling Catch (1933–2006) (by number of whales)

| Year | Catch by Factory Ship | Catch by Other Vessels | Year | Catch by Factory Ship | Catch by Other Vessels |
|------|------------------------|-------------------------|------|------------------------|-------------------------|
| 1933 | (5,241) | | 1975 | 7,423 | 2,941 |
| 1936 | (7,434) | | 1980 | 3,279 | 1,912 |
| 1939 | (9,760) | | 1985 | 429 | 1,941 |
| 1950 | 2,418 | 2,914 | 1990 | 96 | 330 |
| 1955 | 8,606 | 3,258 | 1995 | 174 | 430 |
| 1960 | 15,825 | 3,824 | 2000 | 188 | 527 |
| 1965 | 18,259 | 3,374 | 2003 | 150 | 700 |
| 1970 | 12,143 | 4,744 | 2005 | 121 | 815 |
| | | | 2006 | 87 | 1,214 |

*Source:* Calculated from data in *JSY*, 1949, p. 239, Table 142; *JSY*, 1961, p. 128, Table 67; *JSY*, 1976, pp. 146–47, Table 103; *JSY*, 1985, p. 284, Table 7-15, and p. 304, Table 8-7; *JSY*, 2007, p. 348, Table 10–12, and p. 388, Table 12-7; *JSY*, 2010, p. 274, Table 7-52. Post-1980 categories of catch use other labels.

## FORESTRY

**Table 43:** Forest (*sanrin*) Area by Ownership (1939–2005) (in 1,000 hectares)

| Year | Total | National Government | Other Public Entities | Forestry Households | Other Private Entities | Forest Revival Corporations |
|------|-------|---------------------|------------------------|----------------------|-------------------------|------------------------------|
| 1939 | 23,993 | 7,651 | 1,369 | (14,972) | | – |
| 1946 | 20,400 | 7,562 | 3,041 | (9,798) | | – |
| 1951 | 24,746 | 7,873 | 3,488 | (13,384) | | – |
| 1960 | 24,403 | 7,484 | 2,769 | 6,403 | 7,748 | – |
| 1970 | 24,483 | 7,438 | 2,854 | 6,701 | 7,490 | 291 |
| 1980 | 24,728 | 7,385 | 2,626 | 6,760 | 7,340 | 617 |
| 1990 | 24,621 | 7,301 | 2,681 | 6,752 | 7,042 | 844 |
| 2000 | 24,490 | 7,240 | 2,776 | 5,715 | 7,767 | 994 |
| 2005 | 24,473 | 7,211 | 2,817 | (13,434) | | 1,010 |

"Other Public" = mostly prefectures and municipalities. "Other Private" = mostly corporations, temples and shrines. Totals do not necessarily equal sum of sub-categories.

*Source: JSY*, 1961, pp. 108–9, Table 52; *JSY*, 1985, pp. 174–75, Tables 5-34, 5-36; *JSY*, 2007, pp. 254–55, Tables 7-28, 7-29; *JSY*, 2010, p. 258, Table 7-28.

**Table 44:** Cutover and Reforested Acreage (1913–2006) (in 1,000 hectares*)

| Year | Cutover Acreage | | Reforested Acreage | | | | Artif. Refo. as % of Total Cut |
|---|---|---|---|---|---|---|---|
| | Total | Private | Total | Artificial** | Natural | Private | |
| 1913 | – | – | 149.1 | 149.1 | – | – | |
| 1920 | – | – | 531.6 | 85.1 | 446.5 | – | |
| 1930 | 359.0 | – | 328.5 | 102.1 | 226.4 | – | 28.4 |
| 1940 | 545.1 | – | 396.3 | 152.8 | 243.5 | – | 28.0 |
| 1950 | 539.9 | 290.7 | 536.6 | 249.8 | 286.8 | 343.6 | 46.3 |
| 1955 | 660.8 | 311.8 | 582.7 | 380.3 | 202.4 | 392.6 | 57.6 |
| 1960 | 697.4 | 347.1 | 539.6 | 392.0 | 147.6 | 350.9 | 56.2 |
| 1965 | 485.8 | 230.8 | 469.7 | 362.7 | 107.0 | 256.8 | 74.7 |
| 1970 | 383.1 | 204.3 | 431.3 | 347.8 | 83.7 | 214.8 | 90.8 |
| 1975 | 316.4 | 145.6 | 305.6 | 218.7 | 87.0 | 128.0 | 69.1 |
| 1980 | 253.6 | 118.8 | 250.3 | 162.6 | 87.7 | 89.3 | 64.1 |
| 1983 | 241.0 | 101.5 | 214.8 | 132.2 | 82.6 | 78.6 | 54.9 |
| 1990*** | 243.8 | – | – | 55.4 | – | 48.4 | 22.7 |
| 1995 | 158.2 | – | – | 45.2 | – | 38.4 | 24.3 |
| 2000 | 67.2 | – | – | 31.3 | – | 24.7 | 46.6 |
| 2002 | 33.9 | – | – | 27.3 | – | 21.9 | 80.4 |
| 2003 | 22.2 | – | – | 25.0 | – | 20.3 | 112.5 |
| 2004 | 29.5 | – | – | 25.0 | – | 20.4 | 84.7 |
| 2005 | – | – | – | 25.6 | – | 20.4 | – |
| 2006 | – | – | – | 23.9 | – | 19.4 | – |

\* Pre-1950 acreage figures are in *chô*. One *chô* = 0.992 hectares.

\*\* "Artificial" includes both new and replanted plantation stands.

\*\*\* Record-keeping categories changed during the 1980s.

*Source: JSY*, 1949, pp. 237–38, Tables 140, 141 for pre-1950 figures; *JSY*, 1961, pp. 112–14, Tables 55, 56; *JSY*, 1985, p. 178, Table 5-41; *JSY*, 2007, pp. 255–6, Tables 7-31, 7-32; *JSY*, 2010, pp. 25–60, Tables 7-31, 7-32.

**Table 45:** Wood Production and Imports (1950–2007) (in 1,000 m³)

| Year | Total Supply | Domestic Total | Domestic Logs | Imported Wood |
|------|-------------|----------------|---------------|---------------|
| 1950 | 31,821 | – | 20,338 | – |
| 1955 | 48,029 | – | 42,794 | 2,547 |
| 1960 | 71,467 | 63,762 | 48,515 | 7,705 |
| 1965 | 76,798 | 56,616 | 49,534 | 20,155 |
| 1970 | 106,601 | 49,780 | 45,351 | 56,821 |
| 1975 | 99,303 | 37,113 | 34,155 | 62,190 |
| 1980 | 112,211 | 36,961 | 34,051 | 75,250 |
| 1985 | 95,447 | 35,374 | 32,944 | 60,073 |
| 1990 | 113,242 | 31,297 | 29,300 | 81,945 |
| 1995 | 113,698 | 24,303 | 22,897 | 89,395 |
| 2000 | 101,006 | 19,058 | 17,034 | 81,948 |
| 2005 | 87,423 | 17,900 | 16,166 | 69,523 |
| 2007 | 83,879 | 19,313 | 17,650 | 64,565 |

"Domestic total" combines timber material and wood for other uses.
"Imported wood" includes timber and fuel material.

*Source:* Figures for 1950–55 are from *JSY*, 1961, p. 116, Table 58, and p. 207, Table 109. Later years of "domestic logs" are from *JSY*, 1985, p. 179, Table 5-44; *JSY*, 2010, p. 261, Table 7-34. Post-1955 import figures and "total supply" and "domestic total" are from *JSY*, 1985, p. 180, Table 5-46; *JSY*, 2010, p. 262, Table 7-35.

**Table 46:** Wood Pulp Imports (1930–2008) (in 1,000 tons)

| Year | Tonnage | Year | Tonnage | Year | Tonnage |
|------|---------|------|---------|------|---------|
| 1930 | 80.4 | 1965 | 507 | 1995 | 3,583 |
| 1940 | 175.9 | 1970 | 917 | 2000 | 3,133 |
| 1947 | 2.6 | 1975 | 1,035 | 2005 | 2,360 |
| 1950 | 63.4 | 1980 | 2,216 | 2008 | 2,013 |
| 1955 | 97.0 | 1985 | 2,268 | | |
| 1960 | 147 | 1990 | 2,894 | | |

*Source: JSY*, 1961, p. 249, Table 142; *JSY*, 1976, p. 289, Table 210; *JSY*, 1995, p. 420, Table 12-7; *JSY*, 2010, p. 467, Table 15-6.

**Table 47:** Select Minor Forest Products (1950–2007)

| Year | Bamboo (1,000 bundles) | Charcoal (1,000 t) | Fuel Wood (1,000 m³ stacks) | Imports for Fuel Wood & Charcoal (1,000 m³) |
|---|---|---|---|---|
| 1950 | – | 1,866 | – | – |
| 1955 | 13,900 | 2,089 | – | – |
| 1960 | 13,465 | 1,504 | – | 14,756 |
| 1965 | 12,846 | 593 | 2,957 | 6,241 |
| 1970 | 11,052 | 178 | 1,032 | 1,965 |
| 1975 | 10,494 | 70 | 339 | 398 |
| 1980 | 8,965 | 35 | 151 | 843 |
| 1985 | 7,479 | 32 | 138 | 246 |
| 1990 | 6,822 | 35 | 165 | 152 |
| 1995 | 3,941 | 70 | 161 | 389 |
| 2000 | 2,008 | 57 | 80 | 707 |
| 2004 | 1,372 | 38 | 37 | 859 |
| 2005 | 1,290 | 35 | 37 | 842 |
| 2007 | 1,143 | 30 | 36 | 830 |

*Source: JSY*, 1961, p. 116, Table 58; *JSY*, 1976, p. 129, Table 86; *JSY*, 1995, p. 254, Tables 5-45, 6-46; *JSY*, 2010, pp. 261–62, Tables 7-34, 7-35.

# *Notes*

## CHAPTER 1: JAPAN THE PLACE

1   Two basic texts on the geography of Japan are Glenn T. Trewartha, *Japan, A Physical, Cultural, and Regional Geography* (Madison: University of Wisconsin Press, 1978) and Association of Japanese Geographers (ed.), *Geography of Japan* (Tokyo: Teikoku-Shoin, 1980), p. 440. A richly detailed treatment of Japanese geomorphology is Torao Yoshikawa et al., *The Landforms of Japan* (Tokyo: UTP, 1981).

2   Properly speaking the "Bonins" consist of three island arcs: North to South, the Izu, Ogasawara and Kazan chains. The Ryukyus, properly speaking, are the southern section of the Nansei Islands, with the Satsunan chain, which reaches from Okinawa northward to Kyushu, constituting the northern section. The Ryukyus number some 105 islands. Regarding their history, the classic study is by George H. Kerr, *Okinawa, The History of an Island People* (Boston: Tuttle, originally published in 1958 and reissued in 2000). A recent set of essays is Richard Pearson (ed.), *Okinawa, The Rise of an Island Kingdom* (London: Oxford UP, 2009).

3   Figures are from Rand McNally, *Universal World Atlas, New Census Edition* (Chicago: Rand McNally & Company, 1982), pp. 161–65.

4   Sohei Kaizuka and Yoko Ota, "Land in Torment", in *Geographical Magazine* 51-5 (London: Feb. 1979), p. 345. Because of the complexity of geological processes, the spotty and varied nature of relevant evidence, and the range of interpretive postulates, ample uncertainties surround geological dating. Two helpful texts are Stephen Marshak, *Earth: Portrait of a Planet* (NY: W.W. Norton, 2001), especially Ch. 13, and Frederick K. Lutgens & Edward J. Tarbuck, *Essentials of Geology*, 9th ed. (Upper Saddle River, NJ: Pearson Prentice Hall, 2006), especially Ch. 19.

5   For a summary of this prior history, see Gina L. Barnes, "Origins of the Japanese Islands: The New 'Big Picture'", *Nichibunken Japan Review* No. 15 (2003), pp. 3–50. A detailed treatment is Toshio Kimura et al., *Geology of Japan* (Tokyo: UTP, 1991). Several fascinating essays on the dynamics of geological process, including seven that focus on Japan, appear in J.M. Dickins et al. (eds), "New Concepts in Global Tectonics", a Special Issue of *Himalayan Geology*, Vol. 22, No. 1 (2001). Another bold interpretation is Michihei Hoshi, *The Expanding Earth: Evidence, Causes and Effects* (Tokyo: Tokai UP, 1998). And for a recent interpretive review of geological scholarship and thought,

see Ted Nield, *Supercontinent: Ten Billion Years in the Life of Our Planet* (Cambridge, MA: HUP, 2007).

6    A concise, richly illustrated outline of Pangaea's breakup is Bruno Vrielynck & Philippe Bouysse, *The Changing Face of the Earth: The break-up of Pangaea and continental drift over the past 250 million years in ten steps* (Paris: UNESCO Publishing, 2003).

7    For a diagram of this plate arrangement, see Fig. 3 at p. 9 in Barnes, "Origins of the Japanese Islands: The New 'Big Picture'".

8    An extended treatment of East Sea geology appears in S.K. Chough et al., *Marine Geology of Korean Seas*, 2nd ed. (Amsterdam: Elsevier, 2000). See also Sun Yoon, "Tectonic history of the Japan Sea region and its implications for the formation of the Japan Sea", in Dickins et al. (eds), 2001. For paleomagnetic evidence of the "bending" of Japan, see K. Hirooka, "Paleomagnetic Evidence of the Deformation of Japan and Its Paleogeography during the Neogene", in Ryuichi Tsuchi and James C. Ingle Jr. (eds), *Pacific Neogene: Environment, Evolution, and Events* (Tokyo: UTP, 1992), pp. 151–56.

    On northern Japan and its relationship to Sakhalin Island, see Yasunari Shigeta & Haruyoshi Maeda (eds), *The Cretaceous System in the Makarov Area, Southern Sakhalin, Russian Far East* (Monograph No. 31) (Tokyo: National Science Museum, Dec. 2005). Their bibliography will guide one to earlier works of relevance.

9    For a recent discussion of global cooling ca. 50 myBP, see *Science News*, Vol. 174, No. 8, p. 12 (11 Oct 2008).

10   These climatic oscillations are examined in the essays by L. E. Heusser, I. Koizumi and R. Tsuchi in Tsuchi and Ingle (eds), *Pacific Neogene: Environment, Evolution, and Events*, pp. 3–13, 15–24 and 237–50. On the key role in these developments of the rising Himalayas and resultant changes in atmospheric carbon dioxide, see the essay by M. E. Raymo at pp. 107–16, also in Tsuchi and Ingle. Evidence for a warm period in the Japan area ca. 16–15 myBP is treated by Karyu Tsuda et al., "On the Middle Miocene Paleoenvironment of Japan with Special Reference to the Ancient Mangrove Swamps," in Robert Orr Whyte (ed.), *The Evolution of the East Asian Environment Volume 1 Geology and Palaeoclimatology* (Hong Kong: University of Hong Kong, 1984), p. 388–96.

11   See Figure 3, profiles A, B and C in Yutaka Sakaguchi, "Characteristics of the physical nature of Japan with special reference to landform", in Association of Japanese Geographers (ed.), *Geography of Japan* (Tokyo: Teikoku-Shoin, 1980), pp. 10–11.

12   Sakaguchi, "Characteristics of the physical nature of Japan with special reference to landform", p. 6.

13   Mitsuo Hashimoto (ed.), *Geology of Japan* (Tokyo: Terra Scientific Publishing Company, 1991), pp. 49–52, treats these coal seams.

14   The uplifted ancient rock of paleo-Japan also reveals ample evidence of volcanism in earlier eons, but much of that rock has long since been reworked by subsequent tectonic processes, notably sedimentation and metamorphism.

15   Hashimoto, *Geology of Japan*, p. 136.

16   Hashimoto, *Geology of Japan*, p. 151.

17   See Hashimoto, *Geology of Japan*, pp. 154–55, for an excellent map of volcanic distribution and range of effect.

18   Sakaguchi, "Characteristics of the physical nature of Japan with special reference to landform", p. 4.

19   Sakaguchi, "Characteristics of the physical nature of Japan with special reference to landform", p. 6. Hashimoto, *Geology of Japan*, p. 144.

20   Koji Mizoguchi, *An Archaeological History of Japan 30,000 B.C. to A.D. 700* (Philadelphia: U. Penn. Press, 2002), p. 50. The chronology of the most recent glacial cycle is examined more fully in Yoshinori Yasuda, "Oscillations of Climatic and Oceanographic

Conditions since the Last Glacial Age in Japan", in Robert Orr Whyte (ed.), *The Evolution of the East Asian Environment Volume 1 Geology and Palaeoclimatology* (Hong Kong: University of Hong Kong, 1984), pp. 397–413.

21 On Japan's weather patterns, see Ikuo Maejima, "Seasonal and Regional Aspects of Japan's Weather and Climate", in Association of Japanese Geographers (ed.), *Geography of Japan*, pp. 54–72.

22 The Britain-Japan comparison is explored a bit more fully in Conrad Totman, *Japan's Imperial Forest: Goryôrin, 1889–1946* (Folkestone: Global Oriental, 2007), on pp. xxiv–xxx and 94–97.

23 An old but useful English-language reference work on Japan's woodland is Natural Resources Section, *Important Trees of Japan* (Report no. 119) (Tokyo: General Headquarters, Supreme Commander for the Allied Powers, 1949), and a beautifully illustrated arboreal handbook in Japanese is Kitamura Shirô and Okamoto Shôgo, *Genshoku Nihon jumoku zukan [Illustrated handbook of Japanese trees and shrubs]* (Osaka: Hoikusha, 1959). It gives the Latin binomials of the trees it lists.

## CHAPTER 2: FORAGER SOCIETY TO CA. 500 BCE

1 The term "mesolithic" ("middle stone") is sometimes utilized to denote societies whose tool kit seems to fall between paleolithic and neolithic, and one might wish to apply it here.

2 As noted in the text, the earliest known pottery in Japan dates to about 16,500 yBP. It had simple decorations, not the extensive "cord markings" of Jômon pottery proper. The latter appeared a few thousand years later, ca. 12,000 yBP. Here we are using the term Jômon to encompass both the cord-marked and the simpler pottery that preceded it. However, in calculating total Jômon population in the sub-section titled "Jômon Overall", the period covered is essentially that of cord-marked pottery.

3 These dates are based on Yoshinori Yasuda, "Monsoon Fluctuations and Cultural Changes During the Last Glacial Age in Japan", in *Nichibunken Japan Review*, No. 1 (1990), and Pinxian Wang, "Progress in Late Cenozoic Palaeoclimatology of China: a Brief Review", in Robert Orr Whyte (ed.), *The Evolution of the East Asian Environment Volume 1 Geology and Palaeoclimatology* (Hong Kong: University of Hong Kong, 1984) and for the millennia 15,000 yBP ff, on Habu, 2004, pp. 43–45. The dating in Yoshinori Yasuda, "Oscillations of Climatic and Oceanographic Conditions since the Last Glacial Age in Japan" in Robert Orr Whyte (ed.), *The Evolution of the East Asian Environment Volume 1 Geology and Palaeoclimatology*, pp. 397–413, and in other sources differs somewhat. Dating varies, depending on what "fossil" evidence (such as shellfish or other maritime evidence or pollen or other terrestrial evidence) a researcher is utilizing.

4 Figures are from Matsuo Tsukada, "Vegetation in Prehistoric Japan: The Last 20,000 Years", in Richard J. Pearson et al. (eds), *Windows on the Japanese Past: Studies in Archaeology and Prehistory* (Ann Arbor, MI: Center for Japanese Studies, 1986), p. 81.

5 Two excellent maps showing forest composition of present-day and fully glacial Japan are at Tsukada, "Vegetation in Prehistoric Japan: The Last 20,000 Years", p. 24. A slightly different representation of forest regions at ca. 20,000 yBP is in Keiji Imamura, *Prehistoric Japan* (Honolulu: UHP, 1996), p. 30.

6 Yoshinori Yasuda, "Monsoon Fluctuations and Cultural Changes During the Last Glacial Age in Japan", in *Nichibunken Japan Review*, No. 1 (1990), p. 123.

7   Yasuda, "Monsoon Fluctuations and Cultural Changes During the Last Glacial Age in Japan", pp. 125–29, treats this monsoon topic.

8   Yasuda, "Monsoon Fluctuations and Cultural Changes During the Last Glacial Age in Japan", pp. 125–31, treats this topic. A good map of present-day cryptomeria distribution that relates it to levels of precipitation is at Yoshinori Yasuda, "Oscillations of Climatic and Oceanographic Conditions since the Last Glacial Age in Japan", in Robert Orr Whyte (ed.), *The Evolution of the East Asian Environment Volume 1 Geology and Palaeoclimatology* (Hong Kong: University of Hong Kong, 1984), p. 401.

9   Except as noted in endnotes further on, this summary of early human presence is based on material in Yasuda, "Monsoon Fluctuations and Cultural Changes During the Last Glacial Age in Japan"; the essays by Hanihara Kazurô, Kikuchi Toshihko, and Serizawa Chôsuke in Richard J. Pearson et al. (eds), *Windows on the Japanese Past: Studies in Archaeology and Prehistory*, pp. 75–83; T.E.G. Reynolds and S.C. Kaner, "Japan and Korea at 18,000 BP", in Olga Soffer and Clive Gamble (eds), *The World at 18,000 BP Vol. One: High Latitudes* (London: Unwin Hyman, 1990), pp. 296–311; and Tatsuo Kobayashi (ed. by Simon Kaner with Oki Nakamura), Jômon Reflections: Forager life and culture in the prehistoric Japanese archipelago (Oxford: Oxbow Books, 2004).

10  Matsuo Tsukada, "Vegetation in Prehistoric Japan: The Last 20,000 Years", p. 39.

11  *Science News* 160-13 (29 September 2001), p. 199.

12  Reports of a fossil find dating to some 400,000 yBP were subsequently repudiated amidst allegations of fossil fakery. *Science News* 164–68 (23 August 2003), p. 118.

13  *The New York Times*, 23 December 2010, p. A14.

14  Chôsuke Serizawa, "The Paleolithic Age of Japan in the Context of East Asia: A Brief Introduction", in Richard J. Pearson et al. (eds), *Windows on the Japanese Past: Studies in Archaeology and Prehistory*, pp. 191–92, 202. C. Melvin Aikens and Higuchi Takayasu, *Prehistory of Japan* (NY: Academic Press, 1982), pp. 39–41.

15  Yoshinori Yasuda, "Monsoon Fluctuations and Cultural Changes During the Last Glacial Age in Japan", p. 137.

16  *Science News*, Vol. 171-14 (7 April 2007), p. 211, reports on new fossil finds near Beijing.

17  On the Amur connection, see especially the Hanihara and Kikuchi essays in Richard J. Pearson et al. (eds), *Windows on the Japanese Past: Studies in Archaeology and Prehistory*. On boats, see Fumiko Ikawa-Smith, "Late Pleistocene and Early Holocene Technologies", in Richard J. Pearson et al. (eds), *Windows on the Japanese Past: Studies in Archaeology and Prehistory*, p. 211.

18  The issue of regional difference is explored in Yoshinori Yasuda, "Monsoon Fluctuations and Cultural Changes During the Last Glacial Age in Japan", pp. 138–39; Hanihara Kazurô, "The Origin of the Japanese in Relation to Other Ethnic Groups in East Asia", pp. 80–82; Toshihiko Kikuchi, "Continental Culture and Hokkaido", pp. 149, 154; and Chôsuke Serizawa, "The Paleolithic Age of Japan in the Context of East Asia: A Brief Introduction", pp. 192–95, all in Richard J. Pearson et al. (eds), *Windows on the Japanese Past: Studies in Archaeology and Prehistory*. Also T.E.G. Reynolds and S.C. Kaner, "Japan and Korea at 18,000 BP", in Olga Soffer and Clive Gamble (eds), *The World at 18,000 BP Vol. One: High Latitudes* (London: Unwin Hyman, 1990), p. 302.

19  Except as otherwise noted, this discussion of Jômon society is based on Junko Habu, *Ancient Jômon of Japan* (Cambridge: CUP, 2004).

20  Habu, *Ancient Jômon of Japan*, p. 114. She discusses jade on pp. 224–27, as noted below.

21  On temperature trends, see the graph in Habu, *Ancient Jômon of Japan*, p. 43.

22  On scholarly speculation about pottery's invention, see Tatsuo Kobayashi (ed. by Simon Kaner with Oki Nakamura), Jômon Reflections: Forager life and culture in the prehistoric Japanese archipelago, pp. 19–24, and footnote 3 on p. 190.

23  An entertaining book that explores how these migrants to North America might have crossed the Bering Straits by boat during warmer millennia, rather than on foot during the glacial epoch, is Jon Turk, In the Wake of the Jômon (NY: McGraw-Hill, 2005).

24  Kobayashi Tatsuo (ed. by Simon Kaner with Oki Nakamura), Jômon Reflections: Forager life and culture in the prehistoric Japanese archipelago, p. 10, is citing the archaeologist V. Gordon Childe. Could one argue, however, that the use of fire to cook food, meat in particular, constituted an earlier form of purposeful chemical transformation?

25  Nelly Naumann, Japanese Prehistory (Weisbaden: Harrassowitz, 2000), p. 10. Habu, Ancient Jômon of Japan, passim.

26  Based on Habu, Ancient Jômon of Japan, p. 48. Figures derived from Koyama Shûzo's 1984 study in Japanese, with Habu's explanation of his methodology on pp. 46–50. The yBP dates used here are inserted to represent the mid-points of the five Jômon and two subsequent periods used by Koyama. Also, he broke the data down in terms of four regions from the Kinki area westward and five regions from Chûbu northeastward. Habu, Ancient Jômon of Japan, p. 46, notes that Koyama's "Haji" period covers the "Kôfun, Nara, and Heian periods, ca. AD 250–1150".

27  Given the extremely high rate of infant mortality that is common in simpler societies, an average lifespan of 25 years would still leave a substantial percentage of adults in the 30–60 year range. Insofar as Koyama's basic numbers on population density are an overestimate, however, this Jômon total will be proportionately overstated. The calculations are as follows:

| Jômon Era | A<br>Average Life-span (est.) | B<br>Duration of Era (approx.) | C<br>Number of Generations (B ÷ A) | D<br>Population Density | E<br>Total Population (C × D) |
|---|---|---|---|---|---|
| Initial | 25 | 5,000 | 200 | 20,100 | 4,020,000 |
| Early | 25 | 2,000 | 80 | 105,500 | 8,440,000 |
| Middle | 25 | 1,000 | 40 | 261,300 | 10,452,000 |
| Late | 25 | 1,500 | 60 | 160,300 | 9,618,000 |
| Final | 25 | 500 | 20 | 75,800 | 1,516,000 |
| TOTALS | | 10,000 | | | 34,046,000 |

28  The basic figures used in these calculations are 261,300 people ca. 5,000 yBP, as above. Total land-area figures (from Teikoku-Shoin Co., Teikoku's Complete Atlas of Japan [Tokyo: Teikoku-Shoin, Co., Ltd., 1977], p. 41) are 375,239 km$^2$ for all of Japan proper; 247,150 for eastern Japan (from the Chûbu district eastward); and 128,089 for Japan from the Kinki district westward. Population density figures at 5,000 yBP are 0.7 persons per km$^2$ (1.8/mi$^2$) of total area and, for lowland (20 percent of total area), 3.5 per km$^2$ (9.0/mi$^2$). Population density in eastern Japan would have been substantially greater than in the West: in 5,000 yBP about one person per km$^2$ in the East, but less than one person in 10 km$^2$ in western Japan. By 3,800 yBP, however, there would have been about 1.5 people per 10 km$^2$ in western Japan.

29  Kobayashi (ed. by Simon Kaner with Oki Nakamura), Jômon Reflections: Forager life and culture in the prehistoric Japanese archipelago, passim, provides numerous gorgeous illustrations of jômon pottery. On pp. 30–31 he provides an elaborate diagram of styles and their change through the ages.

30 Kobayashi (ed. by Simon Kaner with Oki Nakamura), *Jōmon Reflections: Forager life and culture in the prehistoric Japanese archipelago*, p. 41.
31 A rich examination of the Jōmon "spiritual world" is Nelly Naumann, *Japanese Prehistory*.
32 A good map of obsidian sources is at p. 222 of Habu, *Ancient Jōmon of Japan*.
33 Habu, *Ancient Jōmon of Japan*, pp. 224–27, discusses jade. Jade (whether jadeite or nephrite) can be confused with agate (a variegated chalcedony). In 1951, Tsunoda reported, perhaps in error, that "jade is not indigenous to Japan". Ryusaku Tsunoda (tr.) and L. Carrington Goodrich (ed.), *Japan in the Chinese Dynastic Histories* (South Pasadena: P.I. & Ione Perkins, 1951), p. 5, footnote 8.
34 Habu, *Ancient Jōmon of Japan*, p. 229, provides a map of the oil deposits and asphalt beds.
35 Examples are illustrated at p. 228 of Habu, *Ancient Jōmon of Japan*.
36 Habu, *Ancient Jōmon of Japan*, p. 214.
37 William Wayne Farris, "Shipbuilding and Nautical Technology in Japanese Maritime History: Origins to 1600", in *The Mariner's Mirror*, Vol. 95, No. 3 (August 2009), p. 261.
38 Habu, *Ancient Jōmon of Japan*, pp. 215–17; Nelly Naumann, *Japanese Prehistory*, pp. 57–59.
39 Habu, *Ancient Jōmon of Japan*, pp. 215–21; Nelly Naumann, *Japanese Prehistory*, pp. 56–57. The lacquer derives from the varnish tree, *urushi* (*Rhus verniciflua*), a species of sumac.
40 Habu, *Ancient Jōmon of Japan*, p. 73.
41 Habu, *Ancient Jōmon of Japan*, p. 250. A recent examination of early Jōmon sites in Kyushu is Richard Pearson, "Jōmon hot spot: increasing sedentism in southwestern Japan in the Incipient Jōmon (14,000–9,250 cal. BC) and Earliest Jōmon (9,250–5,300 cal. BC) periods", in *World Archaeology* Vol. 38-2 (2006), pp. 239–58.
42 See, for example, the illustrations in Kobayashi (ed. by Simon Kaner with Oki Nakamura), *Jōmon Reflections: Forager life and culture in the prehistoric Japanese archipelago*, pp. 105, 121.


## CHAPTER 3: EARLY AGRICULTURAL SOCIETY TO 600 CE

1 Sofus Christiansen, "Wet Rice Cultivation: Some Reasons Why", p. 18, in Irene Nørlund, Sven Cederroth and Ingela Gerdin (eds), *Rice Societies: Asian Problems and Prospects* (London: Curzon Press Ltd., 1986).
2 Of course, even foragers must feed the microbes in their gut to obtain food for themselves, so in that sense their very survival depends on a symbiotic relationship. But those microbes are not "domesticated" creatures in the usual sense of the term.
3 In the case of animal husbandry, when humans feed the animal, they are actually engaging in a "two-stage" level of care because the ingested food must be processed by microbes in the animal's gut before it can be fully utilized by the animal.
4 The Malay term *padi* denotes rice (*Oryza*) in all its forms, wild and domesticated, whether grown in flooded or dry fields. The ambiguous English term "paddy" may refer to either the flooded field (as in rice paddy) or the type of crop grown therein (as in paddy field). To avoid confusion, in this text "paddy" will denote only "irrigated rice", as in "paddy field", meaning a field for growing paddy.
5 Francesca Bray, *The Rice Economies: Technology and Development in Asian Societies* (Oxford: Basil Blackwell, 1986), p. 15.
6 O. s. japonica is sometimes called O. s. sinica. A third type of rice, O. s. javanica, has long been grown in the Java vicinity of Indonesia. A small amount of javanica is grown in Japan today. Ann Kumar, *Globalizing the Prehistory of Japan: Language, Genes and Civilization* (London: Routledge, 2009), p. 68.

7 Kumar, *Globalizing the Prehistory of Japan: Language, Genes and Civilization*, pp. 60–61. On the biology of rice and rice cropping, see D.H. Crist, *Rice* (London: Longmans, Green and Co. Ltd., 1965), pp. 56, 81, and passim. That study is a multi-edition work first published in 1953.

8 Penelope Francks, *Technology and Agricultural Development in Pre-War Japan* (New Haven: YUP, 1984), p. 29.

9 Penelope Francks, *Rural Economic Development in Japan: From the Nineteenth Century to the Pacific War* (London: Routledge, 2006), pp. 30–31. In 1984, p. 61, Francks reported that in the 1880s only about 25 percent of Japan's paddy fields were double-cropped.

10 Kumar, *Globalizing the Prehistory of Japan: Language, Genes and Civilization*, p. 69, reproduces two diagrams showing rice's possible routes through Asia and to Japan.

11 Whereas the term Jômon refers to the "comb pattern" found on pottery of that era, Yayoi is simply a place name, the site in downtown Tokyo (on the Tokyo University campus in Bunkyô-ku) where some of the first archeological evidence of this early agricultural society was found.

12 A recent review of the evidence for Jômon agriculture is Akira Matsui and Masaaki Kanehara, "The question of prehistoric plant husbandry during the Jômon Period in Japan", in *World Archaeology*, Vol. 38-2, 2006.

13 Andrew Cobbing, *Kyushu: Gateway to Japan: A Concise History* (Folkestone: Global Oriental, 2009), p. 56.

14 Tatsuo Kobayashi (ed. by Simon Kaner with Oki Nakamura), *Jômon Reflections: Forager life and culture in the prehistoric Japanese archipelago* (Oxford: Oxbow Books, 2004), pp. 87–88.

15 Junko Habu, *Ancient Jômon of Japan* (Cambridge: CUP, 2004), pp. 69, 117. Akira Matsui and Masaaki Kanehara, "The question of prehistoric plant husbandry during the Jômon Period in Japan", p. 268.

16 Habu, *Ancient Jômon of Japan*, pp. 14, 59, 118, gives the Latin binomials for these plants. The hard, thick shell of the bottle gourd evidently served as a container. Akira Matsui and Masaaki Kanehara, "The question of prehistoric plant husbandry during the Jômon Period in Japan," discuss the evidence for these and other cultivated plants.

17 Many scholars have attempted to make sense of the scattered archeological and literary evidence pertaining to the early centuries of Japan's agricultural society. Two recent works are J. Edward Kidder Jr., *Himiko and Japan's Elusive Chiefdom of Yamatai* (Honolulu: UHP, 2007), and Gina L. Barnes, *State Formation in Japan* (Oxon: Routledge, 2007). A vigorous study is Kumar, *Globalizing the Prehistory of Japan: Language, Genes and Civilization*. Kumar assembles evidence from rice cultivation, skeletal and other archeological remains, DNA analysis and comparative linguistics to argue that migrants from Java established Yayoi culture in Japan. Howells, in Richard J. Pearson et al. (eds), *Windows on the Japanese Past: Studies in Archaeology and Prehistory* (Ann Arbor, MI: Center for Japanese Studies, 1986), pp. 85–99, discusses the physical anthropology of ancient Japan. On language in the archipelago, see Miller, in Richard J. Pearson et al. (eds), *Windows on the Japanese Past: Studies in Archaeology and Prehistory*, pp. 101–20, and Bruce L. Batten, *To the Ends of Japan: Premodern Frontiers, Boundaries, and Interactions* (Honolulu: UHP, 2003), pp. 77–79. Other sources are cited in Conrad Totman, *Pre-industrial Korea and Japan in Environmental Perspective* (Leiden: Brill, 2004), and Conrad Totman, *A History of Japan, Second Edition* (Oxford: Blackwell, 2005). Discussions of continental developments that relate to Japan can be found in various publications, including Charles Holcombe, *The Genesis of East Asia, 221 B.C.–A.D. 907* (Honolulu: UHP, 2001), pp. 183–87, and Crawford, in Miriam A. Stark (ed.), *Archaeology of Asia* (Oxford: Blackwell, 2006),

pp. 77–95. Korea of these centuries is treated by Grace H. Kwon, *State Formation, Property Relations, & the Development of the Tokugawa Economy (1600–1868)* (NY: Routledge, 2002), pp. 29–35, and Sarah M. Nelson, *Korean Social Archaeology: Early Villages* (Seoul: Jimoondang, 2004, pp. 99–109), while Moo-chang Choi, *The Paleolithic Period in Korea* (Seoul: Jimoondang, 2004), reports in detail on paleolithic Korea. A fascinating loyalist Korean interpretation of these centuries can be found in Hyun-hee Lee et al., *A New History of Korea* (Engl. transl.: Seoul: Jimoondang, 2005), Chapters 1–6.

18  A recent study of China's northern rim in prehistoric times is Gideon Shelach, *Prehistoric Societies on the Northern Frontiers of China* (London: Equinox Publishing Ltd., 2009).

19  J. Edward Kidder Jr., *Himiko and Japan's Elusive Chiefdom of Yamatai* (Honolulu: UHP, 2007), pp. 36–49, discusses boats and travel between mainland and archipelago.

20  William Wayne Farris, "Shipbuilding and Nautical Technology in Japanese Maritime History: Origins to 1600", in *The Mariner's Mirror*, Vol. 95, No. 3 (August 2009), 261–63, 270. Richard Pearson (ed.), *Okinawa, The Rise of an Island Kingdom* (London: Oxford UP, 2009), p. vi, citing Habu, forthcoming.

21  Murakami, in Erich Pauer (ed.), *Papers on the History of Industry and Technology of Japan: Volume I: From the Ritsuryô-system to the Early Meiji-Period* (Marburg: Förderverein, 1995), p. 123, says that "The Iron Age in Japan began in the third century B.C.". He reports that the oldest iron items found in Japan are of southern Chinese origin. For a differing view, see Kumar, *Globalizing the Prehistory of Japan: Language, Genes and Civilization*, pp. 31–32.

22  Erich Pauer (ed.), *Papers on the History of Industry and Technology of Japan: Volume I: From the Ritsuryô-system to the Early Meiji-Period*, p. xiii.

23  J. Edward Kidder Jr., *Himiko and Japan's Elusive Chiefdom of Yamatai*, p. 69.

24  On Yoshinogari, see Cobbing, *Kyushu: Gateway to Japan: A Concise History*, Ch. 2. Also, the path-breaking essay by Mark Hudson and Gina Barnes, "Yoshinogari: A Yayoi Settlement in Northern Kyushu", *Monumenta Nipponica* 46/2 (Summer 1991), pp. 211–35.

25  Kidder, *Himiko and Japan's Elusive Chiefdom of Yamatai*, pp. 61–62, and footnote 10, p. 310, discusses this Kyushu volcanism and its ramifications.

26  Hudson, in Peter Bellwood and Colin Renfrew (eds), *Examining the Farming/Language Dispersal Hypothesis* (Cambridge: McDonald Institute, 2002), p. 313, discusses the Ryukyuan-Japanese ethnic relationship.

27  The term Kinai, used extensively in this text, refers imprecisely to the interconnected lowlands that extend southwestward from Lake Biwa to the shoreline of Osaka Bay and to their adjacent uplands. The area mostly lies within the modern prefectures of Osaka and Nara and the southern part of Kyoto. Another, more precise term, Kinki, refers to the Kinki District, the six modern prefectures of Hyôgo, Kyoto, Osaka, Nara, Wakayama and Mie. They lie between the Chûgoku and Shikoku districts to the West and the Chûbu District to the East. Writers sometimes use the term Kinki more narrowly to denote the three modern prefectures of Kyoto, Osaka and Nara.

28  Ryusaku Tsunoda (tr.) and L. Carrington Goodrich (ed.), *Japan in the Chinese Dynastic Histories* (South Pasadena: P.I. & Ione Perkins, 1951), p. 8. These early Chinese records of Wa are also treated in William McOmie (comp.), *Foreign Images and Experiences of Japan: Vol. 1, First Century AD to 1841* (Folkestone: Global Oriental, 2005).

29  Regarding *Wajinden* and Himiko, see Kidder, *Himiko and Japan's Elusive Chiefdom of Yamatai*, Barnes, *State Formation in Japan*, and Ch. 2 of Cobbing, *Kyushu: Gateway to Japan: A Concise History*, for recent treatments.

30 The following quotations come from Tsunoda (tr.) and Goodrich (ed.), *Japan in the Chinese Dynastic Histories*, pp. 11–12.

31 Tsunoda (tr.) and Goodrich (ed.), *Japan in the Chinese Dynastic Histories*, pp. 14, 15. Their text uses the spelling Pimiko, but Himiko is more commonly used now.

32 Hitomi Tonomura, "Black Hair and Red Trousers: Gendering the Flesh in Medieval Japan", *American Historical Review* 99/1 (Feb., 1994), pp. 135–38.

33 Erich Pauer (ed.), *Papers on the History of Industry and Technology of Japan: Volume I: From the Ritsuryô-system to the Early Meiji-Period* (Marburg: Förderverein, 1995), p. xxvi, discussing the Nintoku tumulus near Osaka.

34 Perhaps, however, a Kyushu ruler extended his control eastward and then, with his power base greatly enlarged, engaged in peninsular politics. See Cobbing, *Kyushu: Gateway to Japan: A Concise History*, pp. 49–53.

35 Iwai is treated in Cobbing, *Kyushu: Gateway to Japan: A Concise History*, pp. 57–62, and in Bruce L. Batten, *Gateway to Japan: Hakata in War and Peace, 500–1300* (Honolulu: UHP, 2006), pp. 16, 18, 24.

36 Murakami in Pauer (ed.), *Papers on the History of Industry and Technology of Japan: Volume I: From the Ritsuryô-system to the Early Meiji-Period*, p. 124. On p. 126 he suggests that Chinese-type iron-smelting was introduced to far western Honshu and Izumo "during the early fourth century".

37 Murakami in Pauer (ed.), *Papers on the History of Industry and Technology of Japan: Volume I: From the Ritsuryô-system to the Early Meiji-Period*, pp. 105–7, with photographs of the sedimentation process.


## CHAPTER 4: EARLY AGRICULTURAL SOCIETY, 600–1250

1 A recent study of this imperial ideology and its use from origins to the present is Ben-Ami Shillony, *Enigma of the Emperors: Sacred Subservience in Japanese History* (Folkestone: Global Oriental, 2005). Its bibliography will guide readers to the extensive earlier works.

2 A recent treatment of this culturally uplifting "Sinification" process, with excellent guidance to earlier works, is the essay by Borgen, in David R. Knechtges & Eugene Vance (eds), *Rhetoric and the Discourses of Power in Court Culture; China, Europe, and Japan* (Seattle: U. Washington Press, 2005), pp. 200–38.

3 Andrew Cobbing, *Kyushu: Gateway to Japan: A Concise History* (Folkestone: Global Oriental, 2009), pp. 62–65. Bruce L. Batten, *Gateway to Japan: Hakata in War and Peace, 500–1300* (Honolulu: UHP, 2006), p. 20, cites the Nihon shoki figure of 27,500. William Wayne Farris, *Japan to 1600, A Social and Economic History* (Honolulu: UHP, 2009), p. 29, reports "more than 25,000".

4 A recent study of the role of mythology in the rule of Tenmu and his successors down to about 800 CE is Herman Ooms, *Imperial Politics and Symbolics in Ancient Japan: The Tenmu Dynasty, 650–800* (Honolulu: UHP, 2008).

5 For example, in a meticulous study of the short-lived capital at Nagaoka, 784–94 CE, Ellen Van Goethem, *Nagaoka: Japan's Forgotten Capital* (Leiden: Brill, 2008), pp. 55–68, sees this idea as the reason Kanmu erected a new capital at that site.

6 Donald F. McCallum, *The Four Great Temples: Buddhist Archaeology, Architecture, and Icons of Seventh-Century Japan* (Honolulu: UHP, 2009), pp. 190, 201. Whether Tenmu's capital-city project was meant to deter China's leaders from attempting a conquest or to flatter them and elicit their goodwill is unclear.

7    Kudo, in Kenneth Frampton and Kunio Kudo, *Japanese Building Practice: From Ancient Times to the Meiji Period* (NY: Van Nostrand Reinhold, 1997), p. 48. This work identifies valuable earlier studies of Japanese architecture and carpentry.

8    McCallum, *The Four Great Temples: Buddhist Archaeology, Architecture, and Icons of Seventh-Century Japan*, is a richly detailed study of the archaeological and literary evidence relating to the chronology, architecture, ideological significance and continental linkages of four major temples erected in the Asuka vicinity between the 590s and 690s.

9    On this transport system see the essays by Takeda Sachiko and Hotate Michihisa in Joan R. Piggott (ed.), *Capital and Countryside in Japan, 300–1180* (Ithaca, NY: Cornell East Asian Program, 2006), pp. 147–208.

10   Hotate, in Piggott (ed.), *Capital and Countryside in Japan, 300–1180*, p. 180. Batten, *Gateway to Japan: Hakata in War and Peace, 500–1300*, p. 56, presents a good map of the *ritsuryô* highway system.

11   Figures from Verschuer, in Mikael S. Adolphson et al. (eds), *Heian Japan, Center and Peripheries* (Honolulu: UHP, 2007), p. 307.

12   A recent study of these maritime relations is Batten, *Gateway to Japan: Hakata in War and Peace, 500–1300*. Cobbing, *Kyushu: Gateway to Japan: A Concise History*, also addresses them.

13   William Wayne Farris, "Shipbuilding and Nautical Technology in Japanese Maritime History: Origins to 1600", in *The Mariner's Mirror*, Vol. 95, No. 3 (August 2009), pp. 263–66.

14   Cobbing, *Kyushu: Gateway to Japan: A Concise History*, passim, discusses these people and their history.

15   Takahashi, in Piggott (ed.), *Capital and Countryside in Japan, 300–1180*, pp. 128–45, treats the conquest of Emishi lands. Bay, in Chapter 3 of Gregory M. Pflugfelder and Brett L. Walker (eds), *JAPANimals: History and Culture in Japan's Animal Life* (Ann Arbor MI: Center for Japanese Studies, 2005), discusses the thorny questions of Emishi ethnicity and the relationship of Emishi to the Yamato state during Japan's "medieval" centuries.

16   Koyama, in Piggott (ed.), *Capital and Countryside in Japan, 300–1180*, p. 383.

17   The following paragraphs are mostly based on Conrad Totman, *The Green Archipelago: Forestry in Preindustrial Japan* (Berkeley: UCP, 1989), Chapter One, where footnotes will guide readers to the Japanese sources of information.

18   Temple figures from Conrad Totman, *A History of Japan, Second Edition* (Oxford: Blackwell, 2005), p. 72.

19   Frampton and Kudo, *Japanese Building Practice: From Ancient Times to the Meiji Period*, p. 25.

20   Van Goethem, *Nagaoka: Japan's Forgotten Capital*, pp. 249–51.

21   Verschuer, in Adolphson et al. (eds), *Heian Japan, Center and Peripheries*, p. 310, reports a 10 percent tax rate. However, this figure seems low. Whether it represents what the statutes called for, what the farmer actually provided, the portion of the take that ended up in government warehouses or some other measure is unclear.

22   William Wayne Farris, *Daily Life and Demographics in Ancient Japan* (Ann Arbor: U. Mich. Center for Japanese Studies, 2009), treats this topic, and the book's footnotes identify earlier works.

23   Farris, *Daily Life and Demographics in Ancient Japan*, p. 27.

24   Aspects of these centuries are richly examined in Adolphson et al. (eds), *Heian Japan, Center and Peripheries*. The essays by Adolphson, Batten, Farris and Verschuer are particularly relevant here.

25 A recent study of the role of writing in elite-commoner relations in "early medieval" Japan is Judith Frölich, *Rulers, Peasants and the Use of the Written Word in Medieval Japan* (Bern: Peter Lang, 2007).

26 A recent study of this imperial ideology, which will lead one to the rich earlier literature, is Shillony, *Enigma of the Emperors: Sacred Subservience in Japanese History*.

27 Morita, in Piggott (ed.), *Capital and Countryside in Japan, 300–1180*, pp. 209–66, treats regency rule in detail.

28 A richly detailed study of the technology and techniques of warfare during these centuries is Karl Friday, *Samurai, Warfare, and the State in Early Medieval Japan* (London: Routledge, 2004).

29 The organization and performance of landholding temples during these centuries has recently received closer scrutiny. See Adolphson et al. (eds), *Heian Japan, Center and Peripheries*; Adolphson's essay in op. cit., pp. 212–44; Frölich, *Peasants and the Use of the Written Word in Medieval Japan*; and Motoki, in Piggott (ed.), *Capital and Countryside in Japan, 300–1180*, pp. 298–325.

30 Charlotte von Verschuer, *Across the Perilous Sea: Japanese Trade with China and Korea from the Seventh to Sixteenth Centuries* (Ithaca NY: Cornell UP, 2006), p. 68. She indicates (p. 69) that the Luo tree was *hinoki* (Japanese cypress).

31 Verschuer, *Across the Perilous Sea: Japanese Trade with China and Korea from the Seventh to Sixteenth Centuries*. Chapter 3 discusses these trade commodities at length. Essays in Andrew Edmund Goble et al. (eds), "Tools of Culture: Japan's Cultural, Intellectual, Medical, and Technological Contacts in East Asia, 1000s–1500s", *Asia Past & Present: New Research from AAS*, No. 2 (Ann Arbor: Association for Asian Studies, 2009), notably essay no. 8 by Kosoto Hirose, treat aspects of this continental trade.

32 Farris, *Daily Life and Demographics in Ancient Japan*), p. 73.

33 William Wayne Farris, *Japan's Medieval Population: Famine, Fertility, and Warfare in a Transformative Age* (Honolulu: UHP, 2006, pp. 28–59), treats these events at length.

34 Farris, *Daily Life and Demographics in Ancient Japan*, pp. 66, 68.

35 Farris, *Daily Life and Demographics in Ancient Japan*, p. 69.

36 Fabio Rambelli, *Buddhist Materiality: A Cultural History of Objects in Japanese Buddhism* (Stanford: SUP, 2007), pp. 156–61, examines some instances of temple-woodland despoliation in the Kinai vicinity during later *ritsuryô* centuries, giving particular attention to the rhetoric priests used when opposing such tree-felling.

37 Totman, *The Green Archipelago: Forestry in Preindustrial Japan*, pp. 31, 37. By the later 1400s, *hiratake* was found in Kinai woodland only on protected monastery grounds. *Hiratake* is Agaricus subfunereus; *matsutake* is Armillaria edodes.

38 Totman, *The Green Archipelago: Forestry in Preindustrial Japan*, pp. 45–46, treats this Tôdaiji provisioning.

39 Totman, *The Green Archipelago: Forestry in Preindustrial Japan*, p. 216, footnote 7.

40 Totman, *The Green Archipelago: Forestry in Preindustrial Japan*, p. 55.

41 Farris, *Japan to 1600, A Social and Economic History*, p. 114.

42 Totman, *The Green Archipelago: Forestry in Preindustrial Japan*, pp. 44–45, 55, 69, 105, treats this Kamakura issue.

43 Verschuer, *Across the Perilous Sea: Japanese Trade with China and Korea from the Seventh to Sixteenth Centuries*, p. 69.

## CHAPTER 5: LATER AGRICULTURAL SOCIETY, 1250–1650

1    Charlotte von Verschuer, *Across the Perilous Sea: Japanese Trade with China and Korea from the Seventh to Sixteenth Centuries* (Ithaca NY: Cornell UP, 2006), is a rich treatment of Japan's continental trade relations to the sixteenth century. Andrew Edmund Goble et al. (eds), "Tools of Culture: Japan's Cultural, Intellectual, Medical, and Technological Contacts in East Asia, 1000s-1500s", *Asia Past & Present: New Research from AAS*, No. 2 (Ann Arbor: Association for Asian Studies, 2009), is a recent set of essays on aspects of Japan-mainland contacts during the eleventh to sixteenth centuries. It has an extensive bibliography of earlier titles. Chapter 2 of Louis M. Cullen, *A History of Japan 1582–1941: Internal and External Worlds* (Cambridge: CUP, 2003), treats foreign relations from 1582 onward and guides readers to earlier studies. Part 4 of Stephen R. Turnbull, *Strongholds of the Samurai: Japanese Castles 250–1877* (Oxford: Osprey, 2009), contains a detailed study of the fortification work pursued by Japanese invaders in Korea during the 1590s.

2    In Chapter 3 of Gregory M. Pflugfelder and Brett L. Walker (eds), *JAPANimals: History and Culture in Japan's Animal Life* (Ann Arbor MI: Center for Japanese Studies, 2005), Alexander Bay provides a very good discussion of Emishi society and its relationship to Wa society during Japan's medieval centuries. Brett L. Walker, *The Conquest of Ainu Lands, Ecology and Culture in Japanese Expansion, 1590–1800* (Berkeley: UCP, 2001), pp. 20–34, summarizes what is known of pre-1600 Ainu history. His footnotes will guide readers to other studies.

3    An aspect of the Kinai region's enduring social pre-eminence is nicely explored in John Dougill, *Kyoto: A Cultural History* (NY: Oxford UP, 2006), which treats the elite cultural and entertainment aspects of Kyoto from its origins to today.

4    Pierre François Souyri, *The World Turned Upside Down: Medieval Japanese Society* (NY: Columbia UP, 2001), p. 12.

5    On the Mongol invasions, see Thomas D. Conlan, *In Little Need of Divine Intervention: Takezaki Suenaga's Scrolls of the Mongol Invasions of Japan* (Ithaca, NY: Cornell East Asia Program, 2001), which will guide readers to earlier scholarship. On Japan's "early medieval" warfare more generally, see Karl Friday, *Samurai, Warfare, and the State in Early Medieval Japan* (London: Routledge, 2004), and Thomas D. Conlan, *State of War: The Violent Order of Fourteenth-Century Japan* (Ann Arbor MI: Center for Japanese Studies, 2003).

6    On the Ônin War and Kyoto, see Suzanne Gay, *The Moneylenders of Late Medieval Kyoto* (Honolulu: UHP, 2001), pp. 148–60.

7    Carol R. Tsang, *War and Faith: Ikkô Ikki in Late Muromachi Japan* (Cambridge, MA: HUP, 2007), is a meticulous study of the military-political activity of members of the Buddhist Jôdo Shin (Ikkô) sect from the 1470s to 1570s. Her bibliography will guide readers to earlier studies of this medieval sectarian activism.

8    Gay, *The Moneylenders of Late Medieval Kyoto*, is a fine study of the role of Kyoto moneylenders during the 1350s–1550s. Her bibliography will guide readers to earlier studies of these medieval economic developments.

9    Turnbull, *Strongholds of the Samurai: Japanese Castles 250–1877*, examines these developments in fortification in Part 3 of his gorgeously illustrated study, which brings together in revised form four of his earlier works.

10    On warfare of the decades 1560–1600, two detailed, lavishly illustrated studies are Stephen R. Turnbull, *Nagashino, 1575: Slaughter at the Barricades* (Westport, CT: Praeger, 2005), which treats the 1575 battle of Nagashino; and Anthony Bryant, *Sekigahara, 1600: The Final Struggle for Power* (Westport, CT: Praeger, 2005), which treats Sekigahara.

11  As part of that preparation "for a later day", during the years 1600–15, Japan experienced "the most furious spate of castle-building and redevelopment" in its history, according to Turnbull, *Strongholds of the Samurai: Japanese Castles 250–1877*, p. 143.

12  Lee Butler, *Emperor and Aristocracy in Japan, 1467–1680* (Cambridge, MA: HUP, 2002), is a rich treatment of courtly affairs during these centuries.

13  William Wayne Farris, *Japan's Medieval Population: Famine, Fertility, and Warfare in a Transformative Age* (Honolulu: UHP, 2006), pp. 4–5, 262.

14  Farris, *Japan's Medieval Population: Famine, Fertility, and Warfare in a Transformative Age*, pp. 27–28, 95, 171–72, treats disease during these centuries and will guide readers to earlier works.

15  Quoted in Judith Frölich, *Rulers, Peasants and the Use of the Written Word in Medieval Japan* (Bern: Peter Lang, 2007), p. 155. The landlord being petitioned was the Mt Kôya Shingon temple. Ategawa *shôen* was located nearby in an interior valley of Kii Province.

16  Charlotte von Verschuer, *Across the Perilous Sea: Japanese Trade with China and Korea from the Seventh to Sixteenth Centuries* (Ithaca NY: Cornell UP, 2006), pp. 84–85.

17  Verschuer, *Across the Perilous Sea: Japanese Trade with China and Korea from the Seventh to Sixteenth Centuries*, Chapter 5, examines this trade in detail. See also Andrew Edmund Goble et al. (eds), "Tools of Culture: Japan's Cultural, Intellectual, Medical, and Technological Contacts in East Asia, 1000s-1500s", *Asia Past & Present: New Research from AAS*, No. 2 (Ann Arbor: Association for Asian Studies, 2009), in particular the essays by Saeki on Chinese ceramics and Robinson on trade with Korea.

18  In Chapter 4, Gay, *The Moneylenders of Late Medieval Kyoto*, provides an excellent examination of these debtor protests. See also Souyri, *The World Turned Upside Down: Medieval Japanese Society*, Chapters 10 and 11.

19  Souyri, *The World Turned Upside Down: Medieval Japanese Society*, p. 88.

20  Souyri, *The World Turned Upside Down: Medieval Japanese Society*, pp. 92–95, treats these topics.

21  Souyri, *The World Turned Upside Down: Medieval Japanese Society*, p. 130.

22  Quoted in Souyri, *The World Turned Upside Down: Medieval Japanese Society*, p. 162.

23  Conrad, Totman, *A History of Japan, Second Edition* (Oxford: Blackwell, 2005), p. 150, citing the excellent but unpublished Harvard dissertation (1990) of Kristina Kade Troost.

24  Totman, *A History of Japan, Second Edition*, p. 149.

25  Souyri, *The World Turned Upside Down: Medieval Japanese Society*, p. 87.

26  Farris, *Japan's Medieval Population: Famine, Fertility, and Warfare in a Transformative Age*, p. 132, identifies Champa rice as *Oryza sativa indica*, variety *spontanea* or *perennis*. By the 1600s, he reports on p. 226, there were eight sub-varieties of Champa rice growing in Japan.

27  Sung-je Koh, "A History of the Cotton Trade between Korea and Japan, 1423–1910", *Asian Economies* #12 (March 1975), pp. 5–16, treats this topic of cotton.

28  Conrad Totman, *The Green Archipelago: Forestry in Preindustrial Japan* (Berkeley: UCP, 1989), pp. 46–47.

29  Another practice that spread more widely during medieval centuries was the cremation of human bodies. The process required considerable quantities of wood, in the form of charcoal, firewood and ritual wooden structures. However, the scale of this wood-use and its impact may well be impossible to determine. Karen M. Gerhart, *The Material Culture of Death in Medieval Japan* (Honolulu: UHP, 2009), discusses cremation in the course of examining the funereal practices of the medieval elite.

30  Totman, *The Green Archipelago: Forestry in Preindustrial Japan*, p. 57.

31  Totman, *The Green Archipelago: Forestry in Preindustrial Japan*, p. 48.

32  Turnbull, *Strongholds of the Samurai: Japanese Castles 250–1877*, Part 2, discusses temple fortifications.

33  Souyri, *The World Turned Upside Down: Medieval Japanese Society*, p. 93.

34  Souyri, *The World Turned Upside Down: Medieval Japanese Society*, pp. 92–95, 184–85.

## CHAPTER 6: LATER AGRICULTURAL SOCIETY, 1650–1890

1  Save as otherwise noted, this chapter draws on my earlier writings, several of which focus on the *bakuhan* period, notably Conrad Totman, *Early Modern Japan* (Berkeley: UCP, 1993). Those works, in turn, depended on many excellent earlier studies, which are cited in their notes and bibliographies.

2  Japan's foreign relations during the 1800s have been extensively studied. A recent treatment is Hiroshi Mitani, *Escape from Impasse: The Decision to Open Japan* (Tokyo: International House, 2006), translated from a work published in Japanese in 2003.

3  A recent, richly detailed study of the *sankin kôtai* system is Constantine N. Vaporis, *Tour of Duty: Samurai, Military Service in Edo, and the Culture of Early Modern Japan* (Honolulu: UHP, 2008).

4  In her richly detailed, rehabilitative study of the shogun Tokugawa Tsunayoshi (r. 1680–1709), Beatrice Bodart-Bailey, *The Dog Shogun: The Personality and Politics of Tokugawa Tsunayoshi* (Honolulu: UHP, 2006), chapters 13 and 17 treat these calamities. The quoted fragment is from p. 256.

5  Louis M. Cullen, *A History of Japan 1582–1941: Internal and External Worlds* (Cambridge: CUP, 2003), Ch. 2, treats Japan's foreign relations of this era and provides good bibliographical guidance to earlier works. James B. Lewis, *Frontier Contact between Choson Korea and Tokugawa Japan* (NY: Routledge Curzon, 2003), is a richly illustrated examination of Japan's trade activity in Korea. Bay, in Chapter 3 of Gregory M. Pflugfelder and Brett L. Walker (eds), *JAPANimals: History and Culture in Japan's Animal Life* (Ann Arbor MI: Center for Japanese Studies, 2005), notes the long-standing trade activity between the Ainu of Hokkaido and people in nearby continental areas. In his splendid, ecologically aware study of Ainu history, Brett L. Walker, *The Conquest of Ainu Lands, Ecology and Culture in Japanese Expansion, 1590–1800* (Berkeley: UCP, 2001), treats that trade, as well as other rarely studied aspects of Ainu-Japanese interactions during *bakuhan* centuries.

6  Tsunenari Tokugawa, *The Edo Inheritance* (Tokyo: International House, 2009), p. 131, reports that by 1850, "there were some seven hundred American whalers operating in the Pacific, and of these, some three hundred operated in waters close to Japan".

7  *Kokugaku* has been extensively studied. Two recent works that will guide one to the earlier scholarship are Susan L. Burns, *Before the Nation: Kokugaku and the Imagining of Community* (Durham: Duke UP, 2003), and Mark McNally, *Proving the Way: Conflict and Practice in the History of Japanese Nativism* (Cambridge, MA: HUP, 2005).

8  Mary E. Berry, *Japan in Print: Information and Nation in the Early Modern Period* (Berkeley: UCP, 2006), is a richly illustrated study of the role of literate culture in disseminating awareness of the larger Japanese realm during the 1600s–1700s.

9  Berry, *Japan in Print: Information and Nation in the Early Modern Period*, p. 185. Japanese terms for "our Japan" and "our people" have been omitted here. For more on "feel-good" aesthetics in Japan's "national identity", see Chapter 1 by Ikegami in Joshua A. Fogel (ed.), *The Teleology of the Modern Nation-State: Japan and China* (Philadelphia: U. Penn. Press, 2005).

10  Nam-lin Hur, *Death and Social Order in Tokugawa Japan: Buddhism, Anti-Christianity and the Danka System* (Cambridge, MA: HUP, 2007), Chapter 10, explores how this foreign issue interplayed with tensions between proponents of Buddhism, Confucianism and *Shintô*.

11  A detailed recent study of these treaty developments is William McOmie, *The Opening of Japan, 1853–55* (Folkestone: Global Oriental, 2006).

12  Two recent studies of intellectual aspects of this 1800s foreign problem are Mark Anderson, *Japan and the Specter of Imperialism* (NY: Palgrave, 2009); and Alistair D. Swale, *The Meiji Restoration: Monarchism, Mass Communication and Conservative Revolution* (London: Palgrave, 2009).

13  John H. Sagers, *Origins of Japanese Wealth and Power: Reconciling Confucianism and Capitalism, 1830–1885* (NY: Palgrave, 2006), is a recent study of the reorientation of Satsuma economic policy during the 1800s, with the shift cast in intellectual terms of Confucianism and "capitalism". His bibliography will guide one to earlier works.

14  Andrew Cobbing, *Kyushu: Gateway to Japan: A Concise History* (Folkestone: Global Oriental, 2009), Ch. 11, treats this topic of embittered supporters succinctly, and his bibliography will guide readers to the rich earlier scholarship.

15  In addition to changing the year-period name to Meiji, the new leaders also declared that henceforth *nengô* would change only with a new emperor's accession. Because of that change, emperors in industrial Japan have become known posthumously by their year-period name. Thus, the emperor in 1868, whose personal name was Mutsuhito, became known as the Meiji Emperor. Similarly, his grandson, Hirohito, became known posthumously as the Shôwa Emperor.

16  Edo had good-quality housing facilities available because in 1862 the *sankin kôtai* system had been "reformed" out of existence, and the daimyo exodus led to a massive depopulation of the city. As of 1872 its population numbered some 580,000, about half its earlier number, and it did not reach a million again until about 1890. Mikako Iwatake, "From a Shogunal City to a Life City", p. 237, in Nicolas Fiévé and Paul Waley (eds), *Japanese Imperial Capitals in Historical Perspective: Place, Power and Memory in Kyoto, Edo and Tokyo* (London: Routledge, 2003). The process of dissolving *sankin kôtai* is discussed in Conrad Totman, *The Collapse of the Tokugawa Bakufu, 1862–1868* (Honolulu: UHP, 1980), pp. 18–21, and the city fires of 1866 at pp. 298–99.

17  Earlier generations of *bakuhan* intellectuals had used the *gunken/hôken* construct to contrast the distinctively Japanese *hôken* system with the Chinese – and implicitly less desirable – *gunken* system. Meiji leaders transvalued the two notions.

18  Tessa Morris-Suzuki, *The Technological Transformation of Japan: From the Seventeenth to the Twenty-first Century* (Cambridge: CUP, 1994), p. 85.

19  The writer is Itô Hirobumi, quoted in Morris-Suzuki, *The Technological Transformation of Japan: From the Seventeenth to the Twenty-first Century*, p. 73.

20  A recent examination of intellectual developments that helped shape the Meiji Constitution is Kazuhiro Takii, *The Meiji Constitution: The Japanese Experience of the West and the Shaping of the Modern State* (Tokyo: International House, 2007), a translation of a Japanese-language study published in 2003. A broader-ranging study of early Meiji political thought is Kyu Hyun Kim, *The Age of Visions and Arguments: Parliamentarianism and the National Public Sphere in Early Meiji Japan* (Cambridge, MA: HUP, 2007). And Richard M. Reitan, *Making a Moral Society: Ethics and the State in Meiji Japan* (Honolulu: UHP, 2010) examines intellectual discourse of these decades yet more broadly.

21  Quoted in Ryusaku Tsunoda et al. (comps.), *Sources of the Japanese Tradition* (NY: Columbia UP, 1958), pp. 696–97.

22  The richest study of *bakuhan* population remains Akira Hayami, *The Historical Demography of Pre-modern Japan* (Tokyo: UTP, 2001). Regarding the problematic quality

of *bakuhan* demographic data, an excellent discussion is Cullen, *A History of Japan 1582–1941: Internal and External Worlds*, especially pp. 98–104.

23 Tokugawa, *The Edo Inheritance*, p. 116, reports that "minors below seven years of age" were not counted in Yoshimune's census of 1721. Even around 1890, according to Simon Partner, *The Mayor of Aihara: A Japanese Villager and His Community, 1865–1925* (Berkeley: UCP, 2009), p. 74, "some twenty percent of rural Japanese children died before their tenth birthday".

24 Hayami, *The Historical Demography of Pre-modern Japan*, p. 57.

25 Tokugawa, *The Edo Inheritance*, p. 11, reports that some 5–7 percent of the population were of samurai rank. Court nobles and high clerics added another very small number to the official elite.

26 Ann B. Jannetta, *The Vaccinators: Smallpox, Medical Knowledge, and the "Opening" of Japan* (Stanford: SUP, 2007), p. 179. Mary Louise Nagata, *Labor Contracts and Labor Relations in Early Modern Central Japan* (NY: Routledge, 2005), p. 97, reports that typhus epidemics in Japan date from 1783.

27 Jannetta, *The Vaccinators: Smallpox, Medical Knowledge, and the "Opening" of Japan*, is an excellent study of this topic, and her fine bibliography will direct one to relevant earlier works.

28 Jannetta, *The Vaccinators: Smallpox, Medical Knowledge, and the "Opening" of Japan*, pp. 157–59, discusses the shogunate's posture.

29 Nobuko Iijima (ed.), *Pollution Japan: Historical Chronology* (Elmsford, NY: Pergamon Press, 1979), pp. 17, 20.

30 Regarding entertainers, a recent study of licensed prostitution in *bakuhan* society is William R. Lindsey, *Fertility and Pleasure: Ritual and Sexual Values in Tokugawa Japan* (Honolulu: UHP, 2007), which will also guide readers to earlier works.

31 Daniel V. Botsman, *Punishment and Power in the Making of Modern Japan* (Princeton: PUP, 2005) is a richly detailed and thoughtful study of judicial and criminal practices and trends during these centuries, particularly as they relate to the city of Edo.

32 M. William Steele, *Alternative Narratives in Modern Japanese History* (London: Routledge, 2003), treats aspects of commoner attitudes and behavior during the tumult surrounding the 1868 Restoration.

33 Partner, *The Mayor of Aihara: A Japanese Villager and His Community, 1865–1925*, p. 3.

34 An excellent study of labor organization and utilization during the *bakuhan* centuries is Nagata, *Labor Contracts and Labor Relations in Early Modern Central Japan*.

35 Richard Rubinger, *Popular Literacy in Early Modern Japan* (Honolulu: UHP, 2007), is a richly detailed and thoughtful study of literacy during these centuries.

36 A comprehensive bibliography of 2,849 works on Edo-period thought in European languages is Klaus Kracht, *Japanese Thought in the Tokugawa Era: A Bibliography of Western-Language Materials* (Wiesbaden: Harrassowitz Verlag, 2000). William McOmie (comp.), *Foreign Images and Experiences of Japan: Vol. 1, First Century AD to 1841* (Folkestone: Global Oriental, 2005), examines in rich detail contemporary European writings on *bakuhan* Japan.

37 *Rangaku* has been extensively studied. See, for recent examples, W.F. Vande Walle and Kazuhiko Kasaya (eds), *Dodonaeus in Japan: Translation and the Scientific Mind in the Tokugawa Period* (Leuven: Leuven UP, 2001), and Martha Chaiklin, *Cultural Commerce and Dutch Commercial Culture: The Influence of European Material Culture on Japan, 1700–1850* (Leiden: Leiden UP, 2003).

38 Chinese mathematics (called wasan in Japan) was introduced during the 1600s, as lushly described by Hidetoshi Fukagawa and Tony Rothman, *Sacred Mathematics: Japanese Temple Geometry* (Princeton: PUP, 2008).

39 Rubinger, *Popular Literacy in Early Modern Japan*, pp. 84–85.

40　Tokugawa, *The Edo Inheritance*, p. 117, reports that there were "around 10,000" *terakoya* in the late Edo period.

41　Rubinger, *Popular Literacy in Early Modern Japan*, pp. 113–14.

42　A fine, recent study of the local role of temples in *bakuhan* society is Hur, *Death and Social Order in Tokugawa Japan: Buddhism, Anti-Christianity and the Danka System*, especially Chapter 1. The social role of Sôtô Zen, which flourished during these centuries, is treated in Duncan Ryûken Williams, *The Other Side of Zen: A Social History of Sôtô Zen Buddhism in Tokugawa Japan* (Princeton: PUP, 2005).

43　Edo-period highways and travel have received much attention. For two recent examples, see Herbert Plutschow, *A Reader in Edo Period Travel* (Folkestone: Global Oriental, 2006), and Jilly Traganov, *The Tôkaidô Road: Traveling and Representation in Edo and Meiji Japan* (NY: Routledge, 2004). Marcia Yonemoto, *Mapping Early Modern Japan: Space, Place, and Culture in the Tokugawa Period (1603–1868)* (Berkeley: UCP, 2003), is a richly discursive treatment of maps, map-making and map-usage during these centuries.

44　Brett L. Walker, *The Conquest of Ainu Lands, Ecology and Culture in Japanese Expansion, 1590–1800* (Berkeley: UCP, 2001), treats this topic in rich detail.

45　These figures are simplified from Table 3 on p. 25 of Ryuto Shimada, *The Intra-Asian Trade in Japanese Copper by the Dutch East India Company during the Eighteenth Century* (Leiden: Brill, 2006). On pp. 150–67 he discusses the mechanics of the Dutch trade at Nagasaki.

46　Ryuto Shimada, *The Intra-Asian Trade in Japanese Copper by the Dutch East India Company during the Eighteenth Century*, pp. 47, 61–64, 144–47.

47　Nagata, *Labor Contracts and Labor Relations in Early Modern Central Japan*, p. 80.

48　Aspects of Meiji-era construction and engineering technology are explored in Kenneth Frampton and Kunio Kudo, *Japanese Building Practice: From Ancient Times to the Meiji Period* (NY: Van Nostrand Reinhold, 1997), and Erich Pauer (ed.), *Papers on the History of Industry and Technology of Japan: Volume I: From the Ritsuryô-system to the Early Meiji-Period* (Marburg: Förderverein, 1995). Cobbing, *Kyushu: Gateway to Japan: A Concise History*, pp. 216–21, 227–28, provides a recent treatment of Kyushu's pioneering role in Japan's initiation of industrial technology and techniques. Dan Free, *Early Japanese Railways 1853–1914: Engineering Triumphs that Transformed Meiji-era Japan* (Tokyo: Tuttle, 2008), provides a marvelous array of photographs and drawings of railroad facilities and equipment during the years 1853–1914.

49　Shuzo Teruoka (ed.), *Agriculture in the Modernization of Japan, 1850–2000* (New Delhi: Manohar, 2008), p. 20, reports that ca. 1890–1900, about half the exports were silk while other important ones were "green tea, rice, camphor, mint, shiitake mushrooms, kelp, dried abalone and other agricultural and marine products". Penelope Francks, *Rural Economic Development in Japan: From the Nineteenth Century to the Pacific War* (London: Routledge, 2006), pp. 34–35, discusses silk.

50　A recent collection of essays on Kyoto and Edo/Tokyo is Fiévé and Waley (eds), *Japanese Imperial Capitals in Historical Perspective: Place, Power and Memory in Kyoto, Edo and Tokyo*.

51　Figures from Totman, *Early Modern Japan*, p. 153. Because roughly half of Edo's population was housed in shogunal and baronial mansion sites and because official censuses only counted the producer populace, estimates of Edo's real population vary greatly.

52　Beatrice M. Bodart-Bailey, "Urbanization and the Nature of the Tokugawa Hegemony", in Fiévé and Waley (eds), *Japanese Imperial Capitals in Historical Perspective: Place, Power and Memory in Kyoto, Edo and Tokyo*, p. 119.

53　Tokugawa, *The Edo Inheritance*, p. 85.

54 Bodart-Bailey, *The Dog Shogun: The Personality and Politics of Tokugawa Tsunayoshi*, p. 257.

55 In Chapter 2, Carl Mosk, *Japanese Industrial History: Technology, Urbanization, and Economic Growth* (London: M.E. Sharpe, 2001), examines Osaka of the *bakuhan* era. His study, which focuses on post-1868 economic developments in the Osaka-Tokyo region, provides excellent bibliographical guidance to earlier works.

56 Louis G. Perez, *Daily Life in Early Modern Japan* (Westport, CT: Greenwood Press, 2002), p. 232.

57 Francks, *Rural Economic Development in Japan: From the Nineteenth Century to the Pacific War*, pp. 35–45, discusses the rise of rural industry.

58 Perez, *Daily Life in Early Modern Japan*, is a richly detailed study of commoner life with good treatment of villages.

59 Perez, *Daily Life in Early Modern Japan*, p. 31. On p. 129, he reports that 90 percent of the populace was rural. Francks, *Rural Economic Development in Japan: From the Nineteenth Century to the Pacific War*, p. 26, writes that in 1800, 80–85 percent of the populace lived in villages.

60 Thomas C. Smith, *The Agrarian Origins of Modern Japan* (Stanford: SUP, 1959), p. 56, footnote e.

61 Grace H. Kwon, *State Formation, Property Relations, & the Development of the Tokugawa Economy (1600–1868)* (NY: Routledge, 2002), is a richly detailed study of the changing patterns of village organization during these centuries, particularly in the Kinai vicinity.

62 Penelope Francks, *Technology and Agricultural Development in Pre-War Japan* (New Haven: YUP, 1984), p. 36.

63 Francks, *Rural Economic Development in Japan: From the Nineteenth Century to the Pacific War*, p. 47. Teruoka (ed.), *Agriculture in the Modernization of Japan*, p. 23, gives the 70 percent figure.

64 Francks, *Rural Economic Development in Japan: From the Nineteenth Century to the Pacific War*, p. 46.

65 Partner, *The Mayor of Aihara: A Japanese Villager and His Community, 1865–1925*, pp. 43–44, provides a good example of the annual work cycle in Aihara, a village in the southwest Kantô.

66 In chapters 3 and 4, Tetsuo Najita, *Ordinary Economies in Japan: A Historical Perspective, 1750–1950* (Berkeley: UCP, 2009), discusses *kô* of the 1700s–1800s. Bodart-Bailey, *The Dog Shogun: The Personality and Politics of Tokugawa Tsunayoshi*, pp. 268–70, gives a good example of villagers demanding assistance following Mt Fuji's eruption in 1707.

67 Hur, *Death and Social Order in Tokugawa Japan: Buddhism, Anti-Christianity and the Danka System*, p. 202.

68 Francks, *Rural Economic Development in Japan: From the Nineteenth Century to the Pacific War*, pp. 45, 69.

69 Marius Jansen (ed.), *The Cambridge History of Japan, Vol. 5, The Nineteenth Century* (Cambridge: CUP, 1989), p. 80. The writer was Matsudaira Sadanobu.

70 In chapters 1 and 2, Partner, *The Mayor of Aihara: A Japanese Villager and His Community, 1865–1925*, conveys a sense of how the changing times affected life in Aihara.

71 A richly detailed yet comprehensive study of Japan's technological history from the 1600s to the late 1900s is Morris-Suzuki, *The Technological Transformation of Japan: From the Seventeenth to the Twenty-first Century*.

72 Walker, *The Conquest of Ainu Lands, Ecology and Culture in Japanese Expansion, 1590–1800*, p. 83. The words are those of the Portuguese missionary Diego Carvalho, describing placer mining in the Matsumae domain in Hokkaido.

73   Ryuto Shimada, *The Intra-Asian Trade in Japanese Copper by the Dutch East India Company during the Eighteenth Century* (Leiden: Brill, 2006), pp. 53–54, presents good sketches of this mining technology.

74   Walker, *The Conquest of Ainu Lands, Ecology and Culture in Japanese Expansion, 1590–1800*, pp. 82–84.

75   Iijima, *Pollution Japan: Historical Chronology*, pp. 3–6, specifies mine sites. Shimada, *The Intra-Asian Trade in Japanese Copper by the Dutch East India Company during the Eighteenth Century*, pp. 47–48, reports copper-mine output.

76   Shimada, *The Intra-Asian Trade in Japanese Copper by the Dutch East India Company during the Eighteenth Century*, provides a good discussion of the copper-mining process and the uses of that copper in export trade and currency management.

77   The record of pollution incidents is meticulously presented in Iijima (ed.), *Pollution Japan: Historical Chronology*.

78   Shimada, *The Intra-Asian Trade in Japanese Copper by the Dutch East India Company during the Eighteenth Century*, p. 51, explains that the copper was smelted outside the mine, with the resulting balls of copper sent to Osaka for further refining into diverse forms for export or domestic use.

79   The figures in this table are compiled from annual figures for the years 1874–1908, as given in the Sippel essay in Janet Hunter and Cornelia Storz (eds), *Institutional and Technological Change in Japan's Economy, Past and Present* (London: Routledge, 2006), p. 11. In her essay, Sippel studies technological changes in copper mines of the Akita region.

80   Shimada, *The Intra-Asian Trade in Japanese Copper by the Dutch East India Company during the Eighteenth Century*, p. 47. A long (English or avoirdupois) ton equals 1.016 metric tons.

81   Iijima, *Pollution Japan: Historical Chronology*, passim, records the chronology of the Ashio problem. The topic has been well treated in Kenneth Strong, *Ox Against the Storm; A Biography of Tanaka Shozo: Japan's Conservationist Pioneer* (Tenterden, Kent: Paul Norbury Publishing Ltd., 1977), and Kazuo Nimura, *The Ashio Riot of 1907: A Social History of Mining in Japan* (Durham, NC: Duke UP, 1997).

82   Iijima, *Pollution Japan: Historical Chronology*, p. 3.

83   Totman, *Early Modern Japan*, pp. 271–72.

84   Iijima, *Pollution Japan: Historical Chronology*, p. 16.

85   Unlike most of Hokkaido, the southerly portion of Oshima peninsula (southwestern Hokkaido) was the Matsumae baronial domain and gradually was settled by Japanese. Terrain there was used as the Matsumae regime wished. Walker, *The Conquest of Ainu Lands, Ecology and Culture in Japanese Expansion, 1590–1800*, examines Matsumae-Ainu relations with care.

86   Bodart-Bailey, *The Dog Shogun: The Personality and Politics of Tokugawa Tsunayoshi*, p. 189.

87   Hur, *Death and Social Order in Tokugawa Japan: Buddhism, Anti-Christianity and the Danka System*, pp. 5–6. A similar temple-relocation project followed the 1923 earthquake.

88   This material on *bakuhan* forestry is based on chapters 4 and 5 of Conrad Totman, *The Green Archipelago: Forestry in Preindustrial Japan* (Berkeley: UCP, 1989).

89   Totman, *The Green Archipelago: Forestry in Preindustrial Japan*, p. 124. After ten years, basic de-limbing would have been completed and the nurtured tree would be tall enough to shade out any faster-growing competitors.

90   In chapters 1, 2 and 8, Conrad Totman, *Japan's Imperial Forest: Goryôrin, 1889–1946* (Folkestone: Global Oriental, 2007), briefly sketches these Meiji-era silvicultural developments.

91   Figures compiled from Table 8-1 at p. 107 of Totman, *Japan's Imperial Forest: Goryôrin, 1889–1946*.

92    This section is mostly based on Arne Kalland, *Fishing Villages in Tokugawa Japan* (Honolulu: UHP, 1995), a wonderfully rich study of the coastal villages and fisheries of northwest Kyushu during the Edo period.

93    In Chapter 9 of Pflugfelder and Walker (eds), *JAPANimals: History and Culture in Japan's Animal Life*, Abel touches upon the rise of pelagic whaling, starting in 1861, and her footnotes will guide readers to earlier works in English.

94    Perez, *Daily Life in Early Modern Japan*, p. 172.

95    Kwon, *State Formation, Property Relations, & the Development of the Tokugawa Economy (1600–1868)*, p. 4, reports that during the 1600s, some 900,000 *chô* of land were opened to tillage, mainly by large-scale projects, whereas during the 1700s–1800s, only 200,000 *chô* were added, mostly by small-household projects.

96    Partner, *The Mayor of Aihara: A Japanese Villager and His Community, 1865–1925*, p. 12.

97    Francks, *Rural Economic Development in Japan: From the Nineteenth Century to the Pacific War*, p. 29, reports that whereas paddy fields yielded about 0.7 *koku/tan* during the 1600s, by the 1800s, they nearly doubled the yield to about 1.3 *koku/tan*.

98    Teruoka (ed.), *Agriculture in the Modernization of Japan*, p. 69.

99    Nagata, *Labor Contracts and Labor Relations in Early Modern Central Japan*, p. 80, reports that during the 1700s, "production of raw silk and cotton ... increased by 400 percent". Francks, *Rural Economic Development in Japan: From the Nineteenth Century to the Pacific War*, pp. 33–34, 41, discusses cotton production in the 1800s.

100    Francks, *Rural Economic Development in Japan: From the Nineteenth Century to the Pacific War*, p. 42, notes the fragility of cocoons.

101    Morris-Suzuki, *The Technological Transformation of Japan: From the Seventeenth to the Twenty-first Century*, p. 29.

102    David G. Wittner treats mechanization of silk production in an essay in Morris Low (ed.), *Building a Modern Japan: Science, Technology, and Medicine in the Meiji Era and Beyond* (NY: Palgrave, 2005).

103    Francks, *Rural Economic Development in Japan: From the Nineteenth Century to the Pacific War*, pp. 30–31. Francks, *Technology and Agricultural Development in Pre-War Japan*, p. 61, provides a table of regional rates of single-cropping for the years 1884, 1907 and 1933, and it shows the national average of single-cropped paddy acreage dropping from 73 percent of total paddy land in 1884 to 53–55 percent during the early decades of the 1900s.

104    This section is based on Brett L. Walker, *The Lost Wolves of Japan* (Seattle: U. Washington Press, 2005). His study, which has a good bibliography, is one of the very few English-language works on Japan's ecological history that is well grounded in scientific knowledge. Walker discusses the issue of wolf-wild dog relationship, which is omitted here. In Chapter 5 of Pflugfelder and Walker (eds), *JAPANimals: History and Culture in Japan's Animal Life*, Walker examines the 1749 famine in Hachinohe, in northeast Japan, pointing out how changes in the indigenous animal population contributed to it.

105    Regarding dogs and the problem of rabies, especially during early Meiji, see Chapter 6 by Skabelund, in Pflugfelder and Walker (eds), *JAPANimals: History and Culture in Japan's Animal Life*.

106    One could, of course, argue that the slow and secretive extension of commercial exploitation into the Ainu regions of Hokkaido was simply a continuation of the long-term expansion of the agriculture-based realm into adjoining forager regions, whose process long antedated the emergence of *ritsuryô* governance.

## CHAPTER 7: IMPERIAL INDUSTRIALISM, 1890–1945

1  The ideology of Japanese nationalism has been studied extensively. A recent examination of select thinkers, with good bibliographical guidance to earlier works, is Walter A. Skya, *Japan's Holy War: the Ideology of Radical Shintô Ultranationalism* (Durham: Duke UP, 2009). In Joshua A. Fogel (ed.), *The Teleology of the Modern Nation-State: Japan and China* (Philadelphia: U. Penn. Press, 2005), chapters 3 and 5, Ravina and Howell treat aspects of the development of national identity during the later *bakuhan* and Meiji periods. Kevin M. Doak, *A History of Nationalism in Modern Japan* (Leiden: Brill, 2007), is a richly discursive examination of nationalism in modern Japan.

2  A recent examination of this enduring regional identity is Nanyan Guo et al., *Tsugaru: Regional Identity on Japan's Northern Periphery* (Dunedin NZ: U. of Otago Press, 2005), which reveals the many facets of the "Tsugaru" identity found among residents of the Tsugaru region at the northeastern tip of Honshu. A discursive study of localism, status and regional identity ca. 1600–1900, which examines Ainu-Wajin relations at some length, is David L. Howell, *Geographies of Identity in Nineteenth Century Japan* (Berkeley: UCP, 2005).

3  This national consciousness also found expression in new religious movements of the post-1860s decades. A recent, nicely illustrated study of one such movement, with a good bibliography of earlier works, is Nancy K. Stalker, *Prophet Motive; Deguchi Onisaburô, Oomoto, and the Rise of New Religions in Imperial Japan* (Honolulu: UHP, 2008).

4  The politico/diplomatic history of these decades has been richly treated. A summary can be found in chapters 13 and 15 of Conrad Totman, *A History of Japan, Second Edition* (Oxford: Blackwell, 2005), and its bibliographical references will lead one to the extensive earlier monographic literature. Simon Partner, *The Mayor of Aihara: A Japanese Villager and His Community, 1865–1925* (Berkeley: UCP, 2009), chapters 3–5, conveys nicely how affairs of state and local affairs interplayed in daily life at the local level during ca. 1890–1920 in the village of Aihara in the southwest Kantô.

5  Aspects of 1930s political culture and rhetoric have recently been examined in the 17 essays of Alan Tansman (ed.), *The Culture of Japanese Fascism* (Durham: Duke UP, 2009).

6  A fine, new study of the army's history from the 1850s to 1945 is Edward J. Drea, *Japan's Imperial Army: Its Rise and Fall, 1853–1945* (Lawrence, KN: U.P. of Kansas, 2009). A valuable new study of popular attitudes toward, and relations with, the army, as evidenced in Gifu Prefecture, is Stewart Lone, *Provincial Life and the Military in Imperial Japan: the Phantom Samurai* (London: Routledge, 2010).

7  Louis M. Cullen, *A History of Japan 1582–1941: Internal and External Worlds* (Cambridge: CUP, 2003), chapters 7–8, examines Japan's foreign relations of the decades to 1941.

8  As Cullen, *A History of Japan 1582–1941: Internal and External Worlds*, p. 232, notes, in 1895, China's leaders also ceded Manchuria's Liaotung Peninsula to Japan, but in the so-called Triple Intervention, European powers quickly forced Japan to return it, after which the Russians, Germans and British secured for themselves additional concessions in China. Urs Mattias Zachmann, *China and Japan in the Late Meiji Period: China Policy and the Japanese Discourse on National Identity, 1895–1904* (London: Routledge, 2009), which contains an excellent bibliography of earlier works, is a thoughtful study of the complicated relationship between China and Japan during the Meiji period down to 1905.

9  Phillips Payson O'Brien, *The Anglo-Japanese Alliance, 1902–22* (London: Routledge, 2004), is a collection of 16 essays that examine the origins, logic, content, political significance and cultural ramifications of the alliance, which lasted from 1902 to 1922.

10   The Russo-Japanese War has been treated in detail through the years. Naoko Shimazu, *Japanese Society at War: Death, Memory and the Russo-Japanese War* (Cambridge: CUP, 2009), is a study of Japanese popular experiences, perceptions and later recollections of the war. Joseph Ferguson, *Japanese-Russian Relations, 1907–2007* (London: Routledge, 2008), is a thoughtful examination of Russo-Japanese relations in the century since that war. Both the Shimazu and Ferguson studies offer excellent bibliographies. Recently two two-volume centennial collections of essays also have enriched the corpus. One collection, entitled *The Russo-Japanese War in Global Perspective* is edited (Vol. I) by John W. Steinberg et al., and (Vol. II) by David Wolff et al. The other collection, *Rethinking the Russo-Japanese War, 1904–05*, is edited (Vol. I) by Rotem Kowner and (Vol. II) by John Chapman and Inaba Chiharu.

11   Partner, *The Mayor of Aihara: A Japanese Villager and His Community, 1865–1925*, p. 106. The village was Ayase, in southwestern Kantô.

12   The writer was Nakayama Satoru, as quoted in Eiji Oguma (David Askew, tr.), *A Genealogy of "Japanese" Self-images* (Melbourne: Trans Pacific Press, 2002), p. 140.

13   The rhetorical dimension of imperial Japan's foreign policy has received much attention. A recent study that will guide one to earlier treatments of that complex and ambiguous topic is Eri Hotta, *Pan-Asianism and Japan's War, 1931–1945* (NY: Palgrave, 2007). Another recent work is Sven Saaler and J. Victor Koschmann (eds), *Pan-Asianism in Modern Japanese History: Colonialism, Regionalism and Borders* (London: Routledge, 2007), a collection of 15 essays that explore various aspects of the topic.

14   Partner, *The Mayor of Aihara: A Japanese Villager and His Community, 1865–1925*, pp. 164–74, captures nicely the trauma of the earthquake and its after-effects as experienced by the rural Kantô populace. Louis Frédéric (Käthe Roth, tr.), *Japan Encyclopedia* (Cambridge, MA: HUP, 2002), p. 981, reports 143,000 dead. Nobuko Iijima (ed.), *Pollution Japan: Historical Chronology* (Elmsford, NY: Pergamon Press, 1979), p. 65, reports 100,000 casualties and refers to 3.4 million people being affected by the shock and its aftermath. William L. Langer (comp.), *An Encyclopedia of World History* (Boston: Houghton Mifflin Co., 1952), p. 1125, reports 200,000 estimated dead.

15   In an essay in Christian W. Spang and Ralf-Harald Wippich (eds), *Japanese-German Relations, 1895–1945: War, Diplomacy and Public Opinion* (London: Routledge, 2006), Tajima Nobuo examines the Anti-Comintern Pact and, on pp. 165–66, provides a translation of its clauses.

16   Two recent collections of essays that treat diverse aspects of Japanese-German relations from the 1890s to 1945 are Spang and Wippich (eds), *Japanese-German Relations, 1895–1945: War, Diplomacy and Public Opinion*, and Akira Kudô, Tajima Nobuo and Erich Pauer (eds), *Japan and Germany: Two Latecomers to the World Stage, 1890–1995*, 3 vols. (Folkestone: Global Oriental, 2009).

17   David C. Earhart, *Certain Victory: Images of World War II in the Japanese Media* (Armonk, NY: M.E. Sharpe, 2008) is a vast collection of some 800 images – photographs and art work – that portray the war as experienced by the people of Japan.

18   Hotta, *Pan-Asianism and Japan's War, 1931–1945*, is a fine examination of Pan-Asianist ideology and its antecedent developments.

19   In his essay on emigration to Manchuria, in Ann Waswo and Nishida Yoshiaki (eds), *Farmers and Village Life in Twentieth-Century Japan* (London: Routledge, 2003), p. 179, Mori Takemaro provides an excellent chart showing the population of overseas Japanese by location from 1907 to 1940.

20   Brett L. Walker, *The Conquest of Ainu Lands, Ecology and Culture in Japanese Expansion, 1590–1800* (Berkeley: UCP, 2001), p. 182, reports that the Ainu population of 1807 was

estimated at 26,256, dropping to 17,810 by 1854, probably due mainly to the spread of smallpox. That diffusion of disease appears to have occurred after shogunal authorities intensified their presence in Hokkaido in response to Russian activity there.

21  Totman, *A History of Japan, Second Edition*, pp. 328, 383.

22  Penelope Francks, *Rural Economic Development in Japan: From the Nineteenth Century to the Pacific War* (London: Routledge, 2006), pp. 114, 197.

23  Factory figures are rounded off from numbers in Iijima (ed.), *Pollution Japan: Historical Chronology*, pp. 30–31, 44, 52, 60, 81.

24  Francks, *Rural Economic Development in Japan: From the Nineteenth Century to the Pacific War*, p. 112, for 1890 and 1920 figures; Totman, *A History of Japan, Second Edition*, p. 387, for the 1940 figure.

25  Thus, in 1975, fully 20 percent of Japan's total population resided in its ten largest cities, which numbered 1 million or more apiece. Of these ten, only Kyoto and Sapporo were inland and lacked port facilities. And seven of the ten (with over 85 percent of their combined population) lay in the Osaka-Tokyo industrial heartland.

26  See Nicolas Fiévé and Paul Waley (eds), *Japanese Imperial Capitals in Historical Perspective: Place, Power and Memory in Kyoto, Edo and Tokyo* (London: Routledge, 2003), for 1890 figures; and Totman, *A History of Japan, Second Edition*, p. 382, for 1905 and 1935 figures.

27  Carl Mosk, *Japanese Industrial History: Technology, Urbanization, and Economic Growth* (London: M.E. Sharpe, 2001), p. 245, footnote 5.

28  Totman, *A History of Japan, Second Edition*, p. 466, for 1935 figure; this text, Chapter 6, for *bakuhan* estimate.

29  Francks, *Rural Economic Development in Japan: From the Nineteenth Century to the Pacific War*, pp. 124, 170.

30  Francks, *Rural Economic Development in Japan: From the Nineteenth Century to the Pacific War*, p. 196.

31  Totman, *A History of Japan, Second Edition*, p. 336. After 1920, Hokkaido's arable continued to expand but more slowly, not exceeding a million hectares until the 1970s (1 *chô* = 0.992 hectares).

32  Totman, *A History of Japan, Second Edition*, p. 336.

33  Hiromi Mizuno, *Science for the Empire: Scientific Nationalism in Modern Japan* (Stanford: SUP, 2009), discusses attitudes toward science in Japan, ca. 1910–45.

34  Waswo and Nishida (eds), *Farmers and Village Life in Twentieth-Century Japan*, p. 69.

35  Totman, *A History of Japan, Second Edition*, p. 387. Francks, *Rural Economic Development in Japan: From the Nineteenth Century to the Pacific War*, p. 139, reports that fertilizer use increased at the rate of 1.6 percent per year during 1880–1900, 7.7 percent per year during 1900–20, and 3.4 percent per year during 1920–35.

36  Francks, *Rural Economic Development in Japan: From the Nineteenth Century to the Pacific War*, pp. 113, 124, 207.

37  Francks, *Rural Economic Development in Japan: From the Nineteenth Century to the Pacific War*, p. 53. Totman, *A History of Japan, Second Edition*, p. 435.

38  These and the following figures on pelagic fishing are from Totman, *A History of Japan, Second Edition*, p. 388.

39  Totman, *A History of Japan, Second Edition*, pp. 391–92.

40  A richly detailed study of Japan's economic history is Takafusa Nakamura and Kônosuke Odaka (eds), *The Economic History of Japan: 1600–1990, Vol. 3: Economic History of Japan 1914–1955* (Oxford: Oxford UP, 2003). This four-volume work is the translation of a collection of essays covering facets of economic history from 1600 to 1990, and vol. 3 covers the period 1914–55.

41  Totman, *A History of Japan, Second Edition*, p. 436. The 1936 figure may be a bit deceptive due to earlier devaluation of the yen during the Depression.

42  Two articles (by Hashino and Nakabayashi) in Tetsuji Okazaki, *Production Organization in Japanese Economic Development* (London: Routledge, 2007), examine aspects of the silk industry in Kiryû, not far from Tomioka.

43  Francks, *Rural Economic Development in Japan: From the Nineteenth Century to the Pacific War*, pp. 35, 199. Totman, *A History of Japan, Second Edition*, pp. 314, 336.

44  In her essay in Tetsuji Okazaki, *Production Organization in Japanese Economic Development* (London: Routledge, 2007), Hashino provides (p. 26) a fine chart tracking real wages of female workers in northwest Kantô, showing the steep rise to 1919, the drop and partial recovery by the mid-1920s, and the sharp decline during the later 1920s and 1930s.

45  Totman, *A History of Japan, Second Edition*, pp. 334, 436.

46  Shuzo Teruoka (ed.), *Agriculture in the Modernization of Japan, 1850–2000* (New Dehli: Manohar, 2008), p. 63.

47  Totman, *A History of Japan, Second Edition*, pp. 313, 334, 436.

48  Mosk, *Japanese Industrial History: Technology, Urbanization, and Economic Growth*, p. 183.

49  Teruoka (ed.), *Agriculture in the Modernization of Japan, 1850–2000*, p. 141.

50  The prominence of this femalework force has made it a topic of scholarly attention, and Elyssa Faison, *Managing Women: Disciplining Labor in Modern Japan* (Berkeley: UCP, 2007), provides good guidance to earlier works.

51  Faison, *Managing Women: Disciplining Labor in Modern Japan*, p. 13, gives textile employment statistics. Teruoka (ed.), *Agriculture in the Modernization of Japan, 1850–2000*, p. 57, gives somewhat higher figures for the year 1909.

52  Teruoka (ed.), *Agriculture in the Modernization of Japan, 1850–2000*, p. 141.

53  Mosk, *Japanese Industrial History: Technology, Urbanization, and Economic Growth*, pp. 99–101, 187, discusses shipbuilding.

54  Totman, *A History of Japan, Second Edition*, p. 338.

55  Totman, *A History of Japan, Second Edition*, p. 385.

56  Totman, *A History of Japan, Second Edition*, pp. 313, 617, Table X.

57  Totman, *A History of Japan, Second Edition*, p. 388. The 1894 metric figure is calibrated from the long-ton figure given by Patricia Sippel, "Technology and change in Japan's modern copper mining industry", in Janet Hunter and Cornelia Storz (eds), *Institutional and Technological Change in Japan's Economy, Past and Present* (London: Routledge, 2006), p. 11.

58  The metric figures for 1874 and 1894 are calculated from long-ton figures given by Sippel, "Technology and change in Japan's modern copper mining industry", p. 11. Other figures are from Totman, *A History of Japan, Second Edition*, pp. 388 and 617, Table VIII.

59  Totman, *A History of Japan, Second Edition*, p. 509, also gives post-1945 vehicle figures to 1990.

60  Totman, *A History of Japan, Second Edition*, pp. 389, 617, Table IX.

61  Mosk, *Japanese Industrial History: Technology, Urbanization, and Economic Growth*, chapters 4–5, discusses electrification during the decades to 1940.

62  Partner, *The Mayor of Aihara: A Japanese Villager and His Community, 1865–1925*, passim, shows nicely how the presence of railroads altered lives in the hinterland.

63  On the Russo-Japanese War and Japan's railways, see the essay by Steven J. Ericson in Wolff et al. (eds), *The Russo-Japanese War in Global Perspective: World War Zero, Vol. II*, pp. 225–49.

64 Teruoka (ed.), *Agriculture in the Modernization of Japan, 1850–2000*, p. 49.

65 The recreational culture of the Japanese urban "middle class", especially during the 1920s, has attracted considerable scholarly attention. A recent, richly detailed study with delightful illustrations and an extensive bibliography is Miriam Silverberg, *Erotic Grotesque Nonsense: the Mass Culture of Japanese Modern Times* (Berkeley: UCP, 2006). On women and that culture, see Barbara Sato, *The New Japanese Woman: Modernity, Media, and Women in Interwar Japan* (Durham: Duke U. Press, 2003).

66 E. Patricia Tsurumi, *Factory Girls: Women in the Thread Mills of Meiji Japan* (Princeton: PUP, 1990), p. 94.

67 Totman, *A History of Japan, Second Edition*, p. 345.

68 This section is based primarily on Francks, *Rural Economic Development in Japan: From the Nineteenth Century to the Pacific War*. The chronologically arranged chapters 1–4 in Teruoka (ed.), *Agriculture in the Modernization of Japan, 1850–2000*, treat the agricultural developments of these decades in terms of classical Marxist analytical categories. Most of the themes treated here in general terms are given a local, real-time face in Partner, *The Mayor of Aihara: A Japanese Villager and His Community, 1865–1925*, chapters 3–5. Gail Lee Bernstein et al. (eds), *Public Spheres, Private Lives in Modern Japan, 1600–1950* (Cambridge, MA: HUP, 2005), in her study of a landlord family in southeast Fukushima Prefecture in northeastern Japan, illuminates many aspects of the topic. And Andrew Cobbing, *Kyushu: Gateway to Japan: A Concise History* (Folkestone: Global Oriental, 2009), pp. 241–43, provides a concise description of developments in rural Kyushu.

69 Francks, *Rural Economic Development in Japan: From the Nineteenth Century to the Pacific War*, pp. 194, ftnt 1, 196.

70 Francks, *Rural Economic Development in Japan: From the Nineteenth Century to the Pacific War*, p. 207.

71 Francks, *Rural Economic Development in Japan: From the Nineteenth Century to the Pacific War*, p. 143.

72 Francks, *Rural Economic Development in Japan: From the Nineteenth Century to the Pacific War*, p. 145.

73 Francks, *Rural Economic Development in Japan: From the Nineteenth Century to the Pacific War*, p. 137.

74 Francks, *Rural Economic Development in Japan: From the Nineteenth Century to the Pacific War*, p. 193.

75 Waswo and Nishida (eds), *Farmers and Village Life in Twentieth-Century Japan*, p. 80. In this essay Waswo focuses on tenant matters in the Izumo region of Shimane Prefecture, in southwest Honshu, during the 1920s.

76 Teruoka (ed.), *Agriculture in the Modernization of Japan, 1850–2000*, pp. 118–19.

77 Francks, *Rural Economic Development in Japan: From the Nineteenth Century to the Pacific War*, pp. 156, 237. Teruoka (ed.), *Agriculture in the Modernization of Japan, 1850–2000*, p. 143, Table 4.3, provides more statistical detail on tenancy disputes, 1922–44.

78 Francks, *Rural Economic Development in Japan: From the Nineteenth Century to the Pacific War*, pp. 156, 237.

79 Francks, *Rural Economic Development in Japan: From the Nineteenth Century to the Pacific War*, pp. 118, 210, 212.

80 The quotations that follow come from Partner, *The Mayor of Aihara: A Japanese Villager and His Community, 1865–1925*, pp. 157, 158.

81 Teruoka (ed.), *Agriculture in the Modernization of Japan, 1850–2000*, p. 139.

82 Teruoka (ed.), *Agriculture in the Modernization of Japan, 1850–2000*, p. 140.

83 Francks, *Rural Economic Development in Japan: From the Nineteenth Century to the Pacific War*, p. 137.

84 The workplace role of farm women in Japan, ca. 1915–45, is examined by Ôkado in Waswo and Nishida (eds), *Farmers and Village Life in Twentieth-Century Japan*, pp. 39–51.

85 Francks, *Rural Economic Development in Japan: From the Nineteenth Century to the Pacific War*, pp. 224, 227, 232–33.

86 Teruoka (ed.), *Agriculture in the Modernization of Japan, 1850–2000*, pp. 133–35. This loss of acreage was partially offset by 250,000 hectares that were brought into production by government projects. On p. 133, Teruoka provides a very good table of trends in the major types of agricultural production during 1930–45.

87 The intricacies of technological adoption and innovation during the decades 1868–1945 are examined in rich detail in Chapters 4–6 of Tessa Morris-Suzuki, *The Technological Transformation of Japan: From the Seventeenth to the Twenty-first Century* (Cambridge: CUP, 1994).

88 Iijima (ed.), *Pollution Japan: Historical Chronology*, passim, documents the Besshi problem very nicely.

89 The area being reported was Kurate-gun, an administrative district of Fukuoka Prefecture. The following two quotations come from Iijima, *Pollution Japan: Historical Chronology*, pp. 61–62, 73.

90 The mine figures to 1917 are from Iijima, *Pollution Japan: Historical Chronology*, pp. 30, 44, 57. The figure for 1940, by which time impressed Koreans and various prisoners were working in the mines, is a crude estimate.

91 Iijima, *Pollution Japan: Historical Chronology*, passim, records annual casualties in mining accidents. On p. 102, she notes that the most lethal coal mine explosion occurred in 1942 not in Japan, but in a Manchurian mine controlled by the army. It killed 1,527 and was, she writes, "the worst coal mine disaster in world history".

92 The 180–200 mortality rate is based on data in Statistics Bureau, *Japan Statistical Yearbook (Nihon tôkei nenkan)* (Tokyo: ed. by the Statistical Research and Training Institute; publ. by the Statistics Bureau; both under the Ministry of Internal Affairs and Communications; annual volumes, 1949), p. 114, Table 55. Totman, *A History of Japan, Second Edition*, p. 404, gives higher figures. The etiological agent of TB is the human tubercle bacillus, *Mycobacterium tuberculosis (hominis)*.

93 Iijima, *Pollution Japan: Historical Chronology*, passim, provides a rich chronological listing of factory incidents.

94 Mosk, *Japanese Industrial History: Technology, Urbanization, and Economic Growth*, p. 80.

95 In his study of Japan's economic modernization, Mosk, *Japanese Industrial History: Technology, Urbanization, and Economic Growth*, focuses on Osaka's industrial development to 1945.

96 Iijima, *Pollution Japan: Historical Chronology*, p. 95. The "Osaka vicinity" is commonly called Hanshin, an elision of *kanji* in Osaka and Kobe; "Tokyo vicinity" is similarly called Keihin, from Tokyo and Yokohama.

97 Except as otherwise noted, this material on Osaka pollution summarizes information in Iijima, *Pollution Japan: Historical Chronology*, passim.

98 Mosk, *Japanese Industrial History: Technology, Urbanization, and Economic Growth*, pp. 71, 76, discusses the city's urban expansion. A map on p. 72 shows this (and later) expansion nicely.

99 Iijima, *Pollution Japan: Historical Chronology*, p. 75. The commentator was Murakami Hideo.

100 Iijima, *Pollution Japan: Historical Chronology*, p. 88.

101 Mosk, *Japanese Industrial History: Technology, Urbanization, and Economic Growth*, pp. 217, 223.

102 Mosk, *Japanese Industrial History: Technology, Urbanization, and Economic Growth*, p. 218.

103 David L. Howell, *Capitalism from Within: Economy, Society, and the State in a Japanese Fishery* (Berkeley: UCP, 1995), discusses socio-economic aspects of this fishery at length. On p. 109 he presents a table showing the rise and fall in herring catch, 1871–1958. The Atlantic herring is *Clupea harengus*. The North Pacific herring is the California herring, *Clupea pallasii*.

104 The following material comes from Iijima, *Pollution Japan: Historical Chronology*, passim.

105 Morris-Suzuki, *The Technological Transformation of Japan: From the Seventeenth to the Twenty-first Century*, pp. 203–5, notes the environmental damage done to Kamaishi Bay in Tôhoku and the Yahata (Yawata) vicinity in Kyushu.

106 Mosk, *Japanese Industrial History: Technology, Urbanization, and Economic Growth*, pp. 86–87, 174–77.

107 Teruoka (ed.), *Agriculture in the Modernization of Japan, 1850–2000*, p. 134.

108 Table based on a fuller table at Francks, *Rural Economic Development in Japan: From the Nineteenth Century to the Pacific War*, p. 224.

109 Conrad Totman, *Japan's Imperial Forest: Goryôrin, 1889–1946* (Folkestone: Global Oriental, 2007), p. 3. Another official forest category was temple or shrine woodland, but it only occupied about a quarter of 1 percent of Japan's total woodland.

110 R.T. Fenton, *Japanese Forestry and Its Implications* (Singapore: Marshall Cavendish, 2005), p. 255.

111 Fenton, *Japanese Forestry and Its Implications*, p. 31.

112 Chapter 3 of Conrad Totman, *The Lumber Industry in Early Modern Japan* (Honolulu: UHP, 1995), discusses *bakuhan*-era timber transport.

113 Chapter 4 of Totman, *Japan's Imperial Forest: Goryôrin, 1889–1946*, treats the issue of forest damage in Yamanashi Prefecture, West of Tokyo.

114 Import figures from Totman, *A History of Japan, Second Edition*, p. 388. *Todomatsu* is also known as akatodomatsu.


## CHAPTER 8: ENTREPRENEURIAL INDUSTRIALISM, 1945–2010

1 Regarding the politics of these decades, two richly detailed, standard texts are the updated editions of Louis D. Hayes, *Introduction to Japanese Politics*, 5th ed. (Armonk, NY: M.E. Sharpe, 2009), and J.A.A. Stockwin, *Governing Japan: Divided Politics in a Resurgent Economy*, 4th ed. (Oxford: Blackwell, 2008). On foreign policy, see Richard J. Samuels, *Securing Japan: Tokyo's Grand Strategy and the Future of East Asia* (Ithaca: Cornell UP, 2007). Three recent studies of Japanese nationalism are Alexander Bukh, *Japan's National Identity and Foreign Policy: Russia as Japan's "Other"* (London: Routledge, 2010); Yumiko Iida, *Rethinking Identity In Modern Japan: Nationalism as Aesthetics* (London: Routledge, 2002); and Brian J. McVeigh, *Nationalisms of Japan: Managing and Mystifying Identity* (Oxford: Rowman & Littlefield, 2004). On Japanese law, see Daniel H. Foote, *Law in Japan: A Turning Point* (Seattle: U. Washington Press, 2007), and on social science thought, Andrew Barshay, *The Social Sciences in Modern Japan: The Marxian and Modernist Traditions* (Berkeley: UCP, 2004). Hans Brinckmann, *Showa Japan: The Post-War Golden Age and its Troubled Legacy* (Tokyo: Tuttle, 2008), is a rich treatment of society and culture during the boom years. Marcus Rebick, *The Japanese Employment System: Adapting to a New Economic Environment* (Oxford: Oxford UP, 2005), is an excellent study of the post-boom employment situation. The notes and bibliographies of these works, as well as those of general history textbooks, will guide one to the rich body of earlier works.

2   The three phases are commonly dated 1945–60, 1960–90, 1990ff. These dates are espe-cially appropriate for the study of political history because of the sharp political break in 1960 and the turmoil of 1988–90. From a socio-economic perspective, however, the dates 1955 and 1985 seem better markers of changing phases.

3   Mikio Sumiya (ed.), *A History of Japanese Trade and Industrial Policy* (Oxford: Oxford UP, 2000), p. 200, Table 9-2.

4   Nobuko Iijima (ed.), *Pollution Japan: Historical Chronology* (Elmsford, NY: Pergamon Press, 1979), p. 137. Shuzo Teruoka (ed.), *Agriculture in the Modernization of Japan, 1850–2000* (New Delhi: Manohar, 2008), p. 182, notes that this invoking of creation myths continued, with the booms of 1959–61 and 1965–70 being designated the Iwado (Iwato) and Izanagi boom respectively.

5   The issue of postwar policy planning and implementation has been richly explored. See, for example, the two final essays in Takafusa Nakamura and Kônosuke Odaka (eds), *The Economic History of Japan: 1600–1990, Vol. 3: Economic History of Japan 1914–1955* (Oxford: Oxford UP, 2003), and the many essays in Sumiya (ed.), *A History of Japanese Trade and Industrial Policy*. Laura E. Hein, *Fueling Growth: The Energy Revolution and Economic Policy in Postwar Japan* (Cambridge, MA: HUP, 1990), explores with great thoroughness the key issue of industrial energy policy.

6   Figures from Nakamura and Odaka (eds), *The Economic History of Japan: 1600–1990, Vol. 3: Economic History of Japan 1914–1955*, p. 328, Table 8-13.

7   Nakamura and Odaka (eds), *The Economic History of Japan: 1600–1990, Vol. 3: Economic History of Japan 1914–1955*, p. 331. Also, Sumiya (ed.), *A History of Japanese Trade and Industrial Policy*, p. 200, Table 9-3, reports that between 1946 and 1952 the production of ammonium sulfate, a key fertilizer material, rose more than sevenfold, from 243,000 to 1,860,000 tons.

8   Calculated from figures in Statistics Bureau, *Japan Statistical Yearbook [JSY] (Nihon tôkei nenkan)* (Tokyo: ed. by the Statistical Research and Training Institute; publ. by the Statistics Bureau; both under the Ministry of Internal Affairs and Communications; annual volumes, 1961), pp. 11, 241, 371, Tables 6, 139, 226.

9   Hein, *Fueling Growth: The Energy Revolution and Economic Policy in Postwar Japan*, p. 73, Table 3.

10  Hein, *Fueling Growth: The Energy Revolution and Economic Policy in Postwar Japan*, p. 76.

11  Hein, *Fueling Growth: The Energy Revolution and Economic Policy in Postwar Japan*, p. 67, Table 2.

12  Sumiya (ed.), *A History of Japanese Trade and Industrial Policy*, p. 39, Table 2-5.

13  Nakamura and Odaka (eds), *The Economic History of Japan: 1600–1990, Vol. 3: Economic History of Japan 1914–1955*, p. 373.

14  Hein, *Fueling Growth: The Energy Revolution and Economic Policy in Postwar Japan*, p. 220.

15  Tessa Morris-Suzuki, *The Technological Transformation of Japan: From the Seventeenth to the Twenty-first Century* (Cambridge: CUP, 1994), Part III, is an outstanding study of this topic.

16  Yen figures are derived from *JSY*, 1985, p. 336, Table 10-3, and *JSY*, 2007, p. 456, Table 15-1.

17  Production figures estimated from *JSY*, 1985, p. 255, Table 6-36 and p. 257, Table 6-38, and from *JSY*, 2007, p. 321, Table 8-29, and p. 323, Table 8-31.

18  Automobile figures compiled from *JSY*, 1985, p. 302, Table 8-5, and *JSY*, 2007, p. 386, Table 12-5.

19  Figures in *JSY*, 1961, p. 201, Table 103, on the production and importation of rice, barley and wheat during 1945–60 indicate the trajectory of self-sufficiency during those years.

20 The overwhelming importance of the USA as a source of soybeans is evident in *JSY* tables that break imports down by country of origin.

21 Hein, *Fueling Growth: The Energy Revolution and Economic Policy in Postwar Japan*, is a splendid exploration of the "cultural" factors in this coal-mine story – notably the attitudes and policies of mine operators and miners' unions.

22 See Hein, *Fueling Growth: The Energy Revolution and Economic Policy in Postwar Japan*, p. 67, Table 2, for coal output down to 1960. See *JSY*, 1976, p. 159, Table 115, and *JSY*, 1985, p. 213, Table 6-4, for select years 1965–83; *JSY*, 2007, p. 815, Table 26-21 for 1985ff.

23 These figures on coal production, import and supply are assembled from *JSY*, 1961, p. 202, Table 105; *JSY*, 1995, p. 355, Table 9-16; and *JSY*, 2009, p. 465, Table 15-6, and p. 815, Table 26-21.

24 Crude oil supply figures are from *JSY*, 1985, p. 786, Key Statistics, and *JSY*, 2007, p. 6, Key Statistics. Other tables give slightly different figures. Hein, *Fueling Growth: The Energy Revolution and Economic Policy in Postwar Japan*, p. 76, Table 4, using statistics from *JSY* 1953 and 1961, reports somewhat different oil production and imports, 1930–60. She discusses nicely the role of foreign oil companies in the revived trade after World War II. Natural gas import figures are given in *JSY*, 1985, p. 289, Table 7-21, and p. 347, Table 10-7.

25 Quoted in Iijima, *Pollution Japan: Historical Chronology*, p. 293.

26 Iijima, *Pollution Japan: Historical Chronology*, p. 325.

27 Quoted in Morris-Suzuki, *The Technological Transformation of Japan: From the Seventeenth to the Twenty-first Century*, p. 226.

28 Jeff Kingston, *Contemporary Japan: History, Politics and Social Change Since the 1980s* (Oxford: Wiley-Blackwell, 2010), pp. 14–15, cites the rates of investment inflation.

29 Kingston, *Contemporary Japan: History, Politics and Social Change Since the 1980s*, p. 87.

30 These generalizations about the post-1990 economy are made on the basis of statistical data in *JSY*, 2007, notably the 13 tables numbered 8-6, 8, 10, 17, 28; 12-17, 18, 19, 21; and 13-1, 5, 6, 11.

31 *JSY*, 2007, p. 207, Table 6-12 and passim provide pertinent statistics.

32 *JSY*, 2009, p. 50, Table 2-8.

33 Figures on registered aliens are given in *JSY*, 1985, p. 45, Table 2–15, and *JSY*, 2009, p. 57, Table 2-14. The number of registered aliens surpassed 2 million in 2005. Figures on the overall workforce population and its gender composition are in *JSY*, 2007, pp. 490–91, Table 161.

34 Rebick, *The Japanese Employment System: Adapting to a New Economic Environment*, is a rich and thoughtful examination of the post-1990 labor situation.

35 The relevant statistics are in *JSY*, 1985, pp. 528–29, Table 15-18, and *JSY*, 2007, pp. 604–5, Table 19-2.

36 The *JSY* table on foreign trade cited here also shows a sharp drop in the number of merchant vessels sailing under Japanese registry. But whether this means fewer Japanese vessels and crew or simply more such vessels sailing under foreign "flags of convenience" is unclear.

37 Monetary values for imports and exports are given in *JSY*, 2010, pp. 462–63, Tables 15-3, 15-4.

38 Teikoku-Shoin Co., *Teikoku's Complete Atlas of Japan* (Tokyo: Teikoku-Shoin, Co., Ltd., 1977), p. 41, gives prefectural population figures for 1975.

39 *JSY*, 2010, pp. 37–39, Table 2-3. About 40 km of the mountainous western tip of Tokyo abut the mountainous prefecture of Yamanashi.

40 An excellent study of the tuberculosis epidemic is William Johnson, *The Modern Epidemic: A History of Tuberculosis in Japan* (Cambridge, MA: HUP, 1995). See his graph on p. 39 for prewar mortality rates.

41  *JSY*, 1985, p. 622, Table 18-11; *JSY*, 2007, pp. 684–85, Table 21-15.

42  Iijima, *Pollution Japan: Historical Chronology*, passim, documents this story in rich detail.

43  R.T. Fenton, *Japanese Forestry and Its Implications* (Singapore: Marshall Cavendish, 2005), pp. 168–73, discusses the problem of injury in forestry work.

44  *JSY*, 1985, p. 744, Table 23-9; *JSY*, 1995, p. 778, Table 24-8; *JSY*, 2010, p. 815, Table 26-19. Changes in *JSY* analytical categories make longer-term trends somewhat difficult to assess.

45  *JSY*, 1985, p. 745, Table 23-10, and *JSY*, 2010, p. 816, Table 26-20. Because of insurance arrangements, these injury figures, unlike fatality figures, do not include the agricultural sector.

46  Tiana Norgren, *Abortion before Birth Control: The Politics of Reproduction in Postwar Japan* (Princeton: PUP, 2001), is an excellent study of birth control policy in postwar Japan.

47  Teruoka (ed.), *Agriculture in the Modernization of Japan, 1850–2000*, p. 251. His figures on p. 253 show national trajectories, ca. 1960–2000.

48  Akira Furukawa (tr. by Onoda Kikuko), *Village Life in Modern Japan: An Environmental Perspective* (Melbourne: Trans Pacific Press, 2007), p. 7.

49  Iijima, *Pollution Japan: Historical Chronology*, pp. 145, 147, cites start of construction. *JSY*, 1986, p. 300, Table 82, and p. 306, Table 8-10, and *JSY*, 2009, p. 386, Table 12-2, provide data on roads and railroads.

50  The following land-area figures derive from *JSY*, 1985, p. 9, Table 1-9, and *JSY*, 2010, p. 21, Table 1-9.

51  Figures from *JSY*, 1976, p. 99, Table 63, and *JSY*, 2009, p. 236, Table 7-6.

52  *JSY*, 1985, p. 47, Table 2-17; *JSY*, 2010, p. 59, Table 2-16.

53  Iijima, *Pollution Japan: Historical Chronology*, pp. 187, 201, 205.

54  For details, see *JSY*, 1985, pp. 212–13, Table 6-4, and *JSY*, 2007, p. 286, Table 8-2.

55  The following summary is based on entries in Iijima, *Pollution Japan: Historical Chronology*, pp. 164, 174, 196, 198, 238, 240, 242–4, 252, 260, 273, 288–9, 293, 296–8, 301, 309, 316, 320, 325, 332, 334, 336, 366, 378, 380, 382, 386.

56  Iijima, *Pollution Japan: Historical Chronology*, p. 198.

57  Iijima, *Pollution Japan: Historical Chronology*, pp. 243, 244.

58  Iijima, *Pollution Japan: Historical Chronology*, p. 260.

59  Iijima, *Pollution Japan: Historical Chronology*, pp. 273, 293, 301.

60  Iijima, *Pollution Japan: Historical Chronology*, p. 309. The phrasing is Iijima's.

61  Iijima, *Pollution Japan: Historical Chronology*, p. 386.

62  Morris-Suzuki, *The Technological Transformation of Japan: From the Seventeenth to the Twenty-first Century*, chapters 7–8, examines the technological developments central to this increase in output.

63  Iijima, *Pollution Japan: Historical Chronology*, documents these matters in chronological detail.

64  This section is based on the immense body of information in Iijima, *Pollution Japan: Historical Chronology*, pp. 108–401, which covers the years 1945–75 and mostly reports on damage to humans.

65  Iijima, *Pollution Japan: Historical Chronology*, passim, reports on marine injury in myriad entries. She mentions birds on pp. 128, 168, 212, 234, 306, 308, 330, 350, 374 and 388.

66  Iijima, *Pollution Japan: Historical Chronology*, p. 296.

67  Iijima, *Pollution Japan: Historical Chronology*, p. 228.

68  Iijima, *Pollution Japan: Historical Chronology*, pp. 288, 354. Two fine studies of the Chisso Corporation's pollution record are Timothy S. George, *Minamata: Pollution and the Struggle for Democracy in Postwar Japan* (Cambridge, MA: Harvard U. Asia Center, 2001), and Akio Mishima, *Bitter Sea: The Human Cost of Minamata Disease* (Tokyo: Kosei Publishing Co., 1992).

69   Morris-Suzuki, *The Technological Transformation of Japan: From the Seventeenth to the Twenty-first Century*, p. 187.

70   Iijima, *Pollution Japan: Historical Chronology*, p. 222.

71   Iijima, *Pollution Japan: Historical Chronology*, pp. 222, 224.

72   Iijima, *Pollution Japan: Historical Chronology*, p. 219.

73   Iijima, *Pollution Japan: Historical Chronology*, p. 279.

74   Calculated from data in *JSY*, 2010, p. 354, Table 10-16.

75   Iijima, *Pollution Japan: Historical Chronology*, pp. 302, 303.

76   Iijima, *Pollution Japan: Historical Chronology*, p. 302.

77   Iijima, *Pollution Japan: Historical Chronology*, p. 386.

78   Iijima, *Pollution Japan: Historical Chronology*, pp. 306, 334, 354, 366, 382, 398. The 1973 figure is cited on p. 354.

79   Iijima, *Pollution Japan: Historical Chronology*, passim, has myriad entries on these several topics.

80   Iijima, *Pollution Japan: Historical Chronology*, mentions auto-emissions developments on pp. 145, 219, 335, 336, 370, 381, 400.

81   Numbers of fishermen from *JSY*, 1961, p. 121, Table 59C; *JSY*, 1985, p. 182, Table 5-51; and *JSY*, 2007, p. 260, Table 7-44. Larger catch figures appear in *JSY*, 1985, p. 187, Table 5-58, and *JSY*, 2007, p. 264, Table 7-46. Smaller catch figures appear in the Key Statistics of those volumes.

82   On *konbinato*, see Andrew Gordon, The Wages of Affluence: Labor and Management in Postwar Japan (Cambridge, MA: HUP, 1988), p. 220 and passim.

83   This summary of the Tokyo fisheries problem is based on entries in Iijima, *Pollution Japan: Historical Chronology*, pp. 114, 134, 142–45, 173, 300, 312, 326, 336, 400.

84   Iijima, *Pollution Japan: Historical Chronology*, p. 336.

85   The Chisso affair is treated extensively in Iijima, *Pollution Japan: Historical Chronology*, passim. Also, the affair, particularly its human impact, is richly examined by George, *Minamata: Pollution and the Struggle for Democracy in Postwar Japan* and Mishima, *Bitter Sea: The Human Cost of Minamata Disease*.

86   Iijima, *Pollution Japan: Historical Chronology*, p. 134, quoting the Nishi Nihon Shinbun.

87   Iijima, *Pollution Japan: Historical Chronology*, mentions the Dôkai-wan situation several times, notably at pp. 134, 138, 293 and 301.

88   Iijima, *Pollution Japan: Historical Chronology*, pp. 114, 160, 278.

89   Iijima, *Pollution Japan: Historical Chronology*, p. 256.

90   Iijima, *Pollution Japan: Historical Chronology*, p. 292.

91   Iijima, *Pollution Japan: Historical Chronology*, pp. 380, 386.

92   Iijima, *Pollution Japan: Historical Chronology*, pp. 382, 383.

93   Morris-Suzuki, *The Technological Transformation of Japan: From the Seventeenth to the Twenty-first Century*, p. 203, provides a lucid summary of the devastating impact on fisheries of mining/manufacturing activity above Kamaishi Bay in eastern Tôhoku, 1880s–1960s.

94   *JSY*, 1985, p. 185, Table 5-55, and *JSY*, 2007, p. 263, Table 7-44.

95   Figures calculated from data in *JSY*, 1985, p. 187, Table 5-59, and *JSY*, 2010, p. 268, Table 7-47.

96   Production figures are from *JSY*, 1976, p. 143, Table 100, and *JSY*, 2010, p. 268, Table 7-46.

97   Export and import figures from *JSY*, 1985, p. 201, Table 5-72, and *JSY*, 2010, p. 281, Table 7-60.

98   Teruoka (ed.), *Agriculture in the Modernization of Japan, 1850–2000*, Chapter 5, provides a useful examination of occupation land-reform policy and its outcome. In Chapters 6–7 he follows changes in agriculture during boom and post-boom decades to 2000.

See the essay by Iwamoto Noriaki in Ann Waswo and Nishida Yoshiaki (eds), *Farmers and Village Life in Twentieth-Century Japan* (London: Routledge, 2003), pp. 223–28, for material on legal rationales for postwar land reform.

99   These figures are from Table 9-4, in the essay by Raymond A. Jussaume Jr., in Waswo and Nishida (eds), *Farmers and Village Life in Twentieth-Century Japan*, p. 211.

100  Iijima, *Pollution Japan: Historical Chronology*, p. 165, mentions the "basic law".

101  Teruoka (ed.), *Agriculture in the Modernization of Japan, 1850–2000*, pp. 262–67, 295–301, discusses this trend to large-scale farming.

102  "Raw milk" figures are from *JSY*, 1985, p. 164, Table 5-24, and *JSY*, 2010, p. 248, Table 7-18.

103  *JSY*, 1985, p. 164, Table 5-23; *JSY*, 1995, p. 238, Table 6-23.

104  *JSY*, 1985, p. 154, Table 5-10; *JSY*, 2010, p. 239, Table 7-7.

105  Iijima, *Pollution Japan: Historical Chronology*, reports instances of these problems, as at pp. 190, 212, 219, 248, 277, 278, 281, 297, 301 and 313.

106  Iijima, *Pollution Japan: Historical Chronology*, pp. 225, 288. DDT = dichloro-diphenyl-trichloro-ethane ($C_{14}H_9Cl_5$).

107  Iijima, *Pollution Japan: Historical Chronology*, pp. 130, 132.

108  Iijima, *Pollution Japan: Historical Chronology*, pp. 134, 185, 213, 261, 361.

109  Iijima, *Pollution Japan: Historical Chronology*, pp. 240, 344, 348.

110  Iijima, *Pollution Japan: Historical Chronology*, treats the Annaka and cadmium issues in many entries.

111  Teruoka (ed.), *Agriculture in the Modernization of Japan, 1850–2000*, pp. 312–13, discusses the relatively rapid decline in urban farm lands. Besides Hokkaido and the prefectures of Tôhoku, as of 2005 the prefectures of Ibaraki, Tochigi, Niigata, Fukui, Shiga, Wakayama, Kumamoto and Saga all fared better than the national average in sustaining productive agricultural acreage. (See sources cited in Table 35.)

112  Fenton, *Japanese Forestry and Its Implications*, pp. 58, 157–59, discusses the pine nematode.

113  The 1951 figure is from Yoshiya Iwai (ed.), *Forestry and the Forest Industry in Japan* (Vancouver: U. of British Columbia P., 2002), p. 129. The other figures are from *JSY*, 1985, p. 177, Table 5-39, and *JSY*, 2010, p. 259, Table 7-30. Iwai's figures for later years are slightly higher.

114  Fenton, *Japanese Forestry and Its Implications*, Chapter 7, treats protection forest. He mentions the public-private division on p. 145.

115  Furukawa, *Village Life in Modern Japan: An Environmental Perspective*, p. 225.

116  Fenton, *Japanese Forestry and Its Implications*, pp. 35, 87–88.

117  Iwai (ed.), *Forestry and the Forest Industry in Japan*, pp. 199–200, Table 11-1, gives statistics on housing, 1955–2000. Fenton, *Japanese Forestry and Its Implications*, pp. 200–2, discusses the trajectory of demand for construction timber.

118  Fenton, *Japanese Forestry and Its Implications*, pp. 35, 91–93, 106, 111. His Chapter 6 discusses the techniques of this silviculture; Chapter 10 examines plantation costs. An excellent graph of trends in cutting and reforesting, 1930–95, is in Iwai (ed.), *Forestry and the Forest Industry in Japan*, at p. 298, Figure 17-1. Plantation acreage figures (conifer and broadleafs combined) appear in tables of *JSY* volumes.

119  Fenton, *Japanese Forestry and Its Implications*, p. 196.

120  Fenton, *Japanese Forestry and Its Implications*, discusses thinning in Chapter 7. His plates nos. 34 and 35 show thinning machines. In an essay in Gyorgy Szèll and Ken'ichi Tominaga (eds), *The Environmental Challenges for Japan and Germany* (Frankfurt: Peter Lang, 2004), pp. 285–96, Nishikawa Seiichi stresses the problem of thinning. His essay includes many useful figures.

121  Fenton, *Japanese Forestry and Its Implications*, pp. 173–75.

122 Fenton, *Japanese Forestry and Its Implications*, pp. 180–82.

123 *Webster's Unabridged Dictionary* (1979 edition), p. 1498. The condition is named after the French physician, A.G.M. Raynaud (1834–81).

124 Iijima, *Pollution Japan: Historical Chronology*, reports on chainsaws and Raynaud's Disease at pp. 145, 211, 263, 361, 365, 381, 385 and 401. Fenton, *Japanese Forestry and Its Implications*, mentions the problem on p. 168.

125 Iwai (ed.), *Forestry and the Forest Industry in Japan*, p. 248, has a very good table of wood imports by country of origin, 1960–99.

126 *JSY*, 1985, p. 174, Table 5–34, and *JSY*, 2010, p. 257, Table 7–26.

127 Furukawa, *Village Life in Modern Japan: An Environmental Perspective*, p. 223. This book is a detailed sociological study of a village site on the northwest corner of Lake Biwa.

128 This section on the wood-pulp industry is based on the essay by Noda Hideshi in Iwai (ed.), *Forestry and the Forest Industry in Japan*, pp. 214–29; Fenton, *Japanese Forestry and Its Implications*, pp. 148–51, and data in *JSY*, 1985, pp. 179–80, Tables 5-44, 5-46; and *JSY*, 2007, pp. 257–58, Tables 7-34, 7-35.

129 Noda, in Iwai (ed.), *Forestry and the Forest Industry in Japan* op. cit., discusses recycling. *JSY*, 2010, p. 804, Table 26-6, gives post-2000 recycling figures.

## EPILOGUE

1 Statements in this Epilogue regarding environmental trends since 1990 are based on data in the several tables of *JSY*, 2009, pp. 798–806.

2 According to a *New York Times* article of 4 May 2011, pp. A1, A3, the newest global population projections envisage even more increase than did earlier ones.

3 This quake and its consequences were extensively reported in *The New York Times* from 12 March onward.

4 As an example of human impact on vulnerable species "elsewhere", a recent estimate of non-domesticated bird fatalities in the USA suggests that of the roughly 5 billion bird deaths every year, somewhere between 9 percent and 26 percent are caused by contact with man-made dangers – high-tension lines, pesticides, motor vehicles, domestic cats and buildings. The great range of uncertainty reflects the extremely high but uncertain kill-rate for birds that fly into skyscrapers and other buildings. *The New York Times*, 18 January 2011, p. D4.

# Bibliography

The works listed here are those cited in the endnotes. The list seeks to mention recent works that readers may find useful for further study of Japan's history, particularly those that examine topics with environmental ramifications. Numerous outstanding but older works are not cited. Many of those can be found in the bibliographies of the volumes cited here. For a general introduction to the scholarship on Japanese history, which also cites many of those outstanding earlier works, a useful source may be the bibliographical essay (Appendix D: pp. 631–57) in Conrad Totman, *A History of Japan, Second Edition* (Oxford: Blackwell, 2005).

Abbreviations of publishers are as follows:

| | | | |
|---|---|---|---|
| CUP | Cambridge University Press | UCP | University of California Press |
| HUP | Harvard University Press | UHP | University of Hawaii Press |
| PUP | Princeton University Press | UTP | University of Tokyo Press |
| SUP | Stanford University Press | YUP | Yale University Press |

Adolphson, Mikael S., *The Teeth and the Claws of the Buddha: Monastic Warriors and Sôhei in Japanese History* (Honolulu: UHP, 2007).

Adolphson, Mikael S. et al. (eds), *Heian Japan, Center and Peripheries* (Honolulu: UHP, 2007).

Aikens, C. Melvin and Higuchi Takayasu, *Prehistory of Japan* (NY: Academic Press, 1982).

Anderson, Mark, *Japan and the Specter of Imperialism* (NY: Palgrave, 2009).

Association of Japanese Geographers (ed.), *Geography of Japan* (Tokyo: Teikoku-Shoin, 1980).

Barnes, Gina L., "Origins of the Japanese Islands: The New 'Big Picture,'" *Nichibunken Japan Review*, No. 15 (2003), pp. 3–50.

———, *State Formation in Japan* (Oxon: Routledge, 2007).

Barshay, Andrew, *The Social Sciences in Modern Japan: The Marxian and Modernist Traditions* (Berkeley: UCP, 2004).

Batten, Bruce L., *To the Ends of Japan: Premodern Frontiers, Boundaries, and Interactions* (Honolulu: UHP, 2003).

———, *Gateway to Japan: Hakata in War and Peace, 500–1300* (Honolulu: UHP, 2006).

Bellwood, Peter and Colin Renfrew (eds), *Examining the Farming/Language Dispersal Hypothesis* (Cambridge: McDonald Institute, 2002).

Bernstein, Gail Lee et al. (eds), *Public Spheres, Private Lives in Modern Japan, 1600–1950* (Cambridge, MA: HUP, 2005).

Berry, Mary E., *Japan in Print: Information and Nation in the Early Modern Period* (Berkeley: UCP, 2006).

Bodart-Bailey, Beatrice, *The Dog Shogun: The Personality and Politics of Tokugawa Tsunayoshi* (Honolulu: UHP, 2006).

Botsman, Daniel V., *Punishment and Power in the Making of Modern Japan* (Princeton: PUP, 2005).

Bray, Francesca, *The Rice Economies: Technology and Development in Asian Societies* (Oxford: Basil Blackwell, 1986).

Brinckman, Hans, *Showa Japan: The Post-War Golden Age and its Troubled Legacy* (Tokyo: Tuttle, 2008).

Bryant, Anthony, *Sekigahara, 1600: The Final Struggle for Power* (Westport, CT: Praeger, 2005).

Bukh, Alexander, *Japan's National Identity and Foreign Policy: Russia as Japan's "Other"* (London: Routledge, 2010).

Burns, Susan L., *Before the Nation: Kokugaku and the Imagining of Community* (Durham: Duke UP, 2003).

Butler, Lee, *Emperor and Aristocracy in Japan, 1467–1680* (Cambridge, MA: HUP, 2002).

Chaiklin, Martha, *Cultural Commerce and Dutch Commercial Culture: The Influence of European Material Culture on Japan, 1700–1850* (Leiden: Leiden UP, 2003).

Chapman, John and Inaba Chiharu, *Rethinking the Russo-Japanese War, 1904–05, Vol. II* (Folkestone: Global Oriental, 2007).

Choi, Moo-chang, *The Paleolithic Period in Korea* (Seoul: Jimoondang, 2004).

Chough, S. K. et al., *Marine Geology of Korean Seas*, 2nd ed. (Amsterdam: Elsevier, 2000).

Cobbing, Andrew, *Kyushu: Gateway to Japan: A Concise History* (Folkestone: Global Oriental, 2009).

Conlan, Thomas D., *In Little Need of Divine Intervention: Takezaki Suenaga's Scrolls of the Mongol Invasions of Japan* (Ithaca, NY: Cornell East Asia Program, 2001).

———, *State of War: The Violent Order of Fourteenth-Century Japan* (Ann Arbor MI: Center for Japanese Studies, 2003).

Crist, D. H., *Rice* (London: Longmans, Green and Co. Ltd., 1965).

Cullen, Louis M., *A History of Japan 1582–1941: Internal and External Worlds* (Cambridge: CUP, 2003).

Dickins, J. M. et al. (eds), "New Concepts in Global Tectonics", a Special Issue of *Himalayan Geology*, Vol. 22, No. 1 (2001).

Doak, Kevin M., *A History of Nationalism in Modern Japan* (Leiden: Brill, 2007).

Dougill, John, *Kyoto: A Cultural History* (NY: Oxford UP, 2006).

Drea, Edward J., *Japan's Imperial Army: Its Rise and Fall, 1853–1945* (Lawrence, KN: U.P. of Kansas, 2009).

Earhart, David C., *Certain Victory: Images of World War II in the Japanese Media* (Armonk, NY: M.E. Sharpe, 2008).

Faison, Elyssa, *Managing Women: Disciplining Labor in Modern Japan* (Berkeley: UCP, 2007).

Farris, William Wayne, *Japan's Medieval Population: Famine, Fertility, and Warfare in a Transformative Age* (Honolulu: UHP, 2006).

———, *Daily Life and Demographics in Ancient Japan* (Ann Arbor: U. Mich. Center for Japanese Studies, 2009).

———, *Japan to 1600, A Social and Economic History* (Honolulu: UHP, 2009).

———, "Shipbuilding and Nautical Technology in Japanese Maritime History: Origins to 1600", in *The Mariner's Mirror*, Vol. 95, No. 3 (August 2009), pp. 260–83.

352

Fenton, R.T., *Japanese Forestry and Its Implications* (Singapore: Marshall Cavendish, 2005).

Ferguson, Joseph, *Japanese-Russian Relations, 1907–2007* (London: Routledge, 2008).

Fiévé, Nicolas and Paul Waley (eds), *Japanese Imperial Capitals in Historical Perspective: Place, Power and Memory in Kyoto, Edo and Tokyo* (London: Routledge, 2003).

Fogel, Joshua A. (ed.), *The Teleology of the Modern Nation-State: Japan and China* (Philadelphia: U. Penn. Press, 2005).

Foote, Daniel H., *Law in Japan: A Turning Point* (Seattle: U. Washington Press, 2007).

Frampton, Kenneth and Kunio Kudo, *Japanese Building Practice: From Ancient Times to the Meiji Period* (NY: Van Nostrand Reinhold, 1997).

Francks, Penelope, *Technology and Agricultural Development in Pre-War Japan* (New Haven: YUP, 1984).

——, *Rural Economic Development in Japan: From the Nineteenth Century to the Pacific War* (London: Routledge, 2006).

Frédéric, Louis (Käthe Roth, tr.), *Japan Encyclopedia* (Cambridge, MA: HUP, 2002).

Free, Dan, *Early Japanese Railways 1853–1914: Engineering Triumphs that Transformed Meiji-era Japan* (Tokyo: Tuttle, 2008).

Friday, Karl, *Samurai, Warfare, and the State in Early Medieval Japan* (London: Routledge, 2004).

Frölich, Judith, *Rulers, Peasants and the Use of the Written Word in Medieval Japan* (Bern: Peter Lang, 2007).

Fukagawa, Hidetoshi and Tony Rothman, *Sacred Mathematics: Japanese Temple Geometry* (Princeton: PUP, 2008).

Furukawa, Akira (tr. by Onoda Kikuko), *Village Life in Modern Japan: An Environmental Perspective* (Melbourne: Trans Pacific Press, 2007).

Gay, Suzanne, *The Moneylenders of Late Medieval Kyoto* (Honolulu: UHP, 2001).

George, Timothy S., *Minamata: Pollution and the Struggle for Democracy in Postwar Japan* (Cambridge, MA: Harvard U. Asia Center, 2001).

Gerhart, Karen M., *The Material Culture of Death in Medieval Japan* (Honolulu: UHP, 2009).

Goble, Andrew Edmund et al. (eds), "Tools of Culture: Japan's Cultural, Intellectual, Medical, and Technological Contacts in East Asia, 1000s-1500s", *Asia Past & Present: New Research from AAS*, No. 2 (Ann Arbor: Association for Asian Studies, 2009).

Gordon, Andrew, *The Wages of Affluence: Labor and Management in Postwar Japan* (Cambridge, MA: HUP, 1998).

Guo, Nanyan et al., *Tsugaru: Regional Identity on Japan's Northern Periphery* (Dunedin NZ: U. of Otago Press, 2005).

Habu, Junko, *Ancient Jōmon of Japan* (Cambridge: CUP, 2004).

Hanihara, Kazurô, "The Origin of the Japanese in Relation to Other Ethnic Groups in East Asia", in Richard J. Pearson et al. (eds), *Windows on the Japanese Past: Studies in Archaeology and Prehistory* (Ann Arbor, MI: Center for Japanese Studies, 1986), pp. 75–83.

Hashimoto, Mitsuo (ed.), *Geology of Japan* (Tokyo: Terra Scientific Publishing Company, 1991).

Hayami, Akira, *The Historical Demography of Pre-modern Japan* (Tokyo: UTP, 2001).

Hayes, Louis D., *Introduction to Japanese Politics*, 5th ed. (Armonk, NY: M.E. Sharpe, 2009).

Hein, Laura E., *Fueling Growth: The Energy Revolution and Economic Policy in Postwar Japan* (Cambridge, MA: HUP, 1990).

Hirooka, K., "Paleomagnetic Evidence of the Deformation of Japan and Its Paleogeography during the Neogene", in Ryuichi Tsuchi and James C. Ingle Jr. (eds), *Pacific Neogene: Environment, Evolution, and Events* (Tokyo: UTP, 1992), pp. 151–56.

Holcombe, Charles, *The Genesis of East Asia, 221 B.C.–A.D. 907* (Honolulu: UHP, 2001).

Hoshino, Michihei, *The Expanding Earth: Evidence, Causes and Effects* (Tokyo: Tokai UP, 1998).

Hotta, Eri, *Pan-Asianism and Japan's War, 1931–1945* (NY: Palgrave, 2007).

Howell, David L., *Capitalism from Within: Economy, Society, and the State in a Japanese Fishery* (Berkeley: UCP, 1995).

———, *Geographies of Identity in Nineteenth Century Japan* (Berkeley: UCP, 2005).

Hudson, Mark and Gina Barnes, "Yoshinogari: A Yayoi Settlement in Northern Kyushu", *Monumenta Nipponica* 46/2 (Summer 1991), pp. 211–35.

Hunter, Janet and Cornelia Storz (eds), *Institutional and Technological Change in Japan's Economy, Past and Present* (London: Routledge, 2006).

Hur, Nam-lin, *Death and Social Order in Tokugawa Japan: Buddhism, Anti-Christianity and the Danka System* (Cambridge, MA: HUP, 2007).

Iida, Yumiko, *Rethinking Identity In Modern Japan: Nationalism as Aesthetics* (London: Routledge, 2002).

Iijima, Nobuko (ed.), *Pollution Japan: Historical Chronology* (Elmsford, NY: Pergamon Press, 1979).

Ikawa-Smith, Fumiko, "Late Pleistocene and Early Holocene Technologies", in Richard J. Pearson et al. (eds), *Windows on the Japanese Past: Studies in Archaeology and Prehistory* (Ann Arbor, MI: Center for Japanese Studies, 1986), pp. 199–216.

Imamura, Keiji, *Prehistoric Japan* (Honolulu: UHP, 1996).

Iwai, Yoshiya (ed.), *Forestry and the Forest Industry in Japan* (Vancouver: U. of British Columbia P., 2002).

Jannetta, Ann B., *The Vaccinators: Smallpox, Medical Knowledge, and the "Opening" of Japan* (Stanford: SUP, 2007).

Jansen, Marius (ed.), *The Cambridge History of Japan, Vol. 5, The Nineteenth Century* (Cambridge: CUP, 1989).

*Japan Statistical Yearbook* (annual) (JSY): Statistics Bureau, *Japan Statistical Yearbook (Nihon tôkei nenkan)* [JSY] (Tokyo: ed. by the Statistical Research and Training Institute; publ. by the Statistics Bureau; both under the Ministry of Internal Affairs and Communications; annual volumes).

Johnston, William, *The Modern Epidemic: A History of Tuberculosis in Japan* (Cambridge, MA: HUP, 1995).

JSY (See *Japan Statistical Yearbook*)

Kaizuka, Sohei and Yoko Ota, "Land in Torment", in *Geographical Magazine* 51-5 (London: Feb. 1979), pp. 345–52.

Kalland, Arne, *Fishing Villages in Tokugawa Japan* (Honolulu: UHP, 1995).

Kerr, George H., *Okinawa, The History of an Island People*, rev. ed. (Boston: Tuttle, 2000).

Kidder, J. Edward, Jr., *Himiko and Japan's Elusive Chiefdom of Yamatai* (Honolulu: UHP, 2007).

Kikuchi, Toshihiko, "Continental Culture and Hokkaido", in Richard J. Pearson et al. (eds), *Windows on the Japanese Past: Studies in Archaeology and Prehistory* (Ann Arbor, MI: Center for Japanese Studies, 1986), pp. 149–62.

Kim, Kyu Hyun, *The Age of Visions and Arguments: Parliamentarianism and the National Public Sphere in Early Meiji Japan* (Cambridge, MA: HUP, 2007).

Kimura, Toshio et al., *Geology of Japan* (Tokyo: UTP, 1991).

Kingston, Jeff, *Contemporary Japan: History Politics, and Social Change Since the 1980s* (Oxford: Wiley-Blackwell, 2010).

Kitamura, Shirô and Okamoto Shôgo, *Genshoku Nihon jumoku zukan* [Illustrated handbook of Japanese trees and shrubs] (Osaka: Hoikusha, 1959).

Knechtges, David R. and Eugene Vance (eds), *Rhetoric and the Discourses of Power in Court Culture; China, Europe, and Japan* (Seattle: U. Washington Press, 2005).

Kobayashi, Tatsuo (ed. by Simon Kaner with Oki Nakamura), *Jômon Reflections: Forager life and culture in the prehistoric Japanese archipelago* (Oxford: Oxbow Books, 2004).

Koh, Sung-je, "A History of the Cotton Trade between Korea and Japan, 1423–1910", *Asian Economies* #12 (March 1975), pp. 5–16.

Kowner, Rotem (ed.), *Rethinking the Russo-Japanese War, 1904–05, Vol. I* (Folkestone: Global Oriental, 2007).

Kracht, Klaus, *Japanese Thought in the Tokugawa Era: A Bibliography of Western-Language Materials* (Wiesbaden: Harrassowitz Verlag, 2000).

Kudô Akira, Tajima Nobuo and Erich Pauer (eds), *Japan and Germany: Two Latecomers to the World Stage, 1890–1995*, 3 vols. (Folkestone: Global Oriental, 2009).

Kumar, Ann, *Globalizing the Prehistory of Japan: Language, Genes and Civilization* (London: Routledge, 2009).

Kwon, Grace H., *State Formation, Property Relations, & the Development of the Tokugawa Economy (1600–1868)* (NY: Routledge, 2002).

Kwon, Hack Soo (Hak-su), *A Regional Analysis of the Kaya Polities in Korea* (Seoul: Sowha Publishing Co., 2005).

Langer, William L. (comp.), *An Encyclopedia of World History* (Boston: Houghton Mifflin Co., 1952).

Lee, Hyun-hee et al., *A New History of Korea* (Engl. transl.: Seoul: Jimoondang, 2005).

Lewis, James B., *Frontier Contact between Choson Korea and Tokugawa Japan* (NY: Routledge Curzon, 2003).

Lindsey, William R., *Fertility and Pleasure: Ritual and Sexual Values in Tokugawa Japan* (Honolulu: UHP, 2007).

Lone, Stewart, *Provincial Life and the Military in Imperial Japan: the Phantom Samurai* (London: Routledge, 2010).

Low, Morris (ed.), *Building a Modern Japan: Science, Technology, and Medicine in the Meiji Era and Beyond* (NY: Palgrave, 2005).

Lutgens, Frederick K. and Edward J. Tarbuck, *Essentials of Geology*, 9th ed. (Upper Saddle River, NJ: Pearson Prentice Hall, 2006).

Maejima, Ikuo, "Seasonal and Regional Aspects of Japan's Weather and Climate," in Association of Japanese Geographers (ed.), *Geography of Japan* (Tokyo: Teikoku-Shoin, 1980), pp. 54–72.

Marshak, Stephen, *Earth: Portrait of a Planet* (NY: W.W. Norton, 2001).

Matsui, Akira and Masaaki Kanehara, "The question of prehistoric plant husbandry during the Jômon Period in Japan", in *World Archaeology*, Vol. 38-2, 2006, pp. 259–73.

McCallum, Donald F., *The Four Great Temples: Buddhist Archaeology, Architecture, and Icons of Seventh-Century Japan* (Honolulu: UHP, 2009).

McNally, Mark, *Proving the Way: Conflict and Practice in the History of Japanese Nativism* (Cambridge, MA: HUP, 2005).

McOmie, William (comp.), *Foreign Images and Experiences of Japan: Vol. 1, First Century AD to 1841* (Folkestone: Global Oriental, 2005).

———, *The Opening of Japan, 1853–55* (Folkestone: Global Oriental, 2006).

McVeigh, Brian J., *Nationalisms of Japan: Managing and Mystifying Identity* (Oxford: Rowman & Littlefield, 2004).

Mishima, Akio, *Bitter Sea: The Human Cost of Minamata Disease* (Tokyo: Kosei Publishing Co., 1992).

Mitani, Hiroshi, *Escape from Impasse: The Decision to Open Japan* (Tokyo: International House, 2006).

Mizoguchi, Koji, *An Archaeological History of Japan 30,000 B.C to A.D. 700* (Philadelphia: U. Penn. Press, 2002).

Mizuno, Hiromi, *Science for the Empire: Scientific Nationalism in Modern Japan* (Stanford: SUP, 2009).

Morris-Suzuki, Tessa, *The Technological Transformation of Japan: From the Seventeenth to the Twenty-first Century* (Cambridge: CUP, 1994).

Mosk, Carl, *Japanese Industrial History: Technology, Urbanization, and Economic Growth* (London: M.E. Sharpe, 2001).

Nagata, Mary Louise, *Labor Contracts and Labor Relations in Early Modern Central Japan* (NY: Routledge, 2005).

Najita, Tetsuo, *Ordinary Economies in Japan: A Historical Perspective, 1750–1950* (Berkeley: UCP, 2009).

Nakamura, Takafusa and Kônosuke Odaka (eds), *The Economic History of Japan: 1600–1990, Vol. 3: Economic History of Japan 1914–1955* (Oxford: Oxford UP, 2003).

Natural Resources Section, *Important Trees of Japan* (Report no. 119) (Tokyo: General Headquarters, Supreme Commander for the Allied Powers, 1949).

Naumann, Nelly, *Japanese Prehistory* (Weisbaden: Harrassowitz, 2000).

Nelson, Sarah M., *Korean Social Archaeology: Early Villages* (Seoul: Jimoondang, 2004).

Nield, Ted, *Supercontinent: Ten Billion Years in the Life of Our Planet* (Cambridge, MA: HUP, 2007).

Nimura, Kazuo, *The Ashio Riot of 1907: A Social History of Mining in Japan* (Durham, NC: Duke UP, 1997).

Norgren, Tiana, *Abortion before Birth Control: The Politics of Reproduction in Postwar Japan* (Princeton: PUP, 2001).

Nørlund, Irene, Sven Cederroth and Ingela Gerdin (eds), *Rice Societies: Asian Problems and Prospects* (London: Curzon Press Ltd., 1986).

O'Brien, Phillips Payson, *The Anglo-Japanese Alliance, 1902–22* (London: Routledge, 2004).

Oguma, Eiji (David Askew, tr.), *A Genealogy of "Japanese" Self-images* (Melbourne: Trans Pacific Press, 2002).

Okazaki, Tetsuji, *Production Organization in Japanese Economic Development* (London: Routledge, 2007).

Ooms, Herman, *Imperial Politics and Symbolics in Ancient Japan: The Tenmu Dynasty, 650–800* (Honolulu: UHP, 2008).

Partner, Simon, *The Mayor of Aihara: A Japanese Villager and His Community, 1865–1925* (Berkeley: UCP, 2009).

Pauer, Erich (ed.), *Papers on the History of Industry and Technology of Japan: Volume I: From the Ritsuryô-system to the Early Meiji-Period* (Marburg: Förderverein, 1995).

Pearson, Richard, "Jômon hot spot: increasing sedentism in southwestern Japan in the Incipient Jômon (14,000–9250 cal. BC) and Earliest Jômon (9250–5300 cal. BC) periods," in *World Archaeology*, Vol. 38-2 (2006), pp. 239–58.

Pearson, Richard (ed.), *Okinawa, The Rise of an Island Kingdom* (London: Oxford UP, 2009).

Pearson, Richard J. et al. (eds), *Windows on the Japanese Past: Studies in Archaeology and Prehistory* (Ann Arbor, MI: Center for Japanese Studies, 1986).

Perez, Louis G., *Daily Life in Early Modern Japan* (Westport, CT: Greenwood Press, 2002).

Pflugfelder, Gregory M. and Brett L. Walker (eds), *JAPANimals: History and Culture in Japan's Animal Life* (Ann Arbor MI: Center for Japanese Studies, 2005).

Piggott, Joan R. (ed.), *Capital and Countryside in Japan, 300–1180* (Ithaca, NY: Cornell East Asian Program, 2006).

Plutschow, Herbert, *A Reader in Edo Period Travel* (Folkestone: Global Oriental, 2006).

Rambelli, Fabio, *Buddhist Materiality: a Cultural History of Objects in Japanese Buddhism* (Stanford: SUP, 2007).

Rand McNally, *Universal World Atlas, New Census Edition* (Chicago: Rand McNally & Company, 1982).

Rebick, Marcus, *The Japanese Employment System: Adapting to a New Economic Environment* (Oxford: Oxford UP, 2005).

Reitan, Richard M., *Making a Moral Society: Ethics and the State in Meiji Japan* (Honolulu: UHP, 2010).

Reynolds, T.E.G. and S.C. Kaner, "Japan and Korea at 18,000 BP", in Olga Soffer and Clive Gamble (eds), *The World at 18,000 BP Vol. One: High Latitudes* (London: Unwin Hyman, 1990), pp. 296–311.

Rubinger, Richard, *Popular Literacy in Early Modern Japan* (Honolulu: UHP, 2007).

Saaler, Sven and J. Victor Koschmann (eds), *Pan-Asianism in Modern Japanese History: Colonialism, Regionalism and Borders* (London: Routledge, 2007).

Sagers, John H., *Origins of Japanese Wealth and Power: Reconciling Confucianism and Capitalism, 1830–1885* (NY: Palgrave, 2006).

Sakaguchi, Yutaka, "Characteristics of the physical nature of Japan with special reference to landform", in Association of Japanese Geographers (ed.), *Geography of Japan* (Tokyo: Teikoku-Shoin, 1980), pp. 3–28.

Samuels, Richard J., *Securing Japan: Tokyo's Grand Strategy and the Future of East Asia* (Ithaca: Cornell UP, 2007).

Sato, Barbara, *The New Japanese Woman: Modernity, Media, and Women in Interwar Japan* (Durham: Duke U. Press., 2003).

*Science News* (Washington DC: Science Service), publ. weekly until May 2008, then biweekly.

Serizawa, Chôsuke, "The Paleolithic Age of Japan in the Context of East Asia: A Brief Introduction", in Richard J. Pearson et al. (eds), *Windows on the Japanese Past: Studies in Archaeology and Prehistory* (Ann Arbor, MI: Center for Japanese Studies, 1986), pp. 191–97.

Shelach, Gideon, *Prehistoric Societies on the Northern Frontiers of China* (London: Equinox Publishing Ltd., 2009).

Shigeta, Yasunari and Haruyoshi Maeda (eds), *The Cretaceous System in the Makarov Area, Southern Sakhalin, Russian Far East* (Monograph No. 31) (Tokyo: National Science Museum, Dec. 2005).

Shillony, Ben-Ami, *Enigma of the Emperors: Sacred Subservience in Japanese History* (Folkestone: Global Oriental, 2005).

Shimada Ryuto, *The Intra-Asian Trade in Japanese Copper by the Dutch East India Company during the Eighteenth Century* (Leiden: Brill, 2006).

Shimazu Naoko, *Japanese Society at War: Death, Memory and the Russo-Japanese War* (Cambridge: CUP, 2009).

Silverberg, Miriam, *Erotic Grotesque Nonsense: the Mass Culture of Japanese Modern Times* (Berkeley: UCP, 2006).

Sippel, Patricia, "Technology and change in Japan's modern copper mining industry", in Janet Hunter and Cornelia Storz (eds), *Institutional and Technological Change in Japan's Economy, Past and Present* (London: Routledge, 2006), pp. 10–26.

Skya, Walter A., *Japan's Holy War: the Ideology of Radical Shintô Ultranationalism* (Durham: Duke UP, 2009).

Smith, Thomas C., *The Agrarian Origins of Modern Japan* (Stanford: SUP, 1959).

Soffer, Olga and Clive Gamble (eds), *The World at 18,000 BP Vol. One: High Latitudes* (London: Unwin Hyman, 1990).

Souryi, Pierre François, *The World Turned Upside Down: Medieval Japanese Society* (NY: Columbia UP, 2001).

Spang, Christian W. and Ralf-Harald Wippich (eds), *Japanese-German Relations, 1895–1945: War, Diplomacy and Public Opinion* (London: Routledge, 2006).

Stalker, Nancy K., *Prophet Motive; Deguchi Onisaburô, Oomoto, and the Rise of New Religions in Imperial Japan* (Honolulu: UHP, 2008).

Stark, Miriam A. (ed.), *Archaeology of Asia* (Oxford: Blackwell, 2006).

Steele, M. William, *Alternative Narratives in Modern Japanese History* (London: Routledge, 2003).

Steinberg, John W. et al. (eds), *The Russo-Japanese War in Global Perspective: World War Zero, Vol. I* (Leiden: Brill, 2005).

Stockwin, J. A. A., *Governing Japan: Divided Politics in a Resurgent Economy*, 4th ed. (Oxford: Blackwell, 2008).

Strong, Kenneth, *Ox Against the Storm; A Biography of Tanaka Shozo: Japan's Conservationist Pioneer* (Tenterden, Kent: Paul Norbury Publishing Ltd., 1977).

Sumiya, Mikio (ed.), *A History of Japanese Trade and Industrial Policy* (Oxford: Oxford UP, 2000).

Swale, Alistair D., *The Meiji Restoration: Monarchism, Mass Communication and Conservative Revolution* (London: Palgrave, 2009).

Szèll, Gyorgy and Ken'ichi Tominaga (eds), *The Environmental Challenges for Japan and Germany* (Frankfurt: Peter Lang, 2004).

Takii, Kazuhiro, *The Meiji Constitution: The Japanese Experience of the West and the Shaping of the Modern State* (Tokyo: International House, 2007).

Tansman, Alan (ed.), *The Culture of Japanese Fascism* (Durham: Duke UP, 2009).

Teikoku-Shoin Co., *Teikoku's Complete Atlas of Japan* (Tokyo: Teikoku-Shoin Co. Ltd., 1977).

Teruoka, Shuzo (ed.), *Agriculture in the Modernization of Japan, 1850–2000* (New Delhi: Manohar, 2008).

Tokugawa, Tsunenari, *The Edo Inheritance* (Tokyo: International House, 2009).

Tonomura, Hitomi, "Black Hair and Red Trousers: Gendering the Flesh in Medieval Japan", *American Historical Review* 99/1 (Feb. 1994), pp. 129–54.

Totman, Conrad, *The Collapse of the Tokugawa Bakufu, 1862–1868* (Honolulu: UHP, 1980).

——, *The Origins of Japan's Modern Forests: The Case of Akita* (Asian Studies at Hawaii #31) (Honolulu: UHP, 1985).

——, *The Green Archipelago: Forestry in Preindustrial Japan* (Berkeley: UCP, 1989).

——, *Early Modern Japan* (Berkeley: UCP, 1993).

——, *The Lumber Industry in Early Modern Japan* (Honolulu: UHP, 1995).

——, *Pre-industrial Korea and Japan in Environmental Perspective* (Leiden: Brill, 2004).

——, *A History of Japan, Second Edition* (Oxford: Blackwell, 2005).

——, *Japan's Imperial Forest: Goryôrin, 1889–1946* (Folkestone: Global Oriental, 2007).

Traganov, Jilly, *The Tôkaidô Road: Traveling and Representation in Edo and Meiji Japan* (NY: Routledge, 2004).

Trewartha, Glenn T., *Japan, A Physical, Cultural, and Regional Geography* (Madison: University of Wisconsin Press, 1978).

Tsang, Carol R., *War and Faith: Ikkô Ikki in Late Muromachi Japan* (Cambridge, MA: HUP, 2007).

Tsuchi, Ryuichi and James C. Ingle Jr. (eds), *Pacific Neogene: Environment, Evolution, and Events* (Tokyo: UTP, 1992).

Tsuda, Karyu et al., "On the Middle Miocene Paleoenvironment of Japan with Special Reference to the Ancient Mangrove Swamps", in Robert Orr Whyte (ed.), *The Evolution of the East Asian Environment Volume 1 Geology and Palaeoclimatology* (Hong Kong: University of Hong Kong, 1984), pp. 388–96.

Tsukada, Matsuo, "Vegetation in Prehistoric Japan: The Last 20,000 Years", in Richard J. Pearson et al. (eds), *Windows on the Japanese Past: Studies in Archaeology and Prehistory* (Ann Arbor, MI: Center for Japanese Studies, 1986), pp. 11–56.

Tsunoda, Ryusaku (tr.) and L. Carrington Goodrich (ed.), *Japan in the Chinese Dynastic Histories* (South Pasadena: P.I. & Ione Perkins, 1951).

Tsunoda, Ryusaku et al. (comps.), *Sources of the Japanese Tradition* (NY: Columbia UP, 1958).

Tsurumi, E. Patricia, *Factory Girls: Women in the Thread Mills of Meiji Japan* (Princeton: PUP, 1990).

Turk, Jon, *In the Wake of the Jômon* (NY: McGraw-Hill, 2005).

Turnbull, Stephen R., *Nagashino, 1575: Slaughter at the Barricades* (Westport, CT: Praeger, 2005).

——, *Strongholds of the Samurai: Japanese Castles 250–1877* (Oxford: Osprey, 2009).

Vande Walle, W.F. and Kazuhiko Kasaya (eds), *Dodonaeus in Japan: Translation and the Scientific Mind in the Tokugawa Period* (Leuven: Leuven UP, 2001).

Van Goethem, Ellen, *Nagaoka: Japan's Forgotten Capital* (Leiden: Brill, 2008).

Vaporis, Constantine N., *Tour of Duty: Samurai, Military Service in Edo, and the Culture of Early Modern Japan* (Honolulu: UHP, 2008).

Verschuer, Charlotte von, *Across the Perilous Sea: Japanese Trade with China and Korea from the Seventh to Sixteenth Centuries* (Ithaca NY: Cornell UP, 2006).

Vrielynck, Bruno and Philippe Bouysse, *The Changing Face of the Earth: The break-up of Pangaea and continental drift over the past 250 million years in ten steps* (Paris: UNESCO Publishing, 2003).

Walker, Brett L., *The Conquest of Ainu Lands, Ecology and Culture in Japanese Expansion, 1590–1800* (Berkeley: UCP, 2001).

——, *The Lost Wolves of Japan* (Seattle: U. Washington Press, 2005).

Wang, Pinxian, "Progress in Late Cenozoic Palaeoclimatology of China: a Brief Review", in Robert Orr Whyte (ed.), *The Evolution of the East Asian Environment Volume 1 Geology and Palaeoclimatology* (Hong Kong: University of Hong Kong, 1984), pp. 165–87.

Waswo, Ann and Nishida Yoshiaki (eds), *Farmers and Village Life in Twentieth-Century Japan* (London: Routledge, 2003).

Whyte, Robert Orr (ed.), *The Evolution of the East Asian Environment Volume 1 Geology and Palaeoclimatology* (Hong Kong: University of Hong Kong, 1984) (Vol. 2, *Palaeobotany, Palaeozoology and Palaeoanthropology*).

Williams, Duncan Ryûken, *The Other Side of Zen: A Social History of Sôtô Zen Buddhism in Tokugawa Japan* (Princeton: PUP, 2005).

Wolff, David et al. (eds), *The Russo-Japanese War in Global Perspective: World War Zero, Vol. II* (Leiden: Brill, 2007).

Yasuda, Yoshinori, "Oscillations of Climatic and Oceanographic Conditions since the Last Glacial Age in Japan", in Robert Orr Whyte (ed.), *The Evolution of the East Asian Environment Volume 1 Geology and Palaeoclimatology* (Hong Kong: University of Hong Kong, 1984), pp. 397–413.

——, "Monsoon Fluctuations and Cultural Changes During the Last Glacial Age in Japan", in *Nichibunken Japan Review*, No. 1 (1990), pp. 113–52.

Yonemoto, Marcia, *Mapping Early Modern Japan: Space, Place, and Culture in the Tokugawa Period (1603–1868)* (Berkeley: UCP, 2003).

Yoon, Sun, "Tectonic history of the Japan Sea region and its implications for the formation of the Japan Sea", in J.M. Dickins et al. (eds), "New Concepts in Global Tectonics," a Special Issue of *Himalayan Geology*, Vol. 22, No. 1 (2001), pp. 153–84.

Yoshikawa, Torao et al., *The Landforms of Japan* (Tokyo: UTP, 1981).

Zachmann, Urs Mattias, *China and Japan in the Late Meiji Period: China Policy and the Japanese Discourse on National Identity, 1895–1904* (London: Routledge, 2009).

# Index

agriculture
  defined, 1–4
  early ("one-stage") agriculture, 48–50,
    73–4, 97–103
  in industrial society, 204–7, 209–10,
    215–21, 223–4, 227–32, 239–40,
    252–55, 257, 270–5
  introduced to Japan, 55–7, 60–3
  later ("two-stage") agriculture, 100, 116,
    123–6, 134–5, 166–8, 182–7
  regional variation of, 19, 34, 65–6
*Ainu*, 110, 159, 176
Americans
  and Japan after 2000, 247, 250
  and Japan during 1800s, 144, 147, 148–9,
    182, 187, 196–8
  and Japan during 1900s, 198–202, 239,
    241–2, 244, 247, 249–50
animal husbandry
  in early agricultural society, 48, 55, 62–3,
    66, 69
  in industrial society, 206, 227–30, 272,
    273–4
  in later agricultural society, 101, 120,
    123–4, 134
architecture
  in early agricultural society, 61, 64–5, 69,
    79–81, 103
  in forager society, 39–40
  in industrial society, 257–8
  in later agricultural society, 110, 128–31,
    136–7, 177–8
Ashikaga Takauji, 112

Ashikaga Yoshimitsu, 112
Ashio mine, 173, 222, 226, 259
Asuka, 75, 79

biotic community in Japan
  in early agricultural era, 46–7, 62–3, 88–9,
    103–4
  in industrial era, 19–20, 225–8, 231–2,
    234–5, 256–7, 263, 267–8, 275, 277
  in later agricultural era, 128, 130–1,
    133–5, 138, 172, 175–6, 182–4, 186–7
  in pre-agricultural era, 16, 20, 26–8, 32,
    34
birth control, 168, 208, 248–9, 254
boats *see* maritime travel
Britain, 146, 198, 200–2
British Isles, 16–17, 176
Buddhism, 75, 80, 86, 96, 113, 121–2, 128,
  138, 147, 158
*bunmei kaika*, 151, 154
burial mounds *see* tombs

castles, 110, 129, 131, 136–7
ceramics
  in general, 32–3, 35–6, 40, 64, 100, 319
    n.2
  as roof tile, 80, 177
China
  cultural influence on Japan, 50, 54–5, 57,
    62–3, 75–6, 79, 82, 99, 147, 151, 156
  early human presence, 29–30
  geographical relationship to Japan,
    10–11, 15–16, 18, 25, 33